www.brookscole.com

www.brookscole.com is the World Wide Web site for Brooks/Cole and is your direct source to dozens of online resources.

At *www.brookscole.com* you can find out about supplements, demonstration software, and student resources. You can also send email to many of our authors and preview new publications and exciting new technologies.

www.brookscole.com
Changing the way the world learns®

School Counseling

FOUNDATIONS AND CONTEMPORARY ISSUES

DANIEL T. SCIARRA
Hofstra University

THOMSON

BROOKS/COLE

Australia • Canada • Mexico • Singapore • Spain
United Kingdom • United States

THOMSON

BROOKS/COLE

Executive Editor: Lisa Gebo
Acquisitions Editor: Julie Martinez
Assistant Editor: Shelley Gesicki
Editorial Assistant: Amy Lam
Technology Project Manager: Barry Connolly
Marketing Manager: Caroline Concilla
Marketing Assistant: Mary Ho
Advertising Project Manager: Tami Strang
Project Manager, Editorial Production: Kimberly Adams

Print/Media Buyer: Kristine Waller
Permissions Editor: Sommy Ko
Production Service and Compositor: G & S Typesetters, Inc.
Art Editor: Vernon Boes
Copy Editor: Barbara Bell
Cover Designer: Stanton Design Inc.
Cover Image: Judith L. Harkness
Cover Printer: Thomson/West
Printer: Thomson/West

Printed in the United States
3 4 5 6 7   07

For more information about our products, contact us at:
Thomson Learning Academic Resource Center
1-800-423-0563
For permission to use material from this text, contact us by:
Phone: 1-800-730-2214
Fax: 1-800-730-2215
Web: http://www.thomsonrights.com

Library of Congress Control Number: 2003105422

ISBN-13: 978-0-534-53806-4
ISBN-10: 0-534-53806-1

Brooks/Cole–Thomson Learning
10 Davis Drive
Belmont, CA 94002-3098
USA

Asia
Thomson Learning
5 Shenton Way #01-01
UIC Building
Singapore 068808

Australia/New Zealand
Thomson Learning
102 Dodds Street
Southbank, Victoria 3006
Australia

Canada
Nelson
1120 Birchmount Road
Toronto, Ontario M1K 5G4
Canada

Europe/Middle East/Africa
Thomson Learning
High Holborn House
50/51 Bedford Row
London WC1R 4LR
United Kingdom

Latin America
Thomson Learning
Seneca, 53
Colonia Polanco
11560 Mexico D.F.
Mexico

Spain/Portugal
Paraninfo
Calle/Magallanes, 25
28015 Madrid, Spain

To Brenda,
whose support, encouragement,
and love brought this book to completion

Brief Contents

Contents

Chapter 2

Counseling Services in Schools   22

Chapter 5

Career Counseling and Development   102

Part Two

SPECIAL TOPICS   141

Chapter 6

Multiculturalism in School Counseling   143

Chapter 7

The School Counselor and Students with Disabilities   177

Chapter 8

Separation and Loss in School-Aged Children   217

Chapter 9

Suicide in the School Setting   245

Chapter 10
Sex and Sex-Related Issues in School Counseling   275

Chapter 11

Substance Use and Abuse: Prevention and Intervention 308

Chapter 12

Understanding and Preventing Violence in Schools   340

Chapter 13

Child Maltreatment   379

Appendixes

References   423

Name Index   483

Subject Index   495

Tables

Figures

Preface

This book is written for both school counselors in training and those already in the field. It builds on the work of pioneers in developmental guidance, the likes of Norm Gysbers and Robert Myrick, whose books have changed forever how school counseling is understood and practiced. As developmental guidance has taken hold in the field of school counseling, a frustration around the implementation of developmental guidance programs has grown. In response, this book offers not only the foundation of comprehensive developmental guidance programs but also content that is relevant to young people today. Much of the material here focuses on prevention programs to enhance the development of school-age children and to minimize the risk of factors that could interfere with that development. Also here are interventions for students who are already experiencing obstacles to their development.

A more recent trend in school counseling is an emphasis on promoting academic achievement, especially among underachieving students. Although no one would argue with such a laudable goal, some believe that a focus on academic achievement means that students' psychoemotional and mental health needs are being ignored. That dichotomy is false: Often a psychoemotional problem is responsible for academic underachievement. This book takes seriously the psychoemotional dimensions of school counseling and their relationship to academic achievement.

School Counseling: Foundations and Contemporary Issues can be used as a primary textbook in an introductory course in school counseling or for reference in a practicum, internship, or other advanced courses. The 13-chapter format allows the text to fit nicely into a 15-week semester, with the first and last weeks devoted to the course introduction and evaluation. The book also offers school counselors who are working ways to respond to the challenges facing students today. And although the material here applies to school counselors, the developmental framework makes the book relevant for all counselors who plan to work or are working with school-aged children and adolescents.

The book is divided into two parts. Part One, Foundations, examines the basic functions and roles of school counselors and the fundamental skills they must possess. Chapter 1 is an historical overview of school counseling that ends with a discussion of contemporary movements, including developmental guidance, national standards, and the national model. Chapter 2 describes the basics of individual and group counseling and guidance in schools and the theories that underlie practice. Chapter 3 reviews several basic models of consulting and then focuses on the challenges of and strategies for consulting with parents and teachers. Chapter 4 discusses counselors' use of data to assess students and programs and to hold themselves more accountable. Chapter 5 deals with career counseling and development—theories, standardized assessment, technology, and programs that extend from kindergarten through Grade 12.

Part Two, Special Topics, is designed to help school counselors deal with the issues and challenges facing students today. The selection of topics is somewhat arbitrary, but these are among the most important issues related to the healthy development of children in our schools. Chapter 6 is about multiculturalism in schools. It examines each of the major racial groups in the United States (Whites, Blacks, Hispanics, Asians, and American Indians and Alaskan Natives) and ways to promote academic achievement among students from nondominant cultures. Chapter 7 focuses on another minority culture, students with disabilities. The chapter begins with a discussion of the law that mandates a free appropriate public education for all children, followed by an explanation of the role of the school counselor in inclusive education. The chapter ends with a look at the most common disabilities in our schools today. Chapter 8 deals with separation and loss in children and adolescents, interventions to help youngsters cope with the death of a loved one, a parental divorce or separation, and the many unrecognized losses that are a part of human development. The focus in Chapter 9 is on suicide and a major risk factor for suicide, depression. Suggestions are given for assessing suicidal students, for developing a suicide prevention program, and for dealing with the aftermath of a suicide. Chapter 10 discusses sex and sex-related issues as a natural part of child and adolescent development. Special consideration is given to HIV/AIDS, teenage pregnancy and motherhood, and the role of the school counselor in a comprehensive sex education program. Chapter 11 examines the prevention of substance abuse and interventions for students who use and abuse drugs and alcohol. Chapter 12 is about preventing youth violence. Discussions of the causes and warning signs of violence and of the problems generated by bullying and sexual harassment in schools lead to suggestions for developing a comprehensive violence prevention program. Chapter 13 deals with child abuse and neglect, especially child sexual abuse.

Each chapter ends with questions that can serve as the basis for classroom discussion; or the instructor can assign students the questions to work on for the next class. One of my goals in this book was to be tolerant of different points of view. There are seldom right or wrong answers to the questions at the end of each chapter: They were written to encourage thoughtful and creative responses to the problems school counselors face daily in our schools. Most chapters also end with suggested Internet sites for obtaining more information and resources for the material discussed in the chapter.

I signed the contract for this book six months before being married for the first time. I did it with a certain amount of trepidation, thinking that married life might prevent me from adhering to what seemed to me a demanding writing schedule.

The fact that it did not is a tribute to my wife, Brenda, without whose consideration and support I could not have finished this book. I am deeply grateful to her. I also want to thank my secretary, Adele Piombino, whose dedication and support allowed me time for writing despite my chairing an academic department. I am also grateful to Frank Bowe, Karen De Rosa, Estelle Gellman, Laurie Johnson, Ron McLean, Israel Schwartz, and Estelle Weinstein for reading parts of the manuscript and providing invaluable feedback. And I am indebted to Julie Martinez, former acquisitions editor at Brooks/Cole–Wadsworth, who showed immediate interest in my proposal and provided constant support, guidance, and encouragement through the writing process.

On September 11, 2001, at around 9:15 A.M., while I was working feverishly on the manuscript, my wife walked into my home office and said, "There's been a tragedy." We all know now what she was referring to. After turning on the television and trying to digest what had happened, I saw one and then the other World Trade Center tower collapse, only 60 miles from my home. It took me a while to recover my concentration and return to writing. In the face of that terror and tragedy, this manuscript seemed so much less important. When I did start in again, it was with a new perspective. I didn't have to break ground here: What this book is is nothing more and nothing less than a tool—one of a number of good tools—to help school counselors help children and adolescents deal with the developmental tasks and the psychoemotional challenges that can rob them of the fullness of life.

FOUNDATIONS

HISTORICAL PERSPECTIVES AND CONTEMPORARY TRENDS IN SCHOOL COUNSELING

Counseling in schools dates back to the early 19th century. Since that time, the role of the school counselor has been and continues to be debated. In 1999, the American School Counselor Association (ASCA) adopted a new role definition for professional school counselors:

> The professional school counselor is a certified/licensed educator trained in school counseling. Professional school counselors address the needs of students through the implementation of a comprehensive, standards-based, developmental school counseling program. They are employed in elementary, middle/junior high, and senior high schools, and in post-secondary settings. Their work is differentiated by attention to age-specific developmental stages of student growth, and the needs, tasks and student interests related to those stages. School counselors work with all students, including those who are considered at-risk and those with special needs. They are specialists in human behavior and relationships who provide assistance to students through four primary interventions: counseling (individual and group), large group guidance, consultation, and coordination. (p. 1)

According to this definition, school counselors, sensitive to students' developmental needs, work with them over time with the hope that their efforts will bear fruit at some point. They are held accountable through a standards-based program that promotes "the academic, career, and personal/social development of children and youth" (ASCA, 1999a, p. 2). School counselors are an integral part of the education program, as important to the school as teachers and administrators, and as essential to the main function of the school, academic success. In their role as advocates for students and their families, school counselors employ a variety of prevention and intervention efforts to ensure that all students achieve according to their potential.

The reality, however, is that the role of the school counselor varies greatly from state to state and even from school district to school district. Although some state education departments—Missouri, Tennessee, and Texas to name a few—have adopted standards and guidelines for school counseling programs, more often than not the school counselor's role is defined by the building's lead administrator. As a result, counselors do everything, from leading drug abuse and violence prevention programs to sharpening pencils for standardized tests. An immediate solution may not be in sight, but ASCA (2003) recently developed a national model for school counseling programs that addresses not only the problem of noncounseling responsibilities but also the issues of access, accountability, and underachievement. To appreciate this latest development in school counseling, we begin with a review of the profession from the beginning of the 20th century.

A HISTORY OF COUNSELING IN SCHOOLS

Over the course of its history, school counseling has had four major emphases: vocational guidance, mental health, personal adjustment, and developmental guidance (R. A. Thompson, 2002).[1]

Vocational Guidance, 1900–1925

The Industrial Revolution of the 19th century spurred large-scale migration and immigration to major cities in the United States and resulted in wealth for a few and hardship for many. Exploitative working conditions, along with a lack of adequate housing and social supports, gave rise to the progressive movement, which sought to improve the conditions of the poor. By the turn of the century, a parallel movement had emerged in response to the large number of children who were leaving public school to earn low wages under very unfavorable conditions (C. H. Miller, 1964). The *vocational guidance movement* had two goals: to improve the situation of youngsters who had dropped out of school and to better prepare those in school for the workplace.

Guidance in the Curriculum   In the early decades of the twentieth century, the focus of school counseling was on *guidance,* helping students make educational and job choices through the dissemination of information (Aubrey, 1977). A second component of guidance—which became part of the public school curriculum— was sensitizing students to social ills and contributing to their moral development (Aubrey, 1977; Baker, 2000).

Jesse B. Davis, a high school principal in Grand Rapids, Michigan, is credited with systematically introducing guidance into the schools. At the beginning of the 20th century, Davis set aside one English class period a week "to help high-school students better understand their own characters, emulate good role models, and develop into socially responsible workers" (Baker, 2000, p. 3). Gysbers and Henderson (2000) described Davis's curriculum:

Grade 7: Vocational ambition
Grade 8: The value of education

---

[1] The dates given for each emphasis throughout this section are approximate.

> Grade 9: The elements of character that make for success
> Grade 10: The world's work: a call to service
> Grade 11: Choosing a vocation
> Grade 12: Preparing for one's life work

In the same period, Frank Parsons was working in Boston. Like Davis, Parsons focused on at-risk youngsters, particularly those who had left school and seemed lost in the upheaval caused by the Industrial Revolution. In 1908, Parsons founded the Vocational Bureau, the first institutionalization of guidance in the United States (Ginzberg, 1971).[2] Parsons (1909) believed that careful consideration of each individual's aptitudes, abilities, ambitions, resources, and limitations, and their relation to success in different industries, was the basis of vocational guidance. That theory is still central to many contemporary career guidance programs. Through Parsons's influence, the Boston public schools asked the Vocational Bureau for help in developing and implementing a vocational guidance program (Gysbers & Henderson, 2000). While Parsons was working in Boston, E. W. Weaver was instrumental in establishing a vocational program in the New York City schools. By 1910, approximately 35 cities in the United States had some form of vocational guidance and education in their schools (Aubrey, 1977).

Psychometrics   The vocational guidance movement was not the product of a psychological theory. It originated from a sociological perspective, a response to the social problems of the times, particularly to the exploitation of children and to the perceived lack of direction of youngsters both in and out of school. But shortly after World War I, psychometrics would give vocational guidance a theoretical foundation.

Aubrey (1977) questioned whether the vocational guidance movement would have survived without the support of *psychometrics*, the discipline of testing. The fundamental goal of vocational guidance was to match worker and job. A viable match relied on both the educator's and the student's ability to define "interests, capabilities, strengths, and limitations" (p. 291). Parsons had developed a triadic structure for vocational guidance that combined diagnosis, information, and placement. Although most educators had access to information about jobs, diagnosis and placement seemed to be based more on intuition than knowledge. Binet and Simon (1905), working in Paris, had developed a scale to measure mental abilities; and in 1917 the U.S. Army developed the Army Alpha and Army Beta tests to classify the millions of young men entering military service (Baker, 2000). These instruments would prove extremely useful to vocational guidance educators in search of a systematic means for assessing the key components of vocational choice.

By the 1920s, vocational educators were using psychological testing as a basis for information gathering, assessment and diagnosis, and placement. Like other practitioners of standardized testing, they slipped into the rigid use of tests to label, classify, categorize, and sort individuals. This seemed to fly in the face of vocational guidance's original intent: to promote human dignity and self-determination (Au-

---

[2] In 1913, the bureau gave birth to the National Vocational Guidance Association; two years later, the association began publication of the journal *Vocational Guidance* (Aubrey, 1977).

brey, 1977). Instead, "vocational guidance became problem-oriented, centering on adjustable psychological personal problems—not social moral, religious, ethical, or political problems" (A. H. Johnson, 1973, p. 201).

Mental Health, 1930–1942

During the 1930s, school counseling began to focus less on vocational guidance and more on mental health (Gysbers & Henderson, 2000). Vocational educators, trying to make appropriate job placements, discovered an array of personal problems among their students, including hostility to authority, financial hardship, troubled home life, and indiscriminate sexual relationships (Rudy, 1965). Although practitioners were working with problems beyond career and job, they still functioned primarily as teachers, imparting information to young people (Aubrey, 1977). In his book *How to Counsel Students* (1939), Williamson described the process as "counselor centered": Counselors were charged with diagnosing counselees' problems, enlightening them as to the best course of action, and motivating them to pursue what the counselors believed was in the counselees' best interests.

Personal Adjustment, 1942–1970

The Influence of Carl Rogers   In 1942, Carl Rogers published *Counseling and Psychotherapy: New Concepts in Practice.* The book began a movement away from the counselor-centered mental health model to a client-centered personal adjustment model. The time was right for change. The Depression was over. By the end of World War II, Americans were eager for greater freedom and personal autonomy (Aubrey, 1977). The GI Bill, which made education available to veterans, helped foster the need for freedom and autonomy. The focus of school counseling shifted from identifying problems and solving them, to self-determination and self-actualization. And the counselor's responsibility shifted from finding a solution and convincing the counselee of its worthiness, to creating a climate in which the counselee was free to explore alternatives.

In 1951, Rogers published *Client-Centered Therapy: Its Current Practice, Implications, and Theory,* in which he wrote that testing and diagnosis stifle self-exploration. The book was instrumental in changing the focus of school counseling (Aubrey, 1977). Counselors no longer administered and interpreted vocational tests; instead they learned and practiced the latest therapeutic techniques to help students grow and develop.

Interestingly, as Rogers's influence was deepening in the 1950s, some of the major advances in developmental theory were being made (see, for example, Erikson, 1950; Havighurst, 1952; Imhelder & Piaget, 1958; and Piaget, 1952). Despite the enormous stature of client-centered counseling, developmental theory of the 1950s sowed the seeds that would later flower into comprehensive developmental guidance.

The National Defense Education Act of 1958   Two federal initiatives influenced the development of school counseling. The first was the George-Barden Act of 1946, which appropriated funds for guidance and counseling services in schools and other settings. The second was the National Defense Education Act (NDEA) of 1958. The NDEA appropriated funds in the form of grants for statewide testing and for the development of institutes to train counselors for secondary schools (Herr, 2001). The act was a direct response to the former Soviet Union's launching of Sputnik I. Sputnik had created a fear in the American people that they lagged well behind the Soviets in science and technology. The goal of the NDEA was to improve the testing of students' aptitudes and the identification of their potential, to train counselors who would help students stay in school, and to provide funds for those who were financially unable to attend college (Schmidt, 1999).[3]

We cannot overestimate the influence of the NDEA on the history of school counseling. The act provided $15 million a year to local school systems for the development of counseling services and $7 million to universities for the development of school counselor training institutes. According to F. W. Miller (1968), from 1958 to 1963, the number of full-time counselors increased 126 percent, from 12,000 to 27,180; and more than 400 counseling institutes were funded and trained more than 13,000 counselors.[4]

The curriculum in the training institutes reflected the shift away from guidance as education to guidance as counseling. Guidance came to be seen as an adjunct to teaching, and the role of the counselor as a function of students' needs in a particular school. "As increasing numbers of counselors entered the schools, less emphasis was given to guidance programs and more to the role and functions of the school counselors. In fact, to many individuals, what school counselors did became the guidance program" (Gysbers & Henderson, 2000, p. 19). Programs that could be implemented across many different schools gave way to a wide variety of approaches and roles for school counselors. During this time, the Commission on Guidance in American Schools proposed that the term *guidance* be abandoned and that the services provided by school counselors be subsumed under the broad category *pupil personnel services,* together with the work carried out by school psychologists, school social workers, and attendance and health officers (Wrenn, 1962).

Developmental Guidance, 1970–

In 1962, C. Gilbert Wrenn published his now classic book, *The Counselor in a Changing World.* By the end of the decade, that work had given rise to developmental guidance.

Acknowledging the importance of emerging developmental theories, Wrenn urged that the "primary emphasis in counseling students be placed on the developmental needs and decision points in the lives of the total range of students rather than upon the remedial need and the crisis points in the lives of a few students"

---

[3]The commitment to school counseling was strengthened by James Conant, whose widely read *The American High School Today* (1959) recommended one high school counselor for every 200 to 300 students (Baker, 2000).

[4]The number of counselors trained included many teachers, who quickly amassed enough counseling credits to be certified as school counselors.

(p. 109). With this challenge, Wrenn set off a controversy that has yet to be resolved: Should school counselors focus more on the development of all students, or on remediation for those most at risk?[5] Although various models of school counseling exist today, most can be categorized by their emphasis on either development or mental health.

The controversy has led to debate over terminology. Gysbers and Henderson (2000) use *guidance* to emphasize the importance of development; Baker (2000) uses the term *school counseling* to refer generally to programs and services; Myrick (1997) uses *guidance* and *counseling* interchangeably. In this book we use the terms *school counseling* and *school counselor* much like Baker, as all-inclusive terms for the wide spectrum of programs and activities carried out by counselors in the schools. We use the term *guidance* to refer to a planned program of developmental activities to foster students' academic, career, and personal and social development (ASCA, 1999a).

Two other factors played a part in the growth of developmental guidance over the next few decades. The first was the expansion of school counseling into the elementary schools, a product of 1964 amendments to the NDEA that made funds available for elementary school counseling. In the late 1960s, ASCA began publishing the journal *Elementary School Guidance and Counseling*. By the 1980s, research in child development had increased interest in developmental guidance at the elementary school level (see, for example, Gilligan, 1982; Kegan, 1982; and Kohlberg, 1984).

The second factor was the accountability movement, which began in the late 1960s and intensified in the 1970s. Accountability asked teachers and counselors to set measurable goals and objectives for their students (Gysbers & Henderson, 2000). The services model of school counseling, which focused more on counseling techniques than on outcomes, found it difficult to answer the call to accountability. Developmental counseling, on the other hand, offered curricula with goals and objectives that could be measured. The 1980s and 1990s were marked by the ongoing efforts of proponents of developmental guidance to put those programs into practice across the country.

COMPREHENSIVE DEVELOPMENTAL GUIDANCE: A MAJOR CONTEMPORARY INFLUENCE

Although the term *developmental guidance* was becoming more and more popular during the 1970s and early 1980s, critics claimed it was a program in search of meaning. Two widely read texts were published to answer this criticism: *Developing and Managing Your School Guidance Program* (Gysbers & Henderson, 1988)

---

[5] Between 1976 and 1986, N. S. Wilson (1986a) found 117 articles in the journal *Elementary School Guidance and Counseling* defending developmental guidance and 129 defending remedial counseling. Of the 117 developmental articles, 13 (11.1 percent) documented a positive impact; of the 129 remedial articles, 17 (13.2 percent) documented positive effects.

and *Developmental Guidance and Counseling: A Practical Approach* (Myrick, 1987). Both have gone through several editions. And there have been a significant number of journal articles devoted to developmental guidance programs (for example, see Lapan, Gysbers, & Sun, 1997; Neukrug, Barr, Hoffman, & Kaplan, 1993; and Paisley & Peace, 1995; to name but a few).

Theoretical Foundation

Developmental guidance . . . assumes that human nature moves individuals sequentially and positively toward self-enhancement. It recognizes there is a force within each of us that makes us believe that we are special and there is nobody like us. It also assumes that our individual potentials are valuable assets to society and the future of humanity. (Myrick, 1997, p. 27)

Developmental theories suggest a pattern of growth in a series of *domains*, or dimensions. Among those domains are emotions (Dupont, 1978), psychosocial traits (Erikson, 1950), ethics (Kohlberg, 1981), ego (Loevinger, 1976), thought (Piaget, 1952), and interpersonal skills (Selman, 1980). Developmental guidance programs target certain domains: The programs set goals and objectives for specific areas of development. For example, Missouri has identified three broad domains—career planning and exploration, knowledge of self and others, and educational and vocational development—and has organized its school guidance program around them. Texas has identified seven domains: self-esteem development, motivation to achieve, interpersonal effectiveness, communication skills, cross-cultural effectiveness, decision-making skills, and responsible behavior. ASCA's National Standards for School Counseling make use of three domains: academic development, career development, and personal-social development (Campbell & Dahir, 1997). Choosing the kind and number of domains is simply an organizational strategy through which a state or school district builds a guidance curriculum for all grade levels.

The Guidance Curriculum

According to Gysbers and Henderson (2000, 2001), the choice of developmental domains connects guidance and counseling to the main purpose of schools, life education. They insist that guidance, like math or science or other areas of emphasis, should have a competency-based curriculum, with goals and objectives for every grade level. Table 1.1 shows part of a guidance curriculum. A complete guidance curriculum would identify domains, goals for each domain, grade-level competencies (standards by which each student's success in achieving each goal can be measured), and objectives (the means by which the goals will be reached). For example, objectives for Grade 7 might include an assignment that asks students to compare themselves to a good friend, to describe how they are both the same and different. A guidance curriculum is much like a curriculum for any other subject. And like curricula in other subjects, it is written by someone in the state or district office of education and usually is delivered in the classroom.

TABLE 1.1 SAMPLE GUIDANCE CURRICULUM FOR THE DOMAINS OF SELF-KNOWLEDGE AND INTERPERSONAL SKILLS

Domains	Self-knowledge and interpersonal skills
Goals	Students will develop and incorporate an understanding of their unique personal characteristics and abilities.
Competencies by grade	K: I can tell what I look like and some things I like to do.
	1: I can tell something special about myself.
	2: I can tell something special about myself.
	3: I can describe myself to someone who doesn't know me.
	4: I can tell how people are different and that they have different skills and abilities.
	5: I can tell how my special characteristics and abilities are important to me.
	6: I can tell how my characteristics and abilities change and how they can be expanded.
	7: I can compare the characteristics and abilities of others I know with my own and accept the differences.
	8: I can list the skills I already possess and those I hope to develop in the future.
	9: I can discuss the value of understanding my unique characteristics and abilities.
	10: I can describe and analyze how an individual's characteristics and abilities develop.
	11: I can explain which characteristics and abilities I appreciate most in myself and others.
	12: I can compare my characteristics and abilities with those of others, and appreciate and encourage my uniqueness.

SOURCE: Adapted from *Developing and Managing Your School Guidance Program* (3rd ed.) by N. C. Gysbers and P. Henderson, 2000, p. 70. Copyright by the American Counseling Association. Adapted with permission.

A guidance curriculum has three major implications for school counselors. First, by making guidance a part of the school's overall curriculum, it indicates that guidance is not something ancillary to the main purpose of the school. Second, the guidance curriculum emphasizes the pedagogical and evaluative roles of school counselors. A good deal of counselors' time is spent in the classroom teaching; and, like other teachers, school counselors must evaluate their students' particular competencies. Third, the guidance curriculum makes clear that the school counselor's job is to work with all students, not just those in need of remedial services.

Other Program Components

Although it is recommended that counselors, especially on the elementary level, spend the majority of their time teaching the guidance curriculum, that curriculum is just one component of a developmental guidance program. Gysbers and

TABLE 1.2   **RECOMMENDED TIME ALLOCATIONS FOR SCHOOL COUNSELORS, MISSOURI COMPREHENSIVE GUIDANCE PROGRAM**

	Percent of Time		
Component	**Elementary School**	**Middle School**	**High School**
Guidance curriculum	35–40	35–40	15–25
Individual planning	5–10	15–25	25–35
Responsive services	30–40	30–40	25–35
System support	10–15	10–15	15–20

SOURCE: Adapted from *Developing and Managing Your School Guidance Program* (3rd ed.) by N. C. Gysbers and P. Henderson, 2000, p. 267. Copyright by the American Counseling Association. Adapted with permission.

Henderson (2000) listed three others: individual planning, responsive services, and system support. *Individual planning* involves more-traditional counseling functions: advising, assessment, placement, and follow-up. *Responsive services* include individual counseling, small-group counseling, consulting, and referral for a variety of presenting problems—essentially, remedial services. *System support* includes time spent managing the guidance program, working with other personnel in the school, establishing networks in the community, and engaging in public relations for the program.

School counselors must decide how much time to give to each component and then build their weekly schedule around those time allocations. Table 1.2 shows the recommended allocations for the various components of the Missouri Comprehensive Guidance Program. Notice that the time allocated to each component changes by grade level. In high school, for example, less time is allocated to the guidance curriculum and more time is allocated to individual planning, for helping students with their postsecondary preparations.

Comprehensive developmental guidance programs vary from state to state, district to district, and even school to school. But most programs include teaching, individual planning, response services, and system support. And most suggest that counselors allocate their time much like counselors in Missouri do. Where we find variation is in the goals of the guidance curriculum: Individual districts and schools have different needs and face different challenges. For example, a school with a culturally diverse student population may place more emphasis on getting along with those who are different.

Gysbers and Henderson (2000) acknowledged variations from program to program but insisted that for school counselors to begin, operate, and manage a comprehensive developmental counseling program, they must accept three basic premises:

> *Guidance is a program.* Guidance is a series of activities designed to help students meet defined goals by achieving defined levels of competency. Because guidance is a program, school counselors must continually evalu-

ate its effectiveness for participants. Program evaluation is a key component of developmental guidance programs.

Guidance is comprehensive and developmental. Counselors must conduct program activities on a planned and regular basis to help students master the guidance curriculum competencies. The primary emphasis is on helping all students grow and develop, and programs provide a wide range of activities and services. A secondary emphasis is placed on individual students with special problems.

Guidance is a team effort. The school counselor facilitates and manages the program but must be able to call on other members of the school staff for consultation and collaboration. For example, a number of teachers might work with individual students under the direction of the school counselor. Also important members of the team are parents and the broader community.

The Status of Developmental Guidance Programs

Developmental guidance programs began to emerge in the early 1970s and are widely used today. Some leaders in the field of school counseling believe developmental guidance is the only appropriate focus of school counseling (see, for example, Paisley & Borders, 1995)—a stance endorsed by ASCA (1997). But comprehensive developmental guidance programs across the country have encountered both criticism and obstacles.

Sink and McDonald (1998), in a survey of comprehensive guidance programs in the United States, found that as of March 1, 1997, 24 states had some type of model in place, 10 were developing models, and 7 were encouraging school districts to create their own models.[6] Research shows that a comprehensive guidance program has enhanced student learning in Missouri (Lapan, Gysbers, Hughey, & Arni, 1993; Lapan, Gysbers, & Sun, 1997). More generally, several large-scale studies have demonstrated the positive effects of classroom guidance on behavior and attitudes (Gerler & Anderson, 1986; Myrick, Merhill, & Swanson, 1986); preparation for exams (N. S. Wilson, 1986b); self-care practices for children home alone (Bundy & Boser, 1987); and school attendance for children in kindergarten and Grade 1 (Gerler, 1980). Gerler and Anderson found no significant effects of classroom guidance on achievement in language arts or mathematics.

Sink and McDonald made one disturbing finding: Most of the comprehensive developmental guidance programs lacked theoretical underpinnings for their design. That is, state documents do not make explicit the research or literature on which the programs are based. Many programs seem simply to duplicate Gysbers and Henderson's (1988, 1994, 2000) templates for designing and managing a comprehensive developmental guidance program. A possible explanation is that states have responded to pressure to have a guidance program on paper but have not internalized the need for their program to be informed by the latest developmental theory or the particular challenges their schools face. Sink and Yillik-Downer

---

[6]Since 1997, other states, among them New York, have also adopted models.

(2001) compared the practice to teaching mathematics with models developed years ago, models that have been superseded by newer and more relevant ones. For example, conspicuously absent from the literature on developmental guidance is development theory on racial and cultural identity (Atkinson, Morten, & Sue, 1998; Helms, 1990a, 1995; Rowe, Bennett, & Atkinson, 1994), which is assuming a more prominent place in psychology and counseling to explain behavior as it pertains to racial and cultural diversity. The comprehensive developmental guidance model has also been criticized for being too broad, for adopting a one-size-fits-all approach, and for being insensitive to the needs of diverse populations and at-risk youth (R. A. Thompson, 2002).

School counselors raise another issue: They complain that full-scale implementation of comprehensive programs is unrealistic given a lack of administrative cooperation and the huge amounts of nonguidance work that is thrust on them. In response, efforts continue to be made to reduce the clerical tasks that inundate school counselors.

Finally, some critics argue that developmental guidance pays little or no attention to the mental health needs of students at risk for school failure (Keys, Bemak, & Lockhart, 1998; Lockhart & Keys, 1998).

AMERICAN SCHOOL COUNSELOR ASSOCIATION: THE NATIONAL STANDARDS

The 1980s were marked by concerns that America's schools were lagging behind those of other developed nations. Falling scores in reading and math led to the publication of *A Nation at Risk* (National Commission, 1983), which spoke to the need for improving the quality of education in the United States. The warnings sounded in the 1980s gave rise during the 1990s to the standards movement in education, an effort to increase the schools' accountability for the learning and achievement of their students. In 1994, Congress passed Goals 2000: Educate America Act. The act requires that students meet certain standards for competing in a global economy. But none of these initiatives made mention of school counselors and their role in promoting learning and achievement. In response to that omission, a number of organizations—among them the College Board, the National Association for College Admission Counseling, the American Counseling Association (ACA), and ASCA—began advocating for recognition of the importance of school counselors to educational reform. That advocacy culminated in 1999 in ASCA's redefinition of *school counseling*, which was quoted at the beginning of this chapter.

In the mid-1990s, ASCA also was developing national standards for school counselors. The reasons were twofold: First, the standards would signal the important relationship between school counseling, and student learning and achievement. Second, they would signal that school counselors had become a part of the accountability movement in school reform. To develop the standards, the organization surveyed more than 2,000 school counselors. Results, analysis, and standards were published in *Sharing the Vision: The National Standards for School*

TABLE 1.3 **NATIONAL STANDARDS FOR SCHOOL COUNSELING PROGRAMS**

Academic Development	
Standard A	Students will acquire the attitudes, knowledge, and skills that contribute to effective learning in the school and across the life span.
Standard B	Students will complete school with the academic preparation necessary to choose from a wide variety of substantial postsecondary options, including college.
Standard C	Students will understand the relationship of academics to the world of work and to life at home and in the community.

Career Development	
Standard A	Students will acquire the skills to investigate the world of work in relation to knowledge of self and to make informed career decisions.
Standard B	Students will employ strategies to achieve future career success and satisfaction.
Standard C	Students will understand the relationship between personal qualities, education, and training, and the work world.

Personal and Social Development	
Standard A	Students will acquire the attitudes, knowledge, and interpretation skills to help them understand and respect self and others.
Standard B	Students will make decisions, set goals, and take appropriate action to achieve goals.
Standard C	Students will understand safety and survival skills.

SOURCE: Campbell & Dahir (1997). Copyright by the American School Counselor Association. Reprinted with permission.

Counseling Programs (Campbell & Dahir, 1997). It was a significant moment in the history of school counseling.

The Standards

ASCA identified nine standards, three in each of three areas: academic development, career development, and personal and social development (Table 1.3).

According to Dahir (2001), the three standards for academic development identify attitudes, knowledge, and skills that promote learning both in and out of school. The standards in career development are designed to orient school counseling programs toward strategies and activities that help students acquire the attitudes, knowledge, and skills necessary for postsecondary education and the world of work. Standards in the area of personal and social development are designed to help school counselors create programs that provide personal and social growth experiences through school and into adult life. The standards also connect personal and social development to academic and career success (Campbell & Dahir, 1997).

Competencies

Attached to each standard is a list of competencies, desired learning outcomes. The competencies can be adapted by individual programs to accommodate their special needs. By focusing the standards on outcomes, the competencies play a key role in the accountability of school counselors. The competencies also allow for the marriage of comprehensive and developmental guidance programs. Remember that these programs also are competency based and stress the importance of evaluating outcomes. The competencies serve as a guide for developing "strategies and activities for students to acquire affective, academic, and career competence" (Dahir, 2001, p. 324). Suggested competencies for each standard are listed in Appendix A.

Since their release in 1997, the standards have enjoyed a warm reception in the professional community. More than 400 school districts across the country have developed comprehensive school counseling programs based on the standards (Dahir, 2001). A national survey of school counseling programs found that 14.4 percent used the national standards extensively in their program; 53.8 percent reported moderate use, 12.5 percent minimal use, and 5 percent no use (14.4 percent of the responses were unusable) (Perusse, Goodnough, & Noel, 2001). The organization and content of this book reflect a thorough review and appreciation for the national standards. The challenge remains to fully implement the standards, but they articulate a clear vision for school counseling programs that hope to serve all students.

A NEW INITIATIVE: THE DeWITT WALLACE–*READER'S DIGEST* GRANTS FOR COUNSELOR TRAINING

In early 1997, the Education Trust, a nonprofit organization that promotes high academic achievement for all students, sent a request for proposal (RFP) to more than 400 school counselor training programs in the United States. The RFP was for competitive grants funded by the DeWitt Wallace–*Reader's Digest* Fund that became known as the Transforming School Counseling Initiative (TSCI). Ultimately, six universities received upwards of $500,000 over three years, as part of a six-year initiative to "build new models for graduate-level preparation of school counselors—models that will produce professionals better equipped to serve the diverse student population of the 21st century" (Education Trust, 1997, p. 1).

Targeting Underachieving Students

An article publicizing the seemingly laudable initiative by the Education Trust (Guerra, 1998) set off a firestorm of debate, primarily through CESNET (the Internet listserv for counselor educators). Fueling the debate was the Education Trust's (1997) criticism of the way school counselors were being trained. According to the organization, current programs did not place the academic preparation of all students at the center of the counselor's responsibilities; there was a lack of connection between the way counselors were trained and the services they would need to provide; school counselors were being trained in isolation from other school personnel, a practice that does not promote the concept of school counselor as collaborator; school counselors in training took a core of generic counseling courses, which did not provide them with competencies specific to the school setting; and school counselors were trained primarily through a mental health focus.

Although debate over the role of the school counselor was nothing new, the initiative did delineate the controversy between those who advocate for a mental health model of training and those who favor training to improve the academic preparation of all students. Proponents of the mental health model pointed to, among other things, increased violence in schools, a rising suicide rate among adolescents, and an overwhelming number of child abuse cases—all of which made training in issues of mental health critical. The other side argued that with individual counselor caseloads across the nation of 300 to 500 students, it was impossible for school counselors to provide ongoing mental health counseling. Students in need of mental health services should be referred for long-term counseling in the community; and school counselors should be advocating for students who are underachieving. A major part of the problem, according to the Education Trust, was that school counseling students were being trained in universities by professors who had little or no experience in schools and so taught only from the familiar focus of mental health counseling. In response, one counseling professor compared the Education Trust to a health insurance company that is allowed to dictate patients' treatment because it is paying for it, never mind that it does not have the expertise to make health care decisions.[7]

Interestingly, the proponents of TSCI made no mention of comprehensive developmental guidance programs, although initiative and programs shared certain concerns. For example, both advocated a programmatic approach to school counseling; both connected the function of the school counselor to the main function of the school—education and higher achievement; both minimized the mental health role of the school counselor; and both emphasized the collaborative role of the school counselor. But two key aspects of the initiative differentiated it from developmental guidance. First, the Education Trust did not want to service all students equally; it focused on students who were underachieving. Second, the Education Trust expanded the role of the school counselor to include examination and criticism of systemic forces that prevent some students from achieving to their potential. Ultimately, then, the initiative placed an emphasis on remediation, albeit academic remediation, by having school counselors access whatever resources are necessary to help underachieving children and by working toward changing systems that privilege some students and disadvantage others.

The racial and cultural implications of TSCI were important. African American, Latino, and Native American students continue to lag far behind their White and Asian American peers on many educational measures (College Board, 1999). For example, these three groups make up nearly 33 percent of the under-18 population in the United States (U.S. Bureau of the Census, 2001a); but in academic year

---

[7]The remark was sent across the CESNET listserv on February 17, 1998.

1999–2000, they earned less than 16 percent of the bachelor's degrees awarded in this country.[8] The need to deal with the underachievement of African American, Latino, and Native American youngsters is made more urgent by Census Bureau projections that these three groups will comprise 40 percent of the school-age population by 2030. In other words, if the educational achievement gap is not closed for African Americans, Latinos, and Native Americans, an extraordinarily high percentage of this country's youth will not be prepared to meet the increasingly complex demands of the workplace. The practical consequences are that many young people from these three groups will continue to work in low-paying service jobs and that U.S. companies will have increasing difficulty finding qualified workers. In the absence of academic achievement, access to postsecondary education and, consequently, to high-paying jobs is severely limited.

Traditionally, school counselors acted as gatekeepers, placing some students on the college track and others on remedial or vocational tracks. Underlying the Education Trust initiative was the belief that school counselors trained in areas of learning, cognitive development, and collaboration would be able to function not as gatekeepers, but as advocates, promoting higher achievement for those most at risk in our schools.

The Grants at Work

Six universities received grant money from the Education Trust as part of a six-year initiative.[9] In the fall of 2001, the Center for Applied Research and Educational Improvement (CAREI) issued a report on the early findings from the participating universities (Seashore, Jones, & Seppanen, 2001). Among the changes made by the grant recipients to their school counselor training programs were the following:

- New recruitment efforts aimed at increasing the percentage of minority and male students
- New criteria and admission processes for students willing to work with at-risk populations
- A new curriculum that combines courses in multiculturalism, social advocacy, technology, and data analysis, and that makes use of early field experiences
- The creation of partnerships with local K–12 school districts to provide field experiences consonant with the goals of the TSCI

The six institutions have achieved various levels of success in implementing these changes. Although a final evaluation of the initiative has yet to be published, the Education Trust's strong commitment to underachieving students and the most money ever donated privately to school counselor training programs give the TSCI a significant place in the history of school counseling.

---

[8] In the same period, Whites (45 percent of the under-18 population) earned 75 percent of the bachelor's degrees awarded; and Asian Americans (3 percent) earned almost 7 percent.

[9] California State University, Northridge; Indiana State University; the Ohio State University; the State University of West Georgia; the University of Georgia; and the University of North Florida.

THE ASCA NATIONAL MODEL: A FRAMEWORK FOR SCHOOL COUNSELING PROGRAMS

In March 2002, ASCA's governing board approved the development of a national model for school counseling programs. The project responds to what ASCA continues to see as six fundamental problems in those programs (P. J. Hart & Jacobi, 1992):

- Lack of a basic philosophy
- Poor integration of the school counseling program in the overall mission of the school
- Insufficient student access
- Inadequate guidance for some students (especially minority students)
- Lack of counselor accountability
- The failure to utilize other resources

In addition, ASCA has raised a concern about the number of noncounseling responsibilities—for example, developing a master schedule, coordinating tests, covering classrooms or detention halls, discipline, and clerical responsibilities—school counselors are expected to undertake (Hatch, Kuranz, & Myrick, 2002).

In June 2001, ASCA sponsored a national summit to begin to develop a national model. Using the national standards as a framework, attendees at the meeting outlined the major elements of the model (Table 1.4). The national model reflects components of comprehensive developmental guidance programs (especially

TABLE 1.4 ELEMENTS OF THE ASCA NATIONAL MODEL FOR SCHOOL COUNSELING PROGRAMS

Foundation	Every school counseling program should be based on a set of beliefs, a philosophy, the three domains (academic, career, personal-social), and the national standards for school counseling programs.
Delivery system	Every school counseling program should have a delivery system made up of the guidance curriculum, individual planning, response services, and system support.
Management system	Every school counseling program should have a management system that specifies the counselor's responsibilities, collects and analyzes data for monitoring students and closing the achievement gap between white students and students of color, defines action plans to achieve wanted outcomes, and allocates time to be spent on each area of the delivery system.
Accountability	Every school counseling program should report the results of projects carried out, evaluate the school counselor's performance, have an advisory council to review results and make recommendations, and conduct a program audit to ensure that the program is aligned with the national model.

SOURCE: Adapted from Bowers and Hatch (2002).

Gysbers and Henderson's model), TSCI, and, perhaps most important, the trend toward results-based, data-driven counseling programs. It was expected to serve as a template for counselors to adapt to local needs and political conditions (ASCA, 2001).

In 2003, after the states and national leaders had reviewed and commented on the final draft, ASCA published the model and began a nationwide effort to implement it.

HISTORICAL MANDATE: ETHICAL AND LEGAL PRACTICES

The work school counselors do is governed by ethical codes and laws that in large part evolve from court cases. Ethical and legal practices among school counselors can be challenging, not only because counselees are minors, but also because counseling involves a number of other constituencies—parents, teachers, and school and district administrators (Stone, 2002). When the needs of these constituencies conflict, school counselors are faced with ethical and legal dilemmas. In later chapters we include a section on ethical and legal issues relevant to the chapter content. Here we present an overview of ethical principles and codes.

Ethical Principles

Ethical principles are the underpinning of ethical codes. In developing its ethical codes, the counseling profession relied on five ethical principles:

- *Autonomy* refers to the client's right to self-determination. Counselors respect the right of clients to make their own decisions without interference from or dependence on the counselor. Although they guide and facilitate clients' decision making, counselors understand that in the end, clients are free to do as they choose.
- *Beneficence* refers to counselors' obligation to do good for their clients. Counselors have an ethical responsibility to enhance the well-being of their clients, to help them gain something positive from counseling.
- *Nonmaleficence* refers to the ethical obligation to do no harm to clients or others.
- *Justice* is the ethical principle that obliges counselors to provide equal and fair access and treatment to all students.
- *Fidelity* demands that counselors be honest and truthful, avoid any kind of deception or exploitation, and honor their commitments.

Ethical principles do not define behavior; they are the basis for behavior. Ethical principles can be in conflict with one another. Obviously, a counselor must limit autonomy when students' actions might cause harm to themselves or others. Ethical dilemmas arise when two or more ethical principles conflict with one another and there is no clear best course of action. At this point, counselors must consult with their peers and supervisors to arrive at the best practice in a given situation.

Ethical Codes: Standards of Conduct

Professional and credentialing organizations typically issue ethical codes, or standards of conduct, to suggest appropriate conduct, to provide a mechanism for accountability, and to improve professional practice (Herlihy & Corey, 1996). School counselors who are members of both ASCA and ACA, who are certified by the National Board of Certified Counselors, and who are licensed by a state find themselves under the guidance of four sets of ethical standards (Remley & Huey, 2002). Fortunately, there is a good deal of similarity among the various standards. In this book we rely primarily on ASCA's *Ethical Standards for School Counselors* (1998) because these standards specifically address school counseling (see Appendix B). The eight sections of the code are built around putting "the counselee's best interests first, treating each student as an individual and with respect, involving parents as appropriate, maintaining one's expertise through ongoing professional development and learning, and behaving professionally and ethically" (Linde, 2003, p. 43).

There are times when ethical standards conflict with state laws. Laws tend to be more specific than standards of conduct: They prescribe how professionals should behave in certain situations and what the penalties are for failing to comply. Most counselors find it easier to obey the law unless obeying the law would harm a client. As you move through the rest of this book, you will find many examples of situations in which the ASCA standards can help determine a course of action. Again, certain situations—usually a function of the counselee's being a minor— are less clear than others.

WHERE DO WE GO FROM HERE?

It is an exciting time to be a school counselor. The field has a rich tradition of helping at-risk youngsters; and contemporary theories have extended the counselor's reach to all students. Those theories also encourage school counselors to develop programs and to lead. Fortunately, published materials are available to help them plan and create programs (see, for example, Gysbers & Henderson, 2000; and Van-Zandt & Hayslip, 2001). The national standards and the national model are also important guides for helping school counselors develop programs. This book does not replicate these outstanding efforts. Instead it offers school counselors in training and in the field material they need to implement the national standards: material to help school counselors work with individuals, small groups, and large groups (Chapter 2); consult (Chapter 3); use data to evaluate their programs (Chapter 4); and perform career guidance and development (Chapter 5). In addition, there is material here on multiculturalism (Chapter 6) and a number of personal and social challenges facing students today: disabilities (Chapter 7), separation and loss (Chapter 8), suicide (Chapter 9), sex-related issues (Chapter 10), substance abuse (Chapter 11), violence (Chapter 12), and child maltreatment (Chapter 13). Our focus here is on topics essential to school counseling practice, or, as one reviewer noted, "the meat to cover the bones."

School counselors are a unique group. They understand the power of relationships, that how a child feels with a school staffer is the greatest determinant of change. Few children remember teachers for the content of their classes. Instead they remember how they felt with a particular teacher—motivated, respected, encouraged, affirmed, or special. School counselors understand that regardless of whether they are teaching a guidance lesson or counseling one on one, their ability to establish trusting, nurturing relationships with their students is key to effecting change. In short, counselors must be motivated enough to do all that it takes to help all of their students, humble enough to know they can't do it all, and sensitive enough to reach out to those most at risk for not making dreams a reality.

Questions for Discussion

1. Make a list of the things you would like to accomplish as a school counselor. Now prioritize your list. Suppose you only had time for half of the items. Which activities would you give up? Which would you be unwilling to give up?
2. Contemporary theory suggests that school counseling should be a comprehensive program of planned activities for all children. Some argue that a broad program is very hard to implement because school counselors are pulled in so many directions—by crises, by administrative responsibilities, by paperwork. Do you think a broad program is possible? Do you think there is merit to comprehensive programs?
3. What is your opinion of the Education Trust initiative? Do you think school counselors should target youngsters who underachieve, many of whom happen to be children of color? How do you feel about school counselors' advocating for change so that schools can educate all children, of whatever race?
4. What do you think about accountability? Do you think school counselors should be held accountable in the same way that teachers are? Why or why not? Do you think the national standards are an appropriate tool for increasing the accountability of school counselors? Explain your answer.

Suggested Internet Sites

www.schoolcounselor.org

The official Web site of the American School Counselor Association contains timely resources for school counselors as well as recent developments in the field.

www.counseling.org

The official Web site of the American Counseling Association. Provided are resources and publications. The site also includes a link to the Career Center, which helps members with their job searches.

www.edtrust.org

The official Web site of the Education Trust contains significant information about the TSCI and other programs the organization sponsors to promote student achievement.

COUNSELING SERVICES IN SCHOOLS

School counselors organize their programs around four basic interventions: individual counseling, small-group counseling, large-group guidance, and consultation. In this chapter we discuss the first three interventions; in Chapter 3 we examine consultation.

> Counseling is a confidential relationship which the counselor conducts with students individually and in small groups to help them resolve their problems and developmental concerns. (ASCA, 1999a, p. 1)

INDIVIDUAL COUNSELING

In their training, school counselors take courses in theories and techniques of counseling. But often these courses target a broad group of students, not just school counselors in training. At times it can be difficult to adapt general theories and techniques to the school setting. Here we describe several therapies that are especially useful for counseling individual students. A caution, though: The material here only summarizes the theories. Before implementing any of these techniques, read the sources cited for details.

Person-Centered Counseling

Carl Rogers (1959) had little regard for testing, diagnosis, and intervention techniques. The role of the counselor, he insisted, is to create a therapeutic relationship in which clients can grow and develop through self-exploration. To create that kind of relationship, Rogers argued, the counselor must have three characteristics: congruence, unconditional positive regard, and empathic understanding. Rogers's commitment to nonintervention makes person-centered theory impractical in the school setting today; but the core characteristics he identified are still very important, especially in dealing with children.

Congruence For Rogers, *congruence* meant "genuineness" and "focus," being present in both thought and feeling. Anyone who has worked in a school knows how difficult it can be to stay focused in the midst of distractions. But school counselors must communicate to their students that during a counseling session, the student is the center of the counselor's attention, that there is nowhere else the counselor wants to be. This attention can have a powerful effect on youngsters, especially on children who for one reason or another feel that they are not important.

> *I used to employ a simple technique to communicate congruence to a child in my school office for counseling. Often the phone would ring during the counseling session, and the student would either gesture or suggest that I answer the phone. My response: "You are more important than the phone right now. Whoever it is can call back or leave a message." It was always gratifying to see the look in a child's eye on hearing, perhaps for the first time, how important he or she really is.*

When working one on one with a student, school counselors must create a quiet space in which they can be truly present. Other tasks, clerical and nonclerical, must be set aside. School counselors, simply by being in a state of congruence, can contribute to a child's positive sense of self.

Unconditional Positive Regard By *unconditional positive regard*, Rogers meant "deep and genuine caring for the client." To create an environment in which a child feels secure, school counselors cannot be judgmental, and they cannot personalize the child's successes or failures. Suppose, for example, that a student with behavioral problems is referred to the school counselor. Counseling begins, and the student continues to misbehave. A counselor who has unconditional positive regard for the student does not allow the problem behavior to affect his or her acceptance of the student. Students expect counselors to reprimand them and to be disappointed in them if they continue to get into trouble: that is their experience of authority figures in school. For counselors, this is a wonderful opportunity to act outside the box, to communicate unconditional acceptance and so the student's worth. This doesn't mean that the counselor approves of the bad behavior; it means that the counselor is eager to continue seeing the student despite the unacceptable behavior.

> *I worked alongside a school counselor who every once in a while could be heard yelling at a student. When I investigated, I discovered that the students he yelled at were youngsters whom the principal had reported were in trouble. This counselor was insecure and was personalizing the students' problems—if a student was in trouble, it meant the counselor had failed—which led him to react by disciplining the students. A counselor with unconditional positive regard might have responded like this: "Joe, I don't approve of your fighting, but I very much want to meet with you and see if we can work on this problem behavior together."*

Deep and genuine caring raises the issue of boundaries. Counselors often make one of two mistakes: caring too little or caring too much. Obviously counselors who don't care enough should ask themselves why they are working as school counselors: Caring is essential to effective counseling. The problems with caring too much are more subtle. School counselors are responsible for hundreds of students, many of whom have been victimized in one way or another. Counselors who hold themselves responsible for their students or carry around their students' problems 24 hours a day, 7 days a week, almost inevitably burn out. Second, caring too much skews the limits of the counselor's role. A school counselor's job is to balance caring with respect for each student's autonomy and an understanding of the limited role the counselor plays in light of other social and environmental influences. As a counselor friend once told me, "Good counselors must deeply care and not care at the same time."

Empathic Understanding   The phrase *empathic understanding* implies that empathy is a particular form of understanding. Rogers described *empathy* as feeling "as if one were the other person" (1959, p. 210). Empathy can be communicated nonverbally, with a warm smile or a concerned facial expression; but most counselors communicate empathy verbally. The danger here is saying something superficial, something like "I understand how you feel." A moment of deep and genuine empathy calls for an immediacy response, for the school counselor to share what he or she is feeling that very moment. For example, a counselor might say, "Right now, having listened to all that you've been through, I'm feeling very sad."

Empathic understanding is particularly important in working with children. Few adults understand or appreciate children's feelings. Yet the ability to sense, hear, and validate a child's feelings can transform a relationship. What children commonly hear is "Don't feel that way." What they should be hearing is "I sense that you are very _____ [identify the feeling]; if I were in your situation, I would feel the same way." Children are helped and encouraged by knowing that what they are feeling is okay.

Congruence, unconditional positive regard, and empathic understanding may not be sufficient by themselves to build a working alliance with schoolchildren; but they are essential to that alliance. They also serve as an antidote to the negative responses of other adults at home and in school, to the kinds of responses far too many troubled students have come to expect.

Adlerian School Counseling

The counseling theory of Alfred Adler has had enormous influence on schools in the last quarter century. Central to Adler's theory is the concept of social interest. *Social interest* is a "person's ability to interact in a cooperative way with people that leads to a healthy society" (Pryor & Tollerud, 1999, p. 299). Social interest yields a sense of belonging, and that is the mark of a healthy personality. Adler believed that schools are the primary place where children develop and manifest social interest.

According to Adler, all behavior, even the most negative, has a purpose. In the Adlerian world, negative behaviors are the product of feeling disconnected, the absence of belonging. Adler encouraged teachers and counselors, before reacting to a student's negative behavior, to ask themselves the purpose of the behavior and then to respond accordingly. He believed that if children choose their behaviors to meet their needs, then they can choose alternate behaviors that meet their needs in a less harmful way.

Dinkmeyer and Dinkmeyer (1976) used Adler's behavior-is-chosen principle to help educators deal more "democratically" with students by negotiating new and different behaviors. They argued that it does little good to force a child with behavioral problems to adopt a new behavior, that it is better to allow the child to experience the logical consequences of the behavior and then to negotiate other behaviors that are better suited to meeting the child's needs. The key here is negotiating with the child.

Dreikurs and Soltz (1990) identified four reasons that youngsters misbehave: to get attention, to get power, to take revenge, and to compensate for feelings of inadequacy. Students who want attention behave in ways that distract both teacher and classmates. Power-seeking behaviors are confrontational and disruptive; they usually are manifested through physical and verbal tantrums. Students seeking revenge engage in physical and psychological attacks to hurt others. And students who are compensating for feelings of inadequacy usually display avoidance-of-failure behaviors like frustration tantrums and procrastination.

To recognize the goals of misbehavior, school counselors must pay particular attention to the feelings provoked by the problem behavior. Attention-seeking behavior usually generates feelings of annoyance; power-seeking behavior, the need to control the situation. Revenge-seeking behaviors can produce fear; and avoidance-of-failure behavior can produce feelings of sympathy.

In responding to negative behavior, the first step is to analyze the purpose of the behavior; the second is to react appropriately. For example, when a student acts out to get attention, the teacher or counselor should try to ignore the behavior, giving the child attention only when his or her behavior is more appropriate. By doing so, the adult frustrates the negative behavior (attention is denied) and recognizes the more appropriate behavior (attention is given).

Children who use negative behavior to get power can easily seduce educators into a power struggle that may never end. Instead, Dreikurs and Cassel (1990) recommended that adults suggest ways in which children can use power more appropriately.

> *"Right now I feel that you and I are struggling over whether it's going to be your way or my way. It feels to me like you want some control, which is perfectly okay. But I do have to manage this class. So I would like to have you be the class monitor for today. How does that sound?"*

This intervention recognizes and accepts the purpose of the behavior but tries to redirect the student's need for power into a productive situation.

The third goal of problem behavior, revenge, is very serious because schoolchildren can be vicious and can cause injury. To negotiate this behavior, the adult must set rules in place and then enforce them (Dreikurs & Cassel, 1990). That is, students must suffer the consequences of their actions. The challenge here for counselors and teachers is following through on the punishment while at the same time encouraging the students to behave differently.

Finally, some children misbehave to compensate for feelings of inadequacy, inferiority, or hopelessness. These children can be withdrawn, depressed, and very passive. The necessary response here is to give them lots of encouragement and a sense of belonging by trying to engage them in a group or activity that they value and that will increase their self-esteem.

Table 2.1 summarizes the characteristics and origins of each type of behavior, principles for prevention, and intervention strategies. From the Adlerian perspective, it is important to realize that all of these behaviors stem from undeveloped social interest, a sense of disconnectedness. It is crucial, then, that teachers and counselors choose their interventions by asking, "What will help this child gain a sense of belonging?"

The school can be an invaluable source of social interest. Beyond the concern and intervention of counselors and teachers, the school, by offering different activities, functions as a kind of laboratory in which children can experiment with and eventually gain a sense of connectedness. Of course most children's first experience of belonging is in the family. But for those children whose families frustrate the sense of belonging, the school and the school counselor can play a pivotal role in helping them develop social interest through participation in various forms of group activities—among them clubs, sports, and group counseling.

Reality Therapy

The founder of reality therapy is William Glasser (1965, 1989, 1998, 2000). Like Adler's theory, Glasser's theory has proved particularly useful for school counseling. In fact, the two theories are similar in many ways (Corey, 2001; Nystul, 1995; Whitehouse, 1984).

Like Adler, Glasser believed that all behavior is purposeful. That purpose, Glasser claimed, is to satisfy one of five basic needs: belonging, power, freedom, fun, and survival. Glasser distinguished between wants and needs: *wants* are the individual's unique way of satisfying *needs*. When needs are met, the individual feels good and successful, and has a sense of self-worth; when needs are not met, the individual feels pain and dissatisfaction. In working with a new client, reality therapists make a basic assumption: that the client's particular way of trying to meet his or her needs is not working. The goal of counseling is to help clients find more effective ways to meet their needs. This is possible because all behavior is chosen and can be controlled.

Choice Theory   Choice theory is a foundation of reality therapy. Choice theory is based upon the premise that human beings are born with genetically encoded needs (survival, love and belonging, power, freedom, and fun), and individuals are self determining in that they choose the ways to meet these needs (Corey, 2001; Gladding, 2001). Therefore every behavior, even the most mentally disturbed, is a choice. Because of this theory, Glasser insists that clients express their symptoms in the active voice. For example, instead of "I'm depressed," the client should say

TABLE 2.1   RECOGNIZING AND RESPONDING TO THE GOALS OF MISBEHAVIOR

Characteristics	Behaviors			
	Attention Seeking	**Power Seeking**	**Revenge Seeking**	**Avoidance of Failure**
Active characteristics	Student behaves in ways that distract teacher and classmates.	Temper tantrums: Student is disruptive and confrontational.	Physical and psychological attacks on teacher or classmates.	Frustration tantrums: Student loses control when the pressure to succeed becomes too much.
Passive characteristics	Student exhibits one-pea-at-a-time behavior, operating on slow, slower, slowest speeds.	Quiet noncompliance: Student does his or her own thing, yet often is pleasant and even agreeable.	Student is sullen and withdrawn, and refuses overtures of friendship.	Student procrastinates, fails to complete projects, develops temporary incapacity, or assumes behaviors that resemble a learning disability.
Origins of behavior	Parents and teachers who tend to pay more attention to misbehavior than to appropriate behavior. Failure to teach student how to ask for attention appropriately. Lack of sufficient personal attention.	Changes in society that stress equality in relationships rather than dominant-submissive roles. Society's exaltation of the individual and of achieving personal power.	A reflection of increasing violence in society. Media role models who solve conflicts by force.	Unreasonable expectations of parents and teachers. Student's perfectionism. Star mentality. Emphasis on competition in the classroom.
Silver lining	Student wants a relationship with the teacher and classmates.	Student exhibits leadership potential, assertiveness, and independent thinking.	Student shows a spark of life by trying to protect self from further hurt.	Student may want to succeed if he or she can be sure of not making mistakes and of achieving some status. For some severely discouraged students, there is no silver lining.
Principles of prevention	Give lots of attention for appropriate behavior. Teach student to ask for extra attention when needed.	Avoid and defuse direct confrontations. Grant student legitimate power.	Build caring relationship with student. Teach student to express hurt and hostility appropriately, and ask student to talk to teacher or counselor when student is upset.	Encourage student to change self-perception from "I can't" to "I can." Help end student's social isolation by drawing student into congenial relationships with teacher or counselor and with other students.
Intervention strategies	Minimize the attention. Legitimize the behavior. Do the unexpected. Distract the student. Notice appropriate behavior.	Make a graceful exit. Use time-out. Set the consequences.	Make a graceful exit. Use time-out. Set the consequences.	Modify instructional methods. Provide tutoring. Teach positive self-talk. Make mistakes okay. Build confidence. Focus on past success. Make learning tangible. Recognize achievement.

SOURCE: Adapted from "Four Goals of Misbehavior" from *Cooperative Discipline in the Classroom: A Teacher's Guide to Cooperative Discipline*, pp. 154–155, by Linda Alpert. Copyright 1989 American Guidance Service, Inc., 4201 Woodland Road, Circle Pines, MN 55014-1796. Adapted with permission of publisher. All rights reserved. www.agsnet.com

"I'm depressing" or "I'm choosing to depress"; and instead of "I'm angry," the client should say "I'm angering" or "I'm choosing to anger." This can be especially challenging for school-aged children, who are fond of presenting themselves as victims: "He made me fight; he started it." Glasser would relentlessly confront the students with the fact that it was still their choice to fight, that they could have chosen another behavior to meet the same need for power or survival. For example, they could have walked away, refusing to allow their behavior to be dictated by someone else.

> "Mike [the 'victim'], you must make Jerry [the 'victimizer'] feel really good about himself because he knows he can control you. He knows he can say or do a certain thing, and you are going to respond on cue. When he makes a joke about your family, he knows you're going to get angry and try to hit him, which eventually leads to your getting into trouble. And Jerry is probably laughing all the way home because he knows he can control you like a puppet on a string. He's got your number."

This intervention works because it reframes the child's need for control and power.

The idea that behavior—no matter how pathological—is always a choice is a radical rejection of the medical-genetic model. It also means that the individual can choose to change a problem behavior (Corey, 2001). For change to take place, two conditions must be present: First, the individual must recognize that the current behavior is not working, that it is not satisfying a need. Second, the individual must believe that he or she can choose another behavior.

The Counseling Process   Glasser's counseling process involves four steps: (1) wants, (2) direction and doing, (3) evaluation, and (4) planning. (He used the acronym *WDEP*.) The first step is exploring a client's *wants* by simply asking, "What is it you really want?" Wants can be related to self, to family and friends, or to work. In the second step—*direction and doing*—the counselor explores what the client has done in the past, is doing now, and plans to do tomorrow to get what he or she wants. The third step entails *evaluation*, working with the client to determine whether the present behavior is effective: Does it get the client what he or she wants?

> I will never forget the father of a family I was treating. He walked into the first family counseling session with a belt in his hand. When I asked why he was carrying a belt, he told me he used it to get his son to behave properly. I wanted to talk to him about child abuse; instead I simply asked, "Is it working?" When the father responded with a firm no, I casually suggested, "Then why don't we explore some other ways you can help your son with his behavior?"

The point: However provoking the behavior, counselors should always remember to ask, "Is it helping? How is it helping?"

The last step in the therapeutic process is *planning*. Once a client admits to wanting to change a behavior, counselor and client work together to formulate a plan of action—new ways of behaving that should be more effective at getting the client what he or she wants—and then to carry it out. According to Glasser, a good plan is simple, attainable, measurable, and immediate, and one to which the client is committed.

It is very important for school counselors to follow students through the fourth step, to create opportunities for them to try out their new behavior, and to help them make necessary adjustments (Nystul, 1995).

> *Michael was constantly doing battle with his younger brother, Kevin. When Kevin bothered him, Michael would react by screaming at or hitting Kevin, which inevitably landed him in trouble with his parents. Tired of getting punished, Michael realized he needed a new way to get Kevin to stop pestering him. When Michael understood that he was choosing to hit his brother, he also understood that he could choose another behavior. In our sessions together we practiced two new behaviors: as soon as Kevin began to bother him, Michael would choose to ask him to stop. If that didn't work, he would choose to call his mother for help resolving the conflict. Michael's mother was brought into a session to tell her about the intervention and to elicit her cooperation in practicing the new behaviors at home. With practice, Michael soon was choosing the new behaviors.*

The appeal of reality therapy rests primarily on the directness of the approach and the easy-to-follow therapeutic process. The key to its success is motivating students to change by helping them see first that their behavior is not getting them what they want and second that they can choose to behave differently. The challenge comes when students fail to recognize the costs of behaving badly.

> *I worked in an extremely difficult school in the inner city. There came a point when suspensions for poor behavior simply didn't work. Many of the kids didn't want to be in school and were more than happy to get suspended. What they didn't understand was the cost, the loss of valuable education time. Our solution was in-school suspensions: students who were on suspension had to report to school, where they would serve out their suspension in one room the entire day. Because in-school suspension was much less agreeable than at-home suspension, it was more successful in curtailing problem behaviors.*

When students, with or without counselor facilitation, understand that their behavior is causing them problems, reality therapy can be an effective and efficient way of counseling in the school setting.

Cognitive Behavioral Therapies

People are disturbed not by things but by the view which they take of them.

Epictetus

Cognitive behavioral therapies (CBTs) include Albert Ellis's (1995) rational emotive behavior therapy (REBT), Aaron Beck's (1963, 1993) cognitive therapy, and Donald Meichenbaum's (1977, 1986) cognitive behavioral modification (CBM). All CBTs share two fundamental beliefs: first, that all behavior and feeling are mediated primarily through thought; and second, that active and strategic interventions can modify thought. The CBTs are important to school counseling because they emphasize that how individuals think about themselves and their experiences determines how they feel about themselves, and ultimately how they behave.

Rational Emotive Behavior Therapy   Ellis based REBT on his belief that human beings are self-talking, self-evaluating, and self-sustaining (Corey, 2001). He suggested that everyday life presents us with an ongoing set of experiences, and that we define those experiences by what we tell ourselves about them.

For example, suppose you were expecting an A on a test and got a C. You could have one of two reactions: You could beat yourself up, put yourself down, question your intelligence, and tell yourself that you're not good enough to get an A, that everybody is smarter than you are. All of this self-talk would leave you feeling down and not very good about yourself; it could even leave you unwilling to study for the next test. Or you could tell yourself that you studied hard and deserved an A; that you're still bright and a good student; and that you feel sorry for a professor who doesn't have the ability to evaluate her students accurately! This kind of self-talk would place the problem squarely on the professor's shoulders; and it would leave you feeling good about yourself and motivated to keep studying and perhaps to go and speak with the professor about your grade.

The experience (getting a C when you were expecting an A) triggers a cognitive reaction (you failed or the professor failed), which in turn triggers emotional and behavioral reactions to the event (depression and lack of motivation, or satisfaction and renewed motivation).

According to Ellis, when the cognitive response, or belief, is not rational, the emotional reaction is likely to be depression or anxiety. Irrational beliefs are the result of absolutist, or what Ellis called *mustabatory*, thinking. When people use the words *must, have to,* and *should* in their self-talk, they are setting the stage for depression in reaction to the event and overwhelming anxiety in anticipation of the next event.

If you say, "I absolutely must get an A on this test or else," you make yourself so nervous that you probably won't do well on the test. More rational thinking would be something like this: "It would be nice [helpful? rewarding?] to get an A; but if I don't get an A, it won't be the end of the world. In fact, whether my grade is an A or a B might help me decide if this subject is something I want to major in or not." The second tack substitutes rational thinking for irrational thinking, and lessens your anxiety and depression over an expected result.

The cognitive therapist intervenes at the level of cognition, to change the client's cognitive responses to events. Ellis referred to the process as *disputation:* the counselor disputes the client to get the client to reveal his or her irrational thinking. Beck (1963, 1993) described a less confrontational approach—reflective questioning to help clients recognize their cognitive misconceptions.

According to Ellis, once a client recognizes a cognitive distortion, the counselor can help change the response through any number of behavioral techniques:

- Daily monitoring of absolutist thoughts and of *must, have to,* and *should* in one's self-talk
- Replacing *I should*s with *I want to*s or *I'd rather*s

- Imagining oneself thinking rationally, and feeling and behaving well
- Forcing oneself to engage in behaviors that others might find odd or funny

There's a well-known anecdote about Ellis using the last technique himself. To get over his fear of rejection, he supposedly forced himself to walk into Central Park with the goal of asking 100 women to go out with him.

Cognitive Behavioral Therapies in the School   CBTs can be particularly helpful for children who face certain issues at home and in school. For example, many schoolchildren learn negative self-talk from their experience of parents, teachers, and friends. When a student who feels rejected by adults and peers comes to counseling, it is very important for the counselor to ask: "What are you telling yourself right now?"

> *Kristin came to my office one day in tears. Her friend Laura had just said that she didn't want to be friends anymore. I immediately asked Kristin, "What are you telling yourself right now?" I knew she was feeling depressed because she probably was saying to herself that she wasn't worthy of being Laura's or anyone else's friend. When she admitted that was the case, I asked about other relationships in her life. She immediately described a positive relationship with another friend. That allowed me to reframe the problem for her, making it Laura's problem: "I actually feel sorry for Laura. She has poor judgment and has lost a wonderful friend."*

A negative view of self can translate into a negative interpretation of all experience and a negative vision of the future. Beck (1963) called this the *cognitive triad of depression.* If a child admits to having other positive relationships in his or her life, that knowledge can be used to dispute the irrational thinking, the feeling of worthlessness. Another approach I might have used with Kristin was to talk with her about her other friends and then to acknowledge that the loss of Laura's friendship was sad but certainly not the end of the world, and to think it was would be irrational.

These therapies are also effective for dealing with performance anxiety, another common problem in the school environment. Research has established a curvilinear relationship between performance and anxiety: performance tends to increase with anxiety up to a certain point, but when anxiety becomes too high performance begins to falter (Ashcraft & Kirk, 2001; Humara, 1999). School counselors should be especially alert to performance anxiety among students who are applying to college. The competition for admission into the best schools is fierce. In 1995, New York University received 10,000 applications for a freshman class of about 3,000; in 2000, NYU received 35,000 applications for the same number of freshman seats. Also a source of performance anxiety among students is the standards testing more and more states are requiring at different grade levels to determine promotion, retention, and summer school attendance.

CBTs can help lower students' anxiety to a level where it enhances, not impedes, performance. School counselors should encourage students to do the best they can; at the same time, they should challenge students' irrational thinking by asking: "What would happen if you didn't get into _____ University?" or

"Suppose you don't score 1400 on your SATs, what will happen?" Questions like these can start the disputation process and help students begin using more positive self-talk: "Yeah, if did get into _____ University, it would be nice; but if I don't, I could still go to _____ University, and that would be good too."

Solution-Oriented Therapy

A theoretical orientation, *solution-oriented therapy* (de Shazer 1985, 1988, 1991), has become very popular among school counselors primarily because of its simplicity and novel approach. According to J. J. Murphy (1994, 1997), key to solution-oriented therapy is uncovering and using exceptions. He described a five-step process:

1. *Eliciting.* Many clients, especially those who feel overwhelmed, present as though their problem exists with the same intensity all the time. But no problem is constant. The counselor's first task, then, is to elicit an exception: "When is the problem absent or less noticeable during the school day?" (Murphy, 1997, p. 60). If the client answers "Never," the counselor must challenge the student, insisting that there has to be a time when the problem is less noticeable: "In which classes do you not act out? In which subjects are you having less trouble?" This step ends when the students admits that there is an exception.

2. *Elaboration.* Once an exception is identified, the counselor must begin looking for its cause. For example, a student who is having behavioral problems in all of her classes except social studies should be asked: "How is your social studies class different from your other classes? What is responsible for the difference?" The questioning should continue until the counselor determines that the exception is a function of the teacher or the subject matter or where the student sits or whatever other variable is at work.

3. *Expanding.* Once the variable or variables responsible for the exception have been identified, the counselor must work with the client and others to expand the exception to other situations. If the student behaves better in social studies because the teacher does more small-group activities, the counselor should work with the student's other teachers on allowing her to do more work in small groups.

   > *I once treated a family with a male child who misbehaved constantly, at home and at school. It took some doing, but I finally elicited an exception: the only time the child did not misbehave was when he was helping his father work on the family car. The variables for this child seemed to be spending time with his father and working with his hands. I asked the family to expand the exception by planning other activities for the child and his father, especially activities that include some form of manual labor. I also spoke with the child's teachers, asking them to assign him manual chores to do in the classroom.*

4. *Evaluating.* Evaluation is critical to solution-oriented counseling, and goal setting is its most important component. Goals should be specific, small, and

meaningful (Murphy, 1997). A favorite method for setting goals in solution-oriented counseling is called *scaling*. The counselor asks the client to rate the problem situation on a scale of 1 to 10, with 1 being the very worst and 10 the very best. If the client rates the problem as, say, a 2, the counselor then asks, "What do you think a 3 or a 4 or a 5 would look like?" Scaling allows the client to set incremental goals, based on concrete behaviors, and to evaluate his or her progress continuously (Murphy, 1997). Specificity is key here. It is not enough for a student to say, "My problem will be solved when my behavior is better." The counselor must get the student to describe what the behavior is going to look like or how the student is going to know that the behavior is a 5 or a 6 or a 7 on the scale. The focus is always on progress, and progress is measured by small but concrete changes in behavior.

Another method for establishing goals and focusing on solutions is de Shazer's (1988) *miracle question*. The counselor asks the client: "If a miracle happened and your problem disappeared, how would life be different?" Variations are fine, too. For example, the question might start with "If you could wave a magic wand . . ." or "Suppose your problem suddenly vanished . . ."; and it might end with ". . . how could you tell?" ". . . how would others around you know?" or ". . . what would be different at school?" These kinds of questions help the client define the solution in real-life terms.

5. *Empowerment.* The final step is to help the client maintain change over time. Counseling shouldn't leave the student dependent; it should help the client assume ownership of this and future solutions. One form of empowerment involves practicing relapse prevention with the client. For example, the counselor might ask: "If you find yourself in a class where there is little group activity, how would you go about handling it?" It's important to leave the student with the understanding that reverting back to poor behavior isn't a solution, that he or she can anticipate a solution by asking the teacher for the opportunity to work in a group.

Solution-oriented therapy works well in the school setting. The model focuses on clients' resources, not liabilities; and it evaluates progress strictly in behavioral terms. Also important, the process moves quickly. (De Shazer called it *brief therapy.*) More often than not, problems that come to the school counselor's door are resolved in one or two sessions. Solution-oriented therapy allows school counselors to use limited time productively by helping students define and work on solutions to reduce, if not eradicate, problem behaviors.[1]

Counseling Young Children through Play

Man is perfectly human only when he plays.

Schiller

On November 29, 1999, President Clinton signed the Elementary School Counseling Demonstration Act into law, allocating $20 million for hiring new elementary school counselors. That funding, together with existing commitments by many

---

[1] We have just skimmed the surface of solution-oriented counseling. To learn more about it, read J. J. Murphy's "Solution-Focused Counseling in Middle and High Schools" (1997), an excellent source on the counseling and its applications for preteen and teen students.

states to elementary school counseling, is expected to increase counseling and guidance services for younger children.

For young children (and even for older less verbal children), play is the medium of self-expression. Maria Montessori referred to play as the work of children; and Gary Landreth (1993) explained how children, whose receptive language outpaces their expressive language, use play to communicate what is happening in their world. For elementary school counselors, the question is not whether play counseling should be used but how it should be used (Landreth, 1987). For younger children, play is a developmental necessity.[2]

Yet, despite the widely recognized importance of play in counseling children, a national survey of school counseling training programs found that only 3 percent require a course in play counseling, and just 9 percent offer a course in play counseling as an elective. And only 55 percent of the programs indicated that they offer "some" form of training in play counseling (Cerio, Taggart, & Costa, 1999).

The Various Uses of Play   Fred Rogers, of *Mr. Rogers' Neighborhood,* described how six different types of play can be used in counseling children (F. Rogers & Sharapan, 1993):

> *Making and building.* This kind of activity allows children to feel in control both of the self and of the world outside, and it gives them a sense of mastery. In counseling, children are allowed to make whatever they want.
>
> *Artwork.* Art is a medium through which children express their feelings. The concern here isn't the quality of the work; what matters is what the picture or piece of clay means to the child and how it affects the observer. It is extremely important for counselors to facilitate a child's talking about the work, the details and the interactions of the people or animals depicted. It is equally important for counselors to use their own reactions to the picture to empathize with what the child might be feeling. A picture that a counselor finds frightening may very well indicate deep-seated fears in the child.
>
> *Drama and fantasy.* Children enjoy dressing up and pretending to be other people. Counselors should pay particular attention to the roles that children adopt, especially family roles, and the relationships they play out with their parents and siblings. It is not unusual for children to act out anger toward a particular member of the family.
>
> *Mastery and superheroes.* Playing at being a superhero reflects "children's age-old need to imagine . . . being big and strong in a world where they may often feel little and vulnerable" (p. 8). Counselors can use this type

---

[2] Unfortunately, little empirical research has been done to determine the efficacy of play counseling. A recent study did find that six sessions of client-centered play therapy improved the self-efficacy scores of participants; there was no increase for the control group (Fall, Balvanz, Johnson, & Nelson, 1999). But the literature is sadly lacking research to support practitioners' anecdotal evidence of the effectiveness of play counseling.

of play to communicate a sense of safety, something that is especially important for children whose home life makes them feel insecure.

Toy guns. Many children like to play with toy guns for much the same reason that they like to pretend they are superheroes; it gives them a sense of power and control. Rogers and Sharapan noted that many adults are offended by children's playing with guns and the imagined killing and death. The school counselor must set aside that feeling and recognize the child's need for power and control that is being expressed through the play. At the same time, the counselor must make clear to the child that this is play, not real, and that bad things happen when it is real.

Problem solving. Children use play to both create and solve problems they encounter in their world. In play counseling, it is more effective to allow the child to develop and solve problems on his or her own than to give the child a problem to solve through play. It is important to keep in mind that the driving force behind satisfying play is the child's creativity; the counselor must be careful not to frustrate that creativity.

Client-Centered Play Therapy   There are several theoretical bases underlying play therapies. Client-centered play therapy is based on the principles of Carl Rogers. It was made popular by Virginia Axline (1964) and later Gary Landreth (1991). Today it appears to be the most widely used client-centered approach among elementary school counselors (Stewart, 1998; Watts, 1999).

The counseling gives children the freedom to explore and to expand their sense of self:

> Through the process of play therapy, the unfamiliar becomes familiar, and children express outwardly through play what has taken place inwardly. A major function of play in play therapy is the changing of what may be unmanageable in reality to manageable situations through symbolic representation, which provides children opportunities for learning to cope by engaging in self-directed exploration. (Landreth, 1993, p. 18)

Key to client-centered play therapy is the belief in children's innate capacity to grow, to move toward healthier psychological functioning. The counselor does not have to make things happen because what is necessary for a child's growth is already within (Landreth, 1993).

In 1947, Axline defined eight basic principles for therapeutic contact with children; in 1993, Landreth revised and extended them:

1. The play therapist is genuinely interested in the child and develops a warm and caring relationship.
2. The play therapist experiences unqualified acceptance of the child and does not wish that the child were different in some way.
3. The play therapist creates a feeling of safety and permissiveness in the relationship so the child feels free to explore and express him- or herself completely.

4. The play therapist is always sensitive to the child's feelings and gently reflects those feelings in such a manner that the child develops self-understanding.
5. The play therapist believes deeply in the child's capacity to act responsibly, unwaveringly respects the child's ability to solve personal problems, and allows the child to do so.
6. The play therapist trusts the child's inner direction, allows the child to lead in all areas of the relationship, and resists any urge to direct the child's play or conversation.
7. The play therapist appreciates the gradual nature of the therapeutic process and does not attempt to hurry the process.
8. The play therapist establishes only those therapeutic limits that help the child accept personal and appropriate relationship responsibility. (p. 20)

Most school counselors are drawn to the profession by their deep concern for children. In short order, bureaucratic pulls and scarce resources can make counselors forget why they chose to be school counselors. Client-centered play counseling, at least for elementary school counselors, offers the opportunity to exercise in a very real way their care and concern for children. Play is the language of children, and we are called to listen carefully to that language, to respect it, and to allow it to flourish.

Practical Considerations   There are a number of practical considerations in incorporating play into a school counseling program (Phillips & Mullen, 1999). The first is the *support of other staff members in the school,* especially administrators and teachers. Unfortunately, those who are not familiar with counseling might argue that play is a waste of time, that the counselor is simply having fun with the students. Landreth (1987) recommended that at the beginning of each school year, counselors hold an orientation during a faculty meeting to explain both the importance of and challenges in using play as part of the counseling program.

The second practical consideration is *a designated space appropriate for play counseling.* Even in schools where a lack of space is a serious problem, counselors should lobby for a space that is very different from the classroom, where kids can truly be themselves (Fall, 1994). Landreth (1991) described the ideal playroom as approximately 12 feet by 18 feet, big enough to allow a child (or several children) the freedom to move but small enough to keep the child (or children) relatively close to the counselor. The room should be private; it should have washable walls and floors, and should have or be close to a sink; and, ideally, it should be a distance from classrooms (play counseling can be noisy!) (Phillips & Mullen, 1999).

If a separate play space is not available and counselors choose to use all or part of their office, it is important to keep toys in a locked closet and to take them out only at the appropriate time. Itinerant counselors have to carry a bag of toys with them and set them out in an appropriate place when they arrive at a school.[3]

---

[3] In many school districts throughout the country, elementary school counselors are assigned to more than one school.

Although this can be inconvenient, it should not discourage itinerant counselors from incorporating play into their work.

The third consideration is *setting limits*. Because the playroom represents something so distinct from the classroom, some children, especially those who are angry or aggressive, may overreact to the setting and violate boundaries. Obviously limits need to be set so that children don't hurt themselves (or others). But Guerney (1983) suggests that limits should not be set until necessary and should never be set because of something a child says or feels. The goal is to allow the child to act out through play whatever is troubling him or her. By setting limits too soon, the counselor can frustrate that process.

Whatever boundaries the counselor sets should allow children to continue to act out their feelings through play:[4]

> CLIENT: *"I'm going to draw the outline of my hand on the wall."*
> COUNSELOR: *"The wall is not for drawing; the marker board is for drawing."*
>
> CLIENT: *"Let's play doctor. I want to take off your clothes."*
> COUNSELOR: *"I am not for taking off clothes; the doll is for taking off clothes."*
>
> *The client is really angry with you, and hits and kicks you.*
> COUNSELOR: *"I am not for hitting; Bobo [an inflatable clown] is for hitting."*
>
> CLIENT: *(Playing with a plastic dart gun.) "I'm going to take this home with me."*
> COUNSELOR: *"The gun is not for taking home. The drawing you did is for taking home."* Or, if the child insists: *"If you choose to take the gun home, you choose not to come back to the playroom."*

Some of these responses may seem strange, but they are all designed to set limits while encouraging the child to continue to play and act out conflicts. Feelings are always acceptable and appropriate; yet how they are expressed may require limit setting at times.

Finally, there is the matter of *supplies*. In play counseling, a variety of toys is more important than a large number of toys (Cerio, 1994). The type of toys needed has to do with theoretical orientation. For example, Landreth (1991) recommends three categories of toys: real-life toys, acting-out toys for releasing aggression, and toys for creative expression and emotional release. Adlerians would have five types of toys: family or nurturing toys (for example, dolls, a dollhouse, baby clothes, a bottle, pots and pans); scary toys (plastic snakes, rats, dragons, sharks, alligators); aggressive toys (a punching bag, plastic guns, rubber knives, toy soldiers, plastic handcuffs); expressive toys (crayons, markers, glue, Play-Doh, blunt scissors, tape); and pretend or fantasy toys (masks, a doctor kit, blocks and other building material, cars, trucks, puppets, and at least two telephones) (Kottman, 1995).

Toys to avoid include complex mechanical toys and toys that require an adult's help. These kinds of toys can hinder the child's autonomy and hurt the child's self-

---

[4]These examples are taken from Watts (1999).

concept (Landreth, 1993). All toys should be accessible to the child, and they should be arranged in the same position each week to establish a sense of familiarity and safety in the playroom (Landreth, 1991).

SMALL-GROUP COUNSELING

Group counseling, which involves a number of students working on shared tasks and developing supportive relationships in a group setting, is an efficient and positive way of dealing with students' developmental problems and situational concerns. By allowing individuals to develop insights into themselves and others, group counseling makes it possible for more people to achieve a healthier personal adjustment, handle the stresses of a rapidly changing technological and complex environment and learn to work and live with others (ASCA, 2002, p. 1).

Play is children's natural mode of self-expression, and groups are their natural environment. Much more disturbing than an adult who spends a lot of time alone is a child who appears isolated, withdrawn, and socially disconnected. Groups are a powerful milieu in the lives of all human beings but especially in the lives of children.

Despite the importance of small groups, some school counseling programs lack a small-group counseling component. In elementary and middle schools, counselors' own resistance to the work involved in forming and facilitating groups is the primary obstacle. In high schools, most objections come from teachers and have to do with scheduling: "Our students can't miss class on a regular basis." Yet many schools have overcome the scheduling problem. For example, one high school has its group meet on the same day but during a different period each week, so that the students do not miss the same class every week.

Groups can be difficult to form and challenging to facilitate, but they have enormous potential for helping children help one another deal with the many problems that threaten their studies and their personal and social development. Furthermore, the microcosmic structure of small groups allows counselors to observe students' interactions and to use members' feedback to help individual students strengthen their social skills. Small groups can truly help fulfill students' need for belonging and social purpose when each member believes that he or she can both contribute to and receive from the group's resources.

Research on Children's Groups

For years, school counselors have reported the positive experiences that take place in groups of younger and older children, and many empirical studies have supported that thinking. Riddle, Bergin, and Douzensis (1997) found improvement in self-concept for fourth and fifth graders who were children of alcoholics; and social skills training in small groups was found to improve behavior (Verduyn, Lord, &

Forrest, 1990) and to have a positive impact on children with learning disabilities (Ciechalski & Schmidt, 1995; M. M. Omizo & Omizo, 1988).

Similar results have been shown with older children and adolescents. For example, Tsui and Sammons (1988) found that the small-group format lessens adjustment difficulties for refugees; and Blum and Jones (1993) reported positive retention effects for youngsters at-risk for dropping out of school. And students having difficulty with career decisions reported being helped by group counseling (Barkhaus, Adair, Hoover, & Bolyard, 1985; Glaize & Myrick, 1984).

All of these studies support the idea that small-group counseling is an effective means for helping young people with a variety of problems. They also tell us that the power of groups lies not in format, theory, or type of problem, but in the fundamental nature of group life.

Group Dynamics

We noted above that groups are children's natural environment. It makes sense, then, that their behavior is different—more real—in a group setting, and that counseling in that setting is effective. The problems and goals of a group are less important than the processes that underlie the content. Those processes define the interactions of group members: how they relate to one another and to the group leader. And ultimately they define the effectiveness of the therapy.

Key to the success of group counseling is the members' sense of ownership. This means that the counselor must trust in the power of the group to regulate itself. Certainly a beginning group needs structure and direction; but as time goes on, the counselor should pass ownership of the group to its members. The first step in the process is to include the group's members in developing rules for the group. Adolescents, especially, struggle with issues of autonomy and can react strongly and negatively to authority. They are much more willing to listen to their peers than to a school official.

> *I remember supervising an intern who was working with a small group of high school students, all of whom had failing grades. After facilitating dialogue about the causes of their performance, she discovered that most of them were failing because they were cutting classes, and the reason they gave for cutting classes was that they needed a break. After a while, to move the discussion forward, the intern shared with the group that her son would soon be attending high school. "What should I tell him for him to be successful in high school?" she asked the group members. She was amazed at both the quantity and quality of their answers.*

This is a good example of a group of adolescents struggling with issues of autonomy. When the students talked about needing a break and so giving themselves license to cut classes, they were saying: "We decide when we need a break, not the school. We want to make the rules here." Of course, high school students can't make their own rules. But the intern wisely refrained from saying that. Instead she asked them for advice, in effect feeding their need for power and influence, and the strategy readily elicited their help.

Help is what it's all about: The goal of any group should be getting its members to help one another by exchanging constructive feedback. The intern took the first step by asking the students to help her; the next step was to get the students to help one another. She began to shift the discussion from her problem to a statement one of the students had made, asking the group members for their reactions and suggestions. The intervention works in two ways. First, the students are more willing to listen to what their peers have to say; more important, the experience of helping one another, of having something useful to give, improves the members' self-concept.

Types of School Counseling Groups

Before school counselors can decide on the size and composition of a group, they must decide on the kind and purpose of the group. Myrick (1997) identified three types of small groups: crisis centered, problem centered, and growth centered.

Crisis-Centered Groups   Crisis-centered groups are formed in response to an urgent problem—a trauma, a common loss—and terminate after no more than five sessions, when the situation has stabilized. Usually the groups have just four to six participants, all of whom have been affected in some way by the crisis.[5]

> *The crisis-centered group I remember most clearly was formed after a mass murder. In 1988, a rejected suitor set fire to a Honduran social club in the Bronx section of New York City. Ninety people were killed in the fire. The school in which I was working was not far from the site of the fire and had several Honduran students. Because of the school's proximity to the tragedy and the number of people killed, all of the Honduran students, knew at least one person who had died, and several had lost relatives. I formed two groups, one with five, the other with four Honduran students, and met with them over several sessions to help them process their feelings of sorrow and anger.*

Problem-Centered Groups   Like crisis-centered groups, problem-centered groups focus on a common problem but one that is less urgent. According to Myrick (1997), crisis-centered groups can become problem-centered groups, and vice versa. For example, when a problem-centered group is touched by a crisis, the group can deviate from the problem that brought it into existence, deal with the crisis, and then resume its regular agenda. It also is not unusual for a group that was formed because of a crisis to evolve into a problem-centered group, particularly when the members have had a positive group experience and want to continue meeting.

Problem-centered groups can form to deal with any number of significant difficulties students encounter in school. The most common presenting problems

---

[5] Because a lot of intense work is done in a short time, it is best to keep the number of participants small and to run several groups if need be.

have to do with behavior or academic deficiency. But when counselors interview students, more often than not they discover something in the students' personal lives that could be responsible for the presenting problem. If the underlying problem is shared by more than one student, the nucleus of a problem-centered group is there. Counselors should not limit the kinds of problems for which they are willing to run groups. A basic knowledge of group dynamics and an appreciation for the healing effects of being with others who share the same problem are the only elements necessary for leading a successful group.[6]

> *I worked in a school with an extraordinary number of single-parent, female-headed households. After learning more about the student population, I discovered that many of the students' fathers were in jail, so I decided to run a group for kids whose fathers were incarcerated. I remember searching for material that might help me devise a six- to eight-week curriculum for the small group, but I found nothing. Then I realized that the basic issues facing these children were loss, separation, abandonment, embarrassment, and fear. I didn't need a structured curriculum after all. In the first session, I began by reminding the students why the group was formed and asked each to share his or her story. There was some resistance at first—that's normal in any group—but by the third session, the group had begun to function well. In the following weeks we talked about the effects on the family of having a parent in jail, the experience of visiting a prison, feelings of shame, and dealing with the possibility that a parent will never come home. The curriculum evolved as time went on both from my intuition and from what the children were saying about their situation.*

Growth-Centered Groups   Myrick's (1997) final classification is growth-centered groups. Unlike crisis centered and problem-centered groups, which are formed for just a few students who share a problem, growth-centered groups deal with the developmental needs of all students. This makes growth-centered groups particularly useful for counselors who are managing or implementing a developmental guidance program.

The advantage of growth-centered groups is that they do not single out students who "have a problem" or are "in need of help." The topics—anything from friendship to body image to going to college—affect all students and so tend to be less threatening and to generate less resistance. Myrick (1997) pointed out that growth-centered groups can be used to reach a student who is having problems but has resisted counseling. Putting this individual in a growth-centered group removes the stigma of needing counseling; at the same time, it allows the student to a connect with the counselor. When the group dissolves, the counselor might fol-

---

[6]Later chapters of this book examine specific challenges and problems faced by young people today, and offer content material for individual and small-group counseling and for large-group guidance. Readers in search of specific information about running a small group around a particular problem should find it in those chapters.

low up individually with the student, hoping that the group experience has made the student more amenable to individual counseling.

> *As a middle school counselor, I was very aware of research that suggests that students at risk for dropping out of school report that their problems began with the transition from elementary school. So, throughout the year, I ran a series of small groups for all fifth graders (the school included Grades 5 through 8) that dealt with the differences between elementary and middle school, and the difficulties the students may have been encountering, and used the resources of group members themselves to generate ways of overcoming those difficulties.*

There is no shortage of topics for growth-centered groups. A keen awareness of the developmental challenges young people face today is all that's needed to give birth to a growth-centered group.

Practical Considerations

The success of a small group depends to a large extent on who is in the group. To some degree, the type of group determines its members. But through the recruitment process, counselors can control the makeup of the group. Finding the right mix of students is critical to the success of a small group.

Homogenous versus Heterogeneous Groups   In most if not all of the groups run by school counselors, the members share a difficulty. The three types of groups outlined above all come into being because their members are facing the same crisis, problem, or developmental issue. Therapy groups in clinics and private practice usually form around a variety of presenting problems; school counseling groups are more like support groups, in which kids dealing with similar issues act as a resource and support for one another.

It makes sense, then, that the members of a group should be roughly the same age—no more than a year's difference (Gazda, 1989). Children and adolescents are supersensitive to age differences; they do not have the developmental maturity to think of themselves as equal to someone who is several years younger or older.

There is less agreement about gender. Ginott (1968) believed that mixed-gender groups work fine for preschoolers but not for school-aged children; Gazda (1989) suggested that boys and girls shouldn't be separated until age 9 or 10. Others argue for the inclusion of both sexes at all ages because the group creates a safe place for young people of both sexes to be together (Ohlsen, 1977; C. L. Thompson & Rudolph, 1996). Our recommendation is to separate boys and girls before the onset of puberty, at about age 10. The intimacy of the small-group setting can be provocative and a distraction for members of the group. Later, toward the end of high school, when adolescents have achieved a certain comfort level with their own sexuality, mixed groups can work well again.

In terms of students' personality, heterogeneity is key. Picture a group whose members are all withdrawn or passive, or one whose members all act out. In either case, the members' behavioral style would impede interaction. But if a group includes both types of youngsters, the counselor can use the withdrawn members to temper those who externalize, and can use those who externalize to draw out the passive members.

The difficulty arises when behavioral style is what has brought a group into being. A counselor who is forming a group of children with attention deficit hyperactivity disorder (ADHD) has two options: to include children who do not have an ADHD or to keep the size of the group very small (just three members). The same would be true for a group formed to help children who are withdrawn. In this case, though, a very small group means there's less likelihood of a child's hiding behind others.

Group Size, Frequency, Length, and Duration   Although some argue that group size depends on many variables (Gumaer, 1986), most school counselors would agree that from five to eight students is the ideal number for small-group counseling (Myrick, 1997).[7] Absences and occasional scheduling conflicts make it a good idea to overrecruit: A counselor who would like six in the group, probably should ask eight students to join because on any given day two students probably are going to miss the session.

Small groups should meet once a week at an agreed-on day and time for an entire class period. As noted earlier, the hour can vary, especially at the high school level, where it is difficult to miss the same class each week. This is the most challenging logistical problem for school counselors who run small groups: finding a common hour that does not result in any member's missing important class time. Many counselors run groups during lunch, giving students time to pick up food on the way. This helps with scheduling conflicts; it also seems to increase students' participation (eating can be a good antidote to "emptying" oneself emotionally in a group). Counselors who really want to run groups will find ways to schedule those groups without jeopardizing the academic achievement of a group's members.

Groups for children and adolescents should run between six and twelve sessions. Setting a duration is important: It can act as a catalyst. In fact, the counselor should begin the first group session by saying, "We are going to be together for the next eight weeks for the purpose of _____. During that time, we hope to accomplish _____."

Because they are time limited, small groups, once begun, should be closed to new members. New members can threaten a group's cohesion. Also, a small group takes on a life of its own, moving through stages of development (we discuss them in the next section). Adding new members would cause the group to regress. Instead, the counselor should tell students who want to join an ongoing group about new groups that will be starting in the future. In certain groups, members are free to come and participate for as long as they need to and then leave. Myrick (1997) gave the example of a group for new students. The youngsters would come to the

---

[7] Again, a group of children with special needs—like those with ADHD—should be limited to just three students.

sessions, work through issues of adjustment, and then leave the group when they felt ready.

Recruitment and Screening   There are many different methods for recruiting group members. Sometimes printing up flyers or posting signs around the school is effective. Teachers can be a tremendous source of help in identifying problems students share. Also, counselors who see that their individual caseload is growing should think about forming groups to deal with common problems. This can be tricky: Students who are being counseled individually are accustomed to the counselor's complete attention and can find it difficult to share that attention with others. On the other hand, having developed a trusting relationship with the counselor, individual counselees provide a pool of potential group members.

Whatever the recruitment method, it is very important that school counselors meet individually with potential members before the group begins. This can be difficult because counselors often find that the demands of the job far exceed their available time. Still, individual sessions before the group meets for the first time are important. Several factors are at work here: First, the pregroup interview is a way to screen out students who for one reason or another might have a destructive influence on the group. Second, it is a way to achieve a certain heterogeneity in behavioral styles. Third, it lends formality, seriousness, and commitment to the group process; and it helps the counselor determine whether the student will take the group seriously and commit to it.

The Life Cycle of the Small Group

It is widely recognized that groups move through stages in the journey toward higher functioning and greater learning (Jacobs, Harvill, & Masson, 2002; Mahler, 1969; Wheelan, 1994; Yalom, 1995). Myrick (1997) identified four stages of group life: involvement, transition, working, and ending.[8]

Stage 1: Involvement   The first stage is a kind of orientation: The members clarify the purpose of the group, get acquainted with one another, and begin to build trust by establishing group rules. The most important rule is confidentiality. Other rules might include one member talking at a time, no verbal or physical abuse, and the consequences of violating confidentiality. The counselor should let the members develop rules on their own. Most groups will come up with the important rules after the group leader (the counselor) says something like this: "To be successful, all groups have to have rules. What rules do you think this group should have to reach its goals?" Rulemaking empowers the members, allows them to take ownership of the group, and offers an alternative to their classroom experience, where many times the leader—the teacher—dictates the rules.

---

[8]The duration of each stage is different for every group. Also, the stages are not necessarily linear; they can overlap. And depending on the group's dynamics, a group can even recycle through earlier stages.

Stage 2: Transition   During the transition stage, group members continue to build trust and cohesiveness. Inevitably, the group is tested through a member's sharing something deep and personal. If the group is able to listen and respond appropriately, cohesiveness is strengthened, and the group is well on its way to the next stage. But many group members still need to work through their group-related anxiety: defensiveness, resistance, and what group theoreticians call *storming*, conflicts around structure, direction, control, and interpersonal relationships (Gladding, 2001). A good group leader recognizes that resolving these problems is necessary to the group's growth and trusts in the members' power to self-correct.

Also, group roles begin to develop during the transition stage. A *role* is a "dynamic structure within an individual (based on needs, cognitions, and values), which usually comes to life under the influence of social stimuli or defined positions" (Munich & Astrachan, 1983, as cited in Gladding, 1999, p. 59). Yalom (1995) listed thirty possible roles group members can adopt. Capuzzi and Gross (1992) divided members' roles into three basic categories:

- A *facilitative/building role* helps the group grow and develop; it can take the form of initiator, coordinator, or orienter. The facilitative/building function is essential to the group because it helps the members feel comfortable in the group (Gladding, 1999).
- The *maintenance role* builds cohesiveness in the group by harmonizing, encouraging, compromising, and commentating (Gladding, 1999). This function is most important when the group is strained for some reason.
- The *blocking role,* unlike the facilitative/building and maintenance roles, does not serve the well-being of the group. The blocker can take the form of aggressor, dominator, or monopolizer, or attention seeker. Although the initial reaction may be to remove a blocker, the group leader should facilitate feedback to the blocker from other group members. This helps make the group a social laboratory in which members can learn more about themselves, specifically how their behaviors affect others.

Stage 3: Working   If a group has been able to negotiate the sometimes rough waters of the transition stage, it moves into the working stage, where the group's focus is on accomplishing its goals. Members feel comfortable sharing with and giving feedback to one another, and they feel a real commitment to the group. It is a time when group members are willing to take chances by sharing more fully and experimenting with new behaviors. If the school counselor is using a structured curriculum in the group, he or she can facilitate the members' personal involvement and commitment to the material being presented.

Stage 4: Ending   Groups have a finite life: All counseling groups, even those that are not limited by time, must end eventually. Ending, or *termination*, can cause members to regress (Wheelan, 1994) and to act out their feelings about the relationships that are about to end. The skilled group counselor allows the expression of those feelings, at the same time encouraging group members to recognize and take pleasure in the fruits of their labor (Sciarra, 1999).

LARGE-GROUP GUIDANCE

> Large group guidance is a planned, developmental program of guidance activities designed to foster students' academic, career, and personal/social development. It is provided for all students through a collaborative effort by counselors and teachers. (ASCA, 1999, p. 1)

In Chapter 1 we traced the history of school counseling from its focus on vocational guidance presented as a lesson in a classroom. That format today is called *large-group guidance*.[9] According to Myrick (1997), once a group has more than 10 students, it is no longer a small group. The number is arbitrary. The point is that as the group grows, the group needs more structure, and that means less emphasis on interpersonal processes and group dynamics. In a large group, the counselor still facilitates, but he or she also teaches.

Generally, large-group guidance is proactive (R. S. Lee, 1993): it focuses on preventing problems such as violence in schools or drug use among students. A considerable body of research has shown that large-group guidance has a positive effect on students' achievement (Carns & Carns, 1991; Gerler & Anderson, 1986; Gerler, Drew, & Mohr, 1990; Gerler, Kinney, & Anderson, 1985; Guerrero, Walker, & Langlois, 1987; R. S. Lee, 1993; St. Clair, 1989); multicultural awareness (D'Andrea & Daniels, 1995); and vocational identity (Hughey, Lapan, & Gysbers, 1993). Because of this research and the ability of this modality to reach large numbers of students, large-group guidance may well be the best vehicle for implementing ASCA's National Standards for School Counseling on a schoolwide basis.

The Organization of Large Groups

The section in Chapter 1 on developmental guidance programs explains the importance of the guidance curriculum and the classroom as its primary venue. The curriculum for each grade is made up of lessons appropriate to the emotional, social, and career goals of a certain group of students. Typically, a guidance lesson is in six units, each unit lasting the length of a classroom period.

Unlike small-group counseling, which requires students to leave a class, large-group guidance is scheduled much like a normal class period. Some schools even set aside a period each week for guidance. If a school does not schedule a regular guidance period, the school counselor must coordinate with classroom teachers to find a good time for the guidance units. The guidance units should be seen as complementary to, not as a substitute for, the regular classroom subject. Ideally, within the framework of a comprehensive developmental guidance program, the classroom teacher is involved in planning, implementing, and following up the guidance unit.[10]

---

[9] Large-group guidance typically takes place in a classroom; in some schools, sessions are held in an auditorium.

[10] It is possible to combine the guidance curriculum and the classroom curriculum. S. Borders and

I was always dismayed when I would go into a classroom for a guidance unit, and the teacher would see it as a free period. Although I recognized that some teachers feel uncomfortable with the affective dimensions of certain guidance lessons, I nevertheless insisted that guidance is a collaborative effort and that I needed their help to accomplish the goals of the lesson.

It is imperative that the classroom teacher stay in the classroom during a guidance unit, both for collaborative purposes and to help keep the students' attention. The classroom teacher almost always knows the students better than the counselor and so can be an enormous help in facilitating acceptance of the counselor and in controlling problem students in the class. Teachers who are involved in every step of the guidance process also assume ownership of the guidance curriculum more easily. And that is key if they are going to continue to implement the guidance curriculum once the school counselor leaves the classroom.

The Content of Guidance Lessons

Guidance lessons can be organized around a wide range of topics. Myrick (1997) made several suggestions from a developmental focus:

How to get and hold a job	Resolving conflicts with people
Beating the bullies	How to be more assertive
Human growth and development	School orientation
Choosing a career	How to pick the best college for you
Study habits and time management	Making new friends [11]

School counselors should not limit the large-group guidance lesson to the developmental curriculum. If a school is facing a particular problem, a guidance lesson can be used for intervention as well as for prevention.

A school had a group of female students who were cutting themselves. Most of the other students in the school were distraught just thinking about the students' hurting themselves. The administration balked at first at the counselor's suggestion that she give a three-unit guidance lesson on the behavior to the classes affected by the behavior. But over time she convinced the administration that "mentionable means manageable." In the end, the counselor, with the help of other counselors, provided an intervention in a large-group setting that reached most of the students in the school.

Paisley (1992), for example, suggested using literature as a resource for classroom guidance, which means the school counselor and the classroom teacher would work together in a class where literature is taught.

[11] There are numerous manuals on all of these topics. And, again, in the second half of this book is specific information for both small-group and large-group counseling on some of the most challenging issues facing students in contemporary society.

Facilitating Guidance Lessons

The intention of the guidance unit is to teach something, so the school counselor should prepare a lesson plan with stated goals and objectives for each unit. Because a number of states have eliminated a teaching requirement for school counselors, many now entering the field have little experience writing lesson plans or working in the classroom. The best resource for beginning counselors in the classroom is an experienced teacher. Counselors should ask for feedback and then implement whatever will help them present more effectively in the classroom.

Although large groups demand more structure than small groups do, school counselors should create an atmosphere of acceptance and respect, encourage the participation of all students, and always be ready to go beyond the written curriculum. When presenting group guidance lessons, counselors can follow a simple four-step format:

1. Present the material (videotape, story, behavior simulation).
2. Ask the students to share what they most remember about the material (cognitive component).
3. Ask the students to share their emotional reaction to the presented material (affective component).
4. Ask the students to share any personal experiences they may have had with the presented material (experiential or cathartic component).

School counselors have the unique ability to go beyond the manifest content to respond to the underlying dynamics in the room. Although the large-group format limits the amount of processing that counselors can do, they should be keenly aware of students who are likely to be affected negatively (to become visibly upset or withdrawn) by the presentation. It is important to follow up with those students in an individual session.

ETHICAL AND LEGAL ISSUES

Informed consent, confidentiality, and privileged communication are ethical and legal issues for school counselors. That is, all are governed by professional ethics and by state laws and school district regulations. We examine these issues here just briefly. No textbook can prescribe exactly how counselors should proceed in all ethical situations, or what laws and policies govern those counselors' actions. For that kind of help, school counselors must consult a supervisor or a trusted colleague.

Informed Consent

Age 18 is the legal age of majority in the United States, the age at which society accords individuals certain rights, among them access to health services without parental permission. In fact, many states allow those under age 18 access to outpatient mental health services.[12] What impact do those laws have on school counseling? Can students in a state that allows minors access to health services give their own informed consent for counseling?

Many school districts have established a policy on when parental permission is required for a student to receive counseling. In the absence of a policy, it seems that students can consent to counseling if they have reached the age at which the state's law allows them access to health services on their own. Some schools stipulate that parental permission is required after the first or a certain number of counseling sessions. This avoids the ludicrous situation of a school counselor's having to turn away a student with an immediate need to talk because the student does not have a parent's permission. But after that initial session, if the counselor decides to see the student on an ongoing basis, ethical practice would suggest that informed consent be obtained from a parent.

Informed consent requires disclosure of the purpose, goals, and methods of counseling. Many would argue that students, especially younger students, lack the understanding and experience to give informed consent. They say that minors can assent to counseling, but that only their parents or guardians can give informed consent. The advantage of having parents consent to their child's counseling is that it involves them in the counseling. But this collaboration raises some interesting questions around confidentiality.

Confidentiality

Section A.2 of ASCA's Ethical Standards for School Counselors deals with confidentiality (see Appendix B). Confidentiality is the cornerstone of ethical practice: The guarantee of privacy allows the counselee to build a trusting relationship with the counselor. But school counselors must bear in mind that confidentiality is never absolute, and that parents have a legal right "to control the professional services provided their children and to be involved in planning those services" (Glosoff & Pate, 2002, p. 22).

> *When explaining confidentiality to a minor student, I like to begin by accentuating the positives and then explaining the exception: "Joe, the great thing about counseling is that what you and I speak about here is between us. I am not allowed, unless you give me permission, to go to your parents or teachers or to anyone else for that matter and tell them what goes on here. If I do want to speak to your parents or teachers, I promise to discuss it with you first and go over exactly what I plan to say to them, and you can give me your opinion. But there is one big exception to what I've just said. If I think that you or someone else is in some kind of danger, I would not be able to keep that between us. I would have to act in whatever way necessary to protect you or the other person. How does that sound to you?"*

This kind of statement accomplishes several things. First, it accentuates the positive aspects of counseling and confidentiality; second, it explains the boundary be-

---

[12] See Linde (2003) for a list by state of minors' rights to consent to health care.

tween counselor, and parents and teachers; and third, it highlights the danger exception to confidentiality.

When it comes to issues of confidentiality and parents, school counselors need to be wary of two types of parents: underinvolved and overinvolved. Underinvolved parents are happy to give their informed consent and disengage from the counseling process. They take comfort in the fact that their child is in the hands of a professional and feel relieved of any responsibility. Overinvolved parents, on the other hand, constantly want to know what is going on in counseling sessions and often feel threatened by the counselor's "secret" knowledge of their child. It is crucial to establish a boundary around confidentiality.

> *"Mr. and Mrs. Clark, for me to help your son, he and I need to have a trusting relationship; and the only way to establish that is through confidentiality. You can't expect me to reveal everything Joe and I talk about. But I can't help Joe in isolation. So periodically I will consult with you about him. I expect you will be available so that we can give each other feedback on how Joe is doing. Of course, if I feel Joe is in any kind of danger, you will be the first to know."*

This statement maintains a healthy balance between protecting the confidentiality of the counseling relationship and establishing a collaborative relationship with a child's parents or guardian.

Privileged Communication

Whereas confidentiality is the counselor's ethical responsibility, *privilege* is the client's legal right to ask that information be kept confidential. Over the years, the courts have ruled that information shared with physicians, attorneys, clergy, psychologists, and social workers is privileged. In addition, Glosoff, Herlihy, and Spence (2000) found that 45 of the 46 states that license counselors also have statutes granting privilege to the counselor-client relationship. A licensed counselor cannot be compelled by a court of law to share privileged information unless the client waives the right of privilege. But the states have been reluctant to extend privilege to school counselors: Just 16 states have a statute privileging communications with school counselors who have been certified by the state education department (Fischer & Sorenson, 1996). Even in states without privilege, though, school counselors can argue the confidential nature of the relationship and hope that the presiding judge grants privilege. In counseling minors, it is assumed that the right of privilege belongs to the parents or legal guardian.

CONCLUSION

Over the years, school counseling has moved away from a service model to a program model. The program is delivered through different channels, among them individual, small-group, and large-group sessions. Each sets different goals, draws on different theories and techniques, and demands different skills of the counselor. Yet underlying them all is caring for and a commitment to students.

Counselors hold a unique position in schools, a position that is different from that of teachers and administrators. Although schools have an uncanny way of drawing counselors away from what they have been trained to do and bestowing on them other responsibilities, school counselors should never lose sight of their primary task—the academic, career, and personal and social development of all students. With that focus, and with their training and experience, school counselors can make a real difference in the lives of students.

QUESTIONS FOR DISCUSSION

1. Which theory of individual counseling do you think would be most effective in a school setting? Explain your answer.
2. Suppose you were working in a school where the principal was constantly asking you to take on noncounseling tasks. How would you handle the situation? What strategies would you use to move the principal toward a deeper appreciation for counseling?
3. What do you think are the advantages of small-group counseling? When you imagine yourself leading a small group of students, how do you feel? Does that feeling change when you consider the scheduling and other practical considerations that go into forming and sustaining a small group in a school setting?
4. What kinds of groups would you like to lead? Why? Would your answer change if you were teaching in an elementary school versus a high school? Why or why not? How do you think your background might influence your answers to this question?
5. Large-group guidance involves a pedagogical dimension. What is your reaction to entering a classroom and presenting a guidance lesson? Do you think you need a teaching background to stand up in front of a large group of students? Explain your answer. Are there other experiences beside teaching that could sharpen a counselor's skills at presenting a lesson?

SUGGESTED INTERNET SITES

www.person-centered.org
> This Web site, which is dedicated to the promotion of person-centered counseling, contains information about training, workshops, meetings, and the like for those interested in the work of Carl Rogers.

www.alfredadler.org
> The official Web site of the North American Society of Adlerian Psychology contains information about training, conferences, and workshops for the promotion of Adlerian counseling.

www.rebt.org

The official Web site of the Albert Ellis Institute describes training programs throughout the country and other helpful information for those interested in counseling with REBT.

www.beckinstitute.org

The official Web site of the Beck Institute for Cognitive Therapy and Research. Includes information about training and speakers. Also provides newsletter and recommended reading.

www.wglasser.com

The official Web site of the William Glasser Institute contains information about certificate training programs. Included is recommended reading and criteria for quality schools.

www.coe.unt.edu/cpt

The official Web site of the Center for Play Therapy at the University of North Texas contains information about training, publications, and counseling services. The focus is child-centered play counseling. It also includes resources for students, parents, and professionals.

CONSULTING IN THE SCHOOL SETTING

In 1966, the ACES-ASCA Joint Committee on the Elementary School Counselor named consulting one of the three Cs of the school counselor's role; the other two are counseling and coordination. And in 1999, ASCA again included consulting, with counseling, large-group guidance, and coordination, in its list of primary interventions utilized by school counselors. Over the last 30-plus years, consulting has become an increasingly important part of the school counselor's job. Several factors were at work here. First, the Education for All Handicapped Children Act (Public Law 94-142), which was passed in 1975, mandated school-based consulting for students with special needs. Second, the emphasis on parents as collaborators in the education of their children has led to their consulting with school personnel in general and school counselors in particular. Third, systems theory has made school counselors more aware of the intricate link between a child's academic development and changes in the family system of which the child is a part, and of the need for more systemic interventions, working with teachers, parents, and other health professionals to help overcome these difficulties. Fourth, teachers are consulting with counselors for help dealing with more challenging students (the result of a commitment to reducing the dropout rates for all students) and with adapting teaching styles and methods to a diverse student population (the result of increasing multiculturalism in the school-aged population). Furthermore, research into the role of consulting has revealed that school counselors consider it a major part of their job and rate it as a high priority (Ginter, Scalise, & Presse, 1990; Wilgus & Shelley, 1988).

The material in this chapter acknowledges the importance of consulting to parents, to teachers, and, ultimately, to students. The chapter begins with a brief history of consulting in schools and various definitions of the consulting function. Then the text examines consultation models, focusing on Caplan's mental health model and the behavioral models. The second part of the chapter looks at consulting with parents and teachers, and describes both problems working with and interventions for these two key constituencies.

Of course no one chapter can do justice to all the elements that go into the consulting task; that's a semesterlong course in itself. But if the chapter makes readers aware of the challenges and the rewards of helping the helpers, then it's done its job well.

A HISTORY OF CONSULTING IN SCHOOLS

Consulting in schools dates back to the 1920s, when school psychologists were called on to help parents and teachers of children with learning problems (French, 1990). In 1954, the first Thayer Conference made consulting part of the school psychologist's function (Dougherty, 1995).[1] Twelve years later, the Joint Committee on the Elementary School Counselor made consulting an official function of school counselors.

Also in the 1960s, articles about consulting began to appear in professional counseling journals. One survey of those journals found that 12 articles on the subject were published between 1964 and 1968; by 1972, 27 articles about different models of consulting had appeared (Kahnweiler, 1979). In 1973, Dinkmeyer and Carlson (1973) published *Consulting: Facilitating Human Potential and Change Processes,* which expanded the role of the school consultant to include improving the organizational climate of the school (Dougherty, 1995). And in 1975, Public Law 94-142 was passed: It would dramatically increase consulting services for children with special needs.

Dinkmeyer and Carlson made a convincing case for school-based consulting by underscoring the impossibility of having school counselors, with their enormous caseloads, provide direct services to all students. By working with parents and teachers to improve both home and school environments, counselors could impact a greater number of students. Young children, especially, are dependent on the significant adults in their lives: For school counselors to facilitate the academic, career, and social development of children by working with those adults was logical (Campbell, 1992).

CONSULTING: A DEFINITION

Consulting, like *counseling,* is not easily defined. The difficulty has to do with the many different functions of the school counselor as consultant, which in turn are defined by the many different theoretical models of consulting. In the absence of an operational definition of *consulting,* empirical research into the efficacy of consulting is lacking. In response to this problem, several authors have tried to identify common aspects of consulting, responsibilities and tasks that cut across theoretical lines. For example, Dougherty (1995) noted three common elements:

---

[1] The Thayer Conference was sponsored by the American Psychological Association in response to the shortage of well-trained psychologists to work in schools.

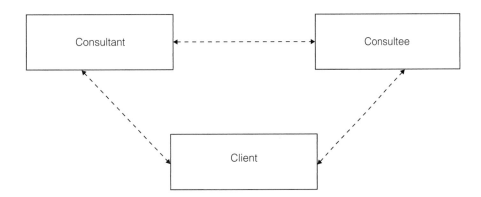

FIGURE **3.1**

CONSULTING: A TRIADIC RELATIONSHIP

SOURCE: Adapted from Dougherty (1995), p. 11.

- Consulting is tripartite: It involves a consultant, a consultee, and a client.
- The goal of all consulting is to solve problems.
- Another goal of consulting is to improve the consultee's work with the client and, in turn, improve the welfare of the client.

Figure 3.1 depicts the tripartite nature of consulting; it also shows the reciprocal nature of the process.

Dougherty then described 11 characteristics of consulting about which the literature is in some agreement (Table 3.1). Because Dougherty was writing about consulting in general, the characteristics as they apply to school counselors need refinement. For example, school counselors usually are internal consultants, part of the system in which the consulting takes place. And although the consultation is always voluntary, there are times when school counselors are proactive, reaching out to parents and teachers, especially when counselors feel that their knowledge and expertise can help. Also, collaboration between consultant and consultee is especially important in the school setting because it eases the burden on the consultant: The problem isn't the consultant's alone; both problem and solution are shared. In fact, when a consultee seems too willing to rely on the consultant's expertise, the consultant must make clear that the two parties have to work on the problem together.

> *When consulting with parents about their child's school-related problem, I always say something like this: "You are the expert on your child. You know him [her] better than anyone else does, and you are with him [her] more than anyone else. All I can do is give you input on how I see the problem and make some suggestions, but you always have the final say."*

This intervention serves two purposes. First, it clarifies the importance of collaboration. Second, it levels the playing field, diminishing the possibility of the parents' feeling threatened by the consultant or the process.

TABLE 3.1   **THE BASIC CHARACTERISTICS OF CONSULTING**

---

1. Either the consultee or the client may have priority over the other at a given time, depending on the consulting approach.

2. The consultant provides indirect service to the client by providing direct service to the consultee.

3. Consultants can be either separate from (external consultant) or part of (internal consultant) the system in which the consulting takes place.

4. The participation of all parties is voluntary.

5. Consultees are free to do whatever they want with the consultant's suggestions. They are under no obligation to follow the consultant's recommendations.

6. In the consulting relationship, consultee and consultant share power equally but not need: That is, the consultee needs help with a problem, and the consultant does not.

7. The consulting relationship is temporary; and when it is over, the consultant does not replace the consultee.

8. Consulting deals exclusively with the consultee's work-related or caretaking-related problems. By definition, it never deals with the personal concerns of the consultee.

9. The consultant can take on a variety of roles in the consulting process, depending on the nature of the problem, the skills of both consultee and consultant, and the purpose and wanted outcomes of the process.

10. Consulting tends to be collaborative in nature; that is, consultant and consultee work together to solve a defined problem. One cardinal exception is in carrying out the agreed-on consultation plan. The consultee carries out the plan, with the consultant typically on call for further help. Another exception is when the consultee has the skills but not the time to do a given task. For example, a consultee might ask a consultant to lead a workshop on substance abuse counseling for the consultee's organization, even though the consultee is skilled in that task.

11. Consulting typically occurs in an organized context. In that context, three key variables can influence the success of the process: the people involved, how the process unfolds, and how change procedures are implemented.

SOURCE: Adapted from Dougherty (1995), pp. 9–10.

There has been controversy in recent years over the effectiveness of the collaborative approach.[2] Several empirical studies support more directive or prescriptive methods for school-based consulting (Erchul, 1987; Erchul & Chewning, 1990; Witt, Erchul, McKee, Pardue, & Wickstrom, 1991). But Gutkin (1999) suggested that *collaborative* is antithetical to *coercive*, not *directive*, that collaborative and directive are two different dimensions (Figure 3.2). According to Gutkin, then, the consultant can use a collaborative-directive approach: always receptive to the consultee's input but prescriptive whenever appropriate.

In what may be the most relevant definition for *school-based consulting*, D. Brown, Pryzwansky, and Schulte (2001) wrote:

> Consultation is defined as a voluntary problem-solving process that can be initiated and terminated by either the consultant or consultee. It is en-

---

[2] See Gutkin (1999) for an excellent review of the literature on this subject.

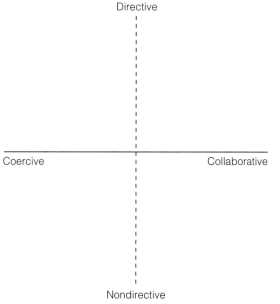

Directive

Coercive   Collaborative

Nondirective

FIGURE **3.2**

THE COLLABORATIVE AND DIRECTIVE DIMENSIONS OF SCHOOL-BASED CONSULTING

SOURCE: Reprinted from the *Journal of School Psychology, 37,* T. B. Gutkin, "Collaborative versus Directive/Prescriptive/ Expert School-Based Consultation: Reviewing and Resolving a False Dichotomy," p. 181. Copyright 1999 with permission from Elsevier Science.

gaged primarily for the purpose of assisting consultees to develop attitudes and skills that will enable them to function more effectively with a client, which can be an individual, group, or organization for which they have responsibility. Thus, the goals of the process are two-fold: enhancing services to third parties and improving the ability of consultees to function in areas of concern to them. (pp. 5–6)

Perhaps the best understanding of consulting comes from a comparison of consulting with other help activities—counseling, teaching, supervising, and mediating, for example.

Counseling and therapy. Individual counseling is dyadic; consulting is always triadic—it involves a third party. Also, counseling deals with the counselee's personal problems; consulting should never deal with the consultee's personal problems. Instead it should be directed toward helping the consultee deal more effectively with the client's problems. In fact, if a consultant discovers that the presenting issue had more to do with the consultee's personal problems than with those of the client, ethical practice would demand the consultee be referred to someone else for counseling.

Teaching. Although consultants do teach—for example, showing a consultee how to perform a certain behavioral intervention—it is much less formal than classroom teaching, and teaching does not form the basis of the relationship (D. Brown, Pryzwansky, & Schulte, 2001). Furthermore, teaching does not usually involve collaboration with those being taught; whereas collaboration with the consultee is at the heart of the consulting process.

Supervising. Although a supervisor, like a consultant, helps a third party work with a client, supervision implies a hierarchical relationship: The supervisor is clearly in a position of authority and at some point must make a formal evaluation of the supervisee. The consultant-consultee relationship is between equals.

Mediating. According to Dougherty (1995), mediation is like consultation in that both have to do with problem solving, involve three parties, and are collaborative. But the mediator must remain neutral at all times, whereas the consultant often makes recommendations. A second distinction has to do with the nature of the problem. Mediation always centers on a conflict; the focus of consultation can be a conflict but more often it is on helping the client.

MODELS OF CONSULTATION

Over the last 30 years, several models of consultation have been described in the literature. Two—the mental health model and the behavioral model—are widely used.[3]

Caplan's Model: A Focus on Emotional Health

Gerald Caplan's experience was rooted in the 1940s, in a child guidance center in Israel, where he worked on a team with other health professionals attending to large numbers of immigrant children. Over time, he began to see common difficulties among the children's caregivers (Dougherty, 1995):

- Many had only a limited range of management strategies.
- Their view of the children and the children's problems tended to be stereotypical.
- The caregivers' personal problems diminished their ability to see the children's problems with any sort of objectivity.

Caplan understood the difficulties the caregivers faced; he also knew that their mental health was crucial to the well-being of the children. His intervention: consultations with the caregivers, sympathetic and objective discussions that helped them see the children in a new light, not as problems themselves, but as individuals *with* problems (Dougherty, 1995). Caplan's insights formed the basis of the mental health model of consultation.

---

[3] An Adlerian model of consultation also is cited frequently in the school counseling literature (see, for example, Dinkmeyer & Carlson, 1973; Dreikurs, 1968; Dreikurs & Cassel, 1990). It relies on many of the principles explained in Chapter 2.

Caplan distinguished four types of consultation, two of which are relevant to school counselors: client-centered case consultation and consultee-centered case consultation.[4]

Client-Centered Case Consultation In this, the most common type of consultation, the focus is on the client. The consultee presents a case about a client who is having or causing a problem, and the consultant designs an intervention to help the consultee help the client.

> *Ms. G., a math teacher, came to talk with me about one of her students. Ramon was performing poorly in ninth-grade Algebra and, two months into the term, had begun acting out for attention. I promised to look into the problem and get back to her.*
>
> *Ramon's record showed that his math grades, although not great, had always been passing. After talking with the boy's other teachers and observing him in math and other classes, I concluded that the problem behavior was specific to the math class. My working hypothesis: Ramon was having difficulty doing more-complex mathematical operations, and his frustration was manifesting in attention-seeking behaviors. I considered two courses of action: the first, a referral for an evaluation by the school psychologist to determine if Ramon had a learning disability in math; the second, tutoring to help the student understand more-complex operations. I decided to recommend tutoring and follow-up. If the tutoring didn't work, I planned to suggest an evaluation.*
>
> *I told Ms. G. all of this at our next meeting. I knew that she was in charge of a number of after-school activities and wouldn't be able to tutor Ramon herself, so I suggested a tutoring program that was being run through a local social services agency. Ms. G. agreed to contact Ramon's mother about the after-school program, and we agreed to meet in a month to assess the effectiveness of the intervention on Ramon's achievement and behavior.*

Notice that before I recommended a course of action, I assessed and diagnosed the situation. I relied on the consultee (Ms. G.) for certain information; but I also collected information from other sources: the boy's record, other teachers, my own observations. Also, integral to the decision-making process—even when consulting is client centered—is an assessment of the consultee's strengths and weaknesses. Knowing that Ms. G. had after-school commitments, I found an alternate source for tutoring. Notice too that the intervention included a scheduled follow-up session to determine the effectiveness of the math tutoring on Ramon's achievement and behavior.

Consultee-Centered Case Consultation In consultee-centered consultation, the focus is on "elucidating and remedying the shortcomings in the consultee's pro-

---

[4]The other two are program-centered administrative consultation and consultee-centered administrative consultation.

fessional functioning that are responsible for" his or her difficulties with a particular case (Caplan & Caplan, 1993, p.101). Because the consultant almost never sees the client in consultee-centered consultation, the consultancy revolves around the consultee's discussion of the case. The consultant listens intently, now and again encouraging the consultee to delve deeper into the problems with the case.

According to Caplan, these sessions give the consultant the necessary information to categorize the consultee's difficulty with the client as a lack of knowledge, skill, self-confidence, or objectivity. Accurate diagnosis of what is causing the consultee's difficulty is key to the process. A consultant would not intervene in the same way for a problem diagnosed as a lack of knowledge as he or she would for a problem diagnosed as a lack of objectivity.

> *Lack of knowledge.* The consultee lacks the factual or theoretical knowledge necessary for dealing more effectively with the client. The consultant's task is to communicate the necessary knowledge to the consultee for use with this client now and with similar clients in the future. Caplan (1970) maintained that when lack of knowledge is pervasive in an organization, the consultant should attempt a systemwide intervention. A school counselor who gets repeated requests for help from teachers who are having discipline problems in the classroom might suggest a workshop on classroom management for the entire staff (D. Brown, Pryzwansky, & Schulte, 2001).
>
> *Lack of skill.* The consultee has the theoretical knowledge but does not have the skill to operationalize that knowledge. In this case, the consultant may teach the needed skill; more often, though, the consultant explores with the consultee ways to get the appropriate training within the school.[5] It can be difficult for a consultee to admit to a lack of skill. It is the consultant's job as well to help teachers see that skill learning is part of their professional development. This is especially important today in schools where the cultural makeup of the student population is shifting, making it crucial for teachers to learn new methods of teaching.
>
> *Lack of confidence.* The consultee does not have confidence in his or her ability to help the client work out the problem. Caplan believed that lack of confidence, like lack of skill, is not ideally suited to consultation. The intervention here is a function of the source of the lack of confidence. If it comes from inexperience—the consultee is a beginner or has never faced the specific problem before—the consultant can provide support and encouragement but also should help the consultee find peer support. If the lack of confidence is a characterological problem, the consultant should work toward referring the consultee for counseling.
>
> *Lack of objectivity.* "The consultee's role functioning, perception, and judgments are impaired by subjective factors that make him or her unable to apply existing knowledge and skills to the case effectively" (Dougherty,

---

[5] Most school counselors, for example, have enough knowledge to identify a problem with teaching methods but do not have the knowledge to train teachers in those methods. For that kind of expertise, they should refer the teachers to a master teacher in the school.

TABLE 3.2   THE CONSULTEE'S LACK OF OBJECTIVITY

Reason	Definition	Example	Intervention
Direct personal involvement	Consultee becomes over-involved with the client.	Teacher becomes friends with the student or the family and socializes outside school.	Consultant emphasizes the need for appropriate boundaries.
Simple identification	Consultee overidentifies with the client and does what is best for him-/herself rather than for the client.	Teacher, when young, also had a speech problem and so assumes that he/she knows what is best for the child.	Consultant models objectivity and helps consultee see the client more objectively.
Transference	Consultee uses past experience to impose roles and expectations on the client.	Teacher, having gone through a difficult divorce, expects difficulties from a student whose parents are divorcing.	Consultant encourages consultee to observe the student more carefully to test the reality of his/her perception.
Characterological distortion	Consultee suffers from a personality problem that interferes with his/her professional functioning.	Teacher engages in sexually inappropriate behavior but accuses student of seduction.	Consultant has little chance of improving consultee functioning, so makes appropriate referral or report.
Theme interference	Consultee engages in stereotyping.	With limited data, teacher assumes that all Latino parents are not concerned about their children's education.	Consultant uses unlinking and theme interference reduction.

SOURCE: Adapted from Caplan and Caplan (1993).

1995, p. 251). Caplan believed that lack of objectivity is the most common cause of consultee difficulties; and he identified five reasons for that lack of objectivity (Table 3.2).

The last reason in Table 3.2, *theme interference,* occupies a good deal of space in Caplan's writings. He considered theme interference the primary cause of lack of objectivity. In this context, a *theme* "represents an unsolved problem or defeat that the consultee has experienced which influences his or her expectations concerning a client" (D. Brown, Pryzwansky, & Schulte, 2001, p. 31). Suppose a teacher believes that Latino parents are not concerned about their children's education. Let's say he developed this theme from two experiences with Latino parents who for whatever reason did not respond to the teacher's efforts to help their underachieving children. That he has generalized from two experiences makes no difference. The next time this teacher comes into contact with a Latino parent, from the outset he is going to believe the situation is hopeless. His theme is going to interfere with his objectivity, and so his performance. Yes, the teacher may make a half-hearted attempt to solve the problem; but it is going to fail, and that is going to confirm the teacher's thinking about Latino parents. When theme interference is operating, the consultee is closed to all but one possible outcome—failure.

According to Caplan, two basic interventions weaken theme interference: unlinking and theme interference reduction (D. Brown, Pryzwansky, & Schulte,

2001). Through *unlinking*, the consultant helps the consultee see that this client is different from previous ones. In our example, the consultant might point out to the teacher that the student has his Latino father's surname, but that he was born and has been raised in the United States by his mother and stepfather, neither of whom is Latino. Do you see the problem with this intervention? Caplan argued that unlinking isn't a good intervention because it leaves the theme intact. The consultation may help this one student, but the teacher is going to finish the session still believing that Latino parents do not care about their children's education.

More effective, according to Caplan, is *theme interference reduction.* In discussions, the consultant encourages the consultee to see that the "inevitable" outcome is actually only one of many possible outcomes. In our example, suppose the consultant knows that this child's mother has agreed to tutoring in the past, so she is likely to agree to it now. The consultant's goal is to help the consultee perceive the present case more realistically. And if the outcome confirms the consultant's prediction, the theme begins to break down and, in time, to disappear.

Theme interference can result in negative stereotypes that contribute to the academic, social, and emotional problems students face. School counselors can make an enormous contribution by working with teachers and other staff members to reduce theme interference. The process is not an easy one. It demands excellent skills and the fortitude to stay calm in the face of what seem to be ridiculous or, even worse, hurtful generalizations. But hard work here pays off: Tolerance and optimism are crucial to learning in schools.

Behavioral Models

Like Caplan's model, behavioral models use problem solving to improve the functioning of both consultee and client (Erchul & Conoley, 1991). Two of the better-known behavioral models are Bergan's (1977) operant-learning model and Brown and Schulte's (1987) social-learning model.[6] In both models the consultant helps develop a behavioral plan, and the consultee is responsible for putting the plan into action.

The Stages of Consultation   The behavioral models divide the consulting process into four steps: (1) problem identification and definition, (2) problem analysis and assessment, (3) intervention, and (4) evaluation and monitoring.

STAGE 1: PROBLEM IDENTIFICATION AND DEFINITION   The goal at this stage is to identify the problem, the discrepancy between the client's actual behavior and the behavior the consultee wants to facilitate (Wallace & Hall, 1996). The method is an interview between consultant and consultee. That interview has six objectives:

1. Target the problems to be solved as a result of consultation. This generally involves asking the teacher about goals and expectations.

---

[6]Operant learning understands behavior as a function of consequences: behaviors (responses) are eliminated or acquired through the use of punishments and rewards. Social learning uses modeling as the primary way of teaching new behaviors (Gladding, 2001).

TABLE 3.3	THE BEHAVIORAL CONSULTATION INTERVIEW: VERBAL COMMUNICATION PROCESSES
Process	**Description**
Specification	The consultant elicits increasingly specific data from the consultee by asking for details. For example: "How often does the behavior occur?"
Evaluation	These communications reveal the consultee's reactions to or feelings about the client's behavior. For example: "I get so annoyed when John just gets up and walks around the room." Evaluation processes can also include positive or negative feedback from consultant to consultee: "You did a good job of positive reinforcement."
Inference	Inferences are judgments based on facts. They can be drawn by consultant or consultee and generally take the form "I think . . ." or "I feel . . ."
Summarization	The consultant restates the problem, focusing on the consultee's core message.
Validation	Agreement between consultant and consultee is critical to the consulting process: The process cannot go forward unless the two agree. Validation indicates agreement. For example, the consultee might answer yes to the consultant's statement: "I believe that you reinforce Tammy's negative behavior."

SOURCE: Adapted from Bergan and Kratochwill (1990).

2. Describe each target problem in behavioral terms rather than with medical model labels so that the exact nature of the problem as well as the course of problem solving can be agreed upon.
3. Identify the environmental conditions surrounding each target behavior. Consultants accomplish this through questioning the teacher with regard to what events come before (antecedents), occur during (sequential), and follow (consequents) the problem behavior.
4. Ask the teacher to estimate the frequency, intensity, and/or duration of each target behavior to determine the severity of the problem and the extent of baseline (pretreatment) data collection procedures.
5. Agree on the type of data collection procedures that will be used and who will collect the data.
6. Arrange a date for the next interview. It is important that an adequate sampling of baseline behavior be obtained before the next interview takes place. (Erchul & Conoley, 1991, p. 208)

Many of these objectives reflect principles of operant learning.

According to Bergan (1977), the consultee's primary function in this stage is to describe the client's problem behavior accurately and specifically. Table 3.3. describes the verbal communication processes that are commonly used in the problem identification interview.[7]

---

[7]These processes are not unique to behavioral consultation. For example, summarization is a common technique in individual counseling.

STAGE 2: PROBLEM ANALYSIS AND ASSESSMENT   The interview continues in the second stage of the consultation process, but now its focus is the variables that influence the problem behavior (Wallace & Hall, 1996). This stage culminates with a plan to correct or eliminate the problem behavior. Erchul and Conoley (1991) describe four objectives for this stage:

1. Document the existence of each target problem by reviewing baseline data with the teacher. Also, the difference between the existing and desired behavior performance of the child must be determined.
2. Specify and analyze the antecedent, sequential, and consequent conditions surrounding the problem.
3. Devise an intervention plan.
4. Arrange a date for the next interview. Also, the consultant should make plans to monitor the teacher's implementation of the plan and make arrangements for teacher training (if necessary). (p. 208)

According to the operant-learning model, the school-based consultant must assess the student's behavioral strengths and weaknesses—intellectual functioning, learning deficits, and physical abilities and limitations, for example—before developing a plan of action. The consultee's primary responsibilities here are to collect information about the client and to design a behavioral plan (Bergan, 1977).

In the social-learning model, it is equally important to assess the student's cognitions, especially the student's "perception of his or her ability to perform in a certain area" (D. Brown, Pryzwansky, & Schulte, 2001, p. 62). This can be done through standardized self-efficacy scales or simply by asking the student (via the consultee), "How confident are you in your ability to _____ [perform in a certain area]?" In addition to self-efficacy, Brown, Pryzwansky, and Schulte suggested that assessments of the client's cognitions include determining the degree to which the client will reinforce appropriate behavior by himself or herself; the extent to which the client expects rewards or punishments for "good" behavior; and the importance the client attaches to performance in the given situation.

The consultee's cognitions are also important. To assess those cognitions, Brown, and his colleagues suggested that the consultant ask a series of questions:

- "How important is your functioning appropriately with the student?"
- "How confident are you that you can deal with the student's problem?"
- "What do you expect in terms of rewards and punishments for the way in which you function with the student?"
- "To what extent would you self-reinforce if you can solve the problem?"

The consultant also must assess the environmental variables that limit what the consultee can do. For example, a teacher may not be able to meet with a student in the early evening if the school's regulations prohibit teacher-student meetings after 5:00 p.m. Or a physical factor—an overcrowded classroom, for example—can make it difficult for a teacher to give sustained individual attention to a particular student.

STAGE 3: INTERVENTION   In the third stage, the plan is implemented. Erchul and Conoley (1991) identified three objectives in this stage:

1. Determine the teacher's ability to implement. If the teacher lacks the appropriate skills, the consultant must decide whether to train the teacher or select an alternate procedure.
2. Monitor the teacher's data collection and plan operations.
3. Determine the need for plan revisions. If the plan is not working, the consultant and teacher must revise it to increase the probability of success. (p. 209)

In the operant-learning model, this is the stage at which many consultations fall apart. This part of the process requires the consultee to implement a behavioral plan using positive and negative reinforcement, punishment, shaping, contingency contracts, rehearsal, and other behavioral techniques. A teacher who lacks the experience, the skill, or just the time to apply those techniques precisely and consistently is going to find it very difficult to implement the behavioral plan.

Social-learning interventions in this stage are designed to increase the self-efficacy of both consultee and client. Table 3.4 lists several of those interventions. The best reinforcement here is *performance accomplishment.* Actually performing

TABLE 3.4   SOCIAL-LEARNING INTERVENTIONS FOR CONSULTEES AND CLIENTS

Intervention	Consultant or consultee . . .*
Symbolic modeling	. . . presents the wanted behavior through videotape, written materials, or observation.
Performance enactment	. . . first models the wanted behavior and then asks the consultee/client to rehearse the behavior. Coaching and feedback are adjuncts to performance enactment.
Covert modeling	. . . asks the consultee/client to imagine someone performing the wanted behavior.
Cognitive modeling	. . . "talks through" the wanted behavior while modeling it.
Cognitive restructuring	. . . identifies thoughts that precede, occur during, or follow a problem situation and suggests replacing them with more appropriate thoughts. This intervention relies on cognitive modeling and feedback.
Systematic desensitization	. . . eliminates phobic responses either by pairing them with a neutral stimulus (e.g., relaxation) or by gradually exposing the consultee/client to the stimulus that precedes the phobic response.
Self-monitoring	. . . has the consultee/client monitor his/her own progress toward some preset goal.

*These interventions are used by consultants with consultees and by consultees with clients.

SOURCE: Adapted from D. Brown, Pryzwansky, and Schulte (2001), p. 65. Published by Allyn and Bacon, Boston, MA. Copyright © 2001 by Pearson Education. Reprinted by permission of the publisher.

the wanted behavior has the greatest impact on the belief in one's ability to repeat the behavior in the future.

Another focus of intervention in the social-learning approach has to do with the consultee's expectations. Much research has been done linking teachers' expectations to their students' performance (Cooper & Moore, 1995; Keneal, Frude, & Shaw, 1991; Kolb & Lee, 1994): If a teacher doesn't expect students to do well, chances are the students won't do well. The consultant's task here is to alter the teacher's expectations. Suppose a teacher believes that students from single-parent households do not learn as well as students from dual-parent households. To alter the teacher's expectations, the consultant might pass along research findings that show no differences in learning ability between the two groups of students. If that doesn't work, the consultant might use any of the interventions listed in Table 3.4.

STAGE 4: EVALUATION AND MONITORING   In the final stage, consultant and consultee meet to evaluate both the consultation process and the behavioral plan. The interview in this stage has four objectives:

1. Determine the extent to which the goals of consultation have been achieved. Different steps must be taken if goal attainment is complete, partial, or non-existent.
2. Determine the effectiveness of the intervention plan.
3. Discuss strategies regarding the continuation, modification, or withdrawal of the intervention plan.
4. Schedule additional interviews (if needed) or terminate the consultation on the problem. (Erchul & Conoley, 1991, p. 209)

In both behavioral models, consultant and consultee use data from observations, rating forms and checklists, and comparisons of pre- and postintervention behaviors to determine the extent to which the client's behavior has changed (Wallace & Hall, 1996). In addition, the social-learning approach assesses cognitive changes in self-efficacy, expectations, and the ability to self-reinforce in both consultee and client.

Problems with the Operant-Learning Model   The behavioral models of consultation have been the subject of a great deal of research, much of it supportive. In recent years, however, critics have begun to be heard on the operant-learning model. For example, Witt, Gresham, and Noell (1996) questioned three aspects of Bergan's model: its overreliance on consultees' description of the problem, consultees' failure to implement interventions, and the effectiveness of collaborative versus directive consultation. Research continues on the model.

Certainly the operant-learning model places a great deal of responsibility on the consultee, not only for assessment, but also for implementation and evaluation. Because precision and consistency are so crucial to the success of behavioral interventions, Witt, Gresham, and Noell have a point: Are teachers in general willing to make the effort required to help students with their problems?

CONSULTING WITH PARENTS

When counselors consult with parents about their children, several issues must be resolved. First, the locus of control in the family must be established. Second, boundaries need setting. And third, specific problems in the family and in the consulting relationship must be addressed.

The Executive Subsystem

The first question is simple: Who is in charge in this family? The *executive subsystem* refers to those in the family with the authority to manage the others. Salvador Minuchin, the founder of structural family therapy, posited that many behavioral problems in children can be traced to a dysfunctional executive subsystem (Minuchin & Fishman, 1981; Minuchin, Montalvo, Guerney, Rosman, & Schumer, 1967). For whatever reason, authority that rightfully belongs to the parent has moved to other parts of the system. When children are given too much power and control in the family, they often develop problems responding to authority in the school setting.

In single-parent households, the parent may be tempted to promote a child to the executive subsystem as a means of replacing the missing parent. In dual-parent households, the source of displaced authority often lies in the parents' inability to work together in dealing with their children. Children quickly learn to play off one parent against the other, a tactic that gives the children too much control in the system.

At the outset, the counselor should look for signs of displaced authority in the parent-child dynamic: Do the parents always take their child's side? Do they seem to give in easily to the child's demands? Another indicator of displaced authority is parenting style. Walton (1980) identified three distinct styles of parenting: autocratic, permissive-indulgent, and authoritative-democratic. Often the consultant can determine parenting style by simply observing the parents interacting with their child. If not, the consultant should ask the parents to describe a typical day in the life of the family, paying close attention to any sign that the parents are unable to set reasonable limits for their child (Nicoll, 1992). Research indicates that autocratic and permissive-indulgent parenting styles are associated with a greater likelihood of learning and behavioral problems (Dornbusch, Ritter, Leiderman, Roberts, & Fraleigh, 1987; Forehand, King, Peed, & Yoder, 1975; Martinez, 1981).

Parents who consciously or unconsciously have ceded authority to their child tend to respond to the school consultant in one of two ways: placing total control in the hands of the consultant or dismissing any suggestions the consultant makes. The consultant has to resist both pulls: He or she must do everything possible to make these parents collaborators in the consulting process. Both consultant and parents must believe that these parents are capable of helping to solve their child's problem. When a parent does not believe in his or her own capabilities, the consultant's first task it to empower the parent: "You know your child better than anyone else";

"I need your help to deal with Tommy's problem"; "You are the authority in this family." Statements like these, repeated often and in front of the child, can help restore power and authority in the executive subsystem to the parents.

The consultant must remember that parents' defensiveness generally signals insecurity. Insecure parents have a difficult time establishing consistent rules and regulations in their household, and the consequences of that difficulty in the school environment can be major. The key to dealing with defensive parents is to recognize the source of their behavior and to respond to it calmly, saying something like "The school needs your help." Remember that the goal is to make these parents collaborators in the process.

Boundaries

A second issue in consulting with parents is *boundaries,* the physical and psychological factors that separate parents from children (Gladding, 2001). Minuchin and Fishman (1981) believed that the boundaries in problematic families are either too diffuse or too rigid. *Diffuse boundaries* lead to enmeshed relationships. Signs of diffuse boundaries include overinvolvement in the lives of other family members, finishing one another's sentences, and a lack of privacy. Parents who are constantly in the school building or calling about their child's welfare may be signaling enmeshment. When diffuse boundaries are a problem, the school consultant has to help the parents set boundaries for their child. Using any of the models described in this chapter, the consultant helps the consultees understand that children, to sustain healthy development, need some space between themselves and their parents.

Rigid boundaries lead to disengaged relationships, to family members being completely separated from one another. Here the problem is a lack of involvement in one another's lives.

> I remember working with a family referred after one of the children had been hospitalized with a psychiatric problem. When I investigated, I discovered that the child had been in the hospital for four days before anyone in her family had visited. When I asked why no one had been to see her sooner, the parents recited a litany of excuses. I ended our meeting by reminding them that the discharge plan for their daughter would include family therapy. They did not seem excited by the idea.

Collaborating with disengaged parents is extremely difficult. Calls to home go unreturned; requests to come to school are met with a host of scheduling conflicts. When disengaged parents finally meet with the consultant, they spend a good part of the session letting the consultant know that the meeting is an intrusion in their very busy and important lives. These parents are not necessarily abusive or neglectful, at least not by state guidelines: They attend to their child's basic physical needs. But they are psychologically and emotionally unavailable to the child.

The key to intervention here is to keep the focus on the source of the problem, the parents. Disengaged parents can seduce the consultant—especially an inexperienced consultant—into thinking that the problem is the school's. It's also important to stay calm.

After several phone calls, Mrs. Jones finally came to school to talk about a problem her son was having. She immediately let me know that she was annoyed at the school's lack of consideration for her busy schedule. I tried my best not to get defensive: "Well, it's great that you came. Some parents are so busy, they never get here. Your coming means that together we have a chance of helping your son. I certainly can't do it without you."

Disengagement can be a defense against feelings of inadequacy; the best way to deal with disengaged parents, then, is around the underlying inadequacy. The intervention with Mrs. Jones worked on two counts: first by relativizing her level of disengagement and second by assuming that she had something to contribute. School counselors may not always be successful at involving disengaged parents, but they must make every effort to return the problem to its rightful place, the parent's authority.

Triangulation

Murray Bowen (1976) introduced the concept of triangles into family counseling to explain a lack of differentiation among family members.[8] He believed that when two undifferentiated people in a relationship face anxiety, they tend to draw in a third party to reduce their own anxiety. In families, triangulation usually takes the form of the child's being drawn into conflicts between the parents. A triangulated child is not allowed to differentiate, which in turn can lead to symptomatic behavior.

Peeks (1992) suggested that eight situations set the stage for triangulation in a family: a natural or uncontrollable disaster, a conflict between the family and a social agency, family transition, confusion in the family hierarchy, marital conflict, parental disagreement over a child's discipline, a family's inability to reorganize after the parents separate or divorce, and the unresolved problems of an individual family member. Edwards and Foster (1995) described the case of a first grader:

Jeff's first-grade teacher referred him because she had noticed he was experiencing a greater amount of frustration over his school work than usual. When she asked why he was having such a difficult time, Jeff said that his divorced parents had a "very big fight" the night before and he could not stop thinking about it. She asked if he would like to talk to the counselor about it, and he said yes. He related that his estranged father had come to the house unexpectedly the previous night and a noisy battle occurred between the parents. I asked Jeff what he did when his parents fought. He explained that he would come downstairs, after being sent to his room, wearing his cap gun and sheriff's badge and say that if his parents did not stop fighting he would arrest them. Then, his parents would scream at him to go back upstairs and to not get involved in their argument. If he did not do as they said he would receive punishment in the form of a spanking or restriction. I asked why he did this, and he replied

---

[8] Actually, Bowen believed all relationships are basically triadic.

that it was his job to stop his parents' fighting. This seemed to be a big responsibility for a 7-year-old. I concluded: "It's no wonder he was having difficulty doing his class work." Perhaps he was busy thinking of other strategies to get his parents to stop fighting. (p. 281)

Some forms of triangulation are less obvious than others. For example, one parent may use generosity to win over the child from the other parent. For the consultant this means asking the parents about problems in the wider context of their lives. When the school consultant discovers a case of triangulation, he or she must try to get the parents to deal directly with their problem and to "detriangulate" the child.

A note of caution: Consultants must be careful not to be triangulated themselves. Remember that triangulation serves a significant purpose: reducing tension between two members of the system. Parents, to reduce the tension intrinsic to the consulting process, can easily triangulate the consultant (Edwards & Foster, 1995), and that's not good. A triangulated consultant loses both objectivity it and focus on the real problem.

Parental Resistance

Engaging the parents is crucial to the success of the consulting process. But parental resistance is common.[9] Few parents want to hear that their child is having a problem in school, and even fewer have the psychological strength to admit that they might be contributing to their child's problem. It's much easier to blame the school.

We talked above about defensiveness, one form of resistance to dealing with a child's problem. Parents also can attack with anger and a great deal of emotion; they can intellectualize, using an eloquent family history, for example, to distract the counselor from the situation at hand; or they can resist by breaking appointments, always with a convincing reason for not being able to make it on a particular day (Campbell, 1993).

Sources of Resistance   Campbell (1993) described eight sources of parental resistance to school-based consulting:

Voluntariness. Ideally consultees are willing participants in the consulting process, but some parents see a request for a conference as a summons. For these parents, power issues can lead to resistance.

Negative association with school. Some parents have painful memories of their own school experience. For these parents, school is not a place where they want to go.

Personal problems. Parents who are so overwhelmed or distracted by their own problems may resist coming to a conference.

---

[9]Actually, consultants can encounter many forms of resistance. For a slightly different taxonomy from the one listed below, see Dougherty, Dougherty, and Purcell (1991).

Fear of personal disclosure. Some parents are reluctant to take part in the consulting process because they are afraid they will have to disclose family secrets.

Philosophical differences. Parents whose parenting style is autocratic may resist meeting with a counselor they believe is going to urge them to be more democratic; these parents also are likely to believe that their child is their business, not the school's.

Sociocultural issues. Differences in race, ethnicity, and social class, and other cultural differences between parents and consultant can contribute to parental resistance. (We talk more about this in Chapter 6.)

Denial. Again, parents in general do not like to admit that their child has a problem. Often denial, and so resistance, stems from parents' inability to separate their child's identity from their own: The child's bad behavior means that they are bad parents.

Impracticality. This takes the form of skepticism about anything the consultant suggests.

How do consultants know that parents are being resistant? Sometimes it's obvious. At other times, consultants must trust their instincts. Good consultants, like good counselors, learn to diagnose problems through their own emotional reactions. When a consultant feels frustrated, impatient, and distracted from any kind of concrete problem solving, it is very likely that he or she is dealing with a resistant consultee.

Reducing Parental Resistance   There are several methods for dealing with parental resistance:

Emphasize collaboration. One of the best ways to reduce parents' resistance is to treat them as experts, to make clear to them and their child that they have special knowledge that is critical to solving the problem. If parents (or any consultee) feel insignificant or left out of the process, their resistance will escalate (Campbell, 1993; Dougherty, Dougherty, & Purcell, 1991).

Refocus. This intervention is especially important with parents who digress from the problem at hand by blaming others for their child's problem (Campbell, 1993).

> *I remember one mother who responded to every statement I made about her child's problem by blaming her ex-husband. Finally, I turned to her and said: "Much of what you say about your ex-husband and his effect on your child could be true. But you are the custodial parent and a very important part of your child's life. So let's see if together we can find a way to get your son to start doing his homework at an appropriate time."*

Reframe. Reframing is a well-known technique in family counseling. It involves giving a positive interpretation to a problem or looking at a mistake as an opportunity for learning (Campbell, 1993). For example, a father who complains that his son is constantly questioning his authority might be told: "It seems that communication with you is very important to your son." Reframing can reduce parents' feelings of anger and frustration and help them focus on possible solutions to the problem at hand.

Use a parable. Campbell suggested that by telling the parents the story of a child with a similar problem, the consultant can introduce new possibilities. This intervention is especially good for consultees whose form of resistance is helplessness.

Use contracts. Once a plan for dealing with the child's problem is agreed on, it can be useful for the consultant and the parents to write down what needs to be done, by whom, and when (Campbell, 1993). Contracts not only clarify the plan; they also help parents take ownership of the plan, which reduces their resistance.

Ask the parents to observe the child at home. Giving the parents a form and asking them to watch their child at home and to note instances of the problem behavior can be especially helpful for parents whose resistance is denial. The consultant also asks the teacher to observe and note the child's behavior in school. Then a meeting can be arranged with parents and teacher to compare their findings and to begin to develop a plan of action together.

CONSULTING WITH TEACHERS

Consulting with teachers is an important part of the curriculum in school counselor training programs. Yet there are few articles on the topic in the literature.[10] How do we explain this apparent contradiction between training and research?

The importance that training programs attach to consulting with teachers is understandable when we consider the potential influence of teachers. The effects of a consultation that helps a teacher learn to deal with a particular student's problem can extend to other students with a similar problem. Teachers, because of the amount of time they spend with their students, can make a real difference in the lives of children, and so can the consultants who work with teachers.

The Challenges

D. Brown, Pryzwansky, and Schulte (2001) identified four major hurdles to consulting with teachers: the training orientation of teachers, time constraints, a lack of administrative support, and professional status.

Training Orientation   Brown and his colleagues pointed out that teachers in this country are trained more in techniques than in decision making. As a result, when teachers are faced with a student who is misbehaving, their reaction is that another or different technique is needed. In a school, this usually means a referral for some form of special service, perhaps a smaller class or individualized instruction.

---

[10] Articles about consulting with parents appear much more frequently than those about consulting with teachers.

I was working as a school counselor in a middle school with a dean of discipline who had taught for a long time before moving into administration. In almost every case involving a behavior problem, her immediate reaction was to refer the child for an evaluation for special education services. With patience and a lot of dialogue, I was able to give her the tools to differentiate between problems that warrant a referral and those that can be addressed by classroom management skills.

Time Constraints   This is perhaps the greatest obstacle to working with teachers. The consultation models described in this chapter take time, a resource teachers sorely lack. Today, with high-stakes testing in the schools, teachers complain that there is pressure from administrators to give every available moment to preparing students for tests. School counselors complain that they are losing classroom periods for guidance activities; and music and art are disappearing from many curricula. Teachers simply don't have the time during the school day for consultation.

Lack of Administrative Support   Some administrators oppose consultation or any kind of in-service training because it takes teachers out of the classroom. Others see the usefulness of in-service training when the subject is instruction and the trainer is a master teacher; but they balk at time spent on the behavior problems of one student. Administrators often do support school counselor-teacher consultations to promote better discipline generally in the classroom or to create a more positive classroom environment. But even that support can stymie the consulting process. The problem: Teachers can react negatively to a process in which they feel pressured to participate, and that means they are not participating voluntarily (D. Brown, Pryzwansky, & Schulte, 2001). In the absence of voluntary participation, consultation cannot work.

Professional Status   The final obstacle to consulting with teachers is their professional status. It can be difficult for someone who is trained in a field to ask for help. Also, insecure teachers, much like insecure parents, can become defensive.

Studies on the help-seeking behaviors of teachers indicate that those who consider themselves good problem solvers or who have high self-efficacy are more likely to ask a consultant for help (Hughes, Grossman, & Barker, 1990; Stenger, Tollefson, & Fine, 1992). In addition, teachers who perceive the consultant's training is different from their own are more amenable to working with a consultant (Stenger et al., 1992). This last finding is interesting, especially when we consider the battle raging over the lack of teacher certification requirements in many states for school counselors. Those who favor certification argue that only a school counselor who has studied to be or worked as a teacher can work and consult with teachers—an argument the Stenger finding appears to call into question.

Consulting Strategies

Although certain obstacles to consulting with teachers—for example, the lack of administrative support—do not have easy solutions, theorists have developed strategies to overcome other obstacles. Both the mental health and behavioral models of consultation are well suited to working with teachers. Also useful are group consultation (Dinkmeyer & Carlson, 1973, 2001) and the 15-minute consultation (D. Brown, Pryzwansky, & Schulte, 2001).

Group Consultation Building on the work of task-oriented groups (T groups), Dinkmeyer and Carlson (1973, 2001) developed *C groups*, consultation groups for teachers. The *C* stands for the functions of the consultant, or group leader: collaboration, consultation, clarification, communication, cohesion, concern, confronting, caring, confidentiality, commitment, and change.

Dinkmeyer and Carlson recommended a five-step process for starting a C group:

1. Select voluntary teachers with similar concerns or, when case-focused, who work with the same students.
2. From this group select teachers who are admired and respected by the majority of the faculty. A favorable report from this group will carry more weight with other faculty members.
3. By interview, narrow this group to five or six members of different ages, levels of experience, and teaching/learning approaches. Greater success is reported with heterogeneous groups.
4. During the interview, clarify the goals of the group. Supply all members with written materials describing purposes, rationale, and benefits of the "C" group experience.
5. With administrative approval and assistance, decide on a time and place for [one-hour] group sessions over a period of six to eight weeks. The "C" group may also be conducted at a one- or two-day retreat away from the school setting. (Wallace & Hall, 1996, pp. 153–154)

The C group is based on Adlerian principles of behavior (see Chapter 2); it is designed to help teachers examine their interactions with students and find ways to improve those interactions. The teachers are given strategies and resources to understand patterns of student behavior and to respond, not just react, to behaviors. Like other small groups, C groups provide mutual support, encouragement, and interpersonal learning.

The C group can be a viable alternative for reaching a number of teachers in a limited time. Of course, scheduling a group during the school day can be a problem. The school counselor should consider running sessions before or after school.

The 15-Minute Consultation Primarily in response to teachers' time constraints, D. Brown, Pryzwansky, and Schulte (2001) developed the 15-minute consultation. The idea is to consult with teachers on the run, for a few minutes between classes or in the lunchroom, for example.

To maximize the use of time, Brown and his colleagues recommended that the consultant determine the type of help the teacher is asking for and the nature of the consulting interaction. For the first, the authors suggested the use of Caplan's typology to identify the consultee's difficulty as a lack of knowledge, skill, self-confidence, or objectivity. For the second, the consultant must determine whether the consultee is more task oriented or process oriented. With teachers who are task oriented, the consultant must maintain a focus on the problem and a concrete solution—a focus that has the consultant functioning more as an expert than a collaborator. The consultant should help the consultee prioritize and identify the specific problem, and ask if the consultee has a hypothesis about the problem and what, if any, interventions he or she has tried. The consultant does not have the luxury of time to talk about alternatives that have already failed.

Next the consultant should make recommendations, but always with a reminder that the recommendations are based on a brief meeting. Finally, the consultant and the consultee agree on their responsibilities for the plan and set a time for their next meeting. If the consultant does not feel comfortable offering a recommendation on the spot, he or she can ask to observe the student in class. But follow-up meetings with the teacher should be held to 15-minute sessions.

Brown and his colleagues did point out the limitations of the 15-minute consultation. For example, brief meetings do not allow contradictions to surface; and a quick diagnosis, based on limited information, may be wrong, which could discourage a teacher from further consultation and could call into question the consultant's credibility. Of course, time is always a problem for school counselors. Schools are hectic, busy places where most of the work is done in a six- or seven-hour day. Often counselors are forced to meet with individual students quickly and between two other urgent tasks. Schools have a way of making almost everything seem urgent. The tension between that urgency and taking time to be fully present for a client or consultee is something with which all school counselors must live.

ETHICAL AND LEGAL ISSUES

When acting as consultants to parents and teachers, school counselors need to be aware of certain ethical guidelines. The key issues in this context are competence, informed consent, confidentiality, protecting the welfare of the client, and maintaining proper boundaries.

Counselors must be reasonably certain that they have the *competence* to give the kind of consulting services needed (ACA, 1995). A school counselor might begin a consultation with a teacher in which the presenting problem appears to be the relational dynamics between the teacher and a student. But after gathering all the necessary information, the counselor-consultant comes to the conclusion that the real problem lies in the teacher's instructional methods. Because instructional methods are beyond the counselor's scope of practice, ethical practice would be to terminate the consultation and refer the teacher to a supervisor or master teacher.

Consultation also requires the *informed consent* of the consultee, which means the consultant must explain the procedure he or she intends to use and any potential risks. Also part of informed consent is an explanation of *confidentiality* and its limits. Consultant and consultee must agree on who will have access to the consultant's findings (Corey, Corey, & Callahan, 2003). And the consultant must make clear that anything discovered during the consultation that jeopardizes the welfare of the client cannot be kept confidential. A school counselor, for example, who discovers in the course of a consulting session with parents that the parents are physically abusing their child would not be able to keep that information secret. Similarly, the discovery that a teacher clearly discriminates against students of color and refuses to change could not be kept confidential. For school counselors acting as consultants, *protecting the welfare of the client* is a very relevant ethical issue.

Finally, school-based consultants must *maintain proper boundaries* in the consulting relationship. It would not be ethical, for example, to be consulting with a teacher in school and to be counseling the same teacher outside school.[11] All ethical codes warn against dual relationships. If in the course of consulting, a teacher asks the consultant for counseling too, the consultant should refer the teacher to someone else for private counseling.

CONCLUSION

School-based consultants are a versatile lot. They draw on counseling, teaching, supervisory, and mediating skills to work with parents and teachers on solving students' problems. What most distinguishes consulting from other counseling and helping services is the collaborative nature of the process: Consultant and consultee must work together to help the client. Collaboration not only defines the consulting process; it also underlies the mental health and behavioral models of consultation. In both client-centered and consultee-centered consultation, determining the consultee's strengths and weaknesses is a first step in the collaborative effort. And at the heart of the behavioral models is a reliance on problem solving to improve the functioning of both consultee and client. The importance of collaboration also is reflected here in the focus on parents and teachers, the two groups from which most consultees in schools come.

School consultants are not magicians: They have no magic power to solve what can seem to be unsolvable problems. But the effects of their work can be magical, as positive relationships multiply through family and school.

QUESTIONS FOR DISCUSSION

1. How important do you think the role of consultant is for school counselors? If you were working as a school counselor, how much of your time would you want to allocate to consulting versus individual counseling, small-group counseling, and large-group guidance? Why?

---

[11] If no other mental health professional is available to counsel the teacher, an argument can be made that the principle of beneficence outweighs the prohibition of dual relationships.

2. What is your reaction to the importance Caplan places on theme interference? Do you agree with him? Is theme interference relevant for schools with students from different cultural backgrounds? Explain your answer.

3. Behavioral models of consultation have the consultant assess the problem, set goals, develop and then implement a plan, and evaluate the plan's success. This problem-solving process takes time, a precious resource in the school setting. Suggest several ways in which a consultant could shorten the process.

4. With which of the models of consultation presented in the chapter are you most comfortable? Explain your answer.

5. In working with an intact family (a family in which the child's biological parents live together), a common assumption is that problems in the marital dyad are responsible for the child's behavioral problems at school. What is your reaction to this structural approach? Be sure to consider the concepts of boundaries and triangulation in your answer.

6. Many families today are not intact. Discuss the different family arrangements school counselors might come across in their role as consultant. Are there any families that you feel would be especially challenging for you to work with? Why?

7. Many states do not require a teaching background for school counselor certification. How much of a problem is a lack of teaching experience when school counselors have to consult with teachers? How would you respond to a teacher who says to you, "How would you know? You haven't been in the classroom as much as I have"?

THE USE OF DATA IN SCHOOL COUNSELING

Schools are results oriented; and today, more than ever before, results are being measured through standardized tests. Politicians call out for accountability, for all students to meet higher standards. The government's mantra "Leave no child behind" has been refashioned by some to "Leave no child untested."

High-stakes testing has become the norm in our schools.[1] And so has anxiety. Administrative and teaching jobs can hang on students' scores on one test. So do students' promotions and graduation. Worse yet, education is suffering: many of our teachers are teaching to the test.

School counselors also are feeling the impact of the new reliance on standardized tests. First, they are dealing with the many schoolchildren who are in need of counseling to reduce their test anxiety. Second, they often are involved in the school's testing program, administering tests and later distributing and explaining the results to students and parents. But school counselors bring to those tasks a history of working with test-generated data. They have long used test scores to help students make decisions about postsecondary education and work; to identify and plan interventions for students at risk for academic failure; and to gauge the effectiveness of counseling activities on students' learning and achievement. The first part of this chapter examines the fundamentals of testing to generate assessment data: both norm-referenced and criterion-referenced tests and the issues of validity and reliability.

In this age of accountability, school counselors are not exempt from having to defend their contribution to the school's primary function: student learning and achievement. From the outset, the pioneers of developmental guidance programs have argued for an evaluative component. More recently, the DeWitt Wallace Foundation, through its grants to improve school counseling (see Chapter 1), also has insisted on the use of data to help counselors evaluate the effectiveness of their programs. And the ASCA National Model for School Counseling (ASCA, 2003) has accountability as one of its four basic elements. In the second part of this chapter,

---

[1] In addition to standardized aptitude and achievement tests, schools also use data generated from observations, interviews, conferences with students and parents, self-reports, and other sociometric methods (S. B. Baker, 2000).

then, we consider program evaluation, ways to generate data to answer a crucial question: "Did the program or activity accomplish what it set out to accomplish?" In effect, "Is what I'm doing working?"

STUDENT ASSESSMENT

We use the word *assessment* here to mean the use of both standardized and non-standardized methods for measuring students' learning (S. B. Baker, 2000). Our focus is on basic measurement principles and the use of standardized test scores and other indicators of academic achievement to evaluate the effectiveness of school counseling programs.[2]

Norm-Referenced Measurement and Testing

Standardized tests are administered under standard directions and conditions. Many of the tests used for educational assessment are *norm referenced*. That means interpretation of the results is based on a comparison of the individual's performance with that of other individuals in a specified group (Drummond, 2000).

Norm-referenced measurement began in the late 19th century with Sir Francis Galton. Galton measured the height and other physical characteristics of 10,000 people and concluded that those characteristics are normally distributed. In a *normal distribution*, the scores of a measure, when plotted, form a bell-shaped curve, with the majority of scores clustered around the middle and the frequency of scores trailing off on either side (Gladding, 2001). Norm-referenced measurement was introduced in schools at the beginning of the 20th century, when the Binet intelligence tests were first used in France to identify children with mental retardation. The tests were further developed and refined at Stanford University, and the Stanford-Binet Intelligence Scale became the benchmark for standardized testing in education. In contrast to its original purpose of identifying children who are mentally retarded, the Stanford-Binet was used in this country to identify the brightest students for special programs. In time, the Stanford-Binet and many other norm-referenced measures (including aptitude and achievement tests) began to be used to assign students to classes by their ability and achievement levels. The fairly strong correlation between aptitude test scores and subsequent school achievement and between achievement test scores and subsequent school performance convinced educators that using norm-referenced measures to make educational decisions was both effective and appropriate.

Scoring and Interpretation   The normal distribution shows a *central tendency:* most of the scores are clustered in the center of the curve. There are three measures

---

[2] In Chapter 5 we explain a number of standardized measures used in career counseling and development, among them aptitude and achievement tests and interest, values, and personality inventories. The focus of that discussion is on measures school counselors can use to enhance individual career planning and development.

of central tendency: the mean (the average score), the mode (the most frequent score), and the median (the middle score). A student's raw score can be converted to a *standard score,* which indicates the student's position in relation to the mean score of the *normative group*—the group on which the test is standardized. The standard score indicates how far above or below the mean an individual score is.

To interpret the results of a test, we must know the mean and standard deviation of the test. For example, the Scholastic Aptitude Test (SAT) uses a mean of 500 and a standard deviation of 100. A score of 650, then, is 1.5 standard deviations above the mean ($+1.5$). In a normal distribution (that is, the bell curve), 68 percent of scores fall within $+1.0$ and -1.0 standard deviations. Standardized scores on educational tests are usually reported in terms of percentiles, grade equivalents, or age norms.

PERCENTILES   Percentile ranks are the most popular method of expressing comparison scores on norm-referenced tests. Percentile ranks range from 1 to 99 and indicate the percentage of those in the normed population who scored at or below a particular score (Drummond, 2000). For example, a score in the 86th percentile means that the test-taker scored the same as or above 86 percent of those who took the test.

GRADE-EQUIVALENT SCORES   Grade-equivalent scores are most often reported on achievement tests. A grade-equivalent score indicates how a student performed in relation to the typical performance of others in the same grade.[3] A fourth grader with a grade score of 6.2 on a reading test, for example, would be performing above average for his or her grade.

Grade-equivalent scores often are misinterpreted. Consider our fourth grader with a grade-equivalent score of 6.2. This does not mean that the child is reading on the sixth-grade level. It means that the child's raw score is equivalent to the mean score of those in the sixth grade (Drummond, 2000). There may have been no sixth-grade-level items on the test; and the child's performance may not have been compared to that of sixth graders.

Adding to the confusion is the fact that many school systems report the percentage of their students who are reading at or above grade level and deplore any percentage of students who score below grade level. The implication is that all students should score at or above grade level. But achievement tests are norm-referenced standardized tests: by design, a percentage of students must score below the average. In fact, it is a statistical necessity that 50 percent score higher and 50 percent score lower than the average (Gredler, 1996). A norm-referenced test that does not yield a normal distribution would have to be renormed.

AGE NORMS   Many intelligence and other cognitive tests report scores in terms of age norms.[4] Age norms are determined from what typical individuals can do at a given age (Drummond, 2000); they are based on developmental criteria. For

---

[3] Grade-equivalent scales typically run from 1 through 12.

[4] Age norms generally are not reported for achievement tests.

example, suppose an 8-year-old gets an age-equivalent score of 10 on an intelligence test. This means that the child's raw score on the test is equivalent to the mean score of 10-year-olds who took the same test. Children who score above their age norm are developing faster than the norm; but that does not necessarily mean that they are able to perform tasks at the older level.

Using Norm-Referenced Measures Appropriately   Norm-referenced measures can be very useful to the school. Students' performance on these tests provide information about new students, about student achievement in different subject areas, and about students' progress from year to year. And when used in conjunction with other measures, norm-referenced measures can help in making good academic decisions.

But norm-referenced tests should never be used as the sole criterion for a placement decision. In some schools, students from nondominant cultures are tracked into lower-level programs based only on the results of a norm-referenced test, with no consideration of other factors—language or educational background, for example. School counselors, in their advocacy role, must be vigilant for this and other improper uses of norm-referenced measures.

When school systems make curriculum decisions or compare classrooms and schools based solely on the results of a norm-referenced test—and many of them do—they are making a serious mistake. One of the problems here has to do with the design of norm-referenced tests. Programs and curriculums have goals and objectives that norm-referenced tests are not designed to measure (Gredler, 1996; Haertel, 1990). Also the multiple-choice items used in most of these tests measure only one limited and rigid form of demonstrated learning. Most important, using norm-referenced testing to make educators accountable for students' learning and achievement encourages teachers to teach to the test. The result: too many drills and practice exercises, too much pressure on students, and too little learning (Gredler; Smith, & Rottenberg, 1991).

The first school I ever worked in had a principal who every morning, from the first day of school, reminded the students about the districtwide reading and math tests that were scheduled for April! He insisted that the constant reminders were working, pointing to the school's relatively high test scores as proof. But another counselor and I saw and understood the negative emotional impact the principal's focus on the tests was having on the students. We decided to speak with him and share our concerns. We knew the meeting would be difficult—the principal was strong willed and authoritarian—so we prepared our intervention carefully, sensitive to his demanding style. At the meeting, we tried to convince him that it was possible to promote student achievement without making the students overanxious, that too much anxiety could actually get in the way of students' performance. I can't say he didn't listen to us, but he certainly looked at us as though we came from another planet. And at one point he insinuated that because we were school counselors, we did not understand the harsh reality of test scores. Of course we did; we simply didn't want to buy into it. Needless to say, the meeting produced no change in the way that principal went about preparing students for the tests.

Again, norm-referenced tests can be a valuable source of information, but that information must be used wisely. For school counselors, that means as input for developing guidance programs and as output for evaluating the effectiveness of interventions. An example: Suppose scores on a math achievement test show that female students in a class are performing below male students in the class. The school counselor might use the scores as *one* basis for developing a math self-efficacy group for female students. Later the counselor would use the results of future math tests as *one* measure of the effectiveness of the intervention. Test results should never be used as the sole criterion for any decision.

Criterion-Referenced Assessment

Criterion-referenced tests are designed to assess students' proficiency in a particular skill, task, or behavior. A score on a criterion-referenced test does not indicate where a test-taker stands in relation to other students who took the test; it simply indicates whether a student has mastered a particular skill. That skill is the criterion on which the test is developed.

There are two kinds of criterion-referenced tests: mastery and minimum competency (Gellman, 1995). In the former, a predetermined level of proficiency defines *mastery*. Students who score at that level are considered to have mastered the particular skill. Usually mastery is designated as a certain percentage of items answered correctly—for example, 70 percent. Unlike norm-referenced tests, criterion-referenced tests do not have a normal distribution. It is possible for the majority of, if not all, students to attain or fail to attain mastery (Gellman, 1995). And scores reflect mastery and nothing more: Let's say on a particular test, 75 percent is the criterion for mastery. If one student scores 75 percent and another scores 95 percent, all we know is that both students have achieved mastery. Criterion-referenced assessments are not designed to compare students with one another but to judge who in the group has achieved mastery and who has not. Teachers typically use mastery tests after the students have completed an instructional unit to see that they've learned the requisite skills.

The second type of criterion-referenced instrument is the *minimum-competency test*. The criterion here is not mastery but minimal competence of the sort many states demand for high school graduation. In this type of test, a certain percentage of test items answered correctly indicates minimal competence. Students who answer more than that percentage of items correctly do not necessarily have more than minimal competence in the subject because all of the items are of equal difficulty.

Some criterion-referenced tests are designed to distinguish different levels of competence by varying the complexity of the items. For example, a teacher might design a midterm or final exam to assess more than minimum competence; in that case, the higher the score, the greater the student's competence. But this kind of test still does not compare students with one another. In criterion-referenced testing, the focus is on what the test-takers know or can do, not on how they compare with others (Anastasi,1988).

Other Sources of Data

In addition to norm- and criterion-referenced tests, school counselors use observation, rating scales, checklists, and teacher judgments as sources of data for developing and evaluating a comprehensive guidance program. Counselors should find the time to observe students who are having difficulty across settings. If a student is receiving help from the counseling program, it can be especially helpful to observe the student at different times to assess differences in behavior. Counselors can use rating scales and checklists to track their observations; these instruments can also be used by teachers to provide feedback to counselors about the behavior of certain students. These evaluations, too, should be made at different times so that counselors can compare pre- and postintervention behaviors. Finally, school counselors spend a lot of time talking with teachers about students and their problems. Informal conversations—no rating scales or checklists—can be very valuable in assessing the effects of counseling program interventions on students. School counselors should always make notes on their conversations with teachers about students' progress.

Validity

It is always interesting to listen to students' comments after an exam "It was so hard." "It was so easy." "Those questions were so stupid." "Nothing I studied was on the test." Was the exam a good one? We might have difficulty getting a consensus from the test-takers. But in fact there are certain elements that go into making a good exam. One of the most important is the test's validity.

A test is considered *valid* if it measures what it is purported to measure. Validity is what allows us to draw inferences from the results of a test. How do we know that a test is a valid measure? There is no single index for validity (Mehrens & Lehman, 1987). In general, a test's validity is a function of three elements: content validity, criterion-related validity, and construct validity.

Content Validity   Content validity is the degree to which the test items are representative of the content area—cognitive or behavioral—that is being assessed (Gellman, 1995). Content validity is determined through expert judgment, not statistical procedures. Developers of educational tests employ university professors, curriculum specialists, and subject-matter teachers to assess whether the test items are an adequate sampling of the content domain (Drummond, 2000).[5]

Content validity is especially important in achievement tests. Of course, national or even statewide achievement tests cannot possibly reflect all of the content

---

[5]Classroom teachers also have to consider content validity when they create a test. Content validity here means that the items on the test adequately represent the content and skills covered in the class (Gellman, 1995).

taught in individual classrooms, and that often leads to some students' complaining that the test did not cover what they learned in class. But this does not necessarily make the test invalid. Of course if all of the students in a class make the same complaint, the school counselor should investigate. A teacher can stray from the curriculum or neglect to teach students how to apply the learning. Many times, an achievement test demands an application of what students learned in class, not rote memorization. Students often mistake this for a lack of validity. If serious concerns persist, the counselor might ask that a specialist review the test and assess its content validity. It's unlikely a problem will be discovered. Test development is a big business, and no company can afford to release a test that lacks content validity. Still, the counselor's advocacy when students insist that a test did not measure their learning can ensure that students are being properly evaluated.

Criterion-Related Validity   Criterion-related validity, or predictive validity, is a measure of the relationship between a test score (known as the *predictor*) and an independent external measure (the *criterion*) (Mehrens & Lehman, 1987). Predictive validity is a key component of aptitude tests. Colleges take SAT scores seriously because those scores are significantly correlated to grade point average (GPA); the higher a student's SAT scores, the more likely that student is to perform well in college (College Board, 2000; Hood & Johnson, 2002). The SAT has predictive validity for achievement in college.[6]

The *correlation coefficient* is the measure of the relationship between two scores, the predictor (for example, the SAT score) and the criterion (GPA) (Gellman, 1995). Correlation coefficients range from $+1.00$ to -1.00. A predictive validity of $+1.00$ would mean that scores on the test are perfect predictors of scores on the criterion, with high scores on one measure associated with high scores on the other. A correlation coefficient of -1.00 also indicates a perfect correlation; in this case, however, high scores on one measure are perfectly correlated with low scores on the other. This is still a very strong correlation, albeit a negative one.

Of course no test has perfect predictive validity. Correlation coefficients between good aptitude tests and student grades generally range from $+.70$ to $+.95$ (Gellman, 1995). This means that to a significant degree, those who score high on the aptitude test also will get high grades. That correlation would not be true for everybody, and the test does not predict exactly what students' grades are or will be. A student whose aptitude scores are very high and whose grades are low is thought of as an underachiever. And a student with low aptitude scores and high grades is thought of as a hard-working overachiever. Those classifications are based on the assumption that both measures (of aptitude and of schoolwork) are relevant, reliable, and unbiased. And the closer the correlation coefficient is to $+1.00$, the more likely those assumptions are true.

Criterion-related validity is particularly important for school counselors who are involved in decisions about students' academic and career plans. Many schools make educational placements based on the predictive validity of a particular test.

---

[6] Predictive validity is also an important component of vocational tests. Companies use these tests for hiring and placement decisions because the tests have proved to have predictive validity for performance on the job.

School counselors should understand a test's predictive validity to help parents and administrators make an informed decision about a student's future. At the same time, counselors should advocate against the misuse of a test's predictive validity to track students, to place them in academic versus vocational programs. Many variables contribute to an individual's future success, and no decision should be reduced to just a single variable.

Construct Validity   The third type of validity is construct validity. A *construct* is what a test is designed to measure; *construct validity* is the degree to which the results of the test are related to the variable or variables the test is designed to measure (Hood & Johnson, 2002). Construct validity pertains especially to tests that measure traits or interests. Intelligence, anxiety, locus of control, and self-esteem are all constructs for which tests have been developed.

Suppose a school counselor wants to identify students with low self-esteem, so she develops a list of items that she believes indicate levels of self-esteem. How does the counselor know for sure that the items actually measure the construct self-esteem? It is not enough for the counselor to simply think the items are valid. She must demonstrate that the items are valid by comparing the measure to other, already validated measures of self-esteem. For example, the counselor could administer the self-developed measure of self-esteem along with the Coopersmith Self-Esteem Inventory, a measure of self-esteem that has been validated in the literature (Coopersmith, 1993). The counselor would then correlate the scores obtained on the self-developed measure and the scores obtained on the Coopersmith inventory. This correlation coefficient is called the *construct validity coefficient,* and it indicates the degree to which the construct of the test is valid. Here, too, the closer the correlation coefficient to +1.00, the greater the validity.

Validity and Educational Decision Making   Again, school districts often use the results of a single test to determine students' placement in programs.[7] And again, the practice is wrong; a single score on a standardized test should never be used to make important educational decisions. No measure is perfectly valid; and no single measure can reflect all the variables that go into students' learning and achievement.

When a school makes placements on the basis of a single score, school counselors must take on their advocacy role. This is especially important when students from nondominant cultures are involved. Language, culture-bound learning styles, and other acculturation issues can call into question the validity of test results for minority students. Counselors' best weapon in this battle is a thorough understanding of the tests, and key to that understanding is the test manual. Test manuals describe the process by which the test was developed and list validity coefficients. They also contain information about the performance of different groups by age, grade, and gender; and the more popular tests provide information about the performance of students by racial and ethnic groups. These data allow counselors to assess variability in validity. Because test developers write the manuals to portray their tests in the best light possible, counselors also should consult inde-

---

[7] Some school districts maintain that the decision to rely on a single score is done in the name of fairness.

pendent reviews of assessment instruments in sources like the *Fourteenth Mental Measurement Yearbook* (Plake & Impara, 2001), *Tests in Print* V (L. L. Murphy, Impara, & Plake, 1999), and *A Counselor's Guide to Career Assessment Instruments* (Kapes & Whitfield, 2001).

Although most test publishers send out a lengthy explanation with students' scores, the school counselor would do well to schedule a yearly workshop for parents on the use of standardized tests and the meaning of the scores. Training in the fundamentals of measurement and sensitivity to the emotions these tests can generate make school counselors uniquely qualified to help parents understand both the testing process and their child's results.

Reliability

Reliability, like validity, is a key element in the development of tests and in the use and evaluation of test data. Reliability contributes to validity; in other words, a test cannot be valid unless it is reliable. *Reliability* is the degree of consistency between two measures of the same thing (Mehrens & Lehman, 1987). A test is considered reliable if, when administered under the same conditions, it produces more or less the same results. Suppose a student takes a test and answers 80 percent of the questions correctly, and then a week later takes the same test and answers 50 percent of the questions correctly. Assuming there were no extenuating circumstances, we would question the test's reliability. Reliability has to do with the consistency, dependability, and repeatability of test results (Gladding, 2001).

No test is perfectly valid, and no test is perfectly reliable. Back to the student who took the test and scored 80 percent. What if the student took the test again a week later and scored 83 percent? Would we say that the test is unreliable? Probably not. How do we explain the discrepancy in the scores? The technical answer is *measurement error*. Every test has a certain degree of error because it cannot demonstrate exactly what a student knows. In our example, the student may have guessed at a couple of questions and answered them correctly. Or a student who really has the ability to answer a question correctly may mark the wrong space on the answer sheet. Any number of factors can contribute to measurement error.

Three broad categories of measurement error have been identified: error caused by the test itself (for example, a typographical error or an item that is poorly written); error caused by the person taking the test (sickness); and error caused by the conditions of testing (a violation of the time limit or unusual distractions).

> *I remember one year, it was the day of the districtwide reading exam. After the start of the test, a construction crew arrived to work on the front doors of the school. First we heard a great deal of drilling and hammering; then we heard the principal yelling at the top of his lungs, demanding that the crew stop working immediately. It was the same principal who used daily reminders to prepare the student body for the districtwide exams. The crew left and came back the next day.*

The principal's intervention was aimed at error caused by the condition of testing.

The Reliability Coefficient   Because no test is error-free or perfectly reliable, every standardized test has a *reliability coefficient,* a correlation coefficient that expresses the estimated reliability of the test. Three methods are used to determine the reliability coefficient of a test

> *Test-retest.* Using the test-retest method, the same students are given the same test on two different occasions, and then the two sets of scores are correlated. If the test is reliable, the students should score more or less the same. The closer the reliability coefficient is to +1.00, the more reliable the test. There are some factors that can affect test-retest reliability. For example, in one of the test administrations, the students may have had more time. Also, if the tests are administered within a very short time of each other, students might recognize the test items and do better the second time around.

> *Alternate forms (parallel forms).* Using this method, the correlation coefficient is derived by giving the same students two equivalent forms of a test several weeks apart. The items on the two tests are different, but they assess the same content and have the same level of difficulty. If the tests are reliable, the correlation of scores from the two tests should be fairly close to +1.00.

> *Split-half.* Unlike the test-retest and alternate-forms methods, split-half reliability is determined in just one test administration. The test is divided into two halves (usually by odd- and even-numbered items). The reliability coefficient is derived by comparing individuals' scores on the two halves. Alternatively, several formulas are available to estimate split-half reliability. Split-half reliability usually yields the highest correlation coefficient; alternate forms, the lowest.

Reliability coefficients are estimates, and because they are obtained through different procedures are not always the same. Still, the reliability coefficients of aptitude and achievement tests should range from +.75 to +.95. Inventories of personality and interests tests tend to have lower reliability coefficients, ranging from +.30 to +.50 (Gellman, 1995). One of the most important factors in the reliability of a test is its length. Generally, the longer a test, the greater its reliability. School counselors should be wary of a standardized test in which the subtests have few items in relation to the overall number of items, yet scores are reported for each of the subtests. Students and parents should know, and the students' records should reflect, that the scores on these subtests are not very reliable.

The Standard Error of Measurement   Because no test is perfectly reliable, a certain amount of error is associated with every student's score. The *standard error of measurement* indicates the range in which a student's true score falls (Drummond, 2000). Let's say that a student scores 86 percent one week and the next week, on the same test, scores 82 percent. A parent may ask "Which is the true score?" The standard error of measurement answers that question by calculating a range within which the student's true score lies. It tells us how much a student's score is likely to vary on subsequent administrations of the same test. The standard error of measurement is a function of reliability: the greater the test's reliability, the lower the standard error of measurement, and vice versa.

The standard error follows a normal distribution. For example, suppose the standard error of an achievement test is 4. If a student's score is 86 on the test, we would conclude that 68 percent of the time (based on a standard deviation of +1.0 and −1.0), the student's score lies between 82 and 90. Similarly, we can say that 95 percent of the time (based on a standard deviation of +2.0 and −2.0), the student's score will fall between 78 and 94.

Counselors should help students and parents understand that scores that fall within 1 standard error of measurement are not really different. If one student scores 86 percent on a test with a standard error of measurement of 4, and another student scores 83 percent, the two students' scores are statistically the same.

Issues of reliability should help school counselors maintain a realistic perspective on standardized testing. The tests are not perfectly reliable, and the test scores do not perfectly assess students' aptitude or achievement. But test scores can help school counselors chart students' progress and identify areas in which students seem likely to excel or to have problems.

Standardized Testing and Accountability

Those who support the high cost of frequent standardized testing justify that cost in the name of accountability. A call has been sounded to measure, measure, and measure some more. And more measurements mean more comparisons of students, teachers, schools, districts, and states. The situation has created special challenges for school counselors. Chief among those is dealing with the anxiety that standardized tests generate. That anxiety is well founded in schools where important educational decisions are based on a single test score. And that, of course, is the second challenge facing school counselors today: advocating for students whose futures are being decided by their performance on a single test.

Again, school counselors' best weapon is knowledge, an understanding of norm-referenced and criterion-referenced tests, of validity and reliability. That knowledge can be used both to calm the anxiety of test-takers and their parents, and to warn against making important educational decisions without considering all the variables that go into students' learning and achievement. It is hard to argue with the call for greater accountability in our schools; but it is the school counselor's job to be sure that accountability is measured accurately and fairly.

COUNSELOR ASSESSMENT

We have been talking about the different ways students are assessed in the school environment. Student assessments are uniquely tied to the functions of school counselors. School counselors are often in charge of the school's standardized testing program. In addition to their administrative responsibilities, counselors help the school community—especially students and parents—be responsible consumers of test results. And they use the results of testing as feedback for program planning and evaluation.

This last function speaks to counselors' own accountability for students' learning and achievement. It is not enough to plan interventions and programs and see them implemented; counselors must also evaluate the effectiveness of their activities. And that evaluation requires data. Standardized tests are just one source of information about the benefits of the counseling program. In this section we examine other sources and the processes school counselors can use to hold themselves accountable for what they do.

School Counselors and Accountability: A Renewed Call to Action

During the last 25 years, many leading figures in the field have called for greater accountability from school counselors (ASCA, 2003; Campbell & Dahir, 1997; Gysbers & Henderson, 2000). That call has been resisted on three fronts. The first has to do with the knowledge and experience of those who would be responsible for evaluating the work counselors do; school administrators generally know very little about school counseling. The second has to do with the difficulty of measuring trust or caring or the many other "non-measurable" variables that contribute to effective counseling. The third also has to do with the nature of counseling, that its effects can be measured only in the long term. Although there is some validity to these arguments, they are simply not sustainable at a time when schools across the country are being forced to take responsibility for what they do. The No Child Left Behind Act of 2001 (U.S. Department of Education, 2001), a federal mandate that students be tested frequently, has created an emphasis on results unparalleled in the history of education in this country. The act also requires school districts to report annually on students' progress and achievement by race, gender, and other criteria (Dahir & Stone, 2003).

The pioneers of developmental guidance have always stressed the importance of evaluation (see, for example, Herr & Cramer, 1972; and A. Mitchell & Gysbers, 1978). Yet a study of research in the field found that between 1988 and 1995, just 50 papers on school counseling outcomes were published (Whitson & Sexton, 1998). This dearth of research is even more remarkable in light of studies that have shown the effectiveness of school counseling (L. Borders & Drury, 1992; Gerler, 1992).

Several reasons have been given for what seems to be a resistance to evaluation among school counselors:

- School counselors are ill prepared in research methodology (Fairchild & Zins, 1986; Myrick, 2003).
- School counselors do not understand the relationships between research methodology and their work (Woolsey, 1986).

- School counselors are uncertain about how to organize a study and collect valid data (C. C. Lee & Workman, 1992; Myrick, 2003).
- School counselors believe that accountability studies are designed to categorize them as good or bad counselors (Myrick, 1990).
- Counselor training courses focus on sophisticated research designs that are difficult for school counselors to apply in the work setting (Keene & Stewart, 1989).
- School counselors lack goals and objectives to evaluate (D. Brown, 1989).
- School counselors have neither the time nor the resources to conduct accountability studies (Fairchild & Zins, 1986; Myrick, 2003; N. S. Wilson, 1985).

In a nationwide survey, Fairchild (1993) found that 67.0 percent of school counselors were involved in some kind of accountability activity—an increase from the 54.8 percent found in an earlier survey (Fairchild & Zins, 1986). Only 34.5 percent of school counselors, however, were involved in collecting outcome data. The majority (62.6 percent) collected only enumerative or descriptive data (time spent on different counseling and guidance activities, number of students seen, and the like). Fairchild found that the greatest obstacle to accountability was attitudinal, and that many school counselors emphasized the need for practical and focused training material on collecting and analyzing data. He went on to suggest that when they leave training programs, school counselors should have the following competencies:

- Methods for developing questionnaires for collecting accountability data
- Specific methods for obtaining information, especially for negotiating process and outcome information
- A comprehensive list of sample instruments and procedures
- Methods for analyzing the data, synthesizing the information, and reporting the findings in understandable ways to different consumer groups
- Comprehensive, time-efficient accountability systems and models
- Exemplary models that are currently being used in the field
- Computer-assisted accountability programs (p. 373)

The following sections operationalize at least some of Fairchild's suggestions. The methods described here are user-friendly, proof that counselors can and should collect outcome data both to evaluate and to defend the things they do.

The Assessment of Need

Underlying all of the work school counselors do is a commitment to meet students' needs. For Myrick (1990), that simple objective defines the evaluation process:

1. Identify the students' needs.
2. Identify what is being done to meet those needs.
3. Determine the difference, if any, that the counselors' intervention is making.

How do counselors know what services, interventions, or programs students need? Counselors identify students' needs in several ways, including observation, information from teachers and parents, and school data (academic, social, and vocational). Many comprehensive school counseling programs are built around children's common developmental needs; but there are times when a school counselor might want to conduct a formal needs assessment either to update a comprehensive guidance program or to uncover less obvious needs. By definition, a comprehensive guidance program must respond to the obvious and less obvious needs of all students.

Here we look at ways for school counselors to keep their programs relevant through the periodic assessment of students' needs. Myrick's second step—*identify what is being done to meet students' needs*—is a matter of tracking the counselor's activities and time spent on those activities. We examine the third step—*determine the difference, if any, that the counselors' intervention is making*—in the sections following this one.

Need: A Definition   *Need* is a discrepancy between what is and what should be (Posavac & Carey, 1997). The discrepancy can be between the actual state and (a) an ideal, (b) a norm, (c) a minimum, (d) a wanted state, or (e) an expected state (Roth, 1990). For a school with a large number of children reading below grade level, the need is defined as a discrepancy between the actual state and the norm— that is, a certain percentage of children reading at grade level. In a school where most children are reading at grade level but the principal believes children should be reading above grade level, the need is defined as the discrepancy between the actual state and a wanted state.[8]

Another way to define needs is in terms of satisfaction: "Need refers to something (*X*) that people must have to be in a satisfactory state. Without *X* they would be in a unsatisfactory state; with *X* they achieve but do not exceed a satisfactory state" (Posavac & Carey, 1997, p. 103). This definition is particularly useful for comprehensive and developmental guidance programs. Schools and counselors create these programs to satisfy students' academic, social, and vocational needs. Anything that impedes the satisfaction of those needs is a problem. Therefore, when school counselors do an assessment of need, they should focus on problems that are interfering with the developmental needs of the student body. In that assessment, it is useful to distinguish between the incidence and prevalence of a problem (Posavac & Carey, 1997). *Incidence* refers to the number of new cases in a given period; *prevalence* refers to the number of existing cases in a period. Incidence and prevalence help the counselor know whether the problem is temporary or longer-term, and how widespread the problem is.

Gathering Information   Once counselors have a working definition of need, they must identify sources for relevant information about students' needs. The first step in this process is to define the population. Does the counselor want to assess

---

[8]This is just an example. Most counselors are too busy to develop programs based on discrepancies between actual and ideal or wanted states.

the entire school? Only students in certain grades? Only female students? Only students of color? Once the population is defined, the counselor can consider any number of sources. Data may already exist in the form of reports by the school, the district, or local, state, and federal governments. Another source of information is the members of the population and those who know them. In addition to the students in the focus population, then, the school counselors can talk with teachers, parents, and key informants in the community (police officers, youth leaders, clergy).

Information can be collected through surveys, focus groups, and community forums. In constructing surveys, counselors should include items that focus first on problems and only secondarily on solutions. They should be careful to avoid leading questions. Questions that require an agree-disagree answer are usually not helpful; but open-ended questions that ask for examples of problems, difficulties, and the like usually are. Assuming a limited number of respondents (40 or less), qualitative answers can be analyzed without taking up too much of the counselor's time. The counselor is looking for answers that are repeated often. The questions should not focus on academic performance; data on that performance are readily available from school records. Instead questions should tap into underlying concerns. Here are examples of several good open-ended questions for students:

- During the last year, what has worried you the most?
- What makes it difficult for you to come to school?
- What do you wish your school would have to help you learn better?
- What would make you feel more connected to your school?
- What is the one thing you would like your school counselor to do for you?

Counselors should adapt questions to students' grade level and to challenges their particular school is facing. If students are too young to read or understand the items, a survey can be given to them orally. Although teachers can administer the survey, it is best for counselors to do it themselves. This is a good way for students to meet the counselor and to begin to understand the importance of the counseling program. Surveys can also be developed for teachers, parents, and community informants.

Focus groups can be arranged for different constituencies: teachers, parents, students, and community informants. The ideal focus group consists of 7 to 10 members, all similar in age, income level, and education (Posavac & Carey, 1997). The leader-counselor must make sure that the group attends to the question at hand; at the same time, he or she must be careful not to influence the group's answers. Focus groups are a good source of information about students' needs, but they are very time consuming. That disadvantage is offset by the counselor's ability to clarify the group's concerns, something that is impossible to do in a survey. Of course a survey can be anonymous, and a focus group is not. So the leader-counselor must try to create a relaxed and trusting atmosphere. If the counselor explains clearly and matter-of-factly the importance of the group's feedback for planning the guidance program, most members are more than willing to share their impressions about the needs of local young people and how the school can respond to those needs.

The failure to examine students' needs and to base programs on them can mean the organization and maintenance of counseling programs that are irrelevant to the school and to the community it serves. Periodic assessments of need are another way counselors can use data constructively in their work and make themselves more accountable to both school and community.

Developing Goals and Objectives

For school counselors to evaluate the outcomes of a specific service or program, they must be clear about what they wanted to achieve. Good evaluation, then, begins with a good design: "The key is to ask what you want to know and what will provide the information you need" (Hughey, Gysbers, & Starr, 1993, p. 35). Goals should be formulated in clear, measurable, and realistic terms. For example, suppose a counselor is planning to run a group on self-esteem and decides to use the Coopersmith Self-Esteem Inventory as a preintervention and postintervention measure. The counselor's goal might be "Participants in the self-esteem counseling group will score 5 basis points higher on the Coopersmith Self-Esteem Inventory after eight sessions of group counseling than they did before starting the group." Or suppose a counselor is setting up a study-skills group. A possible goal for this group would be "Participants in the study-skills group will improve their grades in math and English by 3 percentage points."

Notice that these are outcome goals. *Outcome goals* are the focus of any evaluation of a comprehensive school counseling program. For most schoolwide programs, school counselors also set implementation and intermediate goals. *Implementation goals* are the steps school counselors must take before they can implement a large-scale program such as a schoolwide violence prevention program. For example, teachers are an integral part of any schoolwide program, and they must be trained to work with the counselor in program activities. So an implementation goal might be "By October 1, all ninth-grade teachers will have participated in a half-day training on the violence prevention project for their classrooms." *Intermediate goals* are the tasks that need carrying out en route to the final outcomes (Posavac & Carey, 1997). An intermediate goal for a violence prevention program might be "By the end of the first semester, all ninth-grade students will have received 4 of the 10 lessons in the violence prevention curriculum."

Collecting Data

Before school counselors can collect data, they have to answer three crucial questions: From whom? How? And when?

Data Sources   Posavac and Carey (1997) suggested that *who from* includes program participants, program staff (school personnel who are involved in delivering the program), and observers (experts, trainees, teachers, and parents), and program records (measures taken before, during, and after the program) and artifacts (schoolwork and school records). School counselors can use any or all of these resources, although it is always a good idea to collect data from more than one source. Feedback from students who have participated in the program seems important, and it should be relatively easy to gather. But self-reports have limitations. Program participants can be biased, can have little interest in the evaluation, or may have difficulty recalling their thoughts from weeks before. That's why it is a good idea to collect data from teachers and parents too, and to examine test scores and other indicators of achievement. Counseling programs seldom rely on trained observers, but teachers and parents are excellent sources for information about changes in students who are receiving guidance services.

Data Collection Methods   There are also many ways to collect data, among them tests, interviews, checklists, and written surveys (Posavac & Carey, 1997). Tests can be used after several guidance lessons in the classroom to assess whether the students have learned and understood the material. Formal interviews can be very time consuming, but just talking with teachers and parents works as a way to collect valuable feedback. It's important, however, that the counselor develop a system for documenting informal interviews and incorporating their content into the evaluation. Handing out a checklist to program participants or observers is another method of collecting data.

Written surveys are the most widely used way to collect data in all kinds of settings. A good survey demands careful preparation. The format should make the instrument clear and easy to use. Surveys can be unstructured or structured. In an unstructured survey, the respondent is asked open-ended questions. Although these surveys provide valuable information, their analysis takes time, especially when there are a large number of respondents. Structured surveys are forced choice: that is, the respondent must answer yes or no or choose an answer from several alternatives. A *Likert scale* is a structured survey that measures the degree to which a respondent agrees or disagrees with a statement (Gladding, 2001). Each alternative in a Likert scale is assigned a point value. Table 4.1 shows an item from a Likert scale.

It is not a good idea to mix different formats in a survey. Keeping the same format—for example, all multiple-choice questions—makes it easier for the respondent. If it's necessary to ask questions in different formats, keep all of the same-format questions together. Open-ended questions should be directed questions: "Name one thing you *liked* and one thing you *did not like* about the program" (Posavac & Carey, 1997). This example leaves the choices to the respondent but limits the nature and number of those choices.

TABLE 4.1   A LIKERT SCALE ITEM

The time-management group helped me to complete my homework.

1	2	3	4	5
Strongly disagree	Mildly disagree	Don't know	Mildly agree	Strongly agree

TABLE 4.2	RATING SCALE TO EVALUATE A COUNSELING PROGRAM, FOR STUDENTS IN GRADES 1–6			
Item		**Yes**	**No**	**Not Sure**
1. Do you know who the counselor is?				
2. Do you know what the counselor does?				
3. If you needed help with a problem, would you talk to the counselor?				
4. If you want to see the counselor, do you know how to go about it?				
5. I like talking with the counselor.				
6. I know the counselor keeps our talks private.				
7. The counselor is easy to talk with.				
8. The counselor listens to me.				
9. The counselor understands how I feel.				
10. Talking with the counselor helps me feel better about myself.				
11. The counselor helps me with my problems.				
12. Did you enjoy the classroom activities the counselor provided?				
13. Should these activities continue?				
14. I learned that I am worthwhile and important.				
15. I learned that I am responsible for my behavior.				
16. I learned how to identify and express my feelings.				
17. I learned how to get along with others.				
18. I learned how to solve problems.				

SOURCE: "Evaluation of Counseling Services: Accountability in a Rural Elementary School," by T. N. Fairchild, *Elementary School Guidance and Counseling, 29,* p. 32. Copyright 1994 by the American School Counselor Association. Reprinted with permission.

Tables 4.2 and 4.3 are examples of rating scales for elementary school students and their teachers to evaluate the school counseling program. Because the students are young, their scale uses a simple yes-no-not sure format. The teachers' scale uses a Likert format. Notice that the items on both scales are short, clear, and to the point. Simple scales like these can be adapted for different counseling program activities with different constituencies.

Timing the Data Collection   The answer to the *when* question often is a function of the program's goals. Data on implementation goals have to be collected at various intervals during the program. Data on outcome goals should be collected before the program starts and again after the program ends.[9]

PRETESTING AND POSTTESTING   A relatively easy and time-efficient way to collect accountability data is through pretesting and posttesting; the school counselor

---

[9] Actually, there are instances where outcome goals are measured during the program, too. But we've made a promise to keep the material user-friendly.

TABLE 4.3   RATING SCALE TO EVALUATE A COUNSELING PROGRAM, FOR ELEMENTARY SCHOOL TEACHERS

Item	Level-of-Satisfaction Rating					Does not apply
	1	2	3	4	5	
1. The counselor was visible and accessible to students.						
2. The counselor was willing to work with a wide range of student concerns.						
3. The counselor responded promptly to counseling referrals.						
4. The counselor was sensitive to my schedule when seeing students.						
5. The counselor was readily available for consultation.						
6. The counselor viewed my concerns as important.						
7. The counselor communicated in a clear and understandable manner.						
8. The counselor provided helpful ideas and suggestions.						
9. The counselor was easy to work with.						
10. The counselor kept commitments.						
11. The counselor communicated caring and respect.						

SOURCE: "Evaluation of Counseling Services: Accountability in a Rural Elementary School," by T. N. Fairchild, *Elementary School Guidance and Counseling, 29*, p. 35. Copyright 1994 by the American School Counselor Association. Reprinted with permission.

tests the group members before and after they participate in the program. If the program has been successful, the counselor should see a significant difference between scores on the pretest and posttest. Let's say a counselor decides to run an anger-management group for students. In addition to anecdotal reports, the counselor would like to collect quantitative data for a report to the administration on the success of the group. The first step is for the counselor to select an anger-management scale that is both valid and reliable. The counselor then administers the scale to those selected to participate in the program. This can be done at the very first meeting of the group. Then, at the last meeting, the counselor administers the same scale to determine if participants have improved their anger-management skills.[10]

A posttest obviously shows the short-term effects of a program. The counselor may also want to follow up with a measure several weeks after the program ends to determine the longer-term effects.[11] If counselors can show that their efforts have both short- and longer-term effects, their defense of the program will have greater impact.

---

[10] A counselor who wants to go beyond simply showing the before and after scores of the participants can employ statistical tests like a *t*-test for dependent samples or a nonparametric test (in cases that lack a normal distribution) to support a significant difference in pretest and posttest scores.

[11] For measures related to a specific area, see *Tests in Print* V (L. L. Murphy, Impara, & Plake, 1999), a two-volume set that describes more than 3,000 tests.

| TABLE 4.4 | A RETROSPECTIVE RATING SCALE FOR SCHOOL ACHIEVEMENT RELATED BEHAVIORS |

Directions: Think back to when we first started our group counseling sessions. Now, rate yourself at that point in time, by placing an *O* or circle along the scale (*Very often* to *Very seldom*) for each of the items.

Next, rate yourself now, at this point in time, by placing an *X* along the same scale. If there is no change, put the *X* on top of the *O*.

1. I complete my homework assignments.										
	Very often			Moderate			Very seldom			

2. I participate in classroom discussions.										
	Very often			Moderate			Very seldom			

3. I study for tests.										
	Very often			Moderate			Very seldom			

4. I am punctual to class.										
	Very often			Moderate			Very seldom			

SOURCE: Adapted from "Retrospective Measurement: An Accountability Tool," by R. D. Myrick, *Elementary School Guidance and Counseling, 25*, p. 27. Copyright 1990 by the American School Counselor Association. Reprinted with permission.

The pretest-posttest evaluation is not without problems. One concern centers on the students' understanding of the terms and concepts used in the pretest. If the meaning of those terms and concepts won't become clear until they've participated in the program, clearly the pretest isn't a valid measure. Another concern is the Hawthorne effect, in which students' performance on the posttest is influenced by their awareness that they are being observed.

RETROSPECTIVE MEASUREMENT   The problems with pretesting and posttesting led Myrick (1990) to propose the use of retrospective measurement. "The retrospective method is an attempt to reconstruct the past history of a person by asking for his or her recollections" (p. 25). Retrospective measurement relies on the accuracy of the participants' memory, which raises questions about its reliability. But this simple and time-saving method for gathering outcome data can be quite useful for school counselors in spite of its limitations.

Retrospective measurement asks program participants to remember their perceptions, opinions, judgments, and the like before the intervention and then to describe their perceptions, opinions, judgments, and the like at the time the measure is administered. The participants mark their answers on an interval scale, like the one shown in Table 4.4, using one symbol for what they remember and another for what they are thinking or feeling as they take the measure.

The items on a retrospective measure should be relevant to the program's objectives. Myrick suggested a 10-interval scale. If the difference between *O*s and *X*s on any item is greater than 3 intervals, it is a significant difference. The brief descriptors used to anchor the points can vary. For example, instead of *Very often* to *Very seldom*, the counselor could substitute *Very high, Moderate,* and *Very low.* Myrick (1990) cautioned against using more than three descriptors.

Again, reliability is a concern here. A particular problem is *social desirability:* participants make responses they think will please the counselor. Counselors who want to control for social desirability can also administer a social-desirability scale (Crowne & Marlowe, 1960). But for the majority of school counselors, retrospective measurement can be a valuable tool for evaluating program outcomes. It does not require any special knowledge of research design or statistics, nor is it time consuming to administer and score. Retrospective measurement offers school counselors little room for excuses when it comes to measuring the effectiveness of their programs.

ETHICAL AND LEGAL ISSUES

School counselors are often an integral part of a school's testing program. In many instances, they administer tests and explain scores to students and their parents. At other times, they advocate for students whose academic future has been reduced to their performance on a single test.

Test Security

Whether they are administering a standardized test to an entire class or to one student, counselors have the ethical responsibility to keep tests safe and secure. Violations of test security seem to be on the rise, possibly because more importance is being placed on test scores. Teachers can be tempted to reveal test items to their students, perhaps in a practice session, to ensure good results. Counselors have to be watchdogs here. If they have the tests in their possession before the administration, they must exercise extreme care to prevent theft and to withstand pressure to violate the test administration protocol.

Another type of test security involves allowing a counselee to take a standardized test home. Even if the test is just a personality or interest inventory, the practice is incompatible with the duty to keep tests secure (Welfel, 2002). When a student takes a test home, there is no way for the counselor to know if that student actually took the test or had someone else take it, or if the student made copies of the test. Counselors need to find ways to administer tests in school.

Competence

Administering tests and interpreting the results demand a certain level of competence. For the most part, school counselors administer career-related inventories or scales that measure a single psychological trait; the results of these tests require a minimal amount of interpretation, and most school counselors have no difficulty using them for screening and assessment purposes. But interpretation of scores on more-complex instruments—for example, personality tests like the Minnesota Multiphasic Personality Inventory, the Rorschach, and the Thematic Apperception Test—demands special training. In the absence of that training, it is not ethical for school counselors to use those tests.

Competence is also an issue when school counselors are called on—usually by students or their parents—to interpret the results of standardized tests for aptitude and achievement. Here, too, knowledge is a critical tool. School counselors must be familiar with all the fundamental aspects of standardized tests: the normal distribution, scoring, and validity and reliability. They also should familiarize themselves with each test's objectives and what the research shows about the predictive validity of the instrument.[12] They must know enough about testing in general and this test in particular to be able to explain what students' scores mean clearly and confidently to students and parents. Anything less only escalates the anxiety surrounding standardized testing in schools today. More important, tests are fallible; they cannot predict with certainty how or what an individual student will do in the future. Giving students and parents realistic and informed feedback on test results is both a professional and an ethical responsibility.

Computer-Generated Test Scores and Reports

Increasingly, test publishers offer computer-generated reports that describe and explain students' scores. In the past, the reports followed the administration of a test by several weeks. Now, many tests are administered online, and the reports are generated immediately. These reports raise at least two ethical issues.

The first has to do with the validation criteria: those criteria may not be supported by scientific evidence or reviewed by experts independent from the test publisher (Welfel, 2002). It is the counselor's responsibility to understand and be able to explain any problems with a test's validity. Another ethical issue has to do with the style in which the reports are written. Although most data are open to various interpretations, computer-generated reports tend to suggest just one interpretation of the data. Again, it is the counselor's responsibility to be sure students and parents understand that limitation. Of course in both of these instances, the counselor's ability to explain a test's validity or to clarify a report rests on the counselor's knowledge and competence. It is absolutely crucial that counselors not rely exclusively on computer-generated reports to explain test results to students. If a counselor does not have the expertise to interpret a test independently, he or she should not be using the test.

---

[12] All of this material is in the test manual.

CONCLUSION

Statistics. Just the word can make a perfectly intelligent counselor in training shudder. But statistics can be an important resource for school counselors, a basis for evaluating interventions and programs and for defending them in the age of accountability.

This chapter describes several ways data can be used in the school counseling program. The first is the assessment of students. Here the counselor's primary responsibilities are understanding the fundamentals of standardized testing and advocating for the appropriate use of test scores. When the task is the assessment of counseling activities, the school counselor's focus shifts to generating outcome data to answer a key question: "Is what I am doing effective?"

It may be that counselors are reluctant to ask that question because they simply are not comfortable working with standard deviations or percentile ranks or anything that smacks of statistics. More likely, though, they feel threatened by what they believe the question implies: "If my program is not effective, then I'm a bad counselor and I'm going to lose my job." What they don't realize is that part of being a professional counselor is wanting to do better, and that means being open to feedback and critical assessment. Collecting and interpreting data are professional responsibilities. The school counselor must be able to look at data objectively and say, "This is working, but this is not working and I need to make some changes." In graduate school, counselors in training are taught not to overpersonalize the successes or failures of their clients. Later, when they are working in a school, they must maintain that same distance from the interventions and programs they develop; they must be able to evaluate their efforts and use data constructively. More than that, research over the years has shown that school counseling activities are more successful than not.[13] Counseling programs definitely help children. That's a tradition that should make school counselors proud to stand up and take responsibility for their work.

QUESTIONS FOR DISCUSSION

1. When you hear that you are going to have to do research or testing for a course that involves statistics, what is your first reaction? Discuss with a learning partner your feelings both positive and negative.
2. What do you think about the new reliance on testing in this country as a basis for making academic decisions about students? Discuss the pros and cons of high-stakes testing, being sure to consider the cultural implications of the practice.

---

[13] For an excellent review of outcome evaluations in school counseling, see Whitson and Sexton (1998).

3. Do you think that school counselors, like teachers and administrators, should be held accountable for students' learning and achievement? Explain your answer.
4. School counselors perform many different activities: individual and group counseling, classroom guidance, collaborating and consulting with teachers and parents, interpreting tests for students and parents, and advocacy. How would you determine the effectiveness of each of these activities? Be sure to give concrete examples in your answer.
5. Imagine that you have to defend every one of your professional activities with empirical evidence of their effectiveness. Does this seem more intrusion or opportunity? Discuss your answer.
6. Can you think of other ways school counselors can hold themselves accountable for their work in addition to the methods discussed in the chapter? For example, how would you go about determining the overall effectiveness of a results-based school counseling program?

CAREER COUNSELING AND DEVELOPMENT

Career development has been a part of school counseling programs for a very long time. At the beginning of the 20th century, Jesse Davis began incorporating a class session a week for vocational guidance into his school's curriculum (see Chapter 1). Today, many comprehensive developmental guidance programs include career planning as a major domain.[1] Some basic career development concepts are outlined in Table 5.1.

Career development is a process that combines all of the psychological, sociological, educational, physical, economic, and chance factors that shape the individual's career (NOICC, 1992). That process begins at a very young age and continues for much of the life span. It makes sense, then, that career development should be part of comprehensive guidance programs for all students, from elementary school through high school. Of course the focus of those programs changes at each level: In Grades K through 6, the emphasis is on career exploration, on introducing students to a large number of jobs, and on self-knowledge. In middle school, exploration continues; but programs here also begin to connect educational choices to career choices. In high school, programs help students narrow their choices and give them the skills they need to apply for whatever postsecondary experience they are planning.

Although the focus of vocational guidance programs changes, three elements must be common to all programs. First, they must be integrated into the curriculum, a part of the total educational process. Second, they demand that school counselors, teachers, and other school personnel work together to make students aware of all the possible careers open to them and to help them make wise career choices. And third, ultimately they should help students learn more effectively by helping them understand the link between their studies now and their opportunities tomorrow.

---

[1] For example, Missouri, a pioneer in comprehensive developmental guidance programs, utilizes three domains for the contents of its school counseling programs: career planning and exploration, knowledge of self and others, and educational and vocational development (Starr & Gysbers, 1992). Gysbers and Henderson (2000) suggested an outline for comprehensive developmental guidance programs with three domains: self-knowledge and interpersonal skills; life roles, settings, and events; and life career planning. And career development is the second major area in the national standards (see Appendix A).

TABLE 5.1	A GLOSSARY OF CAREER DEVELOPMENT TERMS
Career	The totality of work one does in his or her lifetime.
Career awareness	The inventory of knowledge, values, preferences, and self-concepts that an individual draws on in the course of making career-related choices.
Career counseling	A one-to-one or small-group relationship between counselor and clients, with the goal of helping the clients integrate and apply an understanding of self and the environment to make the most appropriate career decisions.
Career development	All of the psychological, sociological, educational, physical, economic, and chance factors that combine to shape the career of any given individual over the life span.
Career development theories	Theoretical bases of understanding how individuals develop vocationally. These bases provide guidance specialists with the guidelines necessary to help them solve problems, avoid blocks, and progress with efficiency and satisfaction.
Career education	An effort aimed a refocusing American education and the actions of the broader community in ways that help individuals acquire and utilize the knowledge, skills, and attitudes necessary to make work a meaningful, productive, and satisfying part of life.
Career exploration	One's involvement in trying out a variety of activities, roles, and situations to find out more about aptitude for or interest in an occupation or other career opportunities.
Career guidance	Those activities and programs that help individuals assimilate and integrate knowledge, experience, and appreciations related to <ul><li>self-understanding, which includes a person's relationship to his or her own characteristics and perceptions, and his or her relationship to others and the environment.</li><li>understanding the work of society and those factors that affect its constant change, including workers' attitudes and discipline.</li><li>awareness of the role leisure time can play in one's life.</li><li>understanding the necessity for and the multitude of factors that go into career planning.</li><li>understanding the information and skills necessary to achieve self-fulfillment in work and leisure.</li><li>learning and applying the career decision-making process.</li></ul>
Career information	Information related to the work world that can be useful in the process of career development, including educational, occupational, and psychosocial information related to working (e.g., the availability of training, the nature of the work, and the status of workers in different occupations).
Curriculum infusion	The process of integrating career development objectives and experiences with other subject matter in the ongoing curriculum.
Work	A conscious effort, other than that having as its primary purpose either coping or relaxation, aimed at producing benefits for oneself or for others.

SOURCE: Adapted from the National Occupation Information Coordinating Committee (1992).

TABLE 5.2 **CYCLING AND RECYCLING THROUGH THE LIFE SPAN**

	Developmental Tasks			
Life Stages	Adolescence (ages 14–25)	Early Adulthood (ages 25–45)	Middle Adulthood (ages 45–65)	Late Adulthood (over age 65)
Growth	Developing a realistic self-concept	Learning to relate to others	Accepting one's limitation	Developing non-occupational roles
Exploration	Learning more about more opportunities	Finding opportunity to do wanted work	Identifying new problems to work on	Finding a good retirement spot
Establishment	Getting started in a chosen field	Settling down in a permanent position	Developing new skills	Doing things one has always wanted to do
Maintenance	Verifying current occupational choice	Making occupational position secure	Holding one's own against competition	Keeping up what is still enjoyed
Decline	Giving less time to hobbies	Reducing participation in sports	Focusing on essential activities	Reducing working hours

SOURCE: Adapted from Super (1990), p. 206.

THEORETICAL UNDERPINNINGS

Career development theories lay the foundation for much of career exploration in elementary, middle, and high schools. These theories also suggest ways in which comprehensive developmental guidance programs can be operationalized.

Super's Life-Span, Life-Space Approach

According to Donald Super's theory (1957), work and career are expressions of self-concept, which sets a pattern for career development through the life span. Self-concept develops over time, a product of physical and mental maturation, and "individuals implement their self-concepts into careers that will provide the most efficient means of self-expression" (Zunker, 2002, p. 37).

Table 5.2 outlines Super's life stages and developmental tasks. According to Super an individual can cycle and recycle through any number of stages. A woman in her thirties, for example, who is dissatisfied with her career can recycle through periods of growth and exploration, and change that career. Or an adolescent can go through a period of decline only to recycle through exploration and establishment. Super's concepts of cycling and recycling are important elements in career development even for school-aged children. Often critics object to career counseling in schools because they believe it forces youngsters to decide about a career before they are ready to do so. Cycling and recycling suggest that career development is ongoing, that it is much more circular than linear.

Super theorized that the completion of a developmental task at any age and in any life stage is dependent on the individual's *career maturity*, defined by traits like planning, accepting responsibility, and interest in and knowledge and awareness of an occupation. His research supports a relationship between adolescent career maturity and maturity in later life. Career programs for youngsters are less about having them make a vocational choice and more about promoting certain traits that are appropriate to their developmental level and necessary for making good career decisions. School counselors create career development programs more to help students mature than to have them make a specific vocational choice.

One of the most well-known measures of career maturity is the Career Maturity Inventory (CMI) (Crites & Savickas, 1995). The CMI can be used with students in Grades 6 through12; it yields scores on an attitude scale and a competence test, and for overall career maturity. School counselors can use these instruments to determine students' readiness for career exploration. For example, if an inventory reveals that a student is low on accepting responsibility, the school counselor would have to promote this characteristic to help the student understand the importance and consequences of career choice.

Super's developmental focus is the substance and foundation of many career guidance programs in schools. In today's society, it is not uncommon for people to begin new careers in their fifties and even sixties. Because it provides a framework for looking at career development at all ages, Super's theory continues to provide relevance and substance to career decisions throughout the life span.

Circumspection and Compromise: Gottfredson's Theory of Occupational Aspirations

Like Super, Linda Gottfredson (1981) used self-concept to explain how people become attached to certain occupations. According to Gottfredson, the key determinants of self-concept are socioeconomic background, intellectual level, and experiences with sex typing. She described four stages of development:

1. *Orientation to size and power (ages 3–5).* Although their thought processes are concrete, children develop some sense of what it means to be an adult.
2. *Orientation to sex roles (ages 6–8).* In this stage, self-concept is influenced by gender development.
3. *Orientation to social evaluation (ages 9–13).* In this stage, concepts of social class develop and contribute to the awareness of self-in-situation. Children begin to develop work preferences consistent with their social reference group and perceived abilities.
4. *Orientation to the internal unique self (beginning at age 14).* Introspective thinking promotes greater self-awareness and perceptions of others. The individual comes to understand vocational aspirations in the context of self, sex role, and social class.

Gottfredson believed that career development progresses from the simple and concrete thinking of the child to the more comprehensive, complex, and abstract thinking of the adolescent and the adult (Zunker, 2002). The overarching theoretical idea is that people choose occupations that are consonant with their perceived social space, intellect, and sex type.

Gottfredson also introduced the concept of *compromise* to explain why individuals are not always able to work at what they would most enjoy. For example, a person might compromise his or her vocational interests to accept a job that offers more prestige, or a person might compromise prestige for a job that is more accessible. Although interests would not be sacrificed for a minor trade-off in prestige, Gottfredson believed they could be sacrificed for a major trade-off.

Gottfredson's theory is relevant for school counselors because she believed that occupational stereotypes—children's perceptions of the sex type and the prestige associated with certain occupations—begin to form at an early age, and that through career guidance and counseling, those perceptions can evolve and reconstitute themselves. Take, for example, children from a very low socioeconomic background, whose social space, and so their occupational choice, is restricted because they are uncomfortable interacting with people from other social classes. Career guidance can help these youngsters overcome feelings of rejection and expand their social space, opening up new possibilities for them in terms of career preparation and choice. We know it works. Our society is filled with strong people who have overcome sexism, classism, racism, and ethnocentrism to work in occupations they once thought inaccessible.

Holland's Typology

John Holland (1966, 1985, 1997) believed that career choice is at base an expression of personality, itself the product of heredity and early life experiences. Career satisfaction depends on the degree of congruence between self-image and occupational choice. Holland called this congruence *modal personal style.* Holland identified six personal styles—realistic, investigative, artistic, social, enterprising, and conventional—and suggested that each style "fits" a corresponding occupational environment (Table 5.3). Generally, the stronger an individual's personal style, the better the fit with, the more satisfying, the occupational environment.

The elements of Holland's typology are not mutually exclusive. All personal styles can exist within an individual, but there is a primary, a secondary, and even a tertiary theme. An individual coded SAI (social, artistic, and investigative), for example, would be very much like people in social occupations, somewhat like people in artistic occupations, and a little like people in investigative occupations.

The Self-Directed Search   Several instruments operationalize Holland's theory. He himself developed the Self-Directed Search (SDS) to facilitate self-knowledge and exploration (Holland, 1994). The SDS is one of the most widely used interest inventories. The test measures a respondent's interests in comparison to the interests manifested by a sample of workers in each of the six occupational environments. The score is a personality code consisting of three Holland types. The first

TABLE 5.3   HOLLAND'S TYPOLOGY: THEMES, PERSONAL STYLES, AND OCCUPATIONAL ENVIRONMENTS

Theme	Personal Style	Occupational Environment
Realistic	Aggressive; prefers concrete versus abstract work tasks; not very sociable; poor interpersonal interactions	Skilled trade (plumber, electrician, machine operator) Technician (airplane mechanic, photographer, draftsperson, some service occupations)
Investigative	Intellectual; abstract thinking; analytical; independent; sometimes racial and task oriented	Scientific (chemist, physicist, mathematician) Technical (laboratory technician, computer programmer, electronics worker)
Artistic	Imaginative; values aesthetics; prefers self-expression through the arts; rather independent and extroverted	Artistic (sculptor, artist, designer) Musical (music teacher, orchestra leader, musician) Literary (editor, writer, critic)
Social	Gregarious; concerned with social problems; active in church and community; interested in educational activities	Educational (teacher, school administrator, professor) Social welfare (social worker, sociologist, rehabilitation counselor, nurse)
Enterprising	Extroverted; aggressive; adventurous; prefers leadership roles; dominant; persuasive; has good verbal skills	Managerial (personnel director, production supervisor, sales manager) Sales (insurance agent, realtor, car salesperson)
Conventional	Practical; controlled; sociable; somewhat conservative; prefers structured tasks; conforming	Office and clerical (file clerk, teller, accountant, keypunch operator, secretary, bookkeeper, receptionist, credit manager)

SOURCE: Adapted from J. L. Holland (1997). Copyright 1997 by Psychological Assessment Resources. Reprinted with permission.

type is the most dominant; those that follow are less dominant. The code indicates the degree of similarity and dissimilarity between respondent and sample.

Once the test has been scored, the respondent is referred to the *The Occupations Finder* (Holland, 2001) to see a list of occupations that correspond to the three-letter code. Each occupation listed is cross-referenced to the *Dictionary of Occupational Titles* (U.S. Department of Labor, 1991), where the respondent can find information about the suggested occupations. This system of investigation fulfills the two fundamental criteria for making a satisfying career choice: knowledge of self and knowledge of occupations.[2] Within the Holland framework, personality and interest form the cornerstones of occupational choice; intelligence is not a critical variable.

Caveats   We can't overestimate the influence of Holland's work on career counseling and occupational choice. The user-friendly (and now computerized) SDS is

---

[2] In addition, *The Educational Opportunities Finder for Use with the Self-Directed Search and the Vocational Preference Inventory* (D. Rosen, Holmberg, & Holland, 1997) links the codes with 750 postsecondary fields of study.

an extremely popular instrument in schools, and Holland's typology is a familiar tool. But Holland's model is not without critics. Many of those critics voice concerns about gender bias: The SDS disproportionately places women in three personality types—artistic, social, and conventional (Weinrach, 1984; Weinrach & Srebalus, 1990). In response to this criticism, Holland has suggested that the SDS scores of female participants simply reflect the sexism that exists in our society.

As a first step in making a career decision, Holland's theory and inventory can be very useful because they set students to investigating occupational options. The danger here is of students' believing that the occupations that correspond to their SDS code are the only occupations open to them. School counselors must be alert to the implied limitations of the typology. For example, to a student who scores high on the social personality, the counselor might say, "The results of your inventory suggest that you would like to work with people in a helping capacity. What do you think? Are there any jobs like that that appeal to you?" Counselors must avoid using test results to tell students what they should do. Instead, scores on an interest inventory like the SDS should be a jumping-off point for exploration.

Roe's Needs Approach

Ann Roe (1956) developed a theory of career choice based on Maslow's (1954) hierarchy of needs. In essence, Roe postulated that parenting styles and childhood experiences determine a hierarchy of needs, and that those needs, in turn, are responsible for career choice.

Roe identified three types of relationships between parent and child:

- *Emotional concentration on the child* leads a parent to be overprotective or overdemanding.
- *Avoidance of the child* leads a parent to be neglectful or rejecting.
- *Acceptance of the child* leads a parent to be loving or casual.

Roe pictured a circular relationship among parenting styles and the corresponding behaviors, and she acknowledged that at times the lines separating both styles and behaviors are blurred (Figure 5.1).

According to Roe (1956, 1957), parents who are loving, overprotective, and overdemanding produce children who are oriented toward people; the children of parents who are casual, neglecting, and rejecting are oriented away from people. That orientation is the key to Roe's classification system: She believed all occupations are either person oriented or nonperson oriented. *Person-oriented occupations* include service, business (especially sales), management, general culture (teaching, pastoring), and arts and entertainment. *Nonperson-oriented jobs* include technology (production, maintenance, transportation), work outdoors (agriculture, forestry, mining), and science (research, clinical practice) (Zunker, 2002).

Roe believed that interests and attitudes—and from them occupational choice—develop early on from the individual's needs, which are generated by parenting style. But she insisted that the level of attainment within an occupation is a product of three other factors: ability, socioeconomic background, and need intensity.

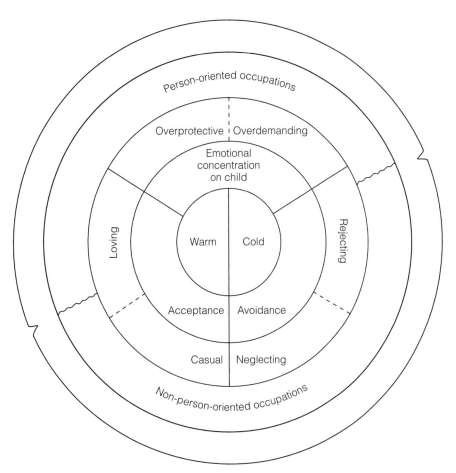

FIGURE **5.1**

**ROE'S HYPOTHETICAL RELATIONSHIP BETWEEN PARENTING
STYLES AND OCCUPATIONAL CHOICE**

Roe's work has been influential, especially in the development of interest inventories. Several widely used inventories, like the Career Occupational Preference System (COPS) (R. R. Knapp & Knapp, 1984, 1985) and the Vocational Interest Inventory (Lunnelborg, 1981), are based on her theory. Yet empirical studies have failed to support Roe's claim that early parent-child interaction is responsible for career choice (L. B. Green & Parker, 1965; Osipow, 1983; D. H. Powell, 1957). For school counselors, though, Roe's needs approach may well explain why some students seem determined to choose any job, just so long as their parents disapprove of it. Perhaps these youngsters felt rejected by their parents. And it is possible that children whose parents are not pressuring them about what to do with their lives come from homes where parents are loving and accepting.

A Social Cognitive Perspective

Albert Bandura's (1986) social cognitive theory has played a major role in furthering the understanding of career choice and has given rise to several theories of career development:

- The social learning approach (Krumboltz, Mitchell, & Jones, 1976; L. K. Mitchell & Krumboltz, 1990, 1996)
- The self-efficacy approach (Hackett & Betz, 1981)
- Social cognitive career theory (Lent, Brown, & Hackett, 1994, 1996)

We focus here on social cognitive career theory (SCCT) because it is rooted in Bandura's social cognitive theory builds on social learning theory and self-efficacy theory, and emphasizes processes that go beyond simple learning and conditioning: "SCCT is more concerned with the specific cognitive mediators through which learning experiences guide career behavior; with the manner in which variables such as interests, abilities, and values interrelate; and with the specific paths by which person and contextual factors influence career outcomes" (Lent, Brown, & Hackett, 1996, p. 377).

More specifically, SCCT builds on three variables from social cognitive theory: self-efficacy, outcome expectations, and choice goals. Self-efficacy is the belief in one's ability to carry out certain behaviors. An *outcome expectation* is a belief about what will happen if a certain behavior is carried out.[3] A *choice goal* is the individual's determination to carry out a particular task or to produce a certain outcome (Bandura, 1986). There is constant and complex interplay among these three variables.

Figure 5.2 shows how person, context, and experience affect career choice. The theoretical path begins with person inputs and contextual inputs, which determine the individual's learning experiences. Learning experiences influence both self-efficacy and outcome expectations, which together are responsible for the development of interests. Notice that in this model, learning experiences do not determine interests directly; instead they are mediated through self-efficacy and outcome expectations. From interests, choice goals develop, which produce choice actions, which in turn lead to performance outcomes. Those outcomes feed back into learning experiences, and from there to self-efficacy and outcome expectations, helping to revise or strengthen them.

To their credit, the authors of SCCT were sensitive to how contextual inputs constantly moderate and influence choice goals and choice actions. For example, an individual's opportunity to develop new skills would affect his or her "ability and willingness to transform career interests into goals and goals into actions" (Lent, Brown, & Hackett, 1996, p. 393).

Social learning theory has made a significant contribution to the understanding of career choice and development. Research consistently supports a stronger link between belief in one's ability (self-efficacy) and vocational interest than be-

---

[3] In this model, outcome expectations include the individual's values.

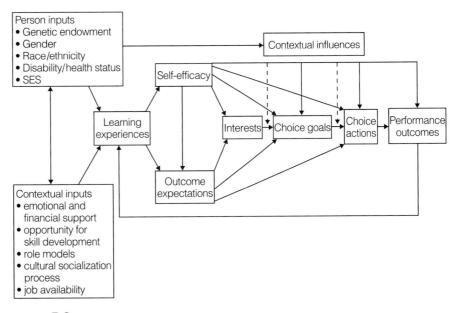

FIGURE **5.2**

SOCIAL COGNITIVE CAREER THEORY:
THE FACTORS THAT AFFECT CAREER CHOICE

NOTE: The figure simplifies the original model somewhat. In that model, self-efficacy and outcome expectations can also act directly on choice goals and actions; in addition, self efficacy can act directly on performance outcomes. The original model also shows the indirect effects of contextual influences.

SOURCE: Adapted from Lent, Brown, and Hackett (1994), p. 93. Reprinted with permission of Robert Lent.

tween measured ability and vocational interest.[4] This has important implications for career counseling in schools because even young children form beliefs about their abilities based on feedback from teachers and parents, and those beliefs play a significant role in the development of vocational interests. For example, poor self-efficacy can prevent an underachieving student from working toward a career that requires a college degree. School counselors can do an enormous service for children by challenging their limiting beliefs about themselves.

> *In my capacity as a faculty member, I have the opportunity to interview prospective students who want to study school counseling. When I ask them why, many answer: "Because of the influence my high school counselor had on me." I usually ask how the counselor influenced them. Many times I get this answer: "By making me believe in myself."*

---

[4] Studies focusing mainly on the relationship between measured abilities and vocational or academic interests have yielded moderate measures of association (Hackett, Betz, O'Halloran, & Romac, 1990; Healy, Tullier, & Mourton, 1990; Lent, Brown, & Larkin, 1987; Lent, Lopez, & Bieschke, 1992, 1993); while studies measuring the relationship between self-efficacy and vocational interests have produced much larger measures of association (see, for example, Coon-Carty, 1995; Multon, Brown, & Lent, 1991; and Sadri & Robertson, 1993).

STANDARDIZED ASSESSMENT AND CAREER DEVELOPMENT

Standardized assessment has been a part of vocational guidance since the beginning of the 20th century. And as is the case in other areas, standardized testing often has been misused and abused in career counseling.

> In the high school I attended, career counseling was required in sophomore year. I remember taking a test, an interest inventory (I don't remember which one), and returning to the counselor several weeks later for the results. The counseling session lasted less than five minutes and consisted of the counselor's informing me that based on the results of the test, I should be a lawyer. Then he asked if I had any questions. When I said no, he told me I could leave.

In years past, it was not uncommon for vocational counselors to rely on the predictive value of a single test score. We talked in Chapter 4 about the danger of doing that. Instead counselors need to administer more than one instrument, preferably a battery of instruments that measure different dimensions. And they have to make clear to students that the tests are just a starting point for an exploration of careers that may go on for a long time.

There is nothing innately wrong with standardized tests; the problem is in how they are used. When they are used appropriately, they can contribute to students' self-awareness of their abilities, interests, and values.

For career counseling, school counselors use several different kinds of standardized tests: aptitude tests, achievement tests, interest inventories, personality inventories, values inventories, and career maturity inventories (Zunker, 2002). Table 5.4 lists the most popular of these tests.

Aptitude Tests

In general, an aptitude test measures an individual's capacity to acquire certain skills and proficiencies (Cronbach, 1990). For example, candidates for a job-training program may be given an aptitude test to see if they have the mental capacity to acquire the skills the program hopes to teach them. In educational settings, aptitude tests abound. Perhaps, the best known are the SAT and the American College Test (ACT), which are used as criteria for college admission. Most general aptitude tests measure verbal and math abilities and other abilities differentially, to indicate strengths and weaknesses. The scores can be used as one of several bases for career decisions. For example, someone with low ability for manual dexterity might think twice before deciding to become a carpenter. High school students who are planning to go to college are encouraged, if not required, to take the SAT or ACT. For other students, a general aptitude test can help them make a more informed choice on postsecondary job training programs.

TABLE 5.4 **STANDARDIZED TESTS FOR CAREER COUNSELING AND DEVELOPMENT**

Test Category	Test	Grade Level	Available From	Notes
Aptitude tests	Armed Services Vocational Aptitude Battery	Designed primarily for Grade 12	ASAVB Career Exploration Program	Both the test and results are available at no charge.
	Differential Aptitude Test	Level 1, Grades 7–9; Level 2, Grades 10–12	Psychological Corporation	Form C has two levels
	General Aptitude Test Battery	Grade 12	U.S. Employment Service	Available from the regional office.
Achievement tests	Educational Testing Service series	Various	Educational Testing Service	Both general survey and single-subject tests.
	Houghton Mifflin series	Various	Houghton Mifflin	Both general survey and and single-subject tests.
	McGraw-Hill series	Various	McGraw-Hill	Both general survey and single-subject tests.
Interest inventories	Career Decision Making 2000: Harrington-O'Shea Decision Making System	Level 1, Grades 7–9; Level 2, Grades 11 and 12	American Guidance Service	Utilizes the Holland codes.
	Geist Picture Interest Inventory	Students with reading difficulties	Western Psychological Services	For nonreaders.
	Kuder Occupational Interest Survey	Form E, junior/senior high school; Form DD, high school	McGraw-Hill	Besides occupational scales, the survey includes scales for college majors.
	Ohio Vocational Interest Survey–II	Grades 8–12	Psychological Corporation	24 general-interest scales related to people data, and things.
	Self-Directed Search	Career Explorer, junior high school; Form R, high school	Psychological Assessment Resources	Based on Holland's theory of career development.
	Strong Interest Inventory	Age 15+	Consulting Psychologists Press	
	Wide Range Interest and Opinion Test	All grades	Guidance Associates of Delaware	For nonreaders; can be used with children who are developmentally delayed.
Values inventories	Career Orientation Placement and Evaluation Survey	Junior high school–community college	EDITS	Results are for 7 work values on a bipolar scale.
	Ohio Work Values Inventory	Grades 4–12	Publishers Test Service	Yields scores on 11 work values.
	Salience Inventory	High school	Consulting Psychologists Press	Measures the importance of life roles according to Super's life-space, life-span model.
	Values Scale	High school	Consulting Psychologists Press	A measure of intrinsic versus extrinsic life-career values.

(continued)

TABLE 5.4 *(continued)*

Test Category	Test	Grade Level	Available From	Notes
Personality inventories	California Test of Personality	Primary, elementary, intermediate, secondary, and adult levels	CTP–Macmillan–McGraw-Hill	Assesses personal worth, and family and school relations.
	Minnesota Counseling Inventory	Grades 9–12	Psychological Corporation	Separate norms for boys and girls.
	Myers-Briggs Type Indicator	High school (7th-grade reading level needed)	Consulting Psychologists Press	Most widely used personality measure in last 20 years.
	Sixteen Personality Factor Questionnaire	Ages 16+	Institute for Personality and Ability Testing	Compares individual profile to samples of occupational profiles.
Career maturity inventories	Career Beliefs Inventory	Grades 8+	Consulting Psychologists Press	Constructed from a social cognitive perspective; designed to identify faulty beliefs that prevent an individual from making appropriate career decisions.
	Career Development Inventory	Form S, middle and high school students	Consulting Psychologists Press	Yields measures of planning orientation, and readiness for exploration, information, and decision making.
	Career Maturity Inventory	Grades 6–12	Psychological Assessment Resources	Measures how ready one is to make a career decision; comes with Career Developer, a resource for acquiring needed skills.

Achievement Tests

Achievement tests are designed to assess the test-taker's level of developed abilities (Zunker, 2002). Aptitude tests measure an individual's potential for learning; achievement tests measure what the individual has learned. As the standards movement takes a firm hold on education across the nation, achievement tests are playing a more important role than ever in the placement and promotion of children in Grades K through 12. The tests can help students going on to college choose a major by indicating the subjects in which students have the most proficiency.

School counselors can easily access students' scores on achievement tests they have already taken, and so rarely need to administer an achievement test for the sole purpose of career exploration. Scores on achievement tests can be used to develop, maintain, or challenge students' career aspirations. At times they function as a reality check for students.

It is not uncommon for middle and high school students to be thinking about a career that demands proficiency in one or more subjects in which they are underachieving. During my years as a school counselor, I had any number of students tell me they hoped to be a doctor. But when I checked their grades and achievement test scores in science, I often found that the students were performing below expected levels of proficiency for admission to a premed program. I never argued with those students about their career aspirations. Instead I would simply talk with them about the apparent contradiction between what they were hoping to do and their academic performance. Then I would issue a challenge: "If you really want to be a doctor, you are going to have to bring up your grades in science." Some students took the challenge, and studied hard to do just that. Others did not, which led me to question their commitment to being a doctor.

Achievement tests generally are divided into two categories: the general-survey battery and single-subject tests. The general-survey battery measures knowledge of most subjects taught in school; the single-subject test measures knowledge of a particular subject or content area.

Interest Inventories

Interest inventories have long been a tool for career counseling. Most inventories list occupations and the activities associated with each of them, and ask the test-taker to respond with a "like" or "don't like" response. The construct validity of interest inventories has been shown by comparing the interest patterns of respondents with those of people already working happily in an occupational group. The objective is to assess the degree of similarity or dissimilarity between individual respondents and a representative sample of an occupational group.

Interest inventories have come under attack for being gender biased—that is, for being constructed in a way that skews responses to a career based solely on gender (Diamond, 1975; Zunker, 2002). Revised versions of the best-known inventories have tried to respond to this criticism.

Interest inventories can be a valuable asset for school counselors as a first step in career development. But even here they should not be used in isolation. And the results should always be discussed with the respondent. That meeting—seeing the student's reaction to his or her results—can yield information even more valuable than the results themselves.

Values Inventories

Although values inventories have been around for many years, their importance of late has waned. That is, interests seem to have superseded values in career development. Of course, if interests alone are considered in a career decision, the potential conflict between the individual's interests and values goes unexplored. An interest inventory, for example, might indicate a good fit with being a lawyer, but a values inventory might reveal that free time with family is important to this student. Lawyers in big law firms have to work long hours, and that restricts their time with family. Armed with that knowledge, the student might reconsider studying law or at least the kind of law he or she wants to practice or where he or she wants to practice it.

Because values inventories reveal how individuals are different in terms of what is and is not important to them, school counselors may find them a good tool to use in small groups. Students' results can set off lively discussions among the group's members, which in turn can help clarify the results.

Not all values inventories are suited to children; those listed in Table 5.4 are appropriate for use with junior high school and high school students.

Personality Inventories

In response to Super's, Holland's, and Roe's theories, that career development is an extension of personality development, personality inventories have become an important part of vocational counseling. The more awareness individuals have of their personality, the more likely they are to make wise and satisfying career choices.

The Sixteen Personality Factor Questionnaire (16PF) (Cattell, Eber, & Tatsuoka, 1970) has enjoyed widespread use among vocational counselors primarily because the inventory matches individual personality traits with occupational profiles (Zunker, 2002). The 16PF can be administered to anyone 16 years old or older who has an average adult vocabulary; and there's a form of the inventory for individuals who have lower reading levels. In addition, there are two forms of the test for students: the Children's Personality Questionnaire for youngsters ages 8 to 12, and the High School Personality Questionnaire for students ages 12 to 18.

As a rule, school counselors do not administer personality inventories to students. But because they are trained in tests and measurement, school counselors should keep available several of the personality inventories listed in Table 5.4. Self-knowledge is often a critical component of the counseling process, and personality inventories are an important way to increase counselees' self-knowledge. In a situation where the counselee's self-knowledge is minimal, a personality profile can be a helpful tool for career exploration and decision making.

Career Maturity Inventories

In recent years, as the belief that the individual's development is a key factor in career exploration and choice has become more popular, so have career maturity inventories. These instruments measure career maturity in terms of a particular dimension derived from a particular career development theory. For example, the Career Beliefs Inventory is constructed from a social cognitive perspective: It is designed to identify faulty beliefs that could prevent an individual from making appropriate career decisions. Recent research shows that lower levels of self-efficacy are related to higher levels of career indecision (Betz & Luzzo, 1996; Betz & Voyten, 1997; Wulff & Steitz, 1999).

Career maturity inventories are a valuable tool for measuring a student's readiness for career exploration and for identifying the developmental level at which to begin the process. They also can be used as pre- and postintervention measures to evaluate the effectiveness of a career guidance program. The three inventories listed in Table 5.4 can be used with middle school and high school students.

Card Sorts

The Vocational Card Sort was developed by Tyler (1961), modified by Dolliver (1967), and further modified by Dewey (1974). The latest version consists of the names of 76 different occupations, each printed on a small piece of paper. The counselee is asked to divide the pieces of paper into two piles: those occupations that are appealing and those that are not. Next the student divides each pile by the reasons the occupations are or are not appealing. Then the counselor conducts a semistructured interview, asking the student to talk about his or her reasons and facilitating an exploration of the student's interests, values, needs, and self-concept.

Over the years, numerous versions of the original card sort have appeared, each emphasizing different aspects of career decision making. Among those tests are Occ-U-Sort (L. K. Jones, 1980), Missouri Occupational Card Sort (Krieschok, Hansen, Johnston, & Wong, 2002), the Career Values Card Sort Planning Kit (Knowdell, 1995), and the Vocational Exploration and Insight Kit (Holland, 1980).

The card sort is to the career counselor what the Rorschach is to the clinical psychologist (Leo Goldman, personal communication, 1993). That is, clients are asked to project onto occupational titles their interests, goals, values, and whatever else they see as a reason for choosing or not choosing an occupation (Goldman, 1983). Unlike the other assessment instruments we describe here, a card sort is not a standardized test; it is a projective technique that can reveal a client's deeper self-concept. And the card sort is a versatile tool: It can be used with individuals or small groups, children or adults; it is inexpensive; and it is easy to administer (Zunker, 2002).

Choosing an Instrument

Standardized assessment has been an integral part of career counseling for many years. To design the best possible career guidance program for their schools, school counselors should be familiar with all of the tests noted in Table 5.4 and with card sorts, should keep at least one test from each category available, and should make use of them as necessary. When choosing a test, counselors should consider the age of the client and the counselor's own evaluation of and level of comfort with the test. One way to sample the different instruments is to go to a career resource center (usually located at a community college or other institution) and take the different tests. Many of these centers are subsidized by government funds and are accessible to anyone who is looking for career information.

Despite the value of many traditional pencil-and-paper tests, the future of assessment in career counseling is electronic, a subject we discuss at length in the next section. Here, we should note that several of the instruments listed in Table 5.4 are available in electronic versions. Also available are all-in-one assessments that measure aptitude, achievement, interests, and values, and combine the results in an *occupational profile*.

USING TECHNOLOGY IN CAREER COUNSELING

Many of the fundamental resources used in career counseling are now available online. In fact, computer-assisted career guidance systems (CACGSs) have already become a mainstay of many school-based vocational guidance programs.

CACGSs are broad in scope, but most share certain components (Zunker, 2002):

Information. About occupations (including careers in the armed services), about postsecondary education (in colleges and universities and in technical and other specialized schools), and about financial aid.

Inventories. Measures of ability, interests, decision-making skills, values, and of likely success in college.

Job-search strategies. How to prepare a résumé and what to expect and do at a job interview.

CACGSs offer tremendous advantages:

1. The interactive capability of computerized systems allows users to become more actively involved in the career guidance process.
2. User motivation is sustained thorough the unique use of immediate feedback.
3. The opportunity to individualize the career exploration process provides opportunities to personalize career search strategies.
4. Computer-assisted career guidance systems provide systematic career exploration and career decision programs.
5. Access to large databases of up-to-date information for local, state, national, and international locations is immediately available. (Zunker, 2002, p. 257)

The immediacy of both information and feedback engages students more readily in the career exploration process than do traditional pencil-and-paper assessments. But that immediacy is also a potential problem. CACGSs run the risk of eliminating the counselor from that process. Students can fill out an inventory and then use the results as a basis—the only basis—for their career decisions. What's missing is the counselor's interpretation of the CACGS profile and his or her explanation of all the variables that can affect the choice of a career. No instrument, whatever its sophistication, is a crystal ball. And whether that instrument is taken with paper and pencil or electronically, the school counselor must be involved in the interpretation and application of its results.

In the following sections, we look at several online career guidance systems. These are the most widely used systems today. That *today* is important. In the rapidly changing world of technology, new products are constantly being added, and old products are constantly being modified.

DISCOVER®

DISCOVER® was released in 1987 and has undergone a number of updates and revisions since.[5] It was designed to help high school and college students make career decisions.

DISCOVER® has three versions: one for middle/junior high school students, one for high school students, and one for college students and adults. The middle/junior high school versions has three modules: (1) You and the World of Work, (2) Exploring Occupations, and (3) Planning Your High School Program. The high school version has seven components:

1. Beginning the Career Journey
2. Learning about the World of Work
3. Learning about Yourself
4. Finding an Occupation
5. Learning about Occupations
6. Making Educational Choices
7. Planning the Next Steps

The college/adult version includes these components and two additional modules:

8. Planning Your Career
9. Making Transitions

Questions in the first module determine the career maturity of the respondent and the level of the exploration. It is recommended that students follow the modules in order. The third component, Learning about Yourself, contains inventories of interests, abilities, and values. After completing the inventories, students are referred to the World-of-Work Map. At various points, respondents are asked about the importance to them of certain occupational characteristics: work setting, compensation, hours, willingness to pursue more education, and the like. Finally, the system generates a list of occupations based on the respondent's profile. By clicking any occupation on the list, the respondent can obtain a description of the occupation and links to more information. Each occupation is cross-referenced to the *Dictionary of Occupational Titles,* a resource we talk about in the O*NET section below.

Career Information Delivery Systems

Most states maintain a career information delivery system (CIDS) that describes educational and vocational information and training options on both a national and state level.[6] These systems are the brainchild of the National Occupational Information Coordinating Committee (NOICC) and the State Occupational Information

---

[5] DISCOVER® is produced by American College Testing. An overview of the system is available on the Web at www.act.org/discover/index.html.

[6] For information about a state's CIDS, see the America's Career InfoNet Web site at www.acinet.org/acinet/.

Coordinating Committees.[7] Because the systems are maintained in large part by government funds, schools can access them relatively cheaply.

Keeping a CIDS up to date is a major undertaking. It's not surprising, then, that the currency and the detail of the state systems can vary.

Several years ago, when I was teaching a course on career counseling, I invited the director of the state CIDS and her assistant to class to talk about and give a demonstration of the system. I was duly impressed by their knowledge and dedication to promoting the computerized career information system. They encouraged all of the school counselors in training to use a CIDS in their future work. I can't vouch for the system in every state, but if school counselors are fortunate enough to work in a state with a well-maintained CIDS, that's very good advice.

Most state systems have four basic parts: assessment, occupational search, occupational information, and educational information. Inventories in the assessment section measure skills, values, interests, aptitudes, and experience. The skills assessment determines not only the respondent's level of skills but also the type and level of skills demanded by a particular job (and information on how to acquire or improve the necessary skills). Like DISCOVER®, these systems generate a list of occupations based on the assessments, along with detailed information about the occupations. The educational component of the systems describe two- and four-year colleges and vocational and technical schools, often with the kind of detail usually found in a school's catalog.

System of Interactive Guidance and Information Plus

The System of Interactive Guidance and Information PLUS (SIGI PLUS®) was developed by Katz (1975, 1993) and is currently owned and administered by the Educational Testing Service (ETS).[8] SIGI PLUS® has nine parts: (1) Introduction, (2) Self-Assessment, (3) Search, (4) Information, (5) Skills, (6) Preparing, (7) Coping, (8) Deciding, and (9) Next Steps. The system is a needs-centered job search: It identifies the respondent's needs and factors those needs into the list of suggested occupations.

SIGI PLUS® was designed mainly for college students and adults in transition. But its user-friendliness and comprehensiveness make it an excellent tool for counseling high schoolers. In fact, for almost three decades, Katz's system has set the standard for CACGSs.

Other Online Resources

The Internet is an enormously important resource for school counselors in search of career guidance information. Best of all, it's free. (All of the CACGSs mentioned

---

[7]The NOICC is no longer functioning. However, much of its work—for example, the CIDS concept and the development of national career guidelines—continues to be very influential in career development programs in both educational and noneducational settings.

[8]Information about the system is available on the Web at www.ets.org/sigi/index.html.

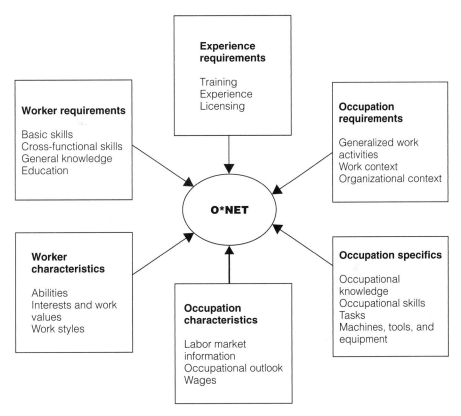

FIGURE 5.3

O*NET: A CONTENT MODEL

above have to be purchased or licensed in some way.) Two of the best sites for career information are O*NET and the *Occupational Outlook Handbook.*[9]

O*NET O*NET (www.doleta.gov/programs/onet) is maintained by the Department of Labor. It is a valuable source of current information about jobs and job markets. Throughout this chapter, we've made references to the *Dictionary of Occupational Titles (DOT)*; O*NET is its online replacement. The *DOT*, currently in its fourth edition (1991), is an official publication of the Department of Labor. It is filled with job classifications and descriptions. That overwhelming amount of information, an onerous classification system, and two heavy volumes make it user-unfriendly. O*NET is much easier to use and is updated much more frequently than the *DOT*, which makes it more relevant to career planning today.

O*NET is organized around six content areas (Figure 5.3). It currently includes information about 1,172 occupations (versus almost 12,000 in the *DOT*). Each occupation is assigned a five-letter code followed by a letter indicating a

---

[9] Other good sites are listed at the end of the chapter.

subdivision with in the occupation. The first number designates one of nine major occupational groups:

1. Executives, managers, and administrators
2. Professional and support specialists (financial specialists, engineers, scientists, mathematicians, social scientists, social services workers, religious workers, and legal workers)
3. Professional support specialties (educators, librarians, counselors, health care workers, artists, writers, performers, and other professional workers)
4. Sales workers
5. Administrative support workers
6. Service workers
7. Agriculture, forestry, and fishing workers
8. Mechanics, installers, repairers, construction trades, extractive trades, metal and plastics working, woodworking, apparel, precision printing, and food-processing workers
9. Machine setters, operators and tenders, production workers, hand workers, plant and system workers, transportation workers, and helpers

Information about jobs is provided by skills, knowledge, work experience, work styles, and work and organizational context variables. In addition, educational requirements are shown on a 12-point scale, with 1 indicating less than a high school diploma and 12 indicating some type of postdoctoral certification. Finally, there is information about earnings, future growth, and supply and demand for workers.

To make full use of the O*NET database, users are encouraged to use companion publications: the O*NET Interest Profiler (measures the Holland's personality types), the O*NET Work Importance Locator (a values inventory), and the O*NET Ability Profiler (measures nine job relevant abilities).

O*NET provides an enormous amount of occupational information for students, just about everything they need to know. (A single entry would take up several pages in a book.) To help students make use of O*NET, school counselors should have good working knowledge of this comprehensive resource.

The *Occupational Outlook Handbook* The *Occupational Outlook Handbook* (*OOH*) is published by the Bureau of Labor Statistics in the Department of Labor. The *OOH* describes the work, working conditions, educational and training requirements, salaries, and the job market for 200 to 300 jobs in 13 general categories, from executive positions to the military. Every job is cross-referenced to the *DOT* and lists additional sources of information. The *OOH* is updated every two years. It is available online at www.bls.gov/oco/.

The principal value of the *OOH* is in its description of employment trends and projections: areas in which jobs are expected to increase or decrease over the next several years, along with projected compensation. The *OOH* can be an important reality check for idealistic students in terms of future job availability and growth.

CAREER DEVELOPMENT IN THE ELEMENTARY SCHOOL

For many years, high school was thought to be the proper and exclusive environment for career counseling and development. But the research that supports career developmental theory has found that much of what adolescents think about careers begins to take shape years earlier, in elementary school (Bailey & Nihlen, 1989; L. Seligman, Weinstock, & Heflin, 1991; Trice & McClellan, 1993). By exposing their students to a wide variety of careers early on, elementary school counselors enable those students to make more-mature career decisions later. That's especially important in our increasingly complex work world.

The NOICC (1992) outlined three areas of career development for students in elementary school:

1. Self-knowledge
   a. Knowledge of the importance of self-concept
   b. Skills to interact with others
   c. Awareness of the importance of growth and change
2. Educational and occupational exploration
   a. Awareness of the benefits of educational achievement
   b. Awareness of the relationship between work and learning
   c. Skills to understand and use career information
   d. Awareness of the importance of personal responsibility and good work habits
   e. Awareness of how work relates to the needs and functions of society
3. Career planning
   a. Understanding of how to make decisions
   b. Awareness of the interrelationship of life roles
   c. Awareness of different occupation and changing male/female roles
   d. Awareness of the career planning process (Zunker, 2002, pp. 435–436)

The National Standards for School Counseling Programs based student competencies for career development on the NOICC guidelines (see Appendix A).

The Role of Gender, Race, and Socioeconomic Status

Over the years, researchers have investigated the influence of several variables on children's career aspirations, but perhaps no other has received more attention than sex-role expectations (Herting-Wahl & Blackhurst, 2000). Early studies (Looft, 1971a, 1971b) found that first- and second-grade girls believed they had far fewer job options than did boys in the same grades. Later studies found that girls were thinking about more jobs, but that they still were not aspiring to high-status or traditional male occupations at the same rate that boys were (Adams & Hicken, 1984; M. J. Miller & Stanford, 1987). More recent research has been inconclusive. Trice (1991) found no differences in the career aspirations of children ages 8 to 11; while

T. M. Phillips, Cooper, and Johnson (1995) found that girls in Grades 4 through 8 identify with a much narrower range of occupations compared with boys in the same grades.

Other studies have examined race as a contributing factor in career development (Carter & Cook, 1992; Carter & Swanson, 1990; Leong & Brown, 1995; Leung, 1995). Criticism has been levied against career development theories that emphasize the individual's control over the decision-making process, citing their inappropriateness for members of racial minorities who experience institutional and social barriers to career choice (Leung, 1995). In addition, researchers have questioned the validity of using standardized tests to make career decisions for students from nondominant racial groups (Carter & Swanson, 1990; Fouad, 1993). The effects of race on career development seem evident. According to Lichter (1988), more than 50 percent of young urban African American men during the 1980s were unemployed, were force to work part-time because they could not get full-time jobs, or earned poverty-level wages. The unemployment rate for African Americans is 2.5 times the rate for Whites, and less than 37 percent of African American men hold professional jobs compared with almost 62 percent of White men (Swinton, 1992). Hispanic Americans are concentrated in lower-paying service jobs; Native Americans living on reservations have an unemployment rate of 45 percent (Herr & Cramer, 1996).[10]

Finally, studies have consistently shown that socioeconomic status is an important variable in determining the occupational aspirations of young children (Herting-Wahl & Blackhurst, 2000). Poor children lack access to resources that can broaden occupational and educational aspirations. In fact, Valadez (1998) found that socioeconomic status mediates the effects of both gender and race: High socioeconomic status tends to mitigate those effects; low socioeconomic status, to make them more severe.

What do these findings mean for school counselors? Clearly they point to the importance of career guidance and development in elementary school. They also indicate that sex-role stereotyping and limited exposure to a wide range of careers can have lasting effects on young children, restricting their future career choices.

The most effective way to combat gender and other stereotypes is to present students with nontraditional role models (K. M. White & Oulette, 1980). Herting-Wahl and Blackhurst (2000) suggested these five methods:

1. Invite speakers with nontraditional occupations.
2. Read stories whose characters hold nontraditional jobs.
3. Take field trips to view workers in nontraditional settings.
4. Depict nontraditional workers on career posters.
5. Establish mentoring programs for children interested in nontraditional careers. (p. 371)

---

[10]The effects of race are explored more fully in Chapter 6.

A Planned Curriculum

Career development is a natural focus for comprehensive guidance programs in schools. The key to success here is twofold: A program must be absorbed into the overall curriculum, and it must be competency based. Today, many programs like this are being implemented. Table 5.5 shows the goals and competencies of one competency-based career guidance program for Grades K through 6.

In the best of all possible worlds, the school counselor would be teaching these competencies to a class of students. And some fortunate elementary school counselors do have classroom time allotted for guidance activities. If not, the counselor must negotiate with the administration and teachers to enter the classroom and implement the curriculum. If the career counseling curriculum is really a part of the school's overall curriculum, the negotiation for classroom time should not be difficult. Again, teachers should remain in the classroom during large-group guidance sessions, both to keep students on task and to be able to integrate the competencies in their teaching.

Using Assessment Instruments

A number of assessment instruments have been designed specifically for elementary school children (Table 5.6). These tests and inventories can be administered to students individually, in small groups, and in large groups. The results can form the basis of discussion and also facilitate an understanding and appreciation of how individuals differ in terms of their interests, values, favorite activities, and needs.

Working with Parents

Ginzberg (1952) believed that youngsters under age 11 fantasize about all different kinds of jobs, their interests changing often. However, more recent research has found that childhood interests may be more stable than once thought (Trice, Hughes, Odom, Woods, & McClellan, 1995; Trice & King, 1991). That stability may well be related to their parents' occupations: Young children want to grow up to be like their parents. One study found a significant relationship between what parents do, especially mothers, and what children hope to do when they grow up (Trice & Knapp, 1992). Another study found that children want to do the same work as the parent they perceive is most satisfied (Trice & Tillapaugh, 1991). We know that collaboration with parents is necessary for the successful development of schoolchildren. But this research on the influence parents have on young children's career development makes parents' involvement in the career development program all the more important.

Many parents may not be aware of their influence on their child's career development. So collaboration should begin with a large-group meeting at which the school counselor introduces the program and explains the important role parents play in their child's career development (Amundson & Penner, 1998). At the

TABLE 5.5	GOALS AND COMPETENCIES IN A CAREER GUIDANCE PROGRAM, GRADES K-6

Overall Goals

- Become aware of personal characteristics, interests, aptitudes, and skills.
- Develop an awareness of and respect for the diversity of the world of work.
- Understand the relationship between school performance and future choices.
- Develop a positive attitude toward work.

Competencies

Kindergarten students will be able to	• identify workers in the school setting.
	• describe the work of family members.
	• describe what they like to do.
Students in Grade 1 will be able to	• describe their likes and dislikes.
	• identify workers in various settings.
	• identify responsibilities they have at home and at school.
	• identify skills they have now that they did not have previously.
Students in Grade 2 will be able to	• describe skills needed to complete a task at home or at school.
	• distinguish which work activities in their school environment are done by specific people.
	• recognize the diversity of jobs in various settings.
Students in Grade 3 will be able to	• define what the term *future* means.
	• recognize and describe the many life roles that people have.
	• demonstrate the ability to brainstorm a range of job titles.
Students in Grade 4 will be able to	• imagine what their lives might be like in the future.
	• evaluate the importance of various familiar jobs in the community.
	• describe workers in terms of work performed.
	• identify personal hobbies and leisure activities.
Students in Grade 5 will be able to	• identify ways that familiar jobs contribute to the needs of society.
	• compare their interests and skills to familiar jobs.
	• compare their personal hobbies and leisure activities to jobs.
	• discuss stereotypes associated with certain jobs.
	• discuss what is important to them.
Students in Grade 6 will be able to	• identify tentative work interests and skills.
	• list elements of decision making.
	• discuss how their parents' work influences life at home.
	• consider the relationship between interests and abilities.
	• identify their own personal strengths and weaknesses.

SOURCE: From *Developmental School Counseling Programs: From Theory to Practice*, by P. O. Paisley and G. T. Hubbard, 1994, pp. 218–219. Copyright 1994 by the American Counseling Association. Reprinted with permission.

TABLE 5.6 CAREER DEVELOPMENT ASSESSMENT INSTRUMENTS, GRADES K–6

Instrument	Beginning Grade	Description	Publisher
Arlin-Hills Attitude Survey	K	Measures attitudes toward teachers, learning, language, and arithmetic	Psychologists and Educators
SCAMIN: A Self-Concept and Preschool-Motivation Inventory	K–3	Assesses achievement investment, role expectations, achievement needs, and self-adequacy	Person-Ometrics
Affective Perception Inventory	1	Measures attitudes toward self and school and specific school subjects	Soares Associates
Martinek-Zaichkowsky Self-Concept Scale for Children	1	Assesses global self-concept and physical, emotional, and behavioral aspects of self-confidence	Psychologists and Educators
Survey of School Attitudes	1	Measures attitudes toward reading and language arts, science, social studies, and mathematics	Psychological Corporation
Values Inventory for Children	1	Assesses children's values and their relationships to other children, parents, and authority figures	Sheridan Psychological Services
Career Awareness Inventory, Level 1	3	Measures how much students know about careers and their own career choices	Scholastic Testing Service
Coopersmith Self-Esteem Inventory—School Form	3	Assesses attitudes toward self, school, family, and peers	Consulting Psychologists Press
Culture Free Self-Esteem Inventory	3	Measures general self-esteem	Special Child Publications
Hall Occupational Orientation Inventory (Intermediate)	3	Assesses psychological needs related to workers' traits and job characteristics	Scholastic Testing Service
Individual Career Exploration	3	Assesses general career areas of interests	Scholastic Testing Service
Explore the World of Work	4	Assesses vocational interests	CFKR Career Material
Piers-Harris Children's Self-Concept Scale	4	Assesses student self-concept in six areas: behavior adjustment, freedom from anxiety, happiness and satisfaction, intellectual and school status, physical appearance and attributes, and popularity.	Psychological Assessment Resources
Safran Student's Interest	5	Measures occupational interests and interest in school subjects	Nelson Canada
Wide Range Interest Opinion Test	5	Assesses perception of ability, aspiration level, and social conformity for use in vocational career planning and counseling	Jastak
Career Maturity Inventory Attitude Scale and Competency Test	6	Assesses attitudes and competencies	CTB/McGraw-Hill
COPSystem Interest Inventory	6	Assesses interests related to occupational clusters	Educational and Industrial Testing Service

SOURCE: Adapted from Herring (1998), pp. 68–69.

meeting, the counselor also should encourage parent-child activities that highlight the different occupations of family members—for example, an occupational family tree or collage. The counselor also might suggest that parents visit the classroom to talk about their jobs or even ask a group of students to visit their workplace (Herting-Wahl & Blackhurst, 2000).

Experiential Activities

Elementary school counselors should keep in mind that the two general goals of their career development efforts are increasing students' self-knowledge and broadening their horizons in terms of career options. Within the curriculum, counselors can have students read and discuss stories about different workers; play "What's My Line"; keep a log of workers they encounter each day or on TV; identify all the workers in the school; or take a field trips to a local pizzeria, for example, and discuss the different roles workers play there (Herr & Cramer, 1984). Counselors also can invite outside speakers and career role models to talk with the class; have the students use puppets to role-play the duties and responsibilities of different occupations; and interview parents in class about their jobs (Drummond & Ryan, 1995).

No textbook can describe all of the creative activities that could be incorporated into a career development program for Grades K through 6. What's important is to stay focused on the program's goals and competencies, and to develop or borrow activities that move children toward achieving those goals and competencies.[11] And what's even more important is the belief that the career development work counselors do with younger students can make a real difference in those students' future career decisions.

CAREER DEVELOPMENT IN THE MIDDLE SCHOOL

Many school systems across the country have moved away from the junior high school model (Grades 7, 8, and 9) to a middle school model (Grades 6, 7, and 8).[12] Career development for middle schoolers should begin with a focus on the developmental issues unique to early adolescence.

Developmental Issues

Many of the issues facing early adolescents stem from the rapid and dramatic physical changes they are undergoing and the feelings of clumsiness and embarrassment

---

[11] There are many books and kits filled with good activities for use with a career development curriculum in the elementary school. See, for example, Career Explorer at www.cx.bridges.com; the *Elementary Career Awareness Guide: A Resource for Elementary School Counselors and Teachers* (North Carolina SOICC, 1999); and *Career Development Activities for Every Classroom: K–3 and 4–6* (Washington State Department of Education, 1998).

[12] Some middle schools also include Grade 5; in this section, we refer to the Grades 6–8 model.

those changes produce. Early adolescents are very concerned about their physical appearance, which can relegate learning to a secondary position. Acceptance by their peers is critical—issues of belonging are primary—and middle schoolers are very susceptible to peer pressure. Erikson (1963) believed the developmental task of adolescence is forging a new identity, which is determined to a large degree by how adolescents feel about themselves. It is important for middle schoolers to experience success, even a small success, because success greatly affects their self-esteem and motivation to learn.

Cognitively, middle school students begin what Piaget (1929) called *formal thinking processes*, the ability to think abstractly and logically, to make connections. Their cognitive development has important consequences for career planning. Middle schoolers are capable of understanding and realizing the effects of an action without doing the action itself. They are capable of reflection, and they can use information to predict the effects of certain decisions.

A Planned Curriculum

Middle school counselors, like elementary school counselors, should develop a curriculum that can be implemented through classroom guidance and small groups. Individual counseling, although sometimes necessary, is not recommended: Most middle schoolers feel more comfortable around their peers than alone with authority figures. In fact, as they strive toward autonomy and independence, some middle schoolers rebel against authority.

Table 5.7 lists the career goals and competencies from a career development curriculum for Grades 6 though 8. Certain themes are crucial for the career development of middle school students. First, students must learn to appraise their own abilities, achievements, and interests realistically (Zunker, 2002). Second, students need to understand the connections between educational decisions and future career plans. The College Board Commission on Precollege and Counseling (1986) found that middle and junior high school students do not understand the consequences of early academic choices. Of those who said they wanted to go to college, only 46 percent were enrolled in an academic versus a vocational curriculum. A middle school career development curriculum should prepare students for the academic decisions they will have to make in high school by connecting those decisions to the students' future career plans. Middle school is a time for exploration, not decision making; still, students need to make a realistic appraisal of their strengths and weaknesses and come to a realistic understanding of what they have to do to achieve their career goals.

Sex Differences and Gender Stereotypes

Dealing with gender stereotypes and broadening the career possibilities for girls are key components of the career development curriculum in elementary schools. They also are important parts of that curriculum in middle schools. Because of inherent sexism in our society and the self-esteem issues of middle schoolers, it is likely that many girls in this group see themselves as incompetent. Young adolescent girls have

TABLE 5.7	CAREER GOALS AND COMPETENCIES, GRADES 6–8

Overall Goals

- Become aware of personal characteristics, interests, aptitudes, and skills.
- Develop an awareness of and respect for the diversity of the world of work.
- Understand the relationship between school performance and future choices.
- Develop a positive attitude toward work.

Competencies

Students in Grade 6 will be able to	• identify tentative work interests and skills.
	• list elements of decision making.
	• discuss how their parents' work influences life at home.
	• consider the relationship between interest and abilities.
	• identify their own personal strengths and weaknesses.
Students in Grade 7 will be able to	• identify tentative career interests and relate them to future planning.
	• recognize the connection between school performance and related career plans.
	• identify resources for career exploration and information.
Students in Grade 8 will be able to	• identify specific career interests and abilities using the results of assessment instruments.
	• consider future career plans in making educational choices.
	• describe their present skills, abilities, and interests.
	• use resources for career exploration and information.

SOURCE: From *Developmental School Counseling Programs: From Theory to Practice*, by P. O. Paisley and G. T. Hubbard, 1994, pp. 219–220. Copyright 1994 by the American Counseling Association. Reprinted with permission.

been found to have a lower self-image than do boys the same age, and a fear of success (Search Institute, 1988). That is, some girls believe that appearing smart and competent makes them less attractive to boys. School counselors should be keenly aware of these issues—and of the fact that between the late 1980s and the year 2000, two-thirds of new entrants into the workforce were women (Niles & Harris-Bowlsbey, 2002)—and develop activities to mitigate this form of sexism.

Some of the strategies suggested for elementary school students work equally well with middle schoolers. Counselors might show videotapes that portray women in nontraditional careers; conduct workshops where girls learn about the lives of famous women; and invite successful working women to speak about their careers (Sears-Jones, 1995).

Culture-based gender roles can also prevent girls in middle school from exploring what have traditionally been male-dominated occupations (Fouad & Bingham, 1995). Acculturative conflict that restricts career exploration may necessitate the involvement of parents in the career development process.[13]

Activities

During middle school, counselors can concentrate on increasing students' awareness of career trends (Herting-Wahl & Blackhurst, 2000). It is an appropriate time to begin using the state CIDS and resources like the *OOH*. To make wise curriculum choices in high school, middle school students need to be aware of the increasing demand for jobs that require postsecondary education. Career days and fairs are very popular in middle school, but counselors must be sure to include speakers whose work breaks with traditional stereotypes (Herring, 1998).

Sears-Jones (1995) suggested the following activities for middle school students:

- Have students spend a half-day on the job with one of their parents.
- Have seventh and eighth graders spend a day on a college campus. Their visit should include time observing a class and visiting the admissions office.
- Promote business-school partnerships that team a business or community agency with the school to provide information and role models for students.

Middle school is an appropriate time for students to begin a *career portfolio* (Bushweller, 1995; Milone, 1995), a record of their career interests, exploratory activities, academic achievements, and extracurricular activities, and their vocational guidance meetings with counselors (Herting-Wahl & Blackhurst, 2000). These portfolios can be an important resource in high school, when students are finalizing their postsecondary plans. More important for middle schoolers, they can point to discrepancies between students' career aspirations and their academic progress, information the school counselor can use immediately to challenge the students: "If you really want to be a _____, you are going to have to bring up your grades in _____."

Career assessment should play a key role in middle school. The results of interest inventories are useful here, along with the results of schoolwide aptitude and achievement tests. Holland's typology (see Table 5.3) can help middle schoolers define their interests. Then, as a follow-up activity, the school counselor could ask each student to interview a worker from each one of his or her Holland types, or could plan field trips to introduce the different types in the workplace (Herring, 1998).

---

[13] It is also important to consider issues of discrimination that prevent students at this age from believing they can work in careers traditionally dominated by Whites. Again, we explore the issues of racism and discrimination in detail in the next chapter.

Middle School: A Turning Point

Middle school can be a turning point in the education of many students. Those who drop out of high school often report that their problems with school began with the transition to middle school (Sciarra, 1998). Early adolescence is a difficult developmental period, which can make the guidance task especially challenging. But it also can make that task especially rewarding. Working with middle school students is an opportunity for school counselors to make connections between the present and the future. By giving students appropriate and accurate information about careers and the requirements to attain them, school counselors can make a significant contribution to students' lives. Too many students enter high school ill informed about the consequences of their academic choices. Middle schoolers are idealistic, and that can prevent them from recognizing that the work they will do in the future very much depends on the work they do in school right now. A solid career development program in middle school can help these students connect their career goals with their educational goals.

CAREER DEVELOPMENT AND GUIDANCE IN HIGH SCHOOL

Career work in high school continues to be competency based (Table 5.8). Although career exploration continues, this is also a time for refinement. By now students should understand their abilities, skills, aptitudes, and interests; and their career choice, although not final, should begin to narrow. The focus of the career development program in high school is on what comes next. Students will be exercising different options: Some will enter the military and others the workforce; and a number of students will go on to college at a two- or four-year institution.

Counselors need to spend equal time with all students: They should not focus on those who plan to go on to college. In fact, students who are making other career decisions probably need *more* attention to be prepared for today's high-tech labor market. Congress recognized a lack of complex skills among high school seniors in 1994, when it passed the School-to-Work Opportunities Act (STWOA).

The School-to-Work Opportunities Act (1994)

The rationale for the STWOA was that in addition to general employability skills (attendance, promptness, motivation, initiative, and the like), graduating seniors need industry-specific skills that make them attractive to employers (Worthington & Juntunen, 1997).[14] The implication was that the current educational system was not providing students with those skills. One section of the act recommends that

---

[14] A detailed description of the act is beyond the scope of this chapter. Our focus here is on the aspects of the act that are particularly relevant for school counselors working with underrepresented youth. For more information about the STWOA, see U.S. Department of Education (1994a, 1994b).

TABLE 5.8 **CAREER GOALS AND COMPETENCIES, GRADES 9–12**

Overall Goals

- Become aware of personal characteristics, interests, aptitudes, and skills.
- Develop an awareness of and respect of the diversity of the world of work.
- Understand the relationship between school performance and future choices.
- Develop a positive attitude toward work.

Competencies

Students in Grade 9 will be able to	• recognize positive work habits. • refine their knowledge of their own skills, aptitudes, interests, and values. • identify general career goals. • make class selections on the basis of career goals. • use career resources in goal setting and decision making.
Students in Grade 10 will be able to	• clarify the role of values in career choice. • distinguish educational and skill requirements for areas or careers of interest. • recognize the effects of job or career choice on other areas of life. • begin realistic assessment of their potential in various fields. • develop skills in prioritizing needs related to career planning.
Students in Grade 11 will be able to	• refine future career goals through synthesis of information concerning self, use of resources, and consultation with others. • coordinate class selection with career goals. • identify specific educational requirements necessary to achieve their goals. • clarify their own values as they relate to work and leisure.
Students in Grade 12 will be able to	• complete requirements for transition from high school. • make final commitments to a career plan. • understand the potential for change in their own interests or values related to work. • understand the potential for change within the job market. • understand career development as a lifelong process. • accept responsibility for their own career directions.

SOURCE: From *Developmental School Counseling Programs: From Theory to Practice,* by P. O. Paisley and G. T. Hubbard, 1994, p. 220. Copyright 1994 by the American Counseling Association. Reprinted with permission.

local industry become more involved in the school system by making curriculum suggestions and offering paid internships to students while they are in school. Critics contended that private industry should not dictate curriculum, and that the act, by forcing decisions early on about who is and who is not college bound, was returning schools to the use of academic and vocational tracking.

Actually, a school-to-work transition does not deny students access to postsecondary education. Today all students take enough academic credits to attend at least a two-year college. What the STWOA does is allow the school to identify at-risk students and better prepare them for quality jobs that do not require a college education. In this sense, the act can make the difference between a minimum-wage job (flipping hamburgers is the common metaphor) and a well-paying job that demands certain academic and technological skills. This is especially important when we consider that African American workers (both men and women) earn 77 percent and Latino workers 67 percent of the median weekly earnings of White workers (U.S. Department of Labor, 1996).

Activities

Classroom guidance sessions in high school do not take place with the same frequency they do in elementary or middle school. High school scheduling is just too inflexible to accommodate classroom guidance activities. Instead, high school counselors work more with individuals and small groups. In these sessions, counselor and students define the students' interests and long-term goals, and identify the learning and skills needed to reach those goals. Each student should record the date and results of each session on a career-planning form like the one in Figure 5.4. This form should be part of the career portfolio the student began compiling in middle school.

Drummond and Ryan (1995) recommended that by the time students are in high school, their career portfolios should include

- a list of school activities (clubs, sports, honors, and so on).
- a list of hobbies and leisure activities.
- profiles from ability, aptitude, achievement, and other tests.
- a list of work experience (part-time and summer jobs).
- a list of courses completed (and grades).
- career plans and information collected on postsecondary programs.
- a record of career-related interviews held with school counselors, teachers, and other advisers.
- a completed résumé.

Assessment activities should continue in high school, especially in Grades 9 and 10. Many of the instruments listed in Table 5.4 are appropriate for this age group. The school counselor also should continue to emphasize the connection between career goals and current academic and vocational choices, that choosing certain courses over others has long-range implications. High school students have the flexibility to change programs or courses to make them consistent with their career goals.

Student _____ Date _____

My career interests: 1. _____ My long-term educational goal: _____

2. _____ _____

3. _____ _____

Course Work Needed to Realize My Goal	Course Taken	Year Completed	Final Grade
Art/music/drama			
Communication skills			
Foreign language			
Literature			
Mathematics			
Sciences			
Social studies			
Statistics and logic			
Technical reading			
Vocational courses			
Other courses			

My extracurricular experiences: _____

_____

_____

My planning conferences with counselor(s), teachers, or advisers:

Date	Decisions/Plans	Counselor/Teacher

Postsecondary tasks I need to accomplish (college applications, scholarship applications, entrance exams, job interviews, résumé, etc.):

Task	Date Completed

SOURCE: Adapted from Schmidt (1999), p. 235.

FIGURE **5.4**

A CAREER-PLANNING FORM

All high school seniors, whatever their plans after graduation, need certain job-search skills, among them writing a résumé, composing a job-application letter, interviewing, and finding a job (Herring, 1998). Some of these skills are taught in the classroom; if not, the counselor must make sure that students have these career-related competencies. Mock interviews, for example, are wonderful practice for students going on a job interview for the first time; and films and videotapes are a good resource for teaching interviewing and other job-search skills.

Developmental Issues

High school students continue to be very much influenced by their peers. It's not unusual for students to plan to do what their friends are planning to do. The school counselor should watch for contradictions between students' career goals and their abilities and skills.

A discrepancy between plans and abilities can also be a product of parental pressure. Some parents live vicariously through their child: They want their child to achieve what they think is important to achieve, or to work at something they were not able to work at. They fail to see that their career goal for their child may not be consistent with the child's interests, skills, or abilities. Although it is always important to involve parents in their child's career decisions, counselors need to be proactive with parents who are pressuring their child to prepare for a career in which the child has no interest.

Most high school students are well aware that educational and vocational decisions have serious consequences, and some may feel overwhelmed and frightened by that. Those students may respond with anxiety, or by being passive or demanding. According to Erikson (1963), occupational decision making can threaten students' acquiring a sense of identity, the major developmental task of adolescents. School counselors should carefully observe how students respond to the challenge of setting career goals and selecting academic options. Some students may need to be taught decision-making skills; others may need assertiveness training. Both interventions can be implemented in small-group meetings.

ETHICAL AND LEGAL ISSUES

Although career counseling might seem exempt from any serious ethical or legal concerns, recent developments prove otherwise. Online career assessments and a 2001 court case in Iowa point to the consequences of students' and counselors' behaving irresponsibly. The preparations and decisions surrounding career choice have real-life consequences for students. School counselors have an ethical and now a legal responsibility to exercise reasonable care and diligence while guiding students through a myriad of educational and vocational options.

Career-Related Assessments

Without question, the most important ethical challenge facing career counselors is the proper use of standardized tests. The problem here is exacerbated by online instruments. Nothing prevents students from logging on to the Internet, accessing a career Web page, completing an assessment, and then accepting without qualification the results of that assessment. The same holds true for students who come to the school counselor wanting to be told what career they should choose.

When they make career assessments, school counselors must follow certain ethical guidelines (National Career Development Association, 1991):

- Be knowledgeable about the assessment instrument being used.
- Talk to students about the assessment results in terms they can understand.
- Ensure that students understand the limitations of career assessment instruments.

Many students take assessment results as gospel; it is the school counselor's ethical obligation to prevent that. It is bad practice when the instrument is published by a reputable testing company and backed by sound validity and reliability correlations; it is worse practice when the instrument is found on a Web site and has not been vetted. Often these online assessments are marketing devices, used to lure the unsuspecting to choose a career that involves expensive training (Niles & Harris-Bowlsbey, 2002). If students share the results of an Internet assessment, the school counselor can caution them and offer to provide an alternate assessment to determine intertest reliability. At the very least, the counselor should issue a general warning to students about Internet-based career assessments.[15]

Negligence

A more recent issue is of a legal nature and involves the liability of school counselors for postsecondary preparation. Stone (2002) described the case of Bruce Sain, who sued the Cedar Rapids Community School District in 2001 for negligence by the school counselor, Larry Bowen.[16] In his senior year, Sain asked Bowen to place him in a different English class. Bowen suggested technical communications, a course being offered for the first time, and said that it eventually would be approved by the National Collegiate Athletic Association's Initial Eligibility Clearinghouse. But the school did not include the course on the list it submitted each year to the NCAA. Sain, who had received a five-year basketball scholarship to Northern Illinois University, was declared ineligible by the NCAA because his English class was not an approved course. The teenager lost his scholarship, and the family sued the school district, claiming that Bowen acted negligently by promising that the course would be approved and then not submitting the course for approval.

---

[15] If the school uses a CAGS, the counselor should encourage the use of that system over a career assessment instrument found by chance on the Internet.

[16] *Sain v. Cedar Rapids Community School District*, 626 N.W.2d 115 (Iowa, 2001).

The legal basis of negligence is one person's breach of duty to another. The lower courts rejected the idea that Sain was owed a duty in terms of academic advising. In an appeal, however, the Iowa Supreme Court found that the charge of negligence against the school had merit and remanded the trial to the lower court. The higher court, in a 5–2 decision, ruled that "school counselors can be held accountable for providing accurate information to student about credits and courses to pursue post–high school goals" (Stone, p. 30). Aware that they might be opening a Pandora's box, the justices in the majority stipulated that for negligence to exist, the student's reliance on the information must be reasonable and the school counselor must be aware that the information is vital (for example, that the information could have an impact on a student's financial situation). In other words, Sain's case had merit because he lost a lucrative scholarship. Implied in the court's decision was a business dimension to the school counselor-student relationship. That dimension was the grounds for duty owed and possible negligence.

Clearly the Iowa court's ruling could have a paralyzing effect on school counselors, making them reluctant to advise students for fear of making a mistake and being found negligent. In light of the decision in *Sain,* Stone made the following recommendations for school counselors:

- Act with reasonable care in advising students. The courts are not asking for extraordinary care.
- Stay current with changes in regulations that might affect counseling students on postsecondary options.
- Work as a team with others who may be as or more knowledgeable about regulations. (In Sain's case, a coach or athletic director might have been a good addition to the counseling team.)
- Make sure that all students and their parents are aware of and understand what students have to do to graduate. It's a good idea to check each student's credits and to give the student a list of the courses and credits still needed.
- Have parents and student sign an acknowledgment when they receive vital information (such as the list of courses or credits still needed).

CONCLUSION

Chapter 5 begins by outlining the developmental theories for children and adolescents that form the basis of career counseling programs in elementary, middle, and high schools. Each of these theories can add coherence and consistency to the career guidance program. More recently, social cognitive theory has introduced the dimension of self-efficacy as a key determinant of career development.

Assessment plays an important role in career counseling and development. The greater their self-knowledge, the better equipped students are to set appropriate career goals and make good career decisions. The text describes standardized instruments for assessing students' aptitude, achievement, interests, values, personality, and career maturity. It also describes several online programs and resources. Whatever the form of assessment, the counselor needs to play a part in interpreting the results. Neither counselors nor students should ever accept the score on a single instrument as definitive.

In the final sections of the chapter we examined the elements and dimensions of career development and guidance programs in elementary, middle, and high schools. In all cases, the programs should be integrated into the school's overall curriculum. Students have an easier time learning academic subjects if they are able to connect their achievement in those subjects to their career goals.

Career counseling has been the mainstay of school counselors for almost a century. This is no accident. Work is part of living, and working at a job one enjoys is part of living fully. Every day, school counselors have a wonderful opportunity through career development programs to help their students live fully.

QUESTIONS FOR DISCUSSION

1. Of the many different theories of career development and planning discussed in this chapter, which one do you think is most appropriate for use with children and adolescents? Explain your answer.
2. Do you believe it's necessary for a school counselor to have a defined theory of career planning? Why or why not?
3. Select one of the career development theories, and apply it to your own career development and choice. Share your analysis with a learning partner.
4. Name two types of standardized tests that you would use to assess a seventh grader's career options. Explain the focus of each type of test and why you would use it. Would your choice of tests change if the student was a high school junior? Why or why not?
5. Computer-assisted career guidance systems are replacing many of the traditional methods of career orientation and planning. Does your local school district use a CACGS? If so, briefly explain the system, and try to find out why the school district chose this particular one. If not, ask why, and then ask what instrument(s) the district does use to promote students' career development and awareness.
6. Proponents of comprehensive developmental guidance programs believe that career development should be a major focus of these programs. In your opinion, should career development be a K–12 endeavor? In other words, should school counselors have a career development curriculum composed of goals and objectives for each grade level with which they work? Why or why not?
7. Explain how you would go about developing a K–12 career guidance curriculum.
8. Community resources can be an enormous asset for a school's career development curriculum. Explain how you could use community resources to enhance a career guidance program.

SUGGESTED INTERNET SITES

www.princetonreview.com

This site is for individuals selecting careers and colleges and also for educators. Provided is The Princeton Review Career Quiz, which allows individuals to search for careers that match interests and ambitions. Helpful information on the interview process can also be found, as well as descriptions of majors and at which colleges they are offered. Educators may find this site useful because it offers free resources that will help students navigate through the admissions process.

www.acinet.org

The Career InfoNet details employment trends, required training, and salaries for the state selected. Included is information for gaining certification training.

www.cdm.uwaterloo.ca/steps.asp

A good all-around site that includes the "Steps to Success"; self-assessment, occupational research, and decision-making strategies; employment contacts; and career life planning.

www.careerbuilder.com

Includes information about jobs, internships, career assessment, and career fairs. It has a college connection page that links career interests with college programs.

www.xap.com

Xap provides a lot of information for students going through the college planning process. The home page links users to a college selection search, financial aid information, and college preparation techniques. Also included are SAT words and questions.

SPECIAL TOPICS

MULTICULTURALISM IN SCHOOL COUNSELING

According to the U.S. Bureau of the Census (2001b), the U.S. population will increase 50 percent by the year 2050, from 255 million people to 383 million people. Most of that growth will be among visible racial and ethnic groups (VREGs). Currently, 45 percent of the public school population comes from VREGs (D. W. Sue et al., 1998). By 2050, well over 50 percent of America's schoolchildren will be children of color. The 1980s witnessed a dramatic rise in the non-White population: The number of African Americans increased over 13 percent, Native Americans 38 percent, Hispanic Americans 53 percent, and Asian Americans 107 percent (D. W. Sue & Sue, 1999). The White population grew just 6 percent over the same period. Lower birthrates among White Americans mean that more and more youngsters in public schools today come from VREGs; and 75 percent of those entering the labor force do as well (D. W. Sue & Sue, 1999). African Americans, Hispanic Americans, and Native Americans currently make up 33 percent of the under-18 population in the United States, and they are projected to make up 40 percent by 2030 (U.S. Bureau of the Census, 2001b).

The increasing diversification of U.S. society has created a challenge for counselors in general and school counselors in particular. In years past, the majority of immigrants to the United States were White Europeans; today, most of the immigrants arriving in the United States are from Asia (34 percent), Latin America (34 percent), and other countries with visible racial or ethnic populations (Atkinson, Morton, & Sue, 1998). They come to a land already diverse, a land in which African Americans make up 12.3 percent of the population and Native Americans another 0.9 percent (U.S. Bureau of the Census, 2000). Our schools were created and are managed for the most part by White Europeans; yet they serve children and families whose racial and ethnic backgrounds are vastly different from those of teachers and school administrators. The potential for problems is clear, and the responsibility for preventing those problems often lies with the school counselor.

This chapter is about school counselors and *multicultural competence,* all the knowledge and understanding and sensitivity that go into working effectively with students from different cultures. It is impossible to write about multicultural competence without sociopolitical overtones. The material here is not meant to offend; but it is meant to challenge members of dominant groups: Whites, males,

TABLE 6.1   A GLOSSARY OF KEY CONCEPTS IN MULTICULTURAL COUNSELING

Concept	Definition
ALANAs	African Americans, Latinos (Latinas), Asian Americans, and Native Americans.
culture	Values, beliefs, language, rituals, traditions, and other behaviors passed from one generation to another in any social group (Helms, 1994).
ethnicity	The specific cultural patterns of a group defined by a specific geographic region of the world (Helms & Cook, 1999).
majority	Used to designate the group with a disproportionate share of power in society; synonymous with dominant and mainstream.
minority	Used to designate the subordinate economic, legal, political, and social position of a particular group (Helms & Cook, 1999); synonymous with nondominant.
multiculturalism	The philosophy of paying careful attention to and treating all aspects of human diversity.
race	A social construct resulting from assumed biological traits based on appearance and used to include and exclude certain peoples from societal resources (Helms & Cook, 1999).
VREG	Visible racial and ethnic group.

SOURCE: From Janet E. Helms & Donelda A. Cook, *Using Race and Culture in Counseling and Psychotherapy: Theory and Process.* Published by Allyn and Bacon, Boston, MA. Copyright © 1997 by Pearson Education. Reprinted by permission of the publisher.

heterosexuals, Christians. It asks them to define membership in their own culture and the consequences of that definition for counseling students from other cultures. It also is meant to challenge members of nondominant cultures, asking them to examine how they have internalized their interactions with the dominant culture and to what degree that internalization determines the counseling relationship with members of both dominant and nondominant groups.

It is also impossible to write about multicultural competence without using an agreed-upon terminology. (Table 6.1 is a glossary of key concepts.) Two of those labels need special mention. When we talk about the *majority group* or the *majority culture*, we are not referring to the relative size of the group or culture. *Majority* in this context means "dominant": this group or culture has a disproportionate share of power in society. In the same way, *minority* means "nondominant": the subordinate economic, legal, political, and social position of a particular group or culture (Helms & Cook, 1999). Our definitions of *majority* and *minority*, then, have to do with power. *Power* is the ability to maintain and influence societal structures that confer privilege. The majority culture obviously has an interest in limiting the power of other cultures. The response of people in minority cultures to the unequal distribution of power varies: some aspire to membership in the dominant culture, while others resent and struggle against the inequality. This dynamic of multiculturalism is a critical factor in society and in our schools.

DIVERSITY: A HUMAN CONDITION

We believe that culture influences every aspect of the individual: thoughts, behaviors, even emotions. The strength of that belief is visible here, in the emphasis on multicultural competence and in the descriptions of the differences among groups of children. But some question a counseling process that responds more to the differences among groups of people than to the similarities. Still others warn that a focus on intergroup differences may obscure individual differences within the group.

The Etic versus Emic Debate

For many years, counselors have struggled with sameness and difference. Is it better to focus on what is the same in all people, on what transcends culture and so is an *etic* approach? Or on their differences, on what is culture specific and so is an *emic* approach? Some argue that when counseling focuses on cultural differences, it loses sight of the sameness in people. They point to counseling practices and interventions as evidence of people's sameness; both are based on general principles that have proved effective over time with people from all different cultural backgrounds. Those who hold what R. T. Carter and Quereshi (1995) call the *universalist position* do not deny cultural differences; but clearly they believe cultural differences are secondary to human similarities.[1]

Critics would argue that looking for the sameness in people really means looking for their "Whiteness." They claim that traditional counseling principles and practices emanate from a particular cultural viewpoint—namely White, male, and Eurocentric. Race-based theorists, for example, insist that the power differential between Whites and people of color intrudes into the counseling process, and that universalists, by ignoring issues of power and race, are advancing an agenda to maintain the status quo.

School counselors must understand the power differential in society and the sociohistorical dimensions of race from which it stems. How the power differential is played out, not only in the counseling process but also in the educational system, has important consequences for school counselors who work with students of color.

It also seems that paying close attention to cultural differences is essential to the counseling process. How can counselors offer good help if they do not understand how a student's culture-based values and behaviors differ from their own? Those who espouse an etic position might argue that a working alliance is necessary for all counseling, whatever a client's cultural background. Although few would argue against the need for a working alliance, all should recognize that how the working alliance is formed—the strategies used to develop it—must vary depending on individual students' cultural background. For example, a young Asian

---

[1] See Carter and Quereshi for a typology of approaches to multicultural counseling.

immigrant might feel uncomfortable with a counselor who freely expresses emotion; a young Latino might be put off by a counselor who does not.

Intragroup Differences

Although it is important to pay attention to intergroup differences—to how cultural groups differ from one another—it is equally important to pay attention to intragroup differences—how members of a particular cultural group differ among themselves. School counselors working across cultures need to ask two questions about every student: What are the broad cultural patterns of this student's racial or ethnic group? And to what extent does this student's behavior reflect those patterns? The first question speaks to intergroup differences; the second, to intragroup differences.

Intergroup differences produce racial and ethnic stereotypes; intragroup differences prove those stereotypes wrong. One primary source of intragroup differences is *second-culture acquisition:* when people from a nondominant culture come into sustained contact with people from the dominant culture, they undergo a process of *cultural adaptation*—learning to live in a culture that is different from their own.[2]

Berry (1980) suggested that the "other culture" is a stimulus that evokes three reactions: moving toward, moving against, or moving away. *Moving toward* the dominant culture means adopting at least some of that culture's characteristics, often as a means of gaining acceptance or privilege. *Moving against* the dominant culture means rejecting that culture, which creates a negative relationship with the dominant culture. *Moving away* from the dominant culture is a form of withdrawal, usually into an ethnic enclave. Members of the nondominant culture who move away from the dominant culture want neither a positive nor a negative relationship with the dominant culture.

More recently, cultural adaptation has been described as a unidirectional, bidirectional, or multidirectional process (LaFromboise, Coleman, & Gerton, 1993). When adaptation is *unidirectional,* members of the nondominant culture move in a single direction, toward the dominant culture and away from their own culture. When adaptation is *bidirectional,* they move back and forth between the two cultures and feel at home in both. When adaptation is *multidirectional,* members of the nondominant culture are capable of participating in various and complex societal structures, made up of multiple cultural groupings, while maintaining a positive identity with their culture of origin.

Clearly youngsters from other cultures must adapt at least to some degree to the dominant culture in the United States. What is crucial for school counselors

---

[2] Members of the dominant culture can also undergo cultural adaptation; but usually the process involves adaptation to the dominant culture—in the United States, the White, male, Eurocentric culture.

Also, there is both disagreement and confusion in the literature about the use of *cultural adaptation* as an umbrella term for all the responses that people from one culture can have to another culture. Some prefer *acculturation,* but we would argue that *acculturation* implies a moving toward and acquisition from another culture. In contrast, *cultural adaptation* allows for those forms of adaptation that do not lead to the acquisition to any real degree of the dominant culture's behaviors or attitudes.

who work with children and their families is an understanding of the process and an awareness that children and their parents may have very different, even conflicting forms of cultural adaptation. It is not uncommon, for example, for children to move toward the dominant culture and for their parents to move against it.

There are several forms of cultural adaptation, each of which involves unidirectional, bidirectional, or multidirectional adaptation:

Assimilation. Here adaptation is unidirectional. The individual adapts by rejecting his or her native culture and trying as much as possible to become like those in the dominant culture.

Integration. The individual retains some aspects of the native culture while he or she also is assuming attributes of the dominant culture.

Biculturalism (alternation). Biculturalism is knowing and understanding two cultures, maintaining a positive relationship with both, and altering one's behavior to fit the particular cultural context (LaFromboise et al., 1993). The relationship is both bidirectional and nonhierarchical.

Rejection. The individual does not seek a positive relationship with the dominant culture; instead he or she continues to identify strongly with the nondominant culture.

Marginality. The individual identifies with neither the dominant culture nor the nondominant culture.

School counselors walk a fine line in the area of cultural adaptation. They want their students to develop and achieve, and the reality is that in this country those processes go on in a White, male, Eurocentric society. At the same time, they recognize the importance of cultural diversity, the flavor diversity adds to the individual, to the school community, and to the larger society. The answer would seem to be adaptation through biculturalism. Certainly the ability to move with comfort between two different cultures is an antidote to cultural imperialism; at the same time, it promotes a sensitivity to and acceptance of different worldviews. Being able to move with comfort in the White culture creates all kinds of opportunities—educational, social, and professional—for youngsters from nondominant cultures. School counselors have a responsibility to facilitate bicultural adaptation; the failure to do so can only limit minority students' options.

That biculturalism promotes understanding of others makes the process equally important for children of the dominant culture. Learning about different cultures teaches flexibility, empathy, and tolerance; it expands the way children think, feel, and behave. An influx of VREG students in a school is an opportunity to enrich the experience of all students.

MULTICULTURAL COUNSELING WITH RACIAL GROUPS

We tread on sensitive ground. *Multicultural counseling* is yet another term that sets off debate in the field of counseling. Some scholars believe that the term should be reserved for working with people of color only (see, for example, Locke, 1997).

Others insist that all counseling is multicultural because everyone is a product of a socialization process based on culture (see, for example, Pederson, 1991). We believe that multicultural counseling considers seriously and sensitively all aspects of human diversity but accords special status to race; that is, race is the primary determinant of culture.[3]

In this section we examine the cultural patterns and their implications for counseling of White Americans, African Americans, Hispanic Americans, Asian Americans, and Native Americans. The organization of the section was not designed to exclude any group. However, it is meant to highlight the primacy of race in multicultural counseling.

White Americans

In my classes, when the issue of race comes up, now and again a VREG student shares an experience with us. When that happens, inevitably two or more White students respond by acknowledging the VREG student's experience and then moving on quickly to describe their own minority experience: growing up poor, growing up an Italian American in an Irish neighborhood, growing up Jewish in a predominantly Christian neighborhood (or the reverse). What the students are doing, I think, is using their memory of discomfort or even oppression to minimize the issue of race and the advantage of having been born White.

A woman I know, a Jewish woman who was born in a Jewish neighborhood in New York City, once told me of a conversation she had with her father when she was a girl, not long after the family had moved to a more diverse neighborhood in the suburbs. He warned her that she probably would encounter anti-Semitism, and that it might bother her, shake her self-confidence, and make her question her ability to achieve what she wanted in life. Then he pinched her gently on the forearm and said, "But remember, you always have this, white skin."

Our discussion of racial groups begins with Whites because it is extremely important to view Whiteness as a culture like other racial cultures. Although in this country, the White culture is dominant, Whiteness is simply another way of being in a world filled with other ways of being. Whites are part of the mosaic of color that makes up American society. Few White people, however, are conscious of themselves as racial beings. Unlike people of color, who are confronted with their racial identity on a daily basis, Whites can easily live their lives without ever reflecting on their Whiteness—on what it means to be White—or on their unique worldview.

Worldview   American culture—acceptable ways of being in the world as defined by Whites of Northern European origin—has been the focus of much research. In one study of the impact and dominance of White culture, Ho (1987) drew comparisons between the values of middle-class White Americans and those of

---

[3] If we accorded all determinants of culture the same significance, all people would in some fashion be members of an oppressed minority, and issues of color would be diluted (Helms & Cook, 1999).

TABLE 6.2   **THE CULTURAL VALUES OF MIDDLE-CLASS WHITE AMERICANS AND OTHER RACIAL GROUPS**

	Racial Group				
Dimension	**Middle-Class White Americans**	**Asian Americans**	**American Indians**	**Black Americans**	**Hispanic Americans**
Relationship of people to nature	Mastery over future	Harmony with past-present	Harmony with present	Harmony with present	Harmony with present
Time orientation	Future	Past-present	Present	Present	Past-present
Definition of self	Individual	Collateral	Collateral	Collateral	Collateral
Preferred mode of activity	Doing	Doing	Being in becoming	Doing	Being in becoming
Nature of the individual	Good and bad	Good	Good	Good and bad	Good

SOURCE: Adapted from M. K. Ho, *Family Therapy with Ethnic Minorities*, p. 232. Copyright 1997 by Sage Publications, Inc. Reprinted by permission of the publisher.

racial or ethnic minority groups. Table 6.2 shows those comparisons along several dimensions.

In a discussion of how worldviews are formed, D. W. Sue (1978) used the concepts of locus of control and locus of responsibility (Rotter, 1966, 1975) to draw comparisons between the mainstream White Euro-American culture and other cultures (also see D. W. Sue & Sue, 2003). Both locus of control and locus of responsibility can be either internal or external. Figure 6.1 shows the four worldviews based on different combinations of internal and external locus of control and locus of responsibility. According to Sue, quadrant 1, in which both the locus of control and the locus of responsibility are internal (IC-IR), represents the worldview of middle-class White culture.

> A high value for solving problems is placed on personal resources: self-reliance, pragmatism, individualism, status achievement through one's own effort, and power or control over others, things, animals, and forces or nature. Democratic ideals such as "equal access to opportunity," "liberty and justice for all," "God helps those who help themselves," and "fulfillment of personal destiny" all reflect this worldview. The individual is held accountable for all that transpires. Constant and prolonged failure or the inability to attain goals leads to symptoms of self-blame (depression, guilt, and feelings of inadequacy). (D. W. Sue & Sue, p. 277)

School counselors, socialized by an IC-IR worldview, must be sensitive when working with students from nondominant cultures whose worldview may be very different. Some youngsters come from countries with totalitarian regimes, places where it is difficult to adopt an internal locus of control. Some people of color, having experienced institutional and societal racism, do not believe in democratic ideals. Education in this country has always been considered a means for achieving more

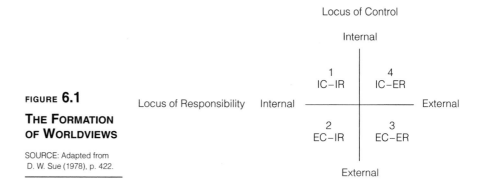

FIGURE 6.1

THE FORMATION OF WORLDVIEWS

SOURCE: Adapted from D. W. Sue (1978), p. 422.

control over one's destiny, and school personnel simply assume that students and their parents do or should buy into that philosophy. Certainly education is a gateway to upward mobility, but school counselors must be sensitive to students whose worldview is formed by an external locus of control or an external locus of responsibility or both. What is all too often perceived to be a lack of motivation among minority students may well be a reflection of a worldview shaped by externalities.

White Racial Identity   *Racial identity* is the combination of attitudes, beliefs, and behaviors that defines the individual as a racial being. All people—whatever their race—have a racial identity. According to Helms and Cook (1999), racial-identity models are psychological models that describe ways to overcome "internalized racism" and achieve "a healthy socioracial self-conception under varying conditions of racial oppression" (p. 81).

Helms (1984, 1990c, 1995) suggested that in a society in which one race is judged "superior" only because another is implicitly or explicitly held to be "inferior," the individual's psychological experience of race necessarily includes attitudes toward his or her own race as well as toward the other race, the partner in the domination-oppression dynamic. She proposed six stages—she called them *statuses*—to explain the White experience of race. Each status represents a cluster of attitudes, beliefs, and values that affects the individual's worldview and influences the way he or she processes information about race:[4]

1. *Contact status.* Contact Whites are oblivious to issues of race and racism. They don't understand that race is a sociopolitical construct that determines the individual's place in society. Contact Whites are fond of their colorblind attitudes ("I don't see color; I look at the person"). They may even point to a Black friend as evidence that they are not racist. Because color doesn't matter, they believe that if people of color work hard, they can get ahead just like everyone else.
2. *Disintegration status.* Disintegrated Whites have become aware of the issues of racism in society. With awareness come feelings of anxiety, guilt, loss, or helplessness. Because they feel unable to do something to reduce the state of conflict, often disintegrated Whites avoid contact with people of color, taking refuge in the comfort of their own racial group.

[4] Based on Helms (1990c, 1995) and Helms and Cook (1999).

3. *Reintegration status.* Reintegrated Whites have come to believe that Whites are superior and people of color are inferior. Passive reintegrated Whites try to avoid people of color; active reintegrated Whites engage in overtly hostile and violent acts against people of color.

4. *Pseudoindependence status.* Pseudoindependent Whites acknowledge racism, accept people of color on an intellectual basis, and would like to help people of color by imposing White standards and White culture on them. Pseudoindependence Whites believe the solution to racism involves changing people of color, not Whites. Although their views are politically correct, pseudoindependence Whites do little to actually combat racism.

5. *Immersion/emersion status.* People in this status are forming a positive White racial identity by learning about being White, about the consequences of being White, and about the relationship of being White to the rest of society. Their focus has shifted from changing people of color to changing themselves. These people seek out others who have also struggled to achieve their own nonracist White identity.

6. *Autonomy status.* Autonomous Whites seek out contact with different cultural groups and experience that contact as mutually enriching. Comfortable in their evolved White identity, they believe they have something to offer as well as something to learn. Committed to working for change, they may be willing to make life choices that reflect that stance.

Each status is increasingly complex; and within each status the individual is able to process race-related information more flexibly. At any given time, one status usually predominates, although some characteristics of others may be present. The individual must integrate the tasks and challenges of each status in turn before progressing to the next status. But in a given situation, he or she may revert to a lower status.

According to Helms, two fundamental processes underlie the individual's progress through increasingly more complex statuses: the abandonment of racism and the development of a positive White racial identity. In the first three statuses — contact, disintegration, and reintegration — the individual abandons racism; in the last three — pseudoindependence, immersion/emersion, and autonomy — the individual develops a positive racial identity.

Helms's theory has particular importance for White school counselors who work with children of color. School counselors must be aware of their own racial-identity status and make every effort to become autonomous. There are several methods for assessing racial identity. In 1996, Helms proposed using the White Racial Identity Attitude Scale (WRIAS) (Helms & Carter, 1990) to generate a profile that shows how the individual's racial identity breaks down by status.[5] Counselors can use the WRIAS to understand their own racial identities and as the basis for consciousness-raising workshops for school personnel and for work with small groups.

---

[5] Helms (1992) developed the scale as a research tool, and it is still used that way. Later she psychometricized the scale in a different way to show results in percentiles and create a racial profile.

African Americans

In the year 2000, African Americans made up just over 12 percent of the U.S. population (U.S. Bureau of the Census, 2000). This racial group is tremendously diverse in terms of socioeconomic class, education, racial-identity status (relationship to the White culture), and family structure. Approximately 35 percent of African Americans are middle class or higher (D. W. Sue & Sue, 2003). This is important because socioeconomic status is an important variable in determining the degree of assimilation into White culture (Hildebrand, Phenice, Gray, & Hines, 1996). Yet African Americans continue to hold minority status in this country. As evidence, Sue and Sue point to the following:

- The rate of African Americans living in poverty is three times higher than that of White Americans.
- The unemployment rate is twice as high among African Americans.
- About one-third of African American men in their twenties are in jail, on probation, or on parole.[6]
- The life span of African Americans is five to seven years shorter than that of White Americans.

Multicultural counseling demands that school counselors see students in the context of their life experience and their cultural history. Certainly not all African American students present for counseling with a lengthy catalog of incidents in which they were the victim of racial discrimination; but no counselor can turn a blind eye to the impact of longstanding discrimination on students of color. Where traditional counseling would look for internal sources of students' problems, multicultural counseling demands that counselors consider societal forces—specifically racism and discrimination—when working with Black students whose response to White authority is rebellion, suspicion, or avoidance.

Cultural Patterns   Before we begin, a warning: Any attempt to describe broad cultural patterns runs the risk of stereotyping, of overlooking individual differences. On the other hand, the failure to consider cultural patterns increases the risk of *dominant-culture imperialism*, an insensitivity to characteristics and behaviors that are related to culture.

According to Helms and Cook (1999), African American culture blends various elements of the many ethnic groups of Africans who have come to the United States over several centuries. Certain characteristics seem to be shared by African cultures, and those characteristics define African American culture today:

Spirituality. The belief that nonphysical forces, especially a Supreme Being who can appear in many manifestations, have the power to determine what happens in people's everyday life.

---

[6]According to the U.S. Department of Justice (2002), just 2 percent of the White population is under correctional supervision.

Harmony. The self and nature are connected and are intended to operate in synchrony.

Movement. Movement and motion complement the spoken word.

Affect-mind-body. The individual's emotions, mind, and body form an interconnected triad that is intended to function in equilibrium. Whatever alters one component of that triad also influences the others.

Communalism. The group plays a significant role in defining the self, and the group is as important as the individual.

Expressiveness. The unique aspects of personality are expressed through the individual's behavior and creativity.

Orality. Knowledge is gained and transmitted orally; and the individual achieves credibility by being an effective oral communicator. Effective communication is rhythmic and symbolic; and it occurs on cognitive, affective, and behavioral levels.

Time. Time is measured by socially meaningful events and customs rather than quantity.

The African American Family   Perhaps the most salient characteristics of the African American family are its structure, an extended network, and its strength, the economic and emotional support that network provides (D. W. Sue & Sue, 2003). Both structure and strength have allowed the African American family to survive even slavery (Gutman, 1977). That a significant number of African American youngsters are raised by family members other than their biological mother or father is not intrinsically wrong. It is only the White Eurocentric culture, with its emphasis on the nuclear family, that tends to pathologize caregiving by someone other than a child's biological mother or father. School counselors inevitably come across African American students who are being raised by grandparents or aunts or uncles or sisters or brothers. The key is to recognize that the practice is both culturally acceptable and a sign of the strength of the African American family.

Working with the parents or guardians of Black students can be a special challenge for school counselors. Years of racism and discrimination can leave parents and guardians mistrustful of White counselors. When faced with this type of suspicion, it is critical that school counselors not replicate the master-slave dynamic by creating the impression that they know what is best for the child. Instead, they have to empower the caregivers and to make their work together a collaboration. The best way to start is by treating parents or caregivers as experts: "You know Michael better than anyone else. We need your help to help him."[7] Only after the parents or caregivers acknowledge a collaboration should a counselor make suggestions for helping the child.

Black Racial Identity   Cross (1971) was one of the first to publish a model of the process by which Black identity develops. He called the process "Nigrescence," and Helms described it as becoming Black "in terms of one's manner of thinking about and evaluating oneself and one's reference groups rather than in terms of skin color per se" (1990b, p. 17).

---

[7] See Chapter 3 for other ways of overcoming parental resistance.

Helms (1984, 1990b, 1994), drawing on Cross's model, developed a Black racial-identity model that has been cited and used widely in the literature.[8] In recent years that model—now called the People of Color Racial Identity Model—was expanded to include all people of color living in the United States (Helms & Cook, 1999):

1. *Conformity status.* Individuals are oblivious to issues of race and their sociopolitical implications. They adhere to White standards of merit.
2. *Dissonance status.* Through an experience of some sort, dissonant individuals become confused and ambivalent about issues of race and their own socioracial group. They begin to question Whiteness as the ultimate standard for judging themselves and others.
3. *Immersion status.* Immersion individuals idealize their own sociracial group and denigrate Whiteness. They define themselves by their racial group and believe that commitment and loyalty to the group are paramount. These people tend to be hypersensitive to and hypervigilant about issues of race.
4. *Emersion status.* People in emersion status derive a sense of well-being from solidarity with their own racial group.
5. *Internalization status.* Internalized people of color are committed to and accepting of their own sociracial group, have redefined their racial attributes themselves, and are able to objectively assess and respond to members of the dominant group.
6. *Integrative-awareness status.* These people value their own collective identities and are able to empathize and work together with members of other minority groups and with Whites. Their life decisions may be motivated by the expression of a global humanism.

Much of what we said in the last section about the dynamics of White racial-identity development can be said about the development of racial identity among people of color. Helms and Cook's model is a fluid model, in which all statuses to one degree or another are present in the individual, but one predominates at a particular time or in a particular situation. In every status, people of color must negotiate their relationship with the dominant culture. For those in conformity status, that means exalting White culture; for those in immersion status, that can mean rejecting White culture; and for those who have reached integrative awareness, that can mean mutual enrichment through interactions with people from all racial groups.

MEASURING BLACK RACIAL IDENTITY The Racial Identity Attitude Scale (RIAS), developed by Parham and Helms (1981), was the first attempt to put Cross's model into practice. The scale consists of 30 items designed to measure

---

[8] Helms's model also draws on the Minority Identity Development Model (Atkinson, Morton, & Sue, 1998), Erikson's collective-identity model, and self-psychology (Kohut, 1971).

an individual's *predominant* racial attitude.[9] The RIAS yields a score on four sub-scales, with higher scores indicating the predominance of a particular racial attitude. Internal consistency reliability coefficients for the RIAS range from .66 to .77. The RIAS has undergone two revisions: the RIAS-B (Helms, 1990a) and the RIAS-L (Helms & Parham, 1996). The RIAS-B consists of the same 30 items as the original RIAS, but some items have been assigned to different subscales. The RIAS-L has an additional 20 items, which were added to improve internal consistency.

COUNSELING IMPLICATIONS   In her seminal article on the development of racial identity, Helms (1984) defined four possible types of relationships between a White counselor and a Black client (or vice versa): parallel, progressive, regressive, and crossed. A *parallel relationship* is one in which counselor and client are at the same level of racial-identity development. For example, a White counselor at the contact status and a Black client at the conformity status would be in a parallel relationship. In a *progressive relationship,* the counselor is at least one level higher than the client. In a *regressive relationship,* the counselor is at least one level lower than the client. Finally, in a *crossed relationship,* counselor and client hold conflicting attitudes: for example, a Black counselor at the immersion status and a White client at the pseudoindependence status. The hypothesis that progressive relationships benefit the counseling process while regressive relationships are detrimental to it has received empirical support (Bradby & Helms, 1990; R. T. Carter, 1988, 1990; R. T. Carter & Helms, 1992; Helms & Carter, 1991). Crossed relationships in counseling are usually antagonistic and short-lived (Helms, 1995). Parallel relationships, on the other hand, can last because of the tendency to avoid tension and maintain harmony, but they do not contribute to the development of racial identity.

The assessment of identity statuses within a counseling relationship can be formal or informal. Formal assessment makes use of racial-identity measures like those we've discussed. An informal assessment requires the counselor to listen for racial-identity themes when counselor and client discuss race or culture and then to gauge the client's racial identity accordingly. Or a White counselor could simply ask a Black client: "How do you deal with living in a White-dominated society?" The day may arrive when counselors can ask a similar question of White clients ("How do you relate to being White?") without the question seeming ludicrous. Certainly this type of question is a fair one. In the assessment process, school counselors freely ask students about their relationship with their parents; it is no less important to ask students about their relationship with their own race.

For school counselors working with students of color, racial identity can clarify the attitudes and behaviors of both students and their parents. For example, conformity-status parents would be much more likely to accept a White counselor's suggestions for their child than immersion-status parents would be. Understanding the source of parents' resistance or even hostility allows the school counselor to devise appropriate interventions for establishing a collaborative relationship with

---

[9] Again, the assumption is that all racial-identity statuses are present to some degree in the individual.

parents. The same dynamics apply when school counselors of color are working with White students and their parents.

Hispanic Americans

Before we discuss the cultural patterns of Hispanic Americans, we should clarify the terms *Hispanic* and *Latino* or *Latina*. The word *Hispanic* means "of Spain." That the term has its origins in an actual place leaves some feeling that it is too narrow to reflect the multiple ancestries and indigenous cultures of Latin people. These people prefer the term *Latino* or *Latina*. Here, we use the term *Hispanic* to refer to all groups who come from Spanish-speaking countries in the Western hemisphere other than Spain, including countries in the Caribbean and in Central and South America.

Demographics   According to the latest U.S. Census figures (2000), there are 32.5 million Hispanic Americans, just under 12 percent of the total U.S. population. Of these, approximately 57 percent are of Mexican ancestry, 10 percent Puerto Rican, and 4 percent Cuban. The rest have roots in other Latin American countries. The number of Hispanic Americans is growing rapidly—a function of a high birthrate. Hispanic Americans are currently the largest minority group in the United States. States with a large Hispanic population include Arizona, California, Colorado, Connecticut, Florida, Illinois, New Mexico, and New York. Most Mexican Americans live in California and Texas; they comprise about 25 percent of the population in both states. Puerto Ricans tend to be clustered in the Northeast; the majority of Cuban Americans in Miami (Gonzalez, 1997).

Hispanic Americans are overrepresented among this country's poor: a third of Hispanic families live below the poverty line. In 2000, the median salary of Hispanic men age 25 and older was $13,000 less than that of White men. Hispanic women in the same age group earned $6,500 less than White women (U.S. Department of Education, 2003). Puerto Ricans are the poorest group of Hispanic Americans; Cubans have the highest incomes, employment rates, and level of education (L. Robinson, 1998). Because of their low-income status, Hispanics suffer from high rates of medical problems, most notably tuberculosis, AIDS, and obesity (D. W. Sue & Sue, 2003). Educational attainment among Hispanics generally continues to be low.

Cultural Patterns   Although we find a tremendous number of differences among Hispanic Americans, we do detect a few broad cultural patterns:

> *Allocentrism.* As a group, Hispanic Americans believe that the individual's center is not the self but the other, or the group. Denial of one's own needs and interests to benefit the group is considered worthy and healthy (Helms & Cook, 1999; Marin, 1994).
>
> *Familialism.* Within Hispanic American culture, the family—the extended family—is preeminent, and there is a very deep sense of loyalty to family. In times of trouble, many Hispanic Americans rely exclusively on their family. The system of *compadrazgo* (coparents) contributes to the ex-

tended family network. The godparents of one's children are *compadres,* members of the extended family (Fitzpatrick, 1987; Rogler, 1983). And anyone who helps raise children can become a *compai* or a *commai* (godfather or godmother).

Personalismo. Hispanic relationships are built around the concept of *personalism,* which in this context has to do with feelings of comfort. How the individual feels in a relationship takes precedence over anything else. So, for example, school counselors cannot assume that their expertise or position is going to help forge a working relationship with Hispanic students or their parents. Cooperation and collaboration come only if counselors can create a sense of warmth and welcome in the relationship.

Roman Catholicism and marianismo. The influence of Roman Catholicism in Hispanic culture is very significant. Devotion to the Virgin Mary shapes the lives of Hispanic women. They are expected to mold their lives after Mary, to be humble, to sacrifice, to be patient, to be submissive, and to devote themselves to family (*marianismo*).

Machismo. Marianismo defines Hispanic women; *machismo* defines Hispanic men. It ties maleness and male pride to control, aggressiveness, strength, and sexual prowess, and to being the sole economic provider for the family. It creates a double standard for males and females. Machismo can make it difficult for Hispanic fathers to actively participate in their children's schooling because this part of parenting is perceived to be the mother's domain.

Fatalism. Fatalism is connected to the issues of locus of control and locus of responsibility we spoke about earlier (see Figure 6.1). It is the belief that the individual's destiny is controlled by external forces: "*Que sera, sera*" ("What will be, will be").

The identity issues faced by Hispanic Americans can be racial or ethnic or both. Most Hispanics self-identify as either White or "other race" (Helms & Cook, 1999). Helms's (1995) racial-identity model can be applied to VREG Hispanic Americans, especially when issues of race take precedence over those of ethnicity. The school counselor should listen carefully to the subtle messages that Hispanic students might give about their relationship with the dominant culture. Often poverty and language combine to marginalize these youngsters. And the counselor should pay special attention to students who are learning English—a process that can heighten acculturative stress—by making the school environment more supportive.

Asian Americans

Asian Americans are the fastest-growing minority population in the United States. Currently there are about 10.6 million Asian Americans (almost 4 percent of the U.S. population); and the population is expected to reach 6 percent by 2010 and 10 percent by 2050 (U.S. Bureau of Census, 2000). Asian Americans are an extremely heterogeneous group, with roots in at least 29 countries in Asia and the Pacific Islands, all with their own languages, customs, and religion (D. Sue, 1998). The largest groups are the Chinese (2,432,585 people in 2000), Filipinos (1,850,314), Asian

Indians (1,678,765), Vietnamese (1,122,528), Koreans (1,076,872), and Japanese (796,700) (U.S. Bureau of the Census, 2000).

The Myth of the Model Minority   In the United States there is a perception that Asian Americans are a "model minority," a group that has attained high educational and employment status. Asian Americans are thought to be intelligent, hardworking, enterprising, and disciplined (Morrissey, 1997). And there are statistics that support this thinking. Forty percent of Asian Americans over age 25 hold a bachelor's degree, compared with about 25 percent of Whites. And Asian Americans make up a disproportionate share of the student body at Berkeley (22 percent), MIT (19 percent), and Harvard (10 percent) (Sandhu, 1997). Low rates of divorce, delinquency, and mental illness also contribute to the model-minority image of Asian Americans (D. Sue, 1998).

But a closer look at the statistics on Asian Americans suggests something other than a model minority. D. W. Sue and Sue (2003) pointed out how average statistics for Asian Americans reflect a bimodal distribution. A small but significant percentage of high wage earners raises the average and disguises the disproportionate percentage of poor in the population. Sandhu reported that the poverty rate among Southeast Asian groups is five times higher than that of the general U.S. population, and that these people are three times more likely to be on public assistance. Furthermore, only 31 percent of Hmongs have finished high school, and only 6 percent of Hmongs, Laotians, and Cambodians hold a bachelor's degree. "Asiantowns" in big cities like New York and San Francisco are known for their overcrowded conditions and for high rates of unemployment, poverty, health problems, and juvenile delinquency (D. W. Sue & Sue, 2003). Many from these neighborhoods work in sweatshops or other exploitative environments. In fact, the statistics probably understate the extent of the problems many Asian Americans face, especially Southeast Asian refugees. Cultural sanctions may well prevent many of those with familial, social, and mental health problems from seeking help from hospitals, community health centers, and other mainstream institutions.

The point: Yes, a small group of Asian Americans is doing very well; but many more are not. School counselors must be careful not to accept the popular stereotype, which could well lead them to minimize the symptoms of problems in this population of students.[10]

Cultural Patterns   Despite the many differences that exist among Asian Americans, several broad cultural patterns have been identified:

> *Allegiance to parents.* Asian American children of all ages are expected to respect and be loyal to their parents. For adolescents, this can mean cultural pressure to choose the career that their parents want for them.
>
> *Familial interdependence.* White Euro-American culture equates maturity with meeting the needs of self; in the Asian American culture, maturity

---

[10]The danger of the Asian American stereotype extends beyond this population to all other people of color. Implicit in the assignment of model-minority status to Asian Americans is the idea that if this group can succeed, then other minority groups can too—and that belief ultimately minimizes the many critical issues of racism.

means responding to the needs of the family. Anything that might disrupt family harmony and functioning is hidden. Furthermore, anything negative about an individual family member brings shame on the entire family. The potential for conflict between children and their parents is especially great when the children are acculturating rapidly.

Patriarchal system. With some exceptions, Asian American culture tends to be patriarchal: more rights and privileges are accorded to males than to females. When consulting with both parents, the school counselor should address the father first in recognition of the patriarchal system (Root, 1998).

Emotional restraint. The culture frowns on displays of emotion or affection, and talk about sex and sexuality is taboo (Root). Although counselors are taught that sexuality is an important area to explore with students, they may find that Asian American students feel very uncomfortable with these kinds of discussions.

High-context communication. Communication among Asian Americans tends to be high context—that is, the situation determines meaning more so than the actual words. For example, the word *no* may mean no or yes depending on the context (tone, intonation, and the nonverbals that accompany the message). Also, the context determines whether a certain kind of verbal message is permissible or not. For example, an Asian American student may say yes to a school counselor out of deference, because the context does not allow the student to say no, even though no is what the student means. Or an Asian American student may avoid eye contact with the counselor, which is a sign of respect in the student's culture; in the dominant culture, of course, it signals disrespect or dishonesty.

Table 6.3 compares the differences in approaches to counseling between Asian American clients and counselors trained in the Western tradition. School counselors must be sensitive to these differences when they work with Asian American students and their parents.

Second-Culture Acquisition and Racial-Identity Issues   There are fewer identity development models for Asian Americans than for Blacks (D. W. Sue & Sue, 1999). The Helms and Cook model (1999) can be used with Asian Americans. In addition, Atkinson et al. (1998) proposed a generic minority identity development (MID) model that can be useful in understanding Asian Americans' relationship with their own and the dominant culture (Table 6.4). The MID model defines the respondent's attitudes not only toward the dominant group but also toward other minority groups. But both this model and Helms and Cook's model show a progression: moving from denigrating the individual's own culture and revering the dominant culture, through revering the individual's culture and denigrating the dominant culture, toward an appreciation of all cultures.

Asian Americans acquire second-culture traits in much the same way that other minority cultures do: through assimilation, integration, biculturalism, rejection, and marginality. Kitano and Maki (1996) developed a typology for resolving conflicts among Asian Americans for issues of both acculturation (the process of becoming Americanized) and ethnic identity (the retention of attitudes, beliefs,

TABLE 6.3 **DIFFERENCES IN APPROACHES TO COUNSELING: ASIAN AMERICAN CLIENTS VERSUS WESTERN-TRAINED COUNSELORS**

Counseling Dimension	Asian American Clients	Western-Trained Counselors
Development of self	Collectivism—family and group focus, interdependence	Individual focus, independence
Counselor-client relationship	Hierarchical	Equal
Psychological maturity	Emotional restraint	Emotional expression
Problem solving	Counselor's responsibility	Client's responsibility by means of introspection
Mental illness	Shameful	A problem like any other problem

SOURCE: Adapted from D. W. Sue and D. Sue (1999), p. 263. Copyright 1999 John Wiley & Sons, Inc. This material is used by permission of John Wiley & Sons, Inc.

TABLE 6.4 **A GENERIC MINORITY IDENTITY MODEL**

Stages of Minority Identity Development	Attitudes toward Self	Attitudes toward		
		Others of the Same Minority	Others of a Different Minority	Dominant Group
1. Conformity	Self-depreciating	Group depreciating	Discriminatory	Group appreciating
2. Dissonance	Conflict between self-depreciating and and self-appreciating	Conflict between group depreciating and group appreciating	Conflict between mainstream views of minority hierarchy and feelings of shared experience	Conflict between group appreciating and group depreciating
3. Resistance and immersion	Self-appreciating	Group appreciating	Conflict between feelings of empathy (shared minority experiences) and culturocentrism	Group appreciating
4. Introspection	Concern with basis of self-appreciation	Concern with nature of unequivocal appreciation	Concern with ethnocentric basis for judging others	Concern with the basis of group depreciation
5. Synergetic articulation and awareness	Self-appreciating	Group appreciating	Group appreciating	Selective appreciation

SOURCE: Adapted from D. R. Atkinson, Morten and Sue (1998), p. 35. Copyright 1998 by McGraw-Hill. Reprinted with permission.

and behaviors of the culture of origin). They noted that conflict can be resolved in one of four ways:

Type A. High in assimilation and low in ethnic identity (very Westernized)
Type B. High in assimilation and high in ethnic identity (bicultural)
Type C. High in ethnic identity and low in assimilation (very Asian)
Type D. Low in ethnicity and low in assimilation (marginalized)

American Indians and Alaskan Natives

The treatment of American Indians at the hands of White settlers in this country was so systematically brutal and destructive that an estimated 90 percent of the American Indian population had been decimated by the end of the 19th century. Yet a century later, that population is increasing dramatically. In fact, between 1980 and 1990, the number of American Indians grew by almost 55 percent, from 1.3 million to just under 2.1 million, the highest rate among racial groups in the United States for that time period (Choney, Berryhill-Paapke, & Robbins, 1995); and the population is expected to reach 4.3 million in the year 2050. Much of the increase comes from those with mixed racial ancestry who identify themselves as Native American. The combined population of American Indians, Eskimos, and Aleuts in 2000 was about 2.4 million, less than 1 percent of the U.S. population. This population is comparatively young—39 percent of it members under age 29, versus 29 percent of the total U.S. population (U.S. Bureau of the Census, 2000).

The terms *Indian, American Indian,* and *Native American* are used interchangeably; they refer to people indigenous to the continental United States. The term *Alaskan Native* is use to refer to the Eskimo and Aleut peoples of Alaska. The federal government has determined that anyone with at least 25 percent Indian blood is an Indian and is eligible for benefits. Others insist that tribal affiliation is the defining characteristic of who is an Indian.[11] According to Trimble (1990), more than 60 percent of American Indians are of mixed heritage, a result of interracial marriages with Blacks, Hispanics, and Whites.

The Native American and Alaskan Native population is extremely diverse: its members come from 542 tribal groups and speak more than 150 Indian languages (Bureau of Indian Affairs, 1993). The five largest groups are the Cherokee (308,000), Navajo (219,000), Chippewa (104,000), Sioux (103,000), and Choctaw (82,000) (U.S. Bureau of the Census, 2000). Approximately 22 percent of Indians live on over 300 reservations; 15 percent live within tribal jurisdiction, Alaskan Native villages, or tribal designated areas; and about 63 percent live in rural and urban areas (Choney et al., 1995).

The American Indian and Alaskan Native population is the poorest of the poor in the United States. Several statistics seem to support that assessment (Atkinson et al., 1998):

- Death from alcoholism in this population is 6 times greater than in the general population, and terminal liver cirrhosis is 14 times greater.
- Suicide rates are twice the national average, with adolescence to adulthood the time of greatest risk.
- The average income of people in this group is some 75 percent less than that of Whites.
- Unemployment is 10 times the national average.
- Infant mortality after the first three months of life is three times the national average.

---

[11] Ken Hanson, chairman of the Samish tribe, cited in D. W. Sue and Sue (2003), p. 312.

- Dropout rates from school are higher and education levels are lower than those of any other ethnic group.
- Rates of delinquency and mental illness far surpass those of most groups in society.

Children and adolescents appear to be particularly at risk. It is estimated that over 34 percent of Indian children are the victims of abuse or neglect (National Indian Justice Center, 1990). A congressional hearing found that 52 percent of adolescents living in cities and 80 percent of those living on reservations engaged in moderate to heavy alcohol or drug abuse, compared with 23 percent of their urban non-Indian counterparts (LaFromboise, 1998). Along with high rates of teenage pregnancies, one study found that one-third of Indian girls report suicidal feelings (Bee-Gates, Howard-Pitney, LaFromboise, & Rowe, 1996). These statistics should alert school counselors to the vital role they can play in helping Native American children and adolescents.

Cultural Patterns   That there are more than 500 identifiable Indian tribes today speaks to the diversity of this population. Yet Helms and Cook (1999), drawing on the work of Locust (1990), identified eight beliefs many Native Americans share:

> *The Supreme Creator is an omnipotent spiritual presence that controls all aspects of existence.*
> *Humans are a composite of spirit, mind, and body.* Of the three components, the spirit (the "I am") is most important because it defines the essence of the person. The physical body, prepared by the individual's parents, is the house in which the spirit dwells; and the mind mediates between spirit and body much like the ego mediates between superego and id.
> *People share a spiritual kinship with all living things because all things originate with the Supreme Creator.*
> *The spirit is immortal.* When the body dies (or is "shed"), the spirit continues to repeat the birth-death process until it reaches perfection and can return to the Supreme Creator.
> *Wellness is harmony of spirit, body, and mind.* Harmony is a state of being that comes from within; it is the individual's goal.
> *Illness is a disruption of the spirit-body-mind harmony.* The cure is to identify whatever circumstance is weakening the spirit and to take steps to correct it.
> *Illness can result from natural or unnatural causes.* Natural illness occurs when one accidentally or intentionally violates a sacred tribal interdiction. Unnatural illness—an accident, depression, irrational thinking, or unusual behavior, for example—results from evil forces that take the form of a bear, an owl, or a snake. (The actual incarnation is tribe specific.)
> *Each person is responsible for her or his own health status.* However, a healer who recognizes the interconnectedness of the human triad (spirit, body, and mind) often can help the individual recover harmony once it is lost.

The contrast between Native American beliefs and White Euro-American beliefs is stark. It is little wonder that many Native Americans find themselves forced to choose between assimilation into or rejection of the dominant culture. And it is

TABLE 6.5	THE SECOND-CULTURE ACQUISITION PROCESS FOR NATIVE AMERICANS: HERITAGE CONSISTENCY AND INCONSISTENCY

Heritage-Consistent Traits

Emphasis on nonverbal communication; limited English proficiency

Socializes only with other Indians; limited contact with non-Indians

Underdeveloped or limited academic skills

Little value placed on education

Behavior assessment in terms of its impact on the tribe and the extended family

Difficulty establishing long-term goals

Places positive value on emotional restraint

External locus of responsibility as a result of government paternalism

Unfamiliar with the expectations of the dominant culture

Heritage-Inconsistent Traits

Denies and lacks pride in being a Native American

Feels pressure to adopt dominant cultural values

Feels guilty for not knowing or participating in Indian culture

Holds negative views of Native Americans

Can suffer from a lack of support or a belief system

SOURCE: Adapted from D. W. Sue and D. Sue (1999).

little wonder that the cultural conflicts are reflected in the school counselor-student relationship. This is a particular problem with youngsters making the transition to middle school, a time when many begin to question the need for school (Wood & Clay, 1996). A focus on the present among Native Americans may make it difficult for students to understand the future value of education. For the school counselor working with an individual student, the task is to connect the value of education with values that are more relevant to Indian culture—for example, sharing, cooperation, and harmony with nature. On a larger scale, the counselor can work toward systemic changes, like the introduction of a biculturally relevant curriculum.

Acculturation among Native Americans   A long history of cruelty and treachery and genocide has left Native Americans justly suspicious of and angry with the White culture. Even their options today reinforce those feelings. When American Indians choose to live outside the reservation, they are forced to assimilate; when a deep reverence for their traditions keeps them on the reservation, they are marginalized. Little wonder that cultural adaptation for this group of people is filled with conflict.

Zitkow and Estes (1981) suggested that the acculturation of Native Americans proceeds along a continuum. At one end of that continuum is *heritage consistency,* adherence to the tribal traditions. At the other is *heritage inconsistency,* a rejection of tribal traditions. Table 6.5 lists the characteristics that mark each end of the continuum.

Native Americans who have characteristics from both groups have adapted somewhat to the White culture and fall somewhere in the middle of the continuum. But this partial adaptation should not be confused with biculturalism, which is the ability to live comfortably in two cultures. In terms of racial/cultural identity development both the Helms (1990b, 1995) model for people of color and the Atkinson et al. (1998) MID model can be applied to Native Americans.

PROMOTING THE ACADEMIC ACHIEVEMENT OF MINORITY STUDENTS: A CASE STUDY

Dan Smith, a longtime math teacher, came to Rachel Goodwin, the ninth-grade school counselor, to talk about one of his students, Carlos Martinez. He said that Carlos is not ready for ninth-grade algebra, that the youngster belongs in remedial math. Mr. Smith went on to say that he has asked Carlos to come for extra help, but that Carlos has not made an appointment. "I don't think that Carlos is capable of keeping up with the rest of the class, and at this rate he's going to get a failing grade." Mr. Smith was troubled by this possibility because he knows that a failure could slow Carlos's educational attainment; and he is aware of the high dropout rate among Hispanics who are failing in school. But, he asserted, he cannot slow the rest of the class because of one student, so it is in the best interest of all that Carlos be moved to the remedial class.

Ms. Goodwin is relatively new at her job, and she felt a bit intimidated by Mr. Smith, a well-respected veteran teacher. On the other hand, her training has made her aware of the long-term consequences of putting a student into remedial math. Yes, Carlos probably would earn a higher grade; but she also knows it may mean tracking him for low math achievement, closing off future educational and job opportunities. Her basic assumption, then, is that given the right conditions, Carlos can learn algebra. She garnered the courage to say that to Mr. Smith and then suggested that she look further into Carlos's situation before changing his class.

Mr. Smith seemed taken aback by her response: "I can't remember the last time a school counselor disagreed with me," he said.

Ms. Goodwin may be young, but she knows the importance of maintaining good working relationships with teachers. She didn't dig in her heels, but she didn't back down. Instead she negotiated: "Mr. Smith, let me have a week to assess Carlos's social and educational history before we make a decision. Is that fair?"

Mr. Smith reluctantly agreed. But he left the counselor's office shaking his head.

Ms. Goodwin felt good about her intervention with the math teacher; she felt less good about the extra work she had given herself. It would have been easier to simply change Carlos's class. But she set aside the pile of folders on her desk, pulled up Carlos's record on her computer, and got to work. The youngster's record showed average grades, with a slight drop-off in middle school. His math grades in particular were not strong, but a comment from a sixth-grade teacher caught Ms. Goodwin's eye: "Carlos seems to perform and learn better in group activities." Most of his teachers noted that Carlos was likable and not a behavioral problem.

The record also gave a brief description of Carlos's family situation. He is the oldest of six children, all being raised by their mother. The family had arrived from Puerto Rico five years earlier.

When she finished reviewing Carlos's record, Ms. Goodwin sent a note to the classroom asking Carlos to come see her during his lunch period. When he walked into her office, he seemed shy and clearly was nervous, afraid that he was in trouble. Ms. Goodwin, drawing on all of her relationship-building skills, explained to Carlos that she wanted to know about his math class, that Mr. Smith had come to the office to talk about his progress.

"I don't like math," Carlos said. Then he added: "And I don't like Mr. Smith. He's always calling on me or sending me to the board when I don't know the answers." Carlos admitted that he often feels embarrassed in the algebra class and asked Ms. Goodwin if she could change his class to an easier one.

Ms. Goodwin immediately recognized the signs of low self-esteem and learned helplessness. It would be so easy just to change Carlos's class. But it's too soon, she told herself. Instead she began to explain to Carlos the importance of learning algebra, how it has been linked to higher SAT scores and to the ability to do the more-complex operations demanded by the current job market.

Carlos wasn't impressed. "I'm not planning to go to college," he said.

"But even if you decide not to go to college, Carlos, algebra can help you get a better job. That's reason enough for us to try to keep you in Mr. Smith's class."

Then Ms. Goodwin laid out her plan for Carlos: "How does this sound? The Math Club meets after school and has tutors who work with two or three students at a time. Most of the kids are Hispanic, so the club also plans activities around the Latino culture." Ms. Goodwin reasoned that the small-group tutoring would be the most effective way to bring Carlos's math grades up, and that the club's activities would help raise his self-esteem.

She went on: "Also, I'll talk to Mr. Smith and ask him about the possibility of your doing more group work in class. And I'll suggest that he call on you only when he is fairly sure you know the answer. And just to be sure that your problem with math has nothing to do with a learning disability, I'm going to ask you to see the school psychologist for testing. What do you think?"

"Okay," Carlos answered. "But I can't do the after-school thing. I've got a part-time job after school—I work at a gas station four afternoons—to help my mom."

Ms. Goodwin felt deflated; the after-school tutoring and activities were a critical part of the plan. She would have to come up with something else that would help Carlos academically and emotionally but that would accommodate his loyalty and responsibility to his family. Then she remembered a letter that had come across her desk a few days before: a local technology company was starting a sort of internship program on Saturdays for students who needed to work and wanted to learn about computer technology. She found the letter in a to-do pile on her desk, scanned it, and then handed it to Carlos to read.

"This may be the answer," she said. "Carlos, I think you would qualify for this program, and, if you do, you could earn almost as much on Saturdays as you are working four days a week at the gas station."

Carlos seemed hesitant: "I'll have to talk with my mom about it."

"Maybe I can help. Would it be okay for me to call and talk to her?"

"Sure, but she doesn't speak English."

"Don't worry. I speak a little Spanish, and we'll find a way to communicate. Now let's schedule our next meeting, and I'll follow up with the school psychologist."

After Carlos left, Ms. Goodwin made the call to his mother. In her broken Spanish, she identified herself, quickly allayed Señora Martinez's fear that Carlos was in trouble, and explained that she simply wanted to discuss how Carlos could do better in school. She finished by asking Carlos's mother to come to the school for a meeting, where a translator could help them talk.

Señora Martinez clearly wanted to help, but she explained that it was very difficult for her to leave the apartment. She had three small children at home, and one of them was chronically ill.

"Puedo visitar su casa?" ("Can I come to your house?") Ms. Goodwin asked.

Señora Martinez responded readily: "Como no! Con eso, no hay problema!" ("Of course! That's no problem!") And they set a date and time.

Ms. Goodwin was smiling as she wrote herself a note to ask Sam Rosario, a teacher's aide who had grown up in the neighborhood and spoke Spanish fluently, to be the translator at her meeting with Carlos's mother.

Consulting with Teachers

The challenge Ms. Goodwin faced in our case study extended beyond Carlos, the student. Integral to the process of helping him was interacting with his teacher.[12] The counselor-teacher relationship is always important when a student is having academic problems. It is even more important when the student is a member of a minority group.

That there is a cultural basis to learning and personality means school counselors must be sensitive to conflicts between the traditional Eurocentric teaching style and the way students from other cultures learn. Vazquez (1998) suggested a three-step procedure for adapting instruction to cultural traits (Figure 6.2). In his model, the teacher first identifies a student trait; then asks a series of questions about the content, context, and mode of instruction that might be changed to address the student trait; and finally develops a new instructional strategy based on the answers to those questions. The school counselor can play a role in each step of the procedure, particularly by helping teachers identify students' cultural traits and then helping them devise ways to adapt context and modes of instruction to those traits.

Of course, the counselor's effectiveness here rests on the relationship he or she has with the teacher. Ms. Goodwin was keenly aware of the need to establish and maintain a good working relationship with Mr. Smith. On the other hand, she felt the need to challenge Mr. Smith's solution: placing Carlos in a remedial math class. The method she chose was negotiation; she bargained for some time to learn about

---

[12] Chapter 3 is a detailed examination of the consulting process.

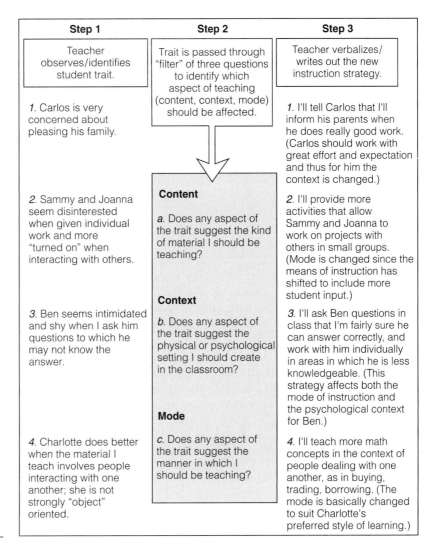

Step 1	Step 2	Step 3
Teacher observes/identifies student trait.	Trait is passed through "filter" of three questions to identify which aspect of teaching (content, context, mode) should be affected.	Teacher verbalizes/ writes out the new instruction strategy.
1. Carlos is very concerned about pleasing his family.		1. I'll tell Carlos that I'll inform his parents when he does really good work. (Carlos should work with great effort and expectation and thus for him the context is changed.)
2. Sammy and Joanna seem disinterested when given individual work and more "turned on" when interacting with others.	**Content** a. Does any aspect of the trait suggest the kind of material I should be teaching?	2. I'll provide more activities that allow Sammy and Joanna to work on projects with others in small groups. (Mode is changed since the means of instruction has shifted to include more student input.)
3. Ben seems intimidated and shy when I ask him questions to which he may not know the answer.	**Context** b. Does any aspect of the trait suggest the physical or psychological setting I should create in the classroom?	3. I'll ask Ben questions in class that I'm fairly sure he can answer correctly, and work with him individually in areas in which he is less knowledgeable. (This strategy affects both the mode of instruction and the psychological context for Ben.)
4. Charlotte does better when the material I teach involves people interacting with one another; she is not strongly "object" oriented.	**Mode** c. Does any aspect of the trait suggest the manner in which I should be teaching?	4. I'll teach more math concepts in the context of people dealing with one another, as in buying, trading, borrowing. (The mode is basically changed to suit Charlotte's preferred style of learning.)

FIGURE **6.2**

A THREE-STEP PROCEDURE FOR ADAPTING INSTRUCTION TO CULTURAL TRAITS

SOURCE: Copyright by Integrated Research Service, *The Prevention Researcher, 5(1),* 1998, p. 3. Reprinted with permission.

Carlos before making a decision. Mr. Smith was surprised that she didn't agree with him from the outset, but she managed to advocate for the student without alienating the teacher.

The key to Ms. Goodwin's future relationship with Mr. Smith—and to his willing cooperation in an intervention for Carlos—lies in her ability to come up with a plan that is good for Carlos and that makes sense to Mr. Smith. Any counselor-teacher collaboration must begin with the assumption that the other party is committed to helping the student. If that commitment is there and the intervention is sound, both counselor and teacher should come away from the process with respect for each other.

Counseling the Student

Ms. Goodwin did a good job of negotiating time for an assessment of Carlos before making a decision that could have serious consequences for his future. And she was right to start her assessment with his record. School records are a valuable source of information not only on achievement, but also on family background, the results of psychological testing, and teachers' assessments of students. In this case, Ms. Goodwin found a note that suggested Carlos works best in small groups. In fact, research suggests that Hispanics, particularly those with lower levels of second-culture acquisition, achieve better in group settings (Avellar & Kagan, 1976; Concha, Garcia, & Perez, 1975; Vazquez, 1979).

In her meeting with Carlos, Ms. Goodwin was immediately struck by his low self-esteem and learned helplessness. But his initial reaction—asking Ms. Goodwin to place him in the remedial math class—alerted her to another problem: Carlos's external locus of control. The youngster believes that his destiny rests on forces outside himself. White Euro-American culture has an IC-IR orientation: the individual controls and is responsible for his or her own behaviors. If Ms. Goodwin had imposed this orientation on Carlos, she would simply have counseled him to work harder at math (D. W. Sue & Sue, 1999). But Ms. Goodwin recognized that when Carlos asked her to change his class, he was saying, "I can't do anything about my problem in math." An external locus of control is all too common among minority students, especially those living in poor socioeconomic conditions. So the counselor promised to speak with Mr. Smith to change some aspects of Carlos's classroom environment. She hopes that Carlos will respond to the changed learning conditions with a good effort to improve his algebra skills.[13]

Consulting with Parents

Consulting with parents provides valuable information about a child's psychosocial history; more important, it involves the parents in their child's education. Research has shown that parents' involvement in their child's education, creation of a positive learning environment at home, and positive academic expectations have a significant impact on student achievement (Henderson, 1987). But when parents are immigrants, poor, or people of color, getting them involved in a collaboration with the school can be challenging.

In the case of Señora Martinez, Carlos's mother, there were two problems: logistics and communication. It can be difficult if not impossible for a low-income single parent to attend an in-school conference. It's easy for school personnel to say that this parent does not care about his or her child's education. But that seldom is true. For example, one study found that parents of Hispanic students at risk of fail-

---

[13] Ms. Goodwin is less concerned about Carlos's locus of responsibility: He works diligently at a part-time job and has clearly accepted the responsibility to help his mother and siblings. In D. W. Sue's (1978) worldview grid, Carlos would fall into quadrant 2, EC-IR (see Figure 6.1).

ing in school had the highest educational aspirations for their children compared with parents of at-risk Anglo students, successful Anglo students, and successful Hispanic students (Casas, Furlong, Carranza, Solberg, & Jamaica, 1986). However, when the same parents were asked about their realistic expectations (versus aspirations) for their children, 43 percent said a high school diploma; 85 percent of the parents of successful Anglo students and 79 percent of the parents of successful Hispanic students expected their children to earn at least a college degree.[14] These findings show that minority parents do care about their children's education; moreover, they point to the importance of school counselors' encouraging the parents of at-risk students to hold high expectations for their children.

In the case study, Ms. Goodwin didn't dismiss Señora Martinez's inability to come to school as evidence that she doesn't care about her son's education; instead she responded to the reality of Señora Martinez's situation by offering to visit her at home. This kind of flexibility on the part of school counselors can be essential to helping minority students achieve academically.

> When I was working as a school counselor in a very poor Latino neighborhood, I often held parent meetings in the community rooms of the large apartment complexes where many of the school's students lived. That flexibility increased the involvement of single parents; it also addressed another problem: the intimidation parents from nondominant cultures often experience in schools that are operated by the dominant culture. I found that the power differential between parents and school was reduced substantially when I met with parents in a place that was familiar to them.[15]

When parents do not speak English and the counselor does not speak their language, obviously there is going to be a communication problem. A more subtle problem is *countertransference*—the tendency to look down on those who do not speak English (D. W. Sue & Sue, 1999). Ideally school counselors who work in a multicultural environment should learn the language of the largest group of minority students they serve. If that isn't feasible, they should at least learn a few words so that they can establish an immediate connection to their students' parents. That's what Ms. Goodwin was doing when she used her limited Spanish to call Señora Martinez—making a connection. But when she actually visits the home to talk with Carlos's mother, Ms. Goodwin plans to bring along a translator.[16] Mr. Rosario is a good choice: he speaks Spanish fluently and he grew up in the neighborhood, which means Ms. Goodwin won't have to navigate an unfamiliar area alone.

---

[14] Research has found that East Asian parents, more than any other group, teach their children that educational success is based more on effort than innate ability (College Board, 1999).

[15] In the same vein, schools in New York City with high achievement profiles hold parent meetings on Saturdays, and one principal told me that he sometimes stays in school as late as 11:00 p.m. if that's the only time a parent can make a conference (B. Lehrer, personal communication, December 1999).

[16] Using a translator can present its own problems—for example, inaccurate translation or the translator's directing the conversation. See Sciarra and Ponterotto (1991) for a discussion of translator pitfalls.

Networking in the Community

Research indicates that immigrant groups, especially Hispanic Americans, utilize informal networks to access services and build relationships (De LaRosa, 1998; Delgado, 1997, 1998; Delgado & Humm-Delgado, 1982).

> *When I was a school counselor in the South Bronx, much of the success I had working with parents came from a network of community leaders involved in churches, social service organizations, and youth groups. These people already had the trust of the community, and I relied on them to help me earn the parents' trust and collaboration in helping their children. One person I remember in particular was a local Catholic priest, Father Joe (el Padre José), who used to visit the school often and enjoyed a close relationship with the principal. Some staff members resented his presence, but I decided to ask him to be a part of my network. Most of the people in the neighborhood's Latino population were Catholic, so I thought Father Joe's help could be particularly valuable. Although certain issues of confidentiality had to be respected, in time Father Joe helped with a number of sensitive interventions for students and their families.*

When Ms. Goodwin asked Mr. Rosario to visit the Martinez home with her, in effect she was forming a community network to help Carlos. The managers of the local technology company, the one offering internships on Saturdays, will also become a part of that network should Carlos start working there. Over time, as Ms. Goodwin becomes more involved in the local community—a must for school counselors—she will add other people with other skills to a network she can rely on for all of her students.

PROMOTING MULTICULTURAL AWARENESS

School counselors, because of their training in and sensitivity to issues of diversity, are particularly well equipped to promote multicultural awareness in the school. Often the process is an informal one, simply introducing issues of race and culture into conversations with teachers and other staff members. The key is to be knowledgeable but nonthreatening. But more important than the opportunities presented by individual encounters are the opportunities to develop programs to enhance multiculturalism throughout the school.

L. S. Johnson (1995) proposed that school counselors help establish a multicultural advisory council in the school system charged with identifying diversity issues. The council should represent a cross-section of racial and ethnic groups and functions (administrators, teachers, parents, students, and community leaders). After the council identifies areas of concern, the members can begin to set goals and objectives and plan activities for meeting them. For example, suppose a council is concerned about multicultural awareness among school staff members. The council might recommend a series of staff development workshops led by an authority on multiculturalism. These workshops could have a two-dimensional goal: knowledge of self and of others. Through racial-identity exercises, teachers and other staff members can come to understand the dynamics of the power differential among races and ethnicities. In addition, they should gain greater knowledge of the cultures with which they are working. For a council to do effective work, it must be sanctioned and supported by the principal and possibly the superintendent of the district. Resistance should be expected from teachers and other school staff members, who ultimately are no different from the rest of society when asked to examine issues of diversity within themselves and the system in which they work.

A host of familiar interventions can help students work through issues of multiculturalism. Johnson suggested conflict mediation and peer mediation programs to give students an alternative to violence for resolving racial conflict. Both small-group counseling and large-group guidance units are excellent modalities for developing multicultural awareness. The composition of small groups should be racially and ethnically diverse, and students should have the opportunity to share their heritage with one another. The curriculum for a classroom program should allow time for students to break up into small groups for discussion and sharing. To lead those groups, the counselor can form multicultural teams made up of professional and nonprofessional staff members who are particularly interested in multicultural issues (T. Robinson, 1992).

> *During my years as a school counselor, I was constantly looking for ways to reach as many students as possible by using multicultural teams. I was particularly proud of one program I developed in a middle school (Grades 5 through 8). I worked with a group of eighth graders who then would mentor incoming fifth graders, to help them adjust to the school. The mentoring program was part of the guidance curriculum for fifth graders.*

School counselors can be overwhelmed by their enormous caseload and the challenge of reaching all of the students in a school; or they can find creative ways of utilizing other resources in the school to multiply their services. Instead of thinking that they have to provide all services to all students, school counselors should think of themselves as program coordinators (Gysbers & Henderson, 2000), who work closely with and supervise others in the school to provide paraprofessional counseling services.

Finally, it is impossible to enhance multiculturalism in the school without educating parents (L. S. Johnson, 1995). We talked earlier about strategies for involving minority parents in their children's education. An even bigger challenge may be working with parents from the dominant culture to help them appreciate the changing population in their children's school and the ways diversity can enrich their children's learning and development. Of course, many of the parents who could benefit from an understanding of diversity no longer send their children to public schools; they've made an educational decision on the basis of race.

> *A White graduate student of mine had always attended racially diverse schools. She remarked recently that she was troubled by the fact that her own children, because of the area in which the family was living, would*

probably attend predominantly White schools. She was lamenting the fact that her children would not have the multicultural experience she had in school, that they would be missing out on something so valuable.

How would a school counselor run a diversity-awareness program for parents? While students are learning in small groups and classrooms, the school counselor can be organizing workshops for parents about the different cultures represented in the school. It makes little sense to teach children multicultural appreciation if their parents are making racist comments at home.

Underlying this discussion of promoting multiculturalism among teachers, students, and parents are the assumptions that school counselors' own racial identity is highly developed, and that they are committed heart and soul to helping others understand cultural diversity as a source of enrichment.

POSTSECONDARY PREPARATION

The postsecondary preparation of students from minority cultural backgrounds presents special challenges. Often these students lack role models and a solid understanding of how to prepare for life after high school. School counselors can play a critical role with these students by providing them with accurate information and showing them how their aspirations can become a reality.

The Need for Accurate Information

An eighth-grade Honduran student came into my office to discuss her career plans. She said she wanted to be a pediatrician. Without thinking, and with my sexism in full flower, I asked if she really meant a medical doctor, or did she mean a pediatric nurse. She answered firmly: "No, not a nurse. A medical doctor." And then, almost in the same breath, she added: "But I don't want to go to college for four years."

Reality has a lot to do with preparing students from low-income and minority groups for life after high school. Some students, like the eighth grader who wanted to be a pediatrician, make no room for reality in their plans for the future. The problem isn't so much that they are denying reality; it is more their lack of accurate information and exposure to real-life role models. My Honduran student probably saw a pediatrician on a TV show. She may never have been to a doctor's office or met a doctor who could explain the years of academic preparation involved in becoming a pediatrician. Other minority students see reality all too clearly. The hardship of their daily lives leaves them feeling hopeless about the future.

It is imperative, then, that school counselors, especially in elementary schools, expose minority students to real people doing a variety of real jobs. Equally important is a visit to a college campus, where youngsters can talk to students and a professor or two.

A friend of mine recently told me about his son. Back in the seventh grade, the boy visited Notre Dame. From that moment, my friend said, he never had to fight with his son about doing homework. Last year, the young man was accepted for early admission to Notre Dame.

School counselors working with students from minority cultures must excite those students about their career opportunities and provide them with accurate information about the work involved in making those opportunities a reality.

School-to-Work Transition

A large number of minority students do not go on to college after graduation. School counselors must be sure that these students leave high school with the knowledge and skills they need to work at good jobs. The School-to-Work Opportunities Act (1994) can be a valuable resource here (see Chapter 5). Of particular interest are the paid internships for low-income youth at local companies. Not only do these internships provide on-the-job training, which increases students' future employability; they also satisfy the immediate pressure many low-income youngsters feel to earn money and help keep those youngsters in school. Critics contend that internship is a variation of the traditional apprenticeship, which tracks students for a particular career. But research has shown that students who go to work after graduation in a field for which they have been trained do better (Stern, Stone, Hopkins, McMillion, & Crain, 1994). School counselors should check with their local district on the availability of internships. The original funds were distributed through state education departments, and all school districts in the state were welcome to apply for a share of the money.

If a student says seriously that he or she wants to go to college, the school counselor and the school should do their utmost to make that happen. But counselor and school also have a responsibility to those who are not college bound. For these students, the STWOA should be part of the overall career development program.

ETHICAL AND LEGAL ISSUES

Much of the material in this chapter is designed to help school counselors understand their own cultural socialization and that of the major racial or ethnic groups in the United States. This understanding is not an option; it is an ethical responsibility:

> The professional school counselor understands the diverse cultural backgrounds of the counselees with whom he/she works. This includes, but is not limited to, learning how the school counselor's own cultural/ethnic/racial identity impacts her or his values and beliefs about the counseling process. (American School Counselor Association, 1998, p. 3)

Arredondo et al. (1996) fleshed out this definition in their description of multicultural counseling competencies. The competencies are organized around three dimensions (beliefs/attitudes, knowledge, and skills), each of which has three characteristics (counselor's awareness of his or her own assumptions, values, and biases; understanding the client's worldview; and developing appropriate intervention strategies and techniques).

Ethical practice obliges counselors to see culture as an important part of the counseling process and to recognize intragroup differences (Welfel, 2002). When counselors fail to recognize the importance of culture, usually they are imposing their own cultural socialization on others, which often leads them to make negative judgments about those who are different—a form of cultural imperialism. And when they fail to see the differences among members of a minority group, in effect they are stereotyping the members of that group. It's fine to look for cultural pattern to explain or understand a student; but it borders on the unethical to ignore the ways in which individual students differ from that pattern. In both White and Black models of racial identity, the highest status combines pride in the individual's racial identity with recognition and appreciation for the differences among people.

Two specific areas that pose ethical challenges for school counselors in schools with a diverse student body are educational assessment and career guidance. We've talked at length about school counselors' responsibility to be sure that the results of standardized tests are not used as the sole basis for educational placement (see Chapter 4). That responsibility becomes even more important when the students are from nondominant cultures. Research has found that standardized tests are biased against minority students (Anastasi & Urbina, 1997). Despite certain improvements, these tests are normed on a population that is not sufficiently diverse, and then are administered to students from diverse cultural backgrounds and interpreted without qualification. A lack of proficiency in English can also affect test results negatively, masking students' aptitude for learning. School counselors cannot allow standardized test results to be used in ways that discriminate against minority students.

The challenge to career guidance is the responsibility children of color often feel toward their parents and family, a responsibility that supersedes their own wants and goals. The counselors' response here must be to respect students' loyalty to their parents while trying to broker a better career fit with the students' own goals.

CONCLUSION

The issues of cultural diversity affect all students. The conflicts between minority students' culture of origin and the dominant culture can have a significant impact on their educational and social experience in school. And by failing to appreciate and learn from the other, White students are denied the richness of a multicultural education. Because the effects of racism and discrimination are so pervasive, school counselors should consider ways to multiply their services by developing programs to reach all children. Of course, if forced to make choices because of overwhelming caseloads, then counselors should focus their energies on those most at risk for not achieving to their potential. In this chapter we've described both the groups most at risk for failure and the long-term consequences of that failure.

Promoting multiculturalism is a challenge. But it also is an opportunity for school counselors to become involved in helping all students, whatever their color or socioeconomic status, to learn and to achieve educationally. And that can make an enormous difference in the life of a child.

QUESTIONS FOR DISCUSSION

1. Carry out an inventory of yourself as a cultural being. Consider the different cultures you belong to and how they have determined your way of being in the world. Think about race, ethnicity, socioeconomic class, gender, sexual orientation, religion, and age. Also think about issues of identity development around your different cultures. Share your cultural inventory with a learning partner.
2. Now think about only the dominant cultures to which you belong. Are you White? Are you male? Are you middle class? Are you straight? Are you Christian? Reflect on your attitudes, feelings, beliefs, and behaviors toward members of the contrasting nondominant culture (females, people of color, gays, Jews and Muslims, for example). With which nondominant cultures would you find it most challenging to work? Explain your answer.
3. Many scholars believe that the public schools in this country are a product of a White Eurocentric culture and so are ill equipped to serve the rapidly increasing population of minority students. What is your reaction to that criticism?
4. Discuss the role of the school counselor in helping students from nondominant cultures achieve their potential. Do you think these students can be helped more by assimilation or biculturalism? Explain your answer.
5. Revisit the case study. What do you think about the way Ms. Goodwin set about working with Carlos? Do you think it was realistic? What would you have done differently? Discuss your answers with a learning partner.

SUGGESTED INTERNET SITES

www.multiculturalcenter.org

The official Web site of the Antioch New England Center for Multicultural Research and Practice, under the direction of Gargi Roysircar-Sodowsy, Ph.D., addresses a number of multicultural topics, including measures, awareness, and support groups.

www.amcd-aca.org

The official Web site of the Association of Multicultural Counseling and Development, a division of the American Counseling Association, lists publications and events and also has good links to other relevant sites.

www.apa.org/divisions/div45

The official Web site for Division 45 (the Society for the Psychological Study of Ethnic Minority Issues) of the American Psychological Association, has comprehensive lists of related societies and professional associations as well as lists of educational and research resources on the Web.

www.edchange.org/multicultural/

The Multicultural Pavilion is a comprehensive site featuring a Teacher's Corner, awareness activities, and links to related Web sites. The site is designed specifically for those working in schools with an interest in multicultural education.

THE SCHOOL COUNSELOR AND STUDENTS WITH DISABILITIES

In 1975, Congress passed Public Law 94-142, the Education for All Handicapped Children Act, which forever changed the face of American education. The law requires that states provide children with disabilities an appropriate education. Those states that comply with the requirements, through the provision of special education services and environments, would receive funds from the federal government. As a result, special education became and continues to be a significant legal and educational challenge for every school district in the country.

In 1990, Congress amended and renamed the Education for All Handicapped Children Act, creating the Individuals with Disabilities Education Act (IDEA) (Public Law 101-476). An obvious change was the replacement in the name of the law and throughout its provisions of the term *handicapped children* with *children with disabilities.* This change was a product of pressure from disability activists and of increasing public awareness that "disability is a natural part of the human experience and in no way diminishes the right of individuals to participate in or contribute to society" (Individuals with Disabilities Education Act, 1997). Then, in 1997, Congress amended IDEA (Public Law 105-17), both to provide additional services and to improve the quality of existing services. This is the law that currently guarantees free appropriate public education (FAPE) for children with disabilities.

Understanding the law that governs special education is fundamental to the school counselor's work with children who are disabled. Therefore, this chapter begins with an explanation of IDEA. The second section describes the population served by the law and educational settings. The inclusion movement, which since 1997 has focused on reinventing schools so that all students—with and without disabilities—are educated together, has made collaboration with teachers and parents a critical component of the school counselor's function. That collaboration and general guidelines for working with special-needs students are the subject of the third section in this chapter. The chapter ends with an examination of students who have specific learning disabilities, speech and language impairments, mental retardation, and emotional disturbance. These children constitute more than 90 percent of those receiving special education services. Also discussed here is attention deficit hyperactivity disorder. Although this disability is not defined as such in IDEA, it is prevalent, and its treatment raises important issues for school counselors.

Many support the notion that disability constitutes a culture (see, for example, Barnartt, 1996; S. E. Brown, 1995; Gill, 1995; Gilson & Depoy, 2000; Ingstad & Whyte, 1995; Middleton, Rollins, & Harley, 1999; and Peters, 2000). Within a cultural context, disability is a nondominant culture vis-à-vis the culture of ability. Many members of this culture share the experience of devaluation and of limited civil rights, along with anger at how their lives are determined by those who belong to the dominant culture.

THE INDIVIDUALS WITH DISABILITIES EDUCATION ACT (AMENDED IN 1997)

Ensuring the rights of all children and their parents and guardians to a FAPE is the cornerstone of IDEA.[1] The operative word here is *all:* Every child has the right to an education regardless of the severity of his or her disability. Table 7.1 outlines the four parts of the act.[2] Our focus here is on Parts A and B, the sections of the law most relevant to the work of school counselors.

Part A: Objectives and Definitions

Part A of the act lists four purposes:

1. To ensure that all children with disabilities have available to them a FAPE that emphasizes special education and related services designed to meet their particular needs
2. To ensure that the rights of children with disabilities and their parents or guardians are protected
3. To assist States and localities to provide for the education of all children with disabilities
4. To assess and ensure the effectiveness of efforts to educate children with disabilities (Individuals with Disabilities Education Act Amendments of 1997, Public Law 105-17, sec. 601)

Part A also defines several important terms:

Child with a disability. A child with a disability is a anyone ages 3 to 21 (or younger, if the individual has finished high school) who has one or more of the following conditions: a specific learning disability, mental retardation,

---

[1] I am deeply grateful to Professor Frank Bowe of Hofstra University. I attended his Introduction to Special Education course and found it invaluable in writing this section.

[2] Public Law 105-17, the most recent amendments to the Individuals with Disabilities Education Act, was passed on June 4, 1997. The discussion here is very limited; a copy of the entire law and information about its provisions is available on the Web at www.ideapractices.org.

TABLE 7.1   **THE INDIVIDUALS WITH DISABILITIES EDUCATION ACT (1997)**

Part	Title	Content
A	General Provisions	States purposes of the act and defines terms
B	Assistance for Education for All Children with Disabilities	States formula grant program, FAPE entitlements, and procedural safeguards
C	Infants and Toddlers with Disabilities	Requires that states serve preschool students with disabilities (ages 3 to 5) and authorizes grants to states to provide early intervention services to infants and toddlers (birth to age 3)
D	National Activities to Improve Education of Children with Disabilities	Describes state improvement grants, technical assistance, dissemination of information, funding for research and demonstration projects, and training for those who educate students with disabilities

an emotional disturbance, a hearing impairment (including deafness), an orthopedic impairment, a visual impairment (including blindness), autism, a traumatic brain injury, or other health impairments.[3] In addition, the disability must create a need for special education or related services. (A student whose visual impairment can be fixed with corrective lenses has no need for special education services.)

Free appropriate public education. FAPE is at the heart of the act. It means the provision of special education services and related services that
- are paid for by the public.
- meet the standards of the state educational agency for preschool, elementary, or secondary school education.
- conform to an individualized education plan.

Related services. These are the noninstructional support services that help a child to learn. Included in related services are psychological services and counseling and transportation.

Transition services. These are services provided to students with disabilities to help them prepare for life after high school—in college or at work—and for independent living.

Part B: Education for Children with Disabilities

Part B of IDEA is the most important for educators because it delineates the legal requirements for appropriately educating students with disabilities. The two most important requirements of Part B are the least restrictive environment and the individualized education program. Other provisions of the law speak to the makeup

---

[3]Those with disabilities who have finished high school or are over age 21 are protected under the Americans with Disabilities Act of 1990 or Section 504 of the Rehabilitation Act of 1973.

Regular Class   Resource Room   Separate Class   Separate School   Home/Hospital

<--->

FIGURE **7.1**

CONTINUUM OF ALTERNATIVE PLACEMENT OPTIONS

of the program team and the right of children with disabilities and their parents to due process protections.

Least Restrictive Environment   According to the act, children with disabilities must be educated in the least restrictive environment (LRE):

> To the maximum extent appropriate, children with disabilities, including children in public or private institutions or other care facilities, are educated with children who are not disabled, and special classes, separate schooling, or other removal of children with disabilities from the regular educational environment occurs only when the nature or severity of the disability of a child is such that education in regular classes with the use of supplementary aids and services cannot be achieved satisfactorily.

Figure 7.1 shows alternative placement options along a continuum. The ideal learning environment for all children is the regular classroom, at the very left of the continuum. If a child's disability makes integration in the regular classroom impossible, then the child must be taught in the least restrictive environment along the continuum.

After the Education for All Handicapped Children Act was passed in 1975, the LRE provision was interpreted to mean *mainstreaming:* "placing handicapped students in regular classes with their non-handicapped peers to the maximum extent appropriate" (Turnbull & Schulz, 1979, p. 52). In practice, special education students were allowed to visit regular education classes for nonacademic parts of the curriculum. Students with disabilities spent most of the school day in separate classrooms.

In 1986, Madeleine Will wrote an article sharply criticizing special education for stigmatizing students with disabilities by separating them from their peers and for failing to adapt general education to accommodate those with special needs.[4] Her criticism strongly influenced the *regular education initiative,* which brought children with mild disabilities into the regular classroom for all subjects (students with severe disabilities continued to be educated in separate environments). The regular education initiative was met by the protests of classroom teachers, who argued that they were being forced into a role that they neither wanted nor were prepared for. Even special educators debated the wisdom of abolishing the placement continuum (Fuchs & Fuchs, 1992). Yet, despite the controversy, Will inspired last-

---

[4]Will's criticism carried the weight of her position: At the time she was the assistant secretary of the Office of Special Education and Rehabilitative Services in the U.S. Department of Education. She was also the mother of a Down syndrome child.

ing change; and she coined a new word, *inclusion* (Turnbull, Turnbull, Shank, & Leal, 1999).

In the late 1980s, inclusion advocates began focusing their efforts on reducing the segregation of students with disabilities from their nondisabled peers. Sailor (1991) identified three components of what came to be called *first-generation inclusion:*

- All students are educated in the school they would attend if they had no disability.
- School and general education placements are age and grade appropriate.
- Special education supports exist within general education classes.

At the heart of the inclusion movement is the belief that the neighborhood school is for everyone, a community that accommodates all students. That accommodation can include special resources or an aide in the regular classroom and even special services in a resource room; but children with disabilities learn with their nondisabled classmates. Advocates insist that inclusion benefits all students—those with disabilities and those without. Critics, although they agree that inclusion is important, contend that it should not be accomplished at the risk of an appropriate education. They insist that LRE is a means toward an appropriate education; it is not an end in and of itself. If a child is not learning to his or her potential in the present educational environment, then, by the provisions of IDEA, the child's education is not appropriate. Still others argue that special attention in the classroom stigmatizes students with disabilities, which is exactly what inclusion advocates were trying to avoid.

Studies on the positive effects of inclusion have produced mixed results. In a review of the literature, Scruggs and Mastropieri (1996) found that teachers in inclusive classrooms

- spend at least an hour a day preparing for students with disabilities.
- lack adequate training, resources, and materials to teach students with disabilities.
- believe that class size should be limited to no more than 20 students if 1 of those students has a disability.
- are more willing to teach students with mild disabilities than those with severe disabilities.

By and large, research shows that inclusion helps students with severe and multiple disabilities learn new skills and establish more friendships better than it does students with less severe disabilities (see, for example, Giangreco, Dennis, Cloninger, Edelman, & Schattman, 1993; Hunt, Alwell, Farron-Davis, & Goetz, 1996; and Staub, Schwartz, Galluci, & Peck, 1994). This somewhat surprising outcome may be explained by the fact that students with severe and multiple disabilities require systemic changes (as opposed to add-on services), and that those changes are the key to the success of inclusion. The positive effects of inclusion on the socialization of students with disabilities are undeniable. In terms of academic success, the research is less conclusive, hampered methodologically by the difficulty of controlling for placements that reflect students' needs.

Second-generation inclusion dates to 1997, when the amendments to IDEA were passed. First-generation inclusion involved *added-on* services: Services were simply added to the regular learning environment. Second-generation inclusion involves *systemic change*—reinventing schools so that they are more accommodating to all students (Ferguson, 1995). In this form of inclusion, teaching for diversity becomes the norm rather than the exception (Turnbull et al., 1999).

Individualized Education Program   Section 614 of IDEA requires that every student with a disability have an individualized education program (IEP). By law, a student's IEP must be updated each year, and it must contain the following eight parts:

1. *The child's needs.* This description of the child's needs is the most important part of the IEP. The description must include the child's current academic performance and an assessment of how the disability affects his or her involvement in general education. Writing this part of the IEP can be an arduous process: It demands the input and agreement of many people. The child's parents are critical here, not only because they are a source of information, but also because this is their best opportunity to advocate for their child's needs. School counselors can play both a contributory and a supportive role in preparing this part of the IEP.
2. *Annual goals.* The goals must be measurable. That is, they should answer two questions: Where do we want this child to be one year from now? And what will the child be able to do one year from now? The goals derive from the needs articulated in the first part of the IEP.
3. *Services.* Part 3 delineates the special education and related services the child will receive to meet the stated goals.
4. *Justification for a separate learning environment.* If the child is going to be removed from the regular classroom for all or even a part of instruction, the law requires an explanation.
5. *Assessment plans.* This part describes the forms of assessment that will be used to gauge the child's achievement, any modifications needed to administer standardized tests or other instruments, and the reasons that alternative assessments or methods are necessary.
6. *Logistics.* This part articulates the projected date on which services will start and the frequency, location, and duration of the services.
7. *Transition plans.* As the child moves closer to graduation (or age 22), the IEP must include transition plans:
   - Beginning at age 14 and updated annually, a statement of the student's transition needs that focuses on his or her course of study (for example, participation in advanced-placement courses or in a vocational education program)
   - Beginning at age 16 (or younger if determined by the IEP team), a statement of transition services that includes, when appropriate, interagency responsibilities or links to other resources

- Beginning at least one year before the student reaches the age of majority under state law (usually age 18), a statement that the child has been informed of his or her rights under IDEA that will transfer to the student from the parents when the student reaches the age of majority

8. *Evaluation.* The last part of the IEP is a statement of how the child's progress toward the annual goals will be measured; the intervals at which the child's parents will be informed about their child's progress toward the annual goals (they must receive reports at least as often as parents of children without disabilities do); and the extent to which current services are sufficient for the child to achieve the goals by the end of the year.

The IEP is the primary vehicle for helping a child with disabilities achieve. The school counselor's role here as a member of the IEP team is to make sure that the plan is meeting the child's needs. The counselor can also be involved in the provision of related services, and so will have input in any modifications to the IEP.

The IEP Team   IDEA requires that a team work on the development and implementation of each child's IEP. The law also mandates that team members include

- the parents of the child.
- at least one of the child's regular education teachers (if the child is or may be participating in the regular classroom).
- at least one special education teacher or provider.
- a representative of the local school board or district who is qualified to provide or supervise instruction to meet the unique needs of students with disabilities; is knowledgeable about the general education curriculum; and is knowledgeable about the resources available from the local system.
- an individual who can interpret the instructional implications of assessment scores (this person may already be a member of the team).
- at the discretion of the parents or the school board, related-services providers or other individuals who have special knowledge of or skills for helping the child.
- whenever appropriate, the child with the disability.

Although the law does not specifically require that the school counselor be a member of the IEP team, the school counselor can join the team as a related-services provider. A counselor who knows or has worked with a student should consider it a duty to be part of the IEP team.

Due Process   Section 615 of IDEA gives the parents of a child with a disability the right to due process if they are not satisfied with their child's IEP or if their request for a special service is denied. The first level of appeal is to an independent hearing officer in the school district. If the concern is not resolved at this level, the case goes to a state review officer. If either party continues to be dissatisfied, the case moves to the courts and requires the involvement of lawyers (whose charges may or may not be reimbursable to the child's parents). A district court ruling can be appealed to the state court of appeals and from there to the state supreme court.

Cases involving IEPs have even been argued before the U.S. Supreme Court. One of the best known was that of Amy Rowley, a child who was deaf.[5] Amy's parents had asked that she have a classroom interpreter, a request that was denied by the local board of education. The Supreme Court ruled in favor of the school district by a vote of 6 to 3. The Court interpreted *appropriate education* as one that benefits the child. Because Amy had passed first grade without a classroom interpreter, the Court argued that she was benefiting from instruction and that the services she was receiving were sufficient.

Although the legal ramifications of the act are important—IDEA is a significant piece of legislation, and compliance with it is monitored by the federal government—and counselors should never lose sight of the fundamental purpose of the act, to ensure that millions of students with disabilities receive a free and appropriate education.

SPECIAL EDUCATION SERVICES TODAY

The data in this section describe the school-aged population served under IDEA and the settings in which students learn.[6]

The Students Served under IDEA

In academic year 1998–99, the number of students ages 6 through 21 who received services through IDEA reached 5,541,166. That number represented a 2.7 percent increase over the previous year and a 30.3 percent increase from the 1989–90 school year.

Population by Disability Category   Table 7.2 shows both the number of students served and the percentage increase between 1989–90 and 1998–99 for the various categories of disabilities. Between 1989–90 and 1998–99, the number of students in all disability categories increased except for those who were deaf and blind, a group that showed a slight decrease. The most dramatic increase was in children with other health impairments, up almost 319 percent over the 10-year period. According to reporting states, the increase in this group of children was a product of an increase in the identification and provision of services to children with attention deficit disorder (ADD) and attention deficit hyperactivity disorder (ADHD).

We have no data for students with autism or traumatic brain injury for the 10-year-period, but we know that large increases have occurred in both groups. In 1991–92, the autistic population served through IDEA was less than 10,000; in

---

[5] *Hendrick Hudson District Board of Education v. Rowley* (458 U.S. 176, 1982).

[6] The data throughout this and the following sections come from the *Twenty-Second Annual Report to Congress on the Implementation of IDEA* (U.S. Department of Education, 2000), the most recent source available at the time this text was written. General population figures come from the U.S. Bureau of the Census (1998).

TABLE 7.2 NUMBER OF STUDENTS SERVED UNDER **IDEA** BY DISABILITY CATEGORY, ACADEMIC YEARS 1989–90 AND 1998–99

Disability Category	Students Served		Percent Change
	1989–90	1998–99	
Specific learning disabilities	2,062,076	2,817,148	36.6
Speech and language impairments	974,256	1,074,548	10.3
Mental retardation	563,902	611,076	8.4
Emotional disturbance	381,639	463,262	21.4
Multiple disabilities	87,957	107,763	22.5
Hearing impairments	57,906	70,883	22.4
Orthopedic impairments	48,050	69,495	44.6
Other health impairments	52,733	220,831	318.7
Visual impairments	22,866	26,132	14.3
Autism	*	53,576	*
Deafness-blindness	1,633	1,609	−1.5
Traumatic brain injury	*	12,933	*
Developmental delay	*	11,910	*
All disabilities	**4,253,018**	**5,541,166**	**30.3**

*Schools were not required to report services for youngsters with autism, traumatic brain injury, or developmental delay until after the 1989–90 school year.

SOURCE: U.S. Department of Education, Office of Special Education Programs, Data Analysis System (DANS).

1998–99, it was more than 53,000. This increase probably reflected better understanding and diagnosis of autistic children (U.S. Department of Education, 2000). Data on students with traumatic brain injury were first reported in the 1992–93 school year. In the next three years, the number of students in the group rose almost 142 percent. Growth in this category has leveled off somewhat: Between 1996–97 and 1998–99, the increase in this population was about 35 percent. Developmental delay was first reported in 1997–98; in the next two years, the population increased 214 percent.

Table 7.3 shows the percentage of students served in each disability category in academic years 1989–90 and 1998–99. In 1998–99, students with specific learning disabilities, speech and language impairments, mental retardation, and emotional disturbance comprised almost 90 percent of the population served under IDEA.

Race and Ethnicity The 1997 amendments to the act require that the states report the number of students with disabilities by race and ethnicity. The data make clear that Black students are overrepresented in special education: Blacks make up just 14.8 percent of the general population between ages 6 and 21, yet they comprise 20.2 percent of students with disabilities. Especially noteworthy is the proportion of Black students among those with mental retardation (34.3 percent) and

TABLE 7.3   PERCENTAGE OF STUDENTS SERVED UNDER IDEA BY DISABILITY CATEGORY, ACADEMIC YEARS 1989–90 AND 1998–99

Disability Category	Percent of Students Served	
	1989–90	1998–99
Specific learning disabilities	48.5	50.8
Speech and language impairments	22.9	19.4
Mental retardation	13.3	11.0
Emotional disturbance	9.0	8.4
Multiple disabilities	2.1	1.9
Hearing impairments	1.4	1.3
Orthopedic impairments	1.1	1.3
Other health impairments	1.2	4.0
Visual impairments	0.5	0.5
Autism	*	1.0
Deafness-blindness	>0.1	>0.1
Traumatic brain injury	*	0.2
Developmental delay	*	0.2

*Schools were not required to report services for youngsters with autism, traumatic brain injury, or developmental delay until after the 1989–90 school year.

SOURCE: U.S. Department of Education, Office of Special Education Programs, Data Analysis System (DANS).

developmental delay (33.7 percent)—more than twice the proportion of Black youngsters in the general population.

There is less of a discrepancy among Hispanic students: 14.2 percent in the general population versus 13.2 percent in special education. These students are overrepresented in the population of children with specific learning disabilities (15.8 percent) and hearing impairments (16.3 percent). American Indian students represent less than 1.0 percent of the general population and make up 1.3 percent of the special education population. They comprise the largest percentage of students who are deaf and blind (1.8 percent) and who have a traumatic brain injury (1.6 percent).

Overall, the percentage of White (non-Hispanic) students in special education is less than their proportion in the general population—63.6 percent versus 66.2 percent—but they are overrepresented in five disability categories: speech and language impairments (68.3 percent), orthopedic impairments (67.2 percent), other health impairments (75.8 percent), visual impairments (69.5 percent), and traumatic brain injury (70.2 percent). Asian American and Pacific Islander students are underrepresented generally in special education (3.8 percent of the general population versus 1.7 percent of the special education population) but overrepresented in three categories: hearing impairments (4.6 percent), autism (4.7 percent), and, most especially, deafness-blindness (11.3 percent).

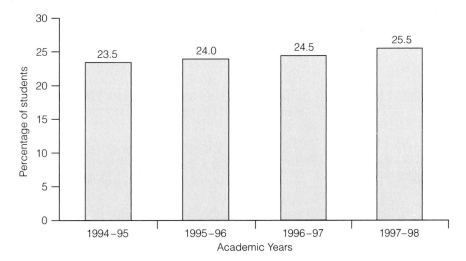

FIGURE **7.2**

**HIGH SCHOOL GRADUATION RATES FOR STUDENTS WITH DISABILITIES,
ACADEMIC YEARS 1994–95 TO 1997–98**

NOTE: These are students ages 17 through 21 who graduated with a standard diploma.

SOURCE: U.S. Department of Education, Office of Special Education Programs, Data Analysis System (DANS).

High School Graduation Rates   A major concern among advocates for special education is the relatively small number of students with disabilities who graduate from high school with a standard diploma. In the 1997–98 school year, only 147,123 students with disabilities ages 17 through 21 graduated with a standard high school diploma, just 25.5 percent of all students with disabilities in that age group.[7] In part the graduation rate among students with disabilities has been affected by the standards movement and high-stakes testing, which are lowering graduation rates across the country. A number of states—among them New York—have done away with local diplomas (diplomas that are recognized by neither the government nor colleges and universities) and now require all students to pass exams to earn an academic diploma.[8]

The good news is that high school completion rates have been improving steadily albeit gradually in recent years among student with disabilities. Figure 7.2 shows the percentage of students with disabilities who graduated with a standard diploma from 1994–95 to 1997–98.

Among those most likely to graduate are students who are deaf and blind (39.2 percent) and those with speech or language impairments (35.0 percent), visual impairments (30.6 percent), and specific learning disabilities (30.5 percent).

---

[7]This figure represented 61.6 percent of students with disabilities who exited the educational system in academic year 1997–98.

[8]The academic diploma-only policy in New York ended a decades-old practice of offering an alternative diploma. Special education advocates raised a hue and cry, claiming that some students, because

Those least likely to graduate are students with mental retardation (13.8 percent), multiple disabilities (10.3 percent), and autism (8.4 percent). Over the four years shown in Figure 7.2, graduation rates improved steadily but very slowly for students in all disability categories except for those with mental retardation (the rate remained stable) and with traumatic brain injury (the rate fluctuated slightly).

Graduation rates for students with disabilities vary considerably from state to state, most likely a function of the different requirements each state has for these students:

- Some states insist that students with disabilities meet all diploma requirements in order to graduate.
- Some states insist that students with mild disabilities meet diploma requirements.
- Some states allow local school boards to determine diploma requirements.
- Some states allow IEP teams to establish diploma requirements for students with severe disabilities.

About 40 states offer something other than a standard diploma—for example, a certificate of completion (Thurlow, Shin, Guy, & Lee, 1999).

Conscious of the importance of a high school diploma in today's society, the Office of Special Education Programs (OSEP) in the U.S. Department of Education is working to increase graduation rates among students with disabilities by funding of dropout prevention projects.

Educational Settings

How has the emphasis on inclusion in the 1990s affected the educational environment of students with disabilities? Over the decade, the percentage of those students who are learning in regular classrooms gradually increased. For example, in the 1988–89 school year, 30 percent of students with disabilities were served outside the regular classroom for less than 21 percent of the day; that rate went up to 47 percent in 1997–98.[9] The rate of special education students served outside the regular classroom for 21 percent to 60 percent of the day fell from 39 percent in 1988–89 to 29 percent in 1997–98. In 1988–89, 25 percent of students with disabilities were served outside the regular classroom for more than 60 percent of the day; in 1997–98, that rate had dropped to 20 percent. There were also modest decreases in those served in separate schools and in residential facilities. Overall, over 46 percent of all students with disabilities in the 1997–98 school year were served outside the regular classroom for less than 21 percent of the school day.

---

of the nature their disability, simply cannot pass the state-mandated exams. The state recently responded by announcing that 2 percent of all special education students would be given an alternative assessment, but that the rest would have to take the state exams. Although the IEP diploma will remain, it is not recognized by the government or by institutions of higher education. (This information was taken from the New York State Education Department's Web site, at www.nysed.gov.)

[9] "Less than 21 percent of the school day" is the most inclusive category in OSEP's continuum of placements.

In all categories of disability, special education students in elementary school are more likely to be mainstreamed than are special education students in middle or high school. In academic year 1997–98, 97.8 percent of students ages 6 to 11 with disabilities were served in the regular classroom, compared with 94.7 percent of students ages 12 to 17 and 87.2 percent of students ages 18 to 21.

The category of disability has a significant impact on the learning environment of students with disabilities. Students with speech and language impairments (87.8 percent) were most likely to be placed in inclusive settings. Students with multiple disabilities (10.0 percent) and mental retardation (12.6 percent) were the least likely to be taught in regular classrooms. Students with language impairments (0.3 percent) or specific learning disabilities (0.8 percent) were the least likely to be educated in a special school or a residential setting. The students most likely to receive services in a separate school or residential settings were those with multiple disabilities (25.2 percent) and those who were deaf and blind (34.7 percent).

THE ROLE OF THE SCHOOL COUNSELOR

To reinvent schools, to create a learning system that accommodates all students, collaboration is essential. Collaboration assumes that the whole is greater than the sum of its parts. It is the recognition among the parties that each has a certain expertise that can be used to generate creative solutions to agreed-on problems (Idol, Paolucci-Whitcomb, & Nevin, 1986). The team in a school working on systemic change draws its members from many groups, among them teachers, parents, students, related-services providers, paraprofessionals, language translators and interpreters, administrators, and, of course, school counselors. In this section we examine the role of the school counselor in collaborating with teachers, parents, and students.

A key task in working with each of these groups is identifying attitudes that consciously or unconsciously could slow the learning or the socialization of students with disabilities. But first school counselors must assess their own attitudes about what is a nondominant culture, to be sure that they are responding without bias to children in need of special education.

Working with Teachers

One manifestation of systemic change in the school is cooperative teaching. *Cooperative teaching* partners a regular education teacher with a special education teacher in the classroom.

Cooperative teaching is a mandate of second-generation inclusion. In some schools, cooperative teaching is working: These schools report that classroom teachers are adapting well to their partnership with special educators. But other schools report that the process is difficult. This is where the school counselor can be especially helpful. The problem usually is resistance: Regular education teachers, angry that inclusion has been imposed on them, are reluctant to reinvent their

TABLE 7.4 **RESPONDING TO THE IN-CLASS BEHAVIORS OF SPECIAL-NEEDS STUDENTS: TIPS FOR TEACHERS**

What You Might See	What You Might Be Tempted to Do	Alternate Responses	Ways to Include the Student's Peers in the Process
Behavior: The student does not cooperate with other students during instructional activities.	Discipline the student for the poor behavior and separate him/her from the rest of the class.	Identify his/her strengths and work together on a list of positive things he/she can say when responding to other students during instructional activities.	Ask the student to identify classmates with whom he/she would like to work. Then work with this small group to practice verbal responses that would be helpful.
Social interactions: The student has few friends and doesn't appear to want any.	Encourage the student to take the initiative toward others but also allow him/her to be by himself/herself whenever he/she chooses.	Collaborate with the school counselor on ways to teach the student specific social skills.	Have the student work with the identified peers to practice the specific social skills in and out of the classroom.
Educational performance: The student's work is acceptable, but he/she needs constant supervision.	Assign an aide to work with the student, and allow him/her to complete unfinished work at home.	Collaborate with the special education teacher to create step-by-step assignments that the student can do on his/her own. Set up a reward system for each layer successfully completed without supervision.	Encourage the student to work with peers to monitor the layered assignments. Ask peers to work with the student to construct a tracking system for class assignments.
Attitude: The student never volunteers answers and is reluctant to participate in class.	Carefully choose activities that allow the student to work alone.	Together with the special education teacher, work with the student ahead of time on the content to be covered, and plan specific things for him/her to contribute.	With peers, plan positive contributions that each can make to upcoming class activities.

SOURCE: Adapted from Turnbull, Turnbull, Shank, and Leal, *Exceptional Lives: Special Education in Today's Schools* (2nd ed.), p. 97. © 1999. Reprinted by permission of Pearson Education, Inc., Upper Saddle River, NJ.

classroom. In the face of that resistance, other members of the team are likely to be defensive. But the school counselor is trained to acknowledge and even join the resistance to help a client or consultee move beyond it.

In addition to empathy, the best tool for overcoming teachers' resistance is information. A growing body of research supports the positive effects of inclusion for both students with disabilities and their nondisabled peers (see, for example, Snell & Eichner, 1989; Stainback & Stainback, 1990; and Stevens & Slavin, 1991). The school counselor should know that research and use it to help regular education teachers adapt to their new roles. The counselor also can offer help by finding the resources and instructional support to deal with teachers' concerns (Tarver-Behring, Spagna, & Sullivan, 1998).

Also helpful is an understanding of effective ways to respond to the behaviors of students with disabilities. Table 7.4 describes four situations teachers may encounter in the inclusive classroom, and possible responses to them.

Students with disabilities belong to a nondominant culture (people who are disabled), and their education is determined, for the most part, by people who belong to the dominant culture (people who are not disabled). The percentage of educators with a disability is very small: Fewer than 14 percent of all special education teachers and just 6 percent of all general education teachers identify themselves as having a disability (Westat, 2002). Teachers' resistance to working with special-needs students, then, may reflect the same kind of bias that made racial integration in the schools a torturous process. A school counselor who is trained in issues of diversity and multiculturalism can be a valuable asset to multidisciplinary team members who find it hard to embrace the culture of disability. The goal is to help teachers understand their own attitudes about and increase their knowledge of those who are "different." To that end, the school counselor can use any of the methods discussed in Chapter 6. In addition, Scarborough and Deck (1998) suggest LaVoie's disability workshop curriculum as an excellent way to sensitize teachers to the culture of disability.

Many children with disabilities also have deficits in problem-solving skills—identifying problems, finding solutions, and evaluating the consequences (Tarver-Behring et al., 1998)—which can lead to behavioral problems in the classroom. The school counselor can help teachers by using peer mentors to provide social skills training in the classroom. The first step in a program like this is to evaluate the attitudes of the mentors and to work with those who may have difficulty interacting with students who are disabled.

Working with the Parents of Children with Disabilities

Stoll-Switzer (1990) identified four factors in the family system that help a child with a disability reach his or her highest level of functioning:

The family's acceptance of the child's learning problem. Children seem to learn more when their family is able to adapt to the fact of their disability.[10]

The family's engagement with the child's learning. Children whose family members help them daily with homework and with learning new tasks develop good study habits and positive attitudes about school.

The parents' method of discipline. Children who understand both the family's rules and the consequences of breaking those rules develop the internal controls necessary to achieve academically.

The role of the child. A healthy family allows the child's role in the system to develop and change as new information about the child or the disability becomes available.

Although this research was done with families of children with learning disabilities, the results may generalize to other kinds of disabilities.

---

[10] Key to the family's acceptance of a child's disability are the early detection and treatment of the disability. Bragg, Brown, and Berninger (1992) found that the family's ability to adapt to a child with a disability was greater for congenital as opposed to acquired disabilities. The severity of the disability did not matter in congenital cases; but the more severe an acquired disability, the greater the disruption in the family.

These findings point to the differences among families in their interactions with a child with a disability. They also generate four questions counselors need answers to for every child with a disability:

- To what extent do the parents accept this child's disability?
- To what degree are they engaged with their child's learning?
- Have the parents made appropriate rules for the child, and have they been clear about the consequences of breaking those rules?
- How open are the parents to learning new information about the child's disability and to trying new approaches to help the child?

Because inclusion demands that parents be fully involved in the placement and education of their children, the counselor's first task is to be sure the parents are engaged in the process. Like teachers, parents can be resistant. They may not be sufficiently engaged with their child, or they may feel that the regular classroom cannot provide their child with the necessary services. Some parents fear that their child will be rejected by classmates and regular education teachers (Tarver-Behring et al., 1998). The school counselor can often act as a broker in the relationship between the parents and the school.

The following are concrete suggestions that schools can employ to work productively and collaboratively with the parents of children with disabilities:

- Establish trusting relationships with parents.
- Obtain accurate and complete information from parents, listen carefully, and value what parents say.
- Help parents acquire more effective ways of handling behavior problems.
- Provide numerous options for parent involvement in the school setting, and keep in mind that involvement may be unfamiliar for parents.
- Provide assurance to those parents who may be fearful of the school bureaucracy.
- Let parents know that the school staff believes that the parents want the best for their children.
- Provide parents with special knowledge to meet the varied needs of children.
- Have parents collaborate in the process to make them more likely to carry out recommendations successfully.
- Think of parents as experts who can contribute knowledge about and insight into their children to enhance educational programs.
- Explain assessment procedures and encourage participation in conference decisions so that parents can help decide on the educational placement of their children.
- Encourage parents to involve themselves in classroom activities whenever appropriate.
- Provide opportunities to work together productively. (Tarver-Behring et al., 1998, p. 55)

Inclusion demands more time and effort from everyone involved in the education of a child with a disability. School counselors, charged with multiple responsibilities, may not have the time to work closely with parents. To deal with the problem of time, school counselors might consider forming parent support groups (Greer, Greer, & Woody, 1995). Besides providing emotional support, these groups can disseminate information to parents about inclusion and other aspects of their child's education.

Some school counselors may find it hard to empathize with the parents of a child with a disability. They should realize that parents may be defensive because they have a child who did not live up to their expectations. The school counselor's primary task is to make the school environment as nonthreatening as possible to these parents. This can help a great deal in meeting the goal of second-generation inclusion, systemic change.

Working with Students

Inclusion provides school counselors with the opportunity to work directly with all students, disabled and nondisabled. In a later section we discuss youngsters who have specific disabilities. Here we examine some general themes that can arise in working with students in inclusive environments.

Students with Mild Disabilities   Students with mild disabilities—learning disabilities, emotional or behavioral disorders, and mild mental retardation—generally experience problems in three areas: a lack of self-direction, social immaturity and inadequacy, and personality difficulties (M. L. Bowen & Glenn, 1998). Many of these students suffer from learned helplessness: They feel they have little control over their environment. Diagnostic labeling can diminish their sense of self-worth, which, along with a lack of social skills, can lead to problems in socialization with peers and teachers. And their frustration with their learning difficulties often manifests in problem behaviors. The school counselor must always be aware of the connection among disability, negative self-image, and disruptive behaviors (Kazdin, 1992). For example, many students with mild disabilities suffer from test anxiety, a function of their lack of confidence, which manifests in disruptive behavior.

School counselors can make a huge difference in the educational life of students with mild disabilities by facilitating a supportive environment in which the fear of failure is reduced (M. L. Bowen & Glenn, 1998; Herring, 1990). Counselors can also help these students communicate their needs to teachers and peers. And they can create socially acceptable ways for these student to release pent-up frustration, anger, and anxiety (W. Steele, 1992).

Using Play   Because many students with disabilities suffer from limited verbal expression, counselors can find play a useful means of working with these students, especially the younger ones.[11] Behavior modification strategies can help change specific behaviors; but counseling through play can access the underlying causes of the behaviors—the issues that come from being different (Ginsberg, 1984). One study found that the use of play with elementary school students with a disability

---

[11] We discussed the fundamentals of play therapy in Chapter 2.

facilitated the expression of feelings, the experience of control, and the development of coping skills (L. Johnson, McLeod, & Fall, 1997).

Working with Nondisabled Peers   Inclusion provides a wonderful opportunity for counselors to work with nondisabled students on their attitudes toward students with disabilities. Inclusion is one more facet of multiculturalism: It brings students into close contact with those who are different. Like all multicultural situations, when students learn to appreciate differences and understand something about the dynamics of dominant versus nondominant cultures, inclusion can be enriching. The philosophy of inclusion rests on the principles of access, acceptance, belonging, security, equity, opportunity, respect, and the absence of stigma (Hibbert & Sprinthall, 1995; York, 1993). These principles can translate into counseling goals for students who are not disabled.

Of course inclusion can also prejudice some students against those with disabilities. The best tool here is information, which appears to weaken stereotypes about people with disabilities (Greer et al., 1995; R. A. Jones, 1982). Children have lots of questions about disabilities (Petrusic & Celotta, 1985), and counselors can help answer them. Accurate information is one way of reducing bias in our schools and in the larger society.

Group Counseling   Group counseling can be an excellent modality for students with disabilities, especially for those with socialization difficulties. Many of the principles common to all group work apply to students with disabilities (see Chapter 2). But there are some special considerations. Table 7.5 lists recommendations for creating a good counseling environment and activities for small groups of students with disabilities.

Vocational Guidance   Among those considered to have a work disability, 33.6 percent are in the labor force and 15.6 percent are unemployed (Isaacson & Brown, 1997). That is to say, more than 50 percent of people with disabilities are not members of the workforce.[12] Clearly, helping students with disabilities prepare for life after high school can be a challenging task for the multidisciplinary team. School counselors, because of their training in vocational assessment and guidance, can make a significant contribution to the school-to-college, -work or -independent living transition.

The career counseling needs of several specific groups of students are examined throughout the next section. In general, though, school counselors should know that there is little reason to exclude students with disabilities from the career component of developmental guidance. Many of the vocational assessment instruments described in Chapter 5 have versions that are appropriate for those with disabilities. Assessment is important because vocational information—the student's interests and aspirations, work history, and work-related habits—should be part of each

---

[12] Some of those not in the workforce are in school, of course. Blackorby and Wagner (1996) found that approximately 14 percent of those with specific learning disabilities matriculated into college within two years of leaving high school and 30 percent had done so within five years. We talk about postsecondary preparation for these students in our examination of students by type of disability.

TABLE 7.5   GUIDELINES FOR DOING GROUP WORK WITH STUDENTS WITH DISABILITIES

Establishing and Maintaining the Counseling Environment

Develop an appropriate setting.	Limit counseling activities to no more than 30 minutes.
	Eliminate distractions.
	Structure tasks, and follow that structure consistently.
	Use multisensory approaches (auditory, visual, tactile, and kinesthetic) while presenting activities to the students.
Communicate concretely.	Do not use generalities or abstract relationships and terms.
	Avoid beginning a question with *how* or *why*.
	Use short, concise, explicit sentences.
Use repetition frequently and consistently.	At the start of each session, review earlier meetings and their objectives.
	Tell students what to expect at each session.
	Present a summary of the activity, and stress what is important for the students to remember.

Creating Appropriate Experiential Situations

Encourage and reinforce students' behavior frequently.	Give out stickers, stamps, and other small rewards.
	Use charts with stickers and stars.
	Make a display of students' projects.
	Praise students; smile; say something kind; or give students a hug.
	Set aside a school day, or part of a day, for a special activity or party.
	Be sure each student has a small job or task.
	Eat lunch with the students.
	Plan a field trip.
Be aware of students' deficits, and compensate for them by presenting stimuli creatively.	Help students express themselves prompting them for appropriate language.
	Model the activity being presented to the group.
	Model appropriate behavior.
	Give examples of concrete projects that group members are expect to do.
	If a student seems confused, rephrase the instruction.
	Use humor to deal with sensitive issues or uncomfortable situations.

SOURCE: Adapted from D. Robinson and Mopsik (1992), pp. 75–76. Copyright 1992 by American School Counselor Association. Reprinted with permission.

student's IEP. In addition, the student's IEP should include a career-vocational profile and the school counselor's "evaluation of the information for decision-making purposes" (S. A. Omizo & Omizo, 1992, p. 40).

IDEA requires that an individual transition plan (ITP) be part of the IEP for students ages 14 to 21 who are still in high school. At age 16, the ITP must also spell out any necessary interagency cooperation. Whether a student plans to go on to college or directly into the workforce, the state rehabilitation agency is often involved in transition planning.[13] A vocational rehabilitation counselor, for example, may attend an IEP team meeting to explain to parents and student the services and financial support available for post–high school job training, and employment qualifications (which can include college).

Often the transition plans are developed haphazardly without full knowledge of the student's skills, interests, and abilities. The school counselor is in the position to be sure each ITP contains appropriate and complete information—the results of vocational assessment and vocational counseling sessions with the student. The counselor should also make an effort to expose students to the many careers that are open to people with disabilities, by inviting speakers to visit the school or showing films. Also, several Web sites offer vocational information for students with disabilities.[14]

STUDENTS WITH DISABILITIES BY GROUP

The following sections discuss students with certain types of disability, groups of students that school counselors are most likely to encounter. The text describes the causes of disability, assessment methods, and interventions for each group of youngsters.

Specific Learning Disabilities

Students with specific learning disabilities accounted for just over half of the student population served under IDEA during the 1998–99 school year. Most of the special-needs students with whom school counselors work have a specific learning disability.

Definition   There is disagreement on the precise meaning of *learning disability*. Public Law 94-142 (1975) suggests that a *learning disability* is a difficulty that creates a need for special education or related services. In 1994, the National Joint Committee on Learning Disabilities developed the following definition:

> *Learning disabilities* is a general term that refers to a heterogeneous group of disorders manifested by significant difficulties in the acquisition and use of listening, speaking, reading, writing, reasoning, or mathematical abilities. These disorders are intrinsic to the individual and presumed to be due to central nervous system dysfunction, and may appear across the life span. Problems in self-regulatory behaviors, social perception, and social interaction may exist with learning disabilities but do not themselves constitute a learning disability. Although learning disabilities may occur

---

[13] The agency's involvement is mandated by the Rehabilitation Act of 1973, which authorizes services for young people with disabilities to help them become employable.

[14] See the list of suggested Internet sites at the end of the chapter.

concomitantly with other handicapping conditions (for example, sensory impairment, mental retardation, serious emotional disturbance) or with extrinsic influences (such as cultural differences, insufficient or inappropriate instruction), they are not the result of the conditions or influences. (p. 3)

According to this definition, learning disorders can manifest in many different ways, and a specific learning disability can cause difficulty in one or more academic areas. That these disorders are *intrinsic* is an important part of the definition. Although poverty, poor schooling, and other extrinsic factors can leave a child with learning difficulties, those difficulties are not classified as learning disabilities. Also, although many students with learning disabilities have behavioral and social problems too, those problems are not the basis of classification.

The strongest criterion in the diagnosis of a learning disability is a severe discrepancy between a student's perceived potential and actual achievement as measured on standardized tests (Turnbull et al., 1999). For example, one or more grossly deviant subscales would raise suspicions of a learning disability. Students with specific learning disabilities usually have average to above-average intelligence, which clearly distinguishes them from those who are mentally retarded.

Categories of Specific Learning Disabilities   The Council for Learning Disabilities (CLD) (1997) divided specific learning disabilities into five categories:

Reading. The most common form of reading disorder is dyslexia, which recent research shows stems from a lack of phonological awareness (CLD, 1997).

Written language. These disorders can take the form of problems with handwriting, spelling, sentence structure, word usage, or composition (Scott, 1991).

Mathematics. Students with a learning disability related to math may have difficulties in visual perception (differentiating numbers and shapes), memory (recalling math facts), motor function (writing numbers legibly), language (understanding the meaning of arithmetic terms), abstract reasoning (solving work problems), and metacognition (using strategies to solve problems) (CLD; Turnbull et al., 1999).

Memory. This kind of learning disability can include problems with either short-term memory (comparing, coding, processing, and organizing information) or long-term memory (accessing stored information) (CLD). A memory learning disability can be extremely frustrating because the student appears to have learned and understood the information but cannot access it when he or she is being tested.

Metacognition. Metacognitive disorders reflect the inability to learn strategies for acquiring, storing, and processing information; understanding when, where, and why these strategies are important; and selecting and monitoring the use of these strategies (CLD).

Causes   As noted in the CLD definition, learning disorders are caused by dysfunction in the central nervous system. Research using brain mapping and other new technology supports the relationship between learning disabilities and abnormalities in the parts of the brain that process language (Dawes, 1996; Manis, 1996). These abnormalities are responsible for problems with storing words and phrases, finding words, and identifying phonemes in spoken words (Manis, 1996). That two or more family members can have the same problem also seems to support a genetic root for learning disabilities (Light & DeFries, 1995; J. M. Oliver, Cole, & Hollingsworth, 1991). Investigation into learning disabilities continues at a rapid pace, but there is a great deal more to learn about these disabilities.

Assessment   Usually a school psychologist diagnoses students with a specific learning disability. The psychologist administers both an IQ test and an achievement test.[15] If a child's scores show a significant discrepancy between aptitude and achievement, between performance and verbal IQ, or between areas of academic achievement, a specific learning disability is indicated (Woodcock, 1990). What constitutes a significant discrepancy? Most states use a measurement from 1.0 standard deviation to 2.0 standard deviations. The subscale standard deviation on the Wechsler IQ and achievement tests is 15 points. So in some states, a 15-point discrepancy leads to a diagnosis of a learning disability; in others, a 30-point discrepancy is needed.

Counseling Issues   Students with specific learning disabilities are at risk for learned helplessness (Turnbull et al., 1999). After failing repeatedly, they can withdraw and simply stop trying. These students need to feel that they are important to the counselor and others, have the power to make choices, are capable of learning, and contribute to the well-being of others (Turnbull et al., 1999).

Students with learning disabilities also are at increased risk for dropping out of high school. Over 40 percent of students with learning disabilities do not complete high school, compared with 25 percent of the general population (Barga, 1996).

Career Counseling   Social immaturity is often a problem for students with learning disabilities, and this can affect their readiness for career exploration. Before implementing any of the career counseling strategies described in Chapter 5, then, the school counselor may need to assess the career maturity of these students (Biller & Horn, 1991). The first step in working with students whose level of career maturity is low is to talk with them about the world of work and help them understand that many exciting careers are open to them despite their disability. Only then should the counselor proceed with a formal career assessment and curriculum.

In choosing an assessment instrument, the counselor should keep in mind that some students with learning disabilities have difficulty reading information on a computer screen or processing the large amount of information that most online instruments generate (Biller & Horn, 1991). The solution is often a paper-and-pencil test.

More and more students with learning disabilities are going on to college. Their admission to colleges and universities is protected by Section 504 of the

---

[15] A popular IQ test is the Wechsler Intelligence Scale for Children–III (WISC–III) (Wechsler, 1991); a widely used achievement test is the Wechsler Individualized Achievement Test (WIAT) (Psychological Corporation, 1992).

Rehabilitation Act of 1973: "No otherwise qualified handicapped individual shall, solely by reason of his handicap, be excluded from participation in, be denied the benefits of, or be subjected to discrimination under any program or activity receiving federal assistance." Although some colleges have adopted a more lenient admissions policy for students with learning disabilities, others evaluate all applicants on the same criteria (Skinner & Schenck, 1992)—a practice in line with Section 504's "otherwise qualified" wording.

The role of the school counselor here is help students plan. First, students with learning disabilities should know that both American College Testing and the Educational Testing Service offer modified versions of standardized college entrance exams. Second, qualified students should know that although the law gives them the right to go to college, it does not promise them the support to help keep them there. What's needed is research into schools that do offer programs and services for students with learning disabilities. For example, many colleges run a summer program for incoming freshmen with disabilities, to prepare them for the college experience and to teach them study skills.[16] Research has shown that students with learning disabilities benefit from being taught organizational and study strategies (Lloyd, Saltzman, & Kaufman, 1981). So a college that offers a study skills course may be a better choice for students with learning disabilities than a college that does not offer that help. Other considerations in choosing a college are the heterogeneity of the student population, academic expectations, and faculty-to-student ratio (Skinner & Schenck, 1992). Finally, the school counselor should prepare students for the social and emotional adjustments they are going to have to make when they go to college. Few colleges monitor students or provide the hands-on services that students with learning disabilities have been accustomed to in high school. These students have to learn to be their own advocates.

Speech and Language Impairments

About 5 percent of the people in the United States have a speech or language disorder. Speech and language impairments in the 1998–99 school year accounted for more than 19 percent of students served under IDEA, 90 percent of them in regular classrooms.

Definitions   A *speech impairment* is a problem in delivering oral messages: repeating words, mispronouncing sounds, or speaking with inadequate breath (Turnbull et al., 1999). Speech disorders are often associated with mental retardation, cerebral palsy, cleft lip or palate, and hearing loss. According to the American Speech-Language-Hearing Association (ASHA, 1993), a *language impairment* is a problem receiving, understanding, or formulating ideas and information.

Causes   Experts recognize two kinds of speech and language disorders: *organic disorders*, which are caused by a neuromuscular problem, and *functional disorders*, which have no physical cause (Turnbull et al., 1999). An impairment that results

---

[16] A list of these programs can be found at the HEATH Resource Center Web site (www.heath.gwu.edu).

from cerebral palsy or cleft palate, for example, would be an organic disorder. Stuttering, which often is the result of emotional stress, is a functional impairment. Very stressful experiences can cause regression, and one symptom of regression is difficulty in speech or language.

Assessment   The assessment of speech and language disorders should be carried out by a qualified speech pathologist. Evaluations are both formal (using diagnostic tools) and informal (through conversation) (J. Morrison & Shriberg, 1992). A primary concern in the diagnosis of speech and language impairments is differentiating an actual disorder from the effects of bilingualism or limited proficiency in English. The key is to test a child's speech and language in the child's native language. The problem is finding a qualified speech pathologist to do the evaluation in that language. Students in the process of learning English pose a major challenge when it comes to being assessed for a disability. They are at constant risk of being misdiagnosed.

Counseling Issues   Students who have communication disorders are very likely to be ridiculed by other students. That treatment, in combination with the difficulty of understanding and being understood, contributes to their alienation and to feelings of frustration, anxiety, and anger (Van Riper & Emerick, 1984). Studies support a relationship between speech and language disorders and behavior problems (Walker, Schwartz, Nippold, Irvin, & Noell, 1994), poor social interaction (Brinton & Fujiki, 1993), and socioemotional problems (Hummel & Prizant, 1993).

Clearly, self-esteem is an issue for many youngsters with communication disorders. Glenn and Smith (1998) suggested a number of self-esteem-building activities for small groups of students with speech and language disorders:[17]

Help students explore their potential. Invite people with the same disability to talk to the group about how their disability does not limit them. The counselor can also suggest books and show videos to further expose students to role models. Students can then explore their personal strengths.

Focus on the positive. Ask students to write an autobiography, a record of their individual achievements. Have each student make a "me basket" filled with paper leaves on which he or she writes down his or her positive characteristics. Ask students to draw a "pride line," where they note how they are improving their communications with other people.

Help students set goals and objectives. Setting goals for one's self is a wonderful way to build self-esteem. Ask the students to choose something about themselves that they would like to change in a month's time, and then have them write a plan for doing that in the form of a self-improvement contract. Reward students who meet their goal.

Teach problem solving. Help students (1) recognize a problem, (2) own the problem, (3) break the problem into smaller parts, (4) gather information,

---

[17]The small group is an excellent format for youngsters with communication disorders: The group can help them feel less alone; it is a forum for sharing their feelings; and it gives them a safe place to develop strategies for coping with a world that often makes fun of them.

(5) formulate alternative solutions, (6) act on one of those solutions, and (7) evaluate the outcome. Have them role-play a conflict situation—someone bullying them, for example—to practice both their communication and problem-solving skills.

Most important the school counselor's caring acceptance of these students can make them feel that despite their difficulties communicating, they truly belong.

Mental Retardation

Definition   The definition of *mental retardation* continues to evolve. In the 1997 amendments to IDEA, the disability is defined this way:

> Mental retardation means significantly subaverage general intellectual functioning existing concurrently with deficits in adaptive behavior and manifested during the developmental period that adversely affects a child's academic performance.

The American Association on Mental Retardation (AAMR) issued its latest definition in 1992:

> Mental retardation refers to substantial limitation in present functioning. It is characterized by significantly subaverage intellectual functioning, existing concurrently with related limitations in two or more of the following applicable adaptive skills areas: communication, self-care, home living, social skills, community use, self-direction, health and safety, functional academics, leisure, and work. Mental retardation manifests itself before age 18. (Luckasson et al., 1992, p. 5)

Finally, in its *Diagnostic and Statistical Manual of Mental Disorders (DSM-IV-TR)* the American Psychiatric Association (2000) suggested that three criteria are necessary for the diagnosis of mental retardation:

A. Significantly subaverage intellectual functioning: an I.Q. approximately 70 or below on an individually administered IQ test (for infants, a clinical judgment of significantly subaverage intellectual functioning).
B. Concurrent deficits or impairments in present adaptive functioning (i.e., the person's effectiveness in meeting the standards expected for his or her age by his or her cultural groups) in at least two of the following areas: communication, self-care, home living, social/interpersonal skills, use of community resources, self-direction, functional academic skills, work, leisure, health, and safety.
C. The onset is before age 18 years. (p. 52)

All three definitions require deficits in both intellectual and adaptive functioning. The diagnosis of mental retardation is never based on IQ alone.

Once a student has been diagnosed with mental retardation, the IEP team must provide a system of support in four areas: intellectual functioning and adaptive skills, psychological and emotional considerations, physical health and etiology, and the learning environment (Turnbull et al., 1999). According to Luckasson et al. (1992), support should be provided in varying intensities:

- *Intermittent support* is provided as needed.
- *Limited support* is provided consistently over time.
- *Extensive support* is provided regularly in at least some environments.
- *Pervasive support* is provided constantly and across environments.

Prevalence   From 1 percent to 3 percent of the U.S. population has been diagnosed with mental retardation. In academic year 1998–99, 11 percent of the students served through IDEA, just over 611,000 students, had been diagnosed with mental retardation. Of those, 8 percent were in the mild category (an IQ between 50 and 69 by the *DSM-IV-TR* criteria). Between 1976 and 1992, the number of students diagnosed with mental retardation fell 39 percent. The reasons for that decrease included more-stringent classification criteria and greater sensitivity to the misdiagnosis of students from minority cultures or with limited proficiency in English (Turnbull et al., 1999). Interestingly, during the same period, diagnoses of specific learning disabilities went up 198 percent.

Causes   The specific cause of mental retardation is known in at most 50 percent of children with the disability, and it is more likely to be known in cases of severe mental retardation (Maxmen & Ward, 1995). The AAMR categorizes the causes of mental retardation by timing (prenatal, perinatal, or postnatal) and type (biomedical or psychosocial disadvantage) (Luckasson et al., 1992). Prenatal causes account for 80 percent to 85 percent of cases; perinatal and postnatal causes each account for between 5 percent and 10 percent of cases. When the cause of mild retardation is known, usually psychosocial and genetic factors are at work (Maxmen & Ward, 1995).

Assessment   Both the AAMR and the APA use IQ scores as a criterion for a diagnosis of mental retardation. The AAMR sets a range—below 70 to 75; the APA uses 70 as its cutoff. Table 7.6 lists the categories of mental retardation based on IQ level. But again, no diagnosis can be made on the basis of IQ score alone; the student also must show significant deficits in adaptive functioning.

For educational purposes, the most important part of the assessment is determining the kind and frequency of services that each student needs. The IEP should reflect the support necessary for an appropriate education.

Counseling Issues   Students diagnosed with mild mental retardation, with training and support, can interact and socialize appropriately with their nondisabled peers. The problem is the willingness of their peers to accept them. Alienation is a very real threat for students with mental retardation. To deal with this challenge, Phillips-Hershey and Ridley (1996) suggested small-group counseling for a mix of students with and without mental retardation. A diverse group can help students with mental retardation feel more secure about their interactions with others; and it can help their nondisabled peers see beyond what is different to what is very much the same.

Counseling a small group of students diagnosed with mental retardation is much like counseling any group of students—with a few special considerations.

TABLE 7.6   **CATEGORIES AND PREVALENCE OF MENTAL RETARDATION ACCORDING TO IQ LEVEL**

Category	Percent of Those with Mental Retardation	IQ Level
Mild	89.0	50–55 to approximately 70
Moderate	6.0	35–40 to 50–55
Severe	3.4	20–25 to 35–40
Profound	1.6	Below 20–25

SOURCE: Adapted from American Psychiatric Association (2000) and Maxmen and Ward (1995).

The first pertains to group rules: Students with mental retardation may have difficulty understanding the guidelines. Rules should be clear, specific, and posted in writing with functional words and pictures illustrating each rule (Phillips-Hershey & Ridley, 1996). In fact, at every stage over the life of the group, the school counselor should use visual aids to help the students who are retarded understand the group process. For example, at the first session, the counselor might use name tags or even T-shirts to help the members remember one another's names. And when students are expressing their feelings, posters showing happy or sad or puzzled faces can help the students identify what they are feeling. Cooperation is an important component of small-group activities for these students. Once the members have achieved a level of coherence, activities should require the members to cooperate. For example, they might plan a field trip, or plant and work in a school garden.

Emotional Disturbance

One of the greatest challenges for schools is to work productively with students who suffer from emotional disturbance. Many of these students act out, which leads the school to punish them, a response that only reinforces the rejection and self-hate that students with emotional disturbance feel.

Definition   The amended IDEA defines *emotional disturbance* this way:

> The term means a condition exhibiting one or more of the following characteristics over a long time and to a marked degree that adversely affects a student's educational performance:
> - An inability to learn that cannot be explained by intellectual, sensory, or other health factors
> - An inability to build or maintain satisfactory interpersonal relationships with peers and teachers
> - Inappropriate types of behavior or feelings under normal circumstances
> - A general pervasive mood of unhappiness or depression

TABLE 7.7	*DSM-IV-TR* DIAGNOSTIC CATEGORIES FOR EMOTIONAL DISTURBANCE

Category of Disorder	Diagnosis
Anxiety disorders	Phobias
	Generalized anxiety disorder
	Panic disorder
	Obsessive-compulsive disorder
	Posttraumatic stress disorder
Mood disorders	Major depression
	Bipolar disorders
Disruptive disorders	Oppositional-defiant disorder
	Conduct disorder
Psychotic disorders	Schizophrenia
Eating disorders	Anorexia nervosa
	Bulimia nervosa

- A tendency to develop physical symptoms or fears associated with personal or school problems

The term includes schizophrenia. The term does not apply to children who are socially maladjusted, unless it is determined that they have an emotional disturbance.

This definition leaves room for disagreement about what constitutes emotional disturbance. In one place it states that the "inability to build or maintain satisfactory interpersonal relationships" is a criterion; in another, it rejects social maladjustment as a criterion. What is clear, however, is that the disturbance must be shown to affect the student's learning.

The use of the term *emotional disturbance* complicates matters. The label is general: It can easily be attached to students who are simply difficult. Table 7.7 lists some of the more common mental health disorders that can qualify as emotional disturbance.

Prevalence In the 1998–99 school year, 463,262 students nationwide were classified as emotionally disturbed and received services under IDEA. That number constituted 8.4 percent of the population served by the act and a little less than 1.0 percent of all school-aged children. Although African American students are overrepresented in this category (26.4 percent of the special education population versus 14.8 percent of the general population ages 6 through 21), there is general consensus that students with emotional disturbance are underidentified and underserved (Burns & Friedman, 1990). Walker and Bullis (1991) suggested five reasons that schools fail to meet the needs of students with emotional disorders:

- Schools are generally reluctant to serve students with conduct disorders. These students are seen as troublemakers rather than disabled by behavioral disturbance.
- Federal constraints make it difficult to discipline students through suspension and expulsion if they are classified as emotionally disturbed.
- Because many students with emotional disturbance are educated in separate settings, there are significant costs associated with labeling a child emotionally disturbed.
- There is a general insensitivity to anxiety, depression, and other mental health disorders.
- The diagnosis of emotional disturbance is often a subjective one, leaving open the possibility of misdiagnosis.

Causes   Most agree that emotional disturbance is caused by genetic, biological, or environmental factors. In roughly 50 percent of cases of mental illness, genetics seems to play a role. Today there is a strong movement to acknowledge a link between emotional disturbance and biological causes, among them a difficult birth, traumatic brain injury, or childhood illness. Certainly the almost immediate use of medication to treat these children and adolescents speaks to a bias in favor of biological causes.

Most experts recognize an interaction between environmental stress and genetics. When a child is genetically predisposed to emotional disturbance, an environmental stressor—for example parental substance abuse, violence, child abuse— can trigger an emotional episode.

Assessment   The assessment of emotional disturbance usually includes a battery of psychological tests. A projective test like the Rorschach, the Thematic Apperception Test, or Tell Me a Story is administered to uncover any internal conflicts that could substantiate emotional disturbance. An achievement test must be administered to provide evidence that the emotional disturbance is affecting learning. Along with formal testing, direct observation of the student's behavior is essential. Behavioral responses need to be assessed for frequency, duration, latency (how long it takes for the behavior to begin), topography (the shape of the response), and magnitude (the intensity of the response) (Turnbull et al., 1999). The student should be observed at different times of the day, in different settings (at school and at home), and interacting with different people (teachers, peers, and parents one on one and in small and large groups).

The assessment of emotional disturbance is a delicate process because the diagnosis involves at least some subjectivity. If school administrators insist that a student is just a troublemaker, they may very well influence the assessment. In the role of advocate, the school counselor must look beyond the negativity often directed at students who act out and make sure that they are receiving necessary and appropriate services.

Counseling Issues   Counseling students with emotional disturbance requires dedication, patience, and unconditional regard. By its very definition, emotional disturbance is chronic, and counselors should not expect a sudden, magical turn-around in the behavior of these students. Many bring with them a history of abuse and other environmental stressors that prevent them from establishing trusting relationships with caring adults.

There are two schools of thought about working with students whose emotional disturbance manifests in inappropriate behaviors. Some believe that this population should be treated with strict behavioral modification. Setting clear limits and enforcing the consequences for bad behavior are crucial to this approach. The perception that this population is extremely manipulative and has great difficulty establishing emotional rapport with anyone means little emphasis on establishing a bond with these youngsters.

Others argue that children with emotional disturbance have a history of behaviors that evoke rejection from those around them. They develop a negative self-image and lose hope that anyone can love or accept them for who they are. In time they may willfully engage in behaviors to elicit responses that confirm their view of self. The solution is not behavior modification, these authorities insist, but a more humanistic approach that focuses on replacing the students' negative self-image with a more positive one. Counselors are encouraged to be patient, to practice unconditional positive regard, and to respond to students' behavior with acceptance and caring. Cochran and Cochran (1997) discovered that students with conduct disorders are not angry so much as fearful, lonely, anxious, and feeling powerless. The key to effective intervention is to understand why these students misbehave and then to respond in an unexpected way. The counseling relationship must provide evidence that the students' beliefs about self ("I'm unlovable"; "I will be rejected") are not correct (Cochran & Cochran, 1999).

Collaboration with teachers and parents is very important in working with students who are emotionally disturbed. They, too, need to analyze the child's behavior and to respond to it in new ways. The parents in particular must set limits for their child and hold the child accountable for the consequences of his or her behavior. Change here can be slow, and the need for consistency, coupled with what seem to be constant complaints from the school, can wear parents down. The school counselor's job is to advocate for the child and to work with the parents to provide needed services to the child and support for the parents.

With the emphasis on inclusion, students who are emotionally disturbed are moving from separate settings into the regular classroom. Still, many of these students are referred for outside counseling. It is important for the school counselor to establish a working relationship with the outside counselor as well, to ensure consistency in the goals and methods of intervention.

Peer mediation is another way to work with youngsters who are emotionally disturbed. Many of these students have serious conflicts with adults, which means it may be easier to reach them through their peers. If the school has a peer mediation program, the school counselor should encourage students with emotional disturbances to take part. If the school does not have a program, the counselor can lobby for one. These programs have proved effective in reducing dropout rates (Millhause, 1989), suspensions (McDonald & Moriarity, 1990), and student assaults (Meek, 1992).

Attention Deficit Hyperactivity Disorder

Attention deficit hyperactivity disorder (ADHD) is now the most common psychiatric disorder diagnosed among children (Bramlett, Nelson, & Reeves, 1997). Professionals journals are filled with articles about ADHD, and controversy abounds around the diagnosis and treatment of the disorder.

ADHD and Special Education   The Individuals with Disabilities Education Act does not list ADHD as a disability that qualifies a student for services. That omission led to a great deal of confusion when the act initially was passed in 1990. In 1991, the U.S. Department of Education issued a policy clarification memorandum, which explained that children diagnosed with ADHD could be eligible for special education services under three categories: other health impairments, specific learning disabilities, and emotional disturbance (Davila, Williams, & McDonald, 1991). The Department of Education maintained then and now that ADHD by itself is not enough to qualify a student for special education services. It must be shown that ADHD prevents the child from benefiting from regular education through one of the three categories.

ADHD is common among children with learning disabilities: It is estimated that 33 percent of those diagnosed with learning disabilities have ADHD (Turnbull et al., 1999), and that between 10 percent and 26 percent of children diagnosed with ADHD also have a specific learning disability (Barkley, 1990). The relationship between ADHD and emotional disturbance is even stronger: Estimates are that between 30 percent and 65 percent of youngsters with ADHD also have a serious emotional disturbance (Turnbull et al., 1999)—most commonly oppositional-defiant disorder, conduct disorder, anxiety and mood disorders, and personality disorders (T. E. Brown, 1994; Stanford & Hynd, 1994).

Those students diagnosed with ADHD who do not qualify for services under IDEA are protected by Section 504 of the Rehabilitation Act of 1973 and the Americans with Disabilities Act (ADA) of 1990. The Rehabilitation Act guarantees "reasonable accommodation" for children with a physical or mental impairment that severely limits one or more major life activities. The ADA also requires reasonable and appropriate accommodations for those with disabilities, and ADHD is considered a disability. To comply with these laws, school districts offer 504 or ADA plans developed by a team that decides what accommodations are necessary (Fossey, Hosie, & Zirkel, 1995). Usually accommodations take the form of a quiet room and unlimited time for taking standardized tests. Protections and services under the Rehabilitation Act and the ADA extend beyond high school into college and graduate school.

Definition   The most widely accepted definition of ADHD is from the *DSM-IV-TR* (American Psychiatric Association, 2000). Table 7.8 lists the diagnostic criteria.

In general, children with ADHD respond to situations based more on feeling than fact (Turnbull et al., 1999). They sense that time is moving more slowly than it actually does, which results in frequent lateness and procrastination. Because they have a difficult time internalizing and privatizing the world around them,

A. Either (1) or (2):

(1) six (or more) of the following symptoms of **inattention** have persisted for at least 6 months to a degree that is maladaptive and inconsistent with developmental level:

Inattention

(a) often fails to give close attention to details or makes careless mistakes in schoolwork, work, or other activities

(b) often has difficulty sustaining attention in tasks or play activities

(c) often does not seem to listen when spoken to directly

(d) often does not follow through on instructions and fails to finish school work, chores, or duties in the workplace (not due to oppositional behavior or failure to understand instructions)

(e) often has difficulty organizing tasks and activities

(f) often avoids, dislikes, or is reluctant to engage in tasks that require sustained mental effort (such as school work or homework)

(g) often loses things necessary for tasks or activities (e.g., toys, school assignments, pencils, books, or tools)

(h) is often easily distracted by extraneous stimuli

(i) is often forgetful in daily activities

(2) six (or more) of the following symptoms of **hyperactivity-impulsivity** have persisted for at least 6 months to a degree that is maladaptive and inconsistent with developmental level:

Hyperactivity

(a) often fidgets with hands or feet or squirms in seat

(b) often leaves seat in classroom or in other situations in which remaining seated is expected

(c) often runs about or climbs excessively in situations in which it is inappropriate (in adolescents or adults, may be limited to subjective feelings of restlessness)

(d) often has difficulty playing or engaging in leisure activities quietly

(e) is often "on the go" or often acts as if "driven by a motor"

(f) often talks excessively

Impulsivity

(g) often blurts out answers before questions have been completed

(h) often has difficulty waiting

(i) often interrupts or intrudes on others (e.g., butts into conversations or games)

B. Some hyperactive-impulsive or inattentive symptoms that caused impairment were present before age 7 years.

C. Some impairment from the symptoms is present in two or more settings (e.g., at school [or work] and at home).

D. There must be clear evidence of clinically significant impairment in social, academic, or occupational functioning.

E. The symptoms do not occur exclusively during the course of a Pervasive Developmental Disorder, Schizophrenia, or other Psychotic Disorder and are not better accounted for by another mental disorder (e.g., Mood Disorder, Anxiety Disorder, Dissociative Disorder, or a Personality Disorder).

SOURCE: Reprinted with permission from the *Diagnostic and Statistic Manual of Mental Disorders, Fourth Edition, Text Revision.* Copyright 2000 American Psychiatric Association.

youngsters with ADHD talk a lot (Barkley, 1995). ADHD children also have difficulty analyzing and synthesizing information and generating a variety of solutions to a problem. On the other hand, people with ADHD can be highly imaginative and intuitive, able to accomplish the extraordinary because they learn, know, and do by touch and feel (Hallowell, 1996). Because they make connections randomly instead of systematically, people with ADHD also are capable of finding unique and innovative solutions to problems (Turnbull et al., 1999).

Prevalence   According to Children and Adults with Attention Deficit Disorders (Ch.A.D.D., 1995), ADHD affects 3 percent to 5 percent of the school-aged population, approximately 2 million children. In years past, boys outnumbered girls nine to one, but more and more girls are being diagnosed with ADHD. Currently, boys outnumber girls three to one. The dramatic increase in children diagnosed with ADHD has evoked responses from two opposing camps. One group argues that the disorder is being overdiagnosed, that the ADHD label has become a catchall for children who are more active than the norm. The other group argues that ADHD, long ignored and misunderstood, is finally being recognized as a legitimate disability that affects learning. In fact, in 1995 the Ch.A.D.D. organization estimated that 50 percent of children with ADHD go undiagnosed. The prevalence of ADHD will continue to be debated as long as there is inconsistency in the identification and diagnosis of the disorder.

Causes   The recent increase in diagnosed cases of ADHD has created an ADHD mythology that blames the disorder on everything from too much sugar to too little sugar, food sensitivity, food additives, lack of vitamins, television, video games, yeast, lightening, and fluorescent lighting (Baren, 1994; Turnbull et al., 1999). Studies have tried to link poor parenting or poor discipline to ADHD but without success (Erk, 1995). Poor parenting seems to be more the result than a cause of ADHD (Barkley, 1995).

Most experts agree that ADHD is probably produced by a combination of biological factors. Turnbull et al. (1999) divided the biological causes of ADHD into three types: genetics; pre-, peri-, and postnatal trauma; and brain differences.

GENETICS   Genetics appears to be a major factor in ADHD. Identical twins have twice the concordance rate for ADHD than do fraternal twins (Ch.A.D.D., 1996), and 30 percent to 40 percent of those diagnosed with ADHD have a relative with the same condition (Baren, 1994). Currently researchers are trying to determine whether a particular gene is responsible for ADHD. If ADHD is seen along a continuum, we all have symptoms of the disorder, but those who exhibit symptoms beyond society's tolerance threshold receive a formal diagnosis (Barkley, 1995).

PRE-, PERI-, AND POSTNATAL TRAUMA   Complications before, during, or after birth contribute to the likelihood of a child's developing ADHD. In cases where the mother has ADHD too, her condition may have inhibited proper care (Barkley, 1995). In these cases, heredity would appear to be the stronger factor than a complication of pregnancy or childbirth (Turnbull et al., 1999). Alcohol and other drugs, smoking, poor nutrition, and exposure to chemical poison during pregnancy can all increase the likelihood of a child's developing ADHD (Baren, 1994). Studies on the relationship between mothers' behaviors during pregnancy and ADHD continue, and firm conclusions have yet to be reached. Postnatal trauma—including brain injuries, exposure to chemicals, infections, and anemia—have all been linked to ADHD (Baren, 1994).

BRAIN DIFFERENCES   The most compelling research in this area in recent years has examined differences in the brains of children with and without ADHD. Several studies have found that the regions of the brain used for paying attention or keeping still are less active in children with ADHD (measured by rate of glucose metabolism) (Barkley, 1990; Goldstein & Goldstein, 1990). Studies also have found that in children with ADHD, there is less blood flow in the premotor and prefrontal areas of the brain, areas that connect to the limbic system (Lou, Henriksen, Bruhn, & Borner, 1989; Riccio, Hynd, Cohen, & Gonzalez, 1993). In addition, electroencephalogram studies have shown that ADHD children have more activity in the right hemisphere of the frontal lobe than in the left (Crawford & Barabasz, 1996). Finally, studies have shown that dopamine and norepinephrine—two neurotransmitters responsible for vigilance and attention—exist in lower levels among children with ADHD than among children without the disorder (Barabasz & Barabasz, 1996). Both stimulants and antidepressants that affect the activity of these neurotransmitters have been shown to improve behavior and concentration (Hallowell & Ratey, 1995).

Assessment   Some children are diagnosed by a pediatrician, a psychiatrist, or a psychologist before they enter school. In those cases, the school's evaluation team must determine how the disorder is affecting the child's learning and socialization. If the team determines that ADHD is having a negative effect on learning, special services are provided. In cases where the school is the first to diagnose ADHD, the student should then be sent to a pediatrician or psychiatrist to confirm the diagnosis and to determine if medication is necessary.

The assessment of ADHD in the school must be multimodal. The formal assessment should include a rating scale that specifically identifies the characteristics of ADHD.[18] In the absence of a standard method for diagnosing ADHD, formal assessment methods are an important means of eliminating subjectivity. But informal assessment—interviews with teachers, parents, peers, and the student, and observation in and out of class (Schwiebert, Sealander, & Tolerud, 1995)—should be used as well.

ADHD has become a popular label, which means school personnel must be careful not to use it haphazardly. When the assessment process indicates that a stu-

---

[18] The Attention Deficit Disorders Evaluation Scale (McCarney, 1989) is designed specifically to assess ADHD. Other scales assess ADHD and other disorders. For example, see the Child Behavior Checklist, Conner's Parent and Teacher Rating Scales, the SNAP Checklist, the Revised Behavior Checklist, and the Comprehensive Behavior Rating Scale (Sealander et al., 1993). Some evaluators also use Continuous Performance Tests (CPTs) to help with the diagnosis of ADHD (Turnbull et al., 1999). These computerized tests, by asking students to repeatedly click the mouse in response to instruction, determine students' capacity for attention.

dent has ADHD, the school counselor should suggest the student have a complete physical and a psychological examination. Only when both confirm the diagnosis should the ADHD label be used.

Treatment   The most common forms of treatment for ADHD are pharmacological and behavioral.

PHARMACOLOGICAL TREATMENT   In recent years, medication has become the treatment of choice for most children diagnosed with ADHD. Studies have shown that between 60 percent and 80 percent of children with ADHD respond favorably to medication (Henker & Whalen, 1989; Reeve, 1990; Whalen et al., 1987). The often dramatic results of drugs have led schools to encourage parents to medicate their children. Many parents who are reluctant to put their children on medication eventually do so, a response to pressure from the school or even to being overwhelmed themselves by their child's behavior. Others simply refuse. It is important to note that not all children with ADHD are helped through pharmacological treatment, and that the medications do have side effects.

According to Dulcan and Lizarralde (2003), the most common drugs used to treat ADHD are methylphenidate (Ritalin, Metadate, Methylin, and Concerta), dextroamphetamine (Dexedrine), and a mixture of amphetamines (Adderall). All are stimulants and are now available in longer-acting forms that can last up to eight hours. Concerta and Adderall XR can last up to 12 hours. Of all of these, Ritalin is the medication of choice for more than 90 percent of the children with ADHD who receive stimulant medication. Antidepressants are used much less frequently, usually only in cases where stimulants have produced serious side effects.

The common side effects of stimulant medication include insomnia, decreased appetite, gastrointestinal pain, irritability, and increased heart rate (not clinically significant). Uncommon side effects include psychosis, feelings of sadness or isolation, major depressive episodes, cognitive impairment, growth retardation, tick disorders, increased heart rate (clinically significant), increased blood pressure, nausea or constipation, dizziness, lethargy or fatigue, rash or hives, heightened hearing, and skin sensation (Sweeney, Forness, Kavale, & Levitt, 1997).

Side effects are one problem with medicating children; another is the tendency for school personnel and parents to use medication as a panacea (Turnbull et al., 1999). Although the short-term effects of stimulants on controlling activity and improving general behavior are well documented, research also suggests that medication as the sole treatment for ADHD is inadequate (Abikoff & Gittelman, 1985; Whalen, Henker, & Hinshaw, 1985). Psychostimulants may control behavior in the short term, but they do not increase academic achievement or antisocial behavior over the long term (Turnbull et al., 1999). Stimulants help children pay attention more, but they do not force them to do their homework or teach them social skills (Koplewicz, 1996).

BEHAVIORAL TREATMENT   Repeatedly, studies have shown that when medication is combined with behavioral management, the results are better than for medication alone (Ajibola & Clement, 1995; Gittelman et al., 1980; Pelham et al., 1988). For example, a system of rewards for on-task behavior, especially when tasks are broken down into manageable subtasks, has proved useful. So have cognitive-behavioral strategies to teach self-monitoring and self-reinforcement along with problem solving (Schwiebert, Sealander, & Tolerud, 1995). The challenge of behavioral treatment is getting all parties—especially teachers and parents—to participate in the program. A teacher or parent who sees the ingestion of psychostimulants as the only way to help a child with ADHD is actually doing a disservice to the child. Behavioral management should be used as an adjunct to medication. Where medication has only a short-term impact, behavioral management teaches skills and strategies that will serve children with ADHD well into their adult years.

Counseling Issues   School counselors can contribute to the education of children with ADHD by working individually or in small groups with the students themselves, their parents, and their teachers. The first task is to become as knowledgeable as possible about ADHD so they can provide information about the disorder to all three groups. In a statewide survey, Kottman, Robert, and Baker (1995) found that the strongest need expressed by parents of children with ADHD was consistent, credible information.[19]

Erk (1999) recommended the following behavioral strategies for parents and teachers to employ with ADHD children:

- Praise the students, especially when they are on task.
- Teach positive self-talk, so that the students learn to reward and praise themselves.
- Have students rehearse appropriate behaviors.
- Use positive reinforcement.
- Use time-outs for inappropriate behavior.
- Allow the students to choose from an agreed-on list of privileges or activities they will forfeit if they don't stay on task or follow rules.
- Let students earn special privileges for their on-task behavior.
- Empathize.
- Model positive behaviors.

In addition to these behavioral interventions, counselors can also work on self-esteem issues and teach basic social skills to children with ADHD. Unfortunately, many of these youngsters don't have friends because their peers find the ADHD behavior intolerable. Of course, this in turn contributes to the youngsters' lack of self-esteem.

Career Counseling   Between 25 percent and 35 percent of students with ADHD fail to complete high school (Barkley, 1990); yet more and more students with ADHD are continuing their education beyond high school. School counselors can play a key role in preparing students with ADHD for college. They should be sure that included in each student's file is an accurate academic summary that focuses on needs and recommendations (Schwiebert, Sealander, & Bradshaw, 1998). That summary both provides evidence of the student's eligibility to the college or

---

[19]See Lucker and Molloy (1995) for an excellent list of books, workbooks, and videos to help parents, teachers, and counselors understand and work with children with ADHD.

university and helps the institution plan for the student's academic accommodations (Richard, 1995). The school counselor should also work with students to be sure they are completing the necessary courses to get into college (Schwiebert, Sealander, & Bradshaw, 1998). Also, some colleges are willing to waive certain academic requirements, and the counselor needs to know what they are.

Through high school, the school system is responsible for identifying and providing services for students with a disability that affects learning. After graduation, this responsibility shifts to the student (Schwiebert, Sealander, & Bradshaw, 1998). Students may be reluctant to reveal their disability and ask for needed accommodations. School counselors can rehearse scenarios with them in which the students practice identifying themselves and asking for what they need.

Role-play can also help students who are making the transition from school to work. In addition to helping students act out situations in which they both listen and then speak persuasively, the school counselor can help students organize their ideas and information. Again, youngsters with ADHD have special talents and capabilities that are often masked by their disability. In providing vocational counseling, the school counselor can help these students reveal their uniqueness to a prospective employer.

ETHICAL AND LEGAL ISSUES

In this chapter we maintain that disability can and should be understood within the context of multicultural counseling. Our premise is that the cultures of ability and disability reflect the same dominant versus nondominant dynamic as cultures of race (White versus People of Color). Much of what was said in Chapter 6, then, about the ethics of multicultural counseling can be applied to counseling students with disabilities.

Counselors who are not disabled are part of the dominant group (that is, the "abled") that has traditionally defined what is best for the nondominant group (the "disabled"). This is especially true in education, where groups of special educators define for parents what is best for their special-needs child. When working with students who have disabilities and their families, a more ethical stance for the school counselor is to treat the collaboration as the coming together of two different cultures, a dominant and a nondominant culture. Within that context, the role of the counselor is to empower the members of the nondominant culture—students with disabilities.

The first step in the empowerment process is to understand and appreciate a different way of being in the world, what life is like for a child with a disability. There is no room here for sympathy: It is impossible to feel sorry for youngsters and at the same time try to empower them. The ethical practitioner must ask, "What can I learn from this student to better understand my own socialization as an able-bodied person so as not to impose a set of values produced by that socialization?"

Compliance with special education laws does not translate into ethical practice. School counselors, trained in issues of cultural diversity, understand that the presence of students with disabilities in their schools is an opportunity for enrichment for themselves and for all of the students with whom they work.

CONCLUSION

The goal of this chapter was to sensitize school counselors in training to the many challenges and rewards in working with students who have disabilities. The starting point: that students with disabilities belong to a nondominant culture and so bring diversity to the school environment that benefits them and their nondisabled peers. That basic understanding colors the counselor's interactions with students with disabilities, their parents, their teachers, and their nondisabled peers.

The chapter began with an examination of the Individuals with Disabilities Education Act, the law that defines the school's responsibilities to students with disabilities, and then a description of the population served under IDEA and the settings in which the members of that population learn.

Inclusion is one of the principles that underlies IDEA. From that commitment to teach all students in the regular classroom, to reinvent the regular classroom, has come an emphasis on collaboration: The school counselor must work with teachers, parents, and students to ensure that the resources and services to help students with disabilities learn are available and provided consistently.

The chapter ends with a discussion of the most prevalent groups of students with disabilities—those with specific learning disabilities, speech and language impairments, mental retardation, emotional disturbance, and ADHD—and a look at the challenges of assessing and counseling the students in each group.

The law in this country mandates special education for students with disabilities. For some, that is an imposition. But for others, it is an opportunity.

Recently a former student of mine, a certified special education teacher, told me about her first-year experience cooperative teaching with a regular education teacher. When they were working in the same classroom, they complemented and reinforced each other, and so showed the students how one person can see and appreciate the gifts of another. Today the two teachers are best friends. I was struck by the fact that their work with two different populations in the same classroom brought the two women together into a friendship, that it was the diversity of their classroom that united them. What a wonderful lesson: Disability brings diversity, and diversity is a gift to all of us.

QUESTIONS FOR DISCUSSION

1. The Individuals with Disabilities Education Act (IDEA) forever changed the face of public education in the United States. Which three changes seem most significant to you? Why?

2. Some insist that IDEA has created a huge and wasteful bureaucracy; others argue that not enough is being done to help children with disabilities. What do you think about special education in this country? How would you improve or change the system?

3. You came to this subject with some understanding of special education. How does the dynamic of dominant culture (the "abled") versus nondominant culture (the "disabled") change that understanding? Discuss practical ways of implementing your new understanding?

4. Discuss the conflict between appropriate education and least restrictive environment. How do you think a school counselor can balance advocacy for these two fundamental principles?

5. Discuss the difference between mainstreaming and inclusion. What is your reaction to the reinvention of schools to allow children with disabilities and their nondisabled peers to be together as much as possible? What do you see as the role of the school counselor in inclusion? In your answers, think about the effects of cultural diversity.

6. Medicating children is a controversial topic in this country. Some argue that drugs are helping children get an education that otherwise would be denied them. Other say that children are being overmedicated to enrich the drug companies and to relieve parents and teachers of the burden of dealing with difficult youngsters. What do you think about using psychostimulants to treat and educate children with ADHD?

7. Suppose a teacher or administrator asked you to talk to the parents of a child with ADHD to convince them to medicate their child. How would you respond? Why? Is there a way to simply present the facts without pressuring the parents to give the child drugs? With a partner, role-play a meeting between counselor and parent.

SUGGESTED INTERNET SITES

www.ed.gov/offices/OSERS/OSEP/

The official Web site of the Office of Special Education Programs contains a simple, easy-to understand summary of the basic special education process under IDEA, including a useful guide to IEPs; a section of frequently asked questions by parents, counselors, and administrators; and information about resources.

www.nichcy.org

The official Web site of the National Information Center for Children and Youth with Disabilities, an information and referral center for families and for educators and other professionals who deal with disability-related issues, offers information on specific disabilities, early intervention, special education and related services, IEPs, family rights, disability organizations, education rights, and transition to adulthood. Links are provided to specific laws, including the Americans with Disabilities Act, and to professional organizations. A comprehensive and useful site.

www.childdevelopmentinfo.com/learning

This site is dedicated to specific learning disabilities. It contains descriptions of disabilities, materials to help children with learning disabilities learn, a list of early warning signs, and suggestions for dealing with the effects on parents of discovering that their child has a learning disability. The site is linked to the Child Development Institute, which offers a wealth of information on development, disorders, learning, parenting, and the health and safety of children with disabilities.

www.chadd.org

The official Web site of Children and Adults with Attention Deficit Disorders, contains a wealth of information and resources related to ADD, as well as links to many online publications. The information is offered in both English and Spanish.

Separation and Loss in School-Aged Children

The impact of loss and separation on children has been underappreciated. One major reason for this is that many adults—parents and counselors alike—have difficulty themselves dealing with death and other forms of loss. But the failure to help children work through their grief has enormous consequences. Studies show that as many as 50 percent of children who need psychological help have experienced a loss (Fox, 1984). Rafael (1983) found that the symptoms of bereaved children five or more years after experiencing a loss included guilt, depressive withdrawal, self-punitive and accident-prone behaviors, fear of death, distorted ideas about illness, and difficulties in cognitive functioning. And the effects of unresolved grief can persist into adulthood. For example, Kastenbaum (1981) found that adults who had experienced the loss of a parent in childhood tend to be more submissive, dependent, introverted, maladjusted, suicidal, and prone to antisocial behaviors (shoplifting and petty theft, for example) compared with those who did not lose a parent. Some studies have even suggested a direct link between cancer and childhood loss (Francis, 1998; Rafael, 1983).

The statistics around separation and loss describe the extent of the problem. In 2000, 22 percent of children lived with their mother only, 4 percent lived with their father only; and 4 percent lived with neither parent (Kids Count, 2002). Approximately, 750,000 children live in a single-parent home because the other parent has died (O'Connell, 1997). The government estimates that each year 228,000 children and young adults die in the United States (Compassionate Friends, 1999); about 40,000 families each year experience the death of a child under the age of 15 (Minino & Smith, 2001). In 1999, 75 percent of all deaths among 15- to 19-year-olds were by accident, homicide, or suicide (Kids Count, 2002). In an early study, Ewalt and Perkins (1979) found that 90 percent of junior and high school students had experienced a death—40 percent had lost a close friend, and 20 percent had witnessed a death.

When we consider other losses, the numbers are even more alarming. For example, 40 percent of all children—about 1.5 million children each year—experience parental divorce (National Institutes of Health, 2002). The rates of loss go up when we include what is called *disenfranchised grief*—the loss of a pet or a

TABLE 8.1   **A GLOSSARY OF TERMS USED IN DISCUSSING LOSS**

Term	Definition
bereavement	The state of being caused by a loss (Wolfelt, 1983).
disenfranchised grief	Grief that people experience from a loss that is not, or cannot be, openly acknowledged, publicly mourned, or socially supported (Doka, 1989; Lenhardt, 1997).
grief	The emotional suffering caused by a death or bereavement (Wolfelt, 1983).
grief work	The activities involved in working through a loss (Wolfelt, 1983).
mourning	Usually, the culture-sanctioned rituals one undertakes after a significant loss (Charkow, 1998; Wolfelt, 1983).

romantic relationship, of having a disability, or of coming from a dysfunctional family. (Table 8.1 defines several terms used in discussions of loss.)

In many ways, loss is part of children's development, and helping them cope with loss is an important part of the school counselor's job. Because of their training, school counselors recognize the devastating consequences of denial around issues of loss and the healthy consequences of allowing children to grieve openly and honestly. But before they can work effectively with students who are grieving, counselors must resolve their own losses. This chapter is written from a double perspective: to help school counselors understand the dynamics of loss for children and for themselves.

LOSS THROUGH DEATH

For many of us, just the mention of death activates a series of mechanisms ranging from avoidance to rationalization. For some, *death* evokes painful memories; for many more, it evokes fear. When death touches children, the pain can be made more intense by the inability to express grief. Children tend to disguise their grief, allowing adults to believe they are unaffected by the loss and coping just fine. But often they are not. In the absence of counseling services that could help them grieve in adaptive ways, much of children's grief around death goes unresolved. A good deal of the blame for this lies with adults who lack the maturity or understanding to recognize children's pain and to talk with them about death. And sometimes circumstances intervene: When a family member dies, for example, the child's parents are also grieving, which can leave them without the emotional strength or the focus to help their child. This is where the school counselor can play a special role: helping children grieve.

Death and Culture

Many of the difficulties we face in dealing with death are cultural: Our culture does not prepare us for death; in fact, it promotes what Ernst Becker (1973) called the *denial of death*. In Chapter 6 we noted how the White, male, Eurocentric culture believes in controlling nature and natural forces. Death is a biological fact and a law of nature. Although intellectually we understand that ultimately we have no control over death, many of us have difficulty accepting that lack of control emotionally.[1] When death touches us, then, we don't experience it as a natural force but as some sort of failure. Death challenges a fundamental assumption in our culture by forcing us to recognize that we do not control our destiny. People from cultures that accept the natural order have an easier time accepting death and the grieving process.

Religion contributes to the cultural differences that surround death and grieving, and counselors should understand and respect families' religious beliefs when counseling children who have lost someone to death:[2]

- Find out from the child's family what its members believe about the nature of death and expectations of an afterlife.
- Learn about the rituals of mourning in the family's faith. Christian religions tend to minimize those rituals; others encourage families to grieve openly and for long periods.
- Find out if there are any gender rules about dealing with death; if there are, respect them.
- Help the child determine his or her own way to commemorate the death of a loved one.

Finally, although religion can be an important source of help for families dealing with a death, it can also contribute to the denial of death. When adults tell children that "Grandpa went to a better place," they communicate to the children that their pain is unwarranted. School counselors can help parents use religion, not to minimize grief, but to find support there for talking about their child's pain.

To work effectively with children who have suffered a loss through death, school counselors must challenge their own cultural assumptions—that is, they have to acknowledge that death is something that they cannot control and to give up the defense mechanisms that prevent them from responding to children's grief.

Childhood Development and Death

As they grow, children's understanding of death changes. There is considerable disagreement among developmentalists about when children acquire the capacity to mourn. According to Bowlby (1963, 1980), infants at 6 months can mirror the grief

---

[1] In today's society, the denial of death is only exacerbated by the miracles of modern medicine and increased longevity.

[2] These recommendations have been adapted from McGoldrick et al. (1991).

reactions of adults. Wolfenstein (1966), on the other hand, believed children do not mourn until adolescence, when the ego is fully differentiated. R. Furman (1964) argued—and his thinking is widely accepted—that children develop the capacity to mourn between the ages of 3½ and 4.

Infants and Toddlers   From birth to about age 5, children do not understand that death is permanent. For them, it is like going to sleep or taking a trip. So they often ask, "When is _____ coming back?" Magical thinking, a component of pre-operational thought, can also be a factor here. Many young children believe that if they simply wish the dead person back, he or she will come back. Children at this age also tend to personalize everything that happens in their life, which can lead them to blame themselves for the absence of the loved one. All of these developmental factors can combine in what seems to be an indifference toward death that puzzles or upsets adults (Costa & Holliday, 1994).

Preoperational children are also very literal, which means they tend to interpret concretely the euphemisms adults typically use to talk about death. To "We lost Grandpa," for example, a young child might respond with "Where did he go?" or "When will we find him?" In response to "Grandpa went to sleep," the child might ask, "When will he wake up?" And if the child is told that Grandpa will not wake up, he or she may be terrified of going to sleep for fear of not waking up.

Jarrat (1994) suggested the following list of important things to say to very young children who have suffered a loss:

- "Someone [name who, preferably] will take care of you. [If it is not going to be you, continue . . .] It will not be me, but I will stay with you until [name] is here to keep you safe."
- "It was not your fault. It was not because you were bad in any way or because you were unlovable. There is nothing you could have done, or can do, to make things different."
- "It is OK for you to know about what happened, to think about it , and to figure it out."
- "You can have your own feelings about what has happened. You may feel differently from other people, even those you live with. No one can tell you what you feel or what you should feel."
- "You can take as much time as you need to figure things out and have your own feelings. You do not have to rush or pretend that you don't think or feel as you do." (pp. 9–10)

Although very young children do not understand that death is permanent, they do experience loss and the changes that take place when a family member dies. According to Grollman (1995), these children may regress to earlier behaviors (thumb sucking or bed-wetting, for example), become irritable, or develop bowel or bladder disturbances. They can also become very fearful, afraid to go to preschool or to sleep, and cling to their caregivers. The children's primary caregiver should watch for these behaviors, understand them as a reaction to loss, and use them as an opportunity to allow the child to grieve openly.

School-Aged Children   From the age of 6 to around the age of 12, children stop thinking magically and begin to think concretely (Imhelder & Piaget, 1958). Youngsters in this stage want to know the details of the death and are apt to ask questions like "What happens to the body?" and "How did they know he was dead?" (Costa & Holliday, 1994). These kinds of questions can be uncomfortable or even difficult for adults to answer, but they need answering. An acceptable way to explain death to children in this age group is to say: "_____'s body stopped working, and it will not work again."

Children at this stage understand that death is final, that it is not simply another form of sleep. But according to Grollman (1995), until age 9, children have difficulty accepting the idea that death happens to everyone, especially themselves. Around age 10, they begin to understand that death is both universal and inevitable, and that can frighten and upset them. When a loved one dies, children at this age "may have difficulty concentrating, exhibit a decline in the quality of their school work, become withdrawn and isolated from family and friends, and seem persistently angry and sad. They often have physical complaints with constant fatigue and frequent drowsiness" (Grollman, 1995, p. 6).

The most effective intervention—before or after symptoms develop—is allowing children to talk about the death and their feelings. Here, too, it is important to avoid euphemism and ambiguity. Phrases like *passed on, was lost,* or *went away on a long journey* are deceptive and confusing for children who are thinking concretely, and are likely to be met with a question like "Why didn't Grandpa say goodbye before he left?"

Theological explanations—"God wanted (needed) Daddy in heaven" can also confuse and even cause resentment or anger in children: "He is *my father.* Why did God want *my* father?" And often they stop youngsters from exploring and revealing their feelings about the death of a loved one.

Most important, the school counselors does well to keep in mind the three questions that children in this stage of development tend to ask themselves when someone they love has died:

- Did I cause it? Is it my fault?
- Who will take care of me?
- Will it happen to me?

Adolescents   Death is no stranger to adolescents in this country. Again, by the time they reach high school, 90 percent of adolescents have experienced death, 40 percent of them the death of a friend or peer.

Complicating the grieving process for adolescents is the variability of their reactions to loss. They are quite capable of understanding, at least intellectually, that death is universal and inevitable; but that understanding contradicts some of what they are feeling—so alive and with so much to live for (Balk & Corr, 1996). Their ambivalence toward death may explain why teenagers engage in high-risk behaviors, almost as though they are trying to "cheat" death. According to Corr (1995), "there are compelling forces at work in adolescent life that militate against the willingness and ability of adolescents to grasp the significance of their own mortality" (p.28). Adolescents may even fantasize about death, seeing it as an adventure from which they will be able to escape in the final minutes (Kandt, 1994).

A major obstacle to helping adolescents cope with death is their tendency to turn to their peers in times of trouble. That adolescents turn away from adults does not mean, however, that they are not aware of them. Quite the contrary. Therefore, school counselors (and parents) can help adolescents cope with death by modeling good coping behaviors. The use of support groups and peer counselors can also be effective because they gratify the adolescent's need to be with his or her peers. Another effective intervention, especially for adolescents who like to read, is bibliotherapy. Corr (1995) suggested the following books to help young adolescents (ages 12 to 15) deal with loss: *Bridge to Terabithia* (Paterson, 1977), *Say Goodnight Gracie* (Deaver, 1988), *Shira: A Legacy of Courage* (Grollman, 1988), *The Sunday Doll* (Shura, 1988), and *Tiger Eyes* (Blume, 1981).

Adolescents seem to experience grief much like adults do, in stages: first shock and denial, then anger and resentment, then disorganization and despair or depression, and finally acceptance and hope. It is important for the school counselor to determine where the student is in the process and respond accordingly.

Another factor that affects both their grieving process and the effectiveness of interventions with adolescents is their exaggerated concern for what their peers think. Adolescents can go to great lengths not to appear different, which can lead them to deny or hide their grief (Kandt, 1994). At work here too is their wanting to appear mature and independent. It is not uncommon for adults to mistake a teenager's outward calm and to rely on him or her for support during the time of bereavement and after.

> Robert was 15 years old when his father died suddenly from a heart attack. When I stopped at his house for a quick visit, I found him putting on a brave front. A few minutes after I got there, a priest from the local parish came by to pay his respects. I heard the priest say to Robert, the only male child in the family, "You're the man of the house, now."

That remark ignored Robert's grief; it also forced him into a role—the head of the house—for which he simply was not ready.

School counselors need to be particularly alert to adolescents who seem "perfectly fine" after the death of a family member or friend. Asking a student to "come see me if you want" only feeds the denial and evasion. School counselors have to be proactive: "I speak to all students who have lost someone through death—there are many in this school—and I would like to talk with you." This kind of statement both initiates the counseling process and normalizes the student's grief.

Interventions

McGlauflin (1998) suggested that the three most important factors in helping schoolchildren grieve are an understanding of the grieving process, an openness to that process, and the integration of that process into the daily operations of the school. There are many ways for counselors and other school personnel to learn about the grieving process. Both workshops and books are good sources of information.[3] Here we examine the other two factors: being open to the grieving process and integrating the process into the educational environment.

Accepting the Grieving Process   Being open to the grieving process means working through any personal issues the school counselor may have with death; it also means making the school environment open to the process. It does students little good for a counselor to be telling them in a counseling session that it is good to cry when they feel sad, if a teacher is telling them an hour later in the classroom that it's time to stop crying and start concentrating on their schoolwork. Every adult in the school should be trained in and accepting of the grieving process.

In a pilot study of teacher's knowledge and awareness of childhood grief and bereavement, Hare and Cunningham (1989) found that teachers

- are unaware of the range of behaviors children manifest in response to a significant death.
- have misconceptions about the duration of childhood grief. Many think it should be over within a few weeks of the death.
- are not clear about how they can help a grieving child.
- have limited awareness of the available resources for helping students deal with grief.
- are unaware of how previous experiences with death can affect a child's current understanding of death.

From their findings, Hare and Cunningham concluded that a death education program for teachers should focus on five areas:

- Awareness of children's bereavement behaviors
- Awareness of children's perceptions of death
- Awareness of personal attitudes toward death
- Exercises for dealing with bereaved children's concerns
- Awareness of curriculum and community resources

To help teachers understand their own attitudes toward death, Cunningham and Hare (1989) suggested the Leming Death Fear Scale (Leming & Dickinson, 1985), a 26-item questionnaire that asks for respondents' reactions to statements about their own death. The responses are grouped into eight areas: fear of being dependent on others while dying; fear of pain; fear of indignity; fear of isolation, separation, or loneliness; fear of an afterlife; fear of the finality of death; fear of leaving loved ones; and fear of the fate of the body. An in-service training program could also make use of role-playing so that teachers and other school personnel can practice their responses to children's feelings and questions about the death of a loved one.

Integrating the Grieving Process   What follow are a number of recommendations for integrating the grieving process into the school:[4]

---

[3] O'Toole (1996–97) has compiled an excellent list of books on the subjects of loss and death.

[4] Much of the material that follows was adapted from McGlauflin (1998). Reprinted by permission of American School Counseling Association.

Look at grieving as a valuable life skill. The goal here is to make teachers and other school personnel comfortable talking about grief and grieving. The basic assumption is that grieving is natural and healthy.

Understand the uniqueness of each student's grief. It has long been held, for example, that men and women grieve differently, that men express grief physically or cognitively and that women are more emotional (Chen et al., 1999; Gilbar & Dagan, 1995; Schut, Stroebe, van den Bout, & de Keijser, 1997; Sigmon, Stanton, & Snyder, 1995; Stroebe, Stroebe, & Schut, 2001). But those generalizations do not apply to grieving children and adolescents. In fact, some experts believe that a third way of grieving—which combines the cognitive and the affective—is possible (see, for example, T. L. Martin & Doka, 2000). The school counselor must understand that each person grieves in his or her own way.

Create and recognize opportunities to help students deal with grief. During the holidays, for example, the school counselor can ask students to contribute to a memorial bulletin board with a photograph or a poem or a story of a loved one who has died. When a student speaks spontaneously about someone who has died, counselor and teachers should be quick to acknowledge the student's sharing by responding with something like "You still think of _____ a lot." This signals the student that it is okay to think and talk about the person who has died.

Respect the disruption of grief. The school environment is built around schedules, but children's grief should not be constrained by time or place. In the aftermath of a death, teachers should expect students now and again to have difficulty staying on task, to make silly mistakes, or to cry or act out. All of these behaviors are a normal part of the grieving process.

Continue with routines, discipline, and high expectations. Death can mean an enormous disruption in a child's home environment. During a time of crisis, the school routine can be comforting; it can even restore the child's sense of safety. School personnel should avoid two extremes: business as usual, which does not recognize the special needs of a grieving child; and misguided sympathy, which removes the structure and routine a grieving child needs to feel safe.

Honor every possible good-bye. As part of their training, counselors are taught the importance of the termination process in counseling. That training should help them recognize the emotional importance of all different types of endings: summer vacations, students' moving, teachers' transferring schools. After a death, any good-bye can evoke painful memories for students. Counselor and teachers need to be aware of this connection and to understand that if students can talk about a loss, they can manage it.

Speak to children about a death or loss. Again, just talking with students about their loss can be the best intervention of all. And the counselor or teacher should initiate the discussion, not wait for the student to do so. A simple acknowledgment of the loss is all that's needed. Even if the student seems to be in denial and does not respond, it is still important that something was said because the action more than the words tells the student that it is all right to talk about death and grief.

Offer children outlets for their grief. Besides talking, school counselors should encourage bereaved children to find other outlets for their grief. Suggestions include keeping a journal, painting, drawing, and, for older children, doing research pertinent to the loss.

Be as honest as possible. Honesty is always a good counseling principle; but honesty around the issues of death and loss is especially important. When kids need and want information, the school counselor and teachers have a responsibility to provide it. The only exceptions: when the details of the death are gruesome, when all the facts are not known, or when the privacy of the family is in question. The best approach is to decide at the outset, with the family if that makes sense, what can be and cannot be shared in the school environment.

Speak with compassion, not pity. In counseling language, this means *empathy*, not *sympathy*.

Don't be afraid to show emotion. This may be the toughest challenge for adults in a school. But the school counselor can help other school staff members to realize that displaying emotion over the loss of a loved one is an honest expression, and that can help children normalize their own emotions in the process. But adults need to be careful not to overwhelm children with their emotions: A teacher's crying profusely in front of the class, for example, might frighten students. And at no time should the adult's emotions leave students feeling that they have to take care of the counselor or the teacher.

Never forget a loss, even years later. Remembering the dead is a healthy and important way of honoring them. Counselor and teachers should mark the anniversary of a student's loss with a simple acknowledgment ("This is an important time of year for you") or encourage the student to share a memory of the person who has died.

Support one another. Working with students who are grieving can be very demanding. It is wise not to take on too many grief cases at one time. Counselors should find support for themselves and other staff members who are dealing with grieving children; and they should be ready and willing to play a supportive role for others who are dealing with a bereaved child.

Group Work

In Chapter 2 we examined the fundamentals of working with students in small groups. Many of those guidelines apply to support groups for students who are grieving. In this section we examine suggestions specific to group work with bereaved children.

Forming a Bereavement Support Group   Before selecting the members of a bereavement support group, school counselors must ask themselves a number of questions. The first is "How do I feel about sitting in a room full of grieving children

TABLE 8.2 A Bereavement Support Group: Themes and Activities

Session Theme	Session Activities
1. Everyone's story	The session begins, as all first group sessions should, with the leader reviewing the group's rules and goals. The emphasis should be on confidentiality, attendance, and members' rights. The focus of this session is each member's experience of death: who died, how it happened, and any other details surrounding the situation. Reluctant members should be encouraged to share by both the leader and the other members. Because this can be an emotional session, the counselor should bring the session to a close by asking members to state any concerns, questions, or reactions. The counselor may choose to close the session with a breathing exercise or some other realization technique (J. Furman & Pratt, 1985).
2–3. From story to feeling	The first session was on the level of fact; these sessions are about the feelings associated with the facts. If the members have difficulty expressing their feelings, the leader might facilitate by explaining the different stages of bereavement, how people can have many different feelings about the death of a loved one. But the leader must be careful not to talk too much about theory: It's important not to limit the spontaneous expression of feelings. The goal of these sessions is to allow the members to identify such varied emotions as anger, sadness, and denial. Although it can be difficult, being able to name feelings is the most important factor in the success of the grieving process. The leader should praise students for their courage in talking about their feelings. Continuous and positive reinforcement at this stage is important. Although the outline suggests two sessions, the counselor can extend the discussion of feelings over however many sessions it takes for the members to access their feelings.
4. What life is like now	In this session, members share how life is different since the death of their loved one. Members can be encouraged to speak primarily about their families: for example, role changes, new responsibilities, and moving (J. Moore & Herlihy, 1993). It is also important to access member's feelings about changes. If the person who died was not a family member, the focus should be on changes that are a direct consequence of the death. For example, if a member of the group lost a close friend, he or she might talk about how playtime or social life is different.
5. The memorial service	It is important during the life of the group to conduct a memorial service. The members are asked to bring something that belonged to or reflects the person who died—a photograph, a piece of jewelry, an article of clothing. Each member is given the opportunity to explain the memento, the circumstances surrounding it, and their feelings about it. If members do not have a memento to share, they are asked to create one by writing a poem or a song, making a drawing, or simply telling a story about the person who died (J. Furman, & Pratt, 1985). This session is designed to communicate to the members that it is perfectly acceptable to remember their loved one, that remembering is a way of honoring someone who has died. This is likely to be a very emotional session, so allotting time for closure is important.
6. Life goes on, and so do I	For this session, members are asked to make a list of special days—holidays, birthdays, vacations—they are going to spend without the person who died and how they are going to spend those days (Kandt, 1994). Then the members share their lists and plans, and discuss how special occasions can evoke painful feelings especially during the first year of bereavement. The first holidays after a death are always difficult, but by planning and listening to one another, group members can feel better prepared to face them.
7. Plans and hopes for the future	This session builds on the previous one, asking members to plan and create strategies for moving ahead (Kandt, 1994). Members should share at least three goals for the short term (and long term if they are older). The purpose is to instill hope for the future. The counselor should watch for members who are unable to generate any plans, something that could signal a serious depression. Also, the leader must remind the group that the next session will be the last, and then should process any feelings members might have about ending the group.

TABLE 8.2 (continued)	
Session Theme	**Session Activities**
8. Termination	The first part of this session should be spent evaluating the group's progress and accomplishments. The leader should ask the members what the group has meant to them and how the process can be improved. It is a time to highlight each member's progress and amplify again the courage and maturity of the group members for sharing around such a difficult topic. They have done what even many adults are not capable of doing. The leader should also try to generalize what has been learned by asking, "What have you learned about living and grieving that will help you cope with your next loss?" Finally, the leader should emphasize that just the formal group is ending, that it is okay if the members continue to grieve and call on the skills they've learned in the group to cope with their pain. If the leader is concerned about any one member, arrangements should be made for a follow-up meeting with the student and an assessment of the need for ongoing services from either the school or an outside agency. The session should end with a celebration of a job well done, with food and possibly entertainment.

and talking with them about the death of a loved one?" As stated throughout this chapter, counselors who are working with death and dying need to take inventory of themselves—of their own childhood, their own issues with death, and their comfort being in and leading a support group for grieving children.

Once counselors have processed and answered the first question, several others remain: Is there a need for a bereavement support group? Have a number of students experienced a major death in their family? (Ideally, bereavement support groups should include five to eight members.) Are teachers and administrators in favor of this kind of group? And, finally, do I feel strongly enough that running this kind of group is a good idea? Only when these questions have been answered positively is the school counselor ready to begin the screening and selection process.

All potential members of the bereavement support group need to be screened, to build a working alliance. The counselor should look for students who are able to sit still, listen to others, and disclose appropriately. And the members should be roughly the same age. Other considerations include the proximity of the death and where the student is in the grieving process.

In the screening interview, the counselor should explain the logistics of the group (time, place, duration), briefly discuss the group process, and dispel any myths about group counseling ("It's for crazy people," "The members have to do weird things"). Certainly the counselor should talk about the group positively. He or she should also alert the potential member that the process—especially the first session—can be painful, but that in the end the student will find it helpful.

The Group Process During the group session, it can be a good idea to offer the members a snack. Food is a great balancer for kids who are being asked to empty themselves emotionally. Also, consider having younger children bring their own security items—a favorite stuffed animal, for example, for comfort when they are being asked to talk about a difficult issue. Table 8.2 is an outline for an eight-session bereavement support group. The content can be adapted to meet the developmental level of the participants.

Specific Deaths

The material in this chapter to this point has been general—that is, it applies to the death of any significant person in the lives of children and adolescents. But there are deaths that young people experience that merit special consideration. In this section we examine the issues specific to the death of a parent, a grandparent, a sibling, or a friend.

The Death of a Parent   One of the major factors in a child's response to death is the significance of the relationship with the person who has died. The loss of a parent is generally the most traumatic loss for children because the loss of emotional and psychological support threatens their emotional and social development (Despelder & Strickland, 1983; Osterweis, Solomon, & Green, 1984). A parent's death also can result in a tremendous loss of self-esteem (Costa & Holliday, 1994): Because parents are an extension of the child's self, their loss is experienced by the child as a loss of self. Crucial to correcting this loss of self is a healthy relationship with the surviving parent or another significant adult (E. Furman, 1974). Therefore, working closely with the surviving parent and even extended family members is important to the success of interventions for the child.

At times, though, the surviving parent is unable or even unwilling to collaborate with the school counselor. The surviving parent is also in mourning, which makes it difficult, despite good intentions, to help the child grieve. Sometimes the surviving parent is so overwhelmed by the child's grief that he or she refuses to mourn, hoping in that way to protect the child. That response, however, only makes it more difficult for the child to work through the grieving process (Miraglia & Samuels, 1988). If the surviving parent acts as though life is unchanged, the child cannot express the emotion he or she is feeling. And the refusal to acknowledge the change and then reassure the child that the family will go on only augments the child's sense of insecurity (Grollman, 1995). In some cases, the surviving parent, wanting to get on with his or her life, becomes impatient with the child's mourning. This factor tends to come into play when the parent has developed a new relationship that he or she believes the child is jeopardizing. Finally, the surviving parent's reactions to the death can complicate the child's bereavement. For example, Worden (1996) found that 42 percent of youngsters in a sample of children who had lost a parent said that they had never seen their surviving parent so upset, and that the strength of the parent's emotions had frightened them. Again, it is good for adults to show emotion but not to the extent that they no longer are a support for the child. "If the parent grieves openly while being consistently loving and reassuring, children will gain the confidence they need to handle the conflicts and changes they are experiencing" (Grollman, p. 12).

The death of a parent also has implications for the school counselor–student relationship. According to Garber (1988), the student's need for a substitute caregiver and the counselor's need to take care of the youngster can overwhelm and violate the boundaries of the counseling relationship. A counselor's wanting to spend more time with a child, perhaps out of school, is a signal of possible overinvolvement. Second, it is not unusual for a counselor, experiencing a child's grief, to get angry at the person who has died and caused that grief. Third, it also is not unusual for a counselor to react negatively to a surviving parent who is in a hurry to restore normalcy to his or her life without considering a grieving child. School counselors involved in grief counseling need to have a mentor or a supervisor with whom they can sort out their own multiple and conflicting reactions to counseling a child who has lost a parent to death.

Worden (1996) offered the following points to remember in dealing with children who have lost a parent through death:

- The emotional responses and behaviors of children are varied around the time of loss but are strongly influenced by the reaction of the surviving parent and other adults.
- Children should be given a choice as to attending the wake, funeral, and burial; but these need to be informed choices, with children prepared for what they will see and experience.
- Children who remain connected after the loss are better able to talk about the dead parent both inside and outside the family and are likely to try and please the dead parent with their behavior.
- An ongoing relationship with the deceased allows the child to engage in a process of "constructing" which involves renegotiating the meaning of the loss rather than letting go of the deceased.
- Children often feel watched by or have dreams about their deceased parent; most realize that these are generated inside themselves.
- Communication with and memories of the deceased parent are important in the mourning process and diminish over time, as does the significance of transitional objects. (pp. 32–34)

Counselors should start working with children who have lost a parent through death from the understanding that the experience is deeply painful and one that can never be totally eradicated (Costa & Holliday, 1994). But with adult support through the grieving process, these children can reconstruct the experience and emerge from their loss emotionally healthy and happy.

The Death of a Grandparent   For many children, the death of a grandparent is their first experience of death and grief. The effect of this loss depends on the closeness of the relationship. In today's world, more and more grandparents are taking over some, if not all, of the primary caregiving for their grandchildren. This means that more and more children are forming the kind of close attachment to their grandparents previously reserved for parents. So the school counselor's first task is to assess the closeness of the relationship to determine the potential severity of the child's grief.

Because grandparents are often old when they die, adults tend to respond to the death of a grandparent with age-related euphemisms—for example, "Well he lived a long life." This kind of response invalidates the child's grief. Also, because this may be the child's first experience with death, school counselors should be quick to talk with the child and to assess his or her need for support services.

The Death of a Sibling   Every year in the United States, 1.8 million children and adolescents experience the death of a brother or sister (Hogan & DeSantis, 1994). This number is expected to go up as social violence escalates, the incidence of HIV/AIDS among teenagers increases, and international ethnic warfare creates a refugee population that has lost siblings. In the natural order, children are not expected to die. When they do, their death creates a crisis for the family, especially for parents who have lost a young child (Grollman, 1995). Because most of the attention and support go to the grief-stricken parents, the grief of the surviving siblings often is ignored or minimized.

Children have strong and sometimes conflicting reactions to the death of a brother or sister. One is fear that they are going to die too, perhaps at the same age their brother or sister died. If the brother or sister died of an illness, adults should reassure the surviving sibling that he or she does not have the illness: "You are fine. There is nothing wrong with you. You do not have the disease that caused your brother's [sister's] death" (Grollman, 1995, p. 13). Counselors must be aware that children's new awareness—that they, too, may die—and fear can produce anxiety that can manifest in phobias (including a phobia of school), overattachment to the primary caregiver, somatic symptoms, and risk-taking behaviors (Worden, 1996).

Survivor guilt is another common reaction to the death of a sibling: "Why did it happen to my brother [sister] and not me?" H. Rosen (1986) found that 50 percent of his sample of survivor siblings admitted to feelings of guilt about their sibling's death. Anger is another common reaction, particularly anger at parents for not protecting the dead brother or sister.

Again, each child's reaction depends on the relationship he or she had with the sibling. A youngster may experience a sense of relief if the dead sibling was perceived as a competitor or if he or she died after a long illness that demanded all of the parents' attention. Research has shown that the closer the relationship with the sibling, the greater the behavioral problems for the survivor in the aftermath of that sibling's death (Davies, 1988, 1995). Problems in school—for example, the inability to concentrate, social withdrawal, and acting out—are common among sibling survivors (Davies, 1995). Some youngsters respond to the loss of a sibling by focusing overmuch on their schoolwork, their perfectionism a way of compensating for the parents' loss. Adults might think these children are handling their loss well, that they don't need support. But school counselors should know better.

Children who have lost a sibling may also be dealing with *replacement:* Parents, trying to "replace" the lost child, force the surviving sibling to take on the dead sibling's role. Replacement can manifest too in constant comparisons to the sibling who has died: "You are so much like him [her]" (Grollman, 1995). And some children place pressure on themselves to be like the lost sibling in an effort to relieve their parents' suffering (Worden, 1996). For example, if the sibling who died was athletic, a surviving sibling may take up sports to try to please his or her parents. Counselors who see children reacting with this kind of replacement behavior can remind them and their parents that the sibling who died cannot be resurrected in the person of someone else (Grollman, 1995).

Most children model their parents in dealing with their grief. Again, if parents do not talk about the death, if they refuse to address the enormous change in the family, neither will their children. In studies of adults who had lost a sibling in childhood, more that half said they had not talked with anyone about their sibling's death (Davies, 1991). That left them ill equipped to manage their grief. And there are some parents who cannot stop talking about their dead child, which over time can affect the surviving sibling's sense of self-importance. The school counselor can be particularly helpful during this sad and confusing time by encouraging parents to adopt healthy ways of dealing with their loss, ways that won't inflict more pain on their surviving child. Parents, in turn, can help the school counselor by communicating the facts surrounding the death and deciding what can and should be revealed to the school's population. Reliable information dispels the rumors that tend to run rampant especially in the case of a sudden death (Davies, 1995).

Of course the school counselor's primary concern is helping the surviving sibling grieve. Another is paying close attention to how the child is being treated by peers. It is especially important that the counselor intervene to ward off peer cruelty, to keep the school a safe place for a child whose home is in crisis.

As difficult as the death of a child can be for a family, something positive can be gleaned from the experience. Davies (1990, 1991) found that most adults who as children lost a sibling reported at least two long-term effects: They had learned to face their own mortality and had developed a deeper understanding of the meaning of life. This is where the school counselor can play a crucial role, facilitating the grieving process so that the surviving child and the parents find comfort.

The Death of a Peer   Estimates of the number of adolescents who will experience the death of a peer vary from 36 percent (McNeil, Silliman, & Swihart, 1991) to 87 percent (Schachter, 1991). Drunk driving, guns in the hands of children, HIV/AIDS, and rising rates of suicide among teenagers are likely to contribute to an increase in the rate of adolescents who lose a friend or schoolmate through death. Like the death of sibling, the death of a peer can generate in children and adolescents a disturbing sense of their own mortality (Grollman, 1995). Adolescents can also feel guilty, fantasizing that there was something they could have done to protect their friend, remembering a recent argument with the youngster who died, or feeling that they should have been the one to die (Oltjenbruns, 1996).[5] Lurie (1993) found that adolescents who had lost a friend to death scored high on anger and hostility.[6] One reason might be that most adolescent deaths are accidental and so preventable.

Oltjenbruns (1996) suggested that when adolescents lose a friend to death, they suffer the initial loss and a *secondary loss,* the support of that friend. That secondary loss is amplified when other friends are also grieving and so cannot be relied on for support; or when they withdraw because they simply don't feel comfortable with the grieving process. School counselors should be aware of how easily adolescents can become isolated in their grief. Adding to that isolation is the fact

---

[5] Survivor guilt is exacerbated for adolescents who actually caused the fatal accident or who survived it. These youngsters may well be in need of support services.

[6] Actually, adolescents who had lost a friend showed more anger and hostility than adolescents who had lost a sibling.

that adolescents seldom turn to their parents for support. And because adolescents as a rule don't confide in their parents, it may well be that the parents don't appreciate the depth of the friendship between their child and the youngster who died. This is another area where school counselors can intervene by alerting parents to the possible consequences of the loss.

The death of a student affects the entire school. When a family member dies, the school can be a haven for children; but when a classmate dies, both students and school personnel are grieving, making it difficult for the school counselor to provide students with support (McNeil, Silliman, & Swihart, 1991). If that happens, the counselor must have the honesty to recognize his or her vulnerability and to arrange for adolescents to receive support services from someone else.[7]

Oltjenbruns (1996) described a series of steps for school counselors to take when dealing with the death of a student:

1. Notify the school community.
2. Communicate with people outside the school who are likely to interact with the bereaved students (for example, parents, clergy, and coaches).
3. Express sympathy to the family and friends of the student has died.
4. Develop a method for providing information and answering questions about the death.
5. Create opportunities for students and others to pay tribute to the youngster who has died and to say good-bye.
6. Create ongoing opportunities for students to share their thoughts and feelings about the loss of their friend and the death itself, and to find support.

Grollman (1995) suggested that a memorial (step 5) take the form of a yearbook dedication, planting a tree, or placing a bookshelf in the school library in the name of the student who died. A memorial of whatever sort can be an excellent way to facilitate the grieving process for a peer, but the school counselor needs to consider both the appropriateness of the ritual and the feelings of the family. Although the circumstances of the death do not lessen the grief students are feeling, it is important that the memorial not idealize or romanticize a death from drugs, alcohol, or suicide. And, of course, the counselor should have the permission of the dead student's family before planning a memorial gesture or event.

Here, too, counseling can produce positive outcomes from tragedy. Oltjenbruns (1991) found that 96 percent of her sample reported at least one good thing that came out of mourning the death of a friend: a deeper appreciation of life, greater emotional strength, increased problem-solving and communication skills, the ability to demonstrate affection, deeper emotional bonds with others, or stronger empathy for others. Grieving is a painful process, but it is the only way to restore adolescents to emotional stability after a friend has died; and it can even enhance their growth and development.

---

[7]The school counselor should be part of a crisis management team that follows a specific protocol (for example, the roles and functions of different members of the school community) in the case of a crisis. The death of a student would be one such crisis.

LOSS THROUGH PARENTAL DIVORCE AND SEPARATION

Again, parental divorce ultimately affects 40 percent of all children. Research consistently documents the short- and long-term effects of divorce on children's emotional, social, and academic functioning: higher levels of aggression and acting-out behavior (Felner, Ginter, Boike, & Cowen, 1981; Felner, Stolberg, & Cowen, 1975); heightened anxiety, anger, loneliness, and somatic complaints (Wallerstein & Kelley, 1976); sadness, fear, and depression (Kelley & Wallerstein, 1977); and overall lowered academic achievement (Cantrell, 1986; Guidubaldi, Perry, Cleminshaw, & Mclaughlin, 1983).

The Variables

Divorce does not affect all youngsters equally. Three major variables moderate the effects of divorce on children: age at the time of the divorce, gender, and the time that has elapsed since the divorce (Richardson & Rosen, 1999).

> *Age.* Younger children (ages 6 to 8) have difficulty understanding the implications of their parents' divorce. Magical thinking keeps alive the fantasy of their parents reuniting. Younger children are more likely to think they are the cause of their parents' breakup (Sanders & Riester, 1996). If they believe they are the cause, they can also feel it is their responsibility to reunite their parents. Typical reactions in this age group include sadness, feelings of loss, and anger (Cantrell, 1986), and anxiety, restlessness, and tantrums (W. F. Hodges, 1986).
>
> Older children (ages 9 to 12) experience many of the same emotions, but their anger often is intense and directed at the parent they believe was responsible for the divorce (Cantrell, 1986; Richardson & Rosen, 1999). Research shows that early adolescents have the most difficult time adjusting to parental divorce (Hetherington, 1993).
>
> *Gender.* In general, boys seem to have more difficulties after divorce than girls do (Doherty & Needle, 1991; Kelley, 1993; Shaw, Emery, & Tver, 1993).[8] Gender differences are most evident immediately after a divorce; then tend to diminish over time (Kelley, 1993; Wallerstein, 1991). There is also some evidence that teachers expect boys to have more problems following a divorce (Ball, Newman, & Scheuren, 1984).
>
> *Time.* Postdivorce stress among children is most severe in the months immediately after the divorce. The divorce triggers a crisis in the family and moderate to severe distress in the child (Chase-Lansdale & Hetherington, 1990; F. F. Furstenberg & Cherlin, 1991). Research into the long-term effects of divorce is not conclusive (Richardson & Rosen, 1999). Wallerstein (1987) found that 10 years after the divorce, children were still having difficulty adjusting and were experiencing greater anxiety around issues of

---

[8] Kelley found that girls have more difficulty before a divorce.

commitment and marriage. But S. F. Allen, Stoltenberg, and Rosko (1990) found no differences between college students from divorced and from intact families. One study found that behavioral problems among boys continued for about six years; girls had their greatest difficulty at the onset of adolescence and then again as adults, with a greater likelihood of divorce themselves (Chase-Lansdale & Hetherington, 1990).

Comparing Death and Divorce

Both death and divorce are losses, and the grieving processes are alike in many ways. But there are some crucial differences.

The Sense of Finality   Although very young children have difficulty accepting the permanence of death, most youngsters do not. Because the separated parent is still alive and often is seen on a regular basis, it is more difficult to accept the divorce as permanent and easier to hope that parents will reunite. This fantasy prevents the grieving process from moving forward. Fantasies of reunion are more likely among children whose parents separated one or more times before finally divorcing.

Adults can help the children of divorce work through their grief by helping them accept the finality of divorce. Parents should be frank and honest with their children: "Mommy and Daddy are never going to live together again." In the same breath, and over and over again, they need to say: "It is not your fault that Mommy and Daddy are not together."

Support   All cultures have rituals surrounding death, but there are no mourning rites for divorce (Jarrat, 1994). Children seldom find the same support after a divorce that they do after the death of a parent. Also, the custodial parent, especially if he or she is in conflict with the ex-spouse, may find the child's expressions of grief difficult (Worden, 1996). Mutual blame, which is common among divorced parents, often prevents them from validating the emotional pain of their children. Despite the alarming divorce rate in this country, there is still a stigma attached to divorce that limits society's response to the needs of children of divorce. That failure is magnified when the parents pressure a child to act as though nothing has changed, to keep the family disruption private. School counselors must learn to recognize those children who are mourning the divorce of their parents, and support them.

Issues of Loyalty   One of the most devastating effects of divorce on children is the feeling that they are caught between two angry parents. Children of divorce tend to blame themselves for their parents' breakup; they also blame their parents but rarely do they accord blame equally or at the same time to both parents. The tendency to blame one parent over the other is fueled by parents' talking badly about each other in front of the child, forcing the child to take a side. When a parent has died, this loyalty conflict is absent and does not obfuscate the grieving process.

Triangulation of children of divorce is most evident when they are asked to carry harsh messages from one parent to the other. Palmatier (1998) suggested that parents communicate in writing. If a child must deliver a message, the message should be placed in a sealed envelope and opened out of sight of the child. Whatever their feelings toward each other, divorced parents need to communicate to their child this way: "Your mother [father] is a good person; I am a good person; our relationship was not good; and you are in no way to blame for that." Here, the parent is saying that it is okay to mourn the loss of the relationship without blaming one parent or the other.

Divorce Is a Choice, Death Is Not   The anger associated with feelings of abandonment is a common response of children who are grieving for a parent who has died. But for most children, this stage of the process is short-lived (Worden, 1996) as they come to realize that the parent did not choose to die.[9] For the children of divorce, however, the anger associated with abandonment and rejection can dominate the grieving process for a long time. Divorce, no matter how painful, is a choice.

Family Restructuring   After the death of a parent, the surviving parent may eventually date and remarry. Although it can be difficult for children to see a dead parent "replaced," replacement can be more difficult to accept for children of divorce. When a divorced parent marries again, the child's reunion fantasies are destroyed (Worden, 1996). The anger that evokes in children is why some stepfamilies have such a difficult adjustment.

Interventions

Counseling children of divorce is a collaborative effort that should involve teachers and parents.

Working with Teachers   Divorce threatens children's emotional security. By providing the children of divorce with emotional security, adults can help reduce their adjustment problems (Davies & Cummings, 1998). The school counselor must work with teachers, encouraging them to communicate with the child of a divorce that the teacher–student relationship is secure (P. A. Miller, Ryan, & Morrison, 1999). Critical to that process is the teacher's understanding when the child exhibits unusual behaviors (including changes in academic performance), and patience in helping the child learn new behaviors. The structure and routine in school contrast sharply with the uncertainty in the child's home. So it also is important for teachers to alert the child well in advance of any changes in scheduling or staffing, to explain those changes as much as possible, and to allow the child to ask questions and process reactions. For example, a teacher might say: "John, I just want to remind you that I won't be in school on Friday and that _____ will be substituting for me. He [she] is very nice. So I don't think you'll have any problems. What is your reaction?"

Because divorce can make children feel as though they have no control over their lives, teachers should be encouraged to provide these youngsters with opportunities for exercising control (P. A. Miller et al., 1999). For example, teachers can allow them to make decisions about classroom activities, assignments, or seating, and can give them leadership roles in the classroom. Teachers also should be aware of the coping strategies that best suit the individual child. So a verbal child might be

---

[9] The exception, of course, is where a parent has committed suicide.

referred to a counseling group; a nonverbal child might be encouraged to keep a diary; and a child who likes physical activity might be given more playground time.

When caring adults see a youngster in emotional pain, their immediate reaction is to make it better. But adults need to know their limitations. For teachers, that means helping the children of divorce in the classroom. P. A. Miller et al. (1999) offered the following guidelines:

1. Focus upon divorce-related problems only as they affect children's classroom behavior and academic performance.
2. Refer general divorce-related problems (e.g., a child chronically stressed by divorce-related events) to the school's counselor/psychologist, and proceed on the basis of that person's recommendations.
3. Discuss divorce-related problems with parents only in terms of how they affect the child's classroom behavior and academic performance.
4. Avoid being drawn into taking sides, or supporting one parent's claims over the other.
5. Be compassionate and a source of support to children, but do not take on a parental role.
6. Facilitate parents' and children's access to relevant resources and information dealing with divorce-related problems, without suggesting that you will be involved in resolving such problems. (p. 288)

Working with Parents   Strangeland, Pellegreno, and Lundholm (1989) found that divorced parents misunderstand their children in a number of areas, from the children's perception of the parents' relationship to the children's sleep patterns (Table 8.3). This is one of the reasons the school counselor should meet with divorced parents: If the parents are not seeing or are seeing but denying a child's grief, clearly they cannot help the child adjust to the divorce. A meeting with the parents is also important to assess the degree of turbulence in the family. The more difficult the divorce, the more support the child is going to need.

Because individual meetings with parents are time consuming and not always practical, Parker (1994) suggested the school counselor run a workshop for divorced parents with school-aged children. The ex-spouses are not advised to attend together unless they have an amicable relationship. The components of the three-hour workshop (plus a 15-minute break) are shown in Table 8.4.

In many divorced families, the mother and father have joint custody. However, if socialized along gender stereotypes, men may find it difficult to ask for help in times of emotional turmoil. Frieman (1994) suggested several ways for the school counselor to involve divorced fathers, including making sure that fathers are on the school's mailing list, keeping them informed of their child's homework assignments, inviting them to use the school counselor as a resource for child-rearing information, warning them about the dangers of triangulation, and reminding them of the need to put their child's problems before their own. Some fathers, angry with their ex-wife, take out that anger on their child by, among other things, refusing to attend school-related activities, no matter how important those activities are to their child. The school counselor should reach out to these fathers with informa-

TABLE 8.3   DIVORCED/SEPARATED PARENTS' MISUNDERSTANDINGS ABOUT THEIR CHILDREN

Item	Child's Response	Parents' Response
The child knows why his/her parents got divorced.	No	Yes
The child knows his/her parents will never live together again.	No	Yes
Since the divorce, the child has had problems in school, including trouble with teachers and poor performance.	Yes	No
Since the divorce, the child has been helping a lot at home, more so than before the divorce.	No	Yes
The child has trouble sleeping.	Yes	No
The child knows he/she will always have someone to take care of him/her.	No	Yes
The child plans to get married in the future.	No	Yes

SOURCE: Adapted from Strangeland, Pellegreno, and Lundholm (1989).

tion, help, and support. It may well be that an angry father will also be angry with the counselor's efforts, but at least contact has been made.

Working with the Children of Divorce   We know that children of divorce can be impulsive, easily distracted, and aggressive, and that they can and do act out. All of these behaviors are manifested in the school environment and can affect their schoolwork. School-based interventions, then, make good sense for the children of divorce (Yauman, 1991).

The most popular school-based intervention for the children of divorce are support groups; and numerous studies confirm their effectiveness (see, for example, Cantrell, 1986; Pedro-Carroll & Alpert-Gillis, 1997; Pedro-Carroll, Alpert-Gillis, & Cowen, 1992; Sanders & Reister, 1996; and Stolberg & Mahler, 1994). Over the years, groups for these children have used a number of techniques, including bibliotherapy (Cantrell, 1986; Snyder, 1985), filmstrips and movies (Wilkinson & Bleck, 1977; B. M. Williams, Wright, & Rosenthal, 1983), board games (Cantrell; Epstein & Borduin, 1986; Titkin & Cobb, 1983), drawings (B. M. Williams et al., 1983), role-playing and skits (Pedro-Carroll & Cowen, 1985; Pfeifer & Abrams, 1984), and the use of puppets (Bonkowski, Bequette, & Boomhower, 1984).

Richardson and Rosen (1999) suggested that all group counseling interventions should focus on three components: peer support, skill building, and flexibility. Groups naturally provide *peer support* by helping children normalize their experiences with divorce, by helping them realize they are not alone. *Skill building* means helping these children to express their feelings, to cope, to solve problems, and to protect and develop interpersonal relationships. *Flexibility* is a key component of any program that must accommodate male and female children and children from different cultures and races and socioeconomic statuses. Table 8.5 is an outline of an eight-session group for the children of divorce that can be adapted to different ages. Before forming a group, the counselor should follow the general guidelines in Chapter 2.

TABLE 8.4   A WORKSHOP FOR DIVORCED PARENTS

Component	Duration (minutes)	Activities
Introduction	10	The discussion focuses on informed consent and on confidentiality.
Changes that accompany separation or divorce	10	Participants are asked to answer two questions:
		1. What physical and emotional changes have you experienced during the process of your separation or divorce?
		2. What physical and emotional changes has (have) your child (children) experienced?
		Responses are recorded on a flip chart and divided into two columns (children and parents), which are further divided according to whether they are positive or negative. Counselors should identify both positive and negative changes that have resulted from the divorce, and discuss them with the group.
Children's reactions to divorce	15	Parents are asked to rank the list of negative changes from most stressful to least stressful for both themselves and their children. The leader should tally up the number of participants who rank a negative change as most stressful. Because commonalties usually exist, the leader should highlight these changes and discuss how the parents' stress affects their children and also how children's stress affects the parents.
Techniques for effective communication	60	The counselor provides the participants with effective communication tools appropriate to their children's ages. For younger children, the counselor should explain play as a displacement activity that helps children verbalize painful feelings. For older and more verbal children, the leader should demonstrate empathy and other techniques for encouraging children to talk about how they feel.
Break	15	Time for refreshments and a look at resources on display—books, videos, and board games for children of divorce in different age groups.
Role-play	20	The counselor divides participants into groups of 3. The members of each group take turns being the parent, the child, and the observer. The groups can choose a play medium from the resources provided by the leader.
Pitfalls and tips	10	Parents are given strategies for minimizing the negative effects of divorce: for example, no fighting in front of the children, no making threats, no denigrating the other parent, no using a child to spy on the other parent, no telling the children that they must choose between one parent and the other, and no trying to buy children's love with material goods. Tips might include promoting open communication, anticipating and addressing fears, confirming and supporting contact with the noncustodial parent, being as consistent as possible in making and enforcing rules, and reassuring the children that both parents do and will continue to love them.
Solutions to specific problems	15	The parents ask questions about specific problems, and the group brainstorms to come up with possible solutions.
Divorce Can Happen to the Nicest People (Mayle, 1987)	30	Participants view an animated film about questions and issues that face children when their parents divorce, and are encouraged to use the material to foster discussion between themselves and their children.*
Evaluation	5	Counselors solicit feedback from parents about the workshop. This can be done by distributing anonymous evaluation forms that have both quantitative and qualitative items.

*Other videos about divorce are readily available in stores and libraries and can be substituted or used in addition to this film.

SOURCE: Adapted from Parker (1994), pp. 140–148. Copyright 1994 by American School Counseling Association. Reprinted with permission.

TABLE 8.5 A SUPPORT GROUP FOR THE CHILDREN OF DIVORCE: THEMES AND ACTIVITIES

Session Theme	Session Activities
1. All about me and my family	This session begins with introductions—first the leader then each member. The leader should reiterate that the group is for children of divorced parents and is designed to help them express their feelings about divorce and to acquire skills to help them deal more effectively with the divorce. The group should establish ground rules, among them the importance of confidentiality, of allowing one person to speak at a time, and of coming to the sessions. Then members are asked to complete an "All About Me and My Family" worksheet by drawing pictures or writing words (depending on the age group) to describe • a good time they had with their family. • a not-good time they had with their family. • why they think their parents got divorced. • what they would like to see happen in the next two years. • something about them that is special. The leader allows time for the group members to share their answers. Then the leader highlights common experiences, congratulate the youngsters for their courage in sharing, and explain that sharing is an important step in helping them cope with their parents' divorce. The leader closes the session by asking members to share any feelings they have and summarizing what happened in the session.
2. Homes my family lives in	The leader begins the discussion by asking members to define *family*. Some members are likely to respond by saying *family* means everyone who lives in the same house. The leader then encourages the children to think about a family member who does not live in the same house, and asks each member to list or draw the number of homes it takes to show his or her family. When the children have finished sharing their list or drawing, the leader asks two more questions: • Can you love someone who lives in a different house as much as you love those who live with you? • Have you ever wished you could live with your other parent? The session ends with the leader's validating members' feelings about family and/or wanting to live somewhere else, again highlighting common situations, and addressing any questions.
3. My feelings about divorce	The counselor asks the students to remember their feelings when they found out their parents were getting a divorce. If the group is small, the counselor can write the feelings on a chalkboard or a large pad of paper; if the groups is large, the members should break up into smaller groups, list their feelings on a piece of newsprint, and then share their lists with the larger group. Here, too, the counselor points out similarities. The leader then asks how members deal with specific feelings: "Do you keep those feelings inside?" If the group is made up of young children, the leader can use a balloon and inflate it a bit each time a child says that he or she keeps a feeling inside. Then the leader should ask the members what is going to happen to the balloon if he or she keeps blowing. A discussion follows about bottled-up feelings and people to talk to about those feelings. The counselor encourages the members to make use of acceptable outlets for the expression of feelings.
4. Stressors in my life	The session begins with the leader reviewing the feelings identified in the last session. Then the leader takes a survey of members' feelings, asking if they have experienced the following: • Fear of failing in school • Hurt from friends or relatives • Sadness about not being with an absent parent • Anger at parents, siblings, and so on • Worry about being taken care of, the situation at home, or an absent parent Members are then given the opportunity to brainstorm sources of stress in families of divorce (e.g., money problems and custody battles). The leader records stressors on newsprint or the chalkboard. The leader closes the session by reminding members that stress is very much a part of divorce and that the group is about learning ways to deal with stress. For the next session, members are asked to think about ways they cope with stress.

(continued)

TABLE 8.5 *(continued)*

Session Theme	Session Activities
5. Recipe for coping	Members are asked to share three positive coping strategies that have helped them deal with stress. Next, the counselor gives each member a 3-inch × 5-inch index card and markers, pencils, or crayons to develop his or her own coping recipe: e.g., "Take 2 cups exercise, 1 cup TV, $\frac{1}{2}$ cup quiet time, and 3 cups talking with a friend, and mix thoroughly for a batch of good feelings." Recipes can be shared with the other members by displaying them on a wall. The leader closes the session by saying that everyone must develop coping mechanisms to deal with stress, and congratulating the members for learning that so young.
6. Stages of divorce	This session helps members understand that many of the feelings and problems they've talked about in earlier sessions are normal in divorce situations and part of what are called the *stages of divorce*. The leader writes the stages on poster board—belief/denial, anxiety, anger, sadness, depression, and acceptance—and then asks the members to identify the times they experienced each of the stages and to share that experience with the group. The leader clarifies that the process is different for everyone, that everyone does not necessarily experience all of the stages, and that some children experience a stage more than once. The session ends with the members sharing their thoughts about the stage they are in at the present.
7. Problem solving	The leader begins by asking students to identify a problem they have had to deal with in the past few weeks and then explaining the steps in the problem-solving process: (1) State the problem; (2) identify your feelings about the problem; (3) talk about the problem with an adult you trust; (4) decide if the problem can be solved; (5) remind yourself that the only person you can change is yourself, and (6) decide what you should do. The group uses some of the problems mentioned at the beginning and applies the problem-solving method. If the group is large, students can be divided into smaller groups, and scenarios are then shared with the larger group. The leader concludes the session by reminding members that although they can't control some of the things that happen to them, they can control their reactions through creative problem solving, and encouraging the students to apply the problem-solving method during the next week.
8. My crystal ball	The last session begins with the members reporting how they used the problem-solving method over the last week. Then the counselor asks the members to look into a crystal ball and take an imaginary trip 5 years, 10 years, 20 years into the future: "What do you see yourself doing? What are your dreams for the future?" Members can talk about their hopes or draw pictures to share with the group. The leader reminds the members that no matter how difficult things are right now, life can and will go on for them, and that they can have hopes and dreams. The session—and the group—ends with the leader recognizing the effort of the members and asking them to say what they liked and did not like about the group. Older students can also evaluate the experience in writing, answering these questions: • Do you feel that participation in the group was helpful to you? Why or why not? • What part of the group did you like the best? The least? • If you had a friend whose parents were divorcing would you recommend that he or she participate in a similar group? Why or why not? • Did you attend all eight sessions? If not, how many did you attend? • Do you have any comments or suggestions?

SOURCE: Adapted from O'Rourke and Worzbyt (1996).

DISENFRANCHISED GRIEF

We have been talking about losses that our culture recognizes. There are other losses, some just as painful as the death of a family member or friend or a parental divorce, that society fails to recognize. Doka (1989) used the term *disenfranchised grief* to describe the pain of these losses and identified four contexts in which grief is disenfranchised: unrecognized relationships, unrecognized losses, unrecognized grievers, and unrecognized deaths.

- Young people's friendships and romantic attachments often are *unrecognized relationships*—that is, many adults don't realize (or remember) how meaningful those relationships are, and how painful the loss of those relationships can be. Glass (1991), in a study of 211 middle school students, found that 55 percent had moved, 52 percent had changed schools, 50 percent had lost a boyfriend or a girlfriend, and 53 percent had lost a best friend. There was little evidence that those youngsters had received any support in dealing with their losses. Instead, adults downplay the importance of these relationships: "You'll make new friends," "You were too young anyway to have a boyfriend." The loss of unrecognized relationships leaves adolescents vulnerable and alone (Lenhardt, 1997).
- *Unrecognized losses* include the death of a pet, abortion, or a separation from family because the incarceration of a parent or placement in foster care. Also included here are the abuse and neglect associated with being in a dysfunctional family. Children are known to form close and important attachments to pets, yet society does not recognize the loss of a pet as significant (Lenhardt, 1997). Pet loss can be children's first experience with death, and the way it is handled can determine how they cope with future losses. Because their psychological needs tell them their family should be otherwise, children from dysfunctional families need to grieve the loss of caring, nurturing parents. Our society has come to recognize abuse as a civil problem, but we rarely treat the loss and grief that the abused child feels. Disability is also an unrecognized loss: Children with disabilities also need to grieve—in this instance, for the loss of self-control or self-direction (Lenhardt, 1997).
- *Disenfranchised grievers* are groups society believes are incapable of grieving—for example, the very young, the very old, and those who are developmentally delayed. But everyone can feel loss, and school counselors, particularly those working in elementary schools, have a responsibility to dispel the myth that certain populations are unable to grieve.
- Finally, *unrecognized deaths* are deaths that society considers shameful: suicide, alcohol- or drug-related deaths, victim-precipitated homicide (someone is killed while committing a crime), and deaths from AIDS (Doka, 1995). The result: No one talks about why the individual died. That repression complicates the grieving process for children and adolescents. Even more confusing is parents' asking them to lie about the cause of death. Honest expression is central to the grieving process.

Disenfranchised grief is common among school-aged students, and counselors should be sensitive to those students who lack a support system for their grief. Lenhardt (1997) advocated strongly for group counseling organized around the themes of disenfranchised loss. Many of the techniques we talked about earlier for dealing with loss through death can also be applied to disenfranchised loss. Most important is for adults to validate the loss and the feelings associated with the loss. Doka (1995) made the point that all grief is the result of broken attachments. If school counselors can adopt that thinking, they can be an important source of support for students suffering from disenfranchised grief.

Ethical and Legal Issues

The most important ethical issue in bereavement counseling is finding a balance between overidentifying with the student who is grieving and disengaging from the student. Overidentification blurs the boundary between counselor and counselee; disengagement avoids the counselee's emotional pain.

> *I have counseled many children who have lost their father through death. My own father died when I was 8 years old, and there is a part of me that still wants to reveal that information to the children I counsel who are suffering the loss of a parent. Of course this kind of disclosure would be a mistake because it would turn the focus of the counseling to me. I have never given in to this impulse, and it has made me realize the potential risk of using grief work to deal with the counselor's own issues.*

Counselors have an ethical responsibility to know themselves and to seek outside counseling for any unresolved losses. The art of grief work is to identify with the counselee just enough to develop empathy but not so much that the counselor loses perspective and crosses a boundary.

In cases of divorce, the courts award either joint or sole parental custody. Joint custody preserves the pre-divorce status held by both parents in terms of decision-making for their children (Arditti, 1992). For school counselors, this means that both parents have equal access to information regarding their children and that both parents have the legal right to make decisions regarding the schooling of their children. In cases of sole parental custody, the court awards only one parent the rights of decision-making, with the non-custodial parent having only the right of access. The divorce decree stipulates the exact nature of the noncustodial parent's involvement with the children (Beis, 1984). The school needs to work out an agreement with the custodial parent as to what can or should be the noncustodial parent's involvement in the child's education. For example, the noncustodial parent may not be allowed to pick up the child from school nor to have access to school records. In cases of sole parental custody, school counselors can help by emphasizing the importance of both parents' involvement (Wilcoxon & Magnuson, 1999) but must be careful not to violate anything stipulated by the legal divorce decree.

It is best to put in writing, signed by the custodial parent, any agreement reached as to the exact nature of the noncustodial parent's involvement in the school life of their children.

CONCLUSION

Loss is a fact of children's lives. This chapter began with an examination of loss through death: how culture and stage of development affect children's responses to the death of a loved one, and how the school counselor can intervene to help students whose parent, grandparent, sibling, or friend has died.

The children of divorce often are caught up in their parents' conflict. To help these youngsters, the school counselor must reach out to the parents and help them understand the consequences of their behavior for their children. Teachers, too, are a critical part of interventions with the children of divorce. In the aftermath of a divorce, children rely on the school for security that's missing from their home. Key to any interventions with these children, then, is making them feel safe again.

Finally, *disenfranchised grief* describes the pain of an unrecognized loss: the death of a pet, the end of a romantic relationship, the abuse and neglect of a dysfunctional family, for example. Because these losses tend to go unnoticed or unappreciated, the school counselor has a special responsibility to help youngsters cope with their very real pain.

Some losses are more important than others. We cannot compare, for example, the loss of a parent to the loss of a boyfriend or girlfriend. But the grieving process is essentially the same. School counselors know that, and they know the consequences of unresolved grief. Their task is to give students the opportunity to grieve and to do that in a way that respects each student's needs. All losses are painful. But if children and adolescents are allowed to grieve, their pain can evolve into strength that will sustain them throughout their lives.

QUESTIONS FOR DISCUSSION

1. Think back on a significant loss in your life. How did you deal with it? In retrospect, what, if anything, would you have done differently to grieve in a more healthy way? What could those around you have done to help you?
2. Grieving children can evoke many emotions in the adults who are trying to help them. What would it be like for you to work with children who are grieving a significant loss? Do you think you are likely to become overinvolved or to be avoidant? Discuss your answer.
3. How do you think schools should deal with a death that affects a large portion of its population? Consider, for example, the death of a teacher, a student, or someone who is well known in the community.

4. Mrs. Clair's father died last week. Her children, both students in your school, were very close to their grandfather, and you had talked with them about their loss. The next day Mrs. Clair came to see you. She was very upset. She feels the best thing for her children is not talk about the loss with anyone because in her experience that only "makes it worse." How would you react to Mrs. Clair? What would you say to her? With a partner, role-play the parts of Mrs. Clair and the counselor.

5. What do you think school counselors can do to minimize the negative effects of divorce on children? Why is the parents' participation in intervention here so important? Discuss the challenges of working with both parents.

SUGGESTED INTERNET SITES

www.grieflossrecovery.com

This site offers emotional support and friendship as well as a haven for people to share their grief. Visitors can access poems, memoirs, and articles about bereavement, and can create an online memorial. Also here are a chat room and links to other Web sites.

www.kidsaid.com

This well-designed forum for children to share and help one another with grief and loss contains an online support group, questions and answers, stories and poems written by youngsters who are grieving, and articles about bereavement in young people. Also included is a section for adults dealing with grieving children.

www.journeyofhearts.org

This is a comprehensive, easy-to-navigate site with an abundance of literature that is both informative and comforting. The site is divided into two sections: One provides information about grief; the other provides support.

www.juliesplace.com

Developed by a bereaved sister, this site is designed for children and teens who have lost a sibling. (There's also a parents-only section that addresses the many questions parents have about children who are grieving.) There is a message board and a Smile List for those in need of immediate cheer.

www.grieflink.asn.au/frameset.html

This Australian Web site offers many resources for professionals, including strategies for dealing with grief and useful ways to help people who are grieving a particular loss. Here, too, are links to other good sites.

SUICIDE IN THE SCHOOL SETTING

Just the word *suicide* can evoke strong reactions: disbelief, a sense of failure, a sense of loss. But for professional helpers today the word also evokes concern about the legal responsibility of protecting clients from harming themselves. This is a very real concern for school counselors. For example, in *Eisel v. Board of Education* (597 A.2d 447, 1991), the Maryland Court of Appeals ruled that school counselors have a legal obligation to protect students if they are aware or should be aware that a student poses a danger to himself or herself (Pate, 1992).

The threat of legal liability does not change the nature of the school counselor's function here: to calmly and knowledgeably do what is necessary to protect students from hurting themselves. Recent studies show that the overwhelming majority of school counselors believe it is their role to recognize students at risk for suicide, but only 38 percent of high school counselors feel competent to do so (King, Price, Telljohann, & Wahl, 1999, 2000). Critical to counselors' competence is knowledge, an understanding of the risk factors for suicide, methods of assessing risk, and effective interventions.

Comprehensive developmental guidance programs focus more on prevention than remediation. Because suicide can be conceived of as a failure in life skills—in building self-esteem, solving problems, and communicating (Kalafat, 1990)—it is appropriate for suicide prevention to find a place in comprehensive guidance programs.

This chapter begins with data that point to an alarming rise in adolescent suicides in the second half of the 20th century and then describes the common myths about suicide. The next sections examine depression and the other risk factors for adolescent suicide, and the verbal and behavioral cues that signal youngsters at risk. Once a counselor is aware that a student may be suicidal—from personal observations or from information gleaned from teachers or other students—he or she must assess the actual risk to the student. Intervention is a function of risk level. Teachers, parents, and peers—because of their close relationships with students who are at risk—are an important part of any schoolwide prevention program. The chapter describes the unique role each of these groups and those in the larger community should play in the prevention program. No matter how good the program or how caring the participants, some students do kill themselves. The chapter concludes with a section on postvention, the issues and problems that inevitably follow a student's suicide.

> *I have dealt with many suicidal adolescents in the school setting. I have never believed that suicide is a normal response, but I have come to understand that suicidal ideation in many adolescents signals a developmental crisis that can be remedied with care and the proper intervention.*

SUICIDE RATES AMONG CHILDREN AND ADOLESCENTS: THE IMPACT OF AGE, RACE, AND GENDER

Several factors affect the rate of suicide and attempted suicide among schoolchildren. The most important is age; but race and gender also can be factors.

> *Age.* Since 1950, the suicide rate for the general population has remained stable. But the suicide rate for those between the ages of 15 and 19 went up more than 300 percent between 1950 and 1990, from 2.7 suicides per 100,000 to 11.1 per 100,000. Suicide is the second leading cause of death for people in this age group, and the third leading cause of death for those between the ages of 15 and 24. There are 100 to 200 suicide attempts for every youth who commits suicide. Approximately 85 percent of the people who commit suicide in this country each year are between ages 15 and 19 (National Center for Health Statistics, 1996). In short, the likelihood of a school counselor's having to deal with a suicide or an attempted suicide is very high. Relatively little is known about attempted and completed suicide among children under age 14, but there is evidence to suggest that suicide is increasing in this age group. School counselors who work in either elementary or middle school are not exempt from being concerned about suicide among the children with whom they work.
>
> *Race.* The group with the highest suicide rate by far is White adolescent males (Metha, Weber, & Webb, 1998). When gender is removed as a variable, Native American adolescents have the highest rate of attempted and completed suicide, nearly twice that of other youngsters of any other racial or ethnic group (Middlebrook, LeMaster, Beals, Novins, & Manson, 2001). There is a great deal of variability across tribes though. For example, Berlin (1987) found little difference in the suicide rate of Navajos and of the general population, but some Apache tribes have a rate about four times the national average. Both Asian Americans and Hispanic Americans have the lowest suicide rates compared with Native Americans, Whites, and African Americans.
>
> *Gender.* Men commit suicide at a higher rate than women, but women attempt suicide four times more often (Capuzzi & Gross, 2000). Among completed suicides, both genders today tend to use firearms. This was not always the case, and many argue that the accessibility of firearms is a

major factor in the frequency of their use. Hanging is the second most common method among male adolescents (Berman & Jobes, 1991); adolescent females are more likely to use gassing and ingestion to complete suicide. There are no gender differences in terms of method among adolescents who attempt suicide. The most common method is overdose through ingestion (Capuzzi & Gross, 2000). In general, males tend to use more violent and lethal methods; females, methods that are more passive (Popenhagen & Qualley, 1998). That distinction probably explains why males have a higher rate of completion and females a higher rate of attempt (Neiger & Hopkins, 1988; Overholser, Evans, & Spirito, 1990).

MYTHS AND MISCONCEPTIONS ABOUT SUICIDE

Schneidman (1981) defined *suicide* as "a conscious act of self-induced annihilation, best understood as a multidimensional malaise in a needful individual who defines an issue for which suicide is perceived as the best solution" (p. 199). Suicide is "a conscious act." Although impulsive individuals are more at risk for suicide, ultimately suicide is a conscious act and so, in many cases, preventable.

There are many myths and misunderstandings about suicide that, if corrected, can solidify prevention efforts:[1]

Suicidal tendencies are inherited. There is no evidence of a genetic basis for suicide. Although more than one member of a family may commit or attempt suicide, the likely explanation is family dysfunction. Also, from a social learning perspective, if a parent chooses suicide, there is a greater likelihood of his or her child's believing suicide is a viable option.

Suicide is a curse of the rich (or of the poor). To date, no research has shown that socioeconomic status is a key variable in suicide. Suicide appears to cut across socioeconomic groups, affecting all of them equally.

Most suicides occur in bad weather (or in the spring, on holidays, or at night). Weather and season and time of day are not what put adolescents at risk for suicide, nor do they augment the risk of suicide.

People who commit suicide are psychotic or mentally ill. Although a history of psychiatric problems is a risk factor for suicide, all suicides are not the result of mental illness. When their coping mechanisms fail them, many people choose to commit suicide.

Every adolescent who commits suicide is depressed. Although depression is often comorbid with suicide, every adolescent who commits suicide is not depressed. Again, suicide is the ultimate failure of the individual's coping mechanisms, not necessarily a consequence of depression.

Once a person is suicidal, he or she is suicidal forever. The good news about suicidal adolescents is that they remain suicidal only for a limited time.

---

[1] The list that follows is adapted from Capuzzi (1989, pp. 5–8). Copyright by ERIC/CASS Clearinghouse. Reprinted with permission.

For most youngsters thoughts of suicide are a response to a crisis; if they get the support they need to face that crisis, they can resume a normal life.

Improvement following a suicidal crisis means the risk is over. That a student seems suddenly energized after a suicidal crisis has ended does not mean the risk of suicide is gone; in fact, increased energy can give the suicidal teenager the strength to complete the suicide.

Suicidal adolescents are intent on dying. The fact of the matter is that most suicidal adolescents do not want to die and do not end up killing themselves. More often than not, suicide is a sign of the adolescent's pain, a cry for help and attention. One of the goals of suicide prevention is to teach young people safe ways of asking for help.

Adolescents who talk about suicide are simply trying to attract attention (or adolescents who really are going to commit suicide don't talk about it). In many cases, suicide is a cry for attention, but that does not mean that those who talk about suicide won't do it. Almost everyone who does commit suicide gives either verbal or behavioral clues about what he or she is planning to do.

Talking about suicide with an adolescent can increase the risk of that teenager's committing suicide. This myth can interfere with suicide prevention. The school counselor should never shy away from asking a student, "Do you ever think about hurting yourself?" If the student does not, he or she simply says no and walks away. But if the student does, the counselor is creating an opening to talk about it. There is simply no truth to the myth that mentioning suicide puts ideas into an adolescent's head.

If an adolescent attempts suicide and survives, he or she probably won't make another attempt. The single greatest factor for putting someone at risk for suicide is a previous attempt. In fact, 80 percent of those who commit suicide have attempted it previously (Hafen & Frandsen, 1986). Working to prevent a first attempt reduces the risk of suicide much more than working with an adolescent who has already attempted to commit suicide.

Professional helpers must keep an adolescent's suicidal intentions confidential. The ethics of their profession—and the law—demand that school counselors do everything possible to protect students from harming themselves or someone else. Maintaining confidentiality is nowhere near as important as keeping students safe.

DEPRESSION: A MAJOR RISK FACTOR IN ADOLESCENT SUICIDE

Not all adolescents who commit suicide are depressed, but a large number of them are. That makes recognizing the symptoms of adolescent depression and helping students who manifest those symptoms all the more crucial.

The Prevalence of Adolescent Depression

Approximately, 10 percent to 15 percent of children and adolescents have some symptoms of depression, and about 5 percent of those between ages 9 and 17 have been diagnosed with major depression (Guida, 2001). These estimates may well understate the prevalence of depression, particularly among adolescents. The problems are twofold: confusion with adolescent turmoil and the failure to recognize masked depression (B. T. McWhirter, McWhirter, Hart, & Gat, 2000). *Adolescent turmoil* (Offer & Sabshin, 1984) is widely used to describe disturbing behaviors—among them the classic symptoms of depression (see Table 9.1)—that are thought to be a normal part of adolescent development. *Masked depression* implies that the symptoms of depression in children and adolescents—among them physical complaints, poor socialization, poor academic performance, school phobia, substance abuse, delinquency, and aggressiveness (Aseltine, Gore, & Colten, 1998; Windle & Windle, 1997)—are different from those of adults and so less likely to be diagnosed. Adding to the confusion is the fact that child and adolescent depression often is comorbid with anxiety, behavior disorders, attention deficit disorder, substance abuse, and eating disorders (Athealth, 2000; Birmaher, Ryan, Williamson, Brent, & Kaufman, 1996).

Treating child and adolescent depression is beyond the purview of the school counselor, but being sensitive to its comorbidity, recognizing symptoms, and consulting with parents to make a referral for help are certainly within the scope of the school counselor's function. Table 9.1 describes the behavioral, emotional, and physical symptoms of depression in children and adolescents.

Types of Depression

The symptoms listed in Table 9.1 can vary in degree, intensity, and duration. This variation has led to the identification of four types of depression (Ramsey, 1994):

Normal depression. This is the least severe type of depression; it interferes only minimally with psychosocial functioning. It affects everyone from time to time, usually in response to some external disappointment. For students, normal depression might be caused by getting into trouble, receiving a poor grade, or having an argument with a friend. Many of the symptoms listed in Table 9.1 can manifest in normal depression, but in a very mild form. This is the kind of depression that the school counselor encounters most often among students; and, with the counselor's support and empathic listening, the students should recover quickly.

Chronic depression. Chronic depression is more trait than state. Students who are chronically depressed often find themselves down in the dumps, either in reaction to an external event of some sort or for no apparent reason.

Crisis depression. Crisis depression is a response to an external event, and it interferes significantly with psychosocial functioning. Students who are in

TABLE 9.1   **THE SYMPTOMS OF DEPRESSION**

Changes in Behavior and Attitude

General slowing down

Neglect of responsibilities and appearance

Poor memory

Trouble concentrating

Irritability (complaints about matters that used to be taken in stride)

Different Feelings and Perceptions

Emotional flatness or emptiness

Inability to find pleasure in anything

Hopelessness

Loss of sexual desire

Loss of warm feelings for family and friends

Extreme self-blame or guilt

Loss of self-esteem

Suicidal thoughts or actions

Physical Complaints

Sleep disturbances (waking up very early, sleeping too much or not enough)

Chronic fatigue and a lack of energy

Loss of appetite or a weight gain

Unexplained headaches or backaches

Digestive upsets (stomach pain, nausea, indigestion, changes in bowel habits)

a crisis depression manifest the symptoms listed in Table 9.1 to a debilitating degree; they may also begin to use alcohol and drugs excessively (Ramsey, 1994). These students feel helpless and hopeless, which can result in thoughts of suicide (Dixon, 1987). The school counselor must support and monitor these students, paying close attention to the duration of the symptoms. If symptoms persist more than two weeks, counselors should start to think about clinical depression and sending the child for help.

Clinical depression. This is the most severe form of depression: The student's psychosocial functioning is significantly impaired and thoughts of suicide are common. Like crisis depression, clinical depression is often caused by an external event; however, unlike crisis depression, it is not clear when or to what degree the student will return to normalcy. When school counselors detect clinical depression, they must refer the student to outside treatment for long-term therapy.

Others have tried to help school counselors detect depression among students by using classifications of the dominant symptoms. Reynolds (1986) advanced the idea that depression could be primarily affective (dominated by worry and anxiety), cognitive (dominated by self-deprecation), motivational (dominated by signs of withdrawal or decreased performance), or vegetative (dominated by physical symptoms). McConville and Bruce (1985), utilizing Reynolds's first three classifications, developed a three-part depression typology for children and adolescents:

- Affective type (dominated by sadness and helplessness)
- Self-esteem type (dominated by discouragement and negative self-esteem)
- Guilt type (dominated by guilt and self-destructive behavior)

Both the affective and self-esteem types are appropriate for school counselors to treat either through individual or small-group counseling, or with classroom interventions. The guilt type is far more serious and demands clinical intervention (S. L. Hart, 1991; McConville & Bruce, 1985).

The Causes of Depression

B. T. McWhirter et al. (2000) divided the causes of depression into five models: biological, psychodynamic, behavioral, cognitive, and family systems. In most of these models, the focus of intervention is on helping the child develop self-esteem.

Biological Models Biological models of depression are of two types: genetic and biochemical (B. T. McWhirter et al., 2000). The *genetic models* derive from research that found that genetic factors account for approximately 50 percent of the variance in mood disorders (Birmaher et al., 1996). A child with a depressed parent is about three times more likely to experience depression.

Biochemical models of depression explain depression as an hormonal imbalance (Puig-Antich, 1985; S. L. Hart, 1991).[2] Biochemical models have become increasingly popular in recent years, as have psychopharmacological interventions for both children and adolescents. Yet studies do not find evidence that medication has a positive effect on young people suffering from depression (Birmaher et al., 1996; Brent et al., 1996; J. Sommers-Flanagan & Sommers-Flanagan, 1996).[3] Still, the drugs are being prescribed, and that means school counselors should know what they are and what kind of side effects they are likely to have (Table 9.2).

Psychodynamic Models Traditional psychoanalytic theory describes depression as anger turned inward, toward the self, and connected to a judging and controlling superego. Because the superego is still forming in children and adolescents, Freudian theorists reasoned that depression is not possible in these age groups

---

[2] Others argue that biochemical imbalances may be less the cause and more the result of depression (Geddes & Butler, 2002; Hazell, 2002).

[3] In contrast, studies do point to the positive effects of antidepressants among adults who are clinically depressed (for examples of those positive effects, see Nemeroff & Schatzberg, 2002).

TABLE 9.2   MAJOR ANTIDEPRESSANTS AND THEIR SIDE EFFECTS

	Side Effects	
Antidepressants	**Anticholinergic***	**Sedative†**
Asendin (amoxapine)	Medium	Low
Aventyl (nortriptyline)	Medium	Medium
Elavil (amitriptyline)	High	High
Norpramin (desipramine)	Low	Low
Paxil (paroxetine)	Low	Very low
Prozac (fluoxetine)	Very low	Low
Sinequan (doxepin)	Medium	Medium
Tofranil (imipramine)	Medium to high	Medium to high
Vivactil (protryptyline)	Medium	Very low
Wellbutrin (bupropion)	Very low	Very low
Zoloft (sertraline)	Very low	Very low

*Anticholinergic side effects include hypotension, dry mouth, constipation, blurred vision, dry eyes, and nasal congestion.

†Sedative side effects include dizziness, unsteadiness, and drowsiness.

SOURCE: Adapted from James and Nims (1996, p. 303).

(S. L. Hart, 1991). More-recent psychodynamic models describe depression among the young in terms of a loss that stems from childhood helplessness and the disruption of emotional bonding with the primary caregiver. The result is a loss of self-esteem. The child or adolescent has no internal sense of self-worth, relying instead on external sources for confirmation of his or her self-worth; when those external sources are lost, the child or adolescent becomes depressed (Capuzzi & Gross, 2000). Although most school counselors do not work from a psychodynamic perspective, understanding depression in terms of a loss of emotional bonding can be helpful. School counselors and teachers, by fostering a nurturing relationship with youngsters who are depressed, can help to counteract the experience of early emotional loss (S. L. Hart, 1991).

Behavioral Models   Behaviorists argue that depression is produced by a lack of positive reinforcement for behaviors that are considered more normal. As time goes on, the depressed youngster manifests behaviors that are less likely to elicit positive reinforcement but that do draw attention to the child and give him or her a sense of control. The symptoms of depression, then, are both cause and consequence of the lack of positive reinforcement. The key for practitioners is not to reinforce the depressed behaviors, to reserve praise and encouragement for those behaviors that show improvement in both task and social functioning (Bauer, 1987). To that end, the school counselor works collaboratively with teachers. Also, the school counselor can form a social skills training group for students who seem isolated and lacking in socialization skills.

M. E. P. Seligman's (1974) learned-helplessness model of depression is based directly on research with behavioral reinforcement. *Learned helplessness* is a response to a series of failures to solve a problem or to improve a situation. In time, the individual becomes convinced that nothing he or she does or tries can make a difference. People with learned helplessness have an external locus of control (their life is controlled by external forces) and an internal locus of responsibility (they blame themselves). Their feelings of hopelessness generalize to most of life's situations. For children and adolescents, learned helplessness often revolves around schoolwork: The student has made numerous attempts and tried numerous means to improve his or her schoolwork without success. So the student gives up, and depression sets in. Schloss (1983) recommended several strategies to help students overcome learned helplessness:

1. Help the child avoid a sense of constant failure by providing work tasks in small incremental steps that give the child a sense of mastery and success.
2. Neutralize helplessness by providing opportunities for choice and power (as in selecting work assignments or self-rewards).
3. Provide increased verbal feedback and explanations to the depressed child who may lack the ability to see cause and effect.
4. Encourage depressed children to identify behaviors and outcomes themselves, for a growing sense of confidence. (quoted in S. L. Hart, 1991, p. 284)

Cognitive Models   According to cognitive theories, depression is the direct result of negative or irrational thoughts. Beck (1967) was the first to develop a cognitive theory of depression; some years later, he and his colleagues described a cognitive triad that they believed is characteristic of people who are depressed (Beck, Rush, Shaw, & Emery, 1979). The triad consists of three negative thought patterns: of self, of the world, and of the future. Over time, these thought patterns develop into *schemas,* frameworks so much a part of the individual's cognitive makeup that they are like personality traits. Environmental stimuli are filtered through these schemas and distorted to conform with the individual's negative view of self, world, and future. Even the most positive experiences are distorted. For example, a depressed child might respond to praise for a good grade with "The teacher probably felt sorry for me." Depressed children often making negative comments about themselves: "I always fail," "I'm not good at anything," "No one likes me."

In the cognitive model, the first step in counseling a student who is depressed is to teach the student to replace negative self-statements with positive self-talk. The counselor usually gives the student a homework assignment: "Every time you say to yourself, 'I'm a bad person,' I want you to correct that statement by saying, 'I'm a good person.'". Other school-based interventions include guidance lessons that teach the relationship between thoughts and feelings and role-play activities that focus on the problems and symptoms of childhood depression (peer rejection, feelings of guilt and failure) (Clarizio, 1985).

Another cognitive model, Rehm's (1977) self-control model, explains depression as the product of deficiencies in three cognitive processes:

Self-monitoring. The child pays attention only to negative events.

Self-evaluation. The child often makes negative self-judgments. He or she sets high standards for positive self-evaluation and low standards for negative self-evaluation.

Self-reinforcement. The child has a negative attribution style: Events are beyond his or her control because external forces control them or because he or she has some sort of internal deficiency.

The broad goal of intervention here is to help the student gain a greater sense of self-control. The school counselor and teachers should begin by assigning the student small, manageable tasks and using positive reinforcement when those tasks are accomplished. Also, there is some evidence that group interventions in schools can increase students' sense of self-control (M. M. Omizo & Omizo, 1987).

The Family Systems Model   Family systems theorists believe that children's behavior—even behavior that is symptomatic of depression—maintains balance (homeostasis) in the family system. Family systems theorists would not approve of treating just the child; they would argue that the family must be treated. Obviously, family counseling is not a school counselor's function, but the school counselor should consider family dynamics in working with a student who is depressed. The counselor can consult with the parents about their child and look for signs during the meeting that the parents are using their child's depression in some way. For example, a child's illness allows parents to focus their psychic energy on the child instead of on other difficulties they should be resolving. If there is evidence that the child's depression is serving some function in the family, the school counselor facilitates a referral for family counseling.

Assessment

School counselors have neither the time nor the training to work with children who show symptoms of severe clinical depression. Those youngsters should be referred for outside counseling. Several assessment instruments are available to help the school counselor determine the need for a referral.

The Reynolds Scales   Reynolds (1987) developed the Reynolds Adolescent Depression Scale (RADS) for young people ages 13 to 18. The scale consists of 30 items derived from symptoms of depression and dysthymia.[4] Responses—*Almost never, Hardly ever, Sometimes, Most of the time*—are weighted from 1 to 4 points, which means scores on the RADS can range from 30 to 120. Higher scores indicate higher levels of depressive symptoms. The RADS takes 5 to 10 minutes to complete. According to Ramsey (1994), the RADS is easy to administer and "provides an efficient and economical method for individual, small, or large group prevention screening" (p. 258).

---

[4]*Dysthymia* is a long-term depressed mood; its symptoms are less severe than those of major depression.

The Reynolds Child Depression Scale (RCDS) was designed for use with children in Grades 3 to 6 (Reynolds, 1989).[5] There is only a slight difference between the formats of the RCDS and the RADS. All but one of the 30 items on the RCDS are rated on a 4-point scale. The last item, a series of faces showing different emotions from happy to sad, is marked on a 5-point scale, so scores on the RCDS can range from 30 to 121. Like the RADS, the RCDS is easy to administer and takes about 10 minutes to complete.

Reynolds (1986) suggested that school counselors undertake a schoolwide multiphase screening for depression early in the school year. Six weeks later, the test should be readministered to all students whose scores indicate a risk for depression (students who score at or above 77). The school counselor can then schedule an interview with any student whose score remains high to plan outside treatment.

Beck Depression Inventory   The Beck Depression Inventory (BDI) is designed to assess the severity of depression in adolescents and adults (Beck & Steer, 1993; Beck, Ward, Mendelson, Mock, & Erbaugh, 1961). The current BDI (it was revised in 1993) consists of 21 items, each a statement related to an affective, cognitive, motivational, or physical symptom of depression. Test-takers are asked to rate each item a 0, 1, 2, or 3 on a severity scale. Scores can range from 0 to 63, with 0 to 9 indicating minimal depression, 10 to 16 mild depression, 17 to 29 moderate depression, and 30 to 63 severe depression. The BDI can be administered individually or in a group, in oral or written form; and it can be scored by hand or by computer.

The Danger of Misdiagnosis   These instruments can help school counselors differentiate depression in children and adolescents from other problems. Again, depression in these populations is easily misdiagnosed. In a breakthrough study with 282 children who had been diagnosed with learning disabilities, the researchers found that 71 percent of the children actually were suffering from depression and that only 7 percent had genuine learning problems (Colbert, Newman, Ney, & Young, 1982). When the 71 percent received treatment for depression, their learning improved dramatically without any kind of academic remediation. In another study, approximately 33 percent of children with conduct problems were found to be depressed; when they were treated for depression, their conduct improved (Puig-Antich, 1985). Our point here: When confronted with students who exhibit learning or behavioral problems, school counselors should be quick to rule out depression as a possible cause of the students' difficulties.

A Group Intervention

Students who are depressed often have poor social skills, a problem for which group counseling can be especially helpful. Table 9.3 is an outline of a 10-session group. Because the group has both cognitive and behavioral components, each session includes a homework assignment to help members put learning into practice.

---

[5] For those with below-grade reading ability, the RCDS can be administered orally.

TABLE 9.3 A SOCIAL-SKILLS GROUP FOR YOUNGSTERS WITH DEPRESSION: THEMES, ACTIVITIES, AND ASSIGNMENTS

Session Themes	Activities and Assignments
1. Introduction	The leader reviews the ground rules and asks the members to make a commitment to learning new and effective ways of dealing with their problems. The homework assignment: to bring to the next session an example of a thought, feeling, or behavior that troubles each member.
2. Mood and focus	The goal of this session is to understand how a problem can spiral downward and become increasingly more difficult to solve. The leader demonstrates the concept by drawing a picture of a tornado on newsprint or the chalkboard. (A tornado is a particularly apt image because its destructive power is greatest at its base.) Members are asked for examples of downward spiraling based on the assignment from the previous session. The homework assignment: to make a list of activities that the member enjoys.
3. Pleasant events	The goal of this session is to help members understand that simply thinking about pleasant things can make them feel happier, that they can control how they feel by using their mind. The homework assignment: to notice during the week someone who seems anxious and to observe how that person handles himself or herself.
4. Reducing tension	The goal is to learn relaxation skills and to learn the connection between being relaxed and being in control. The leader teaches systematic desensitization, then asks the members to participate in relaxation exercises and imagery, and then leads a discussion on the experience.* The homework assignment: to practice a relaxation exercise during the week and record the results in a notebook.
5. Strength bombardment	The goal of this session is to experience both giving and receiving positive feedback. The focus is on the individual strengths of each member. The members choose from a list of positive phrases the ones they feel apply to other members; then the members talk about how it feels to have positive things said about them. The homework assignment: to notice positive things about other people and to give positive feedback to at least three people outside the group.
6. Positive thinking	The goal is to learn the power of internal attention. The leader asks each member to share a negative thought about himself or herself and then explores with the group the consequences of dwelling on negative thoughts. The session ends with the group's revisiting the positive thoughts from the last session. The homework assignment: to find cartoons in newspapers or comic books that show the connections among thoughts, feelings, and behaviors.
7. Problem solving	The goal is to learn problem solving through the use of a group problem-solving activity. The leader presents a situation, for example, getting a bad grade or having an argument with a sibling or friend. Then he or she guides the members through a 5-step problem-solving process: (1) Identify the problem; (2) determine the different things you can do about the problem; (3) decide which solution will work best; (4) try the solution; and (5) evaluate its effectiveness. It is important for the group to reflect on the process. The homework assignment: to notice people who are being treated with respect.
8. Friendly skills	The session begins with the members sharing their examples of people being treated with respect and then brainstorming about different ways to show respect for others. Members then choose one of their own habits that they would like to change. Each student can act out or talk about the habit; then the other students suggest alternative behaviors (which can also be acted out). The homework assignment: to practice any new skills discussed and role-played in the group.
9. Goal setting	The goal is to learn to set short- and long-term goals. Members select a theme or lesson from a previous session and set a goal, along with reasonable objectives, toward improving their skill in the selected area. The homework assignment: to begin implementing at least one objective during the coming week.
10. Closure	The leader asks the members to share their feelings about the end of the group and their thoughts on what they liked and did not like about the group. A follow-up session can be planned for sometime in the future. The leader should point out that although it is sad that the group is ending, congratulations are in order for all the new learning that has taken place and the opportunities that lie ahead to put that learning into practice.

*Systematic desensitization is a stepwise procedure in which anxiety-provoking events—in increasing strength—are paired with relaxation techniques and positive imagery (Gladding, 2001).

SOURCE: Adapted from R. Sommers-Flanagan, Barrett-Hakanson, Clarke, and Sommers-Flanagan (2000).

There are many activities that school counselors can use to expand the themes and ideas in this outline. Remember that the group process alone—simply being and sharing with others—can make students feel happier about themselves.

OTHER RISK FACTORS IN ADOLESCENT SUICIDE

Not all adolescents who attempt or complete suicide manifest signs of clinical depression. Behavioral and personality traits and external events can put young people at risk for suicide.[6]

Behavioral and Personality Traits

Researchers have found a number of behaviors and general personality traits that can help school counselors identify students at risk for suicide:

Hopelessness and helplessness. Ultimately, suicide is an option for those who feel hopeless and helpless about finding any other solution to their problem. Several studies support the connection between suicide and feelings of hopelessness and helplessness (Cull & Gill, 1982; Kovacs, Beck, & Weissman, 1975; Peck, 1983). A good intervention for these students is a group that focuses on problem solving and building self-esteem.

Impulsive and aggressive behavior. Students with a history of impulsive and aggressive behavior are at greater risk for suicide. In adolescence, suicide is often an impulsive act in response to a crisis; but that does not mean that the youngster has not given any warning signs. A history of truancy, running away, and unwillingness to cooperate should alert the school counselor to a possible risk of suicide. Prevention for these students might include an anger control group.

Isolation. The more an adolescent is cut off from his or her peers, the greater his or her risk for suicide. Although many adolescents experience conflicts with their peers, their development at this age dictates that they spend a great deal of time with their peers. Adolescents who have no friends do not have the support system they need in times of trouble; if their own resources are limited, they can be at increased risk of suicide. Small-group counseling is an excellent intervention for improving the socialization skills of adolescents.

Low self-esteem. Again, low or negative self-esteem increases the risk for suicide (Beautrais, Joyce, & Mulder, 1999; Cull & Gill, 1982; Stillion, McDowell, & Shamblin, 1984). A self-esteem group can be of enormous help to these students.

---

[6] Although some of these traits and behaviors are also symptoms of depression, they can exist in isolation and should raise a red flag for the school counselor.

Stress. A combination of high stress and poor management skills can increase the risk for suicide (Capuzzi & Gross, 2000). For these students, the school counselor should consider a stress management group.

Perfectionism. This factor is related to stress. Adolescents who feel they must do everything perfectly or who have an exaggerated need to achieve are at increased risk for suicide. Both perfectionism and overachievement are thought to compensate for feelings of low self-esteem. However, Capuzzi and Gross (2000) rightly pointed out that it would be foolish to consider all high achievers at risk for suicide: Overachievement should be assessed in the context of other observations. For these students, cognitive–behavioral interventions can be effective in altering their thinking that they have to be perfect.

Cognitive deficits. There is concern among experts that learning disabilities may increase the risk of suicide. Certainly if a student thinks of a disability as loss, then depression—and the attendant risk of suicide—is possible. Increasing both the frustration and the risk for students with learning disabilities are deficits in communication skills that can prevent these youngsters from expressing their thoughts and feelings (Capuzzi & Gross, 2000). The school counselor strives to be especially supportive of and nurturing to students with learning disabilities because their self-esteem is so greatly affected by their learning difficulties.

Guilt. Excessive guilt in adolescents, especially if it translates into wanting to be punished, can increase their risk for suicide (Capuzzi & Gross, 2000). Obviously many adolescents experience situational guilt; school counselors need to focus on students whose guilt seems pervasive. These students should be referred for outside counseling because overcoming excessive guilt requires long-term treatment.

Situational Variables

Although behavioral and personality characteristics can contribute to an adolescent's risk for suicide, usually suicide is an immediate response to a crisis of some sort: for example, a broken relationship, a family crisis, the suicide of a relative or a close friend, a significant loss, or the anniversary of a significant loss (M. C. Friedrich, Matus, & Rinn, 1985). Other situational variables that contribute to a suicidal tendency are a previous suicide attempt, a previous attempt to hurt one's self (through self-inflicted behaviors), alcoholism or drug abuse in the family, and being away from home.

THE WARNING SIGNS OF ADOLESCENT SUICIDE

For adolescents who complete or attempt suicide, killing themselves is the only way out of an untenable situation (Peach & Reddick, 1991). Although teenagers may not come right out and ask for help with that situation, they almost always hint at their desperation in words or behavior. It is critical that school counselors be attuned to these cues. One caution though: A determination that a youngster is suicidal cannot be made on the basis of one event or statement or behavior. When adolescents attempt suicide, several of these variables have come together to convince them that suicide is the only way out.

Verbal Cues

Actually, some adolescents do communicate their suicidal intent directly: "I'm going to kill myself," "I just want to die." But most communicate their intentions subtly, often using metaphorical language: "I'd like to go home," "I won't be around much longer," "They'll be sorry for what they did to me," "I'm very tired," "I wonder what death is like," "They'll see how serious I am," "Things are never going to get any better," "I'll always feel this way," "Nobody cares," "People would be better off without me" (Capuzzi & Gross, 2000; Kalafat, 1990). These are just a few examples; there are many others. The point is that when a student says something that strikes the counselor as odd or that can be interpreted in a number of ways, the counselor is quick to ask the student for clarification: "Can you help me understand a bit better what you mean when you say, 'They'll be sorry'?"

Counselors also need to be sensitive to themes that might communicate what an adolescent is thinking. Capuzzi and Gross (2000) listed nine themes that signal thoughts of suicide on the part of adolescents:

- Wanting to escape from a difficult situation
- Wanting to join someone who has died
- Wanting to attract the attention of family and friends
- Wanting to manipulate someone
- Wanting to avoid punishment
- Wanting to be punished
- Wanting to control when and how death will occur (especially for adolescents who have a chronic or terminal illness)
- Wanting to end a conflict that seems unresolvable
- Wanting revenge (p. 328)

According to Capuzzi and Gross, each of these nine motivations can be categorized into one of the three primary functions of suicide: to avoid a difficult situation, to take control of one's life, or to communicate pain. All suicides serve one of the three functions.

Behavioral Cues

The school counselor also must pay attention to behaviors that could signal the intention to commit suicide. Capuzzi and Gross (2000) identified a number of behaviors that are cause for concern:[7]

---

[7] Obviously, school counselors cannot identify all of these behaviors themselves. Often they rely on information from teachers, parents, and even peers.

Lack of concern about personal welfare. At times, adolescents reveal their suicidal tendencies by putting themselves at risk—for example, by driving recklessly, accepting dares from friends, or marking or cutting themselves. The school counselors should understand that these youngsters may be in pain but are unable to express that pain.

Changes in social patterns. The school counselor should notice sudden changes in students' behavior: a socially active student becomes withdrawn and isolated, a normally compliant student become argumentative and rebellious, a student leaves one group of friends and joins another group whose members are more daring or more rebellious.

A decline in school achievement. The counselor should be aware of any good student who suddenly loses interest in schoolwork, itself a symptom of depression in this population. If a student is vague or refuses to talk about the problem, the counselor should not be put off: "For some kids, going from As to Cs means they're giving up. Are you giving up? Have you ever thought about hurting yourself?"

Difficulties concentrating and thinking clearly. Again, these difficulties are symptomatic of depression. They also can indicate that the student is focusing his or her energies on planning a suicide.

Altered patterns of eating and sleeping. Although there can be many causes for disturbances in eating and sleeping, depression and suicidal tendencies are clearly among them. The school counselor should watch for a dramatic loss or gain of weight and should ask teachers to watch for students who are nodding off in class.

Attempts to put personal affairs in order or to make amends. An adolescent's efforts to put his or her affairs in order could signal that the youngster is preparing to die. Often before a suicide attempt, the adolescent repairs a broken relationship, calls old friends, impulsively finishes a project that had been put off, or gives away important personal items.

Alcohol or drug use or abuse. Many adolescents experiment with alcohol and drugs, but sustained use, which leads to abuse, diminishes some of the psychological defenses that protect youngsters from thoughts of suicide. Substance abuse can increase impulsivity and at the same time decrease the adolescent's communications skills. For the substance-abusing adolescent, then, at a particular moment in time suicide can appear to be a viable option.

Unusual interest in how others are feeling. As a defense against their own pain, suicidal adolescents can show an exaggerated interest in and responsiveness to the problems of others. A preoccupation with others serves a dual purpose: It helps suicidal adolescents focus on something other than their own problem, and, paradoxically, it helps them communicate their own pain.

Preoccupation with themes of death and violence. This kind of preoccupation is quite common in suicidal adolescents. Certainly many youngsters are drawn to violence in the media; but when violence becomes a major interest, the school counselor needs to be concerned. Movies, books, music, video games, drawings, and writings that focus on destruction, death, and dying could signal suicidal tendencies.

Sudden improvement after a period of depression. As noted earlier, students who show a sudden improvement after a period of depression may very well be at risk for suicide. Having made the decision to go ahead with the suicide, they are mobilizing themselves to carry out the plan. This is not the gradual improvement that signals a depression is lifting; this is a sudden and drastic change.

Sudden or increased promiscuity. Experimentation with or escalation of sexual activity can be an adolescent's way of diverting attention from suicidal thoughts and feelings. The consequences of promiscuity—for example, an unwanted pregnancy or feelings of guilt—can augment the adolescent's suicidal tendencies.

ASSESSING THE RISK OF SUICIDE

Suicidal adolescents need two types of treatment: acute and long term. Acute treatment is a response to a crisis. Here it is the school counselor's responsibility to assess the risk of suicide (low, moderate, or high) and to design interventions to stabilize the situation.[8] Long-term treatment is not the school counselor's job. When long-term counseling is needed, the counselor must refer the adolescent via the parents for outside therapy.

The Suicide Interview

Some students seek out the school counselor; more often, students who have communicated, verbally or nonverbally, thoughts about suicide are brought to the counselor's attention by teachers or fellow students. To determine appropriate interventions, the school counselor must assess the risk of a suicidal adolescent's taking action. The assessment should cut across four dimensions: ideation, volition, plan, and history. The outline in Table 9.4 is a practical guide for assessing students' risk for suicide. It describes the suicide interview.

This outline will help the school counselors cope in a orderly and professional manner with a suicidal crisis. The goal is to stabilize the situation by choosing an appropriate intervention based on an informed assessment of the risk to the student.

---

[8] If the school has a suicide policy, the counselor should follow the assessment and counseling guidelines described there.

TABLE 9.4 **THE SUICIDE INTERVIEW**

Dimensions	Content
1. Suicidal ideation	Variability in terms of frequency, duration, and intensity of suicidal thoughts is one indicator of risk level. When a student's thoughts of suicide are frequent, last a long time, and interrupt the student's routine, the student is at increased risk of suicide. To determine the frequency, duration, and intensity of suicidal ideation, the counselor should ask the following questions:
	• In the course of a single day, how often do you think about hurting yourself?
	• When the idea of hurting yourself comes to mind, how long does the idea stay with you? How long do you dwell on it?
	• When these thoughts come to you, are you able to continue with what you're doing, or do these thoughts get in the way of your everyday activities?
	If the suicidal ideation is not frequent (e.g., just once a day) and does not last long (e.g., just several minutes), and the student is able to continue with his or her routine, then the student's risk of suicide is low. In this case, the counselor should simply alert the child's parents and give them a list of symptoms to watch for—among them increased isolation, moodiness, or the child's locking himself or herself in a room. When suicidal tendencies remain at the level of ideation, the risk of suicide generally is low.
2. Suicidal volition	The key question here is "Do you want to hurt yourself?" Most students answer no, that they are only thinking about it. When adolescents say they want to hurt themselves, the risk of suicide automatically increases to moderate at least. The counselor must immediately alert the parents, ask them to come to the school, and direct them to take their child to the nearest medical center for a psychiatric evaluation.
3. Suicide plan	Having a plan increases the risk of suicide. The question the counselor needs to ask is "If you did hurt yourself, how would you do it?" If the adolescent answers, "I don't know" or "I haven't really thought about it," the risk is lower than if the student is able to give concrete details about how and when he or she plans to commit suicide. Another factor here is the lethality of the method (e.g., a gun versus pills). Volition plus a plan increase the risk of suicide to high. The counselor should notify the parents at once and, after letting the principal know what's going on, should call 911 to have the student taken for an immediate psychiatric evaluation. In extreme cases, when the counselor has determined that the risk of suicide is imminent, the call to the parents can be made after the student is en route to the hospital.
4. A history of attempted suicide	A history of attempted suicide automatically increases the student's present risk. Spirito, Plummer, Gispert, and Levy (1992) found that 10 percent of those who attempted suicide did so again within a 3-month period. The school counselor should always ask, "Have you ever tried to hurt yourself in the past?" Here, too, the lethality of the earlier attempt should be investigated. There's a significant difference between taking a few pills, and ending up in the hospital with a serious injury. In the presence of ideation and the absence of volition, if a suicidal student has made a serious attempt at some earlier time to hurt himself or herself, the counselor should consider the current risk to be moderate.

The Adapted SAD PERSONS Scale

The Adapted SAD PERSONS Scale (A–SPS) is a formal instrument for assessing the risk of suicide among children and adolescents (Juhnke, 1996).[9] The A–SPS was developed around 10 risk factors for suicide: gender (males are at greater risk for completing suicide), age (older adolescents are at greater risk), depression or

---

[9]The scale is an adaptation of the SAD PERSONS Scale (Patterson, Dohn, Bird, & Patterson, 1983), which was designed for use with both adults and children.

an affective disorder, a previous suicide attempt, alcohol or drug abuse, loss of rational thinking (delusions or hallucinations that result from a physical or psychological disorder), lack of social supports, a suicide plan, family factors (neglect, abuse, suicidal modeling by parents or siblings), and school problems. On each subscale, scores can range from 0 to 10. Males receive a 10 and females a 0 on the dichotomized risk factor of gender. Appropriate interventions are suggested according to categories of total score: 0–29, low risk; 30–49, moderate risk; 50–69, high risk; and 70–100, extreme risk.

Juhnke encourages counseling for low-risk students. He advises that school counselors contact the parents of moderate-risk students to strongly suggest counseling services and a no-suicide contract with the child, and to give them a number to call in a crisis. For a youngster at high risk, the school counselor should contact the parents and instruct them to take their child for an immediate psychiatric evaluation. And, according to Juhnke, a student at extreme risk needs immediate hospitalization. The counselor can make contact with the parents and arrange for the student to be escorted to the hospital; but if the parents fail to follow through or try to obstruct the plan, the counselor should alert child protective services.

Juhnke's suggested interventions based on A–SPS scores parallel those in the previous section with one exception: He stops short of calling 911 for students at extreme risk for suicide. Ideally the school district has a policy that spells out the procedure to follow when the parents of a high-risk child cannot be reached. If not, we strongly urge the school counselor to immediately call 911. The counselor's primary responsibility is to protect the child from imminent danger.

The A–SPS can be a useful tool for screening large numbers of students for suicidal tendencies and for determining the need for and characteristics of a suicide prevention program.

Suicide Ideation Questionnaire

The Suicide Ideation Questionnaire (SIQ) was developed to measure suicidal ideation in adolescents (Reynolds, 1988). Two versions exist: one for students in Grades 7 to 9, which consists of 15 items; the other for students in Grades 10 to 12, which consists of 30 items. The test-taker is asked to rate the frequency with which he or she thought about each item over the last month on a 7-point scale (ranging from *Almost every day* to *I never had this thought*). There are 8 critical items— all related to having a specific suicide plan—that indicate the need for immediate additional screening. The SIQ takes at most 10 minutes to complete. It is only a screening device: That is, the school counselor can use the questionnaire to screen large groups and then follow up with those students whose scores are high. And like the A–SPS, the SIQ can be used to determine the need for a schoolwide suicide prevention program.

DEVELOPING A SCHOOLWIDE
SUICIDE PREVENTION PROGRAM

Much of this chapter has been about helping school counselors detect and respond to suicidal adolescents. Although detection and intervention are certainly important, they are only a part of a suicide prevention program in the school. School counseling programs are comprehensive and proactive, not situational and reactive. According to Malley, Kush, and Bogo (1994), a comprehensive suicide prevention program for adolescents should include the following components:

- A formal suicide policy
- Written procedures to address at-risk students
- In-service training for teachers and other school staff members
- A mental health professional on site
- A mental health team
- Prevention materials for distribution to parents
- Prevention materials for distribution to students
- Screening programs to identify at-risk students
- Prevention discussion in the classroom
- Mental health counseling for at-risk students
- Suicide reference materials for counselors
- Suicide prevention and intervention training for school counselors
- Faculty training in the detection of suicide warning signs
- A statement in writing that describes specific criteria for counselors to use in assessing the lethality of a potential suicide
- A written policy that describes how the comprehensive suicide prevention program should be evaluated
- A postvention component in the event of an actual suicide

What is most important about this list is the idea that suicide prevention is not the sole responsibility of the school counselor. Teachers, parents, and students also play vital roles in a schoolwide program for suicide prevention.

Working with Teachers

Because they are with students during the day more than other adults are, teachers may be the first to recognize the behavioral changes that indicate a student is at risk for suicide. Unfortunately, a national survey of school counselors found that 52 percent of schools do not offer any kind of in-service training in suicide detection and prevention to school staff (Malley et al., 1994).

> *At the beginning of each school year, I always asked the principal to give me 10 to 15 minutes of the agenda for the faculty orientation to talk about the suicide prevention program. In my talk, I emphasized that teachers are more likely to become aware of a suicidal student before the school counselor does because of their close relationship with students. I also men-*

tioned how valuable teachers can be in doing nonprofessional counseling with their students. But I would always remind them that suicide is a problem that must be referred to the school counselor.

Most of the information necessary for teachers to play a key role in preventing adolescent suicide can be communicated in a 1- to 2-hour in-service training (Kalafat, 1990). If the school has a written suicide policy, it should be distributed and explained. Other handouts should address data, myths, risk factors, warning signs, and a general profile of the suicidal adolescent. It is important to emphasize that when teachers feel that a student is at risk for suicide, their first responsibility is to refer the student immediately to the school counselor for assessment.

The training should also stress that a key factor in the prevention of suicide among students is for teachers to develop a positive relationship with students:

- Listen empathetically to students.
- Positively reinforce all students on a regular basis.
- Help students learn better coping and decision-making skills.
- Be aware of their own difficulty discussing suicide, an inability that could hinder their understanding of a child's efforts to communicate suicidal thoughts or behaviors.
- Accept students for who they are; they should not try to impose unrealistic goals on students.
- Recognize the importance of students' problems; never belittle or make light of something that is bothering a student (Popenhagen & Qualley, 1998).

Working with Parents

Parents should be collaborators in any schoolwide suicide prevention program. But the topic of suicide frightens many people, and the school counselor is sensitive to that in talking about suicide and in encouraging parents to talk about it too. Parents must understand that students who can talk through their crisis are more likely to manage that crisis without doing harm to themselves. The golden rule: *If it's mentionable, it's manageable.*

One by-product of the fear that suicide evokes in parents is resistance to suicide prevention efforts in the school. The best tool to use in overcoming that resistance is accurate information. Much of the material described above for the in-service training program for school staff can be used in a workshop with parents. Counselors can also have pamphlets on suicide visible when parents visit the counseling office. It is especially important to disabuse parents of the myths that surround suicide.

Another way to engage parents is to tell them that their knowledge of the risk factors for and warning signs of suicide could help their children's friends. Some teenagers are more likely to share their problems with their friends' parents instead of their own.

Parents who become aware of a suicidal child—their own or someone else's— need to know what to do. They should inform the school counselor if the child is a student in the school, and they also should have a list of resources in the community. Parents must be warned that keeping this kind of information confidential is not helping the child. When someone else's child is at risk, and the child is not a student in the school, they should contact that child's parents and provide them with whatever resources they need to get help for the child. This networking has a significant multiplier effect that both expands prevention efforts in the community and makes the school counselor's job of disseminating information about teenage suicide all the more important.

Working with Peers

We've noted repeatedly that adolescents are more apt to share their problems with their peers than with adults. Their thoughts about suicide are no exception. Therefore, a prevention program must extend to students in the school. Here, too, the most important message is that confidentiality cannot be respected when the issue is suicide. The school counselor must do everything possible to convince students that by keeping a friend's thoughts of suicide secret, they are putting that friend in danger. One effective strategy is to have them imagine that their friend did commit suicide and that they did nothing to try to prevent it. The guilt would be unbearable.

Much like teachers and parents, students can be trained how to identify peers who may be at risk for suicide and how to proceed once they are concerned. The more students know about suicide—the risk factors, the myths, the ways to get help—the more likely they are to ask for help themselves and for their peers (Centers for Disease Control and Prevention, 1992; King et al., 2000). This kind of information is so valuable that it should be offered in a class, so that students do not have to give up free time to have access to it. Adolescent suicide is correlated with other problems—for example, substance abuse, teen pregnancy, and problems with parents—so guidance lessons around those topics also contribute to suicide prevention. But classes in related problems are not a substitute for classes specifically about preventing suicide.

Although the school counselor prepares the classroom session and is there to offer support and expertise, it may well be the classroom teacher who presents the information.[10] In fact, this approach is indicated whenever the teacher has a positive and trusting relationship with the students. Students are more likely to reveal themselves to a teacher they know and trust than to a school counselor with whom they have minimal contact (Kalafat, 1990).

Working with Community Leaders

In addition to working closely with teachers, parents, and students to help them recognize the warning signs of suicide, the school counselor also investigates the community resources that are available to support the school's prevention pro-

---

[10]The teacher should be trained in suicide prevention.

gram. If the counselor discovers that there is little community support for or awareness of suicide prevention, he or she can expand the school's prevention efforts to include youth workers, clergy, and law enforcement officials in the community.[11]

Program Evaluation

Every program school counselors undertake needs evaluating for effectiveness in meeting the program's goals. A suicide prevention program is no different. Table 9.5 is a checklist for school counselors to use in determining the comprehensiveness of their suicide prevention program, identifying components that are missing, and taking steps to modify the program as necessary.

SUICIDE POSTVENTION: WHAT TO DO IN THE AFTERMATH OF A SUICIDE

The harsh reality is that despite the best efforts of school, parents, and community, some youngsters are going to kill themselves.

I always remember my first clinical supervisor, who time and again would tell me that I had to do everything in my power to prevent a client from killing himself or herself. And each time she would add: "Of course, if a client really wants to do it, he or she is going to do it in spite of your best efforts."

The next best thing to preventing all suicides is for the school to have a well-designed postvention plan for dealing with the aftermath of a student suicide. The elements of a good postvention plan include a postvention team, procedures for managing information, appropriate counseling, and appropriate memorial activity.

The Postvention Team

The suicide postvention team should be formed before a suicide happens. Team members can come from inside and outside the school. School members might include the school counselors, the school psychologist, and teachers who have been trained to deal with suicide. Outside members can include representatives from child protective services, the police department, private therapists and psychologists, the community mental health center, and the clergy, again all trained in adolescent suicide (Park & Boyd, 1998).

We cannot emphasize enough the importance of having the team in place and ready to go as soon as the school has been notified of a suicide. There is no time to

---

[11] One example of how school counselors have organized suicide prevention and intervention teams in their community can be found in Smaby, Peterson, Bergmann, Zentner, and Swearingen (1990).

TABLE 9.5 **EVALUATING THE SUICIDE PREVENTION PROGRAM: A COUNSELOR CHECKLIST**

Program Components	Yes	No	Not Sure
Program construction			
Support for the program has been given by the administration.	☐	☐	☐
The district school board has approved the program.	☐	☐	☐
A policy that describes explicit procedures for intervention with potentially suicidal students has been published.	☐	☐	☐
Community mental health resources for referral, training, and consultation have been identified.	☐	☐	☐
A needs assessment has been conducted to determine the knowledge and attitudes of teachers and students regarding youth suicide.	☐	☐	☐
Multidisciplinary teams have been formed as part of the program.	☐	☐	☐
An outside mental health consultant has been made available.	☐	☐	☐
In-service training regarding suicide has been implemented for teachers, counselors, and staff.	☐	☐	☐
Qualified professionals with a special focus on adolescent suicide have been made available in the event of a crisis.	☐	☐	☐
Crisis prevention			
The administration conducts psychometric screening to identify students at risk and conducts an appropriate follow-up of these students.	☐	☐	☐
Students with substance, academic, or family problems are identified.	☐	☐	☐
Supportive counseling for at-risk students is available.	☐	☐	☐
Suicidal students are immediately referred to a mental health professional.	☐	☐	☐
Classroom and group discussions on teen suicide are conducted by mental health professionals competent in suicide prevention skills.	☐	☐	☐
Handouts, pamphlets, and wallet cards with suicide prevention information are distributed to students and parents.	☐	☐	☐
Postvention			
Individual and group counseling will be provided for students.	☐	☐	☐
A specialized consultant will work with the school's prevention team.	☐	☐	☐
A single spokesperson will address the media.	☐	☐	☐
A prepared written statement regarding the death will be read to the students by the teachers.	☐	☐	☐
Memorial activities will not exceed what the school custom is for acknowledging the death of a student.	☐	☐	☐
Assemblies to discuss the death will *not* be held.	☐	☐	☐
Students who want to attend the funeral may do so with parental permission.	☐	☐	☐
The school will stay open for those students not attending the funeral.	☐	☐	☐
Referrals for "survivors of suicide" counseling will be made.	☐	☐	☐

SOURCE: From "Comprehensive and Systemic School-Based Suicide Prevention Programs: A Checklist for Counselors," by P. B. Malley and F. Kush, 1994, *The School Counselor, 41*, pp. 193–194. Copyright 1994 by the American School Counselor Association. Reprinted with permission.

lose in responding to the news and to students' reactions. One fear around adolescent suicide is "contagion," the idea that one suicide can set off a cluster of copycat suicides. That fear is well grounded. We know, for example, that one youngster's suicide can normalize the act for others who are experiencing difficulties (J. J. McWhirter, 1998d). We also know that television programs and movies that depict an adolescent suicide can lead to cluster suicides (Capuzzi & Golden, 1988). And we know that cluster suicides are a particularly relevant problem on Native American reservations (Tomlinson-Keasey & Keasey, 1988).

Managing Information

Once a school learns of a student's suicide, the superintendent or principal should designate one person to be in charge of implementing the postvention plan. That person mobilizes the postvention team and also manages information about the suicide. *Managing information* here means disseminating accurate information to staff, parents, students, and the media in a timely and appropriate way.

The first task is to learn as many details and facts about the death as possible. The best source here is the law enforcement agency that is investigating the case (Roberts, 1995).[12] Once information has been screened for relevance, the team leader prepares written comments—the school's official statement about the suicide. The team leader must consider the family's wishes about what should or should not be said, but the family should also be made to understand the importance of providing accurate information.

Informing Those Outside the School   The team leader should inform the school secretaries about what to say when answering phone calls asking about the death or suicide. Our recommendation is for the secretaries to take down name and number, and to say that someone from the school will get back to the caller. If there are a lot of calls, the team members can divide the callbacks. They should start making those calls as soon as information about the death has been confirmed and the family has agreed to the release of information. It is very important that each team member gives out the same information to everyone: That's the best way to stop rumors.

Informing Faculty   Most student suicides occur in the evenings, on weekends, and on holidays—times when the school is closed. According to Siehl (1990), the principal or team leader should initiate a phone chain to inform teachers and other staff members and to schedule a meeting for the next school day before classes are scheduled to start. At that meeting, teachers and staff are told the facts surrounding the student's death (so they can dispel rumors that crop up during the day) and are given notice of any scheduling changes (Siehl, 1990).

---

[12] In some school districts, the police release information about a suspected suicide only with the family's permission; the person managing information should call the family and ask for that permission and for exactly what can be shared with others in the school community.

All members of the postvention team are present at the meeting. The leader recognizes them and mentions that they are available to teachers and students who need to talk. All of the teachers should receive a list of crisis centers in the school to share with their students.

Informing Students   Armed with the information they received at the early-morning meeting, teachers announce to their classes that the student has died and describe what is known about the death (Siehl, 1990). Teachers answer questions and dispel rumors. Most important, they need to tell the students where to go for help during the day. By this time, the postvention team should have set up crisis centers throughout the school.[13] It is also important to allow students to share their feelings and concerns; but it is a good idea for teachers to set boundaries around the discussion and to return to the educational agenda as soon as possible (Siehl, 1990).

Media Coverage   In dealing with the media, the school has a responsibility to be accurate about the facts of the student's death and about the student who died. Nothing is said about the student that is not true. Under no circumstances should the act or the student be glorified. That would only increase the likelihood of other students hurting themselves.

Again, the family controls the information about the student's death; the school, then, has a responsibility to work with the family to be sure that the information it reports does not hurt the survivors.

Postvention Counseling

Short-Term Services   The goal of short-term counseling for survivors of suicide is to stabilize them by processing their reactions of grief and loss. Many of the interventions described in Chapter 8 can be used in the aftermath of a suicide. Counselors are attuned to feelings of guilt and blame. Some students may feel they could have done something to prevent the death. Others may blame the school. Postvention counselors must be ready to deal with feelings of sadness, anger, and shame too.

It is important that postvention counselors be proactive; do not simply wait for students to come to one of the crisis centers. Many students are reluctant to ask for help, put off by the stigma of needing mental health services (B. F. Carter & Brooks, 1990). Proactive efforts target the dead student's closest friends and classmates (Roberts, 1995).

In talking to students, the counselor needs to be very aware of the contagion factor among teenagers. He or she emphasizes that suicide is a failure in coping mechanisms, that the person who died believed that killing himself or herself was the only way out. Then the counselor asks: "What is your reaction to your friend's way of dealing with his [her] problems?" This question serves a dual purpose: First, the answer can help the counselor detect whether the counselee is at risk for sui-

---

[13]The crisis centers should operate for several days.

cide. Second, it provides an opportunity to discuss suicide and shore up the counselee's coping mechanisms.

Long-Term Services   Short-term counseling for students dealing with the aftermath of suicide can last up to three sessions. If after three sessions a student is still having difficulty, he or she should be referred for long-term services. Those services can be provided individually or in a group, inside or outside the school.

School counselors who have the time and the expertise, and who are comfortable talking about suicide, can consider running a group for students. Counselors should anticipate parental resistance to a survivors-of-suicide group because parents are likely to believe the myth that talking about suicide puts ideas into children's heads (B. F. Carter & Brooks, 1990). The best way to eliminate resistance here is through empathic listening and *psychoeducation*—information shared by a professional to facilitate a greater understanding and appreciation of a psychological difficulty.

Many of the group activities outlined in Chapter 8 are also effective for a postvention group. In addition to coping skills, the groups can focus on decision-making processes. Even after the group ends, counselors should continue to monitor the students, especially those who were very close friends of the student who died, for up to 18 months.

The Memorial Service

There is some disagreement about whether the school should plan a memorial service for a student who died through suicide. Garfinkel et al. (1988) argued that survivors might see a memorial service as a glorification of suicide, which could contribute to the contagion phenomenon. Siehl (1990) disagreed, saying that "a memorial service or special event helps with closure and promotes a healthy feeling with friends, families, and significant others in the life of the deceased child" (pp. 55–56). Capuzzi (2002) recommended that if a memorial service is held, it be held outside the school.

A memorial service can contribute to healthy grieving, but it shouldn't be thought of as a magic potion that can resolve grief with one sip. Grieving is a process, and the friends and classmates of the student who died may need months to work through their loss. And the memorial service, like all of the other postvention activities, should never glorify the act of suicide. The rule here is to grieve the death without condoning the method.

ETHICAL AND LEGAL ISSUES

Many school districts have a policy on suicide that spells out how school counselors must proceed with students at given levels of risk for suicide. Districts that do not have such a policy could be held liable for neglect.

In 1994, Jill Dibley, a student in a Minnesota school, shot herself and died (see Foster, 1996). In 1996, the teenager's parents sued both the school district for not having a policy on suicide and the school counselor for failing to notify them.[14] The school counselor knew that Jill had suicidal tendencies and had notified the parents in the past, but apparently he failed to notify them when their daughter became suicidal again. Although the judge ruled in favor of the school district, saying that neither the district nor the school counselor could be held liable for not having a policy on suicide, the case made clear that a districtwide policy on suicide is an invaluable professional and legal tool for school counselors. School counselors who work in districts that do not have a suicide policy should make it a priority to lobby the administration to develop one.

Much of the material in this chapter is designed to help school counselors meet their ethical and legal responsibilities in working with suicidal students. Counselors who are aware of the myths, risk factors, and warning signs of suicide; who use both assessment and intervention appropriately; and who work with staff, students, and parents to develop a comprehensive suicide prevention program are carrying out their ethical and legal responsibilities.

There are just two other concerns here, both of a legal nature (Capuzzi, 2002). The first is not to do an assessment alone. Having a colleague present reduces the likelihood of questions about the counselor's professional judgment in the event of an actual suicide. A second opinion is always helpful in critical situations. The second has to do with allowing a suicidal student to return to school only after the student has been assessed by a mental health worker outside the school and mental health counseling services have been put into place. More and more school districts are requiring a third-party release as part of their suicide prevention program, a practice that would seem to protect the district from liability should the student later harm himself or herself and the family file a lawsuit. That policy is not without controversy, however. Some argue that keeping a student away from school removes needed structure from the student's life and so increases the likelihood of suicide. If the school does not have a release policy, the school counselor must carefully and clearly document his or her instructions to the parents and perhaps have the parents sign a letter in which they commit to taking their child to a mental health professional for an evaluation and ongoing counseling.

The courts generally have been reluctant to hold school districts liable for student suicide; still, the school counselor must be aware that in the event of a suicide, the parents may very well bring a lawsuit against the school. That awareness makes a second opinion in the assessment of students for risk of suicide or the documentation of interactions with students' parents wise. But it does not change what remains the counselor's primary concern: protecting the life of the student.

CONCLUSION

A key component of a comprehensive developmental guidance program is a suicide prevention program to help prevent suicide, intervene with students who are sui-

---

[14] *Killen v. Independent School District 706*, 547 N.W.2d 113 (Minn. Ct. App. 1996).

cidal, and deal with the aftermath of a student's suicide. Most schools have elaborate plans in place for responding to fires, bomb threats, and natural disasters; but many are reluctant to plan to prevent or cope with student suicide—although statistically suicide is much more likely to occur.

School counselors can play a critical role in reducing the resistance most people have to the topic of suicide. Their most effective tools are facts: data that point to the prevalence of adolescent suicide, and the research findings that dispel the myths of suicide. Information is also the most effective tool in the struggle to identify students who are at risk of hurting themselves. The first step here is understanding the relationship between adolescent suicide, and depression and other risk factors. Armed with that knowledge the school counselor can begin to work with teachers, parents, and students to make them an integral part of the prevention effort. Of course, prevention doesn't always work. A comprehensive program, then, must include activities to help students cope with the aftermath of suicide—to allow them to grieve and to deepen their understanding that suicide is never a viable option.

Perhaps the greatest challenge for the school counselor in dealing with adolescent suicide is coping with the sadness and fear the topic evokes.

I've worked with many suicidal clients in my years as both a clinician and a school counselor. And I can say now that I do not find suicide as threatening as I once did. The difference, I think, is that I know what to do when I'm faced with a suicidal youngster.

QUESTIONS FOR DISCUSSION

1. How do you react when you think about a child or adolescent who wants to commit suicide? Do you think your reactions would help stabilize the crisis? Explain your answer.
2. It is not uncommon for school counselors to meet with resistance from parents and school administrators to the idea of a suicide prevention program. How would you respond to that resistance? In your answer, be sure to consider the common objection, "You'll only put ideas into their heads by talking about it."
3. There is a great deal of secrecy and denial around suicide in our society. How do you think a school should deal with a student's suicide? Some would argue that it's better to fabricate some other cause of death than to admit that a student killed himself or herself. How would you respond to that argument?
4. How comfortable do you feel assessing a student's risk for suicide? What would make you better prepared to deal with a suicidal student? Discuss your ideas with a learning partner.
5. Discuss the ethical and legal responsibilities of school counselors when they discover that a student is having suicidal thoughts.

SUGGESTED INTERNET SITES

www.suicidology.org

The official Web site of the American Association of Suicidology is designed for survivors of suicide, people who are concerned about suicide, and specialists, and contains a referral network for support groups and information about conferences and seminars. Visitors can order informative booklets, pamphlets, and manuals on suicide and depression. There are also links to sites with related information and resources.

www.save.org

This is the official Web site of Suicide Awareness Voices of Education, a group that educates the public about suicide prevention and speaks for suicide survivors. There is a wealth of information about suicide and depression, including symptoms and danger signs by age group. The site also offers a list of suggested books and links to sites for further information.

www.yellowribbon.org

Started by the parents of a boy who committed suicide, the site is an outreach program for the Light of Life Foundation International. The site describes coping strategies and information for arranging training, seminars, and workshops at schools and community centers; it also offers links to more than 50 other sites. The section for teens includes words of wisdom and advice by teens. Parents also have their own section for information, support, and links.

www.bygirlsforgirls.org

The Web site, which was developed by teenage girls to help other teenage girls, contains information about depression, emergency numbers, and links to related sites.

www.livewithdepression.org

The official Web site of the Kristen Brooks Hope Center offers a personal look at depression and suicide and at how they affect others (in letters from family members). There are hotlines, a list of online resources, and links to other sites.

www.afsp.org

The American Foundation for Suicide Prevention Web site offers facts about suicide and depression and information for survivors who have lost a loved one to suicide. Also included are links to the most recent research on suicide and prevention and other relevant sources.

Sex and Sex-Related Issues in School Counseling

Sexuality. It is difficult to think of a topic that can stimulate more interest and, at the same time, more controversy in schools. But sexual development is an overwhelmingly important part of adolescence, which means sexuality is always a presence in middle and high schools. And that means the school counselor must be knowledgeable about the host of problems their developing sexuality creates for young people. More than that, it means the school counselor must be able to talk comfortably about sex-related matters.

For teenagers who choose to be sexually active, more is at stake than the confusing physical and emotional changes that are characteristic of the age group. There are very real risks involved in sexual activity—disease and, of course, pregnancy—that can have life-altering consequences for young people and that demand not only support after the fact but a comprehensive effort at prevention. Also at increased risk—for depression and suicide—are gay and lesbian teenagers, who in many schools are marginalized or are the targets of verbal and physical abuse. These students, too, need the support and protection of the school counselor to challenge institutional homophobia.

When the issue is teenage sexuality, there are no easy answers. This is an area where the counselor's personal mission—to help children—often comes up against school policy or parental rights that would leave a vulnerable population with no information and no support. Policy and parental restrictions may limit the counselor's role here, but the counselor's personal values or reluctance to talk about sex should never be allowed to interfere with his or her work with students. The guiding principle is always *If it's mentionable, it's manageable*. Anything human is mentionable, and issues related to sexuality are at the core of being human.

SEXUAL AWAKENING IN ADOLESCENCE

Adolescence is the developmental stage between the onset of puberty and physical maturity. Over time, the duration of this stage of development has increased. In the United States, the average age for the onset of puberty has fallen, and the entrance into adulthood—marked by steady employment and raising a family—is delayed (Lockhardt & Wodarski, 1990).

Physical Changes

Adolescence begins between the ages of 10 and 11 for girls and 12 and 13 for boys; but it can start as early as age 9. For girls, the physical changes include enlargement of the breasts, the appearance of pubic hair, the beginning of menstruation, and an increase in sex drive. With these changes, adolescent females become overly concerned about how others perceive them. Heterosexual young women are preoccupied with boys and worry about whether boys find them attractive. For boys, physical changes begin with the enlargement of the testes and the penis, the appearance of facial and pubic hair, and voice changes. An increase in testosterone increases sexual drive.

These changes are so sudden and strong that many young adolescents feel as if there is an alien in their bodies (L. J. Bradley, Jarchow, & Robinson, 1999). As youngsters progress through middle adolescence, the intensity of sexual feelings increases, and the heterosexual adolescent begins to experiment with the opposite sex. It is not unusual for an adolescent to fall in love. The preoccupation with appearance is stronger, and both girls and boys can spend hours each day in front of a mirror. Adolescents are constantly comparing themselves physically. Girls worry about breast size; boys, about penis size and their number of erections. Because many of the changes they are undergoing are visible, most adolescents believe that everyone around them is looking at and passing judgment on their physical appearance (L. J. Bradley et al., 1999).

Often what gives adults the patience, the empathy, to deal with the idiosyncratic behavior of adolescents is our memories of the physical changes that were part of our own adolescence, our struggles with appearance, and a growing awareness of our sexuality. But if those memories are painful, if adolescence was a particularly difficult time for us, it may not be easy to work with this volatile and at times provocative population of students.

Cognitive Development

Important cognitive changes take place as adolescents develop formal operational thinking (Imhelder & Piaget, 1958). Adolescents are able to make connections between propositions, to anticipate the consequences of their actions, and to formulate concepts. They can think not only in terms of what is but also in terms of what could be. This kind of cognition is the basis for the lofty ideals and fantastical thinking that are characteristic of many adolescents. It also at times is in conflict with the emotional and sexual needs of adolescents. For example, on the cognitive level adolescents may well understand the negative consequences of being sexually active with a particular partner; but often their emotion overrules their reason. Although they have the capacity to think about the future, their narcissism often keeps them focused on the present, and so they are careless about the consequences of their actions.

This conflict is a factor in the interventions school counselors use with adolescents. An intervention that requires students to consider the consequences of their actions may not be effective if it ignores their emotional and sexual needs. School counselors can develop effective working relationships with adolescents only if they empathize with the students' struggle to balance reason, the need to feel loved and accepted, and their physical drives.

Identity Formation

According to Erikson (1956), the major developmental task of adolescence is exploring and forming identity:

> Identity formation begins where the usefulness of identification ends. It arises from the selective repudiation and mutual assimilation of childhood identifications, and their absorption in a new configuration, which, in turn, is dependent on the process by which a society (often through subsocieties) identifies the young individual, recognizing him as somebody who had to become the way he is, and who, being the way he is, is taken for granted. (p. 113)

Adolescence culminates in the individual's becoming a person in his or her own right (Lidz, 1976). This does not mean that once the individual's identity has formed that he or she stops developing. Instead, the integration of past experiences that is the new identity leads to feelings of security and self-sufficiency that leave the person open to further development.

More-contemporary theories of development recognize a difference between adolescent girls and boys in terms of identity formation (Gilligan, 1982; L. M. Brown & Gilligan, 1992). Research has revealed that adolescent girls are more concerned with establishing, maintaining, and being in relationships; adolescent boys, in individuation and autonomy (B. Miller, 1991; Thomas, 1996; Way, 1995, 1997). Despite these differences, the search for identity can reveal itself in day-to-day changes in appearance, unique clothing and hair, and even body piercings and tattoos. Perhaps more than anything else, sexual activity is part of the search for identity and the development of self-concept, which is why school counselors find themselves exploring sexual issues with students.

As the student population becomes more diverse, counselors also need to explore cultural differences around sexual activity and attitudes. L. J. Bradley et al. (1999) suggested several specific issues to explore with teens:

- How do family members view the teenager's dating?
- How does being male or female influence the rules that the family places on dating, curfew, drinking, and socializing?
- How do members of the student's racial or ethnic group view sexuality among adolescents?
- What do members of the student's racial or ethnic group think about sexual intimacy before marriage?
- Does the student's religion influence his or her views of sexuality?

The need to be their own selves often conflicts with adolescents' cultural socialization around sex. And the rebellion that marks adolescence leads some young people to do the exact opposite of what they were taught by their families. Adding to that likelihood are the influences of contemporary society: It is difficult for adolescents to adhere to what they perceive as rigid and old-fashioned parental mores.

Contemporary Influences on Adolescent Sexuality

Life in the United States today presents unique challenges to teenagers who are constantly negotiating their sexuality:

The media. The media bombard their audiences with sexual content, values, and attitudes. Advertising relies on sex to sell everything from coffee to cars. In the 1990s, evening television offered 8 to 10 sexual situations an hour, and daytime dramas showed sexual situations at a rate more than twice that of 1980 (Greenberg, Brown, & Beurkel-Rothfuss, 1993; Huston, Wartella, Donnerstein, Scantlin, & Kotler, 1998; Lowry & Shidler, 1993). It is almost impossible for adolescents to watch television shows that do not refer to or display sexual situations.

Exposure to pornography. The Internet has made pornography available to anyone with a computer; and the stock of X-rated movies at neighborhood video stores can be another source of pornography for young people. The jury is still out on the effects of pornography on viewers: Does it have a catalytic effect? Does it incite sexual activity with a partner? Or does it have a cathartic effect, providing relief, for example, through self-stimulation? Age seems to be an important variable here. Teenagers generally have a more difficult time than adults do in controlling their sexual impulses, which means that pornography may increase their pursuit of sexual activity. And especially for troubled or aggressive teens, watching pornography can be an antecedent of sexual offense.

Changes in family structure. Changes in the contemporary family have left children and adolescents with more unsupervised time. With the demise of the extended family and the dramatic increase in single-parent households and families with both parents working outside the home, more and more youngsters come home from school to an empty house (Sherwood-Hawes, 2000). McCullough and Scherman (1991) found that adolescents from homes with less adult supervision are more likely to engage in sexual activity.

The Incidence of Teenage Sexual Activity

Sexual activity for both girls and boys often begins in early adolescence, in the form of masturbation. By the time youngsters reach high school, a large number of them have had sexual intercourse: A recent study reported that 43 percent of females and 49 percent of males in high school said they had had sexual intercourse during the past three months (Centers for Disease Control and Prevention, 2002). That rate went up to 61 percent among high school seniors of both genders. Other forms of sexual activity also become more common with age. One study revealed that 44 percent of 15-year-old boys, 62 percent of 16-year-old boys, and 78 percent of boys ages 17 to 19 report some genital sexual activity with a female (Gates & Sonenstein, 2002).

For most teenagers who are sexually active, the decision to become sexually active takes place during high school. For many, it is a decision made complicated by a host of developmental issues. And it is a decision with which the school counselor can help.

Interventions

L. J. Bradley et al. (1999) suggested five general guidelines for school counselors to follow in responding to students' concerns about their sexual development:

Normalize experiences. Adolescents do not fully comprehend what is happening to them emotionally and physically. Often they judge their own behavior according to what they hear from their friends, which may or may not be factual. School counselors can help by normalizing sexual responses—for example, by explaining that wet dreams, spontaneous erections, lighter or heavier menstrual flow are all a normal and healthy part of their development.

Use natural opportunities for interaction. Most teenagers who have questions about their sexuality find it hard to walk into the counselor's office and simply start talking. It's up to the school counselor, then, to build relationships with them outside the office—in the hallways, during extracurricular activities, at lunch breaks. Sexual questions in and of themselves can be threatening to adolescents, so it's important that the counselor create a nonthreatening environment in which youngsters feel encouraged to talk about what's troubling them. It's also important for the school counselor to post informative brochures and information about referrals so that students understand that the counselor is approachable to talk about sexual issues.

Recognize "fishing" expeditions. Again, many adolescents have difficulty talking about sex, so they try to access information indirectly. For example, they might talk about a "friend" whose boyfriend is pressuring her to have sexual intercourse; or they might ask how the counselor would respond if his or her own son was downloading pornography from the Internet. Of course, the counseling relationship is built on honesty, which can make students' dissembling frustrating for the counselor; but the counselor should answer the questions honestly and empathetically, the best way to gain students' trust. Personal questions here, like all personal questions, should be politely turned back to the student: "Gee, I'm not sure what I would do if I caught my son downloading pornography on the Internet. What do you think I should do?"

Encourage conversation. Above all, the counselor has to communicate to adolescents that he or she feels comfortable talking about sexual matters.

One of the ways to do this is not to be put off by even the most provocative questions. The counselor must be careful not to overreact: The last thing a counselor wants is a reputation among students for being prudish. More important, still, is that the counselor not impose his or her own values on students. Instead, the counselor encourages students to talk more about the issue, to explore it more deeply, and to establish their own ways of thinking about sex and sexual activity.

Don't minimize teenagers' experiences. Concerns and conflicts about sexual matters are an extremely important part of adolescent development. Years later many of us look back on our adolescent years and smile at some of the things we thought were so important. But that's a perspective that comes with age; it cannot be used to help adolescents. Instead, the school counselor must empathize with students' emotional intensity. If it is a big deal for the students, then it must be a big deal for the counselor.

Bradley and her colleagues (1999) also identified several interventions to help teenagers negotiate the sometimes choppy waters of their sexuality.

Know How Far Is Enough   Many adolescents struggle with the decision to become sexually active and then with the degree of that activity. They hear their peers talk about their sexual exploits and wonder if there is something wrong because they haven't participated. These youngsters believe there is an external standard to which they are held. The school counselor can intervene here by helping students trust what feels right to them. If they don't feel comfortable, that's perfectly fine. In most cases, adolescents acknowledge there are pros and cons to being sexually active. It is the school counselor's job to help them consider the sufficiency of their reasons for having sex. The counselor cannot control the outcome of a student's decision making, but he or she can support a student who decides it's too soon for sex. Helping students know and trust how much is enough for them also helps maintain their sense of integrity and autonomy.

Reverse the Pressure   It's not uncommon for a partner to pressure a teenager into having sex. For adolescents, who want so much to fit in and be accepted, a partner's challenge can be very persuasive. School counselors can help students who are feeling pressured to do what they aren't comfortable doing by showing them how to reverse the pressure:[1]

- When a partner says, "If you really loved me, you would have sex with me," suggest the teenager respond with "If you really loved me, you wouldn't pressure me to have sex with you."
- When a partner says, "If you really care about me, you wouldn't tell me no," suggest the teenager respond with "Show me you care by not pushing me into having sex with you."

---

[1] These examples are taken from L. J. Bradley et al. (1999), pages 29 and 30.

- When a partner says, "If you don't have sex with me, I'll find someone who will," suggest the teenager respond with "Go ahead and find someone else to have sex with you."
- When a partner says, "Everyone else is doing it," suggest the teenager respond with "If everybody else is doing it, you shouldn't have any problem finding someone else."

If adolescents are certain they do not want to engage in sexual activity, the school counselor can give them strategies to handle the pressures that are a usual part of relationships at this age.

Don't Pressure Others   It is also quite common for teenagers to pressure others into having sex either directly, as described above, or indirectly, by making fun of a peer who decides to abstain. Today, indirect pressure, at least among males, can often take the form of accusing the abstainer of being gay. The school counselor, through small-group counseling and classroom guidance, can help teens understand that everyone develops different values and attitudes, and that those values and attitudes determine whether someone is ready to have sex or not. The counselors should be quick to dispel the many myths about sex that adolescents tend to accept as gospel. One of the most common: "If you're not having sex, there's something terribly wrong with you."

It's Okay to Say No   The school counselor should make this the mantra of students who are struggling to abstain from sexual activity. Teenagers need to develop boundaries around their own bodies and to establish criteria for sharing their body with someone else. The counselor should help them recognize that people can be sexually active and enjoy healthy relationships, but that the reverse is also true: People do not have to be sexually active to enjoy healthy relationships.

To help adolescents develop criteria for participating in sexual activity, the counselor suggests they ask themselves these questions:

- Do I like this person?
- How long have I known this person?
- Do I trust this person?
- Does this person care about me or is he or she faking it?
- Is this person being nice to me because he or she wants me to have sex?
- Do I feel pressured into having sex?
- Am I choosing to have sex to be liked? (L. J. Bradley et al, 1999, pp. 31–32)

UNPROTECTED SEXUAL ACTIVITY: THE RISK OF DISEASE

For adolescents, for anyone, the decision to become sexually active puts them at risk for a sexually transmitted disease (STD). The United States has the highest adolescent STD rate in the developed world (Office of National AIDS Policy, 1996): Approximately, 3 million cases of STDs occur among teenagers (Center for Disease

Control and Prevention, 2001). The most common is chlamydia, but gonorrhea, genital warts, herpes, and syphilis are also common (J. J. McWhirter, 1998c). And then there is AIDS—acquired immune deficiency syndrome. Through December 2001, the Centers for Disease Control and Prevention (2003) reported a total of 4,428 cases of AIDS among individuals between the ages of 13 and 19. But that number is misleading because of the high incidence of HIV infection and the long asymptomatic period (up to 10 years). In 1998, 23,729 Americans had been diagnosed with AIDS, and it is believed that most of them contracted HIV when they were teenagers (Gray, House, & Champeau, 2000). The number of teens with AIDS in this country doubles every year (J. J. McWhirter, 1998c).

Most people are infected with HIV through unprotected sexual contact or shared needles (Gray et al., 2000). All students—male or female; gay, straight, or bisexual; of whatever race and socioeconomic status—are at risk for the virus if they engage in unprotected sexual behaviors in which body fluids are exchanged. The bad news: Statistics vary, but a conservative estimate is that one of every three 15- to 17-year-olds who are sexually active admit that they do not use condoms (Kaiser Family Foundation, 2000). The good news: Knowledge about HIV/AIDS and the use of condoms did increase among adolescents during the 1990s. In a national survey of adolescent males between ages 15 and 19 in 1995, 69 percent reported using a condom at first intercourse, up from 55 percent in 1988 (Sonenstein, Stewart, Lindberg, & Williams, 1998).[2]

HIV/AIDS doesn't discriminate. It infects adolescents across gender, sexual orientation, race, and socioeconomic status. The factors that put young people at risk for the disease are behavioral: Research shows that adolescents who have sex with multiple partners, abuse drugs and alcohol, and generally participate in delinquent behaviors are the least likely to practice safer sex (McCarthy, Brack, Laygo, Brack, & Orr, 1997). HIV/AIDS is not a gay disease. In fact, today, heterosexual transmission accounts for the largest number of AIDS cases in the world (Mann, Tarantola, & Netter, 1992).

What School Counselors Need to Know about HIV/AIDS

HIV compromises the immune system: People don't die from AIDS; they die from the serious illnesses that develop when their immune system fails. According to McFarland and Oliver (1999), school counselors have a responsibility to understand the routes of infection and the rules for practicing safer sex, and the issues surrounding HIV testing.[3]

The Routes of Infection and Safer Sex   The four primary routes of HIV infection are fluid exchange through sexual activity, the use of HIV-contaminated in-

---

[2]The data are somewhat confounded in that adolescents are more aware of HIV/AIDS and are more likely to use condoms when they have sexual intercourse; but the incidence of oral and unprotected anal sex also has increased.

[3]McFarland and Oliver noted that counselors should also be informed about the clinical course of the disease and medical treatment for people with AIDS.

jection needles, mother-to-infant transmission during pregnancy, labor, or delivery, or breast feeding), and transfusion with infected blood or blood products (Keeling, 1993). For teens who are sexually active, the use of condoms is the most effective way to prevent HIV infection.

Any intervention that focuses on safer sex and the use of condoms must start with a disclaimer: The proper use of condoms reduces the risk of infection from vaginal, anal, and oral intercourse but does not eliminate it. Then the counselor can review these guidelines for using condoms (McFarland & Oliver, 1999):

1. Use only latex polyethylene condoms.
2. Use a water-based lubricant (like KY jelly®) to reduce friction on the condom. Be careful not to lubricate the penis, which could cause the condom to slip off.
3. Never use oil-based lubricants (Vaseline, cooking or tanning oils). These lubricants corrode the latex.
4. Pay attention to the expiration date. Old condoms are more likely to break.
5. Use a new condom for each act of sexual intercourse.
6. Keep the condom on for the entire sexual act. Preejaculatory fluid contains HIV.
7. Make a half-inch space between the condom and the head of the penis to collect semen and prevent breaking.
8. Make sure there is no air between the condom and the penis.
9. Withdraw before the erection is lost to prevent spilling. Hold on to the condom when withdrawing.

A definite link between HIV infection and oral–genital contact has not been established.[4] As long as ejaculation does not take place, unprotected oral sex performed on a male *probably* does not transfer the AIDS virus. But it is risky behavior because ejaculation can be difficult to predict and control, and because preejaculatory fluid can also contain the virus. When oral sex is performed on a female, a dental dam should be used to prevent STDs. Many adolescents turn to oral sex as a way of protecting themselves, but the school counselor should emphasize that oral sex is also a risky behavior.

There is no evidence that HIV can be transmitted through casual contact or through tears, urine, or insect bites. There is a question about transmission through saliva. The current thinking is that contact with saliva causes little or no risk of infection unless gums are irritated or there are sores in the mouth.

> Aside from genital sexual contact and shared injection equipment, close contact seems to pose no known risk for HIV transmission. Kissing, touching, hugging, drinking out of the same glass, using the same bathroom and kitchen, breathing the same air, and donating blood do not appear to place a person at risk. The critical message for all people is that it is not who you are that causes HIV infections, but what you do—male or female, gay or straight. (McFarland & Oliver, 1999, p. 270)

---

[4]We do know that using a condom reduces the risk of contracting gonorrhea and syphilis.

HIV Testing   School counselors should also be familiar with HIV testing procedures and policies and with places where students can go to get tested (McFarland & Oliver, 1999). In a national survey, fewer than one-third of teens who said they were sexually active had been tested, and more than half of teens ages 15 to 17 said they were not sure where to go for a test (Kaiser Family Foundation, 2000). HIV antibodies take several weeks to reach detectable levels, and 95 percent of people infected with HIV produce antibodies within six months (Bartlett, 1993). So students who test negative the first time should be retested again after six months. If a student tests negative a second time and has not engaged in risky sexual behavior in that six-month period, the student can be almost certain that he or she is not infected.

The school counselor should know, and students should be told, that HIV test results can be either anonymous or confidential. Anonymous results are tagged to a random number, not a name. Confidential results become part of the individual's medical record but cannot be shared without the written permission of the individual. Students who want to be tested should understand that they may be asked to sign a paper allowing the results to be shared with health care workers, insurance companies, and public health officials. In some states, HIV infection must be reported to the state health department. Home testing kits are available, but they are less reliable than tests performed in a community health clinic. All HIV testing centers also provide important counseling that is not available to those who opt for a home test. Students should understand that the purpose of testing is less to determine their HIV status than it is to receive early treatment for the virus.

Working with Students Who Are HIV-Positive

The American School Counselor Association's position statement on AIDS notes that "the professional school counselor's role is to provide counseling, support and collaboration with school health personnel to provide educational programs for students, staff, and parents" (2001, p. 1). Counseling support for students with AIDS inevitably raises the issue of confidentiality.

Confidentiality   The Rehabilitation Act of 1973 gives students infected with HIV the right to attend school in a regular classroom setting (A. Jones & Bishop, 1990). What should the school counselor do if a student discloses that he or she is HIV-positive? There is no question that school counselors are bound by the ethics of their profession to maintain the confidentiality of information they learn in the counseling relationship with one important exception: when that information puts the client or someone else in imminent danger (ACA, 1995; ASCA, 1992). But the situation is complicated by the fact that some school districts require that staff members disclose a student's HIV-positive status to the principal or some other designated official (Cobia, Carney, & Waggoner, 1998). Furthermore, the American Counseling Association (1995) says that "counselors are justified in disclosing information to an identifiable third party who, by his or her relationship, is at high risk of contracting the disease" (p. 5).

Although we could argue that the school—in the person of the administrator, the classroom teacher, the counselor, or the school nurse—should know about any condition that may require medication or emergency treatment, this does not mean that the counselor is obligated to break the student's confidentiality. The key issue here is the "high risk of contracting the disease." The simple presence of an HIV-positive student in a school does not pose a high risk to others. But if the school counselor learns that a counselee is HIV-positive and is having unprotected sex with a designated partner, the school counselor must inform the partner of the student's HIV-positive status. The legal basis here is *Tarasoff v. Regents of University of California* (17 Cal.3d 425, 1976), in which the California Supreme Court held that a psychologist's failure to warn Tatiana Tarasoff of her boyfriend's plan to kill her was irresponsible.[5] But short of an imminent-danger situation, a school counselor who discloses the HIV-positive status of a counselee without the permission of his or her parents is violating both the student's and the family's privacy.

The decision to disclose medical information to the school is the parents', who may or may not choose to consult with the student's physician. If the parents do make certain school personnel aware of their child's HIV-positive status, they should be assured that the information will be kept confidential, released only with the parents' permission to specific members of the school staff. School officials should never pressure a parent by saying that certain people have a "right to know":

> A decision to increase the number of school staff who know the HIV status of a student or of a member of a student's family to receive support services must rest entirely with the infected student and his or her family. If a family decided to share this information with the school staff member, it is the duty of the staff person to keep the student's identity strictly confidential. (American School Health Association, 1990, p. 250)

If parents choose to disclose their child's condition, the school counselor can guide them through the disclosure process. The discussion should always be about who in the school should know in order to provide the best support services for the child. Again, no one in the school has a right to know.[6] The school should already have procedures and materials in place to protect the well-being of students and staff. For example, teachers should be trained to use latex gloves and the correct cleaning solutions to deal safely with blood spills of *all* students, whatever their HIV status.

Counseling Students with HIV   Elementary school children generally are infected with HIV/AIDS in utero or through a blood transfusion. These youngsters are at risk for developmental delays, psychomotor retardation, and deficits in cognitive functioning (Levenson & Mellins, 1992). In collaboration with the parents, the school psychologist, and the classroom teacher, the school counselors should

---

[5]The boyfriend succeeded, and Tarasoff's family sued both the university, where she was a student, and a psychologist in the university's counseling center.

[6]The exception here: the student's unprotected sexual partner.

gather as much psychological, academic, and family information as possible (Cobia et al., 1998). Particular attention is given to the child's own understanding of and emotional response to his or her illness.

Anyone infected with HIV/AIDS is at increased risk for depression and suicide. In HIV-positive children, physical complaints, anhedonia, withdrawal, and irritability can be evidence of an underlying depression (Cobia et al., 1998; S. L. Hart, 1991). Other emotional reactions can include sadness, confusion, anxiety, fear of isolation, a sense of rejection, and fear of death (Cobia et al., 1998; Spiegel & Mayers, 1991). A child's emotional difficulties may manifest in fighting or in classroom disruption (Pizzo & Wilfert, 1991). The counselor's primary task here is to create an environment in which the child feels safe expressing any and all of his or her emotions. In addition, the school counselor can focus on building the child's self-esteem and problem-solving and conflict-resolution skills, and on the development of self-efficacy (Cobia et al., 1998; Levenson & Mellins, 1992). Play therapy is a recommended modality for children suffering from HIV (Weiner & Septimus, 1991). Another important part of the school counselor's job is environmental engineering—keeping track of the services the child receives, making sure services are not duplicated, and advocating for the child whenever a needed service is lacking.

Many of the guidelines for working with HIV-infected children are also applicable to working with HIV-infected adolescents. In addition, the school counselor must consider the student's ability to form meaningful intimate relationships, issues of sexual orientation, and sexual and other behaviors that could place the student and his or her peers at risk. Suicide is a very real threat for HIV-positive adolescents. Often an adolescent with HIV is grieving the inability to live life as his or her peers do, to form intimate relationships, to take part in physical activities, to plan for the future. And adolescents who are HIV-positive may also be suffering from guilt, especially if they contracted the disease through unprotected sex or intravenous drug use (Cobia et al., 1998).

There are two other areas where the school counselor can make an important difference in the life of students with HIV/AIDS and their family. Even today, many people are ignorant about the disease, and that ignorance can trigger cruel behavior toward children and adolescents who are infected. Educating students about the illness and the facts of transmission is an important first step in making the school a safe place for students with HIV/AIDS. Also, the school counselor can run interference for students whose medications are affecting their academic performance. With the help and support of the school counselor, these youngsters can continue their education side by side with their classmates in an environment that is welcoming and supportive.

TEENAGE PREGNANCY AND MOTHERHOOD

In the United States, about 1 million teenagers become pregnant every year, and about half of those pregnancies result in motherhood (K. A. Moore, Romano, Connon, & Gitelson, 1997). During the 1980s, the birthrate among 15- to 19-year-olds increased dramatically: By 1991, it had reached a high of 62.1 births per 1,000 young women. During the 1990s, the birthrate fell, reaching a low in 2000 of 48.5 births per 1,000. That the number of adolescent abortions also went down over that period means that pregnancy rates in this population fell too (National Center for Health Statistics, 2002). But the rate of nonmarital births to mothers under age 20 rose dramatically between 1960 and 1996, from 15 percent to 76 percent. Although fewer adolescents today are having babies, many more of them are doing so without a stable relationship with the father of their baby.

The United States has the highest rates of adolescent pregnancies, abortions (approximately 400,000 a year), and births of all industrialized countries (Bell, 1997). Yet the rate of sexual intercourse among adolescents is the same as or lower than that in other industrialized nations (Allen-Meares, 1989). Many experts attribute the high incidence of teenage pregnancy in this country to less effective and less consistent use of contraceptives (Christopher & Roosa, 1990; Sherwood-Hawes, 2000). Most adolescents who bring their pregnancy to term keep their babies—90 percent of Whites and 97 percent of African Americans (Sherwood-Hawes). Formal adoption among Hispanics is almost nonexistent, but primary caregiving for the first few years of a baby's life is often provided by a grandmother or other member of the extended family (Sciarra & Ponterotto, 1998).

A Typology of Adolescent Pregnancy

Obviously, adolescents get pregnant because they have sex. But the decision to be sexually active, to carry a fetus to term, and to keep the baby is the product of social, cultural, economic, familial, and biological factors (Brewster, Billy, & Grady, 1993; Sherwood-Hawes, 2000). To understand the complex interactions among these factors, it can be helpful to identify three categories of adolescent pregnancy: intentional, accidental, and uninformed (MacFarlane, 1995).

Intentional Pregnancy   Some adolescent girls want to become pregnant. Within this group are young women whose culture accepts and even rewards early pregnancy, and young women who believe—consciously or unconsciously—that having a baby is a way to fulfill one or more of their psychological needs. In a study of low-income Hispanic families, Sciarra and Ponterotto (1998) found that early pregnancy and motherhood restored a sense of balance and stability. These were families living in inner cities. They looked on early pregnancy and motherhood as a way to keep their daughters off the streets.

According to L. J. Bradley et al. (1999), a number of young women choose to become pregnant to meet one or more of the following needs:

Power. Teens perceive that pregnancy will enhance their power to make choices in their lives by giving them "adult" status.

Control. Teens use pregnancy to control other people. The adolescent may use the pregnancy to force a boyfriend to marry her or compel her parents to comply with her wishes. . . .

Intimacy. Teens equate sex with intimacy. Instead of developing intimacy and then becoming sexually active, teenagers may have the misunderstanding that sexual involvement creates emotional intimacy. Teens believe having a baby will create more intimacy with their sexual partner. Likewise, adolescent females feel their child will help meet their needs for intimacy.

Escape. Teens view pregnancy as an avenue of escape. Adolescents who are experiencing difficulties at home or want to move out of their parents' homes may believe pregnancy will allow them to move into another household or to establish a household of their own. Pregnancy may also allow teenagers to escape the expectations others have for them concerning achievement and status.

Rebellion. Pregnancy is also a means of rebelling against parental authority. If teenagers know their parents dislike their sexual partners, or are opposed to them being sexually active or becoming pregnant, a pregnancy is the ultimate "in your face" act. . . .

Purpose. Pregnancy can be an avenue to form a relationship with someone that will love them and give them a sense of purpose in life.

Procreation. Teens may see pregnancy as a way to pass on part of themselves to the next generation. The infant becomes a symbol of making a lasting legacy or contribution. (pp. 43–44)

It is difficult to determine the number of intentional pregnancies. After the fact, many adolescents insist their pregnancy was intended rather than admit it was a mistake; others may have wanted the pregnancy but refuse to say so. This is especially true in cases where the adolescent decides to bring the "unwanted" pregnancy to term (Sciarra & Ponterotto, 1998).

Accidental Pregnancy   Most adolescent pregnancies appear to be accidental. These adolescents know and understand the proper use of contraceptives but take risks by using them haphazardly or not at all (MacFarlane, 1995). Sometimes drugs or alcohol are involved in clouding judgment.

Uninformed Pregnancy   These pregnant teens report that if information about contraception had been available to them, they would not have become pregnant (MacFarlane, 1995). Or they say that they knowingly had sex without contraception believing that they couldn't get pregnant if it was their first experience or if they had sex only once. These young women know very little about human physiology, and what they do know often is inaccurate.

The Risk Factors

All of the following increase the risk of adolescent pregnancy and motherhood:

- Having a parent who was also a teenage parent
- Having a sibling who is or was a teenage parent
- Coming from a single-parent family
- Coming from a dysfunctional family, in which the parents' marriage is troubled or family members are unable to communicate effectively
- Having few educational or career opportunities

- Poor academic performance
- Ethnicity
- Low socioeconomic status

When several of these factors are present, a young woman is at significantly greater risk of becoming pregnant and bearing a child.

Although the school counselor should keep in mind all of these variables in identifying adolescents who are at risk for pregnancy and motherhood, probably the single most important factor is socioeconomic status: Eighty-three percent of adolescent mothers come from poor and low-income families (Alan Guttmacher Institute, 1994). Those teenagers who choose to abort a pregnancy are more likely to come from higher socioeconomic levels, to be more successful in school, to have parents and friends who support their decision to choose an abortion, to live in communities where access to and funds for abortion are available, and to have few friends or relations who are adolescent parents (F. Furstenberg, Brooks-Gunn, & Chase-Lansdale, 1989; Sherwood-Hawes, 2000).

The Consequences of Early Childbearing

Most of the factors that lead to early pregnancy and motherhood have to do with students' families, with an area of life over which the school counselor has no control. How is it possible, then, to prevent young women from getting pregnant and choosing to raise their child? There is no easy answer to this question. Yet the consequences of early childbearing are so overwhelmingly negative that the school counselor cannot relinquish prevention efforts.

J. J. McWhirter (1998c) identified significant socioeconomic, educational, health-related, and family development consequences for adolescents who bear children:

Socioeconomic consequences. Adolescent mothers are much more likely to live in poverty than are their older counterparts. One study found that the average family income of girls who became mothers at age 16 or younger was 25 percent that of families in which the mothers became pregnant in their late twenties (K. A. Moore, Myers, et al., 1993). Adolescent mothers receive a disproportionate share of public assistance (J. J. McWhirter, 1998c) and are more likely to live in inadequate housing, suffer poor nutrition and health, and be unemployed or underemployed (R. B. Robinson, Watkins-Ferrell, Davis-Scott, & Ruch-Ross, 1993). We know that 83 percent of adolescent mothers come from poor and low-income backgrounds; clearly their own childbearing does nothing to break the cycle of poverty.

Educational consequences. Teen mothers are three times more likely to drop out of school than those who delay childbearing until their twenties (J. J. McWhirter, 1998c). Many schools have begun to offer alternative schools or programs for adolescent mothers. Between 60 percent and 70 percent of teenagers who bear children complete high school, but they are less likely to attend college: Just 29 percent of teen mothers who gave birth in the 1990s were expected to attend college; 70 percent of those who became mothers in their late twenties did go on to college after high school (Hofferth, Reid, & Mott, 2001). The teenage mother's lack of education, in turn, affects her children, who have more behavioral problems in school (Thomson, Hanson, & McLanahan, 1994), more absences, lower grades, and lower scores on standardized tests, and are less likely to attend college (Astone & McLanahan, 1991).

Health-related consequences. Pregnant teenagers have more prenatal, perinatal, and postnatal problems than older mothers do (J. J. McWhirter, 1998c). Only one in five pregnant teens under the age of 15 receives prenatal care during the first trimester.[7] Teen mothers are more likely to give birth prematurely, which increases the likelihood of delivering a low-birth-weight baby, and low-birth-weight children are 2 to 10 times more likely to have academic or behavioral problems (F. Furstenberg, Morgan, Moore, & Peterson, 1987). Children born to mothers under the age of 17 have higher rates of injury, illness, and sudden infant death syndrome (Morris, Warren, & Aral, 1993).

Family development consequences. In general, children born to teenage mothers grow up in families marked by conflict and instability. Again, 76 percent of adolescent child bearers are not married. Many teenage fathers relinquish their responsibilities and do little to provide a secure emotional or financial environment for their children (Kiselica, 1995; Sciarra & Ponterotto, 1998). Single mothers who work are forced to work long hours at low-paying jobs because they lack education. The stress of raising and supporting a child often overwhelms adolescent mothers, increasing the possibility of child abuse (Becker-Lansen & Rickel, 1995). And if they do marry, teen mothers are more likely to divorce within five years (Alan Guttmacher Institute, 1994).

Interventions

School counselors generally work with adolescents who are trying to decide what to do about their pregnancy and with those who have decided to bring their pregnancy to term. They can intervene in ways to help reduce the risk for both the adolescent and her child.

Working with the Undecided Pregnant Teen   Counseling students who are unsure about carrying to term presents the school counselor with two important challenges. The first is the issue of confidentiality. If the student has not informed her parents about the pregnancy and says that she does not want her parents to know, is the counselor obligated to tell the parents? Some school districts give the

---

[7] African American and Hispanic teen mothers are more likely to receive late or no prenatal care than are their White counterparts (J. J. McWhirter).

counselor no choice: Their policy requires the counselor to inform the student's parents. But in the absence of a policy, what is the counselor's responsibility here? In the best of all possible worlds, the student would talk to her parents herself, and the counselor should work with her toward that end. If she refuses, then the imminent-danger rule applies. For example, if the student is having complications from the pregnancy and needs medical attention, the parents may have to be told. In many states minors do not have access to medical services on their own.[8] In the absence of a school policy dictating otherwise, where there are no signs of imminent danger, the school counselor is not obligated to break confidentiality.

The second challenge is giving the student the freedom to consider all of her options, to carefully weigh the pros and cons of each option, without imposing the counselor's own values. That means a counselor who is opposed to abortion must objectively explain that option without trying to influence the student's decision; it also means that a counselor who knows that bearing a child is going to compromise the student's education still must explore with the student the possibility of bringing the pregnancy to term. If the counselor feels unable to talk objectively about all of the student's options, the best decision is to refer the student to a community agency with expertise in counseling pregnant teens and then to follow up regularly with the student. Whenever a counselor makes a referral, there is always the risk of the student's interpreting the action as a rejection. The school counselor must do everything he or she can to convince the student otherwise. The best way to do that is to follow up often with the student and to accept unconditionally her decision about the pregnancy.

Working with the Adolescent Mother-to-Be   In cases where the pregnant teen has made the decision to bring her pregnancy to term, L. J. Bradley et al. (1999) suggested the school counselor take the following steps:

1. *Assess the client's immediate needs.* Many pregnant teens are confused about prenatal care. The counselor can help them see the importance of that care and direct them to places where they can receive it. If the adolescent is afraid to tell her parents or her boyfriend, the school counselor can help her work through the fear. Avoiding disclosure is not going to improve the situation.
2. *Decide whom to notify.* Again, depending on school policy and state laws, the teen's parent may have to be notified. If the student wants to tell her parents but does not know how, the counselor can offer to be part of the meeting with the parents. Role-playing is a good way to anticipate the parents' reactions and to develop strategies for responding to those reactions.
3. *Identify supportive relationships.* Students who are pregnant may be rejected by their peers or feel isolated because of their condition. The counselor will know about and make referrals to community agencies that run support groups for pregnant teens.

---

[8]This situation is complicated by the fact that many other states have an emancipated-minor law that does give pregnant teenagers access to medical services on their own.

4. *Consider long-term options.* As the pregnancy advances, the school counselor can help the adolescent plan her educational future. Will the student stay in the same school or switch to an alternative school? What about child care? Many alternative schools provide day care on-site, which may be a factor in the student's decision. Although the data regarding education and adolescent mothers are not encouraging, the school counselor can help the pregnant teen understand that she can have her baby *and* continue her education. The school counselor can also help with other long-term needs by making sure the adolescent applies for available public assistance, especially the Special Supplemental Food Program for Women, Infants, and Children (WIC).

One adolescent mother had this to say about the importance of education:

> Well, you know, I thought, if I'm being bad like this and am pregnant and am gonna be a mother, I need to give an example to other kids. . . . I changed so I could be an example, a good example. Then when my baby be born, you know, she grows up, they could talk good things about me, not bad. When I wasn't pregnant, I use to not care. But now, you know, 'cause I have a baby, I have to give an example to her, you know, and to other kids, get an education for the baby. So when the baby asks [the mother] something, she'll know what to answer. Or if not, if she don't finish school, she'll be a dropout, the baby's gonna be a dropout. She'll tell her mother, "You were a dropout. Why can't I be too? . . . If you left school, why can't I leave too?" (Sciarra & Ponterotto, 1998, p. 759)

Although most communities offer services to pregnant teenagers and adolescent mothers, often the logistics of getting to and applying for those services can overwhelm a young person. Another task for the school counselor, then, is to be sure the student can get where she needs to go and has all the information she needs to fill out an application (Scherman, Korkanes-Rowe, & Howard, 1990):

1. Does the student have transportation? Is there a bus route or a friend with a car?
2. How much time will it take to apply? How long until the application is approved? What can be done in the meantime?
3. What verification (of income, hours, and child care arrangements) will the student need? (The counselor can help by making copies for the student.) What is the deadline for submitting documents?
4. Does the student have a social security number? Does the student have birth certificates for herself and for the baby? If not, the counselor should be able to tell the student how to get them.

Working with Teen Fathers   Often the teenage father is forgotten in the discussion of adolescent pregnancy and motherhood. A national survey found that school counselors are more likely to refer teen mothers than teen fathers for health and basic living services (Kiselica, Gorczynski, & Capps, 1998). When school counselors do not include teen fathers as part of their intervention with teen mothers, they may well be excluding a source of support for adolescent mothers and their children.

In large part, the extent of a teen father's involvement in the birth and parenting of his child is a function of his personality. In his research on teen fathers, Goodyear (2002) found that they cluster into two groups. One is more predatory, less loving and committed to their partners, less responsible as fathers, and more likely to view the pregnancy as a sign of masculinity. The other group is just the opposite: less predatory, more loving and committed, more responsible, and less likely to see the pregnancy as a symbol of masculinity. Cultural factors may also be involved in the teen father's seeming lack of involvement in the pregnancy and birth of his child (Sciarra & Ponterotto, 1998). For example, in the Latino culture, machismo assigns responsibility for raising children solely to women.

Teen fathers should not be allowed to shirk their responsibility. School counselors must help them understand the consequences of their actions and the responsibility that goes along with fathering a child.[9]

> When I started out as a school counselor, I didn't like to counsel the teen mother and father together. It seemed like couples counseling to me, and I suppose I wasn't ready to accept them as a couple. Over time I realized that by excluding the father, I was helping to marginalize him and perhaps make him feel less responsible. After that, I always encouraged the teen mother to bring the father of her baby in to see me, even if he was not a student in the school: "I would like to meet your boyfriend [or the father of your baby] because it sounds as though he really wants to be with you and the baby." Many of the fathers never came, but some did. And I think their being part of the process helped them and their partner.

SEX EDUCATION: PREVENTING HIV AND TEENAGE PREGNANCY

In most middle and high schools, classes in health offer only a cursory treatment of sex education, the basic anatomy and physiology necessary to meet the state's mandated curriculum. The failure to expand the content here to include the psychological and emotional aspects of sex usually has to do with the social and political ideologies of the individual school district. Where the school district allows a comprehensive program of sex education, the school counselor may be called on to conduct one or more lessons on the nonphysical aspects of sexual activity; where it does not, the counselor can advocate for that kind of program. In either case, the

---

[9] An excellent resource for including young men in a teenage pregnancy and in prevention efforts is *Involving Males in Preventing Teen Pregnancy* (Sonenstein et al., 1998).

counselor must have a thorough understanding of ways to promote safer sex and to prevent teen pregnancy.

Approaches to Sex Education

The literature identifies three basic school programs to promote safer sex and prevent pregnancy: abstinence-only programs, abstinence and contraception programs, and comprehensive programs (J. J. McWhirter, 1998c).

Programs That Teach Abstinence Only   These traditional programs usually are a part of a health education curriculum that focuses on the physiological aspects of sex and reproduction. These programs do not deal with controversial issues like contraception and homosexuality; instead they preach abstinence as the only acceptable way to prevent STDs and pregnancy. There is no research to support the effectiveness of abstinence-only programs on delaying first intercourse or preventing pregnancy; but some abstinence-only programs do promote abstinence attitudes among students (Kirby et al., 1994) and do increase knowledge about reproduction and the biological aspects of sexuality (Barth, Fetro, Leland, & Volkan, 1992; Hofferth, 1991).

Programs That Teach Abstinence and Contraception   These programs provide all the information that traditional programs do, but also discuss contraception and how to get it. Research has been inconclusive about the effectiveness of these programs because knowledge alone is only weakly related to behavior (Kirby, 1999, 2001). Some of these programs have been found to change both attitudes and behavior, while others have not (Kirby et al., 1994). On the other hand, there is no evidence to suggest that a contraception component in sex education programs increases sexual activity among students (Franklin, Grant, Corcoran, Miler, & Bultman, 1997; Kirby, 2001; Sellers, McGraw, & McKinlay, 1994).

There is some evidence that school-based clinics that dispense contraceptives have succeeded in delaying first intercourse and lowering pregnancy rates (Dryfoos, 1994). But according to Kirby (1999), "most studies that have been conducted during the past 20 years have indicated that improving access to contraception did not significantly increase contraceptive use or decrease teen pregnancy" (p. 92). In fact, over the last 10 years, we have seen a decrease in the number of programs allowing access to contraceptives and an increase in the use of contraceptives by adolescents.

Comprehensive Programs   These programs also encourage abstinence or the delay of sexual activity and provide concrete information about contraception; but they also focus on life skills—for example, building students' self-esteem, honing decision-making skills, assertiveness training, and helping students to envision a future in which they are successful and self-sufficient (J. J. McWhirter, 1998c). Much of the information imparted in these programs is applied to each student's personal situation through discussion, role-play, and behavior simulation. The career component of some of these programs provides a part-time work experience along with remedial education in reading and math.

The research on comprehensive prevention programs tends to support their effectiveness. For example, participants in the Youth Incentive Entitlement Employment Program, a program that focuses on job training and employment opportunities as means of preventing risky sexual behavior, had more knowledge about sexual reproduction and contraception and were more likely to delay sexual activity and to use contraception than nonprogram participants (Hofferth, 1991; Olsen & Farkas, 1990). And programs like the Teen Outreach Program, the American Youth and Conservation Corps, the Seattle Social Development Program, and the Quantum Opportunities Program have all been shown to be effective in promoting safer sex and in reducing adolescent pregnancy and childbearing (J. P. Allen, Philliber, Herrlin, & Kuperminc, 1997; Catalano, Hawkins, Kosterman, Abbott, & Hill, 1998; Hahn, Levitt, & Aaron, 1994; Jastrzab, Masker, Blomquist, & Orr, 1996).

Most of the life-skills programs are community based. Counselors who find themselves in schools where only traditional prevention programs are allowed can refer at-risk youngsters to programs in the community. The effectiveness of these programs stems from their comprehensiveness, in particular the focus on providing at-risk youngsters with viable work and career options to offset the attractiveness of early childbearing. This underscores the importance for school counselors of having a strong career development component as part of the overall guidance program: This may well be the best way for the counselor to promote responsible sexual behavior and to prevent teenage pregnancy and childbearing. It is not enough to teach adolescents to say no; they must also have something to say yes to.

Safer Choices: A Comprehensive Program

A comprehensive prevention program must begin in elementary school and continue through middle school and into high school. The focus of the program for younger children should be on issues of self-esteem, on decision-making skills, and on achievement in reading and math—all of which are key to prevention efforts in middle and high school.

Safer Choices (Coyle, Kirby, et al., 1996) is an innovative multicomponent program that was piloted in 20 schools throughout California and Texas. Like other comprehensive prevention efforts, it has been shown to be effective in promoting healthier sexual attitudes and behaviors among participants (Coyle, Basen-Engquist, et al., 1999). Table 10.1 is an overview of the program, a guide school counselors can follow in creating a comprehensive prevention program in their high schools.

An important component of Safer Choices is its inclusion of parents, teachers, and community leaders. The program is a collaboration. Combined with remedial education and career resources for those at risk for school failure, Safer Choices is a good example of how school counselors can manage program activities without having to provide all of the services themselves.

TABLE 10.1   **SAFER CHOICES: AN OVERVIEW**

Program Component	Features
School organization	*School health promotion council.* The council, which involves teachers, students, parents, administrators, and community representatives, plans and conducts program activities.
Curriculum and staff development	*A 20-session classroom curriculum for Grades 9 and 10* (10 lessons at each grade level). The curriculum is implemented by classroom teachers trained by project staff, and peer leaders facilitate selected activities.
Peer resources and the school environment	*A Safer Choices peer team or club.* Club members meet with an adult coordinator to plan schoolwide activities designed to alter the normative culture of the school. Peer teams also run a resource area on-site.
Parent education	*Activities for parents.* Parents receive three newsletters a year that provide information about the program; functional information about HIV/AIDS and other STDs, and pregnancy; and tips on talking with teenagers about these issues. The curriculum includes student–parent homework activities to facilitate communication about STDs and pregnancy. Parents also serve on the health promotion council and help plan events.
School–community linkages	*Activities to enhance students' familiarity with and access to support services outside school.* Homework assignments ask students to gather information about local resources and services. One lesson for Grade 10 brings HIV-positive speakers into the classroom. Students and teachers receive resource guides that list sources for related services for adolescents.

SOURCE: Adapted from Coyle, Basen-Engquist, et al. (1999), p. 182.

SEXUAL ORIENTATION

The general consensus is that about 10 percent of the people in the United States identify themselves as gay or lesbian. That means approximately 3 million young people in high schools are predominantly or exclusively gay. It is quite possible that in any given middle or high school, 1 of every 10 students is in the process of identifying himself or herself as gay or lesbian.[10] These numbers, together with the fact that gay and lesbian youth face all of the challenges any minority group does, make this population a special concern for school counselors.

---

[10] In a survey of gay and lesbian adolescents, Telljohann and Price (1993) found that participants had become aware of their sexual orientation sometime between the ages of 4 and 18. Another study found that the average age for the onset of same-sex experiences for gay males was 14 (Uribe & Harbeck, 1992).

The Challenges Facing Gay and Lesbian Youth

Youngsters who are gay, lesbian, bisexual, or transgendered (GLBT) experience many of the same difficulties that youngsters from any nondominant culture do (see Chapter 6). But the dynamics of their interactions with the dominant culture can have special connotations.

Identity Development   Peer acceptance plays a key role in the adolescent's formation of a positive self-identity. Because gay and lesbian adolescents realize (or are in the process of realizing) that they are different from most of their peers, developing a positive self-identity can be complicated. They know they are different from what the world expects, and that can cause a great deal of confusion. Schools, in particular, can be rigidly heterosexual, even punishing those who have identified themselves as gay. It is not unheard of, for example, for school administrators to harass staff members who are openly gay or lesbian. We can imagine the effect of that harassment on students who are struggling with their own sexual orientation. Because they lack interaction with and the acceptance of their peers, gay and lesbian youngsters may turn elsewhere for and support. For some, this means becoming involved in a relationship with an adult, a situation that further complicates their identity formation (J. Black & Underwood, 1998).

Certainly gay and lesbian adolescents can and do develop positive self-identities. Troiden (1989) outlined a four-stage model of the process:

1. *Sensitization.* This stage is characterized by generalized feelings of marginality, of being different from same-sex peers. In this stage, the young person learns the social identity of being gay.
2. *Identity confusion.* In this stage, the adolescent recognizes the attraction to others of the same sex. At the same time, he or she begins to sort through the many sources of identity and messages that range from social condemnation to misinformation.
3. *Identity assumption.* In this stage the adolescent's gay identity is established and shared with others; the youngster begins associating with other gays and experiments sexually.
4. *Commitment.* For the gay person, this means adopting a way of life by committing to a same-sex relationship and by learning and implementing strategies to manage the stigma of being gay.

Like other identity development models, Troiden's is not really linear. The development of a gay identity can take a long time, during which the individual can cycle in and out of the various stages. But school counselors can use the model to help assess the particular needs of one student and to develop appropriate interventions.

Isolation and Rejection   Often, gay and lesbian adolescents are adjusting to a social stigma (A. Martin & Hetrick, 1988). In and out of the school environment, these students must listen to derogatory jokes and comments about gays and lesbians. Unlike young people of color, gay and lesbian adolescents are not visible to their peers, who freely make insensitive comments that often go uncorrected by the adults around them. It is quite possible for gay youngsters to internalize society's hatred and rejection, for them to think that homosexuality is wrong and sick and that they are unlovable (Cooley, 1998). The extent of their self-hatred is clear in their words:

- "Sometimes I just hate myself and everybody too."
- "I don't know what I did to deserve this."
- "When things go wrong, I sometimes think that it is because I am gay."
- "I feel guilty and don't like myself when I am not honest with people." (M. M. Omizo, Omizo, & Okamoto, 1998, p. 36)

In addition, many gay and lesbian adolescents avoid school dances, proms, and other social activities, feeling unwanted and uncomfortable bringing a same-sex partner. They also have difficulty establishing close relationships for fear their sexual orientation will be discovered (Marinoble, 1998). In a sense, they isolate themselves as a means of protecting themselves from the hurt inflicted on them by school, family, and community (Muller & Hartman, 1998). Two consequences of isolation and rejection among gay youth are "passing" and suicide.

PASSING   Some gay youngsters pretend to be heterosexual. Young men wear very masculine clothes, participate in "manly" activities, flirt with and even date young women, and in general try to appear macho. Young lesbians wear very feminine clothes, flirt with boys, and behave in traditionally feminine ways. These youngsters know what they are doing, and the cost of passing is high levels of anxiety, hyper-vigilance, and self-loathing (J. Black & Underwood, 1998). They set out to minimize their isolation; but, in the end, passing only increases the adolescents' difficulties and prevents them from developing a healthy gay identity.

SUICIDE   Isolation and rejection lead to feelings of anxiety and depression, which increase the risk of suicide for gay and lesbian adolescents . In 1989, a federal task force found that suicide is the leading cause of death among gay and lesbian teens (U.S. Department of Health and Human Services, 1989): These youngsters are two to three times more likely to attempt suicide than are their heterosexual peers (Gibson, 1989). In one survey of 137 gay and bisexual males ages 14 to 21, 30 percent reported at least one suicide attempt (Remafedi, Farrow, & Deisher, 1991). A more-recent study, however, found little difference in suicide rates between GLBT youth and their heterosexual counterparts (DeAngelis, 2002).

The task force report identified a number of factors that put young people at risk for suicide. McFarland (1998) explained how those factors apply to gay and lesbian youth:

Society. Society's attitudes toward homosexuality are often hostile. In 2000, 1,229 incidents of hate crimes based on sexual orientation were reported to the Federal Bureau of Investigation (2001); however, many more go unreported.

Low self-esteem. Gay youngsters tend to have low self-esteem, a product of internalized hostility and rejection.

Family. Gay and lesbian youngsters often experience verbal and physical abuse from family members, along with rejection.

Religion. In many religions, homosexuality is considered a sin.

Schools. Our schools are failing to educate all students about homosexuality and to protect gay and lesbian students from verbal and physical assaults. This is a factor in suicide; it also is a factor in truancy and dropping out. One study found that 25.1 percent of gay, lesbian, and bisexual youngsters do not attend school because of safety concerns, compared with 5.1 percent of their heterosexual counterparts (S. T. Russell & Joyner, 2001).

Social isolation. Gay and lesbian adolescents often encounter rejection after revealing their orientation to their straight peers. It can be equally hard for them to find support from adults, and their contact with other gays and lesbians may be quite limited.

Substance abuse. Many gay teens turn to drugs or alcohol to cope with the challenge they face. In a nonclinical sample of gay and lesbian adolescents, 58 percent reported abusing substances on a regular basis (Whitlock, 1989).

An unwillingness to seek professional help. The perception of these adolescents is that mental health professionals want to pathologize their homosexuality.

The absence of youth programs. Many programs neither accept nor support gay adolescents. The Boy Scouts of America, for example, took its case to the Supreme Court to protect its right to reject gay youngsters.[11]

The inability to form intimate relationships. GLBT youth may not develop intimate relationships as early as heterosexual youngsters do. The reason: They have fewer of the skills needed to maintain relationships. Moreover, when gay youngsters end a relationship, they may internalize the breakup, which confirms their negative self-evaluation.

Homelessness. Gay youngsters often are forced to leave home before they have the educational or work training to support themselves. Many end up homeless.

HIV/AIDS. Because they do not practice safer sex, gay male teenagers are at risk for contracting HIV. In a study by Remafedi (1987), 44 percent of gay adolescents reported that they never use a condom.

Family Issues Alienation from family is a central issue for gay and lesbian youth, especially in terms of coming out. *Coming out* is "the process of identifying and respecting one's homosexuality and disclosing this positive identity to others" (Grace quoted in J. Black & Underwood, 1998, p. 17). Many gay youngsters choose not to come out to their family because they are afraid of rejection, anger, even shame (Hetrick & Martin, 1987). Adolescents need both the financial and emotional support of their parents, and these youngsters know that by admitting their homosexuality to their parents, they run the risk of losing that support. Studies have found that after their family learned of their homosexuality, nearly 50 percent of gay and lesbian youth experienced violence from family members and about 30 percent were forced to leave their homes (Gibson, 1989; Hetrick & Martin, 1987). The family disruption caused by the discovery of a child's homosexuality has a significant

---

[11]*Boy Scouts of America v. Dale,* No. 99–699 (2000).

impact on the child: It can result in anger, hostility, depression, and the inability to concentrate in school (Marinoble, 1998). And when the homosexuality becomes the family's secret, the child also feels inadequate.

Unlike youngsters from other minority cultures, gay and lesbian teens and their parents almost never have the same sexual orientation (K. E. Robinson, 1994). That means they cannot expect the same empathy from their parents that students of color might expect when they talk with their parents about racial discrimination. It is not unusual for gay adolescents to decide to come out to certain groups and not to others, and that decision is one the school counselor must respect.

Institutionalized Homophobia   *Homophobia* is an irrational fear and hatred of gayness (Gramick, 1983) that can be directed at self or others. Homophobia underlies the verbal and physical attacks individuals perpetrate on gays and lesbians; it also underlies institutional discrimination. Schools are among the most homophobic institutions. They ignore homosexuality in sex education curriculums, and they fail to confront the verbal and physical abuse of gay students (K. E. Robinson, 1994). Homophobia often leads to a school's denial of the existence of gay students and so to the denial of needed services for those students (Fontaine, 1998).

Ultimately, of course, an institution is simply a group of people. Well, the people in schools are homophobic. A governor's task force (1988) in New York found higher levels of hostility among junior and high school students toward gays than toward students from racial or ethnic minorities. Other studies consistently show that school administrators and teachers as a group test high on homophobic attitudes and feelings (Dressler, 1985; J. H. Price & Telljohann, 1991; Savin-Williams, 1990; Sears, 1992). Most disappointing of all, school counselors are no better than other members of the school staff. They too tend to test high on homophobic attitudes and feelings. And both counselors and therapists have been found to attribute gay clients' problems to their gayness (Davidson & Friedman, 1981).

Interventions

Before school counselors can effectively intervene with or on behalf of gay and lesbian students, they must confront their own homophobia (Cooley, 1998). The best way to do that is to be aware of the challenges and struggles facing gay and lesbian teens. Without empathy, no amount of intervention can succeed.

Counseling Gay and Lesbian Students Individually   Many students come for counseling because they are not sure they are gay. The first step in helping them is to normalize their confusion and communicate a willingness to work with them to explore their sexual orientation.

J. Black and Underwood (1998) provided the following list of direct intervention strategies for gay and lesbian students:

Be nonjudgmental. Gay youngsters are suspicious, afraid of being judged or attacked by peers and adults. A counselor who is nonjudgmental can be a therapeutic antidote to the hostility these students face from others.

Use the terminology the student uses. One sign of a counselor's comfort in working with gay and lesbian students is his or her use of sexual language. The counselor should use the language the student uses, and should be comfortable doing so. This helps build trust.

Respect confidentiality. In the absence of imminent danger, there is no reason whatsoever for the counselor to break confidentiality around issues of sexual orientation.

Deal with feelings first. Gay and lesbian students are likely to arrive at the counselor's office with a great deal of pent-up feeling. Counselors need to facilitate and be patient with the expression of that feeling.

Anticipate confusion. Again, many students come to the counselor's office confused about their sexual orientation. Under no circumstances should the counselor see confusion as an opportunity to set them "straight."

Help, don't force. The school counselor provides as much information as possible to help gay and lesbian students work through their issues. But students must be allowed to make their own decisions no matter how arduous or lengthy the process.

Don't guess. The school counselor should not try to guess who is really gay and who isn't. Identifying sexual orientation can be a complicated and subtle process; and the counselor must let that process move forward without his or her interference.

Offer to help. The school counselor can help the student work through feelings of self-blame, guilt, and self-hate. The counselor can also help him or her with the coming-out process—role-playing can be effective here. If the student is planning to come out to his or her family, the counselor can also help the family work through its grief over the loss of the image of their child's heterosexuality (Cooley, 1998).

Be alert for depression. Again, gay and lesbian teenagers are at greater risk for depression and suicide. If a student manifests symptoms of depression or suicidal tendencies, the counselor should follow up immediately with an assessment (see Chapter 9).

Provide accurate information on STDs, including AIDS. Gay and lesbian teenagers have health risks, and the counselor should do everything possible to minimize those risks.

Make knowledgeable referrals for community services. Often, a school counselor's interventions can be supplemented by services in the community for gay and lesbian teenagers. But before a counselor refers a student for help, he or she should know how the agency approaches its work with gay and lesbian youngsters and avoid any agency whose goal is to "convert" these teenagers to heterosexuality.

Most important, perhaps, by consistently being there for gay and lesbian students, the school counselor can reduce the isolation so many of those students experience in their schools.

Group Counseling for Gay and Lesbian Students   Group counseling can be an excellent modality for supporting gay and lesbian students and reducing their feelings of isolation.[12] To recruit members, the counselor can speak to students he or she knows, ask a trusted teacher for recommendations, insert a notice in a guidance newsletter ("Anyone with sexuality concerns can speak to me"), or post a notice. Those who reveal their interest in group counseling can be asked to invite other gay and lesbian students to come too. Throughout the process—in conversations and in printed materials—the school counselor promises anonymity for group members.

Muller and Hartman (1998) developed an outline of a support group for gay and lesbian students (Table 10.2). The outline can be expanded or reduced to meet the needs of a particular group. For example, the group can invite additional speakers or dedicate sessions to drug abuse, alcohol abuse, or STDs. If the group is working well, sessions can continue with less structure, allowing members to share interpersonal issues spontaneously.

Schoolwide Interventions   School counselors can also take a role in making the school environment more sensitive to and supportive of the problems gay teenagers face. Schoolwide intervention affects school policies, curriculum, and staff development.

SCHOOL POLICIES   School counselors do not set school policies, but they can advocate for policies that support an inclusive learning environment. According to Marinoble (1998), those policies should include the following provisions:

- The inclusion of sexual orientation in any statement of nondiscrimination, from clauses in teachers' contracts to policies regarding the treatment of students and their parents
- A prohibition—and it must be enforced—against slurs or jokes about homosexuality
- Mandatory human relations sessions for staff and students that include issues of sexual diversity
- The inclusion of books that portray homosexuality in a positive manner in the school library
- The inclusion of gay and lesbian topics in the school newspaper and other school publications

CURRICULUM   Homophobia in schools is supported primarily through neglect and disregard for gay students. The curriculum is a prime example. Although school counselors do not design academic curriculums, they can lobby for the inclusion of gay topics and examples in the classroom. For instance, the school counselor might urge curriculum committees to adopt textbooks that accurately portray gay and lesbian history and culture, encourage teachers to select classroom reading materials that portray gays and lesbians accurately, and help teachers develop lesson plans for discussing gay and lesbian issues in the context of current events and for ac-

---

[12]The school counselor can follow the general guidelines for forming small groups outlined in Chapter 2.

TABLE 10.2 A SUPPORT GROUP FOR GAY AND LESBIAN STUDENTS: THEMES AND ACTIVITIES

Session Themes	Session Activities
1. Introduction and cohesion building	Group rules are discussed; and then the members introduce themselves by writing down on slips of paper three words a friend would use to describe them. The members share what's written on their strips, which are later stapled together to form a chain. The leader explains how their different characteristics unite them.
2. Dear Mom and Dad	After a review of the group rules, the leader starts a discussion on parents. Those who have come out to their parents share their experience and describe their current relationship with their parents. Members who have not come out are asked to discuss what they imagine their parents saying or doing when they learn that their son or daughter is gay.
3 and 4. Stages in the coming-out process	The leader describes Troiden's (1989) stages of coming out. Members are asked to discuss their experiences with the different stages and to identify the stage they currently are going through. Then the members are asked to draw pictures of themselves reflecting their identity as a gay person and to discuss them.
5. People think I am / I think I am	The topic of this session and the next is homophobia. Members begin by sharing all the derogatory names they have been called, and a list is compiled. Next, members receive a worksheet showing two mirrors on it. They are asked to draw two representations: one, the way they feel others see them; and the other, the way they see themselves. The leader facilitates a discussion around the discrepancy between the images in the two mirrors.
6. People think I am / I think I am (continued)	This session begins with more discussion about the images in the two mirrors and then a discussion about anger, self-loathing, pride, and rejection.
7. I wish I could tell you	In this session, members are asked to think of people in their lives with whom they have unfinished business. Then members are encouraged to write a letter—it does not have to be mailed —to one or more of the people who have caused them anger, sadness, and resentment. When they've finished writing, members share their reactions to the activity, and the leader encourages them to use letter writing in the future to work through negative emotions.
8. Field trip	The group takes a field trip to a community gay and lesbian support center. Those members who are not out to their parents can tell their parents they will be visiting a teen counseling center (permission slips are usually needed for offsite activities). If a field trip is not feasible, the group leader may want to ask a representative of the center to speak to the group.
9. Termination	Members are asked to share their feelings—positive and negative—about the group. The leader should explain to the members how they can continue to receive support both inside and outside of school. Finally, the group celebrates its accomplishments with a small party.

SOURCE: Adapted from Muller and Hartman (1998).

knowledging the sexual orientation of people who have made historical contributions (Marinoble, 1998).

STAFF DEVELOPMENT   The school counselor can offer an annual workshop to help teachers and other staff members become more knowledgeable about, sensitive to, and supportive of the issues that pertain to gay and lesbian students. Key to the effectiveness of this type of in-service training is the counselor's response to the inevitable resistance that stems from the staff's homophobia (J. Black & Underwood, 1998). That homophobia should be one focus of the workshop, as should strategies for working with gay youngsters.

ETHICAL AND LEGAL ISSUES

Counseling students on issues related to their sexuality raises ethical and legal concerns especially in the areas of confidentiality and the rights of parents. Some school districts have resolved the problem by adopting policies that prohibit school counselors from discussing contraception, abortion, and sexual activity in general; some districts even require an immediate phone call to parents when a student so much as mentions one of these topics in a counseling session (Stone, 2002). Our first recommendation, then, is for counselors to know their school policy and adhere to it.

Suppose the school does not have a restrictive policy. Does that mean school counselors can discuss sexual activity and abortion with students with no fear of a lawsuit? In 1989, two high school students, Jane and John, and their parents filed a lawsuit against their Alabama school district claiming that the school counselor, along with the assistant principal, forced Jane to have an abortion.[13] Jane's parents also claimed that their privacy rights were violated when the school counselor failed to inform them that their daughter was pregnant. The court's investigation revealed that the two students had told the school counselor that they did not want their parents to know about the pregnancy because they were not supposed to be seeing each other. Fact-finding also revealed that the counselor had presented various options to the students, who rejected all of them except abortion, and that she had repeatedly urged the students to discuss the situation with their parents, which they refused to do. The court concluded that the students had chosen the abortion freely and had made the decision themselves not to inform their parents. The decision implies that the students were of sufficient maturity to decide on an abortion and on keeping the information about the pregnancy from their parents. But what if Jane and John had been younger? Would the court have ruled differently? Our second recommendation, then, is for the school counselor to consider the developmental level of minor students and their ability to make informed choices (Stone, 2002).

---

[13] *Arnold v. Board of Education of Escambia County* (880 F.2d 305, 1989).

In the absence of a school policy forbidding them to discuss issues of abortion and sex or obligating them to inform parents when a student is pregnant, can school counselors work confidentially with students around these issues without fear of liability? The answer is yes, as long as counselors consider certain contextual factors:

The student's health. Is the student in clear and imminent danger?

The student's emotional maturity. Is the student capable of making responsible decisions?

The importance of self-disclosure. The counselor should repeatedly encourage the student to talk with his or her parents, especially in the case of pregnancy.

The counselor's objectivity. The counselor never imposes his or her own values on the student. A counselor who can't be objective can refer the student to a colleague.

The counselor's limited involvement. The counselor's role is to give the student information, explain that information, and then support the student's decision. It is not to physically help the student in any way—for example, by driving the student to a doctor, hospital, or clinic (Stone, 2000).

A second opinion. The counselor should always consult with a supervisor or respected colleague about working with students on sex-related issues.

School counselors cannot allow the fear of liability to stop them from helping students in need of their expertise and training.

CONCLUSION

Adolescence is a time of sexual awakening, a time in which young people become aware of themselves as sexual beings. The struggle to develop identity—what Erikson calls the primary developmental task of adolescence—is made more difficult by the physical and cognitive changes adolescents are undergoing and the value they place on interactions with and the opinions of their peers. The role of the school counselor here is to help students make good decisions for themselves and then to support the decisions they do make. For students who choose not to be sexually active, the counselor helps with strategies to ease the pressure on them. For students who feel ready to take part in sexual activity, the counselor is a source of information about STDs and their prevention, and about contraception.

Another concern when students become sexually active is pregnancy and motherhood. The consequences of early childbearing for young women, and the consequences of HIV/AIDS for any teenager, point to the need for comprehensive sex education programs in the schools.

For some youngsters, with sexual awareness comes the realization that they are attracted to same-sex partners. These adolescents are at risk too, for depression and suicide, in large part because our schools—and the people in them—deny or ridicule or even attack homosexuality. To protect and support gay students, counselors must lobby for policies, curricula, and in-service training that recognize the cultural needs of a sexual minority.

We realize that many of the topics discussed in this chapter are controversial, especially as they pertain to our nation's schools. But sexuality is part of the human condition and a very big part of adolescent development, and these topics need talking about. Unless school policy limits what they can say and do, school counselors have a responsibility to help all students understand, respect, and feel good about their sexuality.

QUESTIONS FOR DISCUSSION

1. Sex education in schools has been a very controversial issue over the last 10 years. What is your opinion about offering comprehensive sex education in schools? How would you respond to a parent who insists that sex education is a parent's responsibility and no one else's?
2. Adolescents take risks; risk-taking behaviors in this population are normal. With that understanding, what responsibility, if any, do schools have to promote safer sex? In your answer, address ethical issues as well as social and other issues.
3. Some say that schools can and should only preach abstinence. How would you respond to this point of view? Explain your answer.
4. Gay, lesbian, bisexual, and transgendered students, confused about their sexual orientation and with few places to go to for help, are turning more frequently to the school counselor. How would you work with a student who came to you questioning his or her sexual orientation? How comfortable are you with allowing students to explore their sexual orientation?
5. You have been given responsibility for developing a sex education program for your elementary, middle, or high school (choose one). With whom would you work? How would you design a program that is ethical, responsible, and comprehensive? How would you develop a curriculum? What are some of the controversial issues you would expect to include? Assuming no restrictive policies in your school, are there any issues you would not include? Share your process and curriculum outline with a study partner.

SUGGESTED INTERNET SITES

www.teenpregnancy.org

The official Web site of the National Campaign to Prevent Teen Pregnancy contains information for teenagers on preventing pregnancy, tips for parents and information for teens who are expecting a baby, and real-life accounts of teen mothers and fathers.

www.siecus.org

This is the official Web site of the Sexuality Information and Education Council of the United States (SIECUS), which develops, collects, and disseminates information;

promotes comprehensive education about sexuality; and advocates the right of individuals to make responsible sexual choices. Included is valuable information on sexually transmitted diseases. The site has sections for educators, parents, and teens.

www.cfoc.org

This is the official Web site of the Campaign for Our Children, a group that encourages healthy, responsible sexual decisions among teens, informed support systems for young people, and public awareness of preventive health issues among adolescents. On the site is a section where teens can ask the "sexpert" questions; and there's a resource center for educators and parents.

www.outproud.org

The Web site of the National Coalition for Gay, Lesbian, Bisexual and Transgendered Youth is broken down into several topic areas, among them personal stories, community role models, resources, support services, and message boards. A good site for parents and educators, too.

www.youthresource.com

The site's mission is to support GLBT teens. It contains information about same-sex dating, violence, sexual health, and GLBT youngsters of color, and personal stories.

Substance Use and Abuse: Prevention and Intervention

There are almost 15 million illicit drug users in the United States today (National Institute on Drug Abuse, 1999a); that number represents approximately 8 percent of the population over age 20, the highest rate of illicit drug use among industrialized nations. Nearly 14 million Americans abuse alcohol or are alcoholic (National Institute on Alcohol Abuse and Alcoholism, 1996). And approximately 48 million adults in the United States smoke cigarettes.

In 1992, the total cost of alcohol and drug abuse in the United States was estimated at $245.7 billion. Taxpayers paid 46 percent of that cost; the rest was borne by the abusers themselves and their families (National Institute on Drug Abuse, 2000b). About half of the cost of substance abuse is related to crime. Alcohol use alone is associated with 25 percent of all victims in general and 67 percent of all crimes against intimate partners (Greenfield, 1998). Smoking-related illnesses cost the nation more than $100 billion each year, and 20 percent of deaths each year in the United States—about 430,000 deaths a year—are attributable to cigarette smoking (Centers for Disease Control and Prevention, 2000).

Substance abuse is like a cancer that the finest health care practitioners and researchers, the most astute policymakers, the most aggressive law enforcement officers, and the most dedicated prevention workers cannot cure. Yet experts agree on two things: The process of addiction begins early in childhood and adolescence, and the risk factors for addiction are clearly identifiable. That knowledge defines both the duration of substance abuse prevention programs—from kindergarten through Grade 12—and the focus of those programs.

The Use and Abuse of Substances Among Young People

Monitoring the Future (MTF) is an annual study of drug abuse nationwide among students in Grades 8, 10, and 12. The *MTF* study collects data on past-month, past-year, and lifetime drug use among students in the three grade levels.[1] It also measures three attitudinal indicators related to drug use: perceived risk of harm, disapproval of others, and perceived availability of a particular drug.

The list that follows summarizes data from the most recent *MTF* study (National Institute on Drug Abuse, 2000d). The information here is to give school counselors a working knowledge of the most popular substances kids are using and abusing, to help counselors speak realistically and convincingly about them to students.

> *Alcohol.* In recent years, alcohol use, though high, has remained stable in the three grades. But the perceived risk of harm in having one or two drinks decreased among 12th graders, from 8.3 percent in 1999 to 6.4 percent in 2000. Binge drinking has been on the rise in all three groups: According to the study, 14.1 percent of 8th graders, 26.2 percent of 10th graders, and 30.0 percent of 12th graders reported having had five or more drinks in a row in the past two weeks. Furthermore, 8.3 percent of 8th graders, 23.5 percent of 10th graders, and 32.3 percent of 12th graders reported having been drunk in the month before the survey. This was the highest percentage of 10th graders reported since the *MTF* study began collecting data for 10th graders in 1991.
>
> *Cigarette use.* In 2000, 14.6 percent of students in Grade 8, 23.9 percent of students in Grade 10, and 31.4 percent of students in Grade 12 reported smoking at least one cigarette in the last month, down from 21.0 percent, 30.4 percent, and 34.0 percent in 1996. Attitudinal changes were also noteworthy: The perceived risk of harm from smoking a pack or more of cigarettes a day increased in the two younger grades, and the perceived availability of cigarettes fell in those groups. Although tobacco use among adolescents remains a grave concern for our society, recent data indicate that antismoking campaigns and high-profile lawsuits against cigarette manufacturers may be reducing tobacco use in this population.
>
> *Marijuana.* Marijuana continues to be the most popular illicit substance among youngsters and adults. Marijuana use among adolescents rose dramatically in the mid-1990s but has leveled off in recent years, especially among students in Grade 8. Past-year use in 2000 fell among 10th graders, to 32.2 percent from a high of 34.4 percent in 1997, and among 8th graders, to 15.6 percent from a high of 18.3 percent in 1996. Still, the use of marijuana remains high among students: In 2000, the *MTF* study reported that more than 48 percent of 12th graders had used marijuana in their lifetime, and 22 percent had used it within the past month.
>
> *Inhalants.* Inhalants continue to be the most popular substance among students in Grade 8. Although the rate fell slightly in 2000, 17.9 percent admitted to inhalant use at least once, and 9.4 percent said they had used inhalants within the last year. Inhalants are also popular among 10th and

---

[1] Occasionally another interval is used too.

12th graders. In the Grade 10 sample, 16.6 percent reported at least one use, and 7.3 percent reported use in the past year; in the Grade 12 sample, 14.2 percent reported at least one use, and 5.9 percent reported use in the past year.

Ecstasy. Ecstasy is one of the street names for the drug methylenedioxy-methamphetamine (MDMA); others are *XTC, Adam, euphoria,* and *X.* The drug combines synthetic mescaline and an amphetamine, and acts as a hallucinogenic, mood-altering stimulant. Users say it produces a sense of great pleasure, heightens sexuality, facilitates emotional insight, and expands consciousness without the loss of control—effects that may explain its growing popularity. In just one year, from 1999 to 2000, the use of ecstasy in the past year increased at all three grade levels: from 1.7 percent to 3.1 percent in Grade 8, from 4.4 percent to 5.4 percent in Grade 10, and from 5.6 percent to 8.2 percent in Grade 12. Attitudinally, the perceived availability of ecstasy among high school seniors increased from 40.1 percent in 1999 to 51.4 percent in 2000. African American students had considerably lower rates of ecstasy use compared to White and Hispanic students.

Steroids. Adolescent use of steroids has been increasing over several years. From 1999 to 2000, rates of use did not change in Grades 8 and 12; but past-year use increased among Grade 10 students from 0.7 percent to 2.2 percent, and lifetime use increased from 2.7 percent to 3.5 percent. More than 500,000 students in Grades 8 and 10 use steroids. Attitudinally, there was a decrease among high school seniors in the perceived risk of harm from using steroids. Anabolic steroids act like the male sex hormone, testosterone; they tend to be abused by athletes and those concerned about body image. Steroid abuse can halt bone growth and cause damage to heart, kidneys, and liver. In males, abuse can lead to impotence, shrunken testicles, and breast enlargement. In females, steroids can cause menstrual irregularities, the growth of body hair and the loss of scalp hair, a deepened voice, and reduction in breast size (National Institute on Drug Abuse, 2001b). Some studies have linked anabolic steroids to increased and unpredictable levels of aggression.

Cocaine and crack. The year 2000 saw the first decrease since the early 1990s in the use of cocaine among 12th graders, from 6.2 percent in 1999 to 5.0 percent; crack use also went down at this grade level. Modest declines were also noted for the two lower grades in all categories of use. Attitudinally, the 2000 study found a decrease among 10th graders in the perceived availability of cocaine and crack but also a decrease in the perceived risk of harm from these drugs.

Heroin. Although less popular than the drugs listed above, the use of heroin among 12th graders increased to its highest level ever in 2000. The use of other opiates also increased to their highest level. In 2000, 10.6 percent of 12th graders reported using opiates at least once, 7 percent reported use in the last year, and 2.9 percent reported use in the last month.

This list describes the most popular substances in use today among teenagers. It might look different five years from now. The popularity of some drugs is influenced by perceived availability, risk, and disapproval. But four substances—alcohol, tobacco, marijuana, and inhalants—are the adolescent's drugs of choice. We come back to them in a later section.

UNDERSTANDING TEENAGE DRUG USE AND ABUSE

The starting point for understanding why anyone, including teenagers, uses and abuses drugs is simple: Drugs have benefits. That is, people who take drugs believe that they produce physiological, emotional, behavioral, or social benefits. Of course those benefits come with costs in each of these dimensions, as well as with financial and legal costs.

Often, counseling professionals have a cost bias; they try to intervene by focusing only on what's bad about a drug. This approach is doomed to fail because it does not consider the benefits that are real to the person using the drug. The only way to stop drug abuse is for the abuser to become convinced that the costs of using outweigh the benefits. For some, this moment never arrives; for others it arrives when something traumatic happens—the death of a loved one; the loss of family, job, possessions—something that is clearly attributable to the abuse.

The challenge in preventing drug use and abuse among adolescents is that they have yet to accumulate the costs of years of abuse; for them, the perceived benefits of drug use clearly outweigh the perceived costs. So any effort to stop drug use among teenagers must begin with an understanding of the benefits they derive from drugs and then focus on alternate ways to attain those benefits.

By age 18, 80 percent of adolescents have used a legal or illegal substance. For some, this is experimentation, nothing more; but for others, it can be the beginning of a serious problem. In a later section we examine the factors that put adolescents at risk for substance use and abuse; here we examine the stages of drug use and the physiological effects of drugs.

The Drug Use Continuum

When does drug use become abuse? Should the school counselor be especially concerned about some students more than others? The fourth edition of the *Diagnostic and Statistical Manual of Mental Disorders Text Revision (DSM-IV-TR)* establishes criteria for substance dependence and abuse but does not make a distinction between children and adolescents (APA, 2000). In the *DSM-IV-TR, substance dependence* is addiction and involves the physiological processes of tolerance and withdrawal. *Substance abuse* refers to the use of substances in a way that interferes with social, school, or occupational functioning. The implication of the *DSM-IV-TR* criteria is that substances can be used in a way that is not pathological. Value judgments about the use of substances are made according to who takes them, why, when and where, and how much (S. E. Robinson, 1989). For example, a drink after work for a middle-aged man is not as much of a problem as a drink every-day after school would be for an adolescent (Gloria & Robinson-Kurpius, 2000). Youngsters who begin experimenting with tobacco and alcohol at a very young age (between 9 and 12) are of greater concern than those who experiment later.

The adolescent chemical use experience (ACUE) is a psychosocial perspective for evaluating drug use by adolescents (Muisener, 1994). It considers social and en-vironmental factors to establish a continuum for understanding the different sub-stance experiences of adolescents. ACUE has four stages:

1. *Experimental use.* Peer pressure can be one factor in adolescents' trying a drug; others are wanting to have fun, being curious, or feeling bored (Jalali, Jalali, Crocette, & Turner, 1981). Experimenters never settle into a drug use pattern (Miziker-Gonet, 1994); they understand the difference between fun and danger; and typically they use only alcohol and marijuana (Gloria & Robinson-Kurpius, 2000). Experimentation implies a limited number of uses: P. H. Miller (1989) sets that number at no more than 5; Avis (1990), at no more than 10.

2. *Social use.* In this stage, adolescents use drugs for the mood swings they ex-perienced during the experimental stage. Youngsters in this stage use drugs regularly in certain situations—at weekend parties, for example. Social users who misuse or overindulge in those situations are at risk for more serious drug use. *Social use* does not imply acceptable use; it is just the term used to describe the frequency of the drug use.

3. *Operational use.* Muisener's *operational use* is synonymous with *abuse:* This stage is marked by a preoccupation with the mood swing. There are two types of operational users: *pleasure-pursuant users,* who use drugs to feel good, and *pain-avoidant* or *compensatory users,* who use drugs to ease pain or to cope with difficult situations. Compensatory users are at greater risk for developing a serious drug problem because drugs have become a coping mechanism.

4. *Dependent use.* According to Muisener (1994), adolescents in this stage use drugs compulsively, urgently seeking the mood swing. These adolescents spend much of their time and energy getting drugs and getting high. Com-pulsive users derive their identity from drugs and often form a subculture that distinguishes them from the mainstream, nonabusing population.

Most adolescents do not progress beyond social use, but current estimates are that more than 1 million teenagers are dependent users (Gloria & Robinson-Kurpius, 2000).

The Physiology of Drug Use

What draws adolescents to the use and abuse of drugs, and ultimately to depen-dence on them, is the mood swing. To understand this effect of drugs, it's impor-tant to understand the physiology of drug use.

TABLE 11.1 MAJOR NEUROTRANSMITTERS AND THEIR EFFECT IN DIFFERENT AREAS OF THE BRAIN

	Effect on Area of the Brain		
Neurotransmitter	Cerebral Cortex (responsible for intellectual functioning)	Limbic System (responsible for emotions)	Brain Stem (responsible for metabolic processes)
Acetylcholine	Affects memory.	Affects perception and creativity.	Affects gross motor functioning.
Dopamine	Affects mental stability: High levels may result in psychosis.	Affects pleasure: Low levels reduce the ability to experience pleasure.	Affects fine motor control: Low levels result in loss of motor control.
Endorphins	Unknown.	Affects reward pathways: Low levels result in loss of interest in eating and sex; high levels have the opposite effect.	Slows heart rate and decreases physical pain.
Norepinephrine	Affects focused thought: Low levels result in reduced concentration.	Affects mood: High levels result in euphoria.	Affects energy level.
Serotonin	Affects processing of sensory information: High levels increase sensory perception.	Affects mood: Low levels result in depression; high levels, in euphoria.	Affects sleep: Low levels result in trouble sleeping; high levels, in too much sleep.

For drugs to have an effect, they must be swallowed, smoked, injected, or snorted. Drugs that are swallowed enter the bloodstream through the walls of the intestines. Smoked and inhaled drugs enter the bloodstream through the lungs. Injected drugs enter the bloodstream directly through a vein. Drugs that are snorted enter the bloodstream through the mucous membranes. From the bloodstream, drug are transported to the central nervous system, which is where drugs have their physiological effect.

How much of an effect a drug has on the user depends on many factors: the type of drug, its potency and purity, the contaminant used to cut the drug, the personality and physiological characteristics of the user, and the environment in which the drug is used (Gloria & Robinson-Kurpius, 2000). The major impact of drugs is on *neurotransmitters,* the chemicals that transmit nerve impulses from one brain cell to another. More than 60 neurotransmitters have been identified; psychoactive substances basically interact with five of them: acetylcholine, dopamine, endorphins, norepinephrine, and serotonin. Table 11.1 explains the effects of these major neurotransmitters in the different parts of the brain. Psychoactive substances produce the mood swing by imitating, blocking, or releasing neurotransmitters. For example, cocaine both releases and blocks the reuptake (the process by which the neurotransmitter returns to its vesicle) of both dopamine and norepinephrine. The excess of these two neurotransmitters produces the euphoria that cocaine users crave.

The same factors that govern the effects of a drug also govern the duration of those effects, at least initially. Over time, as the body gets used to a drug, two processes come into play: tolerance and withdrawal. *Tolerance* is "a diminished biological or behavioral response to repeated administrations of a drug; or the need for an increased amount of the drug to achieve the same, desired level of effect" (Fleming, Potter, & Kettyle, 1996, p. 3). The body responds to the absence of the drug with *withdrawal,* the "physical and/or psychological disturbances that follow the abrupt discontinuation of a drug" p. 4). Withdrawal can be more or less severe depending on the seriousness of the drug use; and its symptoms can be mitigated by absorbing the drug. Withdrawal is itself a symptom of addiction.

ADOLESCENTS' DRUGS OF CHOICE

Here we review the four most common substances abused by children and adolescents: alcohol, nicotine, marijuana, and inhalants. For each substance we examine its general nature along with its physical effects and the health hazards it poses.

Alcohol

The use of alcohol is pervasive in our society. For every person in the United States, 24 gallons of beer, 2 gallons of distilled spirits, and more than 2 gallons of wine are sold each year (Gloria & Robinson-Kurpius, 2000). According to the *MTF* study (National Institute on Drug Abuse, 2000d), 22 percent of 8th graders, 41 percent of 10th graders, and 50 percent of 12th graders reported drinking alcohol within the last month; and binge drinking is on the rise at all three grade levels.

Here are some other facts about alcohol and children:

- Almost 42 percent of 9th graders have consumed alcohol before age 13 (Centers for Disease Control and Prevention, 1997).
- Girls consume alcohol and binge-drink at rates equal to boys (Centers for Disease Control and Prevention, 1997).
- Almost half the children who start drinking before age 15 will become alcoholics at some point in their lives. By delaying the onset of drinking just five years, the risk of alcohol-related problems drops 50 percent (Grant & Dawson, 1997).
- Rates of drinking differ among racial and ethnic groups. For example, in a study of young people between ages 12 and 20, binge drinking was reported by 27.0 percent of Hispanics, 22.6 percent of Native Americans, and 21.9 percent of Whites, but by only 11.6 percent of African Americans and 6.8 percent of Asian Americans (National Institute on Drug Abuse, 1999a).

For many youngsters, what begins as experimental use develops into operational or dependent use: Approximately 14 million Americans—1 in every 13 adults—abuse alcohol or are alcoholic (National Institute on Alcohol Abuse and Alcoholism, 1996).

The Physical Effects of Alcohol   Alcoholic beverages contain the substance ethanol, which depresses the central nervous system and affects the functioning of the cerebral cortex. The effects: decreased alertness, impaired judgment, relaxed inhibitions, increased heart rate, and a general sense of feeling good (Avis, 1990; Gloria & Robinson-Kurpius, 2000; Raskin & Daley, 1991). As alcohol intake increases, blood alcohol level increases, and judgment, reaction time, and sensory and motor capabilities all decrease. Drunkenness in most states is defined as a blood alcohol level of 0.1 percent—in adolescents a level generally reached after just a couple of drinks.

Health Hazards   The physical consequences of alcohol abuse are many and serious. Prolonged use of alcohol has been associated with increased risk for cancer of the liver, esophagus, throat, and larynx. Cirrhosis of the liver, problems with the immune system, brain damage, and harm to the fetus are all associated with alcohol abuse (U.S. Department of Health and Human Services, 2000).

The damage alcohol does to the body happens with prolonged use, so few teenagers manifest long-term problems. But adolescents who abuse alcohol can suffer from withdrawal symptoms—tremors, perspiration, disorientation, agitation, and brief seizures (Gloria & Robinson-Kurpius, 2000). And the temporary effects of alcohol on judgment and reaction time put anyone who drinks at increased risk of accidents at work, at play, and, above all, at the wheel. In 1997, 33 percent of 9th graders reported they had been in a car driven by someone who had been drinking (Centers for Disease Control and Prevention, 1997). And in 1998, 20 percent of the automobile accidents in which children under age 15 were killed were alcohol related (National Highway Traffic Safety Administration, 1999).

Alcohol use also has psychological and behavioral effects:

- Among 12- to 17-year-olds who reported drinking, 31 percent had extreme levels of psychological distress, and 39 percent exhibited serious behavioral problems (Substance Abuse and Mental Health Services Administration, 1999).
- Girls ages 12 to 16, who drink are four times more likely than their non-drinking counterparts to suffer depression (Hanna & Grant, 1999).
- In 1994, suicide or homicide accounted for 18 percent of the alcohol-related deaths of children between ages 1 and 15 (National Institute on Alcohol Abuse and Alcoholism, 1999).

Nicotine

More than 80 percent of smokers start to smoke before age 18 (U.S. Department of Health and Human Services, 1994). Up to age 20, the rate of cigarette smoking increases steadily each year. In 1999, 2.2 percent of 12-year-olds and 43.5 percent of 20-year-olds smoked cigarettes on a regular basis (National Institute on Drug Abuse, 1999a). After age 25, rates gradually fall. Nicotine abuse is clearly a problem that begins in youth. Males are more likely to smoke than females: 36.5 percent versus 24.3 percent. And males are much more likely to use smokeless tobacco. American Indians and Alaskan Natives are more likely to smoke than any other

Today, nearly 3,000 young people across our country will begin smoking regularly. Of these 3,000 young people, 1,000 will lose that gamble to the diseases caused by smoking. The net effect of this is that among children living in America today, 5 million will die an early, preventable death because of a decision made as a child.

Donna E. Shalala, former secretary of the U.S. Department of Health and Human Services racial or ethnic group. In 1999, 43 percent of this group ages 12 and older reported using some form of tobacco, compared to 34 percent of Whites, 32 percent of Hispanics, 22 percent of Blacks, and 19 percent of Asian Americans (National Institute on Drug Abuse, 1999a).

The Physical Effects of Nicotine   In the body, nicotine acts as both a stimulant and a sedative. The drug causes an immediate discharge of epinephrine, which stimulates the sudden release of glucose, giving the user a "kick." But after the glucose is used up, depression and fatigue replace stimulation (National Institute on Drug Abuse, 2000a). As users' tolerance for nicotine increases, they need more and more to achieve the wanted effect.[2]

Quitting smoking is very difficult because nicotine is highly addictive. Studies have shown that when smokers are deprived of nicotine, their levels of hostility, anger, and aggression increase. In addition, during periods of abstinence and craving, nicotine users evidence impaired psychomotor and cognitive functions, among them language comprehension (National Institute on Drug Abuse, 2000a).

Health Hazards   Where do we start? The tar in cigarettes is responsible for lung cancer, emphysema, and bronchial disorders; the carbon monoxide increases the rate of cardiovascular disease. Each year, cigarette smoking kills 430,000 people in the United States: 123,000 from lung cancer, 98,000 from coronary heart disease, 72,000 from chronic lung disease, 32,000 from other cancers, 24,000 from strokes, and 81,000 from other diseases (Centers for Disease Control and Prevention, 2000). Smokeless tobacco and cigars also have deadly effects, including cancer of the lung, larynx, esophagus, and mouth.

The harmful effects of smoking extend beyond smokers themselves. Women who use tobacco during pregnancy are at greater risk for having babies with low birth weight. Each year, environmental tobacco smoke kills 3,000 nonsmokers, causes 300,000 lower-respiratory-tract infections in children, and increases non-smokers' risk of coronary heart disease (Centers for Disease Control and Prevention, 2000).

In addition to coughing, asthma, and other respiratory problems, kids who smoke are more likely to use alcohol and other drugs. Seventy-five percent of adolescent smokers also admit to smoking marijuana (National Institute on Drug Abuse, 1997).

Marijuana

Marijuana (pot, weed, Mary Jane, herb, boom) is the most widely used illegal drug in the United States; and it usually is the first illegal drug that adolescents use (Gloria & Robinson-Kurpius, 2000). The drug is a greenish or grayish mixture of leaves

---

[2] Stress also has been shown to reduce the reward effects of nicotine, which causes users to seek more.

and flowers from the hemp plant *Cannabis sativa.* It contains the active chemical THC (delta-9-tetrahydrocannabinol) and is graded by the relative amount of THC in the drug. Marijuana is usually smoked in cigarette form or in a pipe, although blunts (cigars emptied of tobacco and refilled with marijuana) are growing in popularity (National Institute on Drug Abuse, 2000c). Marijuana can be laced with other drugs, including cocaine, or smoked together with crack.

The Physical Effects of Marijuana   After marijuana is ingested, THC immediately alters the metabolic activity of serotonin and dopamine, creating a dream-like state. The half-life of marijuana is long: Traces can be detected by a standard urine test several days after an individual last ingested the drug. In heavy users, detection can occur after several weeks of not using (National Institute on Drug Abuse, 2003). In fact, daily users may experience a continuous high.

The effect of marijuana on the individual is a function of several factors, including heredity, the availability of the drug, the influence of peers, and the individual's own expectations (National Institute on Drug Abuse, 2000c). Research on the effects of marijuana is ongoing. Scientists have not been able to determine whether marijuana is physiologically addictive; but that it is psychologically addictive is indisputable. More than 120,000 people each year are treated for their addiction to the drug (National Institute on Drug Abuse, 2000c).

Health Hazards   In addition to its affect on the release of serotonin and dopamine, marijuana also acts on the hippocampus, a part of the limbic system. Research has determined that marijuana suppresses neuronal activity in the information-processing system there. As a result, heavy marijuana use has a deleterious effect on memory, certain learned behaviors, and the ability to learn new behaviors (Kingery-McCabe, & Campbell, 1991).

Because marijuana enters the bloodstream almost exclusively through smoking, regular users suffer many of the same respiratory problems tobacco smokers do, including chronic bronchitis and frequent chest colds (National Institute on Drug Abuse, 2000c). The amount of tar and carbon monoxide absorbed by marijuana smokers is three to five times greater than that absorbed by tobacco smokers—probably because marijuana users tend to inhale deeply, hold the smoke in their lungs, and absorb unfiltered smoke (National Institute on Drug Abuse, 2000c).

Longitudinal studies show negative social consequences for heavy users of marijuana. Among adolescents, marijuana use has been associated with lower achievement, high levels of delinquent and aggressive behavior, greater rebelliousness, poor relationships with parents, and having delinquent friends (National Institute on Drug Abuse, 2000c). It also has been linked to decreased motivation (Gloria & Robinson-Kurpius, 2000).

Curbing marijuana use in this population is challenging. The drug does not have the stigma attached to it that most illegal drugs do, and it is readily available. Many adolescents experiment with marijuana and enjoy the experience, particularly when they listen to music—a function of the drug's effect on sensory perception.

Inhalants

Most adults are exposed daily to chemical vapors at home and in the workplace. Because we don't think to inhale them, we don't think of them as drugs. Inhalants are "breathable chemical vapors that produce psychoactive (mind-altering) effects" (National Institute on Drug Abuse, 2001a, p. 1). Inhalants are the most common drugs used by younger adolescents because they are readily available and inexpensive, and because they can be used without parents suspecting.

Inhalants fall into three categories (National Institute on Drug Abuse, 2001a): solvents (paint thinner, degreasers, gasoline, glue, correction fluid, ink); gases (butane, propane, aerosol, spray paint, hair and deodorant sprays, chloroform, and nitrous oxide); and nitrates (cyclohexyl nitrite).[3]

Inhalants can be absorbed through the nose (sniffing) or mouth (huffing). For the most part, they produce a short but intoxicating effect, much like alcohol. Symptoms of intoxication include reduced inhibitions, confusion, disorientation, lack of coordination, and restlessness. Highly concentrated amounts of chemicals can induce delirium coma, heart failure, and even death. Death can also result from suffocation because the chemical displaces oxygen in the lungs. Table 11.2 describes the major health hazards associated with inhalant chemicals and the common products in which they are found.

RISK FACTORS IN CHILD AND ADOLESCENT SUBSTANCE ABUSE

We do not have a profile of the adolescent substance abuser: Substance abuse is most likely the result of a complex interplay of developmental, family, intrapersonal, and cultural factors.

Developmental Factors

Research has identified three factors in the early development of children that put them at risk for substance abuse:

- Chaotic home environments particularly where parents abuse substances or suffer from mental illnesses
- Ineffective parenting, especially with children with difficult temperaments and conduct disorders
- Lack of mutual attachments and nurturing (National Institute on Drug Abuse, 1999b, p. 2)

Because of the primary nature of these factors, many consider them to be the most crucial factors in children's risk for drug abuse.

---

[3]Amyl nitrite is now available only by prescription; butyl nitrite is now an illegal substance.

TABLE 11.2 INHALANTS: COMMON PRODUCTS AND THEIR HEALTH HAZARDS

Chemical	Common Products	Health Hazard
Amyl nitrite, butyl nitrites	—	Kaposi's sarcoma
Benzene (gasoline)	—	Bone marrow damage
Chlorinated hydrocarbons	Correction fluid, dry cleaning fluid	Liver and kidney damage
Hexane	Glue, gasoline	Peripheral neuropathies, limb spasms
Methylene chloride	Paint thinner, varnish remover	Blood oxygen depletion
Nitrous oxide	Aerosol cans, gas cylinders	Neuropathies, limb spasms
Toluene	Spray paint, glue, dewaxers	Hearing loss, brain and nerve damage, liver and kidney damage
Trichloroethylene	Cleaning fluid, correction fluid	Hearing loss

SOURCE: National Institute on Drug Abuse (2001a).

As children begin to interact outside the family, through school and other socializing agents, other risk factors come into play:

- Inappropriate shy [or] aggressive behavior in the classroom
- Failure in school performance
- Poor social coping skills
- Affiliations with deviant peer or peers around deviant behaviors
- Perceptions of approval of drug-using behaviors in the school, peer, and community environments (National Institute on Drug Abuse, 1999b, p. 3)

Research has also identified certain protective factors in the early environment of children that reduce their risk for substance abuse:

- Strong bonds with the family
- Experience of parental monitoring with clear rules of conduct within the family unit
- Involvement of parents in the lives of their children
- Success in school performance
- Strong bonds with prosocial institutions such as the family, school, and religious organizations
- Adoption of conventional norms about drug use (National Institute on Drug Abuse, 1999b, p. 3)

And certain developmental factors make adolescents vulnerable to drug abuse. Again, peers are a significant influence in both the experimental and social use of drugs among adolescents. Other factors are related to dependence and identity.

Peer Group   Their peers are probably the most significant influence on adolescents. In this stage of development, it is normal to transfer dependence needs from parents to peers (Miziker-Gonet, 1994). Adolescents have many ways to connect with a peer group—for example, through sports and clubs. Drug use, unfortunately, is another way for adolescents to belong, especially those who don't fit in with other groups.

Much like a certain height is needed to be on the basketball team, drug use is the requirement for belonging to this particular peer group. Initially, the adolescent experiences real bonding. The price, though, is alienation from a large portion of the population, the nonabusing world (Miziker-Gonet, 1994). And eventually the emotional connections and interactions of group members are masked by the effects of the drug use. No drugs, no friends.

The drug-abusing group can be an attractive substitute for family for adolescents who come from chaotic and disorganized homes (Kamback, Bosma, & D'Lugoff, 1977). But drug use cuts across all kinds of families: That is, any adolescent who turns to drugs regularly is going to seek out drug-abusing peers. In these cases, it is not so much peer influence that draws the adolescent to the group as much as the perception of safety in the group and the need to belong.

Dependence versus Independence   Adolescents need to assert their independence from parents. For some adolescents, using drugs—particularly gateway drugs, like alcohol and tobacco—is a sign of their maturity, of their own adult status. And parental disapproval here may only fuel the fire.

Ironically, habitual drug use promotes dependence, not independence. Sometimes that dependence is physical; it almost always is emotional. Adolescents often resort to drug use in times of conflict or emotional turmoil. The drug becomes a crutch. Preaching this paradox to adolescents may have limited effect; still the school counselor should use the themes of dependence and independence in their talks with adolescents about drugs. A possible approach: The counselor validates the adolescents' need for independence, challenges drugs as a means of being independent, and then facilitates other, less harmful ways for adolescents to achieve their independence. Authority figures run into trouble when they try to impose their authority on adolescents instead of validating the youngsters' need for independence. Helping adolescents understand that drugs actually keep them dependent is a much more effective strategy (Miziker-Gonet, 1994).

Identity   As adolescents work to develop their identity, they often struggle with low self-esteem and feelings of inadequacy. Lacking the coping mechanisms that come with experience, they may well turn to drugs to feel better about themselves. Of course, working through difficult feelings is part of the maturation process, the baptism into adulthood. Adolescents who turn to drugs to negotiate their feelings are in a state of arrested development. The adult drug addict is an adolescent in an adult's body. As drug use evolves into dependence, self-esteem is lowered. Therein lies another paradox. Adolescents who turned to drugs to feel better about themselves instead come to feel worse about themselves (Miziker-Gonet, 1994). Prevention efforts in the schools can use this core relationship between self-esteem and identity to help adolescents see that the solution has become the problem.

Family Factors

The family variable that most influences drug abuse in adolescents is parental use. If parents have a problem with drugs, their children are very likely to have the same problem. Parental use affects genetic disposition and models behavior (Miziker-Gonet, 1994), both of which contribute to children's risk for drug use. The genetic link for drug abuse, especially for alcoholism, is very strong. A groundbreaking study in Denmark found that sons of alcoholics who were raised by nonalcoholic adoptive parents were four times more likely to become alcoholics than were the adopted sons of nonalcoholic parents (Goodwin, 1981). Modeling by adults is also a strong influence because adolescents associate drug use with adult behavior. Adolescents who see their parents using drugs are more likely to use drugs themselves to assert their adult status. Sibling use has also been found to be an important variable in determining adolescent drug use. In addition to their peers, adolescents also use older siblings as a reference group for drug-using behaviors (Brook, Whiteman, Gordon, & Brook, 1990; Gfroerer, 1987).

The way in which family members interact is also an important risk factor for adolescent drug use. Family systems theory sees drug abuse as one by-product of the family's inability to draw appropriate boundaries. When boundaries are blurred, there is little room for the adolescent to grow and become more autonomous. If the absence of boundaries robs the child of his or her development and self-expression, the child may turn to drugs as a way of establishing independence.

In families with rigid boundaries, relationships are distant and alienating. Emotional distance from parents (Stoker & Swadi, 1990); a poor relationship with parents (Pandina & Schuele, 1983), and the child's perception that he or she is not loved (Norem-Hebeisen, Johnson, Anderson, & Johnson, 1984), all have been shown to play a role in adolescent drug use. In addition, drug users are more likely to come from families whose members have difficulty communicating (Tarter, Blackson, Martin, Loeber, & Moss, 1993); in which mistrust is common and discipline punitive (Stoker & Swadi, 1990); and in which parental supervision and praise are lacking, and rules are inconsistent (Hawkins, Lisher, & Catalano, 1987).

Intrapersonal Factors

It can be difficult to identify personality factors here because so many of them are a function of family and environmental influences. But from their work with drug users who come from intact, organized, and high-functioning families, researchers suggest that the following characteristics place adolescents at risk for drug abuse: [4]

- Rebelliousness
- Nontraditionalism
- Tolerance for deviance

---

[4] See, for example, Guy, Smith, and Bentler (1994); Newcomb and McGee (1991); and Shedler and Block (1990).

- Need for excitement
- Need for independence
- Low trust
- Low impulse control
- Poor delay of gratification

Adolescents are more at risk for drug use when psychic pain is high and coping mechanisms are low (J. J. McWhirter, 1998b): Under stress, adolescents can turn to drugs as a means of escape. Also a factor here is difficulty performing well in school, which is associated with delinquent behaviors; previous delinquent behavior is an important risk factor in drug use (Long & Scherl, 1984; Newcomb & Bentler, 1989).

Cultural Factors

Any adolescent who is a member of a minority group is faced with elevated levels of stress, which increase the likelihood of the youngster's turning to drugs. Unfortunately, most of the research on adolescent drug use has been with Whites. In general, more White adolescents use alcohol and other drugs than do Black, Hispanic, and Asian teenagers.[5] Yet, despite their lower rate of drug use, adolescents from these racial and ethnic minorities have higher rates of arrest and violent crimes related to substance abuse than do their White counterparts. It has been suggested that youngsters from minority groups use drugs at a lower rate but do so more heavily (J. J. McWhirter, 1998b). The high number of arrests among these youngsters may also be a function of racial profiling more than drug use.

There is little research on drug and alcohol use among gay and lesbian adolescents. One study of adolescents served at the Hetrick Martin Institute, a resource for gay and lesbian teens in New York City, found that most had used a number of different substances and that a third had frequent and problematic use (Shifrin & Solis, 1992). Certainly the confusion inherent in identifying oneself as gay could contribute to substance use in this population. Other factors here could be the stress of homophobia, and the rejection and ridicule gay teenagers often experience (J. J. McWhirter, 1998b). More research is needed to understand drug and alcohol use among gay and lesbian adolescents and to plan more effective interventions.

PREVENTING SUBSTANCE ABUSE

Choosing and implementing a school-based prevention program present a myriad of challenges. Although a number of programs are available commercially and widely used, there is little or no research to support their effectiveness. This section

---

[5] Native American teenagers have the highest rates of alcohol consumption (Gloria & Robinson-Kurpius, 2000) and the highest rates of illicit drug use (National Institute on Drug Abuse, 1999a).

is designed to help school counselors become critical consumers of prevention programs and to play an active role in the school's efforts to prevent substance abuse.

Choosing an Effective School-Based Program

The 1980s saw important changes in school-based methods of preventing substance abuse. To the knowledge component—increasing students' understanding of drugs and alcohol—most programs added an attitudinal component that considered social and environmental influences on adolescents' drug use. This psychosocial approach to prevention grew out of Bandura's (1977) social learning theory and led to programs like Just Say No and Life Skills Training. In the 1990s came the realization that Just Say No is simplistic: For adolescents to say no, they must have something to which they can say yes. Most newer programs—Adventure Education is one example—offer alternate ways for adolescents to derive some of the same benefits they seek from drugs.

Although the research on the effectiveness of substance abuse prevention programs has been prolific, it is not conclusive. For example, Staulcup, Kenward, and Frigo (1979) evaluated 21 knowledge-based programs and found no connection between knowledge and behavior. Another review of 127 programs found them generally ineffective (Schaps, DiBartolo, Moskowitz, Palley, & Churgin, 1981). And in a metaanalysis of 25 program-effectiveness studies, Kinder, Pape, and Walfish (1980) found increases in basic knowledge but no attitudinal or behavioral changes. Proponents of knowledge-based programs responded by arguing that the programs did effect change, but that poor methodology and a lack of valid measures in the studies included in the metaanalysis may well have concealed that change.

Reviews of psychosocial programs show promising results (Flay, 1985, 1986; W. B. Hanson, 1992; Tobler, 1986, 1992). For example, Flay (1985) found that social influences and life- and social-skills training programs reduce experimental smoking rates among adolescents by as much as 50 percent. These programs were also successful—although to a lesser degree—in reducing alcohol and marijuana use (Botvin, Baker, Dusenbury, Botvin, & Diaz, 1995; Ellickson & Bell, 1990; W. B. Hanson, Johnson, Flay, Graham, & Sobel, 1988). For the most part, these were efficacy studies; but effectiveness studies also have shown positive results for the psychosocial approach (Botvin, Baker, Dusenbury, Tortu, & Botvin, 1990; Pentz et al., 1989).[6]

From years of research into the effectiveness of drug abuse prevention programs, we know that certain approaches simply do not work:

> *Information-only programs.* These programs tend to present the physiological and pharmacological facts about drug use and the legal, social, and psychological consequences (Miziker-Gonet, 1994). Although comprehensive

---

[6]*Efficacy studies* are carried out under controlled conditions and make use of trained program staff; *effectiveness studies* examine programs that have been implemented under real-world conditions—with classroom teachers, for example, as opposed to program staff.

and accurate information is the foundation of good prevention, it simply is not enough to prevent drug abuse.

Scare tactics. Two eggs are frying in a hot skillet, and the voice-over says: "This is your brain on drugs." What's left of a battered car sits at the entrance to the local high school with a sign that reads "They never made it home from the prom." Scare tactics. Prevention programs have been using them since the 1960s. They did not work then, and they do not work now. They make adolescents defensive, which prevents them from taking in the message (Miziker-Gonet, 1994).

One-shot programs. One-time presentations—a guest speaker, a film, a school assembly—are useless; in fact, they may do more harm than good. Students can walk away thinking they now know all there is to know about drugs. But a speaker, a film, or an assembly can be a good way to inaugurate a comprehensive drug prevention program.

Values-clarification programs. The goal of these programs is to help students explore and identify the values they've learned from their families and culture. The programs are not designed to teach new values and so are relatively ineffective in preventing drug abuse.

The research has also taught us what does work. The National Institute on Drug Abuse (1999b) has developed a list of guidelines for choosing an effective school-based prevention program:

- School-based programs should extend from kindergarten through high school. At the very least, they should reach children in the critical middle school and high school years.
- Programs should employ well-tested, standardized interventions with detailed lesson plans and student materials.
- Programs should employ age-appropriate and interactive teaching methods (for example, modeling, role-playing, discussion, group feedback, reinforcement, and extended practice).
- Programs should foster prosocial bonding, identification with and a connection to both school and community.
- Programs should teach social competence (communication, self-efficacy, assertiveness) and drug-resistance skills that are culturally and developmentally appropriate, and promote positive peer influence and antidrug social norms.
- Programs should be delivered in adequate "doses" (10 to 15 sessions a year).
- Programs should be evaluated periodically to determine their effectiveness.

As the list shows, it is not enough to simply focus on saying no. Successful prevention programs must increase students' self-esteem, social skills, decision-making and problem solving skills, and their ability to resist the influence of peers (Botvin, 1986; D. Bradley, 1988). And, as noted above, these programs must offer alternate activities to fill the need for excitement that attracts some adolescents to drugs (J. J. McWhirter, 1998b).

Also, most experts agree that drug prevention is a complex social phenomenon that must involve not only the school but the family and the community as well

(McLaughlin & Vacha, 1993). Parental support of the school's drug education and prevention efforts increases the effectiveness of those efforts (Flay, D'Avernas, Best, Kersell, & Ryan, 1983; Sunseri, Alberti, & Kent, 1983). Many school-based prevention programs include a component for parents to help them improve family communications and relationships. These workshops can be held in the school or in the community.[7]

The National Institute on Drug Abuse (1999b) also has developed guidelines for family-based prevention:

- Programs should train parents in the following behavioral skills: positive reinforcement, listening and communication, problem solving, consistent discipline and rulemaking, and monitoring adolescents' activities.
- Programs should reach families at each stage of their children's development and at all grade levels.
- Programs should provide parents with drug information for them and their children.
- Programs should provide access to counseling services for families at risk.

The community component of a comprehensive program should establish a coalition of community leaders (police, youth directors, church leaders, and the like); should keep the public informed of the program's progress; should incorporate feedback to and from the community into its organizational plan; and should make use of formal evaluations to assess the program's effect on the drug problem in the community.

Of course even the best comprehensive program can't be effective if those who implement it aren't effective. Several studies have found that schools are having problems with implementation (Pentz et al., 1989; Rohrbach, D'Onofrio, Backer, & Montgomery, 1996). The primary problem has to do with those who deliver the programs—often, classroom teachers—and their lack of training in this area. Substance abuse is an emotional issue that touches a large number of people, including teachers. School counselors can help them be more comfortable with the subject matter by offering support and pointing out the pitfalls of transferring resistant feelings to students (McLaughlin & Vacha, 1993). School counselors can also implement the programs themselves and lead workshops for parents.

A K–12 Curriculum

Most states require health education as part of the curriculum, and substance abuse usually is one area of study. But two or three informational lessons in Grade 7 or 8 is not an effective way to prevent drug abuse among adolescents. School counselors need to lobby their school districts for a comprehensive drug prevention program: a program that runs from kindergarten through Grade 12; that targets cognitive and attitudinal changes; that offers students an alternative to drug use; that involves

---

[7]The workshops should be advertised as drug abuse prevention workshops, not parenting workshops, even though they include a parenting-skills component. Parents tend to get defensive around interventions that purport to help them be good parents.

TABLE 11.3 **A K–12 COMPETENCY-BASED CURRICULUM FOR TEACHING ABOUT DRUGS AND FOR PREVENTING DRUG USE**

Grades	Competencies
K–3	1. Understand how foods, poisons, medicines, and illegal drugs differ.
	2. Understand how medicines prescribed by a doctor and administered by a responsible adult may help during illness but can be harmful if misused.
	3. Understand why adults may drink but children may not, even in small amounts, because it is harmful to their brains and developing bodies.
4–6	1. Understand the immediate effects of alcohol, tobacco, and drug use on different parts of the body, including risks of coma or fatal overdose.
	2. Understand the long-term consequences of drug use—how and why drugs can be addicting and make users lose control of their lives.
	3. Understand the reasons why drugs are especially dangerous for growing bodies.
	4. Understand the problems that alcohol and other illegal drugs cause not only the user but also the user's family and the world.
7–9	1. Understand that long-term use of drugs results in the lack of crucial social and emotional skills ordinarily learned during adolescence.
	2. Understand the risk of lung cancer and emphysema from smoking.
	3. Understand that fatal or crippling car accidents and liver damage result from heavy drinking.
10–12	1. Recognize and understand the effects of peer pressure to use drugs.
	2. Understand the potentially deadly effects of combining drugs.
	3. Understand how drug use can ruin plans for college and career.
	4. Understand that choosing to be drug-free reduces the number of innocent victims in their town, in society, and in the world.

SOURCE: Adapted from Partnership for a Drug-Free America (1998).

parents and community members; and that is delivered by properly trained professionals. A K–12 prevention program makes eminent sense from the perspective of comprehensive developmental guidance.

Table 11.3 is an example of a competency-based curriculum for preventing drug and alcohol abuse. The curriculum extends from kindergarten through Grade 12. The actual curriculum would break down each competency into goals and objectives for each grade. The impact of the program is cumulative: Students are exposed to the same themes (for example, the harm drugs cause the body) year after year in age-appropriate ways and at increasing levels of cognitive complexity.

Sample Programs

School counselors should be involved in the adoption of substance abuse prevention programs. They can establish criteria for choosing one program over another and then do their own research to be sure the program they are considering meets those criteria. Drug prevention programs are heavily marketed; it's important that the offerings be examined with a critical eye and with an awareness of the school's special needs.

We can't begin to describe all of the programs that are out there. But here we take a brief look at several programs that adopt a comprehensive psychosocial approach, that are being used by a good number of school systems, and that have proved effective.[8]

Seattle Social Development Project   The Seattle Social Development Project was designed to prevent delinquency and drug abuse by strengthening the variables that protect youngsters from drug use, especially family factors (Hawkins, Catalano, & Miller, 1992). The school-based component relies on interactive teaching strategies and cooperative learning; it is taught by classroom teachers who have been specially trained. Parents are also trained to help their child succeed in school and to improve parenting skills. The program's objectives are to increase children's opportunities and skills, and to reward them for prosocial involvement in school and family.

Project STAR   Project STAR (Students Taught Awareness and Resistance) is a comprehensive drug abuse prevention program that includes a school-based component, a parent program, a media campaign, and community leadership and health policy change (Pentz et al., 1989; Pentz, 1995). The school-based component is a two-year program directed primarily at middle schoolers. The parent program obliges parents and students to work together on homework, to learn communication skills, and to participate in community action. The mass media are used to promote and reinforce the project. Responsibility for the project lies in the community, which organizes and oversees all project-related activities. It is also responsible for implementing change in health policy by developing and implementing alcohol, tobacco, and other drug policies and laws to establish and monitor drug-free sites. Research on STAR has shown both short- and long-term positive effects (Pentz, 1995; Werch et al., 2000). In a follow-up survey of students who participated in STAR, a group of high school seniors reported 30 percent less use of marijuana, 25 percent less use of cigarettes, and 20 percent less use of alcohol than did teenagers who had not participated. The study also found that the most important factor in prevention was the growing perception that friends would not tolerate drug use (National Institute on Drug Abuse, 1999b).

Life Skills Training Program   The Life Skills Training Program (LSTP) is a three-year curriculum for middle school students (Botvin, Baker, Filazzola, & Botvin, 1990; Botvin, Baker, Dusenbury, Botvin, & Diaz, 1995; Botvin, Schinke, Epstein, & Diaz, 1995). The first year consists of 15 sessions; the second year, 10 booster sessions; the third year, 5 more booster sessions.

---

[8] None of these programs extends from kindergarten through Grade 12. There are K–12 programs available, but their effectiveness is questionable. The programs noted here, however, could be incorporated into a K–12 program of the district's design.

LSTP teaches drug-resistance skills along with personal and social skills. The drug-resistance component examines the social influences and misconceptions around drug use; teaches resistance skills and prevention-related information; and promotes antidrug norms. A self-management component teaches skills for increasing independence, personal control, and self-mastery—among them decision making, problem solving, resisting peer and media influences, increasing self-esteem, and adaptive coping mechanisms for dealing with stress and anxiety. The third component, general social skills, includes skills for communicating effectively, overcoming shyness, learning to meet new people, and developing healthy relationships. The skills are learned through demonstration, feedback, behavioral simulation and rehearsal, reinforcement, and homework assignments for practice.

Follow-up data on 6,000 participants in LSTP from 56 schools revealed that their nicotine, alcohol, and marijuana use was 44 percent lower than it was for controls and that their weekly use was 66 percent lower (Botvin, Baker, Dusenbury, Botvin, & Diaz, 1995). Studies also have shown that booster sessions help maintain the program's effects and that the program works equally well with adult or peer providers (Botvin, Baker, Filazzola, & Botvin, 1990). Although most of the research on LSTP has been conducted on White students, one study showed LSTP is also effective with inner-city minority youngsters (Botvin, Schinke, et al., 1995).

The ATLAS Program   The ATLAS (Athletes Training and Learning to Avoid Steroids) Program targets male high school athletes and their use of anabolic steroids and other drugs (Goldberg et al., 1996a, 1996b). As alternatives, it offers strength training and good nutrition. The curriculum begins in Grade 9; it is delivered by peers and coaches in small groups. There are seven 45-minute class sessions and seven physical-training sessions, which involve role-playing and educational games. The program also schedules four booster sessions in each subsequent year of high school. ATLAS teaches about anabolic steroids and the skills to resist drugs, stresses team ethics (including a commitment to stay drug-free), and debunks media images that promote substance abuse. Each participant is asked to set his own goals for nutrition and exercise. Weight-lifting instruction is provided in the school to keep students out of public gyms, where steroids are readily available.

ATLAS is a relatively new program—it was started in 1993—but research supports its effectiveness in keeping high school athletes steroid-free for a full year after participation in the program (Goldberg et al., 1996a, 1996b).

SUBSTANCE ABUSE INTERVENTIONS IN THE SCHOOL

Ideally, prevention is the focus of school counseling programs; but the harsh reality is that counselors are often forced to deal with substance abuse among students. One of the most popular forms of school-based interventions for drug-abusing children and adolescents are student assistance programs; other interventions target adolescents who smoke and the children of drug users.

Student Assistance Programs

Student assistance programs (SAPs) are modeled after employee assistance programs, interventions for workers who are experiencing drug and alcohol problems in the workplace (J. J. McWhirter, 1998b). SAPs typically include four steps: early identification, assessment, referral, and follow-up (Palmer & Paisley, 1991).

Step 1. Early Identification   SAPs are designed on the premise that the earlier schools can identify students who have a substance abuse problem, the better the chances for successful intervention. Among the classic symptoms of adolescent drug abuse are falling grades, changes in physical appearance, sleeping in class, tardiness, and truancy (Palmer & Paisley, 1991). Teachers are with students every day, and they should receive training in identifying these and other early signs of drug abuse.

In addition to the symptoms of substance abuse, in-service training should explain the drug use continuum and the importance of identifying students who have moved beyond experimental use. Teachers also can be trained to confront students whose behaviors indicate drug use and to ask them for a plan for change (Palmer & Paisley, 1991). If the behaviors persist or intensify, teachers refer the students to the school counselor or to the school's drug counselor (if the SAP designates this position) or another designated person in the school. In some schools, students with problems are referred to a multidisciplinary staff team. The team members review each student's "case" and decide on a plan of action. When drug abuse is suspected, the student is referred for assessment.

Step 2. Assessment   The typical SAP provides for a substance abuse specialist who assesses students for drug use. But the assessment can be carried out by the school counselor or anyone with training in substance abuse. Because many referrals are based on suspicion of drug use, the main goal of the assessment is a differential diagnosis, to determine whether the problem is substance abuse or something else that presents similarly. In addition to interviewing the student, the counselor gathers information from as many sources as possible—school records, teachers, coaches, and the like. The counselor may also ask the student's teacher to submit a behavioral checklist or ask the student to complete a formal inventory like the Drug Use Screening Inventory (DUSI) (Tarter, 1990). Finally, the counselor tries to involve the student's family as soon as possible in both assessment and treatment.

The DUSI consists of 149 items and quantifies the severity of problems in 10 domains: substance use, psychiatric disturbance, health, behavior disorder, school adjustment, family adjustment, peer relationships, social competence, work, and leisure/recreation. Each domain yields a score ranging from 0 percent to 100 percent, allowing for easy comparisons across domains. Research on the DUSI has yielded good reliability and validity data (Kirisci, Hsu, & Tarter, 1994; Tarter, Laird, Bukstein, & Kaminer, 1992). The inventory can be administered to individuals or a group, on paper or electronically, and it can be scored manually or by computer.

Step 3. Referral   With an understanding of the severity of the adolescent's drug use, any number of interventions can be planned, from school-based services to in-patient treatment (Palmer & Paisley, 1991). Most SAPs offer a range of school-based services, including individual counseling, short-term family counseling, and support groups for students who are abusing or whose lives have been affected by substance abuse. SAPs may also refer students to groups for other problems that put them at risk for substance abuse—for example, groups for children of divorce, survivors of suicide, social-skills enhancement, adolescent issues, and new students (Miziker-Gonet, 1994).

Although some SAPs are administered by an outside agency, school counselors should consider SAPs a supplement to, not a substitute for, the overall guidance program. If there is an SAP specialist working in the school, he or she should be part of the multidisciplinary team that is responsible for referring students for special services—a structure that avoids the duplication of services.

Step 4. Follow-Up   An important dimension of SAPs is following up with students to determine the effectiveness of interventions and the need for further services. In addition, SAPs provide school-based recovery groups for teens leaving a treatment center and returning to school (J. J. McWhirter, 1998b). These students are very much at risk for relapse when they return to the environment and the factors that contributed to their drug abuse. Recovery groups offer participants peer support for their sobriety.[9]

Interventions for Nicotine Dependence

Students who are addicted to nicotine would also qualify for an SAP; unfortunately, adolescents rarely seek treatment for nicotine dependence because smoking does not have the stigma that the use of illegal substances does. School districts are trying: Almost 98 percent of them have a policy prohibiting tobacco use among students (Ross et al., 1995). But detention and suspension—the usual punishments for violation of the no-smoking policy—do little to help teens deal with their addiction to nicotine.

The American Lung Association (1992) offers a program, Tobacco Free Teens, for helping young people stop smoking. The program runs for eight sessions:

1. Introduction: Do I really want to quit?
2. What kind of a smoker am I?
3. Quit day: What to expect
4. Tempting moments and planning ahead
5. Food for thought
6. A smoker's final lesson
7. High-risk students
8. Panel discussion and celebration

---

[9] M. Hanson and Peterson (1993) have written an excellent manual on how to conduct a school recovery support group.

Smoking cessation can be a long-term process with frequent relapses; so school counselors should not be disappointed when, after an eight-session group, some if not all of the participants are still smoking. The group helps teens examine their tobacco use, which in many instances is the first step toward quitting for good (Mudore, 1997).

Fibkins (1993) designed a smoking-cessation program for high school students based on input from the students themselves. The participants shared a number of characteristics:

- They had started smoking in Grades 6 and 7.
- Their academic performance was poor.
- They felt isolated and not part of the school.
- They looked to one another for support and socialization.
- They had a negative view of their future, with little hope of going to college or getting a good job.
- They had concerns about their general health: They felt they would not live a long life.
- They reported addiction to other drugs, among them alcohol.
- They felt enormous pressure from home and school, and used tobacco and other substances for relief.
- Many reported having tried to quit or cut back but failing each time.
- They enjoyed the game of trying to hide from and outwit school administrators. The game made school more fun for them.

Planning meetings with the students led to the design of a six-session group (Table 11.4). Twenty-seven students volunteered for the group: When they had completed the program, 5 had stopped smoking and 17 had cut back; 5 had made no changes. What is most interesting about this grassroots program is that the students developed a booklet of hints to help themselves and others stop smoking. Here are some of their suggestions:

1. Leave cigarettes where you can't easily get them (e.g., someone's office) — pick them up at the end of the day.
2. Bring only two cigarettes to school and make a promise not to borrow from others.
3. Do not go to places where you can smoke. Instead, go to the health office, the library, or to a friend who will encourage you not to smoke.
4. When under stress, take a deep breath and visualize a peaceful scene like a sunset.
5. If you have a free period, go for a walk without your cigarettes.
6. Keep putting off that cigarette one hour at a time, until it is a challenge to go a longer time.
7. Find ways to occupy your mind and hands. Read, meditate, suck on a lollipop, even do homework. Keep busy.
8. Tell your friends that your goal is to cut back or stop, not to get detention, and not to get suspended. Make a commitment. (Fibkins, 1993, pp. 58–59)

TABLE 11.4 A SMOKING-CESSATION PROGRAM FOR HIGH SCHOOL
STUDENTS: THEMES AND ACTIVITIES

Session Themes	Session Activities
1. Who's in charge of your smoking?	This session deals with the decision to smoke and how it can be reevaluated. Steps to cut back are discussed, and participants are asked to make a commitment not to smoke during school hours.
2. Self-image	This session deals with how smoking becomes a part of self-image and the kind of self-image that participants would like to have.
3. Stress factors and trigger mechanisms	This session focuses on the factors that trigger smoking and on alternatives. Participants are given an assignment: trying out the alternatives.
4. The power of addiction	Participants discuss the power of addiction and the importance of small gains: Change is a slow process, but even the smallest changes are progress.
5. Rewarding ourselves in other ways	This session deals with the use of substances to hide the pain of failure. Participants learn other ways to reward and support themselves.
6. What have we learned?	In the last session, material from the previous five is reviewed along with an evaluation of each participant's progress.

SOURCE: Adapted from Fibkins (1993).

Intervening with the Children of Substance Abusers

SAPs also provide services to students who come from substance-abusing homes. Again, parental substance abuse is the most significant risk factor in children's becoming abusers themselves. Over the last 30 years, children of alcoholics (COAs) have been the focus of a great deal of research on the dynamics of growing up in an alcoholic home. Many of the same issues face youngsters growing up in homes where other substances are abused.

Approximately 44 percent of school-aged children come from families where at least one member abuses substances (G. L. Anderson, 1987; Pilat & Jones, 1985). An estimated 7 million youngsters under age 18 come from homes with at least one alcoholic parent (B. E. Robinson, 1989), and 60 percent of these youngsters eventually abuse alcohol or other substances themselves (G. L. Anderson, 1987). By providing early intervention for COAs—at the elementary school level—school counselors may prevent some of these children from abusing drugs in the future.

Challenges Facing COAs   Self-esteem issues are crucial in the lives of COAs because three key ingredients in developing a sense of self-worth—parental warmth, clearly defined limits, and respectful treatment—usually are lacking in the alcoholic home. COAs also tend to have an external locus of control (Post & Robinson,

1998). J. Wilson and Blocher (1990) identified seven problems that may confront children who live in an alcoholic environment:

Family conflict. COAs are likely to witness their parents arguing, which at times can turn violent. When these youngsters take sides, they add to dissension in the family system. In this environment, COAs find it hard to concentrate on their homework or even to eat dinner.

Abuse and neglect. Alcoholism is involved in 90 percent of child abuse cases (Naiditch & Lerner, 1987), and COAs are twice as likely to be victims of incest (C. Black, 1986). Most COAs, their needs ignored, suffer emotional abuse (Estes & Heinemann, 1977).

Inconsistent discipline and inadequate structure. Boundaries are a problem in the alcoholic family because parental behavior is often unpredictable. The alcoholic parent may alternate between periods of strict supervision and no supervision. Not knowing how their parent is going to behave, children constantly feel off-balance (C. Black, 1984). Said one COA: "You never knew what you would find when you walked in the door. Sometimes he was sober, sometimes he was drunk."

Disruption of family rituals. Celebrating holidays and other special events is also a problem in the alcoholic family. The alcoholic parent often becomes intoxicated on those occasions and causes a scene, embarrassing the child in front of family and friends. Nothing is routine for COAs.

Role reversal and parentification. Alcohol disempowers the parent, often forcing the child to take on the parent's roles and responsibilities. The child may also become the nonalcoholic parent's confidant, listening to complaints about the other parent.

Distortion and the denial of reality. Denial is pervasive in the alcoholic family. The nonalcoholic parent and the children try to make everything seem normal to the outside world by lying and covering up. Worse still is the family in which the children are blamed for their parent's drinking. These youngsters can come to believe that if they change their behavior, the drinking will stop.

Isolation. Because the alcoholic is often a source of hostility and embarrassment, their families isolate themselves. They turn down invitations to functions where the alcoholic might drink and make a scene. And COAs are afraid to bring friends home.

Because of these challenges, COAs can develop cognitive deficits (Bennett, Wolin, & Reiss, 1988; Ervin, Little, Streissguth, & Beck, 1984; Gabrielli & Mednick, 1983); academic problems (Knop, Teasdale, Schulsinger, & Goodwin, 1985; D. Miller & Jang, 1977); behavioral problems (West & Prinz, 1987); emotional difficulties in the form of anxiety and depression (E. Anderson & Quast, 1983; Moos & Billings, 1982; Post & Robinson, 1998; Shuckit & Chiles, 1978; Prewett, Spence, & Chaknis, 1981); and ulcers, obesity, chronic stomachaches, asthma, and other physical problems (C. Black, 1986). However, not all COAs develop serious problems, and some function well (Werner, 1986). The difference may lie in the roles COAs adopt to survive the consequences of parental alcoholism.

The Adaptive Roles of COAs   Wegscheider (1981) identified five typical adaptive roles in alcoholic families:

Chief enabler. This is the alcoholic's confidant, the person on whom he or she relies most. The COA who adopts this role excuses many of the parent's annoying and embarrassing behaviors. The child feels important because the parent has bestowed on him or her a special place in the family. In a sense, the child is receiving certain benefits from the parent's alcoholism.

Family hero. These COAs work hard to make things better for the family. They can become model students and athletes, and all-around good citizens (Glover, 1994). Hero children tend to be controlling, and overachievers (and eventually workaholics) and perfectionists. They also are constantly seeking the approval of others.

Scapegoat. The family troublemaker distracts from the alcoholism. This COA can easily become the "identified patient" for whom the family seeks special services. As long as the family can pay attention to this child, they need not pay attention to the alcoholism. The scapegoat helps the family with its denial.

Lost child. These COAs adapt to the alcoholism by hiding and removing themselves from the chaos. Often they shut down emotionally as a way of coping, and become very self-absorbed. Many have deficits in social skills because they have learned to survive by removing themselves from family interaction.

Mascot. Charm and humor are the major defenses of some COAs. These youngsters cope with their painful family situation by joking and often assume the role of class clown. They have learned to deal with their pain by making people around them laugh.

Working with COAs   The school counselor's most important function here may well be helping teachers identify the 20 percent (J. Wilson & Blocher, 1990) of their students who are COAs. Identifying COAs, especially at the elementary school level, is not easy because these youngsters have learned to hide the family problem. Counselor and teacher should watch for children's reactions to drug and alcohol education classes (O'Rourke, 1990). There also are formal instruments for identifying COAs.[10]

Once a child has been identified, there are several guidelines the teacher can implement in the classroom:

1. Maintain a daily schedule that enables the child to experience order and structure; this may be the only part of the child's life that has order.
2. Allow the child to make choices and decisions, enabling him or her to feel in control of at least part of his or her life.
3. Provide some work time for the child to do homework at school.

---

[10] See, for example, the Family CAGE (A. W. Price & Emshoff, 1997) and the Children of Alcoholics Screening Test (J. Jones, 1982).

4. Be alert to signs of tension and stress in the child and develop a repertoire of relaxation activities. (J. Wilson & Blocher, 1990, p. 102)

The counselor may work with COAs individually; but once a number of these students have been identified, the counselor can consider forming a group.[11] Sessions should focus on information about alcoholism, exploring students' feelings, building self-esteem, developing coping and stress management skills, and rehearsing decision making (O'Rourke, 1990).

Arman and McNair (2000) proposed a nine-session group for elementary school COAs (Table 11.5). The group should have from six to eight members, all within an age range of two years. Each session lasts 30 minutes.

By working with COAs, school counselors in general and elementary school counselors in particular can make a significant contribution to reducing the risk of living in a substance-abusing family system. There are many children of alcoholics, and most go unnoticed. Some learn to handle their pain in resilient and positive ways; but others put themselves on the fast track to substance abuse. School counselors, through individual or group counseling, can help this second group find other solutions.

ETHICAL AND LEGAL ISSUES

Confidentiality is a primary concern in working with students who use and abuse drugs. The federal government has passed two laws that ensure the confidentiality of anyone who is treated for alcohol or drug abuse.[12] Those laws also protect the privacy of youngsters who receive school-based services (Office of Substance Abuse Program, 1992).[13]

But what happens when school policy and the law conflict? Almost all schools prohibit the presence and use of alcohol and other drugs on school grounds, and many require that school personnel inform the administration of any student who has violated the school's policy. Actually, there is no conflict here because the laws of confidentiality apply only to students who are receiving services for drug and al-

---

[11] Ideally students should have the informed consent of a parent to participate in a COA support group (or any group). Obtaining that consent can be difficult if the parents deny that one or both of them are abusing alcohol. We make two suggestions: First, the school counselor can approach the parent who is more likely to be receptive to the idea of group counseling for his or her child. Second, in describing the group, the counselor can focus more on the skills the group will be learning (managing stress, building self-esteem) than on the issue of parental drinking. If asking a parent to consent to a child's participation in a group places the child at risk for abuse, and if the district does not require parental consent for that participation, the child can join the group without parental consent (see Ethical and Legal Issues in Chapter 10).

[12] Both laws—42 USC 290 dd-3 and ee-3 (42 CFR part 2)—were issued by the U.S. Department of Health and Human Services.

[13] Of course confidentiality is waived whenever a school counselor believes that a student's drug use is putting him or her in imminent danger.

TABLE 11.5   A SUPPORT GROUP FOR THE CHILDREN OF ALCOHOLICS

Session 1. Members are introduced to the group structure, logistics, rules, and confidentiality. The leader makes clear the purpose and goal of the group.

Session 2. The leader explains B. E. Robinson and Rhoden's (1998) 10 points about alcoholism:

1. Alcoholism is a disease.
2. Everybody gets hurt in the alcoholic family, including the children.
3. Children whose parents drink too much are not alone.
4. Children do not cause, cannot control, and cannot cure their parent's alcoholism.
5. There are many good ways for kids to take care of themselves when parents drink so that they feel better about themselves.
6. It is healing for children to identify and express their feelings about parental drinking.
7. It is OK for kids to talk about parental drinking to a friend or within the safety of the group.
8. Kids of alcoholics are at high risk of substance abuse themselves.
9. It is important for children to identify and use a trusted support system outside the family.
10. There are many practical ways of problem-solving with parental alcoholism. (quoted in Arman & McNair, 2000, p. 291)

Members discuss the points, and they are posted on a wall, where they should remain until the group ends.

Session 3. Group norms and the 10 points about alcoholism are reviewed. Members are asked to "check in," to tell how things are going at home. The leader supplies crayons, finger paints, and colored pencils, and asks the children to draw a picture of their family. When they've finished, each member is asked to describe his or her picture. The leader's task is to make linkages among the family descriptions so that members understand that they are not alone.

Sessions 4 and 5. The focus of these sessions is exploring how alcoholism affects the members emotionally. The leader can return to some of the family descriptions and ask: "How do you feel when so and so does such and such?" If the members have difficulty expressing their emotions, puppets can be used to act out family situations. Most important, the leader validates and normalizes the variety of emotions the members express in reaction to alcoholism.

Session 6. The goal of this session is to identify members' coping mechanisms for dealing with their alcoholic parent, and to help them create new ones. The leader reviews the emotions and thoughts expressed in previous sessions and asks the members to share how emotions and thoughts affect their behavior. Then the leader should say: "Think about the ways you behave. Would you like to behave differently?" The group explores other behaviors and solutions. Again, puppets or stuffed animals can be used to act out the new behaviors.

Session 7. Working together, the members develop a list of specific coping skills based on the previous session's discussion. The leader explains that coping mechanisms are a shield that people use to defend themselves in difficult situations and then asks: "Are there ways you could make your shields stronger?" Toward the end of the session, the leader gives the members baking clay to make a shield, encouraging them to express themselves freely in their shields.

Session 8. During the first half of this session, members paint their shields using words and symbols to express what they have learned from the group to protect themselves from their parent's alcoholism. In the second half of the session, the members explain their shields to one another. Then the leader explains that the shields are a reminder of the progress they have made in the group and the skills they have learned, and tells them that they can go on learning new skills to protect themselves.

Session 9. Members review what they have learned in the group and talk about their feelings—about the group and the fact that it will no longer meet. The leader explains that ending the group is a sign of progress, that they are better able to protect themselves now, but that the relationships and support they found in the group can and should continue. The leader closes by setting a date for a follow-up session within a couple of months.

SOURCE: Adapted from Arman and McNair (2000). Copyright by the American School Counselor Association. Reprinted with permission.

cohol abuse. As long as students are not being treated, identifying a student who is suspected of having a substance abuse problem does not violate the law. But once a student receives SAP services—even a one-time assessment—the school counselor and other staff members must comply with the federal regulations governing confidentiality.

The difficulty comes in consulting with members of the multidisciplinary team or other colleagues. Certainly team members would need to know who is receiving services. Is that kind of consultation a violation of the law? According to the Office of Substance Abuse Program (1991, 1992), disclosures without the client's consent are permissible in medical emergencies, in cases of child abuse, and *in consultation with team members in a student assistance program.*

The confidentiality ensured by the federal laws extends to students' parents. Even in the case of a student who is being referred for outside services, the client's written consent, not parental consent, is needed. Of course the client can consent, in writing, to his or her parents' being notified; that consent should be kept in the student's record (Coll, 1995).

Finally, there is the issue of confidentiality and crime. Substance use and delinquency correlate significantly: The more serious the involvement with drugs, the more likely the involvement in crime (Huizinga, 1994). Do school counselors have to report crimes committed by students receiving school-based services for drug abuse? According to the Office of Substance Abuse Program (1992), they do not. But in the case of a serious crime—homicide, rape, kidnapping, armed robbery, assault with a deadly weapon, or child abuse and neglect—counselors can report a student to local authorities (Coll, 1995).

What's key here is that school counselors keep in mind the spirit of the federal laws: that young people should be allowed to seek and receive help for substance abuse without fear of reprisal.

Conclusion

The chapter began with the statistics and the frightening story they tell about the prevalence of substance abuse in our society, especially among young people. To prevent that abuse, the school counselor must understand how drugs are used and how they work, the subjects of the next major section. Then the text described the effects and health hazards of the four most popular substances among children and adolescents: alcohol, nicotine, marijuana, and inhalants. An explanation of the complex and broad range of risk factors followed. The final two sections examined school-based prevention and intervention strategies and the role of the school counselor in developing and implementing those strategies as part of the overall comprehensive developmental guidance program.

In the United States today, no one can avoid the subject of substance abuse. It pervades our families, our schools, and our neighborhoods. It comes in all sizes and shapes, in all racial and ethnic and socioeconomic groups. And despite the enormous amounts of money spent in this country, prevention and intervention efforts to date have been only modestly effective at best. The message here: A significant number of students will eventually fall prey to addiction. In the face of that reality, some would throw up their hands and give up the battle. But not school counselors. Giving up on students is not in the nature of our profession. Moreover, schools are where prevention efforts have been working, at least to a degree. If we can reach children when they are young and keep reinforcing the antidrug message as they develop, if we can teach them coping mechanisms and the skills to resist drugs, and if we can offer them alternatives to drug use, we can make a difference in the lives of at least some youngsters. And that makes it all worthwhile.

QUESTIONS FOR DISCUSSION

1. How has substance abuse affected your life? Have you, a family member, or a close friend ever struggled with alcohol, nicotine, or other substances? What do you feel when you remember that experience? What, if anything, helped you deal with the problem? What did not help? What role did you play in relation to the problem?

2. Researchers still do not know why some people who are at risk for drug or alcohol abuse eventually do use and abuse substances, while others do not. Based on what you have read in this chapter and your experience, develop a profile of the student most at risk for future drug or alcohol abuse.

3. There have been many battles over the years about the best way to prevent drug and alcohol abuse. Outline a K–12 program (by school level) for preventing drug and alcohol abuse. Show goals and objectives as well as competencies.

4. A student comes to you, the school counselor, and admits that he is using drugs and wants help, but states firmly that he does not want his parents to know. Would you tell his parents about his drug use? Suppose the student also admits to bringing drugs to school to satisfy his addiction. What would you do with this information?

5. Discuss how you would go about including a substance abuse prevention program in a developmental and comprehensive guidance program. Be sure to explain how you, as a school counselor, might work with different constituencies—for example, parents and community leaders.

6. What criteria would you employ for choosing a substance abuse curriculum for your school? How should the decision be made? Who should make it?

SUGGESTED INTERNET SITES

www.al-anon.alateen.org

This is the official Web site of Al-Anon Family Group Headquarters, an organization that works directly with those affected by someone else's drinking. The site contains literature, professional resources, and information on meetings and programs including Alateen, which is strictly for teenagers.

www.adultchildren.org

Adult Children of Alcoholics World Service Organization targets those who have grown up in an alcoholic or otherwise dysfunctional home. The group's mission: to explain and suggest ways of coping with the problems COAs face as adults. The site contains a wealth of resources, including a support group that addresses the needs of individual members.

www.acde.org

The American Council for Drug Education is committed to preventing substance abuse through school-based programs based on the most-current scientific research. Programs are designed to engage teens, address the needs of parents, and provide employers, educators, and health professionals with information about different types of drugs.

www.ncadd.org

The mission of the National Council on Alcoholism and Drug Dependency is to fight the stigma and disease of alcoholism. The site contains education, information, and resources for obtaining help, including a large number of valuable links to related sites.

www.clubdrugs.org

This site, which is part of the National Institute on Drug Abuse site, contains a wealth of information about the kinds of drugs that are available to children and teens and their effects, and resources both for teens (how to resist drugs) and for parents (how to talk with children about drugs).

www.drugeducation.org

The Drug Education Council is a nonprofit organization dedicated to promoting a drug-free society. Their site includes information about drugs and drug testing, as well as current news and many links to relevant sites.

UNDERSTANDING AND PREVENTING VIOLENCE IN SCHOOLS

By the year 2000, every school in America will be free of drugs and violence and will offer a disciplined environment conducive to learning.

Goals 2000: Educate America Act (1994)

The year 2000 has come and gone, and our schools are not free of violence. On the contrary, school safety has become a major preoccupation throughout the country, the result of school shootings in small towns across America. The violence may have been unpredictable; the reaction of local residents was not: "We never thought it could happen here." The implication: This kind of violence belongs somewhere else. All of the shootings challenged the stereotype of the violent adolescent. In every case, the perpetrators were White boys, and almost all their victims were Whites.[1] The idea that school shootings can take place anywhere has seeped into America's consciousness. The result has been the frantic adoption of safe-school plans and zero-tolerance policies.[2]

The fact of the matter is that school shootings, although terrifying and deserving of attention and prevention measures, are a very rare occurrence. School-aged children are much more likely to be victims of violent crime outside school. Moreover, data show that the incidence of violent crime in schools has fallen steadily in recent years.[3]

This chapter opens with a summary of the statistics on school violence. With an understanding of the extent of the problem, we move to an examination of the factors that put young people at risk for violence and of the warning signs for violent behavior. In the next sections we look at two particular forms of violence in schools: bullying and sexual harassment. The chapter closes with an outline of a broad-based prevention effort.

---

[1] Television, by usually portraying violent offenders as members of minority groups, unemployed and uneducated (Chisolm, 1998), may have reinforced the stereotype that violent offenders are people of color from the inner city.

[2] For example, in 1994 President Bill Clinton signed the Gun-Free Schools Act, which mandates a one-year expulsion for students who bring weapons to school.

[3] There is a question about reporting practices. Many government statistics on violence in the schools are based on incident reports submitted by the schools, which must file an incident report whenever an offense has occurred. The reports are used to determine how well a particular school is functioning, motivation for some administrators to underreport violence.

VIOLENCE IN SCHOOLS: THE STATISTICS

According to the Center for the Prevention of School Violence (2000), school violence is "any behavior that violates a school's educational mission or climate of respect or jeopardizes the intent of the school to be free of aggression against person or property, drugs, weapons, disruptions, and disorder" (p. 2). Under this definition, bullying, sexual harassment, abuse directed at gay and lesbian students—any student behavior that creates a hostile school environment for another student— is school violence. We agree.

Forty percent of teenagers say that the behavior of students in their schools interferes with their performance, and almost 20 percent report threats of physical violence (State of Our Nation's Youth, 2000). School shootings capture headlines, but bullying and harassment are much more pervasive problems. Although both can result in physical violence, the real damage to victims is psychological (for example, depression) and educational (poor attendance or even dropping out).

Table 12.1 is a summary of data on school violence. It helps explain why our schools have become a hostile environment for so many students.

THE ETIOLOGY OF YOUTH VIOLENCE

A discussion of the causes of violent behavior borders on the metaphysical. For every factor—and there are many—there seems to be research that contradicts its significance. Some of the difficulty lies in comparisons across age groups: What might be a factor among younger children may be less of a factor among teenagers, or vice versa. For example, substance use between ages 6 and 11 is a stronger predictor of serious delinquency than it is for youngsters ages 12 to 14. On the other hand, ties to antisocial peers are a stronger predictor of violence for adolescents than they are for children ages 6 to 11.[4] But the real difficulty lies in predicting human behavior: Even expert criminal and forensic psychologists cannot predict with any reliability how an individual at risk for violence will behave.

Why bother then? First, because research methodologies are improving all the time. Today, for example, researchers are better able to separate the effects of age in determining the factors that put young people at risk for violent behavior. Second, because longitudinal studies of violence indicate that certain factors in childhood and early adolescence are predictive of violent acts. That understanding is crucial to planning appropriate interventions.

In this section we examine five categories of factors that contribute to violent behavior in children and adolescents: psychological factors, family factors, school factors, peer-related factors, and community and neighborhood factors. And we look at the controversy that surrounds a possible sixth factor: violence in the media.

---

[4] For a ranking of predictors according to age groups, see, for example, Hawkins et al. (2000).

TABLE 12.1 SCHOOL VIOLENCE: A SUMMARY OF THE DATA

Crime in schools	The most common criminal incidents in schools are theft, larceny, and physical attacks or fights without a weapon.
	Middle school students (ages 12 to 14) are more likely than high school students to be victims of crime at school.
	Between 1993 and 1997, the overall crime rate of school-related crimes was about 155 for every 1,000 students ages 12 to 18; by the end of the 1990s, that rate had dropped to about 102 crimes per 1,000 students.
Teacher victimization	From 1994 to 1998, there were an average of 16,000 serious crimes (e.g., rape, sexual assault, robbery, and aggravated assault) a year against teachers.
	Most crimes against teachers (82%) are neither violent nor serious; 66% involve theft.
	Male teachers are more likely to be the victims of violent crime than are female teachers.
	Teachers in urban schools are more likely to be the victims of violent crime than are teachers in suburban and rural schools.
School environment	In 1999, 1.1 million students reported avoiding some areas of school for fear of their safety.
	That same year, 9% of students ages 12 to 18 reported they feared for their safety at school, up from 5% in 1995.
	In 1999, Black and Hispanic students feared more for their safety than did White students (8% versus 2%).
	Students' reports of street gangs in their schools fell from 29% in 1995 to 17% in 1999.
	In recent years, roughly 10% of students report carrying a weapon (e.g., a gun, a knife, or a club) to school.
	Bullying and sexual harassment are by far the most common forms of school violence reported by students: Seventy-five percent report having been bullied at some point in their schooling, and 81% of female students report some form of sexual harassment in school or on school grounds.
	Gay and lesbian students are the most frequent victims of hate crimes in schools; and they skip school at a rate more than five times that of heterosexual students because of personal-safety concerns.
	About 13% of students experience hate-related words in school, and 36% report having seen hate-related graffiti in school.

SOURCE: U.S. Departments of Education and Justice (2000a, 2000b).

Psychological Factors

Hyperactivity, aggressiveness, early signs of violent behavior, and other antisocial behaviors are all positive predictors of violence in young people.

> *Hyperactivity, concentration problems, and restlessness.* Research consistently reveals a significant correlation between these problems and later violence. One study found that boys who had difficulty concentrating and who were restless were five times more likely to be arrested for violent crimes later in life than were youngsters who did not have attention

problems (Klinteberg, Andersson, Magnusson, & Stattin, 1993; also see Farrington, 1989). It may well be that problems concentrating lead to academic difficulties, which in turn are related to violent behaviors.

Aggressiveness. Numerous studies support the relationship between aggressive behavior, especially in males between ages 6 and 13, to later violence (Loeber, 1990, 1996; Loeber & Hay, 1996; McCord & Ensminger, 1995; Olweus, 1979; Stattin & Magnuson, 1989). The results of studies with aggressive girls are less conclusive.

Early initiation of violent behavior. This is one of the strongest predictors for serious and chronic violence (Farrington, 1991; Piper, 1985; Thornberry, Huizenga, & Loeber, 1995; Tolan & Thomas, 1995; Walker, Colvin, & Ramsey, 1995). One study of boys ages 10 to 16 who had committed an act of violence found that 50 percent of the sample had been convicted of a violent crime by age 24 (versus just 8 percent of the nondelinquent control group) (Farrington, 1995). Blumstein, Cohen, and Farrington (1988) found that from one-half to three-fourths of adolescent delinquents become chronic adult offenders.

Other forms of antisocial behavior. Antisocial behaviors like stealing and property destruction (S. Mitchell & Rosa, 1979) and drug and alcohol use (L. D. Eron, Gentry, & Schlegel, 1994; Maguin et al., 1995) are all associated with a greater risk for violence.

Family Factors

Much has been written about the influence of family on young offenders. Research has identified several family-related factors among violent children and adolescents.

Parental criminality. Actually studies of the relationship between parental criminality and youth violence have been inconsistent. Two studies of sons of criminal fathers found the children were two to four times more likely to commit violent crimes than were those with noncriminal parents (R. L. Baker & Mednick, 1984; Farrington, 1989). But a third study found that adults with criminal fathers are no more likely to be arrested (Moffitt, 1987).

Child maltreatment. Children who have been physically abused or neglected are more likely to commit violent crimes when they get older (C. Smith & Thornberry, 1995; Widom, 1989b; Zingraff, Leiter, Myers, & Johnson, 1993).

Poor family management practices. Inconsistent or severe discipline, poor supervision, and the failure to set clear expectations for children are among the most powerful predictors of later delinquency (Capaldi & Patterson, 1996; Hawkins, Arthur, & Catalano, 1995; McCord, 1979). These practices may also contribute to children's developing emotional problems, which in turn can lead to antisocial and violent behaviors (Steinberg, 2000).

Also, when children are exposed to violence in the home, they come to understand violence as an acceptable way of dealing with conflict and solving problems. Exposure to high levels of family and marital conflict increase the risk for later violence (Elliot, 1994; Farrington, 1989; Maguin et al., 1995).

Low parental involvement. Some research has found a link between disengaged parents and children's risk for future violence, especially among boys (Farrington, 1989; J. H. Williams, 1994). Conversely, strong parental involvement acted as a protective factor against violence.

Parent–child separations. Studies have established a relationship between disruptions in parent–child relationships and later violent behaviors (Farrington, 1989; Henry, Avshalom, Moffitt, & Silva, 1996). Many factors that predict violence may also contribute to parent–child separations. For example, child abuse is a predictive factor and can also lead to a child's removal from the home. More research is needed to understand the interaction of these different factors (Hawkins et al., 2000).

School Factors

The most important school-related factors that contribute to violent behavior are academic failure, low bonding to school, and truancy or dropping out of school.

Academic failure. Research consistently has found a link between poor academic achievement, even in the elementary grades, and later delinquency (Denno, 1990; Farrington, 1989; Maguin & Loeber, 1996; Maguin et al., 1995).[5]

Low bonding to school. This factor has drawn recent attention because school shooters consistently show little connection or commitment to their schools. In fact, school bonding has been shown to be a protective factor against crime and violence (Catalano & Hawkins, 1996; J. H. Williams, 1994), especially for African American students.

Truancy or dropping out of school. In a study by Farrington (1989), high truancy rates at ages 12 to 14 were linked to violent behavior during later adolescence and adulthood; and leaving school before the age of 15 was also a predictor of later violence. Also, it may well be that low bonding to school and truancy are related.

Peer-Related Factors

Having delinquent siblings or delinquent peers and being a member of a gang are all positively linked to violence (Battin, Hill, Abbott, Catalano, & Hawkins, 1998; Farrington, 1989; Maguin et al., 1995; Minden, Henry, Tolan, & Gorman-Smith,

---

[5] In a departure from the norm, the relationship between academic failure and predicted violence is stronger for females than for males (Hawkins et al., 2000).

2000; Moffitt, Caspi, Dickson, Silva, & Stanton, 1996). It seems that delinquent siblings and peers often reinforce antisocial behaviors.

Community and Neighborhood Factors

A number of environmental factors are thought to contribute to violent behavior in children and adolescents:

> *Poverty.* Many studies have found a link between being raised in poverty and youth violence (Elliot, Huizenga, & Menard, 1989; Henry et al., 1996; Sampson & Lauritson, 1994; Wilkstrom, 1985). The interaction of factors here is complex. One possibility is that poor parents often lack education, resources, and problem-solving skills, which means they must work longer hours at low-paying jobs, which in turn means that they are less likely to be available to supervise their children, to be involved in their education, or to positively reinforce their prosocial behaviors (J. J. McWhirter, 1998a).
>
> *Other environmental factors.* Maguin et al. (1995) found that the presence of crime, gangs, and poor housing; the availability of drugs and firearms; and knowing adults who are involved in crime also contribute to youth violence. Racial discrimination may also be a factor here (McCord & Ensminger, 1995).

Violence in the Media

Social scientists and the entertainment industry have been debating the effects of violence in the media since the 1950s, when television first became widely available. That crime rates in this country rose dramatically in 1965 was evidence, some experts claimed, of the impact the medium has on violence in society: That year coincided with the coming of age of the first generation of children raised with TV (Bushman & Anderson, 2001).

By contrast, the entertainment industry has always argued that violence in the media simply reflects the violence already present in society. But in real life, fewer than 1 percent of crimes committed in this country are murders; on television, 50 percent of the crimes shown are murders (M. B. Oliver, 1994). Others argue that watching violence on TV actually has a cathartic effect, that it is a means of purging violent impulses.

The scientific evidence connecting violence in the media to aggression is overwhelming. Although members of the entertainment industry suggest that the correlation is too small to be significant, Bushman and Anderson (2001) found the strength of that link second only to the correlation between smoking and lung cancer. Of course, not everyone who smokes cigarettes develops lung cancer; and not everyone who watches violence on television commits violent acts. But the connection between violence in the media and aggression is undeniable. Some of the variables that turn aggression into violence include the age and predisposition of the viewer, and the amount of viewing (L. D. Eron, 1982): The cumulative effect of watching violence on TV is much more significant than watching a single violent program.[6]

Risk Factors: A Summary

Again, it is impossible to predict human behavior with certainty. But recent research indicates that certain factors are strong predictors of youth violence:

- Hyperactivity or attention deficits
- Parental criminality
- Poor family management practices
- Low bonding to school
- Having delinquent friends
- Gang membership

The strength of a given factor at any time is a function of the youngster's age.

Research is far from complete on youth violence. What is needed in particular is more research on the interaction effects of different factors. We do know that the greater the number of risk factors, the more likely a young person is to behave violently. Farrington (1997), for example, found that the rate of young people convicted of violent crimes rose from 3 percent for those with no risk factors to 31 percent for those with four risk factors. We don't have a profile of the violent offender; but we do know that school counselors need to watch for and reach out to students with multiple risk factors.

WARNING SIGNS AND ASSESSMENT

Recently, the media reported on an elementary school student who was suspended for drawing a military figure with a knife hitched to his belt. When the child was questioned about her drawing, she explained that the drawing was of her uncle, a soldier, who had visited the family over the weekend wearing his fatigues. Despite her parents' protestations, the suspension was upheld.

Hypervigilance is not going to prevent violence in schools. Neither is denial. Somewhere between the two lies a rational response to the reality of youth violence. Key to that response is the knowledge that helps school counselors distinguish students who are at risk of hurting others.

---

[6] It may be impossible to prevent children from watching some violence on television, but the cumulative effect of watching violence means parents should minimize their children's exposure to violence on television, in movies, and in video games.

Watching for Signs of Potential Violence

In 1998, the Department of Education and the Department of Justice published a well-received document titled *Early Warning, Timely Response: A Guide to Safe Schools* (Dwyer, Osher, & Warger, 1998). The document begins by listing 16 early warning signs of aggressive and violent behavior:

- Social withdrawal
- Excessive feelings of isolation and loneliness
- Excessive feelings of rejection
- Being a victim of violence
- A feeling of being picked on or persecuted
- Low interest in school and poor academic performance
- Expressions of violence in writings and drawings
- Uncontrolled anger
- Patterns of impulsive and chronic hitting, intimidating, and bullying
- A history of discipline problems
- A history of violent and aggressive behaviors
- Intolerance and prejudice
- Drug and alcohol use
- Gang membership
- Inappropriate access to, possession of, and use of firearms
- Serious threats of violence

School counselors can list these warning signs on the wall of their office or create a handout for students, teachers, and parents that is available in the literature rack in the counseling office.

Again, none of these signs by itself is an accurate predictor of school violence. School counselors should watch for students who display a number of signs, attempt to engage them, and conduct a more-focused assessment.

The response is very different when a student shows imminent warning signs, signs that indicate the student is close to behavior that is dangerous to self and others:

- Serious physical fighting with peers or family members
- Severe destruction of property
- Severe rage for seemingly minor reasons
- Detailed threats of lethal violence
- Possession and/or use of firearms and other weapons
- Other self-injurious behaviors or threats of suicide (Dwyer et al., 1998, p. 11)

When a student comes to school carrying a weapon and is threatening to use it or describes a detailed plan (time, place, and method) to harm or kill others, the police should be called immediately. In response to other imminent signs, the school should immediately inform the student's parents and help arrange for child and family services and community mental health services.

TABLE 12.2 THE NSSC's CHECKLIST OF CHARACTERISTICS OF YOUTH WHO HAVE CAUSED SCHOOL-ASSOCIATED VIOLENT DEATHS

___	1. Has a history of tantrums and uncontrollable angry outbursts.
___	2. Characteristically resorts to name-calling, cursing, or abusive language.
___	3. Habitually makes violent threats when angry.
___	4. Has previously brought a weapon to school.
___	5. Has a background of serious disciplinary problems at school and in the community.
___	6. Has a background of drug, alcohol, or other substance abuse or dependency.
___	7. Is on the fringe of his/her peer group with few or no close friends.
___	8. Is preoccupied with weapons, explosives, or other incendiary devices.
___	9. Has previously been truant, suspended, or expelled from school.
___	10. Displays cruelty to animals.
___	11. Has little or no supervision and support from parents or a caring adult.
___	12. Has witnessed or been a victim of abuse or neglect in the home.
___	13. Has been bullied and/or bullies or intimidates peers or younger children.
___	14. Tends to blame others for difficulties and problems he/she causes him-/herself.
___	15. Consistently prefers TV shows, movies, or music expressing violent themes and acts.
___	16. Prefers reading materials dealing with violent themes, rituals, and abuse.
___	17. Reflects anger, frustration, and the dark side of life in school essays or writing projects.
___	18. Is involved with a gang or an antisocial group on the fringe of peer acceptance.
___	19. Is often depressed and/or has significant mood swings.
___	20. Has threatened or attempted suicide.

SOURCE: National School Safety Center (1998).

Assessment Instruments

School counselors cannot do a clinical assessment of students' potential aggression and violence; that's a task for psychologists. But school counselors do have at their disposal several simple instruments they can use to substantiate their concerns about a particular student. If those concerns turn out to be valid, counselors can then engage the student's family and make a referral for psychiatric evaluation.

Two instruments are now available for helping school counselors assess a student's potential for violence: the National School Safety Center's (NSSC, 1998) checklist and the VIOLENT STUdent Scale (Juhnke, 2001). The checklist is a by-product of the NSSC's examination of school-related violent deaths since July 1992—a list of 20 behaviors that indicate the likelihood of a student's harming self or others (Table 12.2). If a student presents with one or more of these behaviors, the school counselor should consider one or more of the following courses of action: a meeting with the student's parents, counseling, or referral to appropriate community services, including law enforcement authorities. The NSSC checklist should be part of the school's overall safety plan.

TABLE 12.3 **VIOLENT STUᴅᴇɴᴛ Sᴄᴀʟᴇ Sᴄᴏʀɪɴɢ ᴀɴᴅ Iɴᴛᴇʀᴘʀᴇᴛᴀᴛɪᴏɴ**

Score	Interpretation
0–9	Discussion with appropriate school personnel regarding the incongruence between student's low score and initial concerns about student's risk; single follow-up meeting within 3–5 days to reassess the situation and determine need for further assessment and or intervention.
10–39	Assess danger of harm to identified person(s); establish contact with legal guardians; strongly encourage follow-up counseling and psychological testing; provide crisis intervention access information; utilize "no harm contract."
40–69	Require participation in counseling with close follow-up services; contact legal guardians; require more formalized psychological testing; provide recommendations for treatment and structured living environment; mobilize school interdisciplinary team for academic and social support; notify child protective services if suspected neglect and abuse.
70–100	Remove student immediately from general school environment and transfer to structured living environment; contact legal guardians and facilitate formal evaluation of living environment; notify child protective services if student is deemed to be an immediate danger and guardians are unwilling to appropriately support evaluation for a more structured living environment.

SOURCE: "Assessing Potentially Violent Students Via the *VIOLENT STUdent Scale*," by G. A. Juhnke, W. B. Charkow, R. G. Liles, J. P. Jordan, C. S. Booth, & B. M. Gmutza, 2001. Presentation at the American Counseling Association, San Antonio, TX. Reprinted by authors' permission.

The VIOLENT STUdent Scale is based on 10 risk factors:

Violent or aggressive history
Isolation or feelings of being isolated
Overt aggression toward or torturing of animals
Low school interest
Expressions of violence in drawing or writing
Noted by peers as being "different"
Threats of violence toward others
Social withdrawal
Teased or perception of being teased, harassed, or "picked on"
Use which is inappropriate or inappropriate access to firearms (Juhnke et al., 2001, p. 1)

In a structured interview and using a 10-point scale, the counselor scores the student on each factor. The higher the student's score (to a maximum of 100 points), the greater his or her potential for violence. Table 12.3 shows how the scores on the VIOLENT STUdent Scale are interpreted.[7]

---

[7] Although the scale explains how overall scores should be interpreted, it does not provide guidelines for scoring the individual factors—a major fault according to critics. Ideally the school counselor should consider the frequency, duration, universality, and quality of each factor in assigning a score. So, for example, feeling isolated once in a while as opposed to feeling isolated all the time might warrant a score of 3 points versus a score of 9 points on the isolation factor.

Evaluating and Responding to Threats of Violence

In schools, threats of violence far outnumber violent incidents. But threats can be acted on, which means schools need an informed way of dealing with them. School counselors, because of their unique training, can play a central role in the school's threat assessment policy and plan.

Much of what follows in this section is based on a study published in 2001 by the National Center for the Analysis of Violent Crime (NCAVC). The NCAVC examined 18 schools throughout the country. At 14 of these schools, actual shootings occurred; at the other 4, students made significant preparations but were detected and preempted by the police.

The NCAVC defines a threat as "an expression of intent to do harm or act out violently against someone or something. A threat can be spoken, written, or symbolic—for example, motioning with one's hands as though shooting another person" (p. 6). Again, most threats are not serious; but that some are means each threat must be assessed.

Threats can be direct ("I'm going to place a bomb on the top shelf in the reference section of the library"), indirect ("If I wanted to, I could blow this place up"), veiled ("This place would be much better off if you weren't a teacher here"), and conditional ("If you call my parents, I'm going to shoot you"). Threats are more serious if they contain plausible details, if the student's emotional state is questionable, and if there are identifiable precipitating stressors.

According the NCAVC, threats can be divided into three levels of risk: low (the threat poses minimal risk to the victim and public safety), medium (a threat that could be carried out), and high (a threat that poses an imminent and serious danger to the safety of others):

1. Low-level threat
   - The threat is vague and indirect.
   - The information contained in the threat is inconsistent or implausible, or lacks detail.
   - The threat lacks realism.
   - The content of the threat suggests that the person is unlikely to carry it out.
2. Medium-level threat
   - The threat is more direct and more concrete than a low-level threat.
   - The wording of the threat suggests that the threatener has given some thought to acting on it.
   - The threat may indicate a possible place and time.
   - There is no strong indication that the threatener has taken preparatory steps, although there may be a veiled reference or ambiguous or inconclusive evidence pointing to that possibility—an allusion to a book or movie that shows the planning of a violent act or a general statement about the availability of weapons.
   - There may be a specific statement that the threat is not empty: "I'm serious" or "I really mean this."

3. High-level threat
   - The threat is direct, specific, and plausible.
   - The threat suggests that concrete steps have been taken to carry it out—for example, a statement indicating that the threatener has acquired or practiced with a weapon or has had the planned victim under surveillance.

An example of a high-level threat would be "Tomorrow, at 7:30 in the morning, I'm going to shoot Mrs. Wilson because at that time she is always in her homeroom by herself. I have a 9 mm. Believe me, I'm gonna do it. I'm sick and tired of the way she treats me." The parallels to the assessment for suicide risk are obvious: The more direct and detailed the plan, the more serious the risk.

Threat Management in Schools

To manage threats in a school, NCAVC recommends the following guidelines:

Inform students and parents of school policies. Schools should publicize their threat response and intervention policy at the beginning of each school year. Students and parents should be told that any threat will be reported, investigated, and dealt with efficiently and without compromise.

Designate a threat assessment coordinator. This person oversees and coordinates the school's response to all threats. The school counselor is an ideal choice; or the coordinator can be the school psychologist, a resource officer, or any staff member who has received threat assessment training. Any student who makes a threat is referred to the coordinator, who assesses the level of the threat, evaluates the threatener, and plans and monitors interventions. The coordinator also must maintain close relationships with community resources, including the police.

Encourage students to report threats. Students are in the best position to hear and see signs of potential violence, and schools must encourage them to break the "code of silence." A common strategy to help students understand the importance of revealing threats is to ask them to imagine that the threat is carried out: "If _____ really did _____, and you knew about it and didn't tell anyone, think about the burden you would carry for the rest of your life. Real friends protect other friends from hurting themselves and others."

Consider forming a multidisciplinary team. In addition to the threat assessment coordinator, the school can form a team drawn from school staff and professionals in mental health and law enforcement. The team would review threats, consult with experts, and provide recommendations and advice to the coordinator and/or the school administration. This team can be part of a general crisis-response team that deals with suicide and other problems.

School counselors should be involved in threat assessment management because proper intervention must go beyond disciplinary action to deal with the emotional turmoil that causes a student to make threats:

> It is especially important that a school not deal with threats by simply kicking the problem out the door. Expelling or suspending a student for making a threat must not be a substitute for careful threat assessment and a considered, consistent policy of intervention. Disciplinary action alone, unaccompanied by any effort to evaluate the threat or the student's intent, may actually exacerbate the danger—for example, if a student feels unfairly or arbitrarily treated and becomes even angrier and more bent on carrying out a violent act. (NCAVC, 2001, p. 26)

SCHOOL VIOLENCE AND THE PROBLEM OF BULLYING

Bullying has caught the attention of many school districts because a number of school shooters had a history of being bullied. Although it is true that some victims of bullying turn aggressors, others become withdrawn, truant, and eventually drop out of school.

The Nature of Bullying

One of the leading researchers on bullying is Norwegian John Olweus. According to Olweus (1992), a student is bullied or victimized "when he or she is exposed, repeatedly and over time, to negative actions on the part of one or more other persons" (p. 101). These negative actions are the intentional or attempted infliction of injury or discomfort on another. Bullying behaviors can be physical (hitting, kicking, pushing, choking) or verbal (name-calling, taunting, malicious teasing, threatening, spreading nasty rumors), both forms of *direct bullying*. *Indirect bullying*—making obscene gestures, making faces, or keeping the victim isolated from a group—are more subtle (Olweus, Limber, & Mihalic, 1999). Both boys and girls can be bullies: Boys tend toward direct bullying; girls, toward indirect bullying.

It can be difficult for parents and school personnel to distinguish between normal teasing and bullying. Roberts and Morotti (2000) suggest they ask themselves four main questions:

> *What is the nature of the behavior in question?* Is it age-appropriate? To whom is it directed? Is it specific to one gender or both? Is it directed toward vicinity-aged peers or those younger or older in age? What is the content of the behavior?
>
> *What is the level of intensity of the behavior?* What are the specifics of the behavior? Is the behavior verbal, physical, or psychological? Is the behavior seemingly done in a humorous fashion or with anger, harshness, or malicious intent by the agent?

At what rate does the behavior occur? Is this a frequent occurrence or an isolated incident? Are there times when the behavior occurs more often than others?

How does the target of the agent's behavior respond? Is the target upset or offended by the behavior? Does the target understand the behavior? Does the target reciprocate in-kind to the agent? How does the agent respond to the target's attempts at self-defense against the behavior? (p. 150)

If the child's behavior is age inappropriate, negative, intense, and frequent, then it probably is bullying rather than teasing.

Bullying has both short- and long-term effects on the victim. The short-term effects include unhappiness, pain and humiliation, confusion, distress, loss of self-esteem, anxiety, insecurity, and loss of concentration; and the victim may refuse to go to school. Some victims develop psychosomatic complaints like headaches and stomachaches; others suffer psychological consequences—feeling stupid, ashamed, or unattractive, and seeing themselves as failures (Olweus et al., 1999). The effect on personality and self-esteem can be long lasting: Olweus (1993) found that adults at age 23 who had been bullied in Grades 6 through 9 were more depressed and had lower self-esteem than did their nonvictim counterparts.

Who Bullies and Why

Most bullies share certain psychological characteristics. But the seriousness and pervasiveness of their bullying generally depend on the school's tolerance for bullying behaviors, teachers' attitudes, the arrangement of breaks, and other environmental factors. Also, the influence of the early home environment cannot be underestimated: Bullies come from homes where they are treated harshly (Craig, Peters, & Konarski, 1998; Pepler & Sedighdellami, 1998); homes where criticism, sarcasm, and put-downs are the norm (Greenbaum, Turner, & Stephens, 1989). In the absence of warmth and nurturing, it's not surprising that they come to believe—very young—that intimidation and force are the ways to deal with life's challenges (Roberts & Morotti, 2000). Through the dynamics of *projective identification*, bullies tend to prey on children who are less powerful, children who remind the bullies of their own vulnerability. "Bullies, through attacking the weaknesses of others, are striking out against the shame and humiliation they feel for their own inability to defend themselves against their abusers" (Roberts & Morotti, 2000, p. 151).

Unfortunately, the bully's behavior is often reinforced by parents and peers. Parents frequently defend their child's behaviors: "It's good to stick up for yourself." Because these parents have modeled bullying behaviors, they find it hard to disapprove of them. Peers also tend to be supportive of bullying behavior: They often delight in seeing another student victimized and may even encourage the bully to keep at it (Figure 12.1).

The long-term effects of their behavior on bullies themselves has been well documented. In one study, 60 percent of boys in Grades 6 through 9 who were

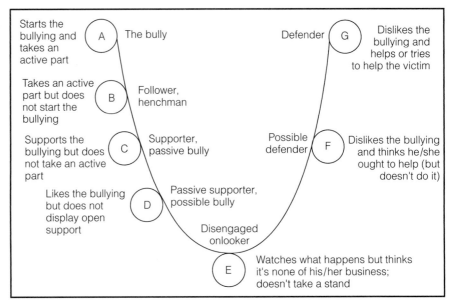

FIGURE **12.1**

THE BULLYING CIRCLE: STUDENTS' REACTIONS TO BULLYING

SOURCE: Adapted from Olweus, Limber, and Mihalic (1999).

characterized as bullies by both teachers and peers had been convicted of at least one crime by age 24, versus just 23 percent of nonbullies (Olweus, 1993). It seems that once the aggressive response develops, it persists into adulthood. A 22-year longitudinal study found that 8-year-olds who were identified as aggressive were more likely at age 30 than their nonaggressive peers to have a criminal conviction, to have been cited for a moving traffic violation, to be aggressive toward their spouse and children, to punish their children more severely or to use physical punishment, and to have children with aggressive behaviors like their own (see D. S. Eron, Walder, & Lefkowitz, 1971; Huesmann, Eron, Lefkowitz, & Walder, 1984; and Lefkowitz, Eron, Walder, & Huesmann, 1977).

Who Gets Bullied and Why

Because bullying affects a large number of students, it can be difficult to profile the typical victim. Hanish and Guerra (2000a) examined the characteristics of children at risk for victimization and grouped them into four categories:

> *Demographic characteristics.* Younger children are more vulnerable to peer victimization than older children because they have yet to develop protection skills. Bullying is more common in elementary school than it is in middle school and high school; but it also is more transient and less

targeted. Fewer older children are victimized; but when they are, the bullying tends to continue over time (Hanish & Guerra, 2000a). Boys are more likely to be bullied physically, while girls are more likely to be gossiped about, excluded, and sexually harassed (Crick & Bigbee, 1998). More research is needed to determine the degree to which race and ethnicity are significant variables in school victimization.[8]

Behavioral characteristics. Some children are victimized because they seem unable to defend themselves: They may be physically weak, submit easily to peer demands, or have few friends (E. V. Hodges, Boivin, Vitaro, & Bukowski, 1999; E. V. Hodges, Malone, & Perry, 1997; Olweus, 1993). Surprisingly, aggressiveness has also been found to increase the likelihood of a youngster's being bullied (E. V. Hodges, Malone, & Perry, 1997; Schwartz, McFadyen-Ketchum, Dodge, Pettit, & Bates, 1999). Aggressive behaviors annoy and alienate others, leaving the student without support and so vulnerable to bullies. Students who are withdrawn, shy, and unsure of themselves, especially older children, are also at risk for being victimized (Younger & Boyko, 1987; Younger, Schwartzman, & Ledingham, 1985). Contrary to popular belief, there is little evidence that students who are fat, wear glasses, speak with an accent, or have a different ethnic background are more likely to be bullied (Olweus, Limber, & Mihalic, 1999).

Peer group dynamics. Peers display a spectrum of reactions to bullying, few of them noble. Estimates are that peers protect the victims of bullying in fewer than 15 percent of incidents (Atlas & Pepler, 1998). In fact, peers are more likely to encourage the bullying; and some youngsters become bullies because they want the influence and power bullying gives them among their peers (Adler & Adler, 1995). In the absence of peer protection, the victim is likely to be bullied over time and so suffer more-significant consequences.

School structure influences. Unfortunately, schools often provide an environment that is conducive to bullying. A lack of supervision allows bullies to prey on their victims: Most incidents take place in hallways, as classes are changing, and in the playground (Atlas & Peper, 1998). In addition, victims are reluctant to report the bully's behavior for fear of reprisal (P. K. Smith & Thompson, 1991). This means that bullying can be going on even on a large scale without the knowledge of teachers and counselors.

The Victim Turned Aggressor

When bullying is intense and sustained, it is impossible for the victim to ignore. Many such victims withdraw, become depressed, drop out of school, or even attempt suicide; but some turn aggressors and, in rare instances, commit deadly

---

[8] Hanish and Guerra (2000b) did find in a study of elementary school students living in disadvantaged communities that Whites and African Americans are more likely to be victimized than Latinos.

school violence. A significant number of school shooters have a history of being bullied. Several experts on violence have suggested that suicide and revenge are both products of the same psychodynamics (see, for example, Carney, 2000; Olweus, 1997; and Rigby & Slee, 1999). In other words, the risk factors for aggression toward self and others are the same. Hazler and Carney (2000) categorized these risk factors as biological, psychological and cognitive, and environmental:

> *Biological risk.* Puberty increases the risk of victims' turning aggressors. Hormonal fluctuations, along with rapid physical and psychological changes, can increase the adolescent's level of hostility and desire for revenge.
>
> *Psychological and cognitive risk.* Victims who are severely depressed are at greater risk for aggression. A victim may reason "Life is not worth living, so what's the difference if I kill myself and those who have been tormenting me?" With depression comes cognitive rigidity: The victim sees revenge as the only option.
>
> *Environmental risk.* Both family and peer dynamics can elevate the risk of aggression. Victims from families whose members lack problem-solving skills and assertiveness have difficulty learning alternate ways of dealing with conflict (Hazler & Carney, 2000). Isolation from peers also increases the risk of victims' turning violent (Hazler, 1996; Olweus, 1996). Many school shooters could not rely on even one friend to prevent the tragedy from occurring.

Intervening to Stop Bullying

The effects of bullying are serious. While others in the school may minimize the behavior, the school counselor cannot. When a student complains about being bullied, the counselor has to investigate.

> *I know all too well the demands of being a school counselor. When a student comes to the office and says, "So and so is bothering me," sometimes it's just easier to say, "Ignore her" or "Don't pay any attention to her." But you have to follow up—if not immediately, as soon as possible—by asking a series of diagnostic questions: "How is he bothering you?" " How long has it been going on?" "Where and when does it usually happen?" "How often does it happen?" "Are you afraid of _____?" "How do you react when he does this to you?" And, as if that's not enough work, counselors also need to ask teachers to make a note of students who complain about being bullied and then follow up with those students too.*

A series of simple questions can help the counselor distinguish between bullying and teasing. If it is bullying, the counselor must attack the problem on three fronts: work with the victim, work with the bully, and work on the school climate and structure.

Working with the Victim   After assessing the magnitude of the problem, the counselor's first task is to ensure the safety of the victim. In some schools, state law or school policy mandates that incidents of victimization be reported (Roberts & Coursol, 1996). Certainly any incidents that endanger the safety of students or have the potential to do so should be reported.[9] Also, public action on behalf of the victim signals the student body that bullying will not be tolerated in the school.

The next step is to help the victim develop the skills he or she needs to stop the bullying. For example, bullies pick on youngsters who are isolated, who don't have friends. These students are bullied because they lack social skills. A good intervention here: involving them in a social-skills training group.[10]

School counselors can also help victims understand that certain reactions reinforce a bully's behavior. If they can learn not to react that way, it is probably only a matter of time before the bully moves on. Role-playing and modeling assertiveness are useful tools to teach new responses to bullying. In the case of verbal harassment, the victim should confront the bully alone—bullies are less likely to show off by being tough when there is not an audience. The victim must be firm: I don't like what you are doing to me, and I want it stopped (Noll & Carter, 2000, p. 2). It is not necessary to spell out what the bully does. If confrontation doesn't work, the counselor can advise the victim first to try to ignore the bully and to keep the counselor informed should the bullying escalate.

Counselors must remember that the primary goal of intervention here is to break victims' sense of powerlessness (Hazler & Carney, 2000). For schools to be safe, students need to feel that they can effectuate change and influence their environment (Olweus et al., 1999). Victims who have convinced themselves that there's nothing they can do to stop being bullied are at risk of hurting themselves or others.

Working with the Bully   Experts on preventing bullying agree that simply working with the victim is not enough. To stop bullying, counselors also must work with the bullies themselves. Roberts and Morotti (2000) suggested a five-step approach for dealing with bullies:

1. *Make nonthreatening contact with the bully.* After learning about an incident, seek out the bully and admit to knowing about the problem between the bully and the victim. Calmly and avoiding any language of blame, spell out the consequences if the problem is not resolved and then ask what victim, bully, and counselor can do to stop the bullying. This intervention is designed to start a dialogue: Bullies seldom have the opportunity to explain their actions.
2. *Listen closely to what the bully has to say.* As the bully explains his or her behavior, pay attention not only to the words but also to clues to the underlying dynamics of the behavior. What cognitive, affective, and behavioral processes are at work? Are there clues about the bully's home life, parental involvement,

---

[9] Counselors must be sensitive to the fact that many victims fear reprisals, so any breach of confidentiality must be warranted and clearly explained to the victim.

[10] See Lochman, Coie, Underwood, and Terry (1993) for a social-relations training program for both aggressive and nonaggressive youngsters.

and discipline? Are there indications of fear, anger, isolation, or low self-esteem? What the bully says about the incident is also important. Does he or she justify the behavior? Own up to it? More important, what emotions does the bully display as he or she recounts the incident? This careful listening and watching helps the counselor assess the causes and the seriousness of the behavior and plan for appropriate intervention.

3. *Create opportunities for the bully to learn about self and to change.* Key to changing the bully's behavior is dispelling the notion that aggression is the only way to deal with peers. Bullies learn, often in the first few years of life, that aggression is an appropriate means of interaction. Behind the aggression is usually anger, so a possible intervention is placement in an anger-management program. If the aggression is a bully's primary way of relating, a social-skills training program is also a possibility. Because of their sociopathic tendencies, some bullies change only by paying the consequences for their behavior. For these youngsters, behavioral contracts that include parents and teachers are a good tool. Because the parents of bullies are often part of the problem, it is extremely important that they be included in the formulation and implementation of the contract: The intervention is much more likely to succeed if school and home act together to curtail the bully's behavior. The behavioral contract should spell out rules of behavior, expectations of compliance, and consequences of noncompliance. Throughout, the counselor must be careful to act, not as a disciplinarian, but as an advocate who is helping by making the bully accountable for the consequences of his or her behavior. It can be hard to empathize with a bully, but remembering that the bully's behavior is symptomatic of his or her turmoil can help.

4. *Provide individual attention and support.* Often bullies do not act in isolation; they are surrounded by peers who are either active or passive participants in the bullying. Counseling the bully in a group setting, with other participants, may only recreate the victimizing group's dynamic and increase the members' bonding around deviant behaviors. The counselor's task is to work individually with the bully and others who want to break away from the bully peer group. These youngsters may well be afraid—of reprisals and of being rejected by another peer group.

5. *Provide long-term follow-up and care.* Changing patterns of behavior is not easy; it is even more difficult for school bullies who return each day to a family environment in which aggressive behaviors are the norm. There may well be instances, then, when the reformed bully regresses. Given the extraordinary demands on their time, school counselors may be tempted to give up when a bully relapses; but they must remember that aggressive behaviors are deeply ingrained, and they must continue to provide support and encouragement for change.

Modifying the School Climate and Structure   The third front in the battle to prevent bullying in school is the school itself. The counselor must work toward a school environment that does not encourage bullying. The attitudes of teachers and other school staff members are key here. Again, school personnel are apt to ignore bullying or to minimize it as teasing. To change those attitudes, the school counselor might run an in-service training for all staff members. The purpose of the training would be twofold: first, to make the adults in the school aware of the extent of bullying and victimization;[11] and second, to engage them—and parents as much as possible—in a schoolwide effort to stop bullying.[12] Once school personnel are sensitized to the problem, the counselor can give them guidelines to recognize bullying, distinguish it from normal teasing, and intervene appropriately.

The school must also do everything possible to develop a warm environment (Hanish & Guerra, 2000a). Adults in the school model positive behaviors by exercising authority in a way that is not oppressive. Signs and posters throughout the school can be used to foster caring and acceptance. School policy should clearly state the consequences for bullying behaviors; it should also state that the school counselor is ready and willing to help change those behaviors. Again, a primary goal here is to communicate to bullies that their way of behaving is not normal, that it runs counter to how most people interact.

SEXUAL HARASSMENT IN SCHOOLS

Of the times I was sexually harassed at school, one of them makes me feel really bad. I was in class and the teacher was looking right at me when this guy grabbed my butt. The teacher saw it happen. I slapped the guy and told him not to do that. My teacher didn't say anything and looked away and went on with the lesson like nothing out of the ordinary had happened. It really confused me because I knew guys weren't supposed to do that, but the teacher didn't do anything. I felt like the teacher (who was a man) betrayed me and thought I was making a big deal out of nothing. But most of all, I felt really bad about myself because it made me feel slutty and cheap. It made me feel mad too because we shouldn't have to put up with that stuff, but no one will do anything to stop it. Now sexual harassment doesn't bother me as much because it happens so much it almost seems normal. I know that sounds awful, but the longer it goes on without anyone doing anything, the more I think of it as just one of those things that I have to put up with. (a 14-year-old quoted in Stein, 1995, p. 146)

Sexual harassment and bullying are the most common forms of violence in schools. That they contribute to an environment in which students feel threatened is one reason—the primary reason—for school counselors to do what they can to

---

[11] Before the training, the counselor can conduct a formal survey—of a particular grade or even the whole student body—to determine the extent of peer victimization in the school. A good instrument for this purpose is the Olweus Bully/Victim Questionnaire (Olweus et al., 1999).

[12] Research shows that the inclusion of parents in schoolwide efforts to prevent bullying makes those efforts more effective in reducing victimization (Olweus, 1992).

prevent sexual harassment. That schools are being held legally responsible for sexual harassment is another.

The Legal Basis of Harassment Policies

Sexual harassment law stems from Title IX of the Education Amendments of 1972, which says that no individual can be discriminated against on the basis of sex in education programs that receive federal funds. In 1986, the Equal Employment Opportunity Commission extended the definition to include sexual advances, requests for sexual favors, and other verbal or physical conduct of a sexual nature when submission to such conduct is a term or condition of an individual's academic advancement; submission to or rejection of such conduct is used as the basis for academic decisions affecting the individual; or such conduct has the purpose or effect of unreasonably interfering with an individual's academic performance or creating an intimidating, hostile, or offensive academic environment (Rowell, McBride, & Nelson-Leaf, 1996). In 1997, the Department of Education's Office for Civil Rights (OCR) added a hostile-environment clause to the definition of *sexual harassment* under Title IX: A *hostile environment* exists when sexual harassment is "sufficiently severe, persistent, or pervasive that it adversely affects a student's education or creates a hostile or abusive educational environment." [13]

Teacher-to-Student Harassment   Several court cases in the 1990s made sexual harassment a top priority for school policymakers. *Franklin v. Gwinnett County Public Schools* (503 U.S. 60, 1992) was a landmark case: In a 9–0 decision, the U.S. Supreme Court established the right to sue a school system for compensatory damages under Title IX in a case of sexual harassment. *Franklin* involved a 15-year-old female student who had sex three times with a teacher on school grounds. The student, Christine Franklin, told both a teacher and a school administrator about the sexual encounters. They told her not to tell anyone and promised they would get rid of the teacher. The offending teacher agreed to resign, and the school agreed not to pursue legal action against him. Franklin sued the school system, claiming that she was entitled to compensatory damages because the school had discriminated against her on the basis of gender. The Court agreed, establishing a parallel between teacher-to-student sexual harassment and supervisor-to-subordinate harassment in the workplace (Marczely, 1999).

Gebser v. Lago Vista Independent School District (524 U.S. 274, 1998) also involved teacher-to-student sexual harassment, in this case a ninth-grade girl who had sexual relations with a teacher for over a year. The relationship was revealed when a policeman discovered them in a parked car. In a 5–4 decision, the Supreme Court ruled that the school district was not liable for compensatory damages, that it could

---

[13] In 2001, the OCR revised its sexual harassment policy. The definition is essentially unchanged, but the new policy distinguishes Title IX regulations from the "standards applicable to private litigation for money damages and clarifies their regulatory basis as distinct from Title VII of the Civil Rights Act of 1964" (p. 1).

be held liable only if school authorities had known about the misconduct and had failed to act on that knowledge.

Student-to-Student Harassment Although *Franklin* involved teacher-to-student sexual harassment, the Court's decision established Title IX as the legal basis for the student-to-student sexual harassment lawsuits that would follow. Since the decision in *Franklin,* 21 sexual harassment cases under Title IX have been filed; all but one of them acknowledged Title IX as the basis for a claim of student-to-student sexual harassment (Stone, 2000).

The most important of those cases was *Davis v. Monroe County Board of Education* (526 U.S. 629, 1999). Here, for the first time, a school district was found liable and was ordered to pay damages under Title IX for student-to-student sexual harassment.

The facts of the case are telling. LaShonda Davis, a fifth grader, complained to her mother that a classmate was bothering her by grabbing her breasts and crotch. The behavior continued over five months, the child reporting each incident to her mother and to her classroom teacher. Mrs. Davis spoke to the teacher and the school principal twice about the abuse, but the boy was never disciplined. After three months of complaints, the teacher's only action was to separate the desks of the two students. Finally Mrs. Davis filed a complaint with the Monroe County, Georgia, Sheriff's Department. The boy pleaded guilty to sexual battery (Stone, 2000). In addition, Mrs. Davis filed a $1 million lawsuit against the Monroe County Board of Education under Title IX's prohibition of sex discrimination in schools (Van Boven, 1999), alleging that her daughter was unable to concentrate on her schoolwork (her grades had fallen significantly) and that her father had found a suicide note LaShonda had written (Stone, 2000). Eventually the case made its way to the U.S. Supreme Court.

Justice Sandra Day O'Connor, writing for the majority in the 5–4 decision, indicated that school districts are liable under Title IX "if they [are] deliberately indifferent to information about severe, pervasive, and objectively offensive harassment among students" (Walsh, 1999, p. 22). *Objectively offensive* means the plaintiff must show that the harassment deprived the victim of access to the educational opportunities provided by the school. The justices were bitterly divided. The dissenting opinion, written by Justice Kennedy and uncharacteristically delivered from the bench, warned of "federal intrusion into the day to day classroom logistics and interactions" and overreactions to behaviors that are "routine problems of adolescence" (Greenhouse, 1999, p. A24). Justice Kennedy characterized the case as "teaching little Johnny a perverse lesson in Federalism," to which Justice O'Connor responded, "It assures that little Mary may attend class" (p. A1).

In an earlier case, *Nabozny v. Podlesny* (92 F.3d 446, 7th Cir. 1996), the Court of Appeals for the Seventh Circuit found that school district administrators had violated the rights of a gay student. In an out-of-court settlement, the Ashland, Wisconsin, school district agreed to pay Jamie Nabozny $900,000 for the harassment he had endured in school for more than four years (Walsh, 1996). Nabozny, who dropped out of school in the 11th grade, had been urinated on and regularly assaulted by boys who held him down and simulated rape. Although Nabozny and his parents complained numerous times to school counselors and principals (McFarland & Dupuis, 2001), school officials either mishandled or ignored the complaints. It was reported that one principal told Nabozny that he should get used to violent behaviors because he was openly gay, and another told Nabozny that he deserved the abuse (Stein, 1999). This case was the first to use the equal protection clause of the Fourteenth Amendment for a gay student. And in March 1997, the OCR issued new guidelines extending Title IX protections to gay and lesbian students. Schools today can be liable if they are deliberately indifferent to the harassment of these students and the harassment interferes with their access to educational opportunity.

The Prevalence of Sexual Harassment in Schools

Sexual harassment in schools became a national issue in the early 1990s with the publication of two nationwide surveys. The first was conducted by the Wellesley College Center for Research on Women and was published in *Seventeen* magazine (LeBlanc, 1992, 1993). The survey, which consisted of 11 multiple-choice and 2 open-ended questions, was administered to a random sample of 4,300 students, ages 9 to 19. About 2,000 surveys were returned and usable, many with notes scribbled on the outside of the envelope: "Open," "Urgent," "Please read" (Stein, 1995).

Answers to the open-ended questions yielded three important findings (Stein, 1999):

- Sexual harassment is often public—that is, often it goes on in front of bystanders, some of whom are adult employees of schools.
- The targets of sexual harassment in schools are not passive, belying the girls-are-passive-victims stereotype.
- When girls told school officials about the harassment incidents, their stories were often dismissed or trivialized.

The survey revealed that the most common forms of harassment were sexual comments, gestures, and looks (89 percent) and being touched, pinched, or grabbed (83 percent). Thirty-nine percent of the respondents said they were harassed on a daily basis over the past year, and 66 percent said that other people were present at the time of the harassment. The harassment occurred most often in classrooms (94 percent), in hallways (76 percent), and in the school parking lot or on playing fields (69 percent).

Louis Harris and Associates conducted the second survey; the American Association of University Women (1993) funded it. Harris surveyed a random sample of 828 boys and 779 girls in Grades 8 through 11.[14] The survey consisted of 40 questions that addressed different areas of sexual harassment. The results revealed that

---

[14]To test for racial differences, the survey oversampled African American and Hispanic students.

TABLE 12.4 TYPE OF SEXUAL HARASSMENT EXPERIENCED IN SCHOOL

Harassment Behaviors	Percentage of	
	Girls (*n* = 779)	Boys (*n* = 828)
Sexual comments, jokes, gestures, or looks	76	56
Touched, grabbed, or pinched in a sexual way	65	42
Intentionally brushed up against in a sexual way	57	36
Flashed or mooned	49	41
Had sexual rumors spread about them	42	34
Had clothing pulled at in a sexual way	38	28
Shown, given, or left sexual pictures, photographs, illustrations, messages, or notes	31	34
Had their way blocked in a sexual way	28	17
Forced to kiss someone	23	14
Had sexual messages/graffiti written about them on a bathroom wall, in locker rooms, etc.	20	18
Called gay or lesbian	10	23
Forced to do something other than kissing	13	9
Spied on while dressing or showering	7	8

SOURCE: *Hostile Hallways* by the American Association of University Women, 1993, p. 9. Copyright 1993 by the American Association of University Women Educational Foundation. Reprinted by permission.

81 percent of the students—girls and boys—had experienced unwanted sexual attention in school: 83 percent of the girls and 60 percent of the boys. Table 12.4 shows the overall results. In almost every area, girls reported a higher incidence of harassment and more-severe harassment, including harassment by a teacher.[15] Blacks and students in higher grades also reported more-severe forms of harassment. About 53 percent of the total sample reported both harassing and being harassed.

A more recent survey by the American Association of University Women (2001) shows that harassment continues to be a serious problem in our schools. In a sample of 2,064 public school students in Grades 8 through 11, 83 percent of girls and 79 percent of boys reported being sexually harassed. Of those, 58 percent experienced physical harassment, and more than 30 percent feared being sexually harassed or hurt in school.

---

[15]The exceptions: being shown, given, or left sexual pictures or notes (34 percent of boys versus 31 percent of girls); being called gay or lesbian (23 percent versus 10 percent); and being spied on while dressing or showering (8 percent versus 7 percent).

Adopting a Sexual Harassment Policy

There are several steps schools can take to make the environment less hostile for students. The most fundamental are to adopt a policy for dealing with the problem and being sure that everyone in the schools—staff and students—knows and understands that policy. In fact, today the OCR requires that school districts adopt and publish a sexual harassment policy and grievance procedures.[16]

According to Webb, Hartwell-Hunnicut, and Metha (1997), a school district's policy on sexual harassment should include the following elements:

1. A statement that the school district is committed to maintaining an educational environment free of sexual harassment.
2. A statement that sexual harassment is illegal, citing Title IX and other relevant state and federal statutes.
3. A definition of *student peer sexual harassment,* with age-appropriate examples.
4. A clear statement that sexual harassment will not be tolerated and guarantees that disciplinary action will be taken against harassers.
5. A detailed grievance procedure for handling complaints that protects all parties involved and guarantees confidentiality. The grievance procedure should provide the name, address, and telephone number of the district Title IX coordinator.
6. The name(s) of the persons on each campus, preferably one person of each gender, to be contacted if a student feels he or she has been a victim of sexual harassment.
7. A list of sanctions for students found guilty of harassment.
8. A statement prohibiting retaliation for submitting a complaint of sexual harassment. (p. 75)

The policy should be widely disseminated: displayed in highly trafficked areas of the school and distributed to parents and other adults connected to the school.

Preventing Sexual Harassment

The legal ramifications of sexual harassment in schools give school counselors a certain leverage in their efforts to sensitize their schools to the problem. There is no room here for a "boys will be boys" attitude. The reason students and their parents are suing schools is that teachers and administrators looked the other way despite repeated evidence of victimization. Although schools may not be able to control the behavior of students who do not respect other students, they can control the way they deal with that behavior.

If the school does not have a policy that speaks explicitly to sexual harassment, the school counselor should advocate for one. We listed the basic elements of that policy above; to expand policy and procedures, the school counselor can administer

---

[16]The OCR rule mandates that policy and procedures be part of each district's Title IX policy. Webb, Hartwell-Hunnicut, and Metha (1997), however, recommend that schools also have a separate policy on sexual harassment to accentuate their concern about the issue.

TABLE 12.5 SEXUAL HARASSMENT: A STUDENT SURVEY

Has any student from school done any of the things listed below to you, which made you feel upset or uncomfortable? If so, please mark an "X" before each of those behaviors that upset you. Mark all that apply.

____ Unwanted physical contact of a sexual nature (for example: grabbing, pushing, pinching, touching, rubbing, pulling or snapping bra straps)

____ "Shucking" or doing "wedgies" (pulling pants up or down)

____ Unwanted sexual comments (for example: name calling, teasing, telling "dirty" or sexual jokes, spreading gossip or rumors)

____ Writing sexual notes or letters or drawing "dirty" pictures

____ Unwanted phone calls of a sexual nature

____ Unwanted pressure for dates

____ Unwanted sexual advances, pressure for sexual activity

____ Sexual assault or attempted rape

We are interested in knowing what you think about the behaviors in the list below. Please indicate to what extent you believe these behaviors are acceptable or unacceptable when directed toward you or any of your classmates. Mark a "1" if *very acceptable;* mark a "2" if *acceptable;* mark a "3" if *unacceptable;* mark a "4" if *very unacceptable.*

____ Unwanted physical contact of a sexual nature (for example: grabbing, pushing, pinching, touching, rubbing, pulling or snapping bra straps)

____ "Shucking" or doing "wedgies" (pulling pants up or down)

____ Unwanted sexual comments (for example: name calling, teasing, telling "dirty" or sexual jokes, spreading gossip or rumors)

____ Writing sexual notes or letters or drawing "dirty" pictures

____ Unwanted phone calls of a sexual nature

____ Unwanted pressure for dates

____ Unwanted sexual advances, pressure for sexual activity

____ Sexual assault or attempted rape

SOURCE: "Sexual Harassment: An Educational Program for Middle School Students," by B. Roscoe, J. S. Strouse, M. P. Goodwin, L. Taracks, & D. Henderson, 1994, *Elementary School Guidance and Counseling, 29,* p. 120. Copyright 1994 by the American School Counselor Association. Reprinted with permission.

a survey to the school population to uncover specific areas of concern (Table 12.5). Survey results also can be used as evidence of the extent and seriousness of the problem. Again, a well-publicized policy on sexual harassment is the foundation of any prevention program.

To help implement the policy, the school counselor must make the counseling office a safe place for students to come to talk about sexual harassment (Stone, 2000). A great deal of empathy is needed to help the victims of sexual harassment with their anxiety and insecurity. Many times students blame themselves for being harassed. The good news is that in recent years, 93 percent of students indicate that they understand what sexual harassment is and 70 percent are aware of school policies on harassment, up from 26 percent in 1993 (American Association of University Women, 2001).

TABLE 12.6 **CORE LESSONS OF A SEXUAL HARASSMENT CURRICULUM**

Lesson Themes	Lesson Activities
1. Flirting versus sexual harassment	This is a teacher-led discussion to raise student awareness about the kinds of sexual harassment that take place all the time; to discern the fluid, subjective line between flirting and harassment; and to encourage open student discussion of a complicated topic. Students are given the assignment of being "anthropologists" and "ethnographers" in their own school by recognizing and taking notes on the sexual harassment that takes place around them.
2. Says who?	In this session, a questionnaire is administered and discussed. The objective is to define *sexual harassment;* to dispel common myths about sexual harassment; and to raise awareness of the prevalence of sexual harassment in school.
3. What are your rights?	This discussion is designed to inform students of their rights; to review school policy and procedures on sexual harassment; and to review possible ways for targets of sexual harassment to respond.
4 and 5. Case studies and role-play	These sessions use case material to generate student discussion and problem solving. Role-play around differing sexual harassment scenarios is also used to help students grapple with the complicated factors involved in incidents of sexual harassment; to try on the roles and respond from the perspectives of various people involved in actual cases of sexual harassment; and to determine responsibility in those cases.
6. Get up, stand up for your rights	This session uses brainstorming and action planning. Members are invited to discuss strategies to eliminate sexual harassment; to explore what it means to be a justice-maker; and to remind students that they have had the experience of responding proactively when a situation needed righting.

SOURCE: Stein and Sjostrom (1994).

Workshops and conferences are a good source of methods and materials both for working with students who have been sexually harassed and for preventing sexual harassment. In turn, a well-trained counselor can provide workshops for school staff and materials for inclusion in the life-skills or health curriculum (Stone, 2000).

A wonderful source for lessons and materials on sexual harassment is Stein and Sjostrom's (1994) guide *Flirting or Hurting.* The book describes six core lessons for boys and girls in Grades 6 through 12 (Table 12.6). The guide also includes supplemental activities. The information is succinct, accurate, and user-friendly. And the activities, both informational and experiential, sensitize students to the psychological, social, and legal consequences of sexual harassment.

A COMPREHENSIVE APPROACH TO SCHOOL-BASED VIOLENCE PREVENTION

Experts agree that violence prevention in schools must be comprehensive and collaborative. *Comprehensive* means that it should target all children—those who show no potential for violence, those who appear to be at risk for violence, and those who show imminent signs of violence. *Collaborative* means that violence prevention efforts must extend beyond the school to family and community.

A number of studies support a multistep approach to preventing violence in schools.[17] They all suggest the same basic outline:

1. Identify and measure the problems.
2. Establish partnerships.
3. Set measurable goals and objectives.
4. Develop a program and strategy for reaching the goals.
5. Implement the plan.
6. Evaluate the plan.

Step 1. Identify and Measure the Problems

The first step in developing a comprehensive violence prevention program is to define and measure the problems. Internal data should be collected from incident reports and school records going back several years. This is not the time for administrators to sugar-coat the facts. For student and staff perspectives, the counselor can conduct a schoolwide survey that asks questions like these (Callahan, 2001):

- How safe do you feel at school?
- How many times have you been harassed, assaulted, physically threatened, attacked, or hurt?
- How many times have you used a weapon?
- How many times have you known about someone else carrying a weapon, stealing, making sexual advances, or being involved in gangs?

For external data, the counselor can turn to national, state, and local government statistics. The local police department and community agencies also can have important data that the school is not privy to and that should be a basis for developing the youth violence prevention program. Also, information sharing is an important first contact with the neighborhood organizations that are a critical component of a collaborative program.

The data the counselor collects at the outset will determine the initial focus of the program. But data collection should be an ongoing process, both to identify new areas for concern and, ultimately, to evaluate the effectiveness of the program.

Step 2. Establish Partnerships

Given the parents' role in the etiology of violence in their children, any comprehensive violence prevention program must include this constituency. If parents are reluctant to take part, the school counselor needs to stress the importance of their influence on their children and the counselor's own need for their help.

All of the resources required to prevent school violence—health and social services agencies, businesses, law enforcement and juvenile justice departments,

---

[17] For example, see Cunningham and Sandhu (2000); Keys, Bemak, Carpenter, and King-Sears (1998); Melaville, Blank, and Asayesh (1993); and U.S. Departments of Education and Justice (2000b).

churches, and civic organizations—already exist in the community. It just takes someone to bring those resources together in a program to reduce school violence.[18]

The place to start is with a planning meeting that includes parents and representatives from the community. The response to the planning meeting indicates the degree to which the community is ready to mobilize its resources for its children. Some communities are always ready for action; others are not. If the turnout at the meeting is poor, or if those who come to the meeting seem reluctant to participate in a violence prevention program, the counselor is going to have to undertake a campaign to sensitize the community to the problems of violence in the school. That campaign should operate on two levels: meetings with community leaders and a grassroots effort to reach out to parents and others in the neighborhood. Holding weeknight meetings in local churches is one good way to announce the campaign; setting up an information and recruitment booth at local fairs is another. The counselor should be armed with statistics on the number and type of violent incidents in the school over the past several years, the results of the schoolwide survey, and the data collected from external sources. But the most effective "marketing" tool here is the counselor's efforts, demonstrating to the community that the school cares about its students (Riley & McDaniel, 1999).

Step 3. Set Measurable Goals and Objectives

With the problems identified and with parents and the community as partners, the school is ready to set goals and objectives. This is a time for team members to develop a shared vision of what they would like their school and community to do to prevent youth violence.

One problem confounding prevention efforts is that for many youngsters, violence is functional; it satisfies their psychological and social needs. In fact, for these youngsters violence may well be the only method they know for getting what they want. To help these students change their behaviors, the prevention program must give them alternate ways of meeting their needs.[19] The Search Institute (1997) came up with a list of what it calls *developmental assets,* factors that help aggressive and violent youngsters respond with less-risky behaviors (also see Leffert et al., 1998). The institute identified 40 internal and external factors (Table 12.7). These developmental assets are a useful framework for designing a comprehensive guidance program in general and a violence prevention program in particular. The more assets students have, the less likely they are to turn to violence as a means of self-expression and fulfillment.

Goals and objectives are the product of a realistic assessment of risk factors and developmental assets in the school and the community. That assessment defines the needs of school and community and so the prevention program's goals. *Goals* are what the program sets out to accomplish; *objectives* are the sequential

---

[18]This is another place where the counselor's understanding of the school's neighborhood and ties to community leaders can be invaluable (see Chapter 6).

[19]This thinking is not unlike the cost–benefit approach to stopping substance abuse that we talked about in Chapter 11.

TABLE 12.7 **DEVELOPMENTAL ASSETS**

External Assets

Support	1. *Family support.* Family provides high levels of love and support.
	2. *Positive family communication.* Young person and his or her parent(s) communicate positively, and young person is willing to seek advice and counsel from parents.
	3. *Other adult relationships.* Young person receives support from three or more non-parent adults.
	4. *Caring neighborhood.* Young person experiences caring neighbors.
	5. *Caring school climate.* School provides a caring, encouraging environment.
	6. *Parent involvement in schooling.* Parents are actively involved in helping young person succeed in school.
Empowerment	7. *Community values youth.* Young person perceives that adults in the community value youth.
	8. *Youth as resources.* Young people are given useful roles in the community.
	9. *Service to others.* Young person serves in the community one hour or more per week.
	10. *Safety.* Young person feels safe at home, school, and in the neighborhood.
Boundaries and expectations	11. *Family boundaries.* Family has clear rules and consequences and monitors the young person's whereabouts.
	12. *School boundaries.* School provides clear rules and consequences.
	13. *Neighborhood boundaries.* Neighbors take responsibility for monitoring young people's behavior.
	14. *Adult role models.* Parent(s) and other adults model positive, responsible behavior.
	15. *Positive peer influence.* Young person's best friends model responsible behavior.
	16. *High expectations.* Both parent(s) and teachers encourage the young person to do well.
Constructive use of time	17. *Creative activities.* Young person spends three or more hours per week in lessons or practice in music, theater, or other arts.
	18. *Youth programs.* Young person spends three or more hours per week in sports, clubs, or organizations at school and/or in community.
	19. *Religious community.* Young person spends one or more hours per week in activities in a religious institution.
	20. *Time at home.* Young person is out with friends with nothing special to do two or fewer nights per week.

Internal Assets

Commitment to learning	21. *Achievement motivation.* Young person is motivated to do well in school.
	22. *School engagement.* Young person is actively engaged in learning.
	23. *Homework.* Young person reports doing a least one hour of homework every school day.
	24. *Bonding to school.* Young person cares about his or her school.
	25. *Reading for pleasure.* Young person reads for pleasure three or more hours per week.
Positive values	26. *Caring.* Young person places high value on helping other people.
	27. *Equality and social justice.* Young person places high value on promoting equality and reducing hunger and poverty.

(continued)

TABLE 12.7 *(continued)*

Positive values (*continued*)	28. *Integrity.* Young person acts on convictions and stands up for her or his beliefs.
	29. *Honesty.* Young person tells the truth even when it is not easy.
	30. *Responsibility.* Young person accepts and takes personal responsibility.
	31. *Restraint.* Young person believes it is important not to be sexually active or to use alcohol or other drugs.
Social competencies	32. *Planning and decision making.* Young person knows how to plan ahead and make good choices.
	33. *Interpersonal competence.* Young person has empathy, sensitivity, and friendship.
	34. *Cultural competence.* Young person has knowledge of and comfort with people of different cultural/racial/ethnic backgrounds.
	35. *Resistance skills.* Young person can resist negative peer pressure and dangerous situations.
	36. *Peaceful conflict resolution.* Young person seeks to resolve conflict.
Positive identity	37. *Personal power.* Young person feels he or she has control over things that happen to him or her.
	38. *Self-esteem.* Young person reports having high self-esteem.
	39. *Sense of purpose.* Young person reports that my life has a purpose.
	40. *Positive view of personal future.* Young person is optimistic about his or her personal future.

SOURCE: *The Assets Approach: Giving Kids What They Need to Succeed.* Copyright 1997 by the Search Institute, Minneapolis, Minnesota. Reprinted with permission.

steps needed to achieve each goal. Goals should be realistic and should be stated more broadly than objectives; objectives should be detailed (who will do what when) and measurable (U.S. Departments of Education and Justice, 2000b). Every goal must have a set of objectives. Table 12.8 shows a sample goal and objectives for reducing crime in schools. The goals and objectives of a violence prevention program should reflect the unique needs of each school and community.

Step 4. Develop a Program and Strategy for Reaching the Goals

There are many commercial and noncommercial programs available for preventing violence in schools and communities. No single program or strategy can meet the needs of all students. What the counselor must look for is the program that best meets the students' needs.

Experts have identified nine critical elements in violence prevention programs that work (Callahan, 2001; Lawler, 2000; Safe schools, safe students, 1998):

Behavioral norms and the consequences of not adhering to them. The program should establish specific behavioral norms. It must make clear that violence is not acceptable and that violation of the school's policy on violence results in very specific consequences.

Skills training strongly based on theory. Violence prevention programs generally focus on anger- and conflict-management skills, peer negotiation skills, and active-listening and communication skills. Whatever the

TABLE 12.8 **SAMPLE GOAL AND OBJECTIVES FOR REDUCING CRIME IN SCHOOL**

Goal	Objectives
Decrease physical fighting on school grounds	1. Professionals from the community will train 90 parents in nonviolent problem-solving and social skills by April 24.
	2. The security officers will teach all school staff proper techniques for intervening in physical fights by November 1.
	3. A subgroup will be established to study and report to the principal by February 2 on how well the school policy on fighting is being communicated and how consistently it is enforced.
	4. The vice principal will notify parents of all students involved in physical fights as participants or as instigators as soon as possible after the fight. All those involved will be provided an information sheet concerning access to due process within the school and courts.
	5. The school will be divided into physically and administratively separate units of no more than 300 students each by June 15.

SOURCE: U.S. Departments of Education and Justice (2000b).

content of the program, it should have a strong theoretical base supported by evidence that this type of skills training does change behavior.

A collaborative effort. Successful programs involve the school, the family, and the community.

Coordination across programs. All of a school's prevention programs must be coordinated. For example, drug abuse prevention programs and violence prevention programs have many elements in common. The school counselor, who coordinates the overall guidance program, should see to it that services are not duplicated in those programs.

Physical and administrative changes. Certain physical changes may be needed to create a safe school environment. Those changes can include locking exterior doors to limit access to the school building, monitoring the school with surveillance equipment, hiring security officers, controlling the number of keys to the building, installing a master phone system, having walkie-talkies available to playground supervisors, better lighting in dark corridors, and staggering class periods to reduce congestion in the hallways.

At least 20 sessions. Research shows that programs should run 10 to 20 sessions the first year followed by 5 to 10 booster sessions in the next two years.

Training for the entire school staff. The more staff members are involved in and understand the program, the greater the probability of its success. Especially important here is that teachers be trained to deliver the violence prevention curriculum.

Multiple teaching methods. Programs that include a variety of teaching methods are more effective than those that rely on just one or two approaches. Among the methods usually used are group work, role-playing, cooperative learning, discussion, and practice of newly learned social skills.

Cultural sensitivity. Any program's material should be adapted to meet the needs of a culturally diverse student body.

TABLE 12.9 VIOLENCE PREVENTION PROGRAMS FOR ELEMENTARY SCHOOL CHILDREN

Program title	Second Step	Promoting Alternative Thinking Strategies (PATHS)	Peace Builders	Bullying Prevention Program	Resolving Conflicts Creatively Program (RCCP)	I Can Problem Solve: An Interpersonal Cognitive Problem-Solving Program
Source and phone number	Kathy Beland, Committee for Children, (800) 634-4449	Developmental Research and Programs, (800) 736-2630	Heartsprings Inc., (520) 299-6770	Center for the Study and Prevention of Violence, (303) 492-8465	RCCP National Center, (212) 509-0022	Research Press, (217) 352-3273
Web site	www .secondstep .com	www.drp.org	www .peacebuilders .com	www.colorado .edu	www .esrnational .org	www .thinkingpreteen .com
Suggested grade level	Pre-K–5	K–5, and special-needs students	K–6+, and families and community	K–6	K–12	Pre-K–6
Program goals	To reduce impulsive and aggressive behavior by teaching students skills in empathy, impulse control, problem solving, and anger management	To promote emotional competence through expression, understanding, and regulation of emotions	To reduce violence by promoting cognitive, social, and emotional competencies	To reduce and prevent bully–victim problems	To reduce violence through skills training in conflict resolution and intergroup relations	To help children resolve interpersonal problems and to prevent antisocial behaviors by teaching thinking skills
Key teaching strategies	Story telling, discussion, modeling, skills, activities, role-play	Didactic instruction, role-play, modeling, social and self-reinforcement	Modeling, recognition, praise, environmental cues and alterations, peer and self-monitoring, Socratic questioning, response cost	n/a	Role-play, interviews, group dialogue, brainstorming	Direct instruction via lesson plans, classroom interaction, and integration into the curriculum
Materials	11 × 17 photo lesson cards, teacher's guide, posters, videos, puppets, song tape	Curriculum with worksheets and posters	Teacher's manual; student, family, mass media, and community resource materials (in English and Spanish)	n/a	K–12 curriculums, videos, resource materials	3 program guides
Duration of instruction	Variable depending on grade and students' needs	60 lessons of increasing difficulty	"It is a way of everyday living, learning, and working"	n/a	15–20 lessons; then infused into all curriculum areas	Varies by grade
Cost	Pre-K: $245; Grades 1–3: $255; Grades 4–5: $235	n/a	$10–$14 per student	n/a	$33 per student	$39.95 per volume
Training	Recommended	Required	Required	n/a	Required	Required

SOURCE: Adapted from Lawler (2000), pages 253–255. Copyright by the American School Counselor Association. Reprinted with permission.

TABLE 12.10 VIOLENCE PREVENTION PROGRAMS FOR MIDDLE AND HIGH SCHOOL STUDENTS

Program title	*Dealing with Anger: Giving It, Taking It, Working It Out*	*Safe Dates*	*Life Skills Training (LST)*	*Project Alert*	*The Prepare Curriculum*	*Responding in Peaceful and Positive Ways (RIPP)*
Source and phone number	Research Press, (217) 352-3273	Vangee Foshee, (919) 966-6616	Institute for Prevention Research, (212) 746-1270	Project Alert, (800) 253-7810	Research Press, (217) 352-3273	Life Skills Center, (888) 572-1572
Web site	www .researchpress .com	n/a	www .preventionnet .com	www .projectalert .best.org	www.uscart .org/prepare %20curric.htm	www .prevention .psu.edu/ripp .htm
Suggested grade level	6–12, African American youngsters	8 and 9	7–9	6–8, ethnically mixed youngsters	6–12	6 and 7
Program goals	To accept angry feelings and criticism, and to negotiate	To change violent dating behaviors and gender stereotyping, and to teach conflict-management skills	To teach self-management, social, and drug-resistance skills, and assertiveness	To teach social-resistance skills	To teach problem solving, interpersonal skills, situational perception, and anger control	To reduce fighting and threats with weapons
Key teaching strategies	Discussion stimulated by videos and role-play	Classroom curriculum, role-play, poster contest	Class sessions taught by adults or peer leaders	Class lessons, home learning with parent involvement	Instruction, modeling, role-play, group discussion	Small groups
Materials	Video and discussion guide	n/a	n/a	n/a	Book	n/a
Duration of instruction	Variable (3 lessons per video set)	10 sessions	Varies by grade	11 weekly lessons in first year, 3 booster sessions in second year	10 weekly sessions	25 sessions
Cost	$405 per set of videos	Free	n/a	n/a	$29.95	$75 for class of 30 students
Training	Required	n/a	n/a	n/a	Required	Strongly recommended

SOURCE: Adapted from Lawler (2000), pages 256–257. Copyright by the American School Counselor Association. Reprinted with permission.

The research also describes what doesn't work: scare tactics and programs that are limited to counseling and peer counseling, that offer only enrichment activities, that lack the support of the school's administration, and that are too brief.

Tables 12.9 and 12.10 offer summaries of a number of violence prevention programs for younger students and for students in middle and high school. All of the programs listed have demonstrated positive short-term and long-term effects.

Step 5. Implement the Plan

Most of the programs in Tables 12.9 and 12.10 involve multiple groups—school, family, and community—performing different yet complementary tasks. Team members must work together to put the comprehensive plan into action. The school is responsible for obtaining district approval of the plan, training staff and peer leaders, and getting parents' approval (U.S. Departments of Education and Justice, 2000b).

In addition to gearing up, procedures must be put in place to monitor the initial response of students, staff, and parents; to deal with unforeseen obstacles; and to defuse any negative consequences of the plan—generally, to make any adjustments that need to be made. Team members should think of problems, not as failures, but as opportunities to make the program better and to work collaboratively. The process behind violence prevention is as important as the content. Any time adults can model collaboration, cooperation, and compromise as means of resolving differences, they strengthen the impact of violence prevention measures in the community.

Step 6. Evaluate the Plan

Evaluation is a critical piece of the violence prevention program. Is the plan working? Most of the programs listed in Tables 12.9 and 12.10 come with instruments for measuring their effectiveness. Some offer technical support for researching the programs' effectiveness both in the short and the long term. Program designers often are willing to consult at no cost because they are interested in monitoring program outcomes. Local colleges and universities can also be a source of support for program evaluation.

The purpose of the evaluation is to determine the effectiveness of the program: Has it reduced students' risk for violent behavior?[20] The process is straightforward: Test the participants before and after the program is implemented.[21] The content of the testing is a function of the program's goals and objectives: That is, the objectives for each goals are stated in measurable terms; they define the substance of the before-and-after comparison. If the program's objectives are clear and a data collection system is in place at the outset, it is a relatively simple matter for the school counselor to determine the program's effectiveness and the need for revisions (Cunningham & Sandhu, 2000).

ETHICAL AND LEGAL ISSUES

Violence in the schools raises all kinds of ethical and legal questions: What is a hostile environment? What is the school's responsibility to the student body? What is

---

[20] Evaluation also ensures accountability.

[21] Where possible, the school counselor can also test a control group for comparison with the intervention group.

its responsibility to students who are at risk for violent behavior? At what point does responsibility become liability? Are there times when breaching student confidentiality is an ethical imperative? A legal imperative? Two areas of special concern here are the assessment of risk factors in students and the confidentiality of student reports of sexual harassment or other acts of violence.

The Threat of Youth Violence

The school has an ethical and legal responsibility to protect students from harm. It also has an ethical and legal responsibility to provide an education for all students. When the school determines that students pose a serious threat to the safety of others, these two principles can come into conflict. Should the school automatically suspend or expel students who are at risk for violent behavior? Don't those students have rights? Can they be suspended simply because someone in the school is afraid of them? The courts have addressed these questions and the liability of school personnel—school counselors in particular—for youth violence in a number of recent cases.

School shootings in West Paducah, Kentucky, and Columbine, Colorado, resulted in lawsuits against school personnel for their failure to recognize warning signs and protect students from harm. In both cases, federal court dismissed the claims. In the Columbine case, a federal district court in Denver recognized the existence of warning signs but ruled that they were not sufficient to predict the eventual shootings (Hermann & Finn, 2002). The families of the victims said they planned to appeal the judge's ruling. In other cases—for example, *Eisel v. Board of Education* (597 A.2d 447, Md. 1991) and *Maynard v. Board of Education* (663 N.Y.S.2d 717, App. Div. 1997)—school counselors were found liable for failing to protect students from harm. In these cases, the courts appeared to base their decisions on two factors: whether the violence was foreseeable and whether school personnel acted with reasonable care.

Foreseeable means that there is an explicit threat of violence and that the perpetrator has a history of violent acts (Hermann & Remley, 2000). In *Lovell v. Poway Unified School District* (90 F.3d 367, 9th Cir. 1996), the court used the true-threat test in determining that a student's constitutional rights were not violated when she was suspended from school for issuing a threat. A *true threat* is "a threat that a reasonable person in the same circumstances would find to be a serious and unambiguous expression of intent to do harm based on the language and context of the threat" (Hermann & Finn, 2002, p. 48). The rulings in two other cases where the true-threat test was applied suggest that schools are within rights to suspend students who appear to pose a serious threat but must allow the students to return to school if a mental health professional from outside the school finds they are not a true threat.[22]

The court addressed reasonable care in *Wyke v. Polk County School Board* (129 F.3d 560, 11th Cir. 1997). The decision there defined *reasonable care* for

---

[22] See *D. G. v. Independent School District No. 11, Tulsa County, Oklahoma* (2000 U.S. Dist. LEXIS 12197, N.D. Okla. 2000) and *Lavine v. Blain School District* (257 F.3d 981, 9th Cir. 2001).

school counselors as "the degree of care that would be exercised by other school counselors with similar education and experience" (Hermann & Finn, 2002, p. 49). One of the best ways for school counselors to protect themselves from liability, then, is to consult with colleagues and supervisors before they act and to carefully document the fact and nature of those consultations.

Student Reports and Confidentiality

When a student reports feeling afraid of or being threatened, harassed, or bullied by another student, the counselor faces an ethical dilemma: the conflict between maintaining confidentiality and protecting the student from harm. For example, suppose a student comes to a counselor to report being bullied. If the counselor breaks confidentiality, the bully's antagonism toward the victim might well escalate. On the other hand, if the counselor does not break confidentiality, the bullying is likely to go on. In the case of reported sexual harassment, the dilemma is all the more difficult because of the legal obligation to maintain a nonhostile environment in the school.

If a student reports sexual harassment to a school counselor but asks that the information stay confidential, what are the counselor's ethical and legal obligations? As always, if the student is in imminent physical danger, the counselor must inform the school administration, law enforcement officials, and the student's parents or legal guardian immediately. In fact, the OCR's guidelines require the counselor to report all instances of sexual harassment. The reasoning: School counselors are employees of the school, so their learning about a case of harassment means the school has received notice and must take corrective action (ACA, 1997; Stone, 2000).

What is less clear is the need to report the source of the information about the harassment—the victim or a concerned peer. Recognizing that a breach of confidentiality here could discourage students from reporting harassment, the OCR gives the school counselor a certain amount of discretion. If the violence can be remedied without revealing the name of the victim or the source of the accusation, then the counselor need not break confidentiality. But if the refusal to name the victim or the accuser impedes the investigation or violates the due process rights of the accused, the counselor must breach confidentiality (OCR, 1997; Stone, 2000). If the victim insists on anonymity, the school may decide to forgo disciplinary action against the accused (Stone, 2000)—that is, the school may decide that the victim's need for confidentiality outweighs the need for disciplinary action against the accused.

CONCLUSION

Youth violence, particularly violence in the form of bullying and sexual harassment, is a pervasive problem in our schools. A large number of factors, working in an even larger number of combinations, makes the task of identifying students at risk for violent behavior very difficult. But laws governing the educational environment and court rulings assigning liability to schools make it imperative that school counselors not only assess students' potential for violent behavior but also take action to prevent that behavior.

Any program to prevent youth violence must be both comprehensive and collaborative. By *comprehensive,* we mean that the program should target all students and that it should attack the problem of youth violence on many fronts and with many methods. Most important, the program should offer students alternatives to violence: developmental assets that mitigate the risk factors for violence. The second critical component of violence prevention programs in schools is the involvement of families and community. It does little good for a school to adopt a violence prevention program if violence is accepted practice in the home and is glorified in the neighborhood and the media. Developing a comprehensive program and involving family and community in that program can be time consuming and challenging. But that time is well spent, and that resolve is crucial. School counselors understand that preventing violence is the cornerstone of a comprehensive developmental guidance program. If schools can play a significant role in reducing violence, the path is clear to address the other problems that children and adolescents face.

One time when I was working as a school counselor, I witnessed a parent come into the cafeteria at lunchtime and, in front of several hundred students, punch a teacher in the face. It seems his daughter didn't like this particular teacher. The teacher was a big strong man, but he did not retaliate—a response that left many students puzzled. For several months afterwards, I worked with a number of students around the incident. We talked about cowardice and manliness and nonviolent ways to resolve conflict. I don't know that the work had a significant impact on the students. I suspect not. But it made clear to me how violence is woven into the fabric of our society and how critical it is that violence prevention efforts involve parents and community.

QUESTIONS FOR DISCUSSION

1. The United States is considered one of the most violent of industrialized nations. Do you think that characterization is accurate? Explain your answer.
2. Identify three ways in which our society reinforces violence. Then describe three interventions in schools that would address those factors.
3. Identifying students who are at risk for violent behavior is a very inaccurate business. Knowing this, what factors or combination of factors would you use in your personal profile of students at risk? Explain your reasons.
4. Bullying in schools is a pervasive problem, and school counselors do not have the time to deal with every complaint. Suppose a student comes to you and says, "_____ is teasing me." What would you look for to determine the seriousness of the problem?

5. Sexual harassment in schools isn't new, but the attention it is garnering is. Why do you think it took so long for schools to deal with the problem? What do you think about changes in the laws and the recent court decisions that hold schools responsible for a hostile learning environment? Do you think schools should be liable for sexual harassment? Why? What factors do you think should determine a school's liability?

Suggested Internet Sites

www.nssc1.org

The official Web site of National School Safety Center contains invaluable information on and strategies for making schools safe. Also here are a number of resources for reporters, educators, and parents.

www.safetyzone.org

The site describes instructional skills and strategies for creating safe schools, with an emphasis on social skills. Of special interest is a sourcebook of prevention practices in four key areas: parents and families, home visits, social and conflict resolution skills, and mentoring.

www.ojp.usdoj.gov/vawo/

The official Web site of the Violence Against Women Office, a Justice Department agency formed in 1995 to stop domestic violence and sexual assault, publishes press releases, provides information about grants, has a section for questions and comments, and offers a link to the National Domestic Violence Hotline.

www.keepschoolssafe.org

This site includes school safety and security information for parents, students, and schools. Parents and schools are provided with information on creating safe schools and dealing with children effectively after a disaster. Students are offered tips for dealing with such issues as bullying and physical fighting.

www.iir.com/nygc

This is the official Web site of the National Youth Gang Center, a resource for the latest information on gang-related demographics, legislation, literature, research, and effective prevention strategies.

www.ncsu.edu/cpsv/

The official Web site of the Center for Prevention of School Violence contains strategies on how to prevent acts of violence, and a calendar of workshops, seminars, and other events having to do with the prevention of violence in schools. Also here is a toll-free number to call in case of an emergency.

CHILD MALTREATMENT

Child maltreatment is a widely documented fact of life. Usually, schools are the first to see evidence of child maltreatment, and school counselors are primarily responsible for working with abused and neglected students. This is not an easy task. It can be very difficult for school counselors to manage their own emotions when confronted with a child who is being abused. Adding to that difficulty are legal implications and the logistics of coordinating with child protective services and law enforcement officials.

> *During my years as a school counselor, I reported many cases of child maltreatment to the authorities. None were more gut-wrenching than the cases of sexual abuse, which often resulted in the child's being removed from home and school. I have vivid memories of child protective services workers coming to the school and taking the child into their custody, and my walking with them to the front door, saying good-bye to an anxious child, and knowing that I most likely would never see her again.*

The law is clear: School counselors must report suspected child abuse. In fact, many states require that counselors in training attend a seminar on reporting before they can be certified. One of the sections in this chapter describes the requirements for and challenges in reporting child abuse.

The chapter begins with definitions of *child maltreatment* and data on its incidence and prevalence. The text then examines the different types of maltreatment, with special emphasis on sexual abuse. The chapter ends with recommendations for including child abuse prevention programs in the comprehensive developmental guidance curriculum.

Always there when we work with children is our own experience of childhood, our memories of good and bad times. Few of us received all that we needed as children on an emotional level. But most of us did receive enough care and nurturing to eventually develop a healthy sense of self and to become productive adults. Abused children do not have enough care and nurturing. Some overcome that developmental challenge; others suffer the effects of abuse and neglect long into adulthood. For these youngsters, school counselors must be a source of support and nurturing.

What Is Child Maltreatment?

In October 1996, the federal government amended and reauthorized the Child Abuse Prevention and Treatment Act (CAPTA).[1] According to the act,

- a child is someone under the age of 18.[2]
- child abuse and neglect are the physical or mental injury, sexual abuse or exploitation, or the negligent treatment or maltreatment of a child by a person responsible for the child's welfare.
- at a minimum, child abuse and neglect are the failure to act on the part of a parent or caregiver that results in death, serious physical or emotional harm, or sexual abuse or exploitation of a child; or any act or failure to act that creates an imminent risk of serious harm to a child.

It remains for each state to define *child abuse and neglect* within civil and criminal contexts. Civil statutes spell out the conditions and circumstances under which certain professionals must report cases of suspected abuse and neglect. Criminal statutes classify the forms of child maltreatment that are punishable by law. All 50 states have reporting laws, and school counselors must know the law in the state in which they work.

Both the federal and state laws recognize three types of child maltreatment: physical abuse; child neglect, which includes emotional or psychological abuse; and sexual abuse:

Physical abuse. Physical abuse is a physical action—punching, kicking, throwing, biting, burning—that harms a child. It also includes severe forms of punishment: for example, extended confinement in a particular space, forcing a child to kneel for a long period of time, or taping a child's mouth. Injuries from physical abuse range from minor bruises and abrasions to lacerations, burns, eye injuries, fractures, and damage to the brain and internal organs. Child abuse–related deaths are most often the result of head and internal injuries (Peterson & Urquiza, 1993).

Child neglect. Child neglect is the failure to provide for a child's basic needs. According to the U.S. Department of Health and Human Services (1988), there are four forms of child neglect (see Table 13.1). *Physical neglect* includes the refusal to seek or a delay in seeking health care for a child, abandonment, expulsion from the home, and the refusal to allow a runaway

---

[1] Public Law 104–235, Section 11; 42 U.S.C. 510g. On April 23, 2002, the House passed, by a vote of 411 to 5, the Keeping Children and Families Safe Act (H.R. 3839), which reauthorizes CAPTA. At this writing, the act is awaiting passage in the Senate; but it is expected to become law sometime in 2003.

[2] For cases of sexual abuse, each state's child protection laws define the term *child*.

TABLE 13.1 FORMS OF CHILD NEGLECT

Physical Neglect

Refusal of health care	Failure to provide or allow needed care (on the recommendation of a health care professional) for a physical injury, illness, or medical condition.
Delay in health care	Failure to seek timely medical care for a serious health problem that any reasonable layperson would recognize needs medical attention.
Abandonment	Desertion of a child without arranging for reasonable care and supervision. Includes cases in which children are not claimed within 2 days and/or cases in which children are left by parents/substitutes who give no or false information about their whereabouts.
Expulsion	Other blatant refusals of custody, including permanent or indefinite expulsion of a child from the home without adequate arrangement for care by others and refusal to accept custody of a returned runaway.
Other custody issues	Other custody-related forms of inattention to a child's needs, including repeated shuttling of a child from one household to another because of an apparent unwillingness to maintain custody, and repeatedly leaving a child with others for days or weeks at a time.
Other physical neglect	Conspicuous inattention to avoidable hazards in the home; inadequate nutrition, clothing, or hygiene; and other forms of reckless disregard of the child's safety and welfare (e.g., driving with the child while intoxicated and leaving a young child unattended in a motor vehicle).

Supervision

Inadequate supervision	Child left unsupervised or inadequately supervised for extended periods of time or allowed to remain away from home overnight without the parents/substitutes knowing (or attempting to determine) the child's whereabouts.

Emotional Neglect

Inadequate nurturing or affection	Marked inattention to the child's needs for affection, emotional support, and attention.
Spousal abuse or domestic violence	Chronic or extreme spousal abuse or other domestic violence in the child's presence.
Permitted drug or alcohol use	Encouraging or allowing the child to use drugs or alcohol, including the failure to intervene when informed of the problem by a third party.
Permitted other maladaptive behaviors	Encouraging or allowing other maladaptive behaviors (e.g., severe assaultiveness and chronic delinquency), including the failure to intervene when parents/guardians have reason to be aware of the existence and seriousness of the problem.
Refusal of psychological care	Refusal to allow needed and available treatment (on the recommendation of a health care professional) for a child's emotional or behavioral impairment or problem.
Delay in psychological care	Failure to seek or provide needed treatment for a child's emotional or behavioral impairment or problem that any reasonable layperson would recognize needs professional psychological attention (e.g., severe depression or a suicide attempt).
Other emotional neglect	Other inattention to the child's developmental or emotional needs not classifiable under any of the other forms of emotional neglect (e.g., overprotective restrictions that foster immaturity or emotional overdependence or expectations that are clearly inappropriate to the child's age or level of development).

Educational Neglect

Failure to enroll or other truancy	Failure to register or enroll a child of mandatory school age for nonlegitimate reasons (e.g., to work or to care for siblings) an average of at least 3 days a month.
Inattention to special education needs	Refusal to allow or failure to obtain recommended remedial educational services, or neglect in obtaining or following through with treatment for a child's diagnosed learning disorder or other special education need without reasonable cause.

SOURCE: Adapted from Gaudin (1993).

to return home.[3] The second form is inadequate *supervision.* Emotional neglect is the most difficult form of child maltreatment to substantiate, but experts confirm its existence (Andreini, 1990; Margolin, 1990; Mugridge, 1991; Wald, 1990). *Emotional neglect* generally refers to the failure to respond to a child's psychological needs for attention, love, and emotional security (Peterson & Urquiza, 1993). It can also include exposure to spousal abuse and allowing the child to engage in illicit activities—drug or alcohol use, for example. Finally, *educational neglect* is the failure of parents or guardian to ensure a child's prompt and regular attendance in school; it also includes the failure to arrange for a child's special educational needs.

Sexual abuse. Sexual abuse includes any sexual activity with a child, including commercial exploitation through prostitution or pornography (Peterson & Urquiza, 1993).

The laws of our society were made to ensure that children's basic physical and psychological needs are met and that they are protected from physical harm and sexual exploitation. If not, schools have an obligation to intervene.

THE INCIDENCE OF CHILD MALTREATMENT

The federal government requires that all states report the number of maltreatment referrals to the National Child Abuse and Neglect Data System (NCANDS). The data that follow come from the NCANDS's 2001 report:

- Almost 2.7 million referrals were made nationwide in 2001. Approximately 67.4 percent of them were referred for investigation; the rest were screened out.
- More than half (56.5 percent) of the referrals were made by professionals; the rest were made by family and community members.
- In 27.5 percent of the total referrals, suspicions of child maltreatment were substantiated. The total number of victims in 2001 was about 903,000, approximately 12.4 children per 1,000 children.[4]
- Of the 903,000 cases nationwide, 57.2 percent involved neglect, 18.6 percent involved physical abuse, 9.6 percent involved sexual abuse, and 26.6 percent involved other types of maltreatment.[5]

---

[3] In its reauthorized form, CAPTA deals with instances where medical treatment is withheld because of the parents' spiritual or religious beliefs by including in its definition of *physical neglect* the failure to respond to a physician's reasonable medical judgment that treatment would save the child's life (not simply prolong the child's dying).

[4] In 2000, the rate was 12.2 children per 1,000 children.

[5] The percentages total to more than 100 percent because children may have been the victims of more than one type of abuse.

The Victims

The NCANDS also analyzes maltreatment data according to the age, gender, race, and ethnicity of the victims, and prior victimization:

- Very young children are at the greatest risk for abuse and neglect. In 2001, children under age 4 had the highest victimization rate and accounted for 27.7 percent of all victims. As children grow older, the rate of victimization falls. Children between the ages of 4 and 7 accounted for 24.1 percent of all victims; ages 8 to 11, 22.8 percent; ages 12 to 15, 19.5 percent; and ages 18 to 21, 0.2 percent.[6]
- In 2001, 48.0 percent of child victims were male, and 51.5 percent of the victims were female.[7]
- In 2001, 50.2 percent of all victims were White; 25.0 percent were African American; and 14.5 percent were Hispanic American. American Indians and Alaskan Natives accounted for 2.0 percent of victims; Asian–Pacific Islanders, 1.3 percent. These rates have remained stable for several years.
- Children who had been victimized before were twice as likely to be victimized again when compared with children who had no history of victimization.

The Perpetrators

According to the 2001 NCANDS report, the perpetrators of child maltreatment had the following characteristics:

- The highest percentage of perpetrators were women under 30: Approximately 60 percent of perpetrators were female. Over 42 percent of female perpetrators were under 30; just over 31 percent of male perpetrators were under 30.
- In 80.9 percent of cases, maltreatment occurred at the hands of one parent. Mothers acting alone were responsible for almost 40.5 percent of all maltreatment: fathers acting alone, for 17.7 percent. In 19.3 percent of cases, maltreatment occurred at the hands of both parents.
- Almost one-third (31.5 percent) of perpetrators in cases of sexual abuse were labeled "Other Relative"; only 4.7 percent of perpetrators in these cases were labeled "Parent."

For almost all categories of perpetrator, neglect was the most common form of maltreatment.

---

[6] In 0.4 percent of cases, the victim's age was unknown.

[7] In 0.5 percent of cases, the victim's gender was unknown or not reported.

Fatalities

NCANDS carefully tracks the child fatalities reported by child protective services (CPS) and other agencies. The numbers are shocking:

- In 2001, an estimated 1,300 children died as a result of abuse and neglect, a rate of 1.8 deaths per 100,000 children.
- Slightly more than 1.5 percent of those fatalities occurred while the children were in foster care.
- Almost 41 percent of the children who died from abuse and neglect in 2001 were under a year old; and over 84 percent were under age 6.
- Neglect caused the largest proportion of deaths—35.6 percent.
- Almost 9 percent of child fatalities occurred in families that had received family services at some point during the five years preceding the death. Just under 1 percent of the children who died had been in foster care and then were returned to their families in the five years preceding their deaths.

The Data: A Summary

Although the statistics indicate a slight drop in recent years, child maltreatment in this country remains a serious problem. Between 1986 and 1993, the number of abused and neglected children doubled, and the number of seriously injured and endangered children quadrupled (Dykeman & Appleton, 2000). The most important factors in child abuse and maltreatment are the child's age and gender (for sexual abuse) and the family's size, structure, and income. Children from large families are neglected at a rate 3 times that of only children. Children from single-parent families are 77 percent more likely to experience physical abuse and 87 percent more likely to experience physical neglect than are children from two-parent households. And children from poor families are 25 times more likely to suffer maltreatment than are children from families living above the poverty line (Sedlak & Broadhurst, 1996).

PHYSICAL ABUSE

Most physical abuse of children stems from punishment, a parent's reacting to a child's misbehavior. Because physical punishment often suppresses the child's behavior for a short time, the parent may believe that it is an appropriate and effective way to discipline the child. But research over the years consistently shows that physical punishment is one of the least successful ways of changing children's behavior.

The Indicators of Physical Abuse

Youngsters who have been physically abused may show physical or behavioral symptoms. Among the physical indicators are

- unexplained bruises and welts on the child's face, torso, buttocks, and thighs in various stages of healing and in clusters. The bruises may reflect the shape

of an electric cord, a belt, or a buckle—anything that might be used to hit a child—and may appear regularly after an absence, a weekend, or a vacation.
- unexplained swelling, dislocation, or sprains of ankles, wrists, or other joints.
- unexplained burns on the palms of the hands, the soles of the feet, or the child's back or buttocks that look as though they were made with a lit cigarette or cigar; or rope burns on the neck, arms, legs, or torso.
- unexplained fractures of the skull, nose, or jaw in various stages of healing.
- unexplained abrasions on the mouth, lips, gums, eyes, or external genitalia.

Physical abuse can also leave behavioral indicators. For example, the school counselor should watch for children who

- are wary of contact with adults.
- are apprehensive when other children cry.
- are extremely aggressive or withdrawn.
- seem frightened of their parents or of going home.
- wear long-sleeved clothing on warm days (possibly to hide their injuries).

And, of course, the counselor should also investigate any reports children make about a parent's injuring them.

The physical abuse of children is pervasive in our society, which means that the school counselor must be alert to the physical and behavioral symptoms of abuse in children and follow up on his or her suspicions. It is never right to minimize the indicators of abuse.

The Consequences of Physical Abuse

Urquiza and Winn (1994) grouped the consequences of physical abuse into five categories: intrapersonal, interpersonal, physical, sexual, and behavioral.[8]

Intrapersonal Consequences   The person most likely to physically abuse a child is the primary caregiver. Because the quality of a child's attachment to the primary caregiver is the most significant factor in the child's development, the effects of that physical abuse are especially significant (Aber, 1989; Crittenden & Ainsworth, 1989). The quality of the primal relationship determines children's perception of their world. Young children who experience physical abuse come to believe that they are incompetent and unworthy of love (Crittenden & Ainsworth, 1989). Also, having experienced injury early on, these children may become wary and suspicious, expecting others to hurt them too (Urquiza & Winn, 1994).

Among older children, the consequences of physical abuse can be affective—depression, sadness, anxiety. Lynch and Roberts (1978) found that physically abused children take significantly less pleasure from their environment than do children from nonabusive environments. Other studies have found that physically abused children have a limited range of emotional expression and difficulty dealing

---

[8] Urquiza and Winn based their classification system on Garbarino's (1992) conceptual framework for the ecology of human development.

with the emotional expression of others. This blunted affective response and difficulty may well be the result of a defense mechanism developed to numb themselves to the psychic pain of being abused (Urquiza & Winn, 1994).

Interpersonal Consequences   Crittenden (1981) found that physically abused infants are more irritable and cry more often than infants who are not abused. By age 1, however, abused children can become cooperative and compliant—superficially, at least—as they try to accommodate their caregiver's behavior. Instead of showing anger, these children become passive, fearful, and vigilant (Crittenden, 1981). According to child abuse experts, children who are physically abused at a young age develop an anxious–avoidant attachment to the abusive parent. They tend to alternate between anger and cooperation, between wanting to be held and nurtured and rejecting attempts by the primary caregiver to hold and nurture them. As they become older, their ambivalence manifests in their wanting to care for their abusive parent and younger siblings (Helfer, 1987). By reversing roles, the youngsters try to acquire positive self-meaning and appreciation to compensate for the negative view of self that results from the physical abuse. Finally, physically abused children have a tremendous need for recognition and attention from adults (Galdston, 1971).

In their peer relationships, physically abused children have been found to be either overly aggressive or excessively withdrawn and avoidant (Urquiza & Winn, 1994). Green (1978) suggested that the aggression is a by-product of identification with the aggressor, a defense mechanism. From a social learning perspective, the aggression is a learned response, the result of parents' modeling aggressive behaviors. Physically abused children have difficulty developing and sustaining peer relationships because the basis for healthy relationships—sharing, equality, nonexploitation—are antithetical to the children's primary experiences of relationship (Mueller & Silverman, 1990).

Physical Consequences   Several studies have documented neurological, sensory, and psychomotor problems in children who have been physically abused (Baron, Bejar, & Sheaff, 1970; Caffey, 1972; Elmer & Gregg, 1967; H. P. Martin, 1976). But research has not established a direct link between physical abuse and developmental delay. Where abused youngsters show signs of developmental delay—for example, in cases of neurological impairment—it is possible that the delay is the direct result of harsh physical punishment. Researchers have also noted that abusive parents can restrict and discourage exploration and normal risk taking in their children, which could cause developmental impairment (H. P. Martin; Urquiza & Winn, 1994).

Sexual Consequences   Little research has been done on the sexual lives of those who were physically abused as children. But we can assume that many of the problems these youngsters develop in peer relationships—issues of trust, aggression, or withdrawal—also are problems in their intimate relationships. Also, in their primal relationship physically abused children experience an abuse of parental authority;

so issues of power and force are likely to play an important role in the sexual lives of these children as adults.

Behavioral Consequences   Again, studies consistently show that victims of physical abuse often become verbally and physically aggressive themselves. From their parents they've learned to use aggression to deal with problems, negative feelings, and conflicts, so abused children have difficulty mastering developmental tasks that demand patience—problem solving, for example, or delayed gratification or impulse control (Helfer, 1987). Although most physically abused children become aggressive, some become fearful, passive, and overcompliant. Others can turn aggression and compliance on and off depending on the situation: For example, they may act aggressively with their peers but be compliant with their parents.

Physical Abuse: A Summary

Children who are physically abused suffer both short- and long-term consequences. They generally experience low levels of self-esteem and trust, quickly become aggressive and hostile, and have difficulty starting and maintaining healthy relationships. Physically abused children employ a number of defense mechanisms to protect themselves from the pain of being abused. Those defense mechanisms can remain well into adulthood.

For school counselors, the important lesson here is that physically abused children are fragile and must be dealt with carefully. This can be a real challenge when a child regularly acts out, as many abused children do. The key is empathy: If counselors can remember that the child's hostility is rarely about them, they are more apt to accept the child unconditionally. It's also important to remember that physically abused children often pull for angry and aggressive reactions from adults, a response the children have come to expect in their interactions with adults. If counselors refuse to react aggressively, if they refuse to be provoked, they can begin teaching these children that other kinds of relationships are possible.

CHILD NEGLECT

All professionals who work with children recognize that neglect is a very real form of maltreatment, but there is considerable disagreement over the way in which *neglect* is defined. Some advocate that the parents' behavior or failure to act must result in identifiable symptoms of physical or emotional damage (Wald, 1976, 1982; Wolock & Horowitz, 1979). Others argue that the focus should be on the parents' behavior, not the consequences (Zuravin, 1991). For example, suppose a parent leaves a child in a locked car for an hour, and the child suffers no apparent physical or emotional damage from the incident. Is this parent neglectful?

Many researchers and child advocates have accepted Polansky's (1987) definition of neglect:

> A condition in which a caretaker responsible for the child, either deliberately or by extraordinary inattentiveness, permits the child to experience avoidable present suffering and/or fails to provide one of more of the ingredients generally deemed essential for developing a person's physical, intellectual, and emotional capacities. (p. 15)

The problem here is the definition of *generally deemed essential:* Even child development experts disagree about what is minimally essential for a child's development (Gaudin, 1993).

Defining *neglect* becomes even more complicated when we add other variables to the mix (Korbin, 1987). Giovannoni and Becera (1979) found significant differences in ratings of abuse and neglect among African American, Hispanic, and White cultures. Socioeconomic variables also complicate the matter. The rate of child neglect is highest among poor families (families that receive Aid to Families with Dependent Children), but this group also has the greatest difficulty finding adequate housing, health care, and child care (Wolock & Horowitz, 1979). Although there are a lot of gray areas in defining and identifying child neglect, most of us would agree that

> infants and young children left without adult supervision, children who are not fed regularly, children who are not taken for necessary medical treatment when ill, chronically dirty, lice-infected children, or chronically truant children are [the victims of] neglect. (Gaudin, 1993, p. 4)

The Types of Neglect

Table 13.1 (see page 381) is a comprehensive list of the different forms of neglect recognized by the U.S. Department of Health and Human Services (1988). Although some types of neglect fall outside the school counselor's domain, the counselor can use the table to assess whether students are receiving what is minimally necessary to develop physical and emotional well-being.

In its national incidence studies, the Department of Health and Human Services (1988, 1996) reported physical neglect to be the most frequent (43.0 percent of all cases) followed by inadequate supervision (36.6 percent) and failure or delay in providing health care (20.8 percent).

It can be difficult to determine when inadequate supervision becomes neglect. In many households where a single parent or both parents work, an older sibling is charged with supervising younger siblings after school, until a parent comes home from work. There is no hard-and-fast rule about the appropriate age for an older sibling to begin caring for younger siblings. A number of variables have to be considered, among them the safety of the environment, the number of siblings, and the maturity and intellectual level of the older sibling (Gaudin, 1993). Cultural differences are also a factor in determining the adequacy of a child's supervision. For example, in Latino families it is very much expected that the oldest female child will care for her younger siblings.

The Indicators of Neglect

There are certain characteristics in both children and parents that indicate neglect.

Children's Characteristics   Children experiencing physical neglect may manifest any of the following signs:

- Consistent hunger, and begging or stealing food
- Poor hygiene
- Inappropriate dress for the season
- Unattended physical problems
- Constant fatigue or listlessness, falling asleep in class
- Alcohol or drug use
- Delinquency (especially theft)
- Extended stays at school
- Early arrival to and late departure from school

Or a child may report that there is no one at home when he or she gets back from school.

Youngsters suffering from emotional neglect and maltreatment may show signs of the following:

- Speech disorders
- Lags in physical development
- Failure to thrive
- Habit disorders (biting, rocking, sucking)
- Conduct disorders (antisocial, destructive)
- Behavioral extremes (very compliant, passive, or shy, or very aggressive and demanding)
- Inappropriate (too adult or infantile) behaviors
- Suicidal tendencies

School personnel, especially classroom teachers, see students every day. They should all be trained to identify the signs of physical and emotional neglect and to refer students if necessary to the school counselor for assessment and services.

Parents' Characteristics   Neglectful parents may also manifest certain characteristics that should alert the counselor to the possibility of neglect:

- Failure to keep appointments
- Lack of cooperation with the school
- Misuse of alcohol or other drugs
- Leaving a child alone or unattended
- Giving a child inappropriate drink or medicine

- Failure to supervise a child's behavior
- Leaving a child isolated for long periods
- Severe criticism of a child
- Calling a child names, scaring or threatening the child, showing no affection for a child, or ignoring a child's bids for affection
- Refusing to listen or talk to the child

The Causes of Neglect

Certain stressors can increase the possibility of parents' neglecting their children. Among the most common are lack of parenting skills, loss of support systems, loss of employment, mental health problems, financial pressure, a history of neglect or maltreatment as a child, chaotic family life, and poor housing. Not all parents who experience these stressors are neglectful; in fact, most are not. But the more stress parents experience, the more likely they are to neglect their children.

Neglectful parents are not a homogenous group, and there is no single cause for inadequate parenting. Sources of stress are only part of the equation. Leading researchers in the field have come to understand parenting within a contextual framework and as a function of several interacting factors (Belsky, 1980; Bronfen-brenner, 1979; Garbarino, 1977). Belsky and Vondra (1989) suggested that parenting style is the result of three principal interacting and reciprocal factors:

- The parent's own developmental history and personality
- Characteristics of the child and family (the child's personality and the marital relationship)
- Environmental sources of stress and support (for example, work and social networks)

Figure 13.1 shows how these determinants of parenting are both interactive and reciprocal. A parent's developmental history influences his or her personality, which in turn influences parenting behavior. Parenting behavior influences the child's characteristics and development, which influence how the parent responds to the child. Finally, both the marital relationship and environmental factors influence and are influenced by the parent's personality; and both contribute to parenting behavior.

The Parent's Background and Personality   Studies have shown that parents who have unresolved feelings about inadequate care or abuse in their own childhood find it difficult to offer their children the nurturance that is fundamental to secure psychological attachment (Crittenden & Ainsworth, 1989; Pianta, Egeland, & Erickson, 1990). The result: A transgenerational cycle of neglect can develop. Not all mothers who were neglected as children are doomed to repeat the cycle of neglect. Certain factors are known to interrupt the cycle, among them fewer life stressors, physically healthier babies, quality relationships with husbands and boyfriends, and less-ambivalent feelings about the child's birth (Egeland & Erickson, 1990; Gaudin, 1993). Other studies suggest that character disorders (W. N. Frie-

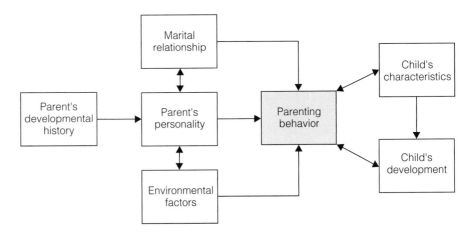

SOURCE: Adapted from Belsky (1984), p. 84. Copyright by the Society for Research in Child Development. Reprinted with permission.

FIGURE **13.1**

A PROCESS MODEL OF THE DETERMINANTS OF PARENTING BEHAVIOR

drich, Tyler, & Clark, 1985; Polansky, 1987), depression (Green, 1980; Zuravin, 1988), poor social skills (Azar, 1984; Larrance & Twentyman, 1983; Polansky, 1987), and substance abuse (Famularo, 1986; M. J. Martin & Walters, 1982) are major contributors to parental neglect.

Child and Family Characteristics   There is no evidence that certain characteristics of the child trigger neglect. Neglect is the product of parents' not attending to the needs of their children. But that lack of attention can produce certain behaviors in children—passiveness, withdrawal, aggressiveness—that do contribute to further neglect (Crittenden, 1988). Most neglected children come from large families headed by a single parent and marked by patterns of communications that are either infrequent or negative (Gaudin, 1993). For example, Polansky (1985, 1987) found that even after controlling for socioeconomic status, neglectful families had, on average, 3.5 more children than did families in which neglect was not a problem. Although neglect is more often a problem in single-parent families, a study of two-parent households in which children were neglected showed that the children tended to have different fathers, which created uncertainty about the family structure (Gaudin, 1993). Stigmatization and chaos are the enduring characteristics of neglectful families.

Environmental Factors   Neglectful parents are more likely to be unemployed, to live in poor neighborhoods, and to believe their community is not supportive; and they are less likely to be involved in religious or community organizations (Gaudin, 1993). In general, neglectful parents do not have informal support networks (Wolock & Horowitz, 1979), and their relatives tend to be more critical than supportive (Gaudin, 1991; Polansky, 1987). Families of color are overrepresented in statistics on neglect; but when socioeconomic status is controlled for, racial and ethnic differences disappear—a fact that suggests poverty, not race or ethnicity, is the overriding variable in situations of neglect (Kadushin, 1988).

The Consequences of Neglect

Like the consequences of physical abuse, the consequences of neglect are felt in both the short and long term. Caregiving that is hostile, rejecting, inconsistent, or inadequate (Gaudin, 1993) can leave young children unable to form attachments to others, anxious, and insecure (Crittenden & Ainsworth, 1989), and can severely threaten their sense of competence (Aber, 1989). Neglected children tend to be more passive and withdrawn in their interactions than are physically abused children, who are more active and aggressive (Hoffman-Plotkin & Twentyman, 1984). When they begin school, neglected children are less prepared for learning (Aber, 1989), manifest signs of inattentiveness, lack initiative and confidence, and have difficulties in comprehension (Egeland, 1988). Learning deficits become more apparent over time. In a comparison with youngsters who have been physically abused, neglected children were found to score lower in reading and math, have more language deficits, and have higher rates of absenteeism and grade repeats (Wodarski, 1990). And in adolescence, neglected children have higher rates of juvenile delinquency than do youngsters who have not been neglected (Widom, 1989a).

The good news is that if the home life of neglected children is stabilized, the negative effects of maltreatment can be modified somewhat (Kurtz, Gaudin, Howing, & Wodarski, 1993). Schools can play a significant role in the lives of neglected children by offering a stable and structured environment to counteract the lack of stability and structure in the home environment. But school counselors also must make sure that everything possible is being done to stabilize the home environment by helping families access needed services and support. Less successful here are parenting workshops, a function of parents' reluctance to admit their neglect.

SEXUAL ABUSE

Child sexual abuse is not the most common form of child maltreatment in this country, but it has become a national issue. So much so that federal legislation was passed in 1996 requiring that the states make available information about convicted sex offenders who, having served their sentences and living anywhere, could pose a threat to a community's children.[9]

---

[9]The national law was modeled after New Jersey's Megan's Law, which requires the police to go door to door in a neighborhood to alert families that a sexual predator has moved into the area. More information about these laws and sex offender registration laws are available online at www .parentsformeganslaw.com.

Legal and Operational Perspectives on Child Sexual Abuse

Child sexual abuse laws are both civil (designed to protect children) and criminal (designed to prohibit certain acts and to punish offenders) (Faller, 1993). Civil laws generally apply to children's caregivers; these are the laws that mandate that school counselors and other professionals report suspected or confirmed cases of child sexual abuse. State civil laws are based on the Child Abuse Prevention and Treatment Act.

The states are also responsible for criminal laws governing child sexual abuse. The laws usually categorize offenses by severity: from sexual misconduct (fondling a child or photographing a child in a sexually explicit pose) to rape, sodomy, sexual abuse, and incest. Also factors in determining the severity of a sex crime are the child's age, the degree of force used, and the relationship between offender and victim (Faller, 1993).

Beyond reporting rules, the terms of child sexual abuse laws have no bearing on the work school counselors do with victims. Their concern, and the basis of deciding among interventions, is the degree of trauma inflicted on the child by the sexual abuse. At work here are three significant variables (Faller, 1993):

- The *power differential* describes the control one party (the offender) has over the other party (the victim) by means of relationship (father, uncle, older brother), authority (teacher, minister, youth group leader), size, or psychological superiority (the offender is able to manipulate the victim).
- The *knowledge differential* describes the difference between the offender's understanding of the significance and implications of the sexual encounter, and the victim's understanding of that encounter. In large part, knowledge is a function of age.[10] In general, the younger the victim and the greater the age differential, the more serious the trauma.
- The third variable is the *gratification differential.* In most sexual abuse cases, the offender is attempting to gratify him- or herself at the expense of the victim. There is no mutual pleasure or satisfaction. This difference in gratification increases the traumatic effect of sexual abuse on children. Some perpetrators need to convince themselves that their victims are actually enjoying the abuse, and use intimidation or force to make their victim admit such gratification.

The Myths

To work effectively with students who have been sexually abused, school counselors must understand not only the trauma involved in the abuse but also the reality of the abusive act. That means being able to distinguish between truth and fiction. Cole (1995) articulated six myths surrounding sexual abuse:

---

[10]The courts would consider a sexual act between a 12-year-old and an 18-year-old more serious than a sexual act between a 12-year-old and a 14-year old. An age differential of more than five years is usually considered predatory.

Incest rarely occurs; but when it does, it is found mainly among poorly edu-cated families of lower socioeconomic status. Child sexual abuse cuts across socioeconomic boundaries. Unlike cases of child neglect, poor children are no more at risk than other children.

Child molesters are sexually attracted to their victims. The key issues in child sexual molestation are power and control, not sexual gratification.

Most child molesters are strangers; their victims do not know them. Most molestation occurs between a parent and a child.

Child sexual abuse is a modern phenomenon, a by-product of the sexual revo-lution. Child sexual molestation is not new; the public's awareness and mandatory requirements for reporting abuse are new. The phenomenon has nothing to do with the sexual revolution: again, the motivation is around power and control more than sexual pleasure.

The sexual abuse of a child is usually a single violent incident. Most child molesters follow a pattern of sexual abuse with their victims over time.

Children frequently make up stories about engaging in sexual activity with adults. Although there is a trend of late to question the credibility of chil-dren who report sexual abuse, most reports by young people are true. Cer-tainly some children do recant, most likely out of fear. But the majority of false reports are instigated by adults who are using the children for their own purposes—to gain custody of a child in a divorce case, for example.

By recognizing these myths, school counselors are less likely to deny the real pos-sibility that students are being sexually abused.

The Risk Factors

Research consistently indicates that preadolescent children (ages 8 to 12) are most at risk for sexual abuse (Finkelhor, 1984; D. E. Russell, 1983; Kendall-Tackett, Meyer-Williams, & Finkelhor, 2001; Wyatt, 1985). Vulnerability increases at age 6 or 7, but the most dramatic increase is at age 10 (the risk drops off after age 12) (Finkelhor & Baron, 1986; Finkelhor, Hotaling, Lewis, & Smith, 1990). And again, girls are four times more likely than boys to be sexually abused. In addition to age and gender, the only other factors strongly associated with child sexual abuse are related to the family. Risk factors include families without a natural father, families in which the mother is employed outside the home, families in which parental con-flict is common, and families in which children have a poor relationship with their parents.

For school counselors, especially those working in middle schools, the crucial factor is age.

The Indicators of Child Sexual Abuse

According to Faller (1993), the indicators of child sexual abuse can be either sex-ual or nonsexual—although they are more likely to be sexual—and vary by the child's age. Table 13.2 lists Faller's indicators. Notice that there are only three sex-

TABLE 13.2   **INDICATORS OF SEXUAL ABUSE**

Age Group	Sexual Indicators	Nonsexual Indicators
Young children (up to age 10)	Statements that include precocious sexual knowledge	Sleep disturbances
		Enuresis and encopresis
	Sexually explicit drawings (that are not open to interpretation)	Fear of being left alone
		Fear of the alleged offender
	Sexual interactions with others (e.g., sexual aggression toward younger children, sexual activity with peers, or sexual gestures or invitations to older persons)	Fear of a specific type of person
		Fire setting (especially in boys)
		Cruelty to animals (especially in boys)
	Sexual interactions involving animals or toys	Role reversal in the family or pseudomaturity
	Excessive masturbation (e.g., many times a day, compulsively, with objects, with groaning, moaning, or thrusting motions)	Problems with peers
		Sudden changes in behavior
	Avoids being touched	Impulsivity
	Unwilling to submit to physical examinations	Distractibility, difficulty concentrating
Older children (over age 10)	Sexual promiscuity	Unwilling to change for gym or participate in activities
	Being sexually victimized by peers or non-family members	Withdrawal, fantasy, or infantile behavior
	Adolescent prostitution	Poor peer relationships
		Delinquent or running away from home
		Eating disturbances
		Depression
		Self-destructive behavior (suicidal gestures or attempts, self-mutilation)
		Substance abuse

SOURCE: Adapted from Faller (1993).

ual indicators in older children. Many indicators of sexual activity in adolescents are normal. Of the three, adolescent prostitution is the strongest indicator. Faller (1990) found that 90 percent of female adolescent prostitutes had been sexually abused. Little research has been done on male adolescent prostitutes, but anecdotal information suggests that they too have high rates of sexual abuse (Campagna & Poffenberger, 1988).

In addition, Faller identified a number of physical indicators of sexual abuse:

- Difficulty walking or sitting
- Pain or itching in the genital area
- Bruises on or bleeding from the penis, vagina, or anal area
- Venereal disease

These indicators are found in younger and older children. Pregnancy, of course, is an indicator in older children.

Although the primary indicators of sexual abuse are visible in children who have been abused, sometime a parent's or caregiver's behaviors can raise suspicion of sexual abuse. Among those indicators are

- being overprotective or jealous of the child.
- failing to keep appointments.
- unwillingness to cooperate.
- discouraging social contacts.
- using different medical facilities.
- keeping the child confined to home for long periods.

Clearly there are a good many indicators of sexual abuse. Counselors should focus on the sexual indicators; a number of the nonsexual indicators can also be symptomatic of other problems. And the most important indicator of all is children's own reports of sexual abuse.

The Effects of Child Sexual Abuse

Finkelhor and Browne (1985, 1986) proposed a conceptual model, a highly regarded explanation of how sexual abuse affects the lives of children in the near and the long term. The model describes the effects of child sexual abuse along four dimensions: traumatic sexualization, betrayal, powerlessness, and stigmatization.

Traumatic Sexualization   *Traumatic sexualization* "refers to a process in which a child's sexuality (including both sexual feelings and attitudes) is shaped in a developmentally inappropriate and interpersonally dysfunctional fashion as a result of sexual abuse" (Finkelhor & Browne, 1985, p. 531). For example, if the offender rewards the child for sexual behavior, the child learns to use sexual behavior as a way of manipulating others to satisfy his or her developmental needs. The dysfunction can also be the result of the offender's fetishizing certain parts of the child's body, the association of frightening memories with sexual activity, and the confusion about sexual behavior and morality usually communicated to the child by the offender. The degree of sexual traumatization depends on a number of variables, including the child's age, the kind of sexual abuse, and the duration of the abuse. Still, all children who have been traumatically sexualized "emerge from their experiences with inappropriate repertoires of sexual behavior, with confusions and misconceptions about their sexual self-concepts, and with unusual emotional associations to sexual activities" (p. 531).

The effects of traumatic sexualization in children and adolescents are the sexual indicators listed in Table 13.2. In adults, traumatic sexualization can result in an aversion to sex, flashbacks to the molestation, difficulties with arousal and orgasm, vaginismus, and negative attitudes toward sexuality (Beitchman et al., 1992; Burgess & Holmstrom, Groth, & Sgroi, 1978; B. Steele & Alexander, 1981; Tsai & Wagner, 1978). All of this leaves the victims of child sexual abuse—now adults—confused about the role of sex in intimate relationships.

Betrayal   The victims of child sexual abuse feel betrayed: Often, someone they trusted and even depended on harmed them, assaulted their body and their dignity.[11] The sense of betrayal can extend to other family members who did not protect them from the abuse. And if the nonoffending caregiver responds to the disclosure of abuse by refusing to believe the child, blaming the child, or even ostracizing the child—as is common—the child's sense of betrayal is even greater.

In children and adolescents, betrayal can produce delinquent and antisocial behaviors. In adults, the manifestation of betrayal can take the form of bad judgment about the trustworthiness of others (Caffaro-Rouget, Lang, & vanSanten, 1989; B. Steele & Alexander, 1981). A number of studies have found that female victims of incest are vulnerable to abusive relationships (Corwin, 1989; De Young, 1982; Fromuth, 1983; Seidner & Calhoun, 1984). The sense of betrayal can also result in hostility, anger, an aversion to intimate relationships, and, in women, antipathy toward men. This negativity serves as a protective shield against future betrayals.

Powerlessness   Child sexual abuse renders the victim powerless: The child's body is being violated, and the child can do nothing to stop it. The child's sense of powerlessness increases when the offender uses force, threats, or manipulation to carry out the abuse. It also increases when the child's reports of sexual abuse are not believed or are met with anger and blame. The child feels trapped, fearing both further abuse and the consequences of disclosure. The silver lining here: When the child is able to end the abuse, the sense of disempowerment can become a sense of empowerment.

The effects of powerlessness are fear, anxiety, and lack of self-efficacy and coping skills (Finkelhor & Browne, 1985, 1986). In younger children, the anxiety is manifested in nightmares, phobias, hypervigilance, clinging behavior, and somatic complaints, symptoms that can extend into adolescence and adulthood. In older children and adults, the lack of self-efficacy and coping skills is associated with despair, depression, suicidality, learning problems, running away, and employment difficulties. Some victims of child sexual abuse compensate for their sense of powerlessness with an exaggerated need to control and dominate others. They may even bully and abuse others as a way to regain the control and power taken from them by their own abusers (Finkelhor & Browne, 1985).

Stigmatization   Stigmatization is the negative self-image the child develops in response to feelings of shame and guilt. It is not unusual for abusers to blame or demean their victims, or to swear them to secrecy, which increases their feelings of shame and guilt. Also a factor here is the reaction of adults to the disclosure of incest or abuse: If adults react with shock and horror, the victims' shame and guilt are exacerbated. Children who are blamed for the abuse are stigmatized much more than those who are told again and again that it was not their fault. That's an important fact for school counselors to remember: They must communicate strongly and often to the victims that the abuse is not their fault. Stigmatization can result in the victims' feeling isolated, turning to alcohol and drugs, and becoming involved in criminal activity and prostitution. Severely low self-esteem can follow these victims

---

[11] The sense of betrayal is strongest when the offender is a family member but can also be felt toward a stranger who seduced the child through trickery.

into adulthood. They may feel damaged and dirty, and believe that no one can truly want or care for them.

ASSESSING THE NEED FOR A REPORT

Most state laws require a "reasonable suspicion" as the foundation for making a report of child abuse. School counselors are not responsible for investigating the abuse or establishing proof that abuse has taken place; they simply have to suspect abuse. In some cases the need for a report is obvious: The child has revealed the abuse to the counselor or the signs of abuse and neglect are clear. But more often than not, the signs of abuse are not clear. In these cases the counselor must interview the child to establish reasonable suspicion.

> *I will never forget an eighth grader who was brought to my attention by a teacher. The student had bruises on her temples, and I knew that her family was not stable. When I asked about the bruises, she told me that she'd hurt herself using a curling iron. When I pressed her, she denied the bruises were the result of physical abuse. I kept tabs on the student for several days, as the bruises faded. During that time I also talked with several female colleagues who confirmed that using a curling iron could lead to bruising. And when I questioned the youngster again, she again denied that she had been hit. In the end, I decided not to make a report. Even today, years later, I wonder if that was the right decision.*

If the interview with the student does not resolve a counselor's questions about the possibility of abuse, it is a good idea for the counselor to consult with his or her colleagues. If that doesn't clarify the situation, then grounds exist for reasonable suspicion, and a report must be filed (Remley & Fry, 1993). School counselors must remember that the burden of proof is *not* on them, that the laws mandating reports were designed in part to relieve counselors of responsibility for deciding whether to report suspected abuse or not. The basic rule here: *When in doubt, report.*

Interviewing the Child

When school counselors interview a student about the possibility of abuse, the goal is to gather information to support a reasonable suspicion of abuse, not to establish proof of abuse (Wilder, 1991). The interview should be held in a private location, a place the child perceives as safe, and there should be no interruptions (Wilder, 1991). Both the counselor's demeanor and the surroundings should make the child feel safe. Even if a teacher or someone else has brought the child to the counselor's attention, just the counselor and the child should be present during the interview. A number of adults in the room can overwhelm the child and increase anxiety.

As a general rule, the counselor should avoid asking leading questions. The more open ended the questions, the more confidence the counselor can have in the child's responses. Faller (1993) and J. Myers (1992) suggested several interview strategies:

Use general questions to start. For example, a good first question is "Do you have any idea why I asked you to come and see me?" A less-helpful beginning would be "Your teacher is concerned that you are being abused at home. Are you being abused in any way?" This question is leading; it also is abrupt, which can make the child feel insecure and less willing to share.

Use focused questions to build on the child's answers to general questions. Focused questions—on people, circumstances, and, in the case of suspected sexual abuse, on body parts—are the most productive; they elicit the most information (Faller, 1993). "How do your parents punish you?" is a good focused question when the counselor suspects physical abuse. "Is there anything your mother's boyfriend does with you that you don't like?" is an example of a focused question when sexual abuse is suspected. Both of these questions focus on people. "What happens when you disobey your parents?" or "What do you do when your uncle baby-sits you?" are questions that focus on circumstances. Questions focused on body parts are usually asked in the context of children's drawings, which we talk about below.

Almost always use open-ended questions. At the outset, the counselor should not ask multiple-choice questions. Once a child has revealed abuse, multiple-choice questions can be helpful in gaining information about the circumstances of the abuse (Faller, 1993). Questions that can be answered yes or no are never a good idea because a child might answer yes or no to a question that he or she really does not understand. And again, leading questions are coercive: They come from the interviewer's interpretation of things, which can influence the child's interpretation.

The child's verbal responses to the counselor are important. Also important is the child's body language during the interview (Hackbarth-James & Burch, 1999). Any nonverbal indication of extreme discomfort, avoidance, or embarrassment should be cause for concern.

The disclosure of sexual abuse by children is generally a five-phase process: (1) denial, (2) tentative disclosure, (3) active disclosure, (4) recantation, and (5) reaffirmation (Sorenson & Snow, 1991). School counselors do not need not wait for active disclosure to make a report to child protective services; reasonable suspicion is enough. Furthermore, counselors should not consider denial or recantation sufficient grounds for not making a report. Other evidence can be a factor here too—sometimes just a gut feeling. If the gray area continues to be gray, the counselor needs to make a report.

Sexualized Behaviors and Drawings

Teachers should notice and tell the school counselor about children's sexualized behaviors or drawings. The counselor then interviews the child to determine whether behaviors or drawings are indicative of sexual abuse.

TABLE 13.3   **SEXUAL DEVELOPMENT AND BEHAVIORS IN CHILDREN**

	Ages		
	0–4 Years	**5–7 Years**	**8–12 Years**
Sexual development	Limited peer contact	Increased peer contact	Increased peer contact
	Self-exploration	Experimental interactions	Experimental interactions
	Self-stimulation	Inhibition	Disinhibition/inhibition
	Disinhibition		
Sexual behaviors	Touches/rubs own genitals (random)	Touches self (specific)	Touches self/others
	Watches, pokes	Watches, asks	Mooning
	Shows genitals	Inhibited (privacy)	Exhibitionistic
	Interested/asks about bathroom functions	Repulsed by/drawn to opposite sex	Kissing/dating
	Uses dirty language	Tells dirty jokes	Petting
	Plays house—mom/dad	Plays house	Touches others' genitals
	Plays doctor (imitative)	Kissing, holding hands	Dry humping
	May insert/stops with pain	May mimic/practice	Digital or vaginal intercourse or oral sex in adolescents

SOURCE: *Sexualized Children: Assessment and Treatment of Sexualized Children and Children Who Molest* by Eliana Gil and Toni Cavanaugh Johnson, 1993, p. 26, Royal Oak, MI: Self-Esteem Shop. Copyright 1993 by Launch Press. Reprinted with permission.

Appropriate versus Inappropriate Child Sexual Behavior   Certain sexual behaviors in young children are perfectly normal. For example, until age 5, children explore their bodies. They may participate in sexual games (playing doctor, for example) and even fondle another child's genitals (Gil & Johnson, 1993; Hackbarth-James & Burch, 1999). After age 5, children tend to become more modest, but they remain curious about human anatomy (Hilman & Solek-Tefft, 1988). Masturbatory activity continues but tends to be done in private. By age 8 or 9, children become quite secretive about sex, and their behavior discreet. Between ages 8 and 12, children begin to experiment sexually by touching, kissing, or petting with a partner (Table 13.3).

Children's sexual play is more symptomatic of abuse when it has the qualities of power and aggression (Dubowitz, Black, Harrington, & Verschoore, 1993; Gil, 1991); is excessive and compulsive (White & Allers, 1994); and is developmentally inappropriate (Sigelman & Shaffer, 1995). Posttraumatic sexual play is anxious, less elaborate, joyless, and constrictive (a single theme is repeated constantly) (Hackbarth-James & Burch, 1999). Gil and Johnson (1993) suggested that counselors consider children's age, size, status, and type of sexual activity to distinguish between age-appropriate sexual play and behavior that is symptomatic of abuse. Differences in age, size, and status all speak to the power differential in sexual play.

When the age difference between two children engaged in sexual play is more than three years, there is cause for concern. Noticeable disparities in size—one child towers over the other, for example—could indicate sexual play that is aggressive and coercive. The same is true for differences in status: an older sibling, for example, who is put in charge of a younger sibling. If the type of sexual activity is not age appropriate, there is a strong possibility of sexual abuse.

Sexualized Drawings   The use of children's drawings in counseling is a widely accepted practice (Powell & Faherty, 1990). Young children especially are more likely to express emotional conflict in art rather than words.

School counselors generally obtain students' drawings from teachers or by asking students, individually or in a group, to make a drawing. The directions can be general or specific. For example, a counselor might ask students to draw whatever is on their minds. Or the counselor could ask the students to draw a picture of their family or of themselves with their father, or of a specific situation—what they do with their family at night or how their family acts (Sadowski & Loesch, 1993).

The interpretation of drawings for clinical diagnoses has a long history in counseling and psychology. Attempts at standardizing the interpretation of house–tree–person drawings, a typical tool in psychological evaluation, have been met with the argument that these drawings cannot and should not be standardized. Certainly school counselors should not be using students' drawings for diagnostic purposes; but they can be useful in determining a reasonable suspicion of sexual abuse.

What should the school counselor look for in a student's drawing? Sadowski and Loesch (1993) suggested starting with the gestalt of the drawing: What does the drawing as a whole say? What words or scenes does it depict? How does it make the counselor feel? Then the counselor should look at the details of the drawing. Is something out of place? Is something overemphasized or underemphasized? Drawings of human figures are especially telling:

- The size and placement of the figures can indicate the child's sense of self-importance.
- The facial expression and affect—tears, frowns, and inappropriate smiles—can indicate underlying conflict.
- Too much hair or the absence of hair indicates a preoccupation with virility, and sexual anxiety, confusion or inadequacy (Ogdon, 1981; Wohl & Kaufman, 1985).[12]
- The treatment of hands in children's drawings expresses their sense of their ability to cope with their environment. The omission of hands symbolizes their lack of control over situations and events (Klepsch & Logie, 1982); an overemphasis on hands suggests anxiety or guilt about sexual behaviors (Sadowski & Loesch, 1993).
- The omission of the lower body is open to two interpretations: Because the lower body supports the upper body, the omission of the lower body could symbolize the child's helplessness or lack of support. Or the omission could

---

[12] In this context, hair is a symbol of masculinity.

TABLE 13.4   INDICATORS OF SEXUAL ABUSE IN HUMAN FIGURE DRAWINGS

Feature	Characteristic	Indication
Eyes	Without pupils Abnormally small Hidden by glasses Totally omitted	Sexual arousal, guilt, shame
Nose	Overemphasized by size or linear contrast	Phallic preoccupation
Mouth	Overly large Emphasized by dark lines Totally omitted	Abused area
Neck	Overemphasized, elongated	Difficulty in maintaining control of sexuality
Midsection	Heavily shaded belt or other emphatic object	Abused area
Genitals	Presence of beings or objects that resemble genitalia Overly detailed Graphic depiction Overemphasized in size Totally omitted	Abused area
Arms/legs	Totally omitted	Helplessness
Figure	Surrounded or enclosed with dark, heavy lines	Entrapment
Color	Red, sickly yellow-green	Anger, fear, dread

SOURCE: "Evidence of Sexual Abuse in Children's Art Products" by R. J. Riordan and A. C. Verdel, 1991, *The School Counselor, 39*, p.119. Copyright 1991 by the American School Counselor Association. Reprinted with permission.

be a denial of the genital area, a coping mechanism of sorts for abuse (Malchiodi, 1990).

- Attention to the midsection of the body—an emphasis on zippers, belts, and belt buckles, for example—could manifest an unusual interest in sex or a psychological conflict about sexuality (Sadowski & Loesch, 1993).
- Even shading—darkened areas of the drawing—can imply anxiety, preoccupation, or fixation. Shading of the genital area is a special cause for concern about possible sexual abuse.

Finally, phallic symbols—chimneys on houses, telephone poles, trees—may be indicative of concerns about sexuality (Hammer, 1988).

Table 13.4 is a summary of the indicators of possible sexual abuse in human figure drawings. If a child's drawing shows one or more indicators, the counselor should follow up by interviewing the child.

The Role of Parents

In making the decision to report reasonable suspicion of child abuse, there is little to be gained in talking with a child's parents. If a child is being abused at home and the parent is aware of it or is the actual perpetrator, he or she likely will deny the abuse. Denial also is the usual response when a child is being abused and the parent is not aware of it. The fact of the matter is that wanting to talk with the parents means the counselor suspects abuse, and that is sufficient grounds to simply make a report.

Once the report has been made, CPS workers notify the parents. But if the counselor knows the parents well and feels comfortable informing them that a report has been made, then the counselor should do so—at least in the case of physical abuse or neglect.[13]

> *In my years as a school counselor, the best scenario in a case of suspected child abuse involved my making a report and then meeting with the parents and telling them that the report had to be made. I would explain exactly what was going to happen in the next 48 hours and that they should look on this intervention as an opportunity to get help. I would emphasize that the purpose of the report and the investigation was not to punish them but to help them and their child. Most parents seemed to understand. And our meeting helped them see the school less as an enemy and more as their advocate.*

After a report of suspected abuse has been made, the school counselor, fearing for the child's safety, may be reluctant to allow the student to return home. Safety is a particular concern in cases of severe physical abuse or sexual abuse. If a report is made early in the school day, the counselor can demand that a CPS worker come to the school and interview the child to determine whether an emergency placement is needed. The CPS worker then deals with the family. In cases of serious abuse, the police are usually involved too, because an arrest may have to be made.

If the report is made late in the day and there are safety concerns, the child should be kept at school until a CPS worker arrives. If the parent calls the school wanting to know the child's whereabouts, he or she should be told the truth: "Your child is being held at school because we had to file a report of suspected abuse. We are waiting for a child protective services worker to come to the school, after which you will be contacted about your child." The school counselor (or a designated adult) must remain with the child until a representative from CPS arrives to interview the child. If the parent asks to come to the school and see the child, it's best to say no. This is a highly charged situation as is. If the parent becomes hostile and threatens to come to the school anyway, the police should be called.

Most important, the school counselor must be extremely sensitive to the student's fears and anxieties. The counselor should explain to the child as clearly as possible what is going to happen in the next few hours. And because the child is probably thinking it was a mistake to tell anyone about the abuse, the counselor

---

[13] Some would argue that it is not a good idea to inform the family that a report of any type of abuse has been made, that the counselor should just let CPS authorities take over. In our experience, when the issue is sexual abuse, it probably is best not to inform the alleged perpetrator that a report has been made. The investigation in cases of sexual abuse is much more invasive than are investigations of other types of abuse; and the perpetrator's anger could well put the counselor at risk of physical injury.

must continuously reinforce to the child that he or she did the right thing, that what was done to the child was not right, that the commotion is about protecting the child and being sure that no harm will come to the child. Empathic listening is especially important in this situation, as is validating the child's feelings.

CHILD ABUSE PREVENTION

Child abuse prevention programs have been in the schools since the 1970s. Today approximately 65 percent of American schoolchildren have been part of a child abuse prevention program (Finkelhor & Dziuba-Leatherman, 1995), and about 88 percent of elementary school districts in the nation offer some sort of child abuse prevention program to their students (Breen, Daro, & Romano, 1991). Yet despite the popularity of these programs, there are few empirical studies to support their effectiveness (Ko & Cosden, 2001). The studies that have looked at child abuse prevention programs, like studies of other prevention programs, tend to focus on comparisons of pre- and postprogram tests of children's knowledge about abuse and abuse prevention (Dhooper & Schneider, 1995; Hazzaard, 1993; Reppucci, Land, & Haugaard, 1998). Whether the change in knowledge also results in behavioral change has largely gone unexamined. One study did attempt to look at the relationship between knowledge about child abuse and behavior. In that study, Finkelhor, Asdigian, and Dzuiba-Leatherman (1995a, 1995b) found the following:

- Those youngsters who participate in child abuse prevention programs know more about the concepts of prevention and abuse than those who do not participate.
- There is no correlation between participating in a program and the incidence of victimization.
- Program participants are more likely to use recommended strategies (yelling, telling others, and the like); but no correlation was found between the use of those strategies and reduction in the seriousness of assault.
- Program participants are more likely to believe that their actions protect them from more-serious consequences.
- Program participants are more likely to disclose an incident of abuse and less likely to blame themselves for the abuse.

Today, child abuse prevention programs—especially those oriented toward sexual abuse—focus on the family, a response to data that show the victimizer is most often a family member or someone known to the child. Both Wolf (1993) and Daro (1993) found that programs that support parents through home visits and that provide modeling and information are the most promising. Ko and Cosden (2001) reported that children abused by a family member are less successful at employing strategies from school-based child abuse prevention programs than are children who are abused by strangers. In light of the research, school-based prevention programs must look to identify and involve parents and siblings from at-risk families.

The Goals of Child Sexual Abuse Prevention Programs

Child sexual abuse prevention programs have two fundamental goals: to keep abuse from occurring and to encourage disclosure of past and ongoing sexual abuse (Reppucci & Haugaard, 1989). To meet these goals, the programs share many of the following objectives:

- The distinctions among good, bad and questionable touching
- The rights of children to control who touches their bodies and where they are touched
- The importance of the child's telling a responsible adult if someone inappropriately touches the child, even if the child was told not to reveal the incident
- Assertiveness skills, ranging from repeatedly saying "no" to the use of self-defense techniques (for example, yelling, kicking, fighting back)
- The existence of support systems to help the child who has experienced any form of maltreatment (Daro & Salmon-Cox, 1994, pp. 1–2)

The curricula for child sexual abuse prevention programs vary according to the participants' age and cognitive level. The material can be presented in books (comic books for young children), videotapes, and theatrical and puppet shows. Also varying among programs are the methods for teaching about sexual abuse. For example, some teach children to distinguish between good touching and bad touching, while others tell children that what feels wrong is wrong. Some programs use anatomically correct names for body parts, while others talk about *private parts* or *parts covered by a bathing suit.*

There is some debate about whether these programs should be taught by school personnel (teachers, counselors, social workers, school nurses) or by a child abuse specialist brought into the school from the community (Daro & Salmon-Cox, 1994). Because of their training in tough-to-talk-about issues, school counselors ought to be involved in facilitating child sexual abuse prevention programs. Even if classes are taught by someone else, the program should be part of the comprehensive developmental guidance curriculum.

Another goal of programs to prevent child sexual abuse is the inclusion of parents, either as participants with their children or in special workshops. It is also important to keep parents informed about the content of the school's program. The better their understanding of the program, the less likely parents are to be anxious about their child's participation. Of course informing parents about the prevention program also runs the risk of having parents who are victimizers prevent their children from taking part in the program.

School counselors can expect some resistance to including a child sexual abuse prevention program as part of developmental guidance. Parents and even school personnel may argue that these programs scare children or encourage them to make false accusations (Daro & Salmon-Cox, 1994). There is evidence that some children do worry about sexual abuse after taking part in a prevention program (Finkelhor, Asdigian, & Dzuiba-Leatherman, 1993; Garbarino, 1987; Reppucci & Haugaard, 1989). But one study indicated that these same children are most likely to utilize the strategies they've learned (Finkelhor, Asdigian, & Dzuiba-Leatherman, 1993).

And anxiety would be a natural response among abused youngsters who are struggling with the need for disclosure that is such an integral part of the prevention taught in these programs (Garbarino, 1987). In response to the second objection, again false accusations are rare, and there is little evidence of children's misinterpreting appropriate adult–child contact as sexual abuse (Conte, 1986).

Choosing a Program

There are several abuse prevention programs from which school counselors can choose. Almost all programs have four basic elements: (1) awareness of body parts; (2) development of decision-making skills; (3) assertiveness training; and (4) how and where to get help (Vernon & Hay, 1988). Research over the years suggests that certain components of child abuse prevention programs are especially helpful in preventing sexual abuse:

- Behavioral rehearsal of prevention strategies
- Curricula tailored to each age group's cognitive characteristics and learning ability
- Material presented in a stimulating and varied manner
- Generic concepts such as assertive behavior and communications skills which children can use in everyday situations, not just to fend off abuse
- Emphasis on the need for children to tell every time someone touches them in a way that makes them feel uneasy
- Longer programs that are better integrated into school curricula (Daro & Salmon-Cox, 1994, p. 7)

School counselors need to remember that school-based prevention programs alone cannot prevent child abuse. By establishing links with parents and community, programs can reach both potential victims and perpetrators.

The School Counselor and Child Abuse Prevention

Besides advocating for and implementing a child abuse prevention program, what else can school counselors do to help protect students from abuse? The following are suggestions for complementing the prevention program: [14]

- Provide in-service training to school personnel with the goals of helping teachers distinguish between normal sexual development and symptoms of sexual abuse and of providing them with an understanding of state laws and reporting procedures.
- Establish a good relationship with local CPS workers. This will make the processes of reporting abuse and following up easier.
- Have a liaison in the community who is a specialist in issues of sexual abuse. School counselors can benefit from the wisdom and experiences of other counselors who have expertise in this area.

---

[14] These suggestions were adapted from Hackbarth-James and Burch (1999) and Wilder (1991).

- Establish a good referral network for parents concerned about abuse. Many parents—including the spouses of sexually abusive parents—are relieved to know where and how to get help for their child.
- Have visible in the school counseling office materials that deal with issues of abuse and trauma.
- Maintain accurate records of students' reports of abuse, and keep them in a confidential file.

ETHICAL AND LEGAL ISSUES

School counselors, like other professionals who work with children, by law must report suspected child abuse. Often they are the appointed liaison between the school and child protective services, which can mean that all child abuse reports are made through the school counselor. That's not a bad thing. Although some might argue that the professional who suspects the abuse—usually the teacher—should make the report, teachers may feel uncomfortable with or insecure about the procedure, which could lead them to put off reporting. By giving teachers a resource, someone they can go to to discuss the situation who will then make a report, teachers are less likely to minimize or ignore a possible problem.

> *I still remember the first child abuse reports I made as a school counselor. I was filled with anxiety, feeling that what I was doing was not quite right. As time went on and I came to understand the reasons for mandated child abuse reporting, my resistance and anxiety disappeared. In time I also was better able to comfort frightened children and deal with their angry parents.*

Most states have enacted laws that protect the anonymity of those who are mandated to report suspected child abuse. The laws are designed to reduce fear of reprisals from angry parents or caregivers, and so to reduce the reporter's reluctance to act. Despite the legal protection, in time the parents or caregivers are likely to discover who instigated the report. Fear of reprisal is no excuse for failing to make a report of suspected child abuse. If the counselor believes that he or she is in some kind of danger, the police should be notified.

> *A number of years ago, a colleague made a report of suspected abuse. A day or two later, the child's father stormed into the school, found the counselor in her office, and threatened her. The next morning, several parents from the neighborhood alerted the school that the father had been out on the streets the night before trying to buy a gun. Although no direct link could be established between the father's looking for a gun and the counselor's being in danger, the information was enough for the school district to transfer my colleague to another school. She returned six months later.*

The primary reason to report suspected abuse is to protect the child. But school counselors should also know that all states penalize professionals who fail to report suspected child abuse. The penalties can be criminal or civil or both (Remley & Fry, 1993). For example, if a child is harmed after the abuse should have been obvious to professionals working with the child, those professionals could be sued for negligence. Some may remember the infamous case of Lisa Steinberg, an elementary school student in New York City, who eventually died from the physical abuse inflicted on her by her father. During the lengthy criminal and civil trials, many wondered how the abuse, which had gone on for years, went unnoticed by school personnel and other professionals involved in Lisa's life. The commission established to investigate the child's death did not take disciplinary action against the teachers who had ignored her bruises and disheveled appearance. But Lisa died in 1987, at a time when school personnel received little or no training in the detection of child abuse, and reporting suspected abuse was not mandatory. The commission felt it would be scapegoating certain individuals for what its members concluded were failures of the system (LISA Organization to Stop Child Abuse, 1989). It was in response to that finding, that schools instituted training for teachers and other staff members and states across the nation revamped and greatly improved their system for reporting child abuse.

CONCLUSION

The sad fact of our wealthy and sophisticated society is that far too many children are neglected and abused. Because schools are the first to confront the problem, the actions of school personnel determine whether children and families receive needed help. That simple fact is key. Child abuse is an offense to civil society. It horrifies us. We don't want to think about it; we find ourselves wishing it out of existence. But if school counselors allow themselves to deny the problem, if they refuse to deal directly and professionally with the problem, they leave children vulnerable, with no protection or support. And that is ethically and legally wrong.

Reporting suspected child abuse is an essential part of the school counselor's job; so is advocating for and implementing school-based prevention programs. Here their training in dealing with the unmentionable stands school counselors in good stead. They can talk honestly and frankly about the need for prevention programs, and they can matter-of-factly teach children to recognize, avoid, and take action when faced with abuse. The skills children need to protect themselves are life skills, skills they can draw on into adulthood. There is no better gift school counselors can give them.

QUESTIONS FOR DISCUSSION

1. As a school counselor, what difficulties do you anticipate in dealing with cases of suspected child abuse? What do you sense within yourself that could be an obstacle to dealing forthrightly with cases of suspected child abuse?

2. Many immigrant parents are not accustomed to the laws in this country that allow the government to intrude on what they see as private family matters. As a school counselor, what could you do to help these parents understand that how they discipline their children is also the business of the state?

3. It is your first year working as a school counselor. You believe you have cause to report a case of suspected child abuse, but the principal of your school tells you not to do so. What would you do?

4. A sixth grader has just revealed to you that her stepfather touches her inappropriately. When you tell her that you are going to have to report the abuse to the authorities, she gets frantic and pleads with you not to do so, saying over and over that she is going to get into big trouble. How would you calm the child down? Would her fears change your decision to report the abuse? With a partner, taking turns as counselor and student, role-play the situation.

5. The secrecy, denial, confusion, collusion, and recantation around children's reports of sexual abuse are well documented. How would you handle the case of a child who first reveals sexual abuse and then denies it? To what degree, if any, would you involve the parents to confirm your suspicions?

6. Some youngsters who are sexually abused at home are removed and placed in foster care, which can create new problems for them. To what degree would this knowledge influence your decision to make a report of suspected abuse? Explain your answer.

7. Parents can be adamant that their children not participate in programs to prevent and stop child sexual abuse. How would you handle that resistance if you felt you needed to include a prevention program as part of the school's comprehensive developmental guidance program?

SUGGESTED INTERNET SITES

www.preventchildabuse.org

The official Web site of the Prevent Child Abuse America organization offers tools and materials for parents, kids, and the media to help prevent child abuse. Although less extensive than other sites, this site is easy to navigate and offers easy-to-implement programs for schools and communities.

www.calib.com/nccanch

The official Web site of the National Clearinghouse on Child Abuse and Neglect offers information on how to start a child abuse prevention program, statistics, state statutes, connections to funding resources, and an explanation for nonprofessionals on how to report child abuse.

www.acf.dhhs.gov

The official Web site of the Administration for Children and Families, the agency responsible for helping the states deliver child welfare services, offers information on laws and policies, initiatives, programs, funding, hot issues, FAQs, and more. An especially good site for those seeking grants or with legal questions about child abuse and neglect.

child.cornell.edu

> The official Web site of the Child Abuse Prevention Network, a network for professionals, offers resources, facts, and statistics on child abuse, and extensive links to related sites. For professionals, there is the opportunity to join a listserv to keep abreast of current news and research.

www.yesican.org

> The official Web site of the International Child Abuse Network, an organization whose mission is to work worldwide to break the cycle of child abuse, is geared to anyone interested in child abuse, especially victims. On the site are a chat room, a bulletin board, articles, suggested books, and the poetry, art, and personal stories of people who have visited the site. A good source of inspiration for professionals who are discouraged by the prevalence of child abuse in this country.

APPENDIXES

APPENDIX A:
NATIONAL STANDARDS FOR SCHOOL COUNSELING
PROGRAMS AND SUGGESTED STUDENT COMPETENCIES

I. Academic development
   A. Students will acquire the attitudes, knowledge, and skills that contribute to effective learning in school and across the life span.
      1. To improve academic self-concept, students will:
         - articulate feelings of competence and confidence as a learner
         - display a positive interest in learning
         - take pride in work and in achievement
         - accept mistakes as essential to the learning process
         - identify attitudes and behaviors which lead to successful learning
      2. To acquire skills for improving learning, students will:
         - apply time management and task management skills
         - demonstrate how effort and persistence positively affect learning
         - use communication skills to know when and how to ask for help when needed
         - apply knowledge of learning styles to positively influence school performance
      3. To achieve school success, students will:
         - take responsibility for their actions
         - demonstrate the ability to work independently, as well as the ability to work cooperatively with other students

Sharing the Vision: The National Standards for School Counseling Programs (pp. 20–31) by C. A. Campbell and C. A. Dahir. Copyright by the American School Counselor Association. Reprinted with permission.

- develop a broad range of interests and abilities
- demonstrate dependability, productivity, and initiative
- share knowledge

B. Students will complete school with the academic preparation essential to choose from a wide range of substantial postsecondary options, including college.

   1. To improve learning, students will:
      - demonstrate the motivation to achieve individual potential
      - learn and apply critical thinking skills
      - apply the study skills necessary for academic success at each level
      - seek information and support from faculty, staff, family, and peers
      - organize and apply academic information from a variety of sources
      - use knowledge of learning styles to positively influence school performance
      - become self-directed and independent learners

   2. To plan to achieve goals, students will:
      - establish challenging academic goals in elementary, middle/ junior high, and high school
      - use assessment results in educational planning
      - develop and implement an annual plan of study to maximize academic ability and achievement
      - apply knowledge of aptitudes and interests to goal setting
      - use problem-solving and decision-making skills to assess progress toward educational goals
      - understand the relationship between classroom performance and success in school
      - identify post-secondary options consistent with interests, achievement, aptitudes, and abilities.

C. Students will understand the relationship of academics to the world of work, and to life at home and in the community.

   1. To relate school to life experiences, students will:
      - demonstrate the ability to balance school, studies, extracurricular activities, leisure time, and family life
      - seek co-curricular and community experiences to enhance the school experience
      - understand the relationship between learning and work
      - demonstrate an understanding of the value of lifelong learning as essential to seeking, obtaining, and maintaining life goals
      - understand that school success is the preparation to make the transition from student to community member
      - understand how school success and academic achievement enhance future career and avocational opportunities

II. Career development
   A. Students will acquire the skills to investigate the world of work in relation to knowledge of self and to make informed career decisions.
      1. To develop career awareness, students will:
         - develop skills to locate, evaluate, and interpret career information
         - learn about the variety of traditional and non-traditional occupations
         - develop an awareness of personal abilities, skills, interests, and motivations
         - learn how to interact and work cooperatively in teams
         - learn to make decisions
         - learn how to set goals
         - understand the importance of planning
         - pursue and develop competency in areas of interest
         - develop hobbies and avocational interests
         - balance between work and leisure time
      2. To develop employment readiness, students will:
         - acquire employability skills such as working on a team, and problem-solving and organizational skills
         - apply job readiness skills to seek employment opportunities
         - demonstrate knowledge about the changing workplace
         - learn about the rights and responsibilities of employers and employees
         - learn to respect individual uniqueness in the workplace
         - learn how to write a resume
         - develop a positive attitude toward work and learning
         - understand the importance of responsibility, dependability, punctuality, integrity, and effort in the workplace
         - utilize time- and task-management skills
   B. Students will employ strategies to achieve future career goals with success and satisfaction.
      1. To acquire career information, students will:
         - apply decision-making skills to career planning, course selection, and career transitions
         - identify personal skills, interests, and abilities and relate them to current career choices
         - demonstrate knowledge of the career planning process
         - know the various ways in which occupations can be classified
         - use research and information resources to obtain career information
         - learn to use the Internet to access career planning information
         - describe traditional and non-traditional occupations and how these relate to career choices
         - understand how changing economic and societal needs influence employment trends and future training

   2. To identify career goals, students will:
      - demonstrate awareness of the education and training needed to achieve career goals
      - assess and modify their educational plan to support career goals
      - use employability and job readiness skills in internship, mentoring, shadowing, and/or other world of work experiences
      - select course work that is related to career interests
      - maintain a career planning portfolio
   C. Students will understand the relationship between personal qualities, education, training, and the world of work.
      1. To acquire knowledge to achieve career goals, students will:
         - understand the relationship between educational achievement and career success
         - explain how work can help to achieve personal success and satisfaction
         - identify personal preferences and interests which influence career choices and success
         - understand that the changing workplace requires lifelong learning and acquiring new skills
         - describe the effect of work on lifestyles
         - understand the importance of equity and access in career choice
         - understand that work is an important and satisfying means of personal expression
      2. To apply skills to achieve career goals, students will:
         - demonstrate how interests, abilities, and achievement relate to achieving personal, social, educational, and career goals
         - learn how to use conflict management skills with peers and adults
         - learn to work cooperatively with others as a team member
         - apply academic and employment readiness skills in work-based learning
         - apply academic and employment readiness skills in work-based learning situations such as internships, shadowing, and/or mentoring experiences
III. Personal/social development
   A. Students will acquire the knowledge, attitudes, and interpersonal skills to help them understand and respect self and others.
      1. To acquire self-knowledge, students will:
         - develop a positive attitude toward self as a unique and worthy person
         - identify values, attitudes, and beliefs
         - learn the goal setting process
         - understand change as a part of growth
         - identify and express feelings
         - distinguish between appropriate and inappropriate behaviors
         - recognize personal boundaries, rights, and privacy needs

- understand the need for self-control and how to practice it
- demonstrate cooperative behavior in groups
- identify personal strengths and assets
- identify and discuss changing personal and social roles
- identify and recognize changing family roles

2. To acquire interpersonal skills, students will:
   - recognize that everyone has rights and responsibilities
   - respect alternative points of view
   - recognize, accept, respect, and appreciate individual differences
   - recognize, accept, and appreciate ethnic and cultural diversity
   - recognize and respect differences in various family configurations
   - use effective communication skills
   - know that communication involves speaking, listening, and nonverbal behavior
   - learn how to make and keep friends

B. Students will make decisions, set goals, and take necessary action to achieve goals.

1. To apply self-knowledge, students will:
   - use a decision-making and problem-solving model
   - understand consequences of decisions and choices
   - identify alternative solutions to a problem
   - develop effective coping skills for dealing with problems
   - demonstrate when, where, and how to seek help for solving problems and making decisions
   - know how to apply conflict resolution skills
   - demonstrate a respect and appreciation for individual and cultural differences
   - know when peer pressure is influencing a decision
   - identify long- and short-term goals
   - identify alternative ways of achieving goals
   - use persistence and perseverance in acquiring knowledge and skills
   - develop an action plan to set and achieve goals

C. Students will understand safety and survival skills.

1. To acquire personal safety skills, students will:
   - demonstrate knowledge of personal information (i.e., telephone number, home address, emergency contact)
   - learn about the relationship between rules, laws, safety, and the protection of an individual's rights
   - learn the difference between appropriate and inappropriate physical contact
   - demonstrate the ability to assert boundaries, rights, and personal privacy
   - differentiate between situations requiring peer support and situations requiring adult professional help

- identify resource people in the school and community, and know how to seek their help
- apply effective problem-solving and decision-making skills to make safe and healthy choices
- learn about the emotional and physical dangers of substance use and abuse
- learn how to cope with peer pressure
- learn techniques for managing stress and conflict
- learn coping skills for managing life events

APPENDIX B:
AMERICAN SCHOOL COUNSELOR ASSOCIATION
ETHICAL STANDARDS FOR SCHOOL COUNSELORS

Preamble

The American School Counselor Association (ASCA) is a professional organization whose members have a unique and distinctive preparation, grounded in the behavioral sciences, with training in clinical skills adapted to the school setting. The school counselor assists in the growth and development of each individual and uses his or her highly specialized skills to protect the interests of the counselee within the structure of the school system. School counselors subscribe to the following basic tenets of the counseling process from which professional responsibilities are derived:

- Each person has the right to respect and dignity as a human being and to counseling services without prejudice as to person, character, belief, or practice regardless of age, color, disability, ethnic group, gender, race, religion, sexual orientation, marital status, or socioeconomic status.

- Each person has the right to self-direction and self-development.

- Each person has the right of choice and the responsibility for goals reached.

- Each person has the right to privacy and thereby the right to expect the counselor-counselee relationship to comply with all laws, policies, and ethical standards pertaining to confidentiality.

In this document, ASCA specifies the principles of ethical behavior necessary to regulate and maintain the high standards of integrity, leadership, and professionalism among its members. The Ethical Standards for School Counselors were developed to clarify the nature of ethical responsibilities held in common by school counseling professionals. The purposes of this document are to:

- Serve as a guide for the ethical practices of all professional school counselors regardless of level, area, population served, or membership in this professional Association;

- Provide benchmarks for both self-appraisal and peer evaluations regarding counselor responsibilities to counselees, parents, colleagues and professional associates, schools, and communities, as well as to one's self and the counseling profession; and

- Inform those served by the school counselor of acceptable counselor practices and expected professional behavior.

Revised June 25, 1998. Copyright by the American School Counselor Association. Reprinted with permission.

A.1. Responsibilities to Students

The professional school counselor:

a. Has a primary obligation to the counselee who is to be treated with respect as a unique individual.

b. Is concerned with the educational, career, emotional, and behavioral needs and encourages the maximum development of each counselee.

c. Refrains from consciously encouraging the counselee's acceptance of values, lifestyles, plans, decisions, and beliefs that represent the counselor's personal orientation.

d. Is responsible for keeping informed of laws, regulations, and policies relating to counselees and strives to ensure that the rights of counselees are adequately provided for and protected.

A.2. Confidentiality

The professional school counselor:

a. Informs the counselee of the purposes, goals, techniques, and rules of procedure under which she/he may receive counseling at or before the time when the counseling relationship is entered. Disclosure notice includes confidentiality issues such as the possible necessity for consulting with other professionals, privileged communication, and legal or authoritative restraints. The meaning and limits of confidentiality are clearly defined to counselees through a written and shared disclosure statement.

b. Keeps information confidential unless disclosure is required to prevent clear and imminent danger to the counselee or others or when legal requirements demand that confidential information be revealed. Counselors will consult with other professionals when in doubt as to the validity of an exception.

c. Discloses information to an identified third party who, by her or his relationship with the counselee, is at a high risk of contracting a disease that is commonly known to be communicable and fatal. Prior to disclosure, the counselor will ascertain that the counselee has not already informed the third party about his or her disease and he/she is not intending to inform the third party in the immediate future.

d. Requests of the court that disclosure not be required when the release of confidential information without a counselee's permission may lead to potential harm to the counselee.

e. Protects the confidentiality of counselee's records and releases personal data only according to prescribed laws and school policies. Student information maintained in computers is treated with the same care as traditional student records.

f. Protects the confidentiality of information received in the counseling relationship as specified by federal and state laws, written policies, and applicable ethical standards. Such information is only to be revealed to others with the informed consent of the counselee, consistent with the counselor's ethical obligation. In a group setting, the counselor sets a high norm of confidentiality and stresses its importance, yet clearly states that confidentiality in group counseling cannot be guaranteed.

A.3. Counseling Plans

The professional school counselor:
works jointly with the counselee in developing integrated and effective counseling plans, consistent with both the abilities and circumstances of the counselee and counselor. Such plans will be regularly reviewed to ensure continued viability and effectiveness, respecting the counselee's freedom of choice.

A.4. Dual Relationships

The professional school counselor:
avoids dual relationships which might impair her or his objectivity and increase the risk of harm to the client (e.g., counseling one's family members, close friends, or associates). If a dual relationship is unavoidable, the counselor is responsible for taking action to eliminate or reduce the potential for harm. Such safeguards might include informed consent, consultation, supervision, and documentation.

A.5. Appropriate Referrals

The professional school counselor:
makes referrals when necessary or appropriate to outside resources. Appropriate referral necessitates knowledge of available resources and making proper plans for transitions with minimal interruption of services. Counselees retain the right to discontinue the counseling relationship at any time.

A.6. Group Work

The professional school counselor:
screens prospective group members and maintains an awareness of participants' needs and goals in relation to the goals of the group. The counselor takes reasonable precautions to protect members from physical and psychological harm resulting from interaction within the group.

A.7. Danger to Self or Others

The professional school counselor:
informs appropriate authorities when the counselee's condition indicates a clear and imminent danger to the counselee or others. This is to be done after careful deliberation and, where possible, after consultation with other counseling professionals. The counselor informs the counselee of actions to be taken so as to minimize his or her confusion and to clarify counselee and counselor expectations.

A.8. Student Records

The professional school counselor:
maintains and secures records necessary for rendering professional services to the counselee as required by laws, regulations, institutional procedures, and confidentiality guidelines.

A.9. Evaluation, Assessment, and Interpretation

The professional school counselor:
a. Adheres to all professional standards regarding selecting, administering, and interpreting assessment measures. The counselor recognizes that computer-based testing programs require specific training in administration, scoring, and interpretation which may differ from that required in more traditional assessments.

b. Provides explanations of the nature, purposes, and results of assessment/ evaluation measures in language the counselee(s) can understand.

c. Does not misuse assessment results and interpretations and takes reasonable steps to prevent others from misusing the information.

d. Uses caution when utilizing assessment techniques, making evaluations, and interpreting the performance of populations not represented in the norm group on which an instrument is standardized.

A.10. Computer Technology

The professional school counselor:
a. Promotes the benefits of appropriate computer applications and clarifies the limitations of computer technology. The counselor ensures that: (1) computer applications are appropriate for the individual needs of the counselee; (2) the counselee understands how to use the application; and (3) follow-up counseling assistance is provided. Members of underrepresented groups are assured equal access to computer technologies and are assured the absence of discriminatory information and values in computer applications.

b. Counselors who communicate with counselees via internet should follow the NBCC Standards for WebCounseling.

A.11. Peer Helper Programs

The professional school counselor:
has unique responsibilities when working with peer helper programs. The school counselor is responsible for the welfare of counselees participating in peer programs under her or his direction. School counselors who function in training and supervisory capacities are referred to the preparation and supervision standards of professional counselor associations.

B. Responsibilities to Parents

B.1. Parent Rights and Responsibilities

The professional school counselor:
a. Respects the inherent rights and responsibilities of parents for their children and endeavors to establish, as appropriate, a collaborative relationship with parents to facilitate the counselee's maximum development.

b. Adheres to laws and local guidelines when assisting parents experiencing family difficulties that interfere with the counselee's effectiveness and welfare.

c. Is sensitive to cultural and social diversity among families and recognizes that all parents, custodial and noncustodial, are vested with certain rights and responsibilities for the welfare of their children by virtue of their role and according to law.

B.2. Parents and Confidentiality

The professional school counselor:
a. Informs parents of the counselor's role with emphasis on the confidential nature of the counseling relationship between the counselor and counselee.

b. Provides parents with accurate, comprehensive, and relevant information in an objective and caring manner, as is appropriate and consistent with ethical responsibilities to the counselee.

c. Makes reasonable efforts to honor the wishes of parents and guardians concerning information that he/she may share regarding the counselee.

C. Responsibilities to Colleagues and Professional Associates

C.1. Professional Relationships

The professional school counselor:
a. Establishes and maintains professional relationships with faculty, staff, and administration to facilitate the provision of optimal counseling services. The relationship is based on the counselor's definition and description of the parameter and levels of his or her professional roles.

b. Treats colleagues with professional respect, courtesy, and fairness. The qualifications, views, and findings of colleagues are represented to accurately reflect the image of competent professionals.

c. Is aware of and optimally utilizes related professions and organizations to whom the counselee may be referred.

C.2. Sharing Information with Other Professionals

The professional school counselor:
a. Promotes awareness and adherence to appropriate guidelines regarding confidentiality; the distinction between public and private information; and staff consultation.

b. Provides professional personnel with accurate, objective, concise, and meaningful data necessary to adequately evaluate, counsel, and assist the counselee.

c. If a counselee is receiving services from another counselor or other mental health professional, the counselor, with client consent, will inform the other professional and develop clear agreements to avoid confusion and conflict for the counselee.

D. Responsibilities to the School and Community

D.1. Responsibilities to the School

The professional school counselor:
a. Supports and protects the educational program against any infringement not in the best interest of counselees.

b. Informs appropriate officials of conditions that may be potentially disruptive or damaging to the school's mission, personnel, and property while honoring the confidentiality between the counselee and counselor.

c. Delineates and promotes the counselor's role and function in meeting the needs of those served. The counselor will notify appropriate officials of conditions which may limit or curtail her or his effectiveness in providing programs and services.

d. Accepts employment only for positions for which he/she is qualified by education, training, supervised experience, state and national professional credentials, and appropriate professional experience. Counselors recommend that administrators hire only qualified and competent individuals for professional counseling positions.

e. Assists in developing: (1) curricular and environmental conditions appropriate for the school and community; (2) educational procedures and programs to meet the counselee's developmental needs; and (3) a systematic evaluation process for comprehensive school counseling programs, services, and personnel. The counselor is guided by the findings of the evaluation data in planning programs and services.

D.2. Responsibility to the Community

The professional school counselor:
collaborates with agencies, organizations, and individuals in the school and community in the best interest of counselees and without regard to personal reward or remuneration.

E. Responsibilities to Self

E.1. Professional Competence

The professional school counselor:
a. Functions within the boundaries of individual professional competence and accepts responsibility for the consequences of his or her actions.

b. Monitors personal functioning and effectiveness and does not participate in any activity which may lead to inadequate professional services or harm to a client.

c. Strives through personal initiative to maintain professional competence and to keep abreast of professional information. Professional and personal growth are ongoing throughout the counselor's career.

E.2. Multicultural Skills

The professional school counselor:
understands the diverse cultural backgrounds of the counselees with whom he/she works. This includes, but is not limited to, learning how the school counselor's own cultural/ethnic/racial identity impacts her or his values and beliefs about the counseling process.

F. Responsibilities to the Profession

F.1. Professionalism

The professional school counselor:
a. Accepts the policies and processes for handling ethical violations as a result of maintaining membership in the American School Counselor Association.

b. Conducts herself/himself in such a manner as to advance individual ethical practice and the profession.

c. Conducts appropriate research and reports findings in a manner consistent with acceptable educational and psychological research practices. When using client data for research or for statistical or program planning purposes, the counselor ensures protection of the individual counselee's identity.

d. Adheres to ethical standards of the profession, other official policy statements pertaining to counseling, and relevant statutes established by federal, state, and local governments.

e. Clearly distinguishes between statements and actions made as a private individual and those made as a representative of the school counseling profession.

f. Does not use his or her professional position to recruit or gain clients, consultees for her or his private practice, seek and receive unjustified personal gains, unfair advantage, sexual favors, or unearned goods or services.

F.2. Contribution to the Profession

The professional school counselor:
a. Actively participates in local, state, and national associations which foster the development and improvement of school counseling.

b. Contributes to the development of the profession through sharing skills, ideas, and expertise with colleagues.

G. Maintenance of Standards

Ethical behavior among professional school counselors, Association members and nonmembers, is expected at all times. When there exists serious doubt as to the ethical behavior of colleagues,

or if counselors are forced to work in situations or abide by policies which do not reflect the standards as outlined in these Ethical Standards for School Counselors, the counselor is obligated to take appropriate action to rectify the condition. The following procedure may serve as a guide:

1. The counselor should consult confidentially with a professional colleague to discuss the nature of a complaint to see if she/he views the situation as an ethical violation.

2. When feasible, the counselor should directly approach the colleague whose behavior is in question to discuss the complaint and seek resolution.

3. If resolution is not forthcoming at the personal level, the counselor shall utilize the channels established within the school, school district, the state SCA, and ASCA Ethics Committee.

4. If the matter still remains unresolved, referral for review and appropriate action should be made to the Ethics Committees in the following sequence:
    - state school counselor association
    - American School Counselor Association

5. The ASCA Ethics Committee is responsible for educating— and consulting with—the membership regarding ethical standards. The Committee periodically reviews and recommends changes in code. The Committee will also receive and process questions to clarify the application of such standards. Questions must be submitted in writing to the ASCA Ethics Chair. Finally, the Committee will handle complaints of alleged violations of our ethical standards. Therefore, at the national level, complaints should be submitted in writing to the ASCA Ethics Committee, c/o the Executive Director, American School Counselor Association, 801 North Fairfax, Suite 310, Alexandria, VA 22314.

H. Resources

School counselors are responsible for being aware of, and acting in accord with, standards and positions of the counseling profession as represented in official documents such as those listed below:

American Counseling Association. (1995). *Code of ethics and standards of practice.* Alexandria, VA. (5999 Stevenson Ave., Alexandria, VA 22034) 1 800 347 6647 www.counseling.org.

American School Counselor Association. (1997). *The national standards for school counseling programs.* Alexandria, VA. (801 North Fairfax Street, Suite 310, Alexandria, VA 22314) 1 800 306 4722 www.schoolcounselor.org.

American School Counselor Association. (1998). *Position Statements.* Alexandria, VA.

American School Counselor Association. (1998). *Professional liability insurance program.* (Brochure). Alexandria, VA.

Arrendondo, Toperek, Brown, Jones, Locke, Sanchez, and Stadler. (1996). Multicultural counseling competencies and standards. *Journal of Multicultural Counseling and Development.* Vol. 24, No. 1. See American Counseling Association.

Arthur, G.L. and Swanson, C.D. (1993). *Confidentiality and privileged communication.* (1993). See American Counseling Association.

Association for Specialists in Group Work. (1989). *Ethical guidelines for group counselors.* (1989). Alexandria, VA. See American Counseling Association.

Corey, G., Corey, M.S. and Callanan. (1998). *Issues and ethics in the helping professions.* Pacific Grove, CA: Brooks/Cole. (Brooks/Cole, 51 Forest Lodge Rd., Pacific Grove, CA 93950) www.thomson.com.

Crawford, R. (1994). *Avoiding counselor malpractice.* Alexandria, VA. See American Counseling Association.

Forrester-Miller, H. and Davis, T.E. (1996). *A practitioner's guide to ethical decision making.* Alexandria, VA. See American Counseling Association.

Herlihy, B. and Corey, G. (1996). ACA ethical standards casebook. Fifth ed. Alexandria, VA. See American Counseling Association.

Herlihy, B. and Corey, G. (1992). *Dual relationships in counseling.* Alexandria, VA. See American Counseling Association.

Huey, W.C. and Remley, T.P. (1988). *Ethical and legal issues in school counseling.* Alexandria, VA. See American School Counselor Association.

Joint Committee on Testing Practices. (1988). *Code of fair testing practices in education.* Washington, DC: American Psychological Association. (1200 17th Street, NW, Washington, DC 20036) 202 336 5500

Mitchell, R.W. (1991). *Documentation in counseling records.* Alexandria, VA. See American Counseling Association.

National Board for Certified Counselors. (1998). *National board for certified counselors: code of ethics.* Greensboro, NC. (3 Terrace Way, Suite D, Greensboro, NC 27403-3660) 336 547 0607 www.nbcc.org.

National Board for Certified Counselors. (1997). *Standards for the ethical practice of webcounseling.* Greensboro, NC.

National Peer Helpers Association. (1989). *Code of ethics for peer helping professionals.* Greenville, NC. PO Box 2684, Greenville, NC 27836. 919 522 3959. nphaorg@aol.com.

Salo, M. and Schumate, S. (1993). *Counseling minor clients.* Alexandria, VA. See American School Counselor Association.

Stevens-Smith, P. and Hughes, M. (1993). *Legal issues in marriage and family counseling.* Alexandria, VA. See American School Counselor Association.

Wheeler, N. and Bertram, B. (1994). *Legal aspects of counseling: avoiding lawsuits and legal problems.* (Videotape). Alexandria, VA. See American School Counselor Association.

References

Aber, J. L. (1989). The effects of maltreatment on development and during early child-hood: Recent studies and their theoretical, clinical, and policy implications. In D. Ci-cchetti & V. Carlson (Eds.), *Child maltreatment: Theory and research on the causes and consequences of child abuse and neglect* (pp. 579–619). New York: Cambridge University Press.

Abikoff, H., & Gittelman, R. (1985). Hyperactive children treated with stimulants: Is cog-nitive training a useful technique? *Archives of General Psychiatry, 42*, 953–961.

ACES–ASCA Joint Committee on the Elementary School Counselor (1966). The elemen-tary school counselor: Preliminary statement. *Personnel and Guidance Journal, 61*, 658–661.

Adams, G. R., & Hicken, M. (1984). Historical–cultural change in the expression of voca-tional preference and expectation by preschool and elementary school aged children. *Family Relations, 33*, 301–307.

Adler, P. A., & Adler, P. (1995). Dynamics of inclusion and exclusion in preadolescent cliques. *School Psychology Quarterly, 58*, 145–162.

Ajibola, O., & Clement, P. (1995). Differential effects of methylphenidate and self-reinforcement on attention-deficit/hyperactivity disorder. *Behavior Modification, 19*, 211–233.

Alan Guttmacher Institute. (1994). *Sex and America's teenagers.* New York: Author.

Albert, L. (1989). *Cooperative discipline in the classroom: A teacher's guide to cooperative discipline.* Circle Pines, MN: American Guidance Service.

Allen, J. P., Philliber, S., Herrling, S., & Kuperminc, G. P. (1997). Preventing teen preg-nancy and academic failure: Experimental evaluation of a developmentally-based ap-proach. *Child Development, 64*, 729–742.

Allen, S. F., Stoltenberg, C. D., & Rosko, C. K. (1990). Perceived psychological separation of older adolescents and young adults from their parents: A comparison of divorced versus intact families. *Journal of Counseling and Development, 69*, 57–61.

Allen-Meares, P. (1989). Adolescent sexuality and premature parenthood: Role of the Black church in prevention. *Journal of Social Work and Human Sexuality, 8*, 133–142.

American Association of University Women (1993). *Hostile hallways: The AAUW survey on sexual harassment in America's schools.* Washington, DC: Author.

American Association of University Women (2001). *Hostile hallways: Bullying, teasing, and sexual harassment in school.* Washington, DC: Author.

American Counseling Association (1995). *Code of ethics and standards of practice.* Alexandria, VA: Author.

American Counseling Association (1997). *Sexual harassment in the schools. Background on Title IX of the Education Amendments of 1972 and guidance issued by the Office for Civil Rights.* Alexandria, VA: Author.

American Lung Association (1992). *Tobacco free teens.* St. Paul, MN: Author.

American Psychiatric Association (2000). *Diagnostic and statistical manual of mental disorders* (4th ed., text revision). Washington, DC: Author.

American School Counselor Association (1990). *Role statement: The school counselor.* Alexandria, VA: Author.

American School Counselor Association (1992). *Ethical standards for school counselors.* Alexandria, VA: Author.

American School Counselor Association (1997). *Definition of school counseling.* Alexandria, VA: Author.

American School Counselor Association (1999a). *ASCA role statement: The role of the professional school counselor.* Alexandria, VA: Author.

American School Counseling Association (1999b). *Position statement: The professional school counselor and comprehensive school counseling programs* (Revised). Alexandria, VA: Author.

American School Counselor Association (2001). *ASCA national model for school counseling programs.* Alexandria, VA: Author.

American School Counselor Association (2002). *Position statement: The professional school counselor and group counseling* (Revised). Alexandria, VA: Author.

American School Counselor Association (2003). *The ASCA national model: A framework for school counseling programs.* Alexandria, VA: Author.

American School Health Association (1990). Guidelines for HIV and AIDS student support services. *Journal of School Health, 60,* 249–255.

American Speech-Language-Hearing Association (1993). Definitions of communications disorders and variations. *ASHA, 35*(Suppl. 10), 40–41.

Amundson, N. E., & Penner, K. (1998). Parent involved career exploration. *Career Development Quarterly, 47,* 135–144.

Anastasi, A. (1988). *Psychological testing.* New York: Macmillan.

Anastasi, A., & Urbina, S. (1997). *Psychological testing* (7th ed.). New York: Macmillan.

Anderson, E., & Quast, W. (1983). Young children in alcoholic families: A mental health needs–assessment intervention prevention strategy. *Journal of Primary Prevention, 3,* 174–187.

Anderson, G. L. (1987). *When chemicals come to school: The student assistance program model.* Greenfield, WI: Community Recovery Press.

Andreini, M. (1990, September). *Chronic neglect: Diagnosis and treatment.* Paper presented at the Eighth International Congress on Child Abuse and Neglect, Hamburg, Germany.

Arditti, J. A. (1992). Differences between fathers with joint custody and noncustodial fathers. *American Journal of Orthopsychiatry, 62,* 186–195.

Arman, J. F., & McNair, R. (2000). A small group model for working with elementary school children of alcoholics. *Professional School Counseling, 3,* 290–293.

Arredondo, P., Toporek, R., Brown, S., Jones, J., Locke, D. C., Sanchez, J., & Sandler, H. (1996). *Operationalization of the multicultural counseling competencies.* Alexandria, VA: Association for Multicultural Counseling and Development.

Aseltine, R. H., Gore, S., & Colten, M. E. (1998). The co-occurrence of depression and substance abuse in late adolescence. *Development and Psychopathology, 10,* 549–570.

Ashcraft, M., & Kirk, E. P. (2001). The relationships among working memory, math anxiety, and performance. *Journal of Experimental Psychology, 130,* 224–237.

Astone, N., & McLanahan, S. (1991). Family structure, parental practices, and high school completion. *American Sociological Review, 56,* 309–320.

Athealth (2000). Depression in children and adolescents. Available online at www.athealth.com/consumer/disorders/childdepression.html.

Atkinson, D. R., Morten, G., & Sue, D. W. (1998). *Counseling American minorities* (5th ed.). Boston: McGraw-Hill.

Atlas, R. S., & Pepler, D. J. (1998). Observations of bullying in the classroom. *Journal of Educational Research, 92,* 86–99.

Aubrey, R. (1977). Historical development of guidance and counseling and implications for the future. *Personnel and Guidance Journal, 55,* 288–295.

Avellar, J., & Kagan, S. (1976). Development of competitive behaviors in Anglo-American and Mexican-American children. *Psychological Reports, 39,* 191–198.

Avis, H. (1990). *Drugs and life.* Dubuque, IA: Brown.

Axline, V. (1947). *Play therapy: The inner dynamics of childhood.* Cambridge, MA: Houghton Mifflin.

Axline, V. (1964). *Dibbs: In search of self.* New York: Ballantine.

Azar, S. T. (1984). Unrealistic expectations and problem-solving ability in maltreating and comparison mothers. *Journal of Consulting and Clinical Psychology, 52,* 687–690.

Bailey, B. A., & Nihlen, A. S. (1989). Elementary school children's perceptions of the world of work. *Elementary School Guidance and Counseling, 24,* 135–145.

Baker, R. L., & Mednick, B. R. (1984). *Influences on human development: A longitudinal perspective.* Boston: Kluer–Nijhoff.

Baker, S. B. (2000). *School counseling for the twenty-first century* (3rd ed.). Englewood Cliffs, NJ: Prentice Hall.

Balk, D. E., & Corr, C. A. (1996). Adolescents, developmental tasks, and encounters with death and bereavement. In C. A. Corr & D. E. Balk (Eds.), *Handbook of adolescent death and bereavement* (pp. 3–41). New York: Springer-Verlag.

Ball, D. W., Newman, J. M., & Scheuren, W. J. (1984). Teachers' generalized expectations of children of divorce. *Psychological Reports, 54,* 347–353.

Bandura, A. (1977). *Social learning theory.* Englewood Cliffs, NJ: Prentice Hall.

Bandura, A. (1986). *Social foundations of thought and action: A social cognitive theory.* Englewood Cliffs, NJ: Prentice Hall.

Barabasz, M., & Barabasz, A. (1996). Attention deficit disorder: Diagnosis, etiology, and treatment. *Child Study Journal, 26,* 1–38.

Baren, M. (1994). *Hyperactivity and attention disorders in children.* San Ramon, CA: Health Information Network.

Barga, N. K. (1996). Students with learning disabilities in education: Managing a disability. *Journal of Learning Disabilities, 29,* 413–421.

Barkhaus, R. S., Adair, M. K., Hoover, A. B., & Bolyard, C. W. (1985). *Threads* (3rd ed.). Dubuque, IA: Kendall/Hunt.

Barkley, R. A. (1990). *Attention-deficit hyperactivity disorder: A handbook for treatment.* New York: Guilford.

Barkley, R. A. (1995). *Taking charge of ADHD: The complete, authoritative guide for parents.* New York: Guilford.

Barnartt, S. N. (1996). Disability culture or disability consciousness. *Journal of Disability Policy Studies, 7*(2), 1–19.

Baron, M. A., Bejar, R. L., & Sheaff, P. J. (1970). Neurological manifestations of the battered child syndrome. *Pediatrics, 45,* 1003–1007.

Barth, R., Fetro, J., Leland, N., & Volkan, K. (1992). Preventing adolescent pregnancy with social and cognitive skills. *Journal of Adolescent Research, 7,* 208–232.

Bartlett, J. G. (1993). *The Johns Hopkins Hospital guide to medical care of patients with HIV infection* (3rd ed.). Baltimore: Williams & Wilkins.

Battin, S. R., Hill, K. G., Abbott, R. D., Catalano, R. F., & Hawkins, J. D. (1998). The contribution of gang membership to delinquency beyond delinquent friends. *Criminology, 36,* 93–115.

Bauer, A. M. (1987). A teacher's introduction to childhood depression. *Clearing House, 61,* 81–84.

Beautrais, A. L., Joyce, P. R., & Mulder, R. T. (1999). Personality traits and cognitive styles as risk factors for serious suicide attempts among young people. *Journal of Suicide and Life-Threatening Behavior, 17,* 218–232.

Beck, A. T. (1963). Thinking and depression. Idiosyncratic content and cognitive distortions. *Archives of General Psychiatry, 9,* 324–333.

Beck, A. T. (1967). *Depression: Causes and treatment.* Philadelphia: University of Pennsylvania Press.

Beck, A. T. (1993). Cognitive therapy: Past, present, and future. *Journal of Consulting and Clinical Psychology, 61,* 194–198.

Beck, A. T., Rush, A. G., Shaw, B. F., & Emery, G. (1979). *Cognitive therapy of depression.* New York: Guilford.

Beck, A. T., & Steer, R. A. (1993). *Beck Depression Inventory.* San Antonio, TX: Psychological Corporation.

Beck, A. T., Ward, C. H., Mendelson, M., Mock, J., & Erbaugh, J. (1961). An inventory for measuring depression. *Archives of General Psychiatry, 4,* 561–571.

Becker, E. (1973). *The denial of death.* New York: Free Press.

Becker-Lansen, E., & Rickel, A. U. (1995). Integration of teen pregnancy and child abuse research: Identifying mediator variables for pregnancy outcome. *Journal of Primary Prevention, 16*(8), 39–53.

Bee-Gates, D., Howard-Pitney, B., LaFromboise, T., & Rowe, W. (1996). Help-seeking behavior of Native American Indian high school students. *Professional Psychology: Research and Practice, 27,* 495–499.

Beis, E. B. (1984). *Mental health law.* Rockville, MD: Aspen.

Beitchman, J. H., Zucker, K. J., Hood, J. E., daCosta, G. A., Akman, D., & Cassavia, E. (1992). A review of the long-term effects of child sexual abuse. *Child Abuse and Neglect, 16,* 101–118.

Bell, A. (1997). Pregnant on purpose. *Teen Magazine, 41,* 106.

Belsky, J. (1980). Child maltreatment: An ecological integration. *American Psychologist, 4,* 320–335.

Belsky, J. (1984). Determinants of parenting: A process model. *Child Development, 55,* 83–96.

Belsky, J., & Vondra, J. (1989). Lessons from child abuse: The determinants of parenting. In D. Cicchetti & V. Carlson (Eds.), *Child maltreatment: Theory and research on the causes and consequences of child abuse and neglect* (pp. 153–202). New York: Cambridge University Press.

Bennet, L. A., Wolin, S. J., & Reiss, D. (1988). Cognitive, behavioral, and emotional problems among school-age children of alcoholic parents. *American Journal of Psychiatry, 145,* 185–190.

Bergan, J. R. (1977). *Behavioral consultation.* Columbus, OH: Merrill.

Bergan, J. R., & Kratochwill, T. R. (1990). *Behavioral consultation and therapy.* New York: Plenum.

Berlin, I. N. (1987). Suicide among American Indian adolescents. An overview. *Journal of Suicide and Life-Threatening Behavior, 29,* 37–47.

Berman, A. L., & Jobes, D. A. (1991). *Adolescent suicide: Assessment and intervention.* Washington, DC: American Psychological Association.

Berry, J. W. (1980). Acculturation as variety of adaptation. In A. M. Padilla (Ed.), *Acculturation: Theory, models and some new findings.* Washington, DC: American Association for the Advancement of Science.

Betz, N. E., & Luzzo, D. A. (1996). Career assessment and the Career Decision-Making Self-Efficacy Scale. *Journal of Career Assessment, 4,* 413–428.

Betz, N. E., & Voyten, K. K. (1997). Efficacy and outcome expectations influence career exploration and decidedness. *Career Development Quarterly, 46,* 179–189.

Biller, E. F., & Horn, E. E. (1991). A career guidance model of adolescents with learning disabilities. *School Counselor, 38,* 279–286.

Binet, A., & Simon, T. Methodes nouvelles pour le diagnostic du niveau intellectual des anormaux. *Anne Psychologique, 11,* 191–244. (1905).

Birmaher, B., Ryan, N. D., Williamson, D. E., Brent, D. A., & Kaufman, J. (1996). Childhood and adolescent depression: A review of the past 10 years. Part II. *Journal of the American Academy of Child and Adolescent Psychiatry, 35,* 1575–1583.

Black, C. (1984). *Changing legacies: Growing up in an alcoholic home.* Pompano Beach, FL: Health Communications.

Black, C. (1986). Claudia Black: Children of alcoholics. *Journal of Child and Adolescent Psychotherapy, 3,* 311.

Black, J., & Underwood, J. (1998). Young, female, and gay: Lesbian students and the school environment. *Professional School Counseling, 1,* 15–20.

Blackorby, J., & Wagner, M. (1996). Longitudinal postschool outcomes of youth with disabilities: Findings from the National Longitudinal Transition Study. *Exceptional Children, 62,* 399–413.

Blum, D. J., & Jones, L. A. (1993). Academic growth group and mentoring program for potential dropouts. *School Counselor, 40,* 207–217.

Blume, J. (1981). *Tiger eyes.* Scarsdale, NY: Bradbury.

Blumstein, A., Cohen, J., & Farrington, D. P. (1988). Criminal career research: Its value for criminology. *Criminology, 26,* 1–35.

Bonkowski, S. E., Bequette, S. Q., & Boomhower, S. (1984). A group design to help children adjust to parental divorce. *Social Casework, 65,* 131–137.

Borders, L., & Drury, S. M. (1992). Comprehensive school counseling programs: A review for policy makers and practitioners. *Journal of Counseling and Development, 70,* 487–498.

Borders, S., & Paisley, P. O. (1992). Children's literature as a resource for classroom guidance. *Elementary School Guidance and Counseling, 27,* 131–139.

Botvin, G. J. (1986). Substance abuse prevention efforts: Recent developments and future directions. *Journal of School Health, 56,* 369–374.

Botvin, G. J., Baker, E., Dusenbury, L., Botvin, E. M., & Diaz, T. (1995). Long-term follow-up results of a randomized drug abuse prevention trial in a White middle-class population. *Journal of the American Medical Association, 273,* 1106–1112.

Botvin, G. J., Baker, E., Dusenbury, L., Tortu, S., & Botvin, E. M. (1990). Preventing adolescent drug abuse through a multimodal cognitive–behavioral approach: Results of a 3-year study. *Journal of Counseling and Clinical Psychology, 58,* 437–446.

Botvin, G. J., Baker, E., Filazzola, A. D., & Botvin, E. M. (1990). A cognitive behavioral approach to substance abuse prevention: One-year follow-up. *Addictive Behaviors, 15,* 47–63.

Botvin, G. J., Schinke, S. P., Epstein, J. A., & Diaz, T. (1995). Effectiveness of culturally focused and generic skills training approaches to alcohol and drug abuse prevention among minority adolescents: Two-year follow-up results. *Psychology of Addictive Behaviors, 9,* 183–194.

Bowen, M. (1976). Theory in the practice of psychotherapy. In P. J. Guerin (Ed.), *Family therapy: Theory and practice.* New York: Gardner.

Bowen, M. L., & Glenn, E. E. (1998). Counseling interventions for students who have mild disabilities. *Professional School Counseling, 2,* 16–25.

Bowers, J. L., & Hatch, P. A. (2002). *The national model for school counseling programs* (Draft). Alexandria, VA: American School Counseling Association.

Bowlby, J. (1963). Pathological mourning and childhood mourning. *Journal of the American Psychoanalytic Association, 11,* 500–541.

Bowlby, J. (1980). *Attachment and loss: Loss, sadness, and depression.* New York: Basic Books.

Bradby, D., & Helms, J. E. (1990). Black racial identity attitudes and White therapist cultural sensitivity in cross-racial therapy dyads: An exploratory study. In J. E. Helms (Ed.), *Black and White racial identity: Theory, research, and practice* (pp. 165–175). Westport, CT: Greenwood.

Bradley, D. (1988). Alcohol and drug education in the elementary school. *Elementary School Guidance and Counseling, 23,* 99–105.

Bradley, L. J., Jarchow, E., & Robinson, B. (1999). *All about sex: The school counselor's guide to handling tough adolescent problems.* Thousand Oaks, CA: Corwin Press.

Bragg, R. M., Brown, R. L., & Berninger, V. W. (1992). The impact of congenital and acquired disabilities on the family system: Implications for school counseling. *School Counselor, 39,* 292–299.

Bramlett, R. K., Nelson, P., & Reeves, B. (1997). Stimulant treatment of elementary school children: Implications for school counselors. *Elementary School Guidance and Counseling, 31,* 243–250.

Breen, M., Daro, D., & Romano, N. (1991). *Prevention services and child abuse: A comparison of services availability in the nation and Michigan.* Chicago: National Committee to Prevent Child Abuse.

Brent, D. A., Roth, C. M., Holder, D. P., Kolko, D. J., Birmaher, B., Johnson, B. A., & Schweers, J. A. (1996). Psychosocial interventions for treating adolescent suicidal depression: A comparison of three psychosocial interventions. In E. D. Hibbs & P. S. Jensen (Eds.), *Psychosocial treatments for child and adolescent disorders: Empirically based strategies for clinical practice* (pp. 187–206). Washington, DC: American Psychological Association.

Brewster, K., Billy, J., & Grady, W. (1993). Social context and adolescent behavior. The impact of community on the transition to sexual activity. *Social Forces, 71,* 713–740.

Brinton, B., & Fujiki, M. (1993). Clinical forum: Language, social skills, and socioemotional behavior. *Language, Speech, and Hearing Services in Schools, 24,* 194–198.

Bronfenbrenner, U. (1979). *The experimental ecology of human development.* Cambridge, MA: Harvard University Press.

Brook, J. S., Whitman, M., Gordon, A. S., & Brook, D. W. (1990). The role of older brothers in younger brothers' drug use viewed in the context of parent and peer influences. *Journal of Genetic Psychology, 151,* 59–75.

Brown, D. (1989). The perils, pitfalls, and promises of school counseling program reform. *School Counselor, 37,* 47–53.

Brown, D., Pryzwansky, W. B., & Schulte, A. C. (2001). *Psychological consultation: Introduction to theory and practice* (5th ed.). Boston: Allyn & Bacon.

Brown, D., & Schulte, A. (1987). A social learning model of consultation. *Professional Psychology: Research and Practice, 18,* 283–287.

Brown, D., Spano, D. B., & Schulte, A. C. (1988). Consultation training in master's level counselor education programs. *Counselor Education and Supervision, 27,* 323–330.

Brown, L. M., & Gilligan, C. (1992). *Meeting at the crossroads: Women's psychology and girls' development.* Cambridge, MA: Harvard University Press.

Brown, S. E. (1995). Disability culture: Here and now. *Disability Studies Quarterly, 15*(4), 2–3.

Brown, T. E. (1994). The many faces of ADD: Comorbidity. *Attention!, 1*(2), 29–36.

Bundy, M. L., & Boser, J. (1987). Helping latchkey children: A group guidance approach. *School Counselor, 35,* 58–65.

Bureau of Indian Affairs (1993, October). Indian entities recognized and eligible to receive services from the United States Bureau of Indian Affairs, 58 Fed. Reg. 54,364.

Burgess, A., & Holmstrom, L., Groth, A. N., & Sgroi, S. M. (1978). Accessory to sex: Pressure, sex, and secrecy. In A. Burgess (Ed.), *Sexual assault of children and adolescents* (pp. 85–98). Lexington, MA: Lexington Books.

Burns, B. J., & Friedman, R. M. (1990). Examining the research base for child mental health services and policy. *Journal of Mental Health Administration, 17*(1), 87–98.

Bushman, B. J., & Anderson, C. A. (2001). Media violence and the American public. *American Psychologist, 56,* 477–489.

Bushweller, K. (1995). The high-tech portfolio. *Executive Educator, 17,* 19–22.

Caffaro-Rouget, A., Lang, R. A., & vanSanten, V. (1989). The impact of child sexual abuse. *Annals of Sex Research, 2,* 29–47.

Caffey, J. (1972). On the theory and practice of shaking infants: Its potential residual effects of permanent brain damage and mental retardation. *American Journal of Diseases of Childhood, 124,* 161–169.

Callahan, C. J. (2001). *Predicting and preventing violence in schools: The counselor's role.* Workshop conducted at the annual meeting of the American Counseling Association, San Antonio, TX.

Campagna, D., & Poffenberger, D. (1988). *Sexual trafficking in children.* Dover, MA: Auburn House.

Campbell, C. A. (1992). The school counselor as consultant: Assessing your aptitude. *Elementary School Guidance and Counseling, 26,* 237–250.

Campbell, C. A. (1993). Strategies for reducing parent resistance to consultation in the schools. *Elementary School Guidance and Counseling, 28,* 83–91.

Campbell, C. A., & Dahir, C. A. (1997). *Sharing the vision: The national standards for school counseling programs.* Alexandria, VA: American School Counselor Association.

Cantrell, R. G. (1986). Adjustment to divorce: Three components to assist children. *Elementary School Guidance and Counseling, 20,* 162–173.

Capaldi, D. M., & Patterson, G. R. (1996). Can violent offenders be distinguished from frequent offenders? Predictors from childhood to adolescence. *Journal of Research in Crime and Delinquency, 33,* 206–231.

Caplan, G. (1970). *Theory and practice of mental health consultation.* New York: Basic Books.

Caplan, G., & Caplan, R. B. (1993). *Mental health consultation and collaboration.* San Francisco: Jossey-Bass.

Capuzzi, D. (1989). *Adolescent suicide prevention: Counseling and intervention strategy* (2nd ed.). Ann Arbor, MI: ERIC Counseling and Personnel Services Clearinghouse.

Capuzzi, D. (2002). Legal and ethical challenges in counseling suicidal students. *Professional School Counseling, 6,* 36–45.

Capuzzi, D., & Golden, L. (Eds.). (1988). *Preventing adolescent suicide.* Muncie, IN: Accelerated Development.

Capuzzi, D., & Gross, D. R. (1992). Group counseling: Elements of effective leadership. In D. Capuzzi & D. R. Gross (Eds.), *Introduction to group counseling* (pp. 39–57). Denver: Love.

Capuzzi, D., & Gross, D. R. (2000). I don't want to live: The adolescent at risk for suicidal behavior. In D. Capuzzi & D. R. Gross (Eds.), *Youth at risk: A prevention resource for counselors, teachers, and parents.* (3rd ed.) (pp. 319–352). Alexandria, VA: American Counseling Association.

Carney, J. V. (2000). Bullied to death: Perceptions of peer abuse and suicidal behavior during adolescence. *School Psychology International, 21,* 44–54.

Carns, A. W., & Carns, M. R. (1991). Teaching study skills, cognitive strategies, and metacognitive skills through self-diagnosed learning styles. *School Counselor, 38,* 341–346.

Carter, B. F., & Brooks, A. (1990). Suicide postvention: Crisis or opportunity? *School Counselor, 37,* 378–390.

Carter, R. T. (1988). An empirical test of a theory on the influence of racial identity attitudes on the counseling process within a workshop setting. *Dissertation Abstracts International, 49,* 431-A.

Carter, R. T. (1990). Does race or racial identity attitudes influence the counseling process in Black and White dyads? In J. E. Helms (Ed.), *Black and White racial identity: Theory, research and practice* (pp. 145–163). Westport, CT: Greenwood.

Carter, R. T., & Cook, D. A. (1992). A culturally relevant perspective for understanding the career paths of visible racial/ethnic group people. In H. D. Lea and Z. B. Leibowitz (Eds.), *Adult career development* (2nd ed.) (pp. 192–217). Tulsa, OK: National Career Development Association.

Carter, R. T., & Helms, J. E. (1992). The counseling process as defined by relationship types: A test of Helms's interactional model. *Journal of Multicultural Counseling and Development, 20,* 181–201.

Carter, R. T., & Quereshi, A. (1995). A typology of philosophical assumptions in multicultural counseling and training. In J. G. Ponterotto, J. M. Casas, L. A. Suzuki, & C. M. Alexander (Eds.), *Handbook of multicultural counseling* (pp. 239–262). Thousand Oaks, CA: Sage.

Carter, R. T., & Swanson, J. L. (1990). The validity of the Strong Interest Inventory with Black Americans: A review of the literature. *Journal of Vocational Behavior, 36,* 195–209.

Casas, J., Furlong, M., Carranza, O., Solberg, S., & Jamaica, P. (1986). *Santa Barbara student success study.* Unpublished manuscript. University of California, Santa Barbara.

Catalano, R. F., & Hawkins, J. D. (1996). The social development model: A theory of antisocial behavior. In J. D. Hawkins (Ed.), *Delinquency and crime: Current theories* (pp. 149–197). New York: Cambridge University Press

Catalano, R. F., Hawkins, J. D., Kosterman, R., Abbott, R. D., & Hill, K. G. (1998). *Long-term effects of the Seattle Social Development Project: Implications for theory and practice.* Paper presented at the annual meeting of the Society for Research on Adolescence, San Diego, CA.

Cattell, R. B., Eber, H. W., & Tatsuoka, M. M. (1970). *Handbook for the Sixteen Personality Factor Questionnaire (16PF).* Champaign, IL: Institute for Personality and Ability Testing.

Center for the Prevention of School Violence (2000). *Stats 2000: Selected school violence research findings.* Available online at www.cpsv.org.

Centers for Disease Control and Prevention (1992). *Youth suicide prevention programs: A resource guide.* Atlanta: Author.

Centers for Disease Control and Prevention (1997). Youth risk behavior surveillance—United States, 1997. *Morbidity and Mortality Weekly Report: CDC Surveillance Summaries, 47*(No. SS-3), 1–89.

Centers for Disease Control and Prevention (1998, June). *HIV/AIDS Surveillance Report, 10,* 1–40.

Centers for Disease Control and Prevention (2000). *Targeting tobacco use: The nation's leading cause of death.* Available online at www.cdc.gov/tobacco/overview/oshaag.htm (retrieved February 14, 2001).

Centers for Disease Control and Prevention (2002). Trends in sexual risk behaviors among high school students—United States, 1991–2001. *Morbidity and Mortality Weekly Report, 51*(38), 856–859.

Centers for Disease Control and Prevention (2003). *Divisions of HIV/AIDS prevention: Basic statistics.* Available online at www.cdc.gov/hiv/stats.htm (retrieved June 1, 2003).

Cerio, J. (1994). Play therapy: A brief primer for school counselors. *Journal for the Professional Counselor, 9,* 73–80.

Cerio, J., Taggart, T., & Costa, L. (1999). Play therapy training practices for school counselors: Results of a national study. *Journal for the Professional Counselor, 14,* 57–67.

Charkow, W. B. (1998). Inviting children to grieve. *Professional School Counseling, 2,* 117–122.

Chase-Lansdale, P. L., & Hetherington, E. M. (1990). The impact of divorce on life-span development: Short and long term effects. In P. B. Baltes, D. L. Featherman & R. M. Lerner (Eds.), *Life-span development and behavior Vol. 10* (pp. 105–151). Hillsdale, NJ: Erlbaum.

Chen, J. H., Bierhals, A. J., Prigerson, H. G., Kasl, S. V., Mazure, C. M., & Jacobs, S. (1999). Gender differences in the effects of bereavement-related psychological distress in health outcomes. *Psychological Medicine, 29,* 367–380.

Children and Adults with Attention Deficit Disorders (1995). *The disability named ADD.* Available online at www.chadd.org/fact1.htm.

Children and Adults with Attention Deficit Disorders (1996). ADD research: A look at today and tomorrow: An interview with Richard D. Todd. *Attention! 3*(2), 46–47.

Chisolm, J. F. (1998). Understanding violence in the school: Moral and psychological factors. *Journal of Social Distress and the Homeless, 7,* 137–157.

Choney, S. K., Berryhill-Paapke, E., & Robbins, R. R. (1995). The acculturation of American Indians: Developing frameworks for research and practice. In J. G. Ponterotto, J. M. Casas, L. A. Suzuki, & C. M. Alexander (Eds.), *Handbook of multicultural counseling* (pp. 73–92). Thousand Oaks, CA: Sage.

Christopher, R., & Roosa, M. (1990). An evaluation of an adolescent pregnancy prevention program: Is "Just say no" enough? *Family Relations, 39,* 68–72.

Ciechalski, J. C., & Schmidt, M. W. (1995). The effects of social skills training on students with exceptionalities. *Elementary School Guidance and Counseling, 29,* 217–222.

Clarizio, H. F. (1985). Cognitive–behavioral treatment of childhood depression. *Psychology in the Schools, 22,* 308–322.

Cobia, D. C., Carney, J. S., & Waggoner, I. M. (1998). Children and adolescents with HIV disease. *Professional School Counseling, 1,* 41–45.

Cochran, J. L., & Cochran, N. H. (1997, March). *Counseling children with conduct disorder.* Preconference learning institute conducted at the American Counseling Association World Conference, Orlando, FL.

Cochran, J. L., & Cochran, N. H. (1999). Using the counseling relationship to facilitate change in students with conduct disorder. *Professional School Counseling, 2,* 395–403.

Colbert, P., Newman, B., Ney, P., & Young, J. (1982). Learning disabilities as a symptom of depression in children. *Journal of Learning Disabilities, 15,* 333–336.

Cole, C. V. (1995). Sexual abuse of middle school students. *School Counselor, 42,* 239–245.

Coll, K. M. (1995). Legal challenges in secondary prevention programming for students with substance abuse problems. *School Counselor, 43,* 35–41.

College Board (1999). *Reaching the top: A report of the National Task Force on Minority High Achievement.* New York: Author.

College Board (2000). *Taking the SAT I: Reasoning test.* New York: Author.

College Board Commission on Precollege and Counseling. (1986, January). *Keeping the options open: An overview.* New York: College Board.

Compassionate Friends (1999). *When a child dies: A study of bereaved parents.* Available from www.compassionatefriends.org/survey.shtml (retrieved May 27, 2003).

Conant, J. B. (1959). *The American high school today.* New York: McGraw-Hill.

Concha, P., Garcia, L., & Perez, A. (1975). Cooperation versus competition: A comparison of Anglo-American and Cuban-American youngsters in Miami. *Journal of Social Psychology, 95,* 273–274.

Conte, J. (1986). *A look at child sexual abuse.* Chicago: National Committee for the Prevention of Child Abuse.

Cooley, J. J. (1998). Gay and lesbian adolescents: Presenting problems and the counselor's role. *Professional School Counseling, 1,* 30–34.

Coon-Carty, H. M. (1995). *The relation of work-related abilities, vocational interests, and self-efficacy beliefs: A meta-analytic investigation.* Unpublished master's thesis, Loyola University, Chicago.

Cooper, H., & Moore, J. C. (1995). Teenage motherhood, mother-only households, and teacher expectations. *Journal of Experimental Education, 63,* 231–248.

Coopersmith, S. (1993). *Self-Esteem Inventories (SEI).* Palo Alto, CA: Consulting Psychologists Press.

Corey, G. (2001). *Theory and practice of counseling and psychotherapy* (6th ed.). Pacific Grove, CA: Brooks/Cole.

Corey, G., Corey, M., & Callahan, P. (2003). *Issues and ethics in the helping professions* (6th ed.). Pacific Grove, CA: Brooks/Cole.

Corr, C. A. (1995). Entering into adolescent understandings of death. In E. A. Grollman (Ed.), *Bereaved children and teens: A support guide for parents and professionals* (pp. 21–35). Boston: Beacon Press.

Corwin, D. L. (1989). Early diagnosis of child sexual abuse: Diminishing the lasting effects. In G. E. Wyatt & G. J. Powell (Eds.), *Lasting effects of child sexual abuse* (pp. 251–270). Newbury Park, CA: Sage.

Costa, L., & Holliday, D. (1994). Helping children cope with the death of a parent. *Elementary School Guidance and Counseling, 28,* 206–213.

Council for Learning Disabilities (1997). *Infosheet: What do we know about the characteristics of learning disabilities?* Available online at www.winthrop.edu/cld/Infosheet%20characteristics.html.

Coyle, K., Basen-Engquist, K., Kirby, D., Parcel, G., Banspach, S., Harrist, R., Baumler, E., & Weil, M. (1999). Short-term impact of Safer Choices: A multicomponent, school-based HIV, other STD, and pregnancy prevention program. *Journal of School Health, 69,* 181–188.

Coyle, K., Kirby, D., Parcel, G., Basen-Engquist, K., Banspach, S., Rugg, D., & Weil, M. (1996). Safer Choices: A multicomponent school-based HIV/STD and pregnancy prevention program for adolescents. *Journal of School Health, 66,* 89–94.

Craig, W. M., Peters, R. D., & Konarski, R. (1998). *Bullying and victimization among Canadian school children.* Available online at www.hrdc-drhc.ca/arb/publications/research/abw-98-28e.html.

Crawford, H. J., & Barabasz, M. (1996). Quantitative EEG magnitudes in children with and without attention deficit disorder. *Child Study Journal, 26,* 71–86.

Crick, N. R., & Bigbee, M. A. (1998). Relational and overt forms of peer victimization: A multi-informant approach. *Journal of Consulting and Clinical Psychology, 66,* 337–347.

Crites, J. O., & Savickas, M. L. (1995). *The Career Maturity Inventory—Revised form.* Ontario, Canada: Bridges.com.

Crittenden, P. M. (1981). Abusing, neglecting, problematic, and adequate dyads: Differentiating by patterns of interactions. *Merrill–Palmer Quarterly, 27,* 1–18.

Crittenden, P. M. (1988). Family and dyadic patterns of functioning in maltreating families. In K. Browne, C. Davies, & P. Stratton (Eds.), *Early prediction and prevention of child abuse* (pp. 161–189). New York: Wiley.

Crittenden, P. M., & Ainsworth, M. D. (1989). Child maltreatment and attachment theory. In D. Cicchetti & V. Carlson (Eds.), *Child maltreatment: Theory and research on the causes and consequences of child abuse and neglect* (pp. 432–464). New York: Cambridge University Press.

Cronbach, L. J. (1990). *Essentials of psychological testing* (5th ed.). New York: Harper & Row.

Cross, W. E. (1971). The Negro-to-Black conversion experience. *Black World, 20,* 13–27.

Crowne, D. P., & Marlowe, D. (1960). A scale of social desirability independent of psychopathology. *Journal of Consulting Psychology, 24,* 349–354.

Cull, J., & Gill, W. (1982). *Suicide Probability Scale manual.* Los Angeles: Western Psychological Services.

Cunningham, B., & Hare, J. (1989). Essential elements of a teacher in-service program on child bereavement. *Elementary School Guidance and Counseling, 23,* 175–182.

Cunningham, N. J., & Sandhu, D. S. (2000). A comprehensive approach to school–community violence. *Professional School Counseling, 4,* 126–133.

Dahir, C. A. (2001). The national standards for school counseling programs: Development and implementation. *Professional School Counseling, 4,* 320–327.

Dahir, C. A., & Stone, C. B. (2003). Accountability: A M.E.A.S.U.R.E. of the impact school counselors have on student achievement. *Professional School Counseling, 6,* 214–221.

D'Andrea, M., & Daniels, J. (1995). Helping students learn to get along: Assessing the effectiveness of a multicultural guidance project. *Elementary School Guidance and Counseling, 30,* 143–154.

Daro, D. (1993). Child maltreatment research: Implications for program design. In D. Cicchetti & S. L. Toth (eds.), *Child abuse, child development and social policy* (pp. 331–368). Norwood, NJ: Ablex.

Daro, D., & Salmon-Cox, S. (1994). *Child abuse prevention programs. Do they work?* Washington, DC: U.S. Department of Health and Human Services, National Center on Child Abuse and Neglect.

Davidson, G. C., & Friedman, S. (1981). Sexual orientation stereotyping in the distortion of clinical judgment. *Journal of Homosexuality, 6,* 37–44.

Davies, B. (1988). The family environment in bereaved families and its relationship to surviving sibling behavior. *Children's Health Care, 17,* 22–31.

Davies, B. (1990). Long-term follow-up of bereaved siblings. In J. Morgan (Ed.), *The dying and bereaved teenager* (pp. 78–89). Philadelphia: Charles Press.

Davies, B. (1991). Long-term outcomes of adolescent sibling bereavement. *Journal of Adolescent Research, 6,* 83–96.

Davies, B. (1995). Toward siblings' understanding and perspectives of death. In E. A. Grollman (Ed.), *Bereaved children and teens: A support guide for parents and professionals* (pp. 61–74). Boston: Beacon Press.

Davies, B., & Cummings, E. M. (1998). Exploring children's emotional security as a mediator of the link between marital relations and child adjustment. *Child Development, 69,* 124–139.

Davila, R. R., Williams, M. L., & McDonald, J. T. (1991, September 16). *Clarification of policy to address the needs of children with attention deficit disorders within general and/or special classrooms.* Unpublished memorandum. Available online at www.add.org/contents/legal/memo.htm.

Dawes, C. (1996). Learning disabilities research encompasses education and biology. *CHDD Outlook, 9*(2), 1–3.

DeAngelis, T. (2002). New data on lesbian, gay, and bisexual mental health. *APA Monitor, 33,* 46–47.

Deaver, J. R. (1988). *Say goodnight, Gracie.* New York: Harper & Row.

De LaRosa, M. (1998). Natural support systems of Puerto Ricans: A key dimension to well-being. *Health and Social Work, 13,* 181–190.

Delgado, M. (1997). Role of Latina-owned beauty parlors in a Latino community. *Social Work, 42,* 445–453.

Delgado, M. (1998). Puerto Rican elders and merchant establishments. *Journal of Gerontological Social Work, 30,* 33–45.

Delgado, M., & Humm-Delgado, M. (1982). Natural support systems: Source of strength in Hispanic communities. *Social Work, 27,* 83–89.

Denno, D. W. (1990). *Biology and violence: From birth to adulthood.* Cambridge, England: Cambridge University Press.

de Shazer, S. (1985). *Keys to solutions in brief therapy.* New York: Norton.

de Shazer, S. (1988). *Clues: Investigating solutions in brief therapy.* New York: Norton.

de Shazer, S. (1991). *Putting difference to work.* New York: Norton.

Despelder, L. A., & Strickland, A. L. (1983). *The last dance: Encountering death and dying.* Mountain View, CA: Mayfield.

Dewey, C. R. (1974). Exploring interests: A non-sexist method. *Personnel and Guidance Journal, 52,* 311–315.

De Young, M. (1982). *Sexual victimization of children.* Jefferson, NC: McFarland.

Dhooper, S. S., & Schneider, P. L. (1995). Evaluation of a school-based child abuse prevention program. *Research on Social Work and Practice, 5,* 36–46.

Diamond, E. E. (1975). Overview. In E. E. Diamond (Ed.), *Issues of sex bias and sex fairness in career interest measurement* (pp. xiii–xxi). Washington, DC: Department of Health, Education, and Welfare.

Dinkmeyer, D., & Carlson, J. (1973). *Consulting: Facilitating human potential and change processes.* Columbus, OH: Merrill.

Dinkmeyer, D., & Carlson, J. (2001). *Consultation: Creating school-based interventions.* Philadelphia: Bruner-Routledge.

Dinkmeyer, D., & Dinkmeyer, D. (1976). Logical consequences: A key to the reduction of disciplinary problems. *Phi Delta Kappa, 57,* 663–666.

Dixon, S. L. (1987). *Working with people in crisis* (2nd ed.). Columbus, OH: Merrill.

Doherty, W., & Needle, R. (1991). Psychological adjustment and substance use among adolescents before and after a parental divorce. *Child Development, 62,* 328–337.

Doka, K. J. (1989). *Disenfranchised grief: Recognizing hidden sorrow.* Lexington, MA: Lexington Books.

Doka, K. J. (1995). Friends, teachers, movie star: The disenfranchised grief of children. In E. A. Grollman (Ed.), *Bereaved children and teens: A support guide for parents and professionals* (pp. 37–45). Boston: Beacon Press.

Dolliver, R. H. (1967). An adaptation of the Tyler Vocational Card Sort. *Personnel and Guidance Journal, 45,* 916–920.

Dornbusch, S., Ritter, P., Leiderman, H., Roberts, D., & Fraleigh, M. (1987). The relation of parenting style to adolescent school performance. *Child Development, 58,* 1244–1257.

Dougherty, A. M. (1995). *Consultation: Practice and perspectives in school and community settings* (2nd ed.). Pacific Grove, CA: Brooks/Cole.

Dougherty, A. M., Dougherty, L. P., & Purcell, D. (1991). The sources and management of resistance to consultation. *School Counselor, 38,* 178–186.

Dreikurs, R. (1968). *Psychology in the classroom* (2nd ed.). New York: Harper & Row.

Dreikurs, R., & Cassel, P. (1990). *Discipline without tears* (2nd ed.). New York: Dutton.

Dreikurs, R., & Soltz, V. (1990). *Children: The challenge.* New York: Plume.

Dressler, J. (1985). Survey of school principals regarding alleged homosexual teachers in the classroom: How likely (really) is discharge? *University of Dayton Law Review, 10,* 599–620.

Drummond, R. J. (2000). *Appraisal procedures for counselors and helping professionals* (4th ed.). Upper Saddle River, NJ: Merrill.

Drummond, R. J., & Ryan, C. W. (1995). *Career counseling: A developmental approach.* Columbus, OH: Merrill.

Dryfoos, J. G. (1994). *Full-service schools: A revolution in health and social services for children, youth and families.* San Francisco: Jossey-Bass.

Dubowitz, H., Black, M., Harrington, D., & Verschoore, A. (1993). A follow-up study of behavior problems associated with child sexual abuse. *Child Abuse and Neglect, 17,* 743–754.

Dulcan, M.K.,& Lizarralde, C. (2003). *Helping parents, youth, and teachers understand medications for behavioral and emotional problems: A resource book of medication information handouts* (2nd ed.). Washington, DC: American Psychiatric Publishing.

Dupont, H. (1978). Meeting the emotional–social needs of students in a mainstream environment. *Counseling and Human Development, 10,* 1–11.

Dwyer, K., Osher, D., & Warger, C. (1998). *Early warning, timely response: A guide to safe schools.* Washington, DC: U.S. Department of Education.

Dykeman, C., & Appleton, V. E. (2000). The impact of dysfunctional family dynamics on children and adolescents. In D. Capuzzi & D. R. Gross (Eds.), *Youth at risk: A prevention resource for counselors, teachers, and parents.* (3rd ed.) (pp. 81–108). Alexandria, VA: American Counseling Association.

Education Trust (1997). *Transforming school counseling: Request for planning grant proposals.* Washington, DC: Author.

Edwards, D. L., & Foster, M. A. (1995). Uniting the family and school systems: A process of empowering the school counselor. *School Counselor, 42,* 277–282.

Egeland, B. (1988). The consequences of physical and emotional neglect on the development of young children. In U.S. Department of Health and Human Services, National Center on Child Abuse and Neglect (Ed.), *Research symposium on child neglect* (pp. 34–48). Washington, DC: Author.

Egeland, B., & Erickson, M. F. (1990). Rising above the past: Strategies for helping new mothers break the cycle of abuse and neglect. *Zero to Three, 11,* 29–35.

Ellickson, P. L., & Bell, R. M. (1990). Drug prevention in junior high: A multi-site longitudinal test. *Science, 247,* 1299–1305.

Elliot, D. S. (1994). Serious violent offenders: Onset, developmental course, and termination—The American Society of Criminology 1993 presidential address. *Criminology, 32,* 1–21.

Elliot, D. S., Huizenga, D., & Menard, S. (1989). *Multiple problem youth: Delinquency, substance use and mental health problems.* New York: Springer-Verlag.

Ellis, A. (1995). Rational emotive behavior therapy. In R. J. Corsini & D. Wedding (Eds.), *Current psychotherapies* (5th ed.) (pp. 162–196). Itasca, IL: Peacock.

Elmer, E., & Gregg, G. S. (1967). Developmental characteristics of abused children. *Pediatrics, 40,* 596–602.

Epstein, Y. M., & Borduin, D. M. (1986). Could this happen? A game for children of divorce. *Psychotherapy, 22,* 770–773.

Equal Employment Opportunity Commission (1986). Guidelines on discrimination because of sex, 29 C.F.R. § 1604.11, 25 C.F.R. § 700.561.

Erchul, W. P. (1987). A relational communication analysis of control in school consultation. *Professional School Psychology, 2,* 113–124.

Erchul, W. P., & Chewning, T. G. (1990). Behavioral consultation from a request-centered relational communication perspective. *School Psychology Quarterly, 5,* 1–20.

Erchul, W. P., & Conoley, C. W. (1991). Helpful theories to guide counselor's practice of school-based consultation. *Elementary School Guidance and Counseling, 25,* 204–211.

Erikson, E. H. (1950). *Childhood and society.* New York: Norton.

Erikson, E. H. (1956). The problem of ego identity. *Journal of the American Psychoanalytic Association, 4,* 56–121.

Erikson, E. H. (1963). *Childhood and society* (2nd ed). New York: Norton.

Erk, R. R. (1995). A diagnosis of attention deficit disorder: What does it mean for school counselors? *School Counselor, 42,* 292–299

Erk, R. R. (1999). Attention deficit hyperactivity disorder: Counselors, laws, and implications for practice. *Professional School Counseling, 2,* 318–326.

Eron, D. S., Walder, L. O., & Lefkowitz, M. M. (1971). *Learning of aggression in children.* Boston: Little, Brown.

Eron, L. D. (1982). Parent–child interaction, television violence, and aggression of children. *American Psychologist, 37,* 197–211.

Eron, L. D., Gentry, J. H., & Schlegel, P. (1994). *Reason to hope: A psychosocial perspective on violence and youth.* Washington, DC: American Psychological Association.

Ervin, C. S., Little, R. E., Streissguth, A. P., & Beck, D. E. (1984). Alcoholic fathering and its relation to child's intellectual development: A pilot investigation. *Alcoholism: Clinical and Experimental Research, 8,* 362–365.

Estes, N. J., & Heinemann, M. E. (1977). *Alcoholism: Development, consequences, and interventions.* St. Louis, MO: Mosby.

Ewalt, P. L., & Perkins, L. (1979). The real experience of death among adolescents: An empirical study. *Social Casework, 60,* 547–551.

Fairchild, T. N. (1993). Accountability practices of school counselors: 1990 national survey. *School Counselor, 40,* 363–374.

Fairchild, T. N., & Zins, J. E. (1986). Accountability practices of school counselors: A national survey. *Journal of Counseling and Development, 65,* 196–199.

Fall, M. (1994). Self-efficacy: An additional dimension in play therapy. *International Journal of Play Therapy, 3,* 21–32.

Fall, M., Balvanz, J., Johnson, L., & Nelson, L. (1999). A play therapy intervention and its relationship to self-efficacy and learning behaviors. *Professional School Counseling, 2,* 194–204.

Faller, K. C. (1990). *Understanding child sexual maltreatment.* Thousand Oaks, CA: Sage.

Faller, K. C. (1993). *Child sexual abuse and treatment.* Washington, DC: U.S. Department of Health and Human Services, Administration for Children and Families.

Famularo, R. (1986). Alcoholism and severe child maltreatment. *American Journal of Orthopsychiatry, 53,* 481–485.

Farrington, D. P. (1989). Early predictors of adolescent aggression and adult violence. *Violence and Victims, 4,* 79–100.

Farrington, D. P. (1991). Childhood aggression and adult violence: Early precursors and later-life outcomes. In D. J. Pepler & K. H. Rubin (Eds.), *The development and treatment of childhood aggression* (pp. 5–29). Hillsdale, NJ: Erlbaum.

Farrington, D. P. (1995). Key issues in the integration of motivational and opportunity-reducing crime prevention strategies. In P. O. Wilkstrom, R. V. Clarke, & J. McCord (Eds.), *Integrating crime prevention strategies: Propensity and opportunity* (pp. 333–357). Stockholm: National Council for Crime Prevention.

Farrington, D. P. (1997). Early prediction of violent and nonviolent youthful offending. *European Journal on Criminal Policy and Research, 5,* 51–66.

Federal Bureau of Investigation (2000). *Hate crime statistics, 2000.* Available online at www.fbi.gov/ucr/cius_00/hate00.pdf (retrieved January 23, 2003).

Felner, R. D., Ginter, M. A., Boike, M. F., & Cowen, E. L. (1981). Parental death or divorce and the school adjustment of young children. *American Journal of Community Psychology, 9,* 181–191.

Felner, R. D., Stolberg, A. L., & Cowen, E. L. (1975). Crisis events and school mental health referral patterns of young children. *Journal of Consulting and Clinical Psychology, 43,* 305–310.

Ferguson, D. L. (1995). The real challenge of inclusion: Confessions of a "rabid inclusionist." *Phi Delta Kappan, 77,* 281–287.

Fibkins, W. L. (1993). Combating student tobacco addiction in secondary schools. *NAASP Bulletin, 77,* 51–59.

Finkelhor, D. (1984). *Child sexual abuse: New theory and research.* New York: Free Press.

Finkelhor, D., Asdigian, N., & Dzuiba-Leatherman, J. (1993). *Victimization prevention training in action: A national survey of children's experiences coping with actual threats and assaults and reactions* (Final report of the National Youth Victimization Prevention Study funded by the Boy Scouts of America). Durham, NH: University of New Hampshire.

Finkelhor, D., Asdigian, N., & Dzuiba-Leatherman, J. (1995a). The effectiveness of victimization prevention instruction: An evaluation of children's threats and assaults. *Child Abuse and Neglect, 19,* 141–153.

Finkelhor, D., Asdigian, N., & Dzuiba-Leatherman, J. (1995b). Victimization prevention programs for children: A follow-up. *American Journal of Public Health, 85,* 1684–1689.

Finkelhor, D., & Baron, L. (1986). High-risk children. In D. Finkelhor (Ed.), *Sourcebook on child sexual abuse* (pp. 60–88). Newbury Park, CA: Sage.

Finkelhor, D., & Browne, A. (1985). The traumatic impact of child sexual abuse: A conceptualization. *American Journal of Orthopsychiatry, 55,* 530–541.

Finkelhor, D., & Browne, A. (1986). Initial and long-term effects: A conceptual framework. In D. Finkelhor (Ed.), *Sourcebook on child sexual abuse* (pp. 180–198). Newbury Park, CA: Sage.

Finkelhor, D., & Dzuiba-Leatherman, J. (1995). Victimization prevention programs: A national survey of children's exposure and reactions. *Child Abuse and Neglect, 19,* 129–139.

Finkelhor, D., Hotaling, G., Lewis, I. A., & Smith, C. (1990). Sexual abuse in a national study of adult men and women: Prevalence, characteristics, and risk factors. *Child Abuse and Neglect, 14,* 19–28.

Fischer, L., & Sorenson, G. P. (1996). *School law for counselors, psychologists, and social workers* (3rd ed.). New York: Longmans.

Fitzpatrick, J. P. (1987). *Puerto Rican Americans* (2nd ed.). Englewood Cliffs, NJ: Prentice Hall.

Flay, B. R. (1985). Psychosocial approaches to smoking prevention. A review of findings. *Health Psychology, 4,* 449–488.

Flay, B. R. (1986). Efficacy and effectiveness trials (and other phases of research) in the development of health promotion programs. *Preventive Medicine, 15,* 451–474.

Flay, B. R., D'Avernas, J. R., Best, J. A., Kersell, M. W., & Ryan, R. B. (1983). Cigarette smoking and why young people do it and ways to prevent it. In P. McGrath & P. Firestone (Eds.), *Pediatric and adolescent behavioral medicine* (pp. 132–183). New York: Springer-Verlag.

Fleming, N. F., Potter, D., & Kettyle, C. (1996). What are substance abuse and addiction? In L. Friedman, N. F. Fleming, D. H. Roberts, & S. E. Hyman (Eds.), *Sourcebook of substance abuse and addiction* (pp. 1–15). Baltimore: Williams & Wilkins.

Fontaine, J. H. (1998). Evidencing a need: School counselor's experiences with gay and lesbian students. *Professional School Counseling, 1,* 8–14.

Forehand, R., King, H. E., Peed, S., & Yoder, P. (1975). Comparisons of noncompliant clinic group and non-clinic group. *Behavior Research and Therapy, 13,* 79–84.

Fossey, R., Hosie, T., & Zirkel, P. (1995). Section 504 and "front line" educators: An expanded obligation to serve students with disabilities. *Preventing School Failure, 39,* 10–14.

Foster, S. (1996, July). Minnesota court rules in school's favor after student suicide. *Counseling Today, 39*(2), 19–21.

Fouad, N. A. (1993). Cross-cultural vocational assessment. *Career Development Quarterly, 42,* 4–13.

Fouad, N. A., & Bingham, R. P. (1995). Career counseling with racial/ethnic minorities. In W. B. Walsh & S. H. Osipow (Eds.), *Handbook of vocational psychology* (2nd ed., pp. 331–365). Hillsdale, NJ: Erlbaum.

Fox, S. S. (1984). Children's anniversary reactions to the death of a family member. In R. A. Kalish (Ed.), *The final transition* (pp. 87–101). New York: Baywood.

Francis, J. (1998). Death and childhood grief. In L. L. Palmatier (Ed.), *Crisis counseling for a quality school community* (pp. 401–438). Washington, DC: Accelerated Development.

Franklin, C., Grant, J., Corcoran, J., Miler, P., & Bultman, L. (1997). Effectiveness of prevention programs for adolescent pregnancy: A meta-analysis. *Journal of Marriage and the Family, 59,* 551–567.

French, J. L. (1990). History of school psychology. In T. B. Gutkin & C. R. Reynolds (Eds.), *The handbook of school psychology* (2nd ed.) (pp. 3–20). New York: Wiley.

Friedrich, M. C., Matus, A. L., & Rinn, R. (1985). *An interdisciplinary supervised student program focused on depression and suicide awareness.* New York: Department of Education.

Friedrich, W. N., Tyler, J. D., & Clark, J. A. (1985). Personality and psychophysiological variables in abusive, neglectful, and low-income control mothers. *Journal of Nervous and Mental Disease, 173,* 449–460.

Frieman, B. B. (1994). Children of divorced parents: Action steps for the counselor to involve fathers. *Elementary School Guidance and Counseling, 28,* 197–205.

Fromuth. M. E. (1983). *The long-term psychological impact of childhood sexual abuse.* Unpublished doctoral dissertation, Auburn University, Auburn, AL.

Fuchs, D., & Fuchs, L. (1992). Framing the REI debate: Abolitionists versus conservationists. In J. W. Lloyd, N. N. Singh, & A. C. Repp (Eds.), *The regular education initiative: Alternative perspectives on concepts, issues, and models* (pp. 241–255). Sycamore, IL: Sycamore.

Furman, E. (1974). *A child's parent dies.* New Haven, CT: Yale University Press.

Furman, J., & Pratt, P. (1985, January). *Coping with the ultimate change, death of a family member: A support group for bereaved adolescents.* Paper presented at the meeting of the National Association of Social Workers, New Orleans. (ERIC Document Reproduction Service No. ED259239)

Furman, R. (1964). Death and the young child: Some preliminary considerations. *Psychoanalytic Study of the Child, 19,* 321–333.

Furstenberg, F., & Cherlin, A. J. (1991). *Divided families: What happens to children when parents part.* Cambridge, MA: Harvard University Press.

Furstenberg, F., Brooks-Gunn, J., & Chase-Lansdale, L. (1989). Teenaged pregnancy and childbearing. *American Psychologist, 44,* 313–320.

Furstenberg, F., Morgan, S., Moore, K. A., & Peterson, J. L. (1987). Race differences in the timing of adolescent intercourse. *American Sociological Review, 52,* 511–518.

Gabrielli, W. F., & Mednick, S. A. (1983). Intellectual performance in children of alcoholics. *Journal of Nervous and Mental Disease, 171,* 444–447.

Galdston, R. (1971). Psychiatric treatment of abused children. *Journal of the American Academy of Child Psychiatry, 10,* 336–350.

Garbarino, J. (1977). The human ecology of child maltreatment: A conceptual meld of research. *Journal of Marriage and the Family, 39,* 7221–7235.

Garbarino, J. (1987). Children's response to a sexual abuse prevention program: A study of the Spider-Man comic. *Child Abuse and Neglect, 11,* 143–148.

Garbarino, J. (1992). *Children and families in the social environment* (2nd ed.). New York: Aldine de Gruyter.

Garber, B. (1988). Some common transference–countertransference issues in the treatment of parental loss. In S. Altschul (Ed.), *Childhood bereavement and its aftermath* (pp. 145–163). Madison, CT: International Universities Press.

Garfinkel, B. D., Crosby, E., Herbert, M., Matus, A., Pfeifer, J., & Sheras, P. (1988, September). *Responding to adolescent suicide: The first 48 hours.* Bloomington, IN: Phi Delta Kappa Educational Foundation.

Gates, G. J., & Sonenstein, F. L. (2000). Heterosexual genital sexual activity among adolescent males: 1988 and 1995. *Family Planning Perspectives, 32*(6), 295–304.

Gaudin, J. M. (1991). Remedying child neglect: Effectiveness of social network interventions. *Journal of Applied Social Sciences, 15,* 97–123.

Gaudin, J. M. (1993). *Child neglect: A guide for interventions.* Washington, DC: U.S. Department of Health and Human Services, Administration for Children and Families.

Gazda, G. M. (1989). *Group counseling: A developmental approach* (4th ed.). Boston: Allyn & Bacon.

Geddes, J. & Butler, R. (2002). Depressive disorders. *Clinical Evidence, 7,* 74–89.

Gellman, E. S. (1995). *School testing: What parents and educators need to know.* Westport, CT: Praeger.

Gerler, E. R. (1980). A longitudinal study of multimodal approaches to small group psychological education. *School Counselor, 27,* 184–190.

Gerler, E. R. (1992). What we know about school counseling: A reaction to Borders and Drury. *Journal of Counseling and Development, 70,* 499–501.

Gerler, E. R., & Anderson, R. F. (1986). The effects of classroom guidance on children's success in school. *Journal of Counseling and Development, 65,* 78–81.

Gerler, E. R., Drew, N. S., & Mohr, P. (1990). Succeeding in middle school: A multimodal approach. *Elementary School Guidance and Counseling, 24,* 263–271.

Gerler, E. R., Kinney, J., & Anderson, R. F. (1985). The effects of counseling on counseling performance. *Journal of Humanistic Education and Development, 23,* 155–165.

Gfroerer, J. (1987). Correlation between drug use by teenagers and drug use by older family members. *American Journal of Drug and Alcohol Abuse, 13,* 95–108.

Giangreco, M. F., Dennis, R., Cloninger, D., Edelman, S., & Schattman, R. (1993). "I've counted Jon": Transformational experiences of teachers educating students with disabilities. *Exceptional Children, 59,* 359–372.

Gibson, P. (1989). Gay male and lesbian youth suicide. In G. Remafedi (Ed.), *Death by denial: Studies of suicide in gay and lesbian teenagers* (pp. 15–68). Boston: Alyson.

Gil, E. (1991). *The healing power of play.* New York: Guilford.

Gil, E., & Johnson, T. C. (1993). *Sexualized children: Assessment and treatment of sexualized children and children who molest.* Rockville, MD: Launch Press.

Gilbar, O., and Dagan, A. (1995). Coping with loss: Differences between widows and widowers of deceased cancer patients. *Omega, 31,* 207–220.

Gill, C. (1995). A psychological view of disability culture. *Disability Studies Quarterly, 15*(4), 16–19.

Gilligan, C. (1982). *In a different voice: Psychological theory and women's development.* Cambridge, MA: Harvard University.

Gilson, S. F., & Depoy, E. (2000). Multiculturalism and disability: A critical perspective. *Disability and Society, 15,* 207–218.

Ginott, H. (1968). Group therapy with children. In G. Gazda (Ed.), *Basic approaches to group psychotherapy and group counseling* (pp. 176–194). Springfield, IL: Thomas.

Ginsberg, B. (1984). Beyond behavior modification: Client-centered play therapy with the retarded. *Academic Psychology Bulletin, 6,* 321–324.

Ginter, E. J., Scalise, J. J., & Presse, N. (1990). The elementary school counselor's role: Perceptions of teachers. *School Counselor, 38,* 19–23.

Ginzberg, E. (1952). Toward a theory of occupational choice. *Occupations, 30,* 491–494.

Ginzberg, E. (1971). *Career guidance.* New York: McGraw-Hill.

Giovannoni, J. M., & Becera, R. M. (1979). *Defining child abuse.* New York: Free Press.

Gittelman, R., Abikoff, H., Pollack, E., Klein, D., Katz, S., & Mattes, J. (1980). A controlled trial of behavior modification and methyphenidate in hyperactive children. In C. Whalen & B. Henker (Eds.), *Hyperactive children: The social ecology of identification and treatment* (pp. 221–243). New York: Academy Press.

Gladding, S. T. (1999). *Group work: A counseling specialty* (3rd ed.). Upper Saddle River, NJ: Merrill.

Gladding, S. T. (2001). *The counseling dictionary: Concise definitions of frequently used terms.* Upper Saddle River, NJ: Prentice Hall.

Glaize, D. L., & Myrick, R. D. (1984). Interpersonal groups or computers? A study of career maturity and career decidedness. *Vocational Guidance Quarterly, 32,* 168–176.

Glass, J. C. (1991). Death, loss, and grief among middle school children: Implications for the school counselor. *Elementary School Guidance and Counseling, 26,* 139–148.

Glasser, W. (1965). *Reality therapy: A new approach to psychiatry.* New York: Harper & Row.

Glasser, W. (1989). Control theory in the practice of reality therapy. In N. Glasser (Ed.), *Control theory in the practice of reality therapy: Case studies* (pp. 1–15). New York: Harper & Row.

Glasser, W. (1998). *Choice theory: A new psychology of personal freedom.* New York: HarperCollins.

Glasser, W. (2000). *Reality therapy in action.* New York: HarperCollins.

Glenn, E. E., & Smith, T. T. (1998). Building self-esteem in children and adolescents with communication disorders. *Professional School Counseling, 2,* 39–46.

Gloria, A. M., & Robinson-Kurpius, S. E. (2000). I can't live without it: Adolescent substance abuse from a cultural and contextual framework. In D. Capuzzi & D. R. Gross (Eds.), *Youth at risk: A prevention resource for counselors, teachers, and parents* (3rd ed.) (pp. 409–439). Alexandria, VA: American Counseling Association.

Glosoff, H. L., & Pate, R. H. (2002). Privacy and confidentiality in school counseling. *Professional School Counseling, 6,* 20–27.

Glosoff, H. L., Herlihy, B., & Spence, B. (2000). Privileged communication in the counselor–client relationship: An analysis of state laws and implications for practice. *Journal of Counseling and Development, 78,* 454–462.

Glover, G. J. (1994). The hero child in the alcoholic home: Recommendations for counselors. *School Counselor, 41,* 185–190.

Goldberg, L., Elliot, D. L., Clarke, G. N., MacKinnon, D. P., Zoref, L., Moe, E., Green, C., & Wolf, S. (1996a). The Adolescents Training and Learning to Avoid Steroids (ATLAS) prevention program: Background and results of a model intervention. *Archives of Pediatric and Adolescent Medicine, 150,* 713–721.

Goldberg, L., Elliot, D. L., Clarke, G. N., MacKinnon, D. P., Zoref, L., Moe, E., Green, C., & Wolf, S. (1996b). Effects of a multidimensional anabolic steroid prevention intervention: The A.T.L.A.S. (Adolescents Training and Learning to Avoid Steroids) Program. *Journal of the American Medical Association, 276,* 1555–1562.

Goldman, L. (1983). The Vocational Card Sort technique: A different view. *Measurement and Evaluation in Guidance, 16,* 107–109.

Goldstein, S., & Goldstein, M. (1990). *Managing attention disorders in children.* New York: Wiley.

Gonzalez, G. M. (1997). The emergence of Chicanos in the 21st century: Implications for counseling, research, and policy. *Journal of Multicultural Counseling and Development, 25,* 94–106.

Goodwin, D. W. (1981). *Alcoholism: The facts.* New York: Oxford University Press.

Goodyear, R. (2002). A concept map of male partners in teenage pregnancy: Implications for school counselors. *Professional School Counseling, 5,* 186–193.

Gottfredson, L. S. (1981). Circumspection and compromise: A developmental theory of occupational aspirations. *Journal of Counseling Psychology, 28,* 545–579.

Governor's Task Force on Biased-Related Violence (1988). *Final Report 2*(1), 77–79. (Available from Division of Human Rights, 55 W. 125th St., New York, NY 10027)

Gramick, J. (1983). Homophobia: A new challenge. *Social Work, 28,* 137–141.

Grant, B. F., & Dawson, D. A. (1997). Age at onset of alcohol use and association with *DSM-IV* alcohol abuse and dependence: Results from the National Longitudinal Alcohol Epidemiological Survey. *Journal of Substance Abuse, 9,* 103–110.

Gray, L. A., House, R. M., & Champeau, D. A. (2000). A future in jeopardy: Adolescents and AIDS. In D. Capuzzi & D. R. Gross (Eds.), *Youth at risk: A prevention resource for counselors, teachers, and parents* (3rd ed.) (pp. 281–317). Alexandria, VA: American Counseling Association.

Gredler, M. E. (1996). *Program evaluation.* Englewood Cliffs, NJ: Prentice Hall.

Green, A. H. (1978). Psychiatric treatment of abused children. *Journal of the American Academy of Child Psychiatry, 17,* 356–371.

Green, A. H. (1980). Psychological assessment of child-abusing, neglecting, and normal mothers. *Journal of Nervous and Mental Diseases, 168,* 356–360.

Green, L. B., & Parker, H. J. (1965). Parental influence upon adolescents' occupational choice: A test of an aspect of Roe's theory. *Journal of Counseling Psychology, 12,* 379–383.

Greenbaum, S., Turner, B., & Stephens, R. (1989). *Set straight on bullies.* Malibu, CA: National School Safety Center.

Greenberg, B. S., Brown, J. D., & Buerkel-Rothfuss, N. L. (Eds.). 1993. *Media, sex, and the adolescent.* Cresskill, NJ: Hampton Press.

Greenfield, J. A. (1998). *Alcohol and crime: An analysis of national data on the prevalence of alcohol involvement in crime.* Report prepared for the Assistant Attorney General's National Symposium on Alcohol Abuse and Crime. Washington, DC: U.S. Department of Justice.

Greenhouse, L. (1999, May 25). Sex harassment in class is ruled schools' liability. *New York Times,* pp. A1, A24.

Greer, B. B., Greer, J. G., & Woody, D. E. (1995). The inclusion movement and its impact on counselors. *School Counselor, 43,* 124–132.

Grollman, E. A. (1988). *Shira: A legacy of courage.* New York: Doubleday.

Grollman, E. A. (1995). Explaining death to young children: Some questions and answers. In E. A. Grollman (Ed.), *Bereaved children and teens: A support guide for parents and professionals* (pp. 3–19). Boston: Beacon Press.

Guerney, L. (1983). Client-centered (non-directive) play therapy. In C. Schaefer & K. O'Connor (Eds.), *Handbook of play therapy* (pp. 21–64). New York: Wiley.

Guerra, P. (1998, February). Revamping school counselor education: The DeWitt Wallace–*Reader's Digest* Fund. *CTOnline.* Available online at www.counseling.org.

Guerrero, F., Walker, S., & Langlois, C. (1987). *Chapter 1 clinical and guidance program 1985–1986.* Brooklyn: New York City Board of Education. (ERIC Document Reproduction Service No. ED293025)

Guida, A. (2001). Depression . . . or just the blues? *School Counselor, 39*(2), 11–13.

Guidubaldi, J., Perry, J. D., Cleminshaw, H. K., & Mcloughlin, C. S. (1983). The impact of parental divorce on children: Report of a nationwide NASP study. *School Psychology Review, 12,* 300–323.

Gumaer, J. (1986). Working in groups with middle graders. *School Counselor, 33,* 230–238.

Gutkin, T. B. (1999). Collaborative versus directive/prescriptive/expert school-based consultation: Reviewing and resolving a false dichotomy. *Journal of School Psychology, 37,* 161–190.

Gutman, H. G. (1977). *The Black family in slavery and freedom, 1750–1925.* New York: Pantheon.

Guy, S. M., Smith, G. M., & Bentler, P. M. (1994). The influence of adolescent substance use and socialization on deviant behavior in young adulthood. *Criminal Justice and Behavior, 21,* 236–255.

Gysbers, N. C., & Henderson, P. (1988). *Developing and managing your school guidance program.* Alexandria, VA: Association for Counseling and Development.

Gysbers, N. C., & Henderson, P. (1994). *Developing and managing your school guidance program* (2nd ed.) Alexandria, VA: Association for Counseling and Development.

Gysbers, N. C., & Henderson, P. (2000). *Developing and managing your school guidance program* (3rd ed.). Alexandria, VA: American Counseling Association.

Gysbers, N. C., & Henderson, P. (2001). Comprehensive guidance and counseling programs: A rich history and a bright future. *Professional School Counseling, 4,* 246–256.

Hackbarth-James, S., & Burch, K. M. (1999). School counselors' roles in cases of child sexual behavior. *Professional School Counseling, 2,* 211–217.

Hackett, G., & Betz, N. E. (1981). A self-efficacy approach to the career development of women. *Journal of Vocational Behavior, 18,* 326–329.

Hackett, G., Betz, N. E., O'Halloran, S. M., & Romac, D. S. (1990). Effects of verbal and mathematics task performance on task and career self-efficacy and interest. *Journal of Counseling Psychology, 37,* 169–177.

Haertel, E. H. (1990). Achievement tests. In H. J. Walberg & G. D. Haertel (Eds.), *The international encyclopedia of educational evaluation* (pp. 485–489). Oxford, England: Pergamon Press.

Hafen, B. Q., & Frandsen, K. J. (1986). *Youth suicide: Depression and loneliness.* Provo, UT: Behavioral Health Associates.

Hahn, A., Levitt, T., & Aaron, P. (1994). *Evaluation of the Quantum Opportunities Program (QOP): Did the program work?* Waltham, MA: Center for Human Resources.

Hallowell, E. M. (1996). *When you worry about the child you love: Emotional and learning problems in children.* New York: Simon & Schuster.

Hallowell, E. M., & Ratey, J. J. (1995). *Driven to distraction.* New York: Simon & Schuster.

Hammer, E. F. (1988). *The house–tree–person (HTP) clinical research manual.* Los Angeles: Western Psychological Services.

Hanish, L. D., & Guerra, N. G. (2000a). Children who get victimized at school: What is known? What can be done? *Professional School Counseling, 4,* 113–119.

Hanish, L. D., & Guerra, N. G. (2000b). The roles of ethnicity and school context in predicting children's victimization by peers. *American Journal of Community Psychology, 28,* 201–223.

Hanna, E. Z. (1999, November). *Drinking, smoking, and blood pressure: Do their relationships among youth foreshadow what we know among adults?* Paper presented at the annual meeting of the American Public Health Association, Chicago.

Hanna, E. Z., & Grant, B. F. (1999). Parallels to early onset alcohol use in the relationship of early onset smoking with drug use and *DSM-IV* drug and depressive disorders: Findings from the National Longitudinal Epidemiologic Survey. *Alcoholism: Clinical and Experimental Research, 23,* 513–522.

Hanson, M., & Peterson, D. S. (1993). *How to conduct a school recovery support group.* Portland, ME: Walch.

Hanson, W. B. (1992). School-based substance abuse prevention: A review of the state of the art in curriculum, 1980–1990. *Health Education Research, 7,* 403–430.

Hanson, W. B., Johnson, C. A., Flay, B. R., Graham, J. G., & Sobel, J. (1988). Affective and social influences approaches to the prevention of multiple substance abuse among seventh grade students: Results from Project SMART. *Preventive Medicine, 17,* 1–20.

Hare, J., & Cunningham, B. (1988). Effects of child bereavement training program for teachers. *Death Studies, 12,* 345–353.

Hart, P. J., & Jacobi, M. (1992). *From gatekeeper to advocate: Transforming the role of the school counselor.* New York: College Board.

Hart, S. L. (1991). Childhood depression: Implications and options for school counselors. *Elementary School Guidance and Counseling, 25,* 227–289.

Hatch, T., Kuranz, M., & Myrick, R. (2002). *School counselors: Partners in student achievement.* Symposium conducted at the annual meeting of the American Counseling Association, New Orleans.

Havighurst, R. J. (1952). *Developmental tasks and education.* New York: Longmans, Green.

Hawkins, J. D., Arthur, M. W., & Catalano, R. F. (1995). Preventing substance abuse. In M. Tonry & D. P. Farrington (Eds.), *Building a safer society: Strategic approaches to crime prevention: Vol. 19. Crime and justice: A review of research* (pp. 343–427). Chicago: University of Chicago Press.

Hawkins, J. D., Catalano, R. F., & Miller, J. Y. (1992). Risk and protective factors for alcohol and other drug problems in adolescence and early adulthood: Implications for substance abuse prevention. *Psychological Bulletin, 112,* 64–105.

Hawkins, J. D., Herrenkohl, T. I., Farrington, D. P., Brewer, D., Catalano, R. F., Harachi, T. W., & Cothern, L. (2000, April). Predictors of youth violence. *Office of Juvenile Justice and Delinquency Prevention,* pp. 1–7.

Hawkins, J. D., Lisher, D. M., & Catalano, R. F. (1987). Childhood predictors and the prevention of adolescent substance abuse. *National Institute on Drug Abuse Research Monograph Series, 56.*

Hazell, P. (2002). Depression in children and adolescents. *Clinical Evidence, 7,* 67–73.

Hazler, R. J. (1996). *Breaking the cycles of violence: Interventions for bullying and victimization.* Washington, DC: Accelerated Development.

Hazler, R. J., & Carney, J. V. (2000). When victims turn aggressors: Factors in the development of deadly school violence. *Professional School Counseling, 4,* 105–112.

Hazzaard, A. (1993). Psychoeducational groups to teach children sexual abuse prevention skills. *Journal of Child and Adolescent Group Therapy, 3,* 13–23.

Healy, C. C., Tullier, M., & Mourton, D. M. (1990). My vocational situation: Its relation to concurrent career and future academic benchmarks. *Measurement and Evaluation in Counseling and Development, 23,* 100–107.

Helfer, R. E. (1987). The developmental basis of child abuse and neglect: An epidemiological approach. In R. E. Helfer & R. S. Kempe (Eds.), *The battered child* (4th ed.) (pp. 60–80). Chicago: University of Chicago Press.

Helms, J. E. (1984). Toward a theoretical explanation of the effects of race on counseling. A Black and White model. *Counseling Psychologist, 13,* 153–165.

Helms, J. E. (1990a). The measurement of Black racial identity attitudes. In J. E. Helms (Ed.), *Black and White racial identity: Theory, research, and practice* (pp. 33–47). Westport, CT: Greenwood Press.

Helms, J. E. (1990b). An overview of Black racial identity theory. In J. E. Helms (Ed.), *Black and White racial identity: Theory, research, and practice* (pp. 9–32). Westport, CT: Greenwood Press.

Helms, J. E. (1990c). Toward a model of White racial identity development. In J. E. Helms (Ed.), *Black and White racial identity: Theory, research, and practice* (pp. 49–66). Westport, CT: Greenwood Press.

Helms, J. E. (1992). *Race is a nice thing to have.* Topeka, KS: Content Communications.

Helms, J. E. (1994). Racial identity and other "racial" constructs. In E. J. Trickett, R. Watts, & D. Birman (Eds.), *Human diversity* (pp. 285–311). San Francisco: Jossey Bass.

Helms, J. E. (1995). An update on Helms's White and people of color racial identity models. In J. G. Ponterotto, J. M. Casas, L. A. Suzuki, & C. M. Alexander (Eds.), *Handbook of multicultural counseling* (pp. 181–198). Thousand Oaks, CA: Sage.

Helms, J. E. (1996). Toward a methodology for assessing "racial identity" as distinguished from "ethnic identity." In G. R. Sodowsky & J. Impara (Eds.), *Multicultural assessment* (pp. 143–192). Lincoln, NE: Buros Institute of Mental Measurement.

Helms, J. E., & Carter, R. T. (1990). Development of the White Racial Identity Inventory. In J. E. Helms (Ed.), *Black and White racial identity: Theory, research, and practice* (pp. 67–80). Westport, CT: Greenwood Press.

Helms, J. E., & Carter, R. T. (1991). Relationships of White and Black racial identity attitudes and demographic similarity to counselor preferences. *Journal of Counseling Psychology, 38,* 446–457.

Helms, J. E., & Cook, D. A. (1999). *Using race and culture in counseling and psychotherapy.* Needham Heights, MA: Allyn & Bacon.

Helms, J. E., & Parham, T. A. (1996). The development of the Racial Identity Attitude Scale. In R. L. Jones (Ed.), *Handbook of tests and measurements for Black populations* (Vol. 2) (pp. 167–174). Hampton, VA: Cobb & Henry.

Henderson, A. T. (1987). *The evidence continues to grow: Parent involvement in education.* Columbia, MD: National Committee for Citizens in Education.

Henker, B., & Whalen, C. K. (1989). Hyperactivity and attention deficits. *American Psychologist, 44,* 216–223.

Henry, B., Avshalom, C., Moffitt, T. E., & Silva, P. A. (1996). Temperamental and familial predictors of violent and non-violent criminal convictions: Age 3 to age 18. *Developmental Psychology, 32,* 614–623.

Herlihy, B., & Corey, G. (1996). *ACA ethical standards casebook* (5th ed.). Alexandria, VA: American Counseling Association.

Hermann, M. A., & Finn, A. (2002). An ethical and legal perspective on the role of school counselors in preventing violence in schools. *Professional School Counseling, 6,* 46–54.

Hermann, M. A., & Remley, T. P. (2000). Guns, violence, and schools: The results of school violence—Litigation against educators and students shedding more constitutional rights at the school house gate. *Loyola Law Review, 46,* 389–439.

Herr, E. L. (2001). The impact of national policies, economics, and school reform on comprehensive guidance programs. *Professional School Counseling, 4,* 236–245.

Herr, E. L., & Cramer, S. H. (1972). *Vocational guidance and career development in schools: Toward a systems approach.* Boston: Houghton Mifflin.

Herr, E. L., & Cramer, S. H. (1984). *Career guidance and counseling through the life span.* Boston: Little Brown.

Herr, E. L., & Cramer, S. H. (1996). *Career guidance and counseling through the lifespan* (5th ed.). New York: HarperCollins.

Herring, R. D. (1990). Suicide in the middle school: Who said kids will not? *Elementary School Guidance and Counseling, 25,* 129–137.

Herring. R. D. (1998). *Career counseling in schools: Multicultural and developmental perspectives.* Alexandria, VA: American Counseling Association.

Herting-Wahl, K., & Blackhurst, A. (2000). Factors affecting the occupational and educational aspirations of children and adolescents. *Professional School Counseling, 3,* 367–374.

Hetherington, E. M. (1993). An overview of the Virginia longitudinal study of divorce and remarriage with a focus on early adolescence. *Journal of Family Psychology, 7,* 39–56.

Hetrick, E. S., & Martin, A. D. (1987). Developmental issues and their resolution for gay and lesbian adolescents. *Journal of Homosexuality, 14,* 25–43.

Hibbert, M. T., & Sprinthall, N. A. (1995). Promoting social and emotional development of preschoolers: Inclusion and mainstreaming for children with special needs. *Elementary School Guidance and Counseling, 30,* 131–142.

Hildebrand, V., Phenice, L. A., Gray, M. M., & Hines, R. P. (1996). *Knowing and serving diverse families.* Englewood Cliffs, NJ: Prentice Hall.

Hilman, D., & Solek-Tefft, J. (1988). *Spiders and flies: Help for parents and teachers of sexually abused children.* Lexington, MA: Lexington Books.

Ho, M. K. (1987). *Family therapy with ethnic minorities.* Newbury Park, CA: Sage.

Hodges, E. V., Boivin, M., Vitaro, F., & Bukowski, W. M. (1999). The power of friendship: Protection against an escalating cycle of peer victimization. *Developmental Psychology, 35,* 94–101.

Hodges, E. V., Malone, M. J., & Perry, D. G. (1997). Individual risk and social risk as interacting determinants of victimization in the peer group. *Developmental Psychology, 33,* 1032–1039.

Hodges, W. F. (1986). *Interventions for children of divorce.* New York: Wiley.

Hofferth, S. L. (1991). Programs for high-risk adolescents: What works? *Evaluation and Program Planning, 14,* 3–16.

Hofferth, S. L., Reid, L., & Mott, F. L. (2001). The effects of early childbearing on schooling over time. *Family Planning Perspectives, 33,* 259–267.

Hoffman-Plotkin, D., & Twentyman, C. (1984). A multimodal assessment of behavioral and cognitive deficits in abused and neglected preschoolers. *Child Development, 55,* 794–802.

Hogan, N. S., & DeSantis, L. (1994). Things that help and hinder adolescent sibling bereavement. *Western Journal of Sibling Research, 16,* 132–153.

Holland, J. L. (1966). *The psychology of vocational choice.* Waltham, MA: Blaisdell.

Holland, J. L. (1980). *Vocational Exploration and Insight Kit (VEIK).* Odessa, FL: Psychological Assessment Resources.

Holland, J. L. (1985). *Making vocational choices. A theory of careers* (2nd ed). Englewood Cliffs, NJ: Prentice Hall.

Holland, J. L. (1994). *Self-directed search (SDS), Form R.* Odessa, FL: Psychological Assessment Resources.

Holland, J. L. (1997). *Making vocational choices* (3rd ed.). Odessa, FL: Psychological Assessment Resources.

Holland, J. L. (2001). *The occupations finder* (4th ed.). Odessa, FL: Psychological Assessment Resources.

Hood, A. B., & Johnson, R. W. (2002). *Assessment in counseling* (3rd ed.). Alexandria, VA: American Counseling Association.

Huesmann, L. R., Eron, L. D., Lefkowitz, M. M., & Walder, L. O. (1984). Stability of aggression over time and generations. *Developmental Psychology, 20,* 1120–1134.

Hughes, J. N., Grossman, P., & Barker, D. (1990). Teachers' expectancies participation, in consultation, and perceptions of consultant helpfulness. *School Psychology Quarterly, 5,* 167–179.

Hughey, K. F., Gysbers, N. C., & Starr, M. (1993). Evaluating comprehensive school guidance programs: Assessing the perceptions of students, parents, and teachers. *School Counselor, 41,* 31–35.

Hughey, K. F., Lapan, R. T., & Gysbers, N. C. (1993). Evaluating a high school guidance–language arts career unit: A qualitative approach. *School Counselor, 41,* 31–35.

Huizinga, D. (1994). *Urban delinquency and substance abuse: Initial findings* (NCJ Publication No. 143454). Washington, DC: Office of Juvenile Justice and Delinquency Prevention.

Humara, M. (1999). The relationship between anxiety and performance: A cognitive–behavioral perspective. *Athletic Insight: Online Journal of Sport Psychology, 1*(2). Available online at www.athleticinsight.com.

Hummel, L., & Prizant, B. (1993). A socioemotional perspective for understanding social difficulties of school-age children with language disorders. *Language, Speech, and Hearing Services in Schools, 24,* 216–224.

Hunt, P., Alwell, M., Farron-Davis, F., & Goetz, L. (1996). Creating socially supportive environments for fully included students who experience multiple disabilities. *Journal of the Association for Persons with Severe Handicaps, 21*(2), 53–71.

Huston, A. C., Wartella, E., Donnerstein, E. I., Scantlin, R., & Kotler, J. (1998). *Measuring the effects of sexual content in the media: A report to the Kaiser Family Foundation.* Menlo Park, CA: Kaiser Foundation.

Idol, L., Paolucci-Whitcomb, P., & Nevin, A. (1986). *Collaborative consultation.* Austin, TX: Pro-Ed.

Imhelder, B., & Piaget, J. (1958). *The growth of logical thinking from childhood to adolescence.* New York: Basic Books.

Ingstad, B., & Whyte, S. R. (1995). *Disability and culture.* Los Angeles: University of California Press.

Isaacson, L. E., & Brown, D. (1997). *Career information, career counseling, and career development* (6th ed.). Needham Heights, MA: Allyn & Bacon.

Jacobs, E. E., Harvill, R. L., & Masson, R. L. (2002). *Group counseling: Strategies and skills* (4th ed.). Pacific Grove, CA: Brooks/Cole.

Jalali, B., Jalali, M., Crocette, G., & Turner, F. (1981). Adolescents and drug use: Toward a more comprehensive approach. *American Journal of Orthopsychiatry, 51,* 120–130.

James, S. H., & Nims, D. R. (1996). A catalogue of psychiatric medications used in the treatment of child and adolescent mental disorders. *School Counselor, 43,* 299–307.

Jarrat, C. J. (1994). *Helping children cope with separation and loss.* Boston: Harvard Common Press.

Jastrzab, J., Masker, J., Blomquist, J., & Orr, L. (1996). *Evaluation of national and community service programs: Impacts of service. Final report on the evaluation of the American Youth and Conservation Service Corps.* Cambridge, MA: Abt Associates.

Johnson, A. H. (1973). Changing conceptions of vocational guidance and concomitant value-orientations, 1920–1930. *Dissertation Abstracts International, 33,* 3292A.

Johnson, L., McLeod, E. H., & Fall, M. (1997). Play therapy with labeled children in the schools. *Professional School Counseling, 1,* 31–34.

Johnson, L. S. (1995). Enhancing multicultural relations: Intervention strategies for the school counselor. *School Counselor, 43,* 103–113.

Jones, A., & Bishop, P. (1990). Policy making by the lower federal courts and the bureaucracy: The genesis of national AIDS policy. *Social Science Journal, 27,* 273–288.

Jones, J. (1982). *Preliminary test manual. The Children of Alcoholics Screening Test.* Chicago: Family Recovery Press.

Jones, L. K. (1980). Issues in developing an occupational card sort. *Measurement and Evaluation in Guidance, 12,* 200–213.

Jones, R. A. (1982). Perceiving other people: Stereotyping as a process of social cognition. In A. G. Miller (Ed.), *In the eye of the beholder: Contemporary issues in stereotyping* (pp. 41–91). New York: Praeger.

Juhnke, G. A. (1996). The Adapted–SAD PERSONS: A suicide assessment scale designed for use with children. *Elementary School Guidance and Counseling, 30,* 252–258.

Juhnke, G. A., Charkow, W. B., Liles, R. G., Jordan, J. P., Booth, C. S., & Gmutza, B. M. (2001, March). *Assessing potentially violent students via the VIOLENT STUdent Scale.* Workshop conducted at the annual meeting of the American Counseling Association, San Antonio, TX.

Kadushin, A. (1988). Neglect in families. In E. Nunally, C. Chilman, & F. Cox (Eds.), *Families in trouble series: Vol. 4. Mental illness, delinquency, addictions, and neglect* (pp. 147–156). Newbury Park, CA: Sage.

Kahnweiler, W. M. (1979). The school counselor as consultant. A historical review. *Personnel and Guidance Journal, 57,* 374–379.

Kaiser Family Foundation (2000). *National survey of teens on HIV/AIDS.* Available online at www.kff.org (retrieved March 19, 2002).

Kalafat, J. (1990). Adolescent suicide and the implications for school response programs. *School Counselor, 37,* 359–369.

Kamback, M. C., Bosma, W. G., & D'Lugoff, B. C. (1977). Family surrogates: The drug culture or the methadone maintenance programme. *British Journal of Addiction, 72,* 171–176.

Kandt, V. E. (1994). Adolescent bereavement: Turning a fragile time into acceptance and peace. *School Counselor, 41,* 203–211.

Kapes, J. T., & Whitfield, E. A. (Eds.). (2001). *A counselor's guide to career assessment instruments* (4th ed.). Columbus, OH: National Career Development Association.

Kastenbaum, R. J. (1981). *Death, society and human experience* (3rd ed.). Columbus, OH: Merrill.

Katz, M. R. (1975). *SIGI: A computer-based system of interactive guidance and information.* Princeton, NJ: Erlbaum.

Katz, M. R. (1993). *Computer-assisted career decision-making: The guide in the machine.* Hillsdale, NJ: Erlbaum.

Kazdin, A. F. (1992). Overt and covert antisocial behavior: Child and family characteristics among psychiatric inpatient children. *Journal of Child and Family Studies, 1,* 3–20.

Keeling, R. (1993). HIV disease: Current concepts. *Journal of Counseling and Development, 71,* 261–273.

Keene, K. M, & Stewart, N. R. (1989). Evaluation: Rx for counseling program growth. *School Counselor, 37,* 62–66.

Kegan, R. (1982). *The evolving self.* Cambridge, MA: Harvard University Press.

Kelley, J. B. (1993). Current research of children's postdivorce adjustment. *Family and Conciliation Courts Review, 31,* 29–49.

Kelley, J. B., & Wallerstein, J. S. (1977). Brief interventions with children in divorcing families. *American Journal of Orthopsychiatry, 47,* 23–39.

Kendall-Tackett, K. A., Meyer-Williams, L., & Finkelhor, D. (2001). Impact of sexual abuse on children: A review and synthesis of recent empirical studies. In R. Bull (Ed.), *Children and the law: Essential readings in developmental psychology* (pp. 31–76). Oxford, England: Blackwell.

Keneal, P., Frude, N., & Shaw, W. (1991). Teacher expectations as predictors of academic success. *Journal of Social Psychology, 131,* 305–306.

Keys, S. G., Bemak, F., Carpenter, S. L., & King-Sears, M. E. (1998). Collaborative consultant: A new role for counselors serving at-risk youths. *Journal of Counseling and Development, 76,* 123–133.

Keys, S. G., Bemak, F., & Lockhart, E. J. (1998). Transforming school counseling to serve the mental health needs of at-risk youth. *Journal of Counseling and Development, 76,* 381–388.

Kids Count (2000). Percent of families with children headed by a single parent. *Data Book Online.* Available online at www.aecf.org/kidscount/kc2002/summary (retrieved May 24, 2003).

Kinder, B., Pape, N., & Walfish, S. (1980). Drug and alcohol education programs: A review of outcome studies. *International Journal of Addiction, 15,* 1035–1054.

King, K. A., Price, J. H., Telljohann, S. K., & Wahl, J. (1999). How confident do high school counselors feel in recognizing students at risk for suicide? *American Journal of Health Behavior, 23,* 457–467.

King, K. A., Price, J. H., Telljohann, S. K., & Wahl, J. (2000). Preventing adolescent suicide: Do high school counselors know the risk factors? *Professional School Counseling, 3,* 255–263.

Kingery-McCabe, L. G., & Campbell, F. A. (1991). Effects of addiction on the addict. In D. C. Daley & M. S. Raskin (Eds.), *Treating the chemically dependent and their families* (pp. 57–78). Newbury Park, CA: Sage.

Kirby, D. (1999). Reflections on two decades of research on teen sexual behavior and pregnancy. *Journal of School Health, 69,* 89–94.

Kirby, D. (2001). *Emerging answers: Research findings on programs to reduce teen pregnancy* [Summary]. Washington, DC: National Campaign to Prevent Teenage Pregnancy.

Kirby, D., Short, L., Colins, J., Rugg, D., Kolbe, L., Howard, M., Miller, B., Sonenstein, F., & Zabi, L. S. (1994). School-based programs to reduce sexual risk behaviors: A review of effectiveness. *Public Health Report, 109,* 339–360.

Kirisci, L., Hsu, T. C., & Tarter, R. (1994). Fitting a two-parameter logistic item response model to clarify the psychometric properties of the Drug Use Screening Inventory for adolescent alcohol and drug abuse. *Alcoholism: Clinical and Experimental Research, 18,* 1335–1341.

Kiselica, M. S. (1995). *Multicultural counseling with teen fathers: A practical guide.* Newbury Park, CA: Sage.

Kiselica, M. S., Gorczynski, J., & Capps, S. (1998). Teen mothers and fathers: School counselor perceptions of service needs. *Professional School Counseling, 2,* 146–152.

Kitano, H. H. L., & Maki, M. T. (1996). Continuity, change, and diversity: Counseling Asian Americans. In P. B. Pederson, J. G. Draguns, W. J. Lonner, & J. E. Trimble (Eds.), *Counseling across cultures* (4th ed.) (pp. 124–145). Thousand Oaks, CA: Sage.

Klepsch, M., & Logie, L. (1982). *Children draw and tell: An introduction to the projective uses of children's human figure drawings.* New York: Brunner/Mazel.

Klinteberg, B. A., Andersson, T., Magnusson, D., & Stattin, H. (1993). Hyperactive behavior in childhood as related to subsequent alcohol problems and violent offending: A longitudinal study of male subjects. *Personality and Individual Differences, 15,* 381–388.

Knapp, R. R., & Knapp, L. (1984). *COPS interest inventory technical manual.* San Diego, CA: EDITS.

Knapp, R. R., & Knapp, L. (1985). *California occupational preference system: Self-interpretation profile and guide.* San Diego, CA: EDITS.

Knop, J., Teasdale, T. W., Schulsinger, F., & Goodwin, D. W. (1985). A prospective study of young men at high risk for alcoholism: School behavior and achievement. *Journal of Studies on Alcohol, 46,* 273–278.

Knowdell, R. L. (1995). *Career Values Card Sort planning kit.* San Jose, CA: Career Research and Testing.

Ko, S. F., & Cosden, M. A. (2001). Do elementary school-based child abuse prevention programs work? A high school follow-up. *Psychology in the Schools, 38,* 57–66.

Kohlberg, L. (1981). *The philosophy of moral development: Moral stages and the idea of justice.* San Francisco: Harper & Row.

Kohlberg, L. (1984). *The psychology of moral development: The nature and validity of moral stages.* San Francisco: Harper & Row.

Kohut, J. (1971). *Analysis of the self.* New York: International University Press.

Kolb, K. J., & Lee, J. (1994). Teacher expectations and underachieving gifted children. *Roeper Review, 17,* 26–30.

Koplewicz, H. S. (1996). *It's nobody's fault: New hope and help for difficult children and their parents.* New York: Times Books.

Korbin, J. (1987). Child abuse and neglect: The cultural context. In R. E. Helfer & R. S. Kempe (Eds.), *The battered child* (4th ed.) (pp. 23–41). Chicago: University of Chicago Press.

Kottman, T. (1995). *Partners in play: An Adlerian approach to play therapy.* Alexandria, VA: American Counseling Association.

Kottman, T., Robert, R., & Baker, D. (1995). Parental perspectives on attention deficit hyperactivity disorder: How school counselors can help. *School Counselor, 43,* 142–150.

Kovacs, M., Beck, A., & Weissman, A. (1975). The use of suicidal motives in the psychotherapy of attempted suicides. *American Journal of Psychotherapy, 29,* 363–368.

Krieschok, T. S., Hansen, R. N., Johnston, J. A., & Wong, S. C. (2002). *Missouri Occupational Card Sort.* Columbia, MO: Career Center, University of Missouri.

Krumboltz, J. D., Mitchell, A. M., & Jones, G. B. (1976). A social learning theory of career selection. *Counseling Psychologist, 6,* 71–81.

Kurtz, D. P., Gaudin, J. M., Howing, P. T., & Wodarski, J. S. (1993). The consequences of physical abuse and neglect on the school-age child: Mediating factors. *Children and Youth Services Review, 15,* 85–104.

LaFromboise, T. (1998). American Indian mental health policy. In D. R. Atkinson, G. Morten, & D. W. Sue (Eds.), *Counseling American minorities* (5th ed.) (pp. 137–158). Boston: McGraw-Hill.

LaFromboise, T., Coleman, H. L., & Gerton, J. (1993). Psychological impact of biculturalism: Evidence and theory. *Psychological Bulletin, 114,* 395–412.

Landreth, G. L. (1987). Play therapy: Facilitative use of child's play in elementary school counseling. *Elementary School Guidance and Counseling, 21,* 253–261 [Special issue: *Counseling with Expressive Arts*].

Landreth, G. L. (1991). *Play therapy: The art of the relationship.* Muncie, IN: Accelerated Development.

Landreth, G. L. (1993). Child-centered play therapy. *Elementary School Guidance and Counseling, 28,* 17–29.

Lapan, R. T., Gysbers, N. C., Hughey, K., & Arni, T. J. (1993). Evaluating a guidance and language arts unit for high school juniors. *Journal of Counseling and Development, 71,* 444–452.

Lapan, R. T., Gysbers, N. C., & Sun, Y. (1997). The impact of more fully implemented guidance programs on the school experiences of high school students: A statewide evaluation study. *Journal of Counseling and Development, 75,* 292–302.

Larrance, D. T., & Twentyman, C. T. (1983). Maternal attributions and child abuse. *Journal of Abnormal Psychology, 92,* 449–457.

LaVoie, R. D. (1990). *How difficult can this be? (The F.A.T. City Learning Disability Workshop)* [Videotape]. (Available from PBS Video, 1320 Braddock Place, Alexandria, VA 22314)

Lawler, M. K. (2000). School-based violence prevention programs: What works. In D. S. Sandhu & C. B. Aspy (Eds.), *Violence in American schools: A practical guide for counselors* (pp. 247–266). Alexandria, VA: American Counseling Association.

LeBlanc, A. (1992, September). Harassment in the halls. *Seventeen,* pp. 162–165, 170.

LeBlanc, A. (1993, May). Harassment at school: The truth is out. *Seventeen,* pp. 134–135.

Lee, C. C., & Workman, D. J. (1992). School counselors and research: Current status and future direction. *School Counselor, 40,* 15–19.

Lee, R. S. (1993). Effects of classroom guidance on student achievement. *Elementary School Guidance and Counseling, 27,* 163–171.

Leffert, N., Benson, P. L., Scales, P. C., Sharma, A. R., Drake, D. R., & Blythe, D. A. (1998). Developmental assets: Measurement and prediction of risk behaviors among adolescents. *Applied Developmental Science, 2,* 209–230.

Lefkowitz, M. M., Eron, L. D., Walder, L. O., & Huesmann, L. R. (1977). *Growing up violent: A longitudinal study of the development of aggression.* New York: Pergamon Press.

Leming, R., & Dickinson, G. (1985). *Understanding death, dying, and bereavement.* New York: Holt, Rinehart, & Winston.

Lenhardt, A. C. (1997). Disenfranchised grief/hidden sorrow: Implications for the school counselor. *School Counselor, 44,* 264–270.

Lent, R. W., Brown, S. D., & Hackett, G. (1994). Toward a unified theory of career and academic interests, choice, and performance. *Journal of Vocational Behavior, 45,* 79–122.

Lent, R. W., Brown, S. D., & Hackett, G. (1996). Career development from a social cognitive perspective. In D. Brown, L. Brooks, & Associates (Eds.), *Career choice and development* (3rd ed., pp. 373–416). San Francisco: Jossey-Bass.

Lent, R. W., Brown, S. D., & Larkin, K. C. (1987). Comparison of three theoretically derived variables in predicting career and academic behavior: Self-efficacy, interest congruence, and consequence thinking. *Journal of Counseling Psychology, 34,* 293–298.

Lent, R. W., Lopez, F. G., & Bieschke, K. J. (1992). Mathematics self-efficacy: Sources and relations to science-based career choice. *Journal of Counseling Psychology, 38,* 424–430.

Lent, R. W., Lopez, F. G., & Bieschke, K. J. (1993). Predicting mathematics-related choices and success behaviors: Test of an expanded social cognitive model. *Journal of Vocational Behavior, 42,* 223–236.

Leong, F. T. L., & Brown, M. T. (1995). Theoretical issues in cross-cultural development: Cultural validity and cultural specificity. In W. B. Walsh & S. H. Osipow (Eds.), *Handbook of vocational psychology: Theory, research, and practice* (2nd ed.) (pp. 143–180). Mahwah, NJ: Erlbaum.

Leung, S. A. (1995). Career development and counseling: A multicultural perspective. In J. G. Ponterotto, J. M. Casas, L. A. Suzuki, & C. M. Alexander (Eds.), *Handbook of multicultural counseling* (pp. 549–566). Thousand Oaks, CA: Sage.

Levenson, R. L., & Mellins, C. A. (1992). Pediatric HIV disease: What psychologists need to know. *Professional Psychology and Practice, 23,* 410–415.

Lichter, D. (1988). Race, employment hardship and inequality in American non-metropolitan South. *American Sociological Review, 54,* 436–446.

Lidz, T. (1976). *The person.* New York: Basic Books.

Light, J. G., & DeFries, J. C. (1995). Comorbidity of reading and mathematics disabilities: Genetic and environmental etiologies. *Journal of Learning Disabilities: Genetic and Environmental Etiologies, 28,* 96–106.

Linde, L. (2003). Ethical, legal, and professional issues in school counseling. In B. T. Erford (Ed.), *Transforming the school counseling profession* (pp. 39–62). Upper Saddle River, NJ: Merrill/Prentice Hall.

LISA Organization to Stop Child Abuse (1989). *The LISA Report: A report on the prevention and treatment of child abuse and neglect in New York State.* New York: Author.

Lloyd, J., Saltzman, N. J., & Kaufman, J. M. (1981). Predictable generalization in academic learning as a result of preskills and strategy training. *Learning Disability Quarterly, 4,* 203–216.

Lochman, J. E., Coie, J. D., Underwood, M. K., & Terry, R. (1993). Effectiveness of a social relations intervention program for aggressive and nonaggressive, rejected children. *Journal of Consulting and Clinical Psychology, 61,* 1053–1058.

Locke, D. C. (1997). *Increasing multicultural understanding.* Thousand Oaks, CA: Sage.

Lockhardt, L. L., & Wodarski, J. S. (1990). Teenage pregnancy: Implications for social work practice. *Family Therapy, 17,* 32–47.

Lockhart, E. J., & Keys, S. G. (1998). The mental health role of school counselors. *Professional School Counseling, 1,* 3–6.

Locust, C. (1990). Wounding the spirit: Discrimination and traditional American Indian belief systems. In G. E. Thomas (Ed.), *U.S. race relations* (pp. 219–232). New York: Hemisphere.

Loeber, R. (1990). Development and risk factors of juvenile antisocial behaviors and delinquency. *Clinical Psychology Review, 10,* 1–41.

Loeber, R. (1996). Developmental continuity, change and pathways in male juvenile problem behaviors and delinquency. In J. D. Hawkins (Ed.), *Delinquency and crime: Current theories* (pp. 1–27). Cambridge, England: Cambridge University Press.

Loeber, R., & Hay, D. F. (1996). Key issues in the development of aggression and violence from childhood to early adulthood. *Annual Review of Psychology, 48,* 371–410.

Loevinger, J. (1976). *Ego development.* San Francisco: Jossey-Bass.

Long, J. V., & Scherl, D. J. (1984). Developmental antecedents of compulsive drug use: A report on the literature. *Journal of Psychoactive Drugs, 16,* 169–182.

Looft, W. R. (1971a). Sex differences in the expression of vocational aspirations by elementary school children. *Developmental Psychology, 5,* 366.

Looft, W. R. (1971b). Vocational aspirations of second-grade girls. *Psychological Reports, 28,* 241–242.

Lowry, D. T., & Shidler, J. A. (1993). Prime time TV portrayals of sex, safe sex, and AIDS: A longitudinal analysis. *Journalism Quarterly, 70,* 628–637.

Luckasson, R., Coulter, D. L., Polloway, E. A., Reiss. S., Schalock, R. L., Snell, M. E., Spitalnik, D. M., & Stark, J. A. (1992). *Mental retardation: Definition, classification, and systems of supports.* Washington, DC: American Association on Mental Retardation.

Lucker, J .R., & Molloy, A. T. (1995). Resources for working with children with attention-deficit/hyperactivity disorder (ADHD). *Elementary School Guidance and Counseling, 29,* 260–277.

Lunneborg, P.W. (1981). *The Vocational Interest Inventory (VII) manual.* Los Angeles: Western Psychological Services.

Lurie, C. (1993). *The death of friends vs. family members in late adolescence: The role of perceived social support and self-worth.* Unpublished master's thesis, Colorado State University, Fort Collins.

Lynch, M. A., & Roberts, J. (1978). *Consequences of child abuse.* New York: Academic Press.

MacFarlane, R. (1995). Adolescent pregnancy research: Implications for prevention. In M. W. O'Hara, R. C. Reiter, S. R. Johnson, A. Milburn, & J. Engeldinger (Eds.), *Psychological aspects of women's reproductive health* (pp. 248–264). New York: Springer-Verlag.

Maguin, E., Hawkins, J. D., Catalano, R. F., Hill, K., Abbott, R., & Herrenkohl, T. (1995, November). *Risk factors measured at three ages for violence at age 17–18.* Paper presented at the meeting of the American Society of Criminology, Boston.

Maguin, E., & Loeber, R., (1996). Academic performance and delinquency. In M. Tonry (Ed.), *Crime and justice: A review of research* (Vol. 20) (pp. 145–264). Chicago: University of Chicago Press.

Mahler, C. (1969). *Group counseling in the schools.* Boston: Houghton Mifflin.

Malchiodi, C. A. (1990). *Breaking the silence: Art therapy with children from violent homes.* New York: Brunner/Mazel.

Malley, P. B., & Kush, F. (1994). Comprehensive and systemic school-based suicide prevention programs: A checklist for counselors. *School Counselor, 41,* 191–194.

Malley, P. B., Kush, F., & Bogo, R. J. (1994). School-based adolescent suicide prevention and intervention programs: A survey. *School Counselor, 42,* 130–136.

Manis, F. R. (1996). Current trends in dyslexia research. In B. J. Cratty & R. L. Goldman (Eds.), *Learning disabilities: Contemporary viewpoints* (pp. 27–42). Amsterdam: Harwood Academic.

Mann, J., Tarantola, D. J., & Netter, T. W. (1992). *A global report: AIDS in the world.* New York: Oxford University Press.

Marczely, B. (1999). Mixed messages: Sexual harassment in the public schools. *Clearing House, 72,* 315.

Margolin, L. (1990). Fatal child neglect. *Child Welfare, 69,* 309–319.

Marin, G. (1994). The experience of being a Hispanic in the United States. In W. J. Lonner & R. Malpass (Eds.), *Psychology and culture* (pp. 23–27). Boston: Allyn & Bacon.

Marinoble, R. M. (1998). Homosexuality: A blind spot in the school mirror. *Professional School Counseling, 1,* 4–7.

Martin, A., & Hetrick, E. (1988). The stigmatization of the gay and lesbian adolescent. *Journal of Homosexuality, 15,* 163–183.

Martin, H. P. (1976). *The abused child: A multidisciplinary approach to developmental issues and treatment.* Cambridge, MA: Ballinger.

Martin, M. J., & Walters, J. (1982). Familial correlates of selected types of child abuse and neglect. *Journal of Marriage and the Family, 44,* 267–276.

Martin, T. L., & Doka, K. J. (2000). *Men don't cry—women do: Transcending gender stereotypes of grief.* Frederick, MD: Hood College.

Martinez, P. (1981). *The home environment and academic achievement: There is a correlation.* (ERIC Document Reproduction Service No. 212421)

Maslow, A. H. (1954). *Motivation and personality.* New York: Harper & Row.

Maxmen, J. S., & Ward, N. G. (1995). *Essential psychopathology and its treatment* (2nd ed.). New York: Norton.

Mayle, P. (1987). *Divorce can happen to the nicest people* [Videotape].

McCarney, S. B. (1989). *Attention Deficit Disorders Evaluation Scale.* Columbia, MO: Hawthorne Educational Services.

McCarthy, C. J., Brack, C. J., Laygo, R. M., Brack, G., & Orr, D. P. (1997). A theory based investigation of adolescent risk behaviors and concern about AIDS. *School Counselor, 44,* 185–197.

McConville, B. J., & Bruce, R. T. (1985). Depressive illnesses in children and adolescents: A review of current concepts. *Canadian Journal of Psychiatry, 30,* 119–129.

McCord, J. (1979). Some child-rearing antecedents of criminal behavior in adult men. *Journal of Personality and Social Psychology, 37,* 1477–1486.

McCord, J., & Ensminger, M. (1995, November). *Pathways from aggressive childhood to criminality.* Paper presented at the meeting of the American Society of Criminology, Boston.

McCullough, M., & Scherman, A. (1991). Adolescent pregnancy: Contributing factors and strategies for prevention. *Adolescence, 26,* 809–816.

McDonald, S., & Moriarty, A. (1990). The Rich East High School Mediation Project. *School Social Work Journal, 14,* 25–32.

McFarland, W. P. (1998). Gay, lesbian, and bisexual student suicide. *Professional School Counseling, 1,* 26–29.

McFarland, W. P., & Dupuis, M. (2001). The legal duty to protect gay and lesbian students from violence in school. *Professional School Counseling, 4,* 171–179.

McFarland, W. P., & Oliver, J. (1999). Empowering professional school counselors in the war against AIDS. *Professional School Counseling, 2,* 267–274.

McGlauflin, H. (1998). Helping children grieve at school. *Professional School Counseling, 1,* 46–49.

McGoldrick, M., Almeida, R., Moore-Hines, P., Garcia-Preto, N., Rosen, E., & Lee, E. (1991). Mourning in different cultures. In F. Walsh & M. McGoldrick (Ed.), *Living beyond loss* (pp.176–206). New York: Norton.

McLaughlin, T. F., & Vacha, E. F. (1993). Substance abuse prevention in the schools: Roles for the school counselor. *Elementary School Guidance and Counseling, 28,* 124–132.

McNeil, J. N., Silliman, B., & Swihart, J. J. (1991). Helping adolescents cope with the death of a peer. *Journal of Adolescent Research, 6,* 132–145.

McWhirter, B. T., McWhirter, J. J., Hart, R. S., & Gat, I. (2000). Preventing and treating depression in children and adolescents. In D. Capuzzi & D. R. Gross (Eds.), *Youth at risk: A prevention resource for counselors, teachers, and parents.* (3rd ed.) (pp. 137–165). Alexandria, VA: American Counseling Association.

McWhirter, J. J. (1998a). Delinquency and problems of violence. In J. J. McWhirter, B. T. McWhirter, A. M. McWhirter, & E. H. McWhirter, (Eds.), *At-risk youth: A comprehensive response* (2nd ed.) (pp. 158–178). Pacific Grove, CA: Brooks/Cole.

McWhirter, J. J. (1998b). Substance use and addiction. In J. J. McWhirter, B. T. McWhirter, A. M. McWhirter, & E. H. McWhirter (Eds.), *At-risk youth: A comprehensive response* (2nd ed.) (pp. 114–132). Pacific Grove, CA: Brooks/Cole.

McWhirter, J. J. (1998c). Teenage pregnancy and risky sexual behavior. In J. J. McWhirter, B. T. McWhirter, A. M. McWhirter, & E. H. McWhirter (Eds.), *At-risk youth: A comprehensive response* (2nd ed.) (pp. 133–157). Pacific Grove, CA: Brooks/Cole.

McWhirter, J. J. (1998d). Youth Suicide. In J. J. McWhirter, B. T. McWhirter, A. M. McWhirter, & E. H. McWhirter (Eds.), *At-risk youth: A comprehensive response* (2nd ed.) (pp. 179–199). Pacific Grove, CA: Brooks/Cole.

Meek, M. (1992). The peacekeepers. *Teaching Tolerance, 1,* 46–52.

Mehrens, W. A., & Lehman, I. J. (1987). *Using standardized tests in education* (4th ed.). New York: Longmans.

Meichenbaum, D. (1977). *Cognitive behavior modification. An integrative approach.* New York: Plenum.

Meichenbaum, D. (1986). Cognitive behavior modification. In F. H. Kanker & A. P. Goldstein (Eds.), *Helping people change: A textbook for methods* (pp. 346–380). New York: Pergamon Press.

Melaville, A., Blank, M., & Asayesh, G. (1993). *Together we can: A guide for crafting a pro-family system of educational and human services* (No. PIP 93-1103). Washington, DC: U.S. Department of Education, Office of Educational and Research Improvement, and U.S. Department of Health and Human Services, Office of the Assistant Secretary for Planning and Evaluation.

Metha, A., Weber, B., & Webb, L. D. (1998). Youth suicide prevention: A survey and analysis of policies in the 50 states. *Journal of Suicide and Life-Threatening Behavior, 28,* 150–164.

Middlebrook, D.L., LeMaster, P.L., Beals, J., Novins, D.K., & Manson, S.M.. (2001). Suicide prevention in American Indian and Alaskan Native communities: A critical review of programs. *Suicide and Life-Threatening Behavior, 31,* 132–149.

Middleton, R. A., Rollins, C. W., & Harley, D. A. (1999). The historical and political context of the civil rights of persons with disabilities: A multicultural perspective for counselors. *Journal of Multicultural Counseling and Development, 27,* 105–120.

Miller, B. (1991). *Adolescents' relationships with their friends.* Unpublished doctoral dissertation, Harvard Graduate School of Education, Cambridge, MA.

Miller, C. H. (1964). Vocational guidance in the perspective of cultural change. In H. Borow (Ed.), *Man in a world at work* (pp. 3–23). Boston: Houghton Mifflin.

Miller, D., & Jang, M. (1977). Children of alcoholics: A 20-year longitudinal study. *Social Work Research & Abstracts, 13,* 23–29.

Miller, F. W. (1968). *Guidance: Principles and services.* Columbus, OH: Merrill.

Miller, M. J., & Stanford, J. T. (1987). Early occupational restriction: An examination of elementary school children's expression of vocational preferences. *Journal of Employment Counseling, 24,* 115–121.

Miller, P. A., Ryan, P., & Morrison, W. (1999). Practical strategies for helping children of divorce in today's classroom. *Childhood Education, 75,* 285–289.

Miller, P. H. (1989). *Theories of developmental psychology* (2nd ed.). New York: Freeman.

Millhause, M. (1989). Gladiators and conciliators. *Legal Reformer, 9*(2), 17–20.

Milone, M. N. (1995). Electronic portfolios: Who's doing them and how? *Technology and Learning, 16,* 28–36

Minden, J., Henry, D. B., Tolan, P. H., & Gorman-Smith, D. (2000). Urban boys' social networks and school violence. *Professional School Counseling, 4,* 95–104.

Minino, A. M., & Smith, B. L. (2001). Deaths: Preliminary data for 2000. *National Vital Statistics Reports, 49 (12).*

Minuchin, S., & Fishman, H. C. (1981). *Family therapy techniques.* Cambridge, MA: Harvard University Press.

Minuchin, S., Montalvo, B., Guerney, B., Rosman, B., & Schumer, F. (1967). *Families of the slums.* New York: Basic Books.

Miraglia, K., & Samuels, A. (1988). The influence of the recent death of a spouse on the parenting function of the surviving parent. In S. Altschul (Ed.), *Childhood bereavement and its aftermath* (pp. 37–63). Madison, CT: International Universities Press.

Mitchell, A., & Gysbers, N. C. (1978). Comprehensive school guidance and counseling programs: Planning, design, implementation, and evaluation. In American Personnel and Guidance Association (Ed.), *The status of guidance and counseling in the schools* (pp. 23–39). Washington, DC: American Personnel and Guidance Association.

Mitchell, L. K., & Krumboltz, J. D. (1990). Social learning approach to career decision making: Krumboltz's theory. In D. Brown & L. Brooks (Eds.), *Career choice and development: Applying contemporary theories to practice* (2nd ed.) (pp. 145–196). San Francisco: Jossey-Bass.

Mitchell, L. K., & Krumboltz, J. D. (1996). Krumboltz's learning theory of career choice and counseling. In D. Brown, L. Brooks, & Associates (Eds.), *Career choice and development* (3rd ed.) (pp. 233–276). San Francisco: Jossey-Bass.

Mitchell, S., & Rosa, P. (1979). Boyhood behavior problems as precursors of criminality: A fifteen-year follow-up. *Journal of Child Psychology and Psychiatry, 22,* 19–33.

Miziker-Gonet, M. (1994). *Counseling the adolescent substance abuser: School-based intervention and prevention.* Thousand Oaks, CA: Sage.

Moffitt, T. E. (1987). Parental mental disorder and offspring criminal behavior: An adoption study. *Psychiatry, 50,* 346–360.

Moffitt, T. E., Caspi, A., Dickson, N., Silva, P., & Stanton, W. (1996). Childhood-onset versus adolescent-onset antisocial conduct problems in males: Natural history from ages 3 to 18 years. *Development and Psychopathology, 8,* 399–424.

Moore, J., & Herlihy, B. (1993). Grief groups for students who have had a parent die. *School Counselor, 41,* 54–59.

Moore, K. A., Myers, D. E., Morrison, D. R., Nord, C. W., Brown, B., & Edmonston, B. (1993). Ages at first childbirth and later poverty. *Journal of Research on Adolescents, 3,* 393–342.

Moore, K. A., Romano, A., Connon, L .C., & Gitelson, L. B. (1997, October). *Facts at a glance: Annual newsletter on teen pregnancy.* Washington, DC: Child Trends.

Moos, R. H., & Billings, A. G. (1982). Children of alcoholics during the recovery process: Alcoholics and matched control families. *Addictive Behaviors, 7,* 155–163.

Morris, L., Warren, C. W., & Aral, S. O. (1993). Measuring adolescent sexual behaviors and related health outcomes. *Public Health Report, 108*(Suppl. 1), 31–36.

Morrison, J., & Shriberg, L. (1992). Articulation testing versus conversational speech sampling. *Journal of Speech and Hearing Research, 35,* 259–273.

Morrissey, M. (1997, October). The invisible minority: Counseling Asian Americans. *Counseling Today,* pp. 1, 21–22.

Mudore, C. F. (1997). Assisting young people in quitting tobacco. *Professional School Counseling, 1,* 61–62.

Mueller, E., & Silverman, N. (1989). Peer relations in maltreated children. In D. Cicchetti & V. Carlson (Eds.), *Child maltreatment: Theory and research on the causes and consequences of child abuse and neglect* (pp. 529–578). New York: Cambridge University Press.

Mugridge, G. B. (1991, September). *Reducing chronic neglect.* Paper presented at the Ninth National Conference on Child Abuse and Neglect, Denver.

Muisener, P. P. (1994). *Understanding and treating adolescent substance abuse.* Thousand Oaks, CA: Sage.

Muller, L. E., & Hartman, J. (1998). Group counseling for sexual minority youth. *Professional School Counseling, 1,* 38–41.

Multon, K. D., Brown, S. D., & Lent, R. W. (1991). Relation of self-efficacy beliefs to academic outcomes: A meta-analytic investigation. *Journal of Counseling Psychology, 38,* 30–38.

Murphy, J. J. (1994). Working with what works: A solution-focused approach to school behavior problems. *School Counselor, 42,* 59–65.

Murphy, J. J. (1997). Solution-focused counseling in middle and high schools. Alexandria, VA: American Counseling Association.

Murphy, L. L., Impara, J. C., & Plake, B. S. (1999). *Tests in print V* (Vols. 1–2). Lincoln, NE: Buros Institute of Mental Measurements.

Myers, J. (1992). *Legal issues in child abuse and neglect.* Newbury Park, CA: Sage.

Myrick, R. D. (1987). *Developmental guidance and counseling: A practical approach.* Minneapolis: Educational Media.

Myrick, R. D. (1990). Retrospective measurement: An accountability tool. *Elementary School Guidance and Counseling, 25,* 21–29.

Myrick, R. D. (1997). *Developmental guidance and counseling: A practical approach* (3rd ed.). Minneapolis: Educational Media.

Myrick, R. D. (2003).Accountability: Counselors count. *Professional School Counseling, 6,* 174–179.

Myrick, R. D., Merhill, H., & Swanson, L. (1986). Changing student attitudes and behavior through classroom guidance. *School Counselor, 33,* 244–252.

Naiditch, B., & Lerner, R. (1987, January–February). The next generation. *Changes: For and about Children of Alcoholics,* pp. 36–38.

National Career Development Association (1991). *Ethical standards.* Columbus, OH: Author.

National Center for Health Statistics (1996). Advance report of final mortality statistics, 1994. *NCHS Monthly Vital Statistics Report, 45*(Suppl. 3). Hyattsville, MD: Author.

National Center for Health Statistics (2002). Teen birth rates decline in all states during the 1990's. *2002 Fact Sheet.* Available online at www.cdc.gov/nchs/releases/02facts/teenbirths.htm (retrieved July 13, 2003).

National Center for the Analysis of Violent Crime (2001). *The school shooter: A threat assessment perspective.* Available online at www.fbi.gov/library/schools/school2.

National Child Abuse and Neglect Data System (2001). *Child maltreatment 2001.* Washington, DC: Department of Health and Human Services, Administration for Children and Families.

National Commission on Excellence in Education (1983). *A nation at risk.* Washington, DC: U.S. Government Printing Office.

National Highway Traffic Safety Administration (1999). *Traffic safety facts 1998—Children.* Washington, DC: U.S. Department of Transportation.

National Indian Justice Center. (1990). *Child abuse and neglect in American Indian and Alaska Native communities and the role of the Indian Health Service* (Unpublished final report, Indian Health Service Contract No. 282-90-036). Washington, DC: U.S. Department of Health and Human Services.

National Institute on Alcohol Abuse and Alcoholism (1996). *Alcoholism: Getting the facts.* Available online at www.niaaa.nih.gov/publications/booklet.htm (retrieved February 14, 2001).

National Institute on Alcohol Abuse and Alcoholism (1999). Estimates for alcohol-related deaths by age and cause based on National Center for Health Statistics. *1994 mortality data.* Washington, DC: U.S. Government Printing Office.

National Institute on Drug Abuse (1997). *1996 national household survey on drug abuse.* Rockville, MD: U.S. Department of Health and Human Services.

National Institute on Drug Abuse (1999a). *National household survey on drug abuse.* Available online at www.health.org/govstudy/bkd376/Chapter2.htm (retrieved February 14, 2001).

National Institute on Drug Abuse (1999b). *Preventing drug use among children and adolescents: A research-based guide.* Washington, DC: Author.

National Institute on Drug Abuse (2000a). *Cigarettes and other nicotine products.* Available online at www.drugabuse.gov/tobacco.html (retrieved February 22, 2001).

National Institute on Drug Abuse (2000b). *Costs to society.* Available online at www.nida.nih.gov/Infofax/costs to society.html (retrieved February 14, 2001).

National Institute on Drug Abuse (2000c). *Marijuana.* Available online at www.drugabuse.gov/tobacco.html (retrieved February 22, 2001).

National Institute on Drug Abuse (2000d). *Monitoring the Future Study.* Available online at www.drugabuse.gov/Infofax/HSYouthtrends.html (retrieved December 14, 2000).

National Institute on Drug Abuse (2001a). *Inhalants.* Available online at www.drugabuse.gov/inhalants/html (retrieved February 22, 2001).

National Institute on Drug Abuse (2001b). *NIDA initiative targets increasing teen use of anabolic steroids.* Available online at www.drugabuse.gov/NIDA_NotesNNVil15N3/Initiative.html (retrieved February 14, 2001).

National Institutes of Health (2002, October 15). *Preventive sessions after divorce protect children into teens* [News release]. Available online at www.nih.gov/news/pr/oct2002/nimh-15.htm (retrieved May 27, 2003).

National Joint Committee on Learning Disabilities (1994). Learning disabilities: Issues on definition, a position paper of the National Joint Committee on Learning Disabilities. In National Joint Committee on Learning Disabilities, *Collective perspectives on issues affecting learning disabilities: Position papers and statements* (pp. 3–8). Austin, TX: Pro-Ed.

National Occupational Information Coordinating Committee, U.S. Department of Labor. (1992). *The National Career Development Guidelines Project.* Washington, DC: U.S. Department of Labor.

National School Safety Center (1998). *Checklist of characteristics of youth who have caused school-associated violent deaths.* Available online at www.nssc1.org/reporter/checklist.htm (retrieved March 21, 2001).

Neiger, B. L., & Hopkins. R. W. (1988). Adolescent suicide: Character traits of high-risk teenagers. *Adolescence, 23,* 469–475.

Nemeroff, C.B., & Schatzberg, A.F. (2002). Pharmacological treatments for unipolar depression. In P.E. Nathan & J.M. Gorman (Eds.), *A guide to treatments that work* (2nd ed.)(pp. 229–243). New York: Oxford University Press.

Neukrug, E. S., Barr, C. G., Hoffman, L. R., & Kaplan, L. S. (1993). Developmental counseling and guidance: A model for use in your school. *School Counselor, 40,* 356–362.

Newcomb, M. D., & Bentler, P. M. (1989). *Consequences of adolescent drug use.* Newbury Park, CA: Sage.

Newcomb, M. D., & McGee, L. (1991). Influence of sensation seeking on general deviance and specific problem behaviors from adolescence to young adulthood. *Journal of Personality and Social Psychology, 61,* 614–628.

Nicoll, W. G. (1992). A family counseling and consultation model for school counselors. *School Counselor, 39,* 351–361.

Niles, S. G., & Harris-Bowlsbey, J. (2002). *Career development interventions in the 21st century.* Upper Saddle River, NJ: Merrill/Prentice Hall.

Noll, K. (2000). *Empowering kids to deal with bullies and low self-esteem.* Available online at www.members.aol.com/_ht_a/kthynoll/bullies.htm (retrieved March 25, 2001).

Noll, K., & Carter, J. (1998). *Taking the bully by the horns.* Wyomissing, PA: Unicorn Press.

Norem-Hebeisen, A., Johnson, D. W., Anderson, D., & Johnson, R. (1984). Predictors and concomitants of changes in drug use patterns among teenagers. *Journal of Social Psychology, 124,* 43–50.

North Carolina State Occupational Information Coordinating Committee. (1999). *Elementary career awareness guide: A resource for elementary school counselors and teachers.* Raleigh, NC: Author.

Nottingham, J., & Gulec, J. (n.d.). *Prototype development of the O*NET: The occupational information network.* Raleigh, NC: North Carolina Occupational Analysis Field Center.

Nystul, M. S. (1995). A problem-solving approach to counseling: Integrating Adler's and Glasser's theories. *Elementary School Guidance and Counseling, 29,* 297–302.

O'Connell, M. T. (1997). *Children with single parents—How they fare* (Census Brief CENBR/97-1). Washington, DC: U.S. Census Bureau.

Offer, D., & Sabshin, M. (1984). *Normality and the life cycle: A critical integration.* New York: Basic Books.

Office for Civil Rights (1997). *Sexual harassment policy guidance: Harassment of students by school employees, other students, or third parties.* Washington, DC: U.S. Department of Education.

Office for Civil Rights (2001). *Revised sexual harassment policy guidance: Harassment of students by school employees, other students, or third parties.* Available online at www.ed.gov/offices/OCR/shguide/index.html (retrieved June 13, 2003).

Office of National AIDS Policy (1996). *Youth and HIV/AIDS: An American agenda.* Washington, DC: Author.

Office of Substance Abuse Program (1991). *Legal issues for alcohol and other drug use prevention and treatment programs serving high-risk youth* (Rep. No. 1). Rockville, MD: U.S. Department of Health and Human Services.

Office of Substance Abuse Program (1992). *Legal issues for alcohol and other drug use prevention and treatment programs serving high-risk youth* (Rep. No. 2). Rockville, MD: U.S. Department of Health and Human Services.

Ogdon, D. P. (1981). *Psychodiagnostics and personality assessment: A handbook* (2nd ed.). Los Angeles: Western Psychological Services.

Ohlsen, M. M. (1977). *Group counseling* (2nd ed.). New York: Holt, Rinehart, & Winston.

Oliver, J. M., Cole, N. H., & Hollingsworth, H. (1991). Learning disabilities as functions of familial learning problems and developmental problems. *Exceptional Children, 57,* 427–440.

Oliver, M. B. (1994). Portrayals of crime, race, and aggression in "reality-based" police shows: A content analysis. *Journal of Broadcasting and Electronic Media, 38,* 179–192.

Olsen, R., & Farkas, G. (1990). The effects of economic opportunity and family background on adolescent cohabitation and childbearing among low-income Blacks. *Journal of Labor Economics, 8,* 341–362.

Oltjenbruns, K. A. (1991). Positive outcomes of adolescents' experience with grief. *Journal of Adolescent Research, 6,* 43–53.

Oltjenbruns, K. A. (1996). Death of a friend during adolescence. In C. A. Corr & D. E. Balk (Eds.), *Handbook of adolescent death and bereavement* (pp. 196–215). New York: Springer-Verlag.

Olweus, D. (1979). Stability of aggressive reaction patterns in males: A review. *Psychological Bulletin, 100,* 674–701.

Olweus, D. (1992). Bullying among school children: Intervention and prevention. In R. Peters, R. J. McMahon, & V. L. Quinsey (Eds.), *Aggression and violence throughout the life span* (pp. 100–125). Newbury Park, CA: Sage.

Olweus, D. (1993). Victimization by peers: Antecedents and long-term outcomes. In K. H. Rubin & J. B. Asendorpf (Eds.), *Social withdrawal, inhibition, and shyness in childhood* (pp. 315–341). Hillsdale, NJ: Erlbaum.

Olweus, D. (1996). Bully/victim problems at school: Facts and effective intervention. *Journal of Emotional and Behavioral Problems, 5,* 15–22.

Olweus, D. (1997). Tackling peer victimization with a school-based intervention program. In D. P. Fry, & K. Bjorkqvist (Eds.), *Cultural variation in conflict resolution: Alternatives to violence* (pp. 215–234). Mahwah, NJ: Erlbaum.

Olweus, D., Limber, S., & Mihalic, S. (1999). *Blueprints for violence prevention, book nine: Bullying prevention program.* Boulder, CO: Center for the Study and Prevention of Violence.

Omizo, M. M., & Omizo, S. A. (1987). Group counseling with children of divorce: New findings. *Elementary School Guidance and Counseling, 22,* 46–52.

Omizo, M. M., & Omizo, S. A. (1988). Group counseling's effects on self-concept and social behavior among children with learning disabilities. *Journal of Humanistic Education and Development, 26,* 109–117.

Omizo, M. M., Omizo, S. A., & Okamoto, C. M. (1998). Gay and lesbian adolescents: A phenomenological study. *Professional School Counseling, 1,* 35–37.

Omizo, S. A., & Omizo, M. M. (1992). Career and vocational assessment information for program planning and counseling for students with disabilities. *School Counselor, 40,* 32–39.

O'Rourke, K. (1990). Recapturing hope: Elementary school support groups for children of alcoholics. *Elementary School Guidance and Counseling, 25,* 107–114.

O'Rourke, K., & Worzbyt, J. C. (1996). *Support groups for children.* Washington, DC: Taylor & Francis.

Osipow, S. H. (1983). *Theories of career development* (3rd ed.). New York: Appleton-Century-Crofts.

Osterweis, M., Solomon, F., & Green, M. (Eds.). (1984). *Bereavement: Reactions, consequences and care.* Washington, DC: National Academy Press.

O'Toole, D. (Cataloger) (1996–1997). *Compassion books catalog.* Burnsville, NC: Rainbow Connection.

Overholser, J., Evans, S., & Spirito, A. (1990). Sex differences and their relevance to primary prevention of adolescent suicide. *Death Studies, 14,* 391–402.

Paisley, P. O., & Borders, L. D. (1995). School counseling: An evolving specialty. *Journal of Counseling and Development, 74,* 150–153.

Paisley, P. O., & Hubbard, G. T. (1994). *Developmental school counseling programs: From theory to practice.* Alexandria, VA: American Counseling Association.

Paisley, P. O., & Peace, S. D. (1995). Developmental principles: A framework for school counseling programs. *Elementary School Guidance and Counseling, 30,* 85–93.

Palmatier, L. L. (1998). Parental involvement with certain school problems. In L. L. Palmatier (Ed.), *Crisis counseling for a quality school community* (pp. 439–464). Washington, DC: Accelerated Development.

Palmer, J. H., & Paisley, P. O. (1991). Student assistance programs: A response to substance abuse. *School Counselor, 38,* 287–293.

Pandina, R., & Schuele, J. A. (1983). Psychosocial correlates of alcohol and drug use of adolescent students and adolescents in treatment. *Journal of Studies on Alcohol, 44,* 950–973.

Parham, T. A., & Helms, J. E. (1981). The influence of Black students' racial identity attitudes on preferences for counselor's race. *Journal of Counseling Psychology, 28,* 250–257.

Park, J. C., & Boyd, A. O. (1998). Depression and suicide: Injecting hope. In L. L. Palmatier (Ed.), *Crisis counseling for a quality school community* (pp. 207–225). Washington, DC: Accelerated Development.

Parker, R. J. (1994). Helping children cope with divorce: A workshop for parents. *Elementary School Guidance and Counseling, 29,* 137–146.

Parsons, F. (1909). *Choosing a vocation.* Boston: Houghton Mifflin.

Partnership for a Drug-Free America (1998). *Growing up drug-free: A parent's guide to prevention.* Pueblo, CO: Author.

Pate, R. H. (1992). Are you liable? *American Counselor, 31,* 116–118.

Paterson, K. (1977). *Bridge to Terabithia.* New York: Crowell.

Patterson, W. M., Dohn, H. H., Bird, J., & Patterson, G. A. (1983). Evaluation of suicidal patients: The SAD PERSONS Scale. *Psychosomatics: Journal of Consultation Liaison Psychiatry, 24,* 343–349.

Peach, L., & Reddick, T. L. (1991). Counselors can make a difference in preventing adolescent suicide. *School Counselor, 39,* 107–110.

Peck, D. (1983). The last moments of life. Learning to cope. *Deviant Behavior, 4,* 313–342.

Pederson, P. B. (1991). Multiculturalism as a generic approach to counseling. *Journal of Counseling and Development, 70,* 6–12.

Pedro-Carroll, J. L., & Alpert-Gillis, L. J. (1997). Prevention interventions for children of divorce: A developmental model for 5 and 6 year old children. *Journal of Primary Prevention, 18,* 5–23.

Pedro-Carroll, J. L., Alpert-Gillis, L. J., & Cowen, E. L. (1992). An evaluation of the efficacy of a preventive intervention for 4th–6th grade urban children of divorce. *Journal of Primary Prevention, 13,* 115–130.

Pedro-Carroll, J. L., & Cowen, E. L. (1985). The Children of Divorce Intervention Project: An investigation of the efficacy of a school-based prevention program. *American Journal of Consulting and Clinical Psychology, 53,* 603–611.

Peeks, B. (1992). Protection and social context: Understanding a child's problem behavior. *Elementary School Guidance and Counseling, 26,* 295–304.

Pelham, W. E., Schnedler, R. W., Bender, M. E., Nilsson, D. E., Miller, J., Budrow, M. S., Ronnei, M., Paluchowski, C., & Marks, D. A. (1988). The combination of behavior therapy and methylphenidate in the treatment of attention deficit disorders: A therapy outcome study. In L. M. Bloomingdale (Ed.), *Attention deficit disorder: Vol. 3. New research in attention, treatment, and psychopharmacology* (pp. 28–48). Oxford, England: Pergamon Press.

Pentz, M. A. (1995). The school–community interface in comprehensive school health education. In S. Stansfield (Ed.), *1996 Institute of Medicine annual report, Committee on Comprehensive School Health Programs.* Washington, DC: National Academy Press.

Pentz, M. A., Dwyer, J. H., MacKinnon, D. P., Flay, B. R., Hansen, W. B., Wang, E. Y., & Johnson, C. A. (1989). A multi-community trial for primary prevention of adolescent drug use: Effects on drug use prevalence. *Journal of the American Medical Association, 261*, 3259–3266.

Pepler, D. J., & Sedighdellami, F. (1998). *Aggressive girls in Canada.* Available online at http://www.hrdc-drhc.gc.ca/sp-ps/arb-dgra/publications/research/abw-98-30e.shtml.

Perusse, R., Goodnough, G. E., & Noel, C. J. (2001). Use of the national standards for school counseling programs in preparing school counselors. *Professional School Counseling, 5*, 49–55.

Peters, S. (2000). Is there a disability culture? A syncretisation of three possible world views. *Disability and Society, 15*, 583–601.

Peterson, M. S., & Urquiza, A. J. (1993). *The role of mental health professionals in the prevention and treatment of child abuse and neglect.* McLean, VA: Circle.

Petrusic, J., & Celotta, B. (1985). What children want to know about their disabled peers: An exploratory study. *School Counselor, 32*, 39–46.

Pfeifer, G., & Abrams, L. (1984). School-based discussion groups for children of divorce: A pilot program. *Group, 8*, 22–28.

Phillips, E., & Mullen, J. (1999). Client-centered play therapy techniques for elementary school counselors: Building the supportive relationship. *Journal for the Professional Counselor, 14*, 25–36.

Phillips, T. M., Cooper, W. E., & Johnson, J. T. (1995). Listen to the children: Where adolescents obtain their role models. *Rural Educator, 17*(1), 24–26.

Phillips-Hershey, E. H., & Ridley, L. L. (1996). Strategies for acceptance of diversity of students with mental retardation. *Elementary School Guidance and Counseling, 30*, 282–290.

Piaget, J. (1929). *The child's conception of the world.* New York: Harcourt Brace.

Piaget, J. (1952). *The origins of intelligence in children.* New York: International Universities Press.

Pianta, R., Egeland, B., & Erickson, M. F. (1989). The antecedents of maltreatment: Results of the mother–child interaction project. In D. Cicchetti & V. Carlson, *Child maltreatment: Theory and research on the causes and consequences of child abuse and neglect* (pp. 203–253). New York: Cambridge University Press.

Pilat, J. M., & Jones, J. W. (1985). A comprehensive treatment program for children of alcoholics. In E. M. Freeman (Ed.), *Social work practice with clients who have alcohol problems* (pp. 141–159). Springfield, IL: Thomas.

Piper, E. (1985). Violent recidivism and chronicity in the 1958 Philadelphia cohort. *Journal of Quantitative Criminology, 1*, 319–344.

Pizzo, P. A., & Wilfert, C. M. (1991). *Pediatric AIDS: The challenge of HIV infection in infants, children, and adolescents.* Baltimore: Williams & Wilkins.

Plake, B. S., & Impara, J. C. (Eds.). (2001). *The fourteenth mental measurements yearbook.* Lincoln, NE: Buros Institute of Mental Measurements.

Polansky, N. A. (1985). The psychological ecology of the neglectful mother. *Child Abuse and Neglect, 9*, 265–275.

Polansky, N. A. (1987). *Damaged parents.* Chicago: University of Chicago Press.

Popenhagen, M. P., & Qualley, R. M. (1998). Adolescent suicide: Detection, intervention, and prevention. *Professional School Counseling, 1*, 30–35.

Posavac, E. J., & Carey, R. G. (1997). *Program evaluation methods and case studies* (5th ed.). Upper Saddle River, NJ: Prentice Hall.

Post, P., & Robinson, B. E. (1998). School-age children of alcoholics and non-alcoholics: Their anxiety, self-esteem, and locus of control. *Professional School Counseling, 1,* 36–40.

Powell, D. H. (1957). Careers and family atmosphere: An empirical test of Roe's theory. *Journal of Counseling Psychology, 4,* 212–217.

Powell, L., & Faherty, S. L. (1990). Treating sexually abused latency age girls: A 20 session treatment plan utilizing group process and the creative arts therapies. *Arts in Psychotherapy, 17,* 35–47.

Prewett, M. J., Spence, R., & Chaknis, M. (1981). Attribution of causality by children with alcoholic parents. *International Journal of the Addictions, 16,* 367–370.

Price, A. W., & Emshoff, J. G. (1997). Breaking the cycle of addiction: Prevention and intervention with children of alcoholics. *Alcohol Health and Research World, 21,* 241–246.

Price, J. H., & Telljohann, S. K. (1991). School counselors' perceptions of adolescent homosexuals. *Journal of School Health, 61,* 433–438.

Pryor, D. B., & Tollerud, T. R. (1999). Applications of Adlerian principles in school settings. *Professional School Counseling, 2,* 299–304.

Psychological Corporation (1992). *Wechsler Individual Achievement Test.* San Antonio, TX: Author.

Puig-Antich, J. (1985). Biological factors in prepubertal major depression. *Psychiatric Annals, 15,* 390–397.

Rafael, B. (1983). *The anatomy of bereavement.* New York: Basic Books.

Ramsey, M. (1994). Student depression: General treatment dynamics and symptom specific interventions. *School Counselor, 41,* 256–262.

Raskin, M. S., & Daley, D. C. (1991). Introduction and overview of addiction. In D.C. Daley & M. S. Raskin (Eds.), *Treating the chemically dependent and their families* (pp. 1–21). Newbury Park, CA: Sage.

Reeve, R. E. (1990). ADHD: Facts and fallacies. *Intervention in School and Clinic, 26*(2), 70–78.

Rehm, L. P. (1977). A self-control model of depression. *Behavior Therapy, 8,* 787–804.

Remafedi, G. (1987). Adolescent homosexuality: Psychosocial and medical implications. *Pediatrics, 79,* 331–337.

Remafedi, G., Farrow, J. A., & Deisher, R. W. (1991). Risk factors for attempted suicide in gay and bisexual youth. *Pediatrics, 87,* 869–875.

Remley, T. P., & Fry, L. J. (1993). Reporting suspected child abuse: Conflicting roles for the counselor. *School Counselor, 40,* 253–259.

Remley, T. P., & Huey, W. C. (2002). An ethics quiz for school counselors. *Professional School Counseling, 6,* 3–11.

Reppucci, N. D., & Haugaard, J. J. (1989). Prevention of child sexual abuse: Myth or reality. *American Psychologist, 44,* 1266–1275.

Reppucci, N. D., Land, D., & Haugaard, J. J. (1998). Child abuse prevention programs that target young children. In P. K. Trickett & C. J. Schellenbach (Eds.), *Violence against children in the family and the community* (pp. 317–337). Washington, DC: American Psychological Association.

Reynolds, W. M. (1986). A model for the screening and identification of depressed children and adolescents in school settings. *Professional School Psychology, 1,* 117–129.

Reynolds, W. M. (1987). *RCDS manual.* Odessa, FL: Psychological Assessment Resources.

Reynolds, W. M. (1988). *The Suicide Ideation Questionnaire.* Odessa, FL: Psychological Assessment Resources.

Reynolds, W. M. (1989). *RADS manual.* Odessa, FL: Psychological Assessment Resources.

Richard, M. (1995). Students with attention deficit disorders in post-secondary education: Issues in identification and accommodation. In K. Nadeau (Ed.), *A comprehensive guide to attention deficit disorders in adults* (pp. 284–307). New York: Brunner/Mazel.

Richardson, C. D., & Rosen, L. A. (1999). School-based interventions for children of divorce. *Professional School Counseling, 3,* 21–26.

Riddle, J., Bergin, J. J., & Douzensis, C. (1997). Effects of group counseling on the self-concept of children of alcoholics. *Elementary School Guidance and Counseling, 31,* 192–303.

Rigby, K., & Slee, P. (1999). Suicidal ideation among adolescent school children, involvement in bully–victim problems, and perceived social support. *Journal of Suicide and Life-Threatening Behavior, 29,* 119–130.

Riley, P., & McDaniel, J. 1999. *Youth out of the education mainstream: A North Carolina profile.* Rockville, MD: Juvenile Justice Clearinghouse.

Riordan, R. J., & Verdel, A. C. (1991). Evidence of sexual abuse in children's art products. *School Counselor, 39,* 116–121.

Roberts, W. B. (1995). Postvention and psychological autopsy in the suicide of a 14-year-old public school student. *School Counselor, 42,* 322–330.

Roberts, W. B., & Coursol, D. (1996). Strategies for intervention with childhood and adolescent victims of bullying, teasing, and intimidation. *Elementary School Guidance and Counseling, 30,* 204–212

Roberts, W. B., & Morotti, A. A. (2000). The bully as victim: Understanding bully behaviors to increase the effectiveness of interventions in the bully–victim dyad. *Professional School Counseling, 4,* 148–155.

Robinson, B. E. (1989). *Working with children of alcoholics: The practitioner's handbook.* Lexington, MA: Lexington Books.

Robinson, B. E., & Rhoden, J. L. (1998). *Working with children of alcoholics: The practitioner's handbook* (2nd ed.). Thousand Oaks, CA: Sage.

Robinson, D., & Mopsik, W. (1992). An environmental–experiential model for counseling handicapped children. *Elementary School Guidance and Counseling, 27,* 73–78.

Robinson, K. E. (1994). Addressing the needs of gay and lesbian students: The school counselor's role. *School Counselor, 41,* 326–332.

Robinson, L. (1998, May 11). "Hispanics" don't exist. *U.S. News & World Report, 124,* 26–32.

Robinson, R. B., Watkins-Ferrell, P., Davis-Scott, P., & Ruch-Ross, H. S. (1993). Preventing teenage pregnancy. In D. S. Glenwick & L. A. Jason (Eds.), *Promoting health and mental health in children, youth, and families* (pp. 99–124). New York: Springer-Verlag.

Robinson, S. E. (1989). Preventing substance abuse among teenagers. A school and family responsibility. *Counseling and Human Development, 34,* 130–137.

Robinson, T. (1992). Transforming at-risk educational practices by understanding and appreciating differences. *Elementary School Guidance and Counseling, 27,* 84–95.

Roe, A. (1956). *The psychology of occupations.* New York: Wiley.

Roe, A. (1957). Early determinants of vocational choice. *Journal of Counseling Psychology, 4,* 212–217.

Rogers, C. R. (1942). *Counseling and psychotherapy: New concepts in practice.* Boston: Houghton Mifflin.

Rogers, C. R. (1951). *Client-centered therapy: Its current practice, implications, and theory.* Boston: Houghton Mifflin.

Rogers, C. R. (1959). A theory of therapy, personality and interpersonal relationships as developed in the client-centered framework. In S. Koch (Ed.), *Psychology: A study of a science* (Vol. 3) (pp. 184–256). New York: McGraw-Hill.

Rogers, F., & Sharapan, H. (1993). Play. *Elementary School Guidance and Counseling, 28,* 5–9.

Rogler, L. (1983). A conceptual framework for mental health research on Hispanic populations. *Hispanic Research Center Monograph, 10* (Fordham University).

Rohrbach, L. A., D'Onofrio, C. N., Backer, T. E., & Montgomery, S. B. (1996). Diffusion of school-based substance abuse prevention programs. *American Behavioral Scientist, 39,* 919–934.

Root, M. P. P. (1998). Facilitating psychotherapy with Asian American clients. In D. R. Atkinson, G. Morten, & D. W. Sue (Eds.), *Counseling American minorities* (5th ed., pp. 214–234). Boston: McGraw-Hill.

Roscoe, B., Strouse, J. S., Goodwin, M. P., Taracks, L., & Henderson, D. (1994). Sexual harassment: An educational program for middle school students. *Elementary School Guidance and Counseling, 29,* 110–120.

Rosen, D., Holmberg, K, & Holland, J. L. (1997). *The educational opportunities finder for use with the self-directed search and the vocational preference inventory.* Odessa, FL: Psychological Assessment Resources.

Rosen, H. (1986). *Unspoken grief: Coping with childhood sibling loss.* Lexington, MA: Lexington Books.

Ross, J. G., Einhaus, K. E., Hohenemser, L. K., Greene, B. Z., Kann, L., & Gold, R. S. (1995). School health policies prohibiting tobacco use, alcohol and other drug use, and violence. *Journal of School Health, 65,* 333–338.

Roth, J. (1990). Needs and the needs assessment process (reprinted from 1978). *Evaluation Practice, 11,* 141–143.

Rotter, J. (1966). Generalized expectancies for internal versus external control of reinforcement. *Psychological Monographs, 80,* 1–28.

Rotter, J. (1975). Some problems and misconceptions related to the construct of internal versus external control of reinforcement. *Journal of Consulting and Clinical Psychology, 43,* 56–67.

Rowe, W., Bennett, S. K., & Atkinson, D. R. (1994). White racial identity models: A critique and alternative proposal. *Counseling Psychologist, 22,* 129–146.

Rowell, L. L., McBride, M. C., & Nelson-Leaf, J. (1996). The role of the school counselor in confronting peer sexual harassment. *School Counselor, 43,* 196–207.

Rudy, W. S. (1965). *School in the age of mass culture.* Englewood Cliffs, NJ: Prentice Hall.

Russell, D. E. (1983). The incidence and prevalence of intrafamilial and extrafamilial sexual abuse and female children. *Child Abuse and Neglect, 7,* 133–146.

Russell, S. T., & Joyner, K. (2001). Suicide attempts more likely among adolescents with same-sex sexual orientation. *American Journal of Public Health, 91,* 1276–1281.

Sadowski, P. M., & Loesch, L. C. (1993). Using children's drawings to detect potential child sexual abuse. *Elementary School Guidance and Counseling, 28,* 115–123.

Sadri, G., & Robertson, L. T. (1993). Self-efficacy and work-related behavior: A review and meta-analysis. *Applied Psychology: An Internal Review, 42,* 139–152.

Safe schools, safe students. (1998). (Available from Drug Strategies, 2445 M Street, NW, no. 480, Washington, DC 20037)

Sailor, W. (1991). Special education in the restructured school. *Remedial and Special Education, 12*(6), 8–22.

Sampson, R., & Lauritson, J. (1994). Violent victimization and offending: Individual-, situational-, and community-level risk factors. In A. J. Reiss & J. A. Roth (Eds.), *Understanding and preventing violence: Vol. 3. Social influences* (pp. 1–114). Washington, DC: National Academy Press.

Sanders, D. R., & Riester, A.E. (1996). School-based counseling groups for children of divorce: Effects on the self-concepts of 5th grade children. *Journal of Child and Adolescent Group Therapy, 6,* 147–156.

Sandhu, D. S. (1997). Psychocultural profiles of Asian and Pacific Islander Americans: Implications for counseling and psychotherapy. *Journal of Multicultural Development and Counseling, 25,* 7–22.

Savin-Williams, R. C. (1990). Gay and lesbian adolescents. *Marriage and Family Review, 14,* 197–216.

Scarborough, J. L., & Deck, M. D. (1998). The challenges of working for students with disabilities: A view from the front lines. *Professional School Counseling, 2,* 10–15.

Schachter, S. (1991). Adolescent experiences with the death of a peer. *Omega, 24,* 1–11.

Schaps, E., DiBartolo, R., Moskowitz, J., Palley, C., & Churgin, S. (1981). A review of 127 drug abuse prevention evaluations. *Journal of Drug Issues, 11,* 17–43.

Scherman, A., Korkanes-Rowe, D., & Howard, S. S. (1990). An examination of the living arrangements and needs expressed by teenage mothers. *School Counselor, 38,* 133–141.

Schloss, P. J. (1983). Classroom-based interventions for students exhibiting depressive reactions. *Behavioral Disorders, 8,* 231–236.

Schmidt, J. J. (1999). *Counseling in schools: Essential services and comprehensive programs* (3rd ed.). Boston: Allyn & Bacon.

Schneidman, E. (1981). Suicide. *Journal of Suicide and Life-Threatening Behavior, 11,* 198–220.

Schut, H. A. W., Stroebe, M., van den Bout, J., & de Keijser, J. (1997). Gender differences in the efficacy of grief counseling. *British Journal of Clinical Psychology, 36,* 63–72.

Schwartz, D., McFadyen-Ketchum, S. A., Dodge, K. A., Pettit, G. S., & Bates, J. E. (1999). Early behavior problems as a predictor of later peer group victimization: Moderators and mediators in the pathways of social risk. *Journal of Abnormal Child Psychology, 27*, 191–201.

Schwiebert, V. L., Sealander, K. A., & Bradshaw, M. L. (1998). Preparing students with attention deficit disorders for entry into the workplace and postsecondary education. *Professional School Counseling, 2*, 26–32.

Schwiebert, V. L., Sealander, K. A., & Tolerud, T. R. (1995). Attention-deficit hyperactivity disorder: An overview for school counselors. *Elementary School Guidance and Counseling, 29*, 249–259.

Sciarra, D. T. (1999). *Multiculturalism in counseling.* Itasca, IL: Peacock.

Sciarra, D. T., & Ponterotto, J. G. (1991). Counseling the Hispanic bilingual family: Challenges to the therapeutic process. *Psychotherapy, 28*, 473–479.

Sciarra, D. T., & Ponterotto, J. G. (1998). Adolescent motherhood among low-income urban Hispanics: Familial considerations of mother–daughter dyads. *Qualitative Health Research, 8*, 751–763.

Scott, C. M. (1991). Problem writers: Nature, assessment, and intervention. In A. G. Kamhi & H. W. Catts (Eds.), *Reading disabilities: A developmental language perspective* (pp. 303–344). Boston: Allyn & Bacon.

Scruggs, T. E., & Mastropieri, M. A. (1996). Teacher perceptions of mainstreaming/inclusion, 1958–1995: A research synthesis. *Exceptional Children, 63*, 59–74.

Sealander, K., Bush, J., Chen, J., Henning, M., Tragash, J., & Ross, J. (1993). Attention deficit disorder: A primer for parents and professionals. *Multidisciplinary Diagnostic Training Program (MDTP) Monograph Series* (University of Florida, College of Medicine, Department of Pediatrics).

Search Institute (1988). The risky business of growing up female. *Sources, 1*, 1–4.

Search Institute (1997). *The assets approach: Giving kids what they need to succeed.* Minneapolis: Author.

Sears, J. T. (1992). Educators, homosexuality, and homosexual students: Are personal feelings related to professional beliefs? In K. M. Harbeck (Ed.), *Coming out of the classroom closet: Gay and lesbian students, teachers, and curricula* (pp. 29–79). Binghamton, NY: Harrington Park Press.

Sears-Jones, S. (1995). Career and educational planning in the middle level school. *NASSP Bulletin, 79*, 36–42.

Seashore, K. R., Jones, L.M., & Seppanen, P. (2001). *Transforming school counseling: A report on early evaluation findings.* Minneapolis, MN: Center for Applied Research and Educational Improvement.

Sedlak, A., & Broadhurst, D. (1996). *Third national incidence study of child abuse and neglect: Final report.* Washington, DC: U.S. Department of Health and Human Services, Administration for Children and Families.

Seidner, A. L., & Calhoun, K. S. (1984, August). *Childhood sexual abuse: Factors related to differential adult adjustment.* Paper presented at the Second National Conference for Family Violence Researchers, Durham, NH.

Seligman, L., Weinstock, L., & Heflin, E. N. (1991). The career development of 10 year olds. *Elementary School Guidance and Counseling, 25*, 172–181.

Seligman, M. E. P. (1974). Depression and learned helplessness. In R. J. Friedman & M. M. Katz (Eds.), *The psychology of depression: Contemporary theory and research* (pp. 83–113). New York: Wiley.

Sellers, D., McGraw, S., & McKinlay, J. (1994). Does the promotion and distribution of condoms increase teen sexual activity? *American Journal of Public Health, 84,* 1952–1959.

Selman, R. (1980). *The growth of interpersonal understanding.* New York: Academic Press.

Shaw, D., Emery, R., & Tver, M. (1993). Parental functioning and children's adjustment in families of divorce. *Journal of Abnormal Child Psychology, 21,* 119–134.

Shedler, J., & Block, J. (1990). Adolescent drug use and psychological health: A longitudinal study. *American Psychologist, 45,* 612–630.

Sherwood-Hawes, A. (2000). Children having children: Teenage pregnancy and parenthood. In D. Capuzzi & D. R. Gross (Eds.), *Youth at risk: A prevention resource for counselors, teachers, and parents.* (3rd ed.) (pp. 243–280). Alexandria, VA: American Counseling Association.

Shifrin, F., & Solis, M. (1992). Chemical dependency in gay and lesbian youth. *Journal of Chemical Dependency Treatment, 5,* 67–76.

Shuckit, M. A., & Chiles, J. A. (1978). Family history as a diagnostic aid in two samples of adolescents. *Journal of Nervous and Mental Disease, 166,* 165–176.

Shura, M. F. (1988). *The Sunday doll.* New York: Dodd Mead.

Siehl, P. M. (1990). Suicide postvention: A new disaster plan—What a school should do when faced with a suicide. *School Counselor, 38,* 52–57.

Sigelman, C. K., & Shaffer, D. R. (1995). *Life-span human development.* Pacific Grove, CA: Brooks/Cole.

Sigmon, S. T., Stanton, A. L., & Snyder, C. R. (1995). Gender differences in coping: A further test of socialization and role constraint theories. *Gender Roles, 33,* 25–35.

Sink, C. A., & McDonald, G. (1998). The status of comprehensive guidance and counseling in the United States. *Professional School Counseling, 2,* 88–94.

Sink, C. A., & Yillik-Downer, A. (2001). School counselors' perceptions of comprehensive guidance and counseling programs: A national survey. *Professional School Counseling, 4,* 278–288.

Skinner, M. E., & Schenck, S. J. (1992). Counseling the college-bound student with a learning disability. *School Counselor, 39,* 369–376.

Smaby, M. H., Peterson, T. L., Bergmann, P. E., Zentner, K. L., & Swearingen, S. (1990). School-based community intervention: The school counselor as lead consultant for suicide prevention and intervention programs. *School Counselor, 37,* 370–377.

Smith, C., & Thornberry, T. P. (1995). The relationship between childhood maltreatment and adolescent involvement in delinquency. *Criminology, 33,* 451–481.

Smith, M., & Rottenberg, C. (1991). Unintended consequences of external testing in elementary schools. *Educational Measurement: Issues and Practice, 10,* 7–11.

Smith, P. K., & Thompson, D. (1991). Dealing with bully/victim problems in the U.K. In P. K. Smith & D. Thompson (Eds.), *Practical approaches to bullying* (pp. 1–2). London: Fulton.

Snell, M. E., & Eichner, S. J. (1989). Integration for students with profound disabilities. In F. Brown & D. H. Lehr (Eds.), *Persons with profound disabilities* (pp. 109–138). Baltimore: Brookes.

Snyder, K. A. (1985). An intervention program for children of separated or divorced parents. *Techniques, 1,* 286–296.

Sommers-Flanagan, J., & Sommers-Flanagan, R. (1996). Efficacy of antidepressant medication with depressed youth: What psychologists should know. *Professional Psychology: Research and Practice, 27,* 145–153.

Sommers-Flanagan, R., Barrett-Hakanson, T., Clarke, C., & Sommers-Flanagan, J. (2000). A psychoeducational school-based coping and social skills group for depressed students. *Journal for Specialists in Group Work, 25,* 170–190.

Sonenstein, F. L., Stewart, K., Lindberg, L., & Williams, S. (1998). *Involving males in preventing teen pregnancy.* Washington, DC: Urban Institute.

Sorenson, T., & Snow, B. (1991). How children tell: The process of disclosure in child sexual abuse. *Child Welfare, 70,* 3–15.

Spiegel, L., & Mayers, A. (1991). Psychosocial aspects of AIDS in children and adolescents. *Pediatric Clinics of North America, 38,* 153–167.

Spirito, A., Plummer, B., Gispert, M., & Levy, S. (1992). Adolescent suicide attempts: Outcomes at follow-up. *American Journal of Orthopsychiatry, 62,* 464–468.

Stainback, W., & Stainback, S. (1990). *Support networks for inclusive schooling.* Baltimore: Brookes.

Stanford, L. D., & Hynd, G. W. (1994). Congruence of behavioral symptomatology in children with ADD/H, ADD/WO, and learning disabilities. *Journal of Learning Disabilities, 27,* 243–253.

Starr, M., & Gysbers, N. C. (1992). *Missouri comprehensive guidance: A model for program development, implementation, and evaluation.* Jefferson City, MO: Missouri Department of Elementary and Secondary Education.

State of Our Nation's Youth (2000). *The Horatio Alger Association of Distinguished Americans, 2000.* Available online at www.horatioalger.com/pubmat/surpro.htm.

Stattin, H., & Magnusson, D. (1989). The role of early aggressive behavior in the frequency, seriousness, and types of later crime. *Journal of Counseling and Clinical Psychology, 57,* 710–718.

Staub, D., Schwartz, I. S., Galluci, C., & Peck, C. (1994). Four portraits of friendship at an inclusive school. *Journal of the Association for Persons with Severe Handicaps, 19,* 314–325.

Staulcup, H., Kenward, K., & Frigo, D. (1979). A review of federal primary alcoholism prevention projects. *Journal of Studies in Alcohol, 40,* 943–968.

St. Clair, K. L. (1989). Middle school counseling research: A resource for school counselors. *Elementary School Guidance and Counseling, 23,* 219–226.

Steele, B., & Alexander, H. (1981). Long-term effects of sexual abuse in childhood. In P. Marazek & C. Kempe (Eds.), *Sexually abused children and their families* (pp. 223–233). Oxford, England: Pergamon Press.

Steele, W. (1992). *Preventing self-destruction: A manual for school crisis teams.* Holmes Beach, FL: Learning Publications.

Stein, N. (1995). Sexual harassment in school: The public performance of gendered violence. *Harvard Educational Review, 65,* 145–162.

Stein, N. (1999). *Classrooms and courtrooms: Facing sexual harassment in K–12 schools.* New York: Teachers College Press.

Stein, N., & Sjostrom, L. (1994). *Flirting or hurting: A teacher's guide on student-to-student sexual harassment in schools.* Washington, DC: National Education Association.

Steinberg, L. (2000, April). Youth violence: Do parents and families make a difference? *National Institute of Justice Journal,* pp. 30–38.

Stenger, M. K., Tollefson, N., & Fine, M. J. (1992). Variables that distinguish elementary teachers who participate in school-based consultation from those who do not. *School Psychology Quarterly, 7,* 271–284.

Stern, D., Stone, J., Hopkins, C., McMillion, M., & Crain, R. (1994). *School-based enterprise: Productive learning in American high schools.* San Francisco: Jossey-Bass.

Stevens, R. J., & Slavin, R. E. (1991). When cooperative learning improves the achievement of students with mild disabilities: A response to Tateyama-Sniezek. *Exceptional Children, 57,* 276–280.

Stewart, A. L. (1998). *It's child play: Facilitating children's emotional growth through play.* Workshop conducted at the annual meeting of the American Counseling Association, Indianapolis.

Stillion, J., McDowell, E., & Shamblin, J. (1984). The suicide attitude vignette experience: A method for measuring adolescent attitudes toward suicide. *Death Education, 8,* 65–81.

Stoker, A., & Swadi, H. (1990). Perceived family relationships in drug abusing adolescents. *Drug and Alcohol Dependence, 25,* 293–297.

Stolberg, A. L., & Mahler, J. (1994). Enhancing treatment gains in a school-based intervention for children of divorce through skill training, parental involvement, and transfer procedures. *Journal of Consulting and Clinical Psychology, 62,* 147–156.

Stoll-Switzer, L. (1990). Family factors associated with academic progress for children with learning disabilities. *Elementary School Guidance and Counseling, 24,* 200–206.

Stone, C. (2000). Advocacy for sexual harassment victims: Legal support and ethical aspects. *Professional School Counseling, 4,* 23–30.

Stone, C. (2002). Negligence in academic advising and abortion counseling: Court rulings and implications. *Professional School Counseling, 6,* 28–35.

Strangeland, C. S., Pellegreno, D. D., & Lundholm, J. (1989). Children of divorced parents: A perceptual comparison. *Elementary School Guidance and Counseling, 23,* 167–174.

Stroebe, M., Stroebe, W., & Schut, H. (2001). Gender differences in adjustment to bereavement: An empirical and theoretical review. *Review of General Psychology, 5,* 62–83.

Substance Abuse and Mental Health Services Administration (1999). *The relationship between mental health and substance abuse among adolescents.* Rockville, MD: Author.

Sue, D. (1998). The interplay of sociocultural factors on the psychological development of Asians in America. In D. R. Atkinson, G. Morten, & D. W. Sue (Eds.), *Counseling American minorities* (5th ed.) (pp. 205–213). Boston: McGraw-Hill.

Sue, D. W. (1978). Eliminating cultural oppression in counseling: Toward a general theory. *Journal of Counseling Psychology, 25,* 419–428.

Sue, D. W., Carter, R. T., Casas, J. M., Fouad, N. A., Ivey, A. E., Ponterotto, J. G., & Vazquez-Nutall, E. (1998). *Multicultural counseling competencies: Individual and organizational development.* Thousand Oaks, CA: Sage.

Sue, D. W., & Sue, D. (1999). *Counseling the culturally different: Theory and practice* (3rd ed.). New York: Wiley.

Sue, D. W., & Sue, D. (2003). *Counseling the culturally diverse: Theory and practice* (4th ed.). New York: Wiley.

Sunseri, A. J., Alberti, J. M., & Kent, N. O. (1983). Reading, demographic, social, and psychological factors related to pre-adolescent smoking and non-smoking behaviors and attitudes. *Journal of School Health, 53,* 257–263.

Super, D. E. (1957). *The psychology of careers.* New York: Harper & Row.

Super, D. E. (1990). A life-span, life-space approach to career development. In D. Brown, L. Brooks, & Associates (Eds.), *Career choice and development: Applying contemporary theories to practice* (pp. 197–261). San Francisco: Jossey-Bass.

Sweeney, D. P., Forness, S. R., Kavale, K. A., & Levitt, J. G. (1997). An update on psychopharmacologic medication: What teachers, clinicians, and parents need to know. *Intervention, 23*(1), 4–21.

Swinton, D. H. (1992). The economic status of African Americans: Limited ownership and persistent inequality. In B. J. Tidwell (Ed.), *The state of Black America* (pp. 61–117). New York: Urban League.

Tarter, R. E. (1990). Evaluation and treatment of adolescent substance abuse. A decision tree method. *American Journal of Drug and Alcohol Abuse, 16,* 1–46.

Tarter, R. E., Blackson, T., Martin, C., Loeber, R., & Moss, H. B. (1993). Characteristics and correlates of child discipline practices in substance abuse and normal families. *American Journal on Addictions, 2,* 18–25.

Tarter, R. E., Laird, S., Bukstein, O., & Kaminer, Y. (1992). Validation of the Adolescent Drug Use Screening Inventory: Preliminary findings. *Psychology of Addictive Behaviors, 6,* 233–236.

Tarver-Behring, S., Spagna, M. E., & Sullivan, J. (1998). School counselors and full inclusion for children with special needs. *Professional School Counseling, 1,* 51–56.

Telljohann, S. K., & Price, J. H. (1993). A quantitative examination of adolescent homosexuals' life experiences: Ramifications for secondary school personnel. *Journal of Homosexuality, 26,* 41–56.

Thomas, M. (1996, March). *Diversity in women's friendships.* Paper presented at the annual meeting of the Association for Women in Psychology, Portland, OR.

Thompson, C. L., & Rudolph, L. B. (1996). *Counseling children* (4th ed.). Pacific Grove, CA: Brooks/Cole.

Thompson, R. A. (2002). *School counseling: Best practices for working in the schools* (2nd ed.). New York: Brunner-Routledge.

Thomson, E., Hanson, T., & McLanahan, S. (1994). Family structure and child well-being: Economic resources vs. parental behaviors. *Sociological Forces, 73,* 221–242.

Thornberry, T. P., Huizenga, D., & Loeber, R. (1995). The prevention of serious delinquency and violence: Implications from the Program of Research on the Causes and Correlates of Delinquency. In J. C. Howell, B. Krisberg, J. D. Hawkins, & J. J. Wilson (Eds.), *Sourcebook on serious, violent, and chronic juvenile offenders* (pp. 213–237). Thousand Oaks, CA: Sage.

Thurlow, M., Shin, H., Guy, B., & Lee, S. Y. (1999). *State graduation requirements for students with and without disabilities.* Minneapolis: National Transition Network. (ERIC Document Reproduction Service No. ED431284)

Titkin, E. A., & Cobb, C. (1983). Treating post-divorce adjustment in latency age children: A focused group paradigm. *Social Work with Groups, 6,* 53–66.

Tobler, N. S. (1986). Meta-analysis of 143 adolescent drug prevention programs: Quantitative outcome results of program participants compared to a control or a comparison group. *Journal of Drug Issues, 16,* 537–567.

Tobler, N. S. (1992). Drug prevention programs can work: Research findings. *Journal of Addictive Diseases, 11(3),* 1–28.

Tolan, P. H., & Thomas, P. (1995). The implications of age of onset for delinquency risk: II. Longitudinal data. *Journal of Abnormal Child Psychology, 23,* 157–181.

Tomlinson-Keasey, C., & Keasey, C. B. (1988). "Signatures" of suicide. In D. Capuzzi & L. Golden (Eds.), *Preventing adolescent suicide* (pp. 213–245). Muncie, IN: Accelerated Development.

Trice, A. D. (1991). Stability of children's career aspirations. *Journal of Genetic Psychology, 152,* 137–139.

Trice, A. D., Hughes, M. A., Odom, C., Woods, K., & McClellan, N. C. (1995). The origins of children's career aspirations: IV, Testing hypotheses from four theories. *Career Development Quarterly, 43,* 307–322.

Trice, A. D., & King, R. (1991). Stability of kindergarten children's career aspirations. *Psychological Reports, 68,* 1378.

Trice, A. D., & Knapp, L. (1992). Relationship of children's career aspirations to parents' occupations. *Journal of Genetic Psychology, 153,* 355–357.

Trice, A. D., & McClellan, N. (1993). Do children's career aspirations predict adult occupations? An answer from a secondary analysis of a longitudinal study. *Psychological Reports, 72,* 368–370.

Trice, A. D., & Tillapaugh, P. (1991). Children's estimates of their parents' job satisfaction. *Psychological Reports, 69,* 63–66.

Trimble, J. E. (1990). Application of psychological knowledge for American Indians and Alaska Natives. *Journal of Training and Practice in Professional Psychology, 4,* 45–63.

Troiden, R. R. (1989). The formation of homosexual identities. *Journal of Homosexuality, 17,* 43–74.

Tsai, M., & Wagner, N. (1978). Therapy groups for women sexually molested as children. *Archives of Sexual Behavior, 7,* 417–429.

Tsui, A. M., & Sammons, M. T. (1988). Group intervention with adolescent Vietnamese refugees. *Journal for Specialists in Group Work, 13,* 90–95.

Turnbull, A., & Schulz, J. B. (1979). *Mainstreaming handicapped students: A guide for the classroom teacher.* Boston: Allyn & Bacon.

Turnbull, A., Turnbull, R., Shank, M., & Leal, D. (1999). *Exceptional lives: Special education in today's schools* (2nd ed.). Upper Saddle River, NJ: Merrill.

Tyler, L. E. (1961). Research explorations in the realm of choice. *Journal of Counseling Psychology, 8,* 195–202.

U.S. Bureau of the Census (1995). *Population profile of the United States.* Washington, DC: U.S. Government Printing Office.

U.S. Bureau of the Census (1998). *Current population reports.* Washington, DC: U.S. Government Printing Office.

U.S. Bureau of the Census (2000). *Table DP-1: Profile of general demographic characteristics for the United States: 2000.* Available online at www.census.gov (retrieved October 14, 2001).

U.S. Bureau of the Census (2001a). Population projections of the U.S. by age, sex, race, and Hispanic origin: 1995–2030. *Statistical abstract of the United States: 2001* (121st ed.). Washington, DC: U.S. Government Printing Office.

U.S. Bureau of the Census (2001b). *Statistical abstract of the United States* (121st ed.). Washington, DC: U.S. Government Printing Office.

U.S. Department of Education (1994a). *Creating a school-to-work opportunities system.* Washington, DC: Author.

U.S. Department of Education (1994b). *School-to-work opportunities: An owner's guide.* Washington, DC: Author.

U.S. Department of Education (2000). *Twenty-second annual report to Congress on the implementation of the Individuals with Disabilities Education Act.* Washington, DC: Author.

U.S. Department of Education (2001). *No Child Left Behind Act of 2001 (H.R. 1).* Washington, DC: Author.

U.S. Department of Education, National Center for Education Statistics (2003). *Status and trends in the education of Hispanics* (NCES 2003-008). Washington, DC: Author.

U.S. Department of Health and Human Services (1984). *Alcohol and health: Fifth special report to the U.S. Congress* (Publication No. ADM 84-1291). Washington, DC: Author.

U.S. Department of Health and Human Services (1988). *Study of national incidence and prevalence of child abuse and neglect.* Washington, DC: Author.

U.S. Department of Health and Human Services (1989). *Report of the secretary's task force on youth suicide.* Washington, DC: Author.

U.S. Department of Health and Human Services (1994). *Preventing tobacco use among young people: A report of the surgeon general.* Washington, DC: Author.

U.S. Department of Health and Human Services (1996). *Study of national incidence and prevalence of child abuse and neglect.* Washington, DC: Author.

U.S. Department of Health and Human Services (2000). *Tenth special report to the U.S. Congress on alcohol and health.* Washington, DC: Author.

U.S. Department of Justice, Bureau of Justice Statistics (2002). *Key facts at a glance: Demographic trends in correctional populations.* Available online at www.ojp.usdoj.gov/bjs/glance/tables/cpracepttab.htm (retrieved May 20, 2003).

U.S. Department of Labor (1991). *Dictionary of occupational titles.* Washington, DC: U.S. Government Printing Office.

U.S. Department of Labor (1996). *Employment and earnings: Annual report.* Washington, DC: Author.

U.S. Departments of Education and Justice (2000a). *Indicators of school crime and safety 2000.* Available online at www.nces.ed.gov/pubsearch/pubsinfo.asp?pubid=2001017.

U.S. Departments of Education and Justice (2000b). *2000 annual report on school safety.* Available online at www.ed.gov/offices/OESE/SDFS/annrept00.pdf.

Uribe, V., & Harbeck, K. M. (1991). Addressing the needs of lesbian, gay, and bisexual youth: The origin of PROJECT 10 and school-based interventions. *Journal of Homosexuality, 22,* 9–28.

Urquiza, A. J., & Winn, C. (1994). *Treatment of abused and neglected children: Infancy to age 18.* McLean, VA: Circle.

Valadez, J. R. (1998). Applying to college: Race, class, and gender differences. *Professional School Counseling, 1,* 14–20.

Van Boven, S. (1999, January 25). Playground justice. *Newsweek,* p. 33.

Van Riper, C., & Emerick, L. (1984). *Speech correction: An introduction to speech pathology and audiology* (7th ed.). Englewood Cliffs, NJ: Prentice-Hall.

VanZandt, Z., & Hayslip, J. (2001). *Developing your school counseling program: A handbook for systemic planning.* Belmont, CA: Brooks/Cole.

Vazquez, J. A. (1979). Motivation and Chicano students. *Bilingual Resources, 2,* 2–5.

Vazquez, J. A. (1998). Three-step procedure for adapting instruction to cultural traits. *Prevention Researcher, 5*(1), 1–5.

Verduyn, C. M., Lord, W., & Forrest, G. C. (1990). Social skills training in schools: An evaluation study. *Journal of Adolescence, 13,* 3–16.

Vernon, A., & Hay, J. (1988). A preventative approach to child sexual abuse. *Elementary School Guidance and Counseling, 22,* 306–312.

Wald, M. S. (1976). State intervention on behalf of neglected children: Standards for removal of children from their homes, monitoring the status of children in foster care and termination of parental rights. *Stanford Law Review, 28,* 637.

Wald, M. S. (1982). State intervention on behalf of endangered children: A proposed legal response. *Child Abuse and Neglect, 6,* 3–45.

Wald, M. S. (1990). Risk assessment: The emperor's new clothes? *Child Welfare, 69,* 483–511.

Walker, H. M., & Bullis, M. (1991). Behavior disorders and the social context of regular class integration: A conceptual dilemma? In J. W. Lloyd, N. N. Singh, & A. C. Repp (Eds.), *The regular education initiative: Alternative perspectives on concepts, issues, and models* (pp. 75–93). Sycamore, IL: Sycamore.

Walker, H. M., Colvin, G., & Ramsey, E. (1995). *Antisocial behavior in schools: Strategies and best practices.* Pacific Grove, CA: Brooks/Cole.

Walker, H. M., Schwarz, L. E., Nippold, M. A., Irvin, L. K., & Noell, J. W. (1994). Social skills in school-age children and youth: Issues and best practices in assessment and intervention. *Topics in Language Disorders, 14*(3), 70–82.

Wallace, W. A., & Hall, D. L. (1996). *Psychological consultation: Perspective and applications.* Pacific Grove, CA: Brooks/Cole.

Wallerstein, J. S. (1987). Children of divorce: Report of a ten-year follow-up of early latency-age children. *American Journal of Orthopsychiatry, 57,* 199–211.

Wallerstein, J. S. (1991). The long-term effects of divorce on children: A review. *Journal of the American Academy of Child and Adolescent Psychiatry, 30,* 349–360.

Wallerstein, J. S., & Kelley, J. B. (1976). The effects of parental divorce: Experiences of the child in early latency. *American Journal of Orthopsychiatry, 46,* 20–32.

Walsh, M. (1996, May 8). Districts cannot be held liable for student harassment, court rules. *Education Week, 15*(33), 7.

Walsh, M. (1999, June 2). Harassment ruling poses challenges. *Education Week, 18*(38), 1, 22.

Walton, F. X. (1980). *Winning teenagers over in home and school: A manual for parents, teachers, counselors, and principals.* Chicago: Practical Psychology Associates.

Washington State Department of Education (1998). *Career development activities for every classroom: K–3 and 4–6.* Olympia, WA: Author.

Watts, R. E. (1999, March). *Basic principles and procedures in play therapy.* Workshop conducted at the annual meeting of the American Counseling Association, San Diego, CA.

Way, N. (1995). "Can't you hear the strength, the courage I have." Listening to urban adolescent girls speak about their relationships. *Psychology of Women Quarterly, 19,* 107–128.

Way, N. (1997). Using feminist research methods to understand the friendships of adolescent boys. *Journal for Social Issues, 53,* 703–723.

Weaver, E. (1918). *Choosing a career.* Brooklyn, NY: Brooklyn Vocational Guidance Association.

Webb, L. D., Hartwell-Hunnicut, K., & Metha, A. (1997). What schools can do to combat student-to-student sexual harassment. *NASSP Bulletin, 81,* 72–78.

Wechsler, D. (1991). *Wechsler Intelligence Scale for Children–III.* San Antonio, TX: Psychological Corporation.

Wegscheider, S. (1981). *Another chance: Hope and health for the alcoholic family.* Palo Alto, CA: Science and Behavior Books.

Weiner, L., & Septimus, A. (1991). Psychological considerations and support for the child and family. In P. A. Pizzo & C. M. Wilfert (Eds.), *Pediatric AIDS: The challenge of HIV infection in infants, children, and adolescents* (pp. 577–594). Baltimore: Williams & Wilkins.

Weinrach, S. G. (1984). Determinants of vocational choice: Holland's theory. In D. Brown & L. Brooks (Eds.), *Career choice and development: Applying contemporary theories to practice* (pp. 61–93). San Francisco: Jossey-Bass.

Weinrach, S. G., & Srebalus, D. J. (1990). Holland's theory of careers. In D. Brown & L. Brooks (Eds.), *Career choice and development: Applying contemporary theories to practice* (2nd ed., pp. 37–67). San Francisco: Jossey-Bass.

Welfel, E. (2002). *Ethics in counseling and psychotherapy* (2nd ed.). Pacific Grove, CA: Brooks/Cole.

Werch, C. E., Pappas, D. M., Carlson, J. M., Edgemon, P., Sinder, J. A., & DiClemente, C. C. (2000). Evaluation of a brief alcohol prevention program for urban school youth. *American Journal of Health Behavior, 24,* 120–131.

Werner, E. E. (1986). Resilient offspring of alcoholics: A longitudinal study from birth to age 18. *Journal of Studies on Alcohol, 47,* 34–40.

West, M. O., & Prinz, R. J. (1987). Parental alcoholism and childhood psychopathology. *Psychological Bulletin, 102,* 204–218.

Westat (2002). Percent of service providers who consider themselves or are considered by others to have a disability, by type of service provider. Retrieved May 20, 2003 from www.spense.org.

Whalen, C. K., Henker, B., & Hinshaw, S. P. (1985). Cognitive–behavioral therapies for hyperactive children: Premises, problems, and prospects. *Journal of Abnormal Child Psychology, 13,* 391–410.

Whalen, C. K., Henker, B., Swanson, J., Granger, D., Kliewer, W., & Spencer, J. (1987). Natural social behaviors in hyperactive children: Dose effects of methylphenidate. *Journal of Consulting and Clinical Psychology, 55,* 187–193.

Wheelan, S. A. (1994). *Group processes: A developmental perspective.* Boston: Allyn & Bacon.

White, J., & Allers, C. T. (1994). Play therapy with abused children: A review of the literature. *Journal of Counseling and Development, 72,* 390–394.

White, K. M., & Oulette, P. L. (1980). Occupational preferences. Children's projections for self and opposite sex. *Journal of Genetic Psychology, 136,* 37–44.

Whitehouse, D. G. (1984). Adlerian antecedents to reality therapy and control theory. *Journal of Reality Therapy, 3*(2), 10–14.

Whitlock, K. (1989). *Bridges of respect: Creating support for lesbian and gay youth.* Philadelphia: American Friend's Service Committee.

Whitson, S. C., & Sexton, T. L. (1998). A review of school counseling outcome research: Implications for practice. *Journal of Counseling and Development, 76,* 412–426.

Widom, C. S. (1989a). Child abuse, neglect, and violent criminal behavior. *Criminology, 1,* 251–271.

Widom, C. S. (1989b). The cycle of violence. *Science, 24*(4), 160–166.

Wilcoxon, S. A., & Magnuson, S. (1999). Considerations for school counselors serving noncustodial parents: Premises and suggestions. *Professional School Counseling, 2,* 275–279.

Wilder, P. (1991). A counselor's contribution to the child abuse referral network. *School Counselor, 38,* 203–214.

Wilgus, E., & Shelley, V. (1988). The role of the elementary school counselor: Teacher perceptions, expectations, and actual functions. *School Counselor, 35,* 259–266.

Wilkinson, G. S., & Bleck, R. T. (1977). Children's divorce groups. *Elementary School Guidance and Counseling, 11,* 205–213.

Wilkstrom, P. O. (1985). *Everyday violence in contemporary Sweden.* Stockholm: National Council for Crime Prevention.

Will, M. C. (1986). Educating children with learning problems: A shared responsibility. *Exceptional Children, 52,* 411–415.

Williams, B. M., Wright, D., & Rosenthal, D. (1983). A model for intervention with latency aged children of divorce. *Family Therapy, 10,* 111–124.

Williams, J. H. (1994). *Understanding substance use, delinquency involvement, and juvenile justice system involvement among African-American and European-American adolescents.* Unpublished doctoral dissertation, University of Washington, Seattle.

Williamson, E. H. (1939). *How to counsel students.* New York: McGraw-Hill.

Wilson, J., & Blocher, L. (1990). The counselor's role in assisting children of alcoholics. *Elementary School Guidance and Counseling, 25,* 98–106.

Wilson, N. S. (1986a). Developmental versus remedial guidance: An examination of articles in *Elementary School Guidance and Counseling, volumes 8–18. Elementary School Guidance and Counseling, 20,* 208–214.

Wilson, N. S. (1986b). Effects of a classroom guidance unit on sixth graders' examination performance. *Journal of Humanistic Education and Development, 25,* 70–79.

Windle, R. C., & Windle, M. (1997). An investigation of adolescents' substance use behaviors, depressed affect, and suicidal behaviors. *Journal of Child Psychology and Psychiatry, 38,* 921–929.

Witt, J. C., Erchul, W. P., McKee, W. T., Pardue, M. M., & Wickstrom, K. F. (1991). Conversational control in school-based consultation: The relationship between consultant and consultee topic determination and consultation outcome. *Journal of Educational and Psychological Consultation, 2,* 101–116.

Witt, J. C., Gresham, F. M., & Noell, G. H. (1996). What's behavioral about behavioral consultation? *Journal of Educational and Psychological Consultation, 7,* 327–344.

Wodarski, J. S. (1990). Maltreatment and the school-age child: Major academic, socioemotional, and adaptive outcomes. *Social Work, 35,* 506–513.

Wohl, A., & Kaufman, B. (1985). *Silent screams and hidden cries: An interpretation of artwork by children from violent homes.* New York: Brunner/Mazel.

Wolf, D. (1993). Child abuse intervention research: Implications for policy. In D. Cicchetti & S. L. Toth (Eds.), *Child abuse, child development, and social policy* (pp. 369–398). Norwood, NJ: Ablex.

Wolfelt, A. (1983). *Helping children cope with grief.* Muncie, IN: Accelerated Development.

Wolfenstein, M. (1966). How is mourning possible? *Psychoanalytic Study of the Child, 21,* 93–123.

Wolock, I., & Horowitz, B. (1979). Child maltreatment and material deprivation among AFDC-recipient families. *Social Service Review, 53,* 175–194.

Wood, P. B., & Clay, W. C. (1996). Perceived structural barriers and academic performance among American Indian high school students. *Youth and Society, 28,* 40–61.

Woodcock, R. W. (1990). Theoretical foundations of the WJ-R measures of cognitive ability. *Journal of Psychoeducational Assessment, 8,* 231–258.

Woolsey, L. K. (1986). Research and practice in counseling. A conflict in values. *Counselor Education and Supervision, 26,* 84–94.

Worden, J. W. (1996). *Children and grief.* New York: Guilford.

Worthington, R. L., & Juntunen, C. L. (1997). The vocational development of non–college bound youth: Counseling psychology and the school-to-work transition movement. *Counseling Psychologist, 25,* 323–363.

Wrenn, C. G. (1962). *The counselor in a changing world.* Washington, DC: American Personnel and Guidance Association.

Wulff, M. B., & Steitz, J. A. (1999). A path model of the relationship between career indecision, androgyny, self-efficacy and self-esteem. *Perceptual and Motor Skills, 88,* 935–940.

Wyatt, G. (1985). The sexual abuse of Afro-American and White American women in childhood. *Child Abuse and Neglect, 9,* 507–519.

Yalom, D. (1995). *The theory and practice of group psychotherapy* (3rd ed.). New York: Basic Books.

Yauman, B. E. (1991). School-based group counseling for children of divorce: A review of the literature. *Elementary School Guidance and Counseling, 26,* 130–138.

York, J. (1993, Fall). What does inclusion really mean? *Exceptional Children's Assistance Center News Line,* p. 12.

Younger, A. J., & Boyko, K. A. (1987). Aggression and withdrawal as social schemas underlying children's peer perceptions. *Child Development, 58,* 1094–1100.

Younger, A. J., Schwartzman, A. E., & Ledingham, J. E. (1985). Age-related changes in children's perceptions of aggression and withdrawal in their peers. *Developmental Psychology, 21,* 70–75.

Zingraff, M. T., Leiter, J., Myers, K. A., & Johnson, M. (1993). Child maltreatment and youthful problem behavior. *Criminology, 31,* 173–202.

Zitkow, D., & Estes, G. (1981). The heritage consistency continuum in counseling Native American children. In Spring Conference on Contemporary American Issues (Ed.), *American Indian issues in higher education* (pp. 133–139). Los Angeles, CA: American Indian Studies Center.

Zunker, V. G. (2002). *Career counseling: Applied concepts of life planning* (6th ed). Pacific Grove, CA: Brooks/Cole.

Zuravin, S. J. (1988). Child abuse, child neglect, and maternal depression: Is there a connection? In U.S. Department of Health and Human Services, National Center on Child Abuse and Neglect (Ed.), *Research symposium on child neglect* (pp. 34–48). Washington, DC: U.S. Department of Health and Human Services, National Center on Child Abuse and Neglect.

Zuravin, S. J. (1991). Suggestions for operationally defining child physical abuse and physical neglect. In R. H. Starr & D. A. Wolfe (Eds.), *The effects of child abuse and neglect* (pp. 100–128). New York: Guilford.

Name Index

Subject Index

Italic page numbers indicate material in tables or figures.